DATE DUE

2/16/86

Demco No. 62-0549

For Better, For Worse

For Better, For Worse
British Marriages, 1600 to the Present

JOHN R. GILLIS

New York   Oxford
OXFORD UNIVERSITY PRESS
1985

Oxford University Press

Oxford   New York   Toronto
Delhi Bombay   Calcutta   Madras   Karachi
Kuala Lumpur   Singapore   Hong Kong   Tokyo
Nairobi   Dar es Salaam   Cape Town
Melbourne   Auckland

and associated companies in
Beriut   Berlin   Ibadan   Nicosia

Library of Congress Cataloging-in-Publication Data
Gillis, John R.
  For better, for worse.

  Bibliography: p. Includes index.
  1. Marriage—Great Britain—History.
2. Courtship—Great Britain—History.   I. Title.
HQ613.G55   1986   306.8'1'0941   85-13701
ISBN 0-19-503614-X

Printing (last digit): 9 8 7 6 5 4 3 2 1

Printed in the United States of America

To One Spouse
and Many Friends

List of Figures

1. Courting couple in the sixteenth century   24
2. Love tokens   32
3. *Jealousy and Frustration*   41
4. *The Refusal*   49
5. Welsh wedding   61
6. Riding from church   65
7. Chaining custom at Coxwold   67
8. Riding the stang   78
9. *Off She Goes*   91
10. Fleet wedding   95
11. Age of marriage, prenuptial pregnancy, illegitimacy, and common-law marriage in Britain, 1550–1900   111
12. Wensley Dale knitters   120
13. *Happy Is the Bride*   146
14. Welsh bidder   154
15. Bidding letter   155
16. Bidding wedding   157
17. *Penny Wedding*   158
18. *The Tailor's Wedding*   188
19. *Gretna Green Wedding*   197
20. *A Seamans Wifes Reckoning*   202
21. Wife sale   212
22. The women of Moss Alley, London   250
23. *Hampstead Heath on the August Bank Holiday*   273
24. *Yarmouth Beach*   277
25. *The Proposal*   280
26. White wedding, 1961   295
27. East End white wedding, 1970   312

Contents

List of Figures   xi

Introduction   3

Part I
Courtship and Marriage in the Sixteenth and Seventeenth Centuries   9

1. Neither Single nor Actually Married: Courtship and Betrothal in a Homosocial World   11

2. A Maie Game of Marriage: The Politics of Big Weddings   55

3. Neither Birth nor Portion Shall Hinder the Match: Clandestine Marriage and Sexual Nonconformity   84

Part II
Conflict and Change in the Age of Agrarian and Industrial Revolution, 1750–1850   107

4. The Better Man of the Two: Changing Relations between the Sexes, 1750–1850   109

5. Time Changes Fau'k an' Manners: Private Marriages versus Public Bridals   135

6. The Last Stage of Their Hope: From the Celibate to the Conjugal City   161

7. Married but not Churched: Common-Law Marriage and the Renewal of Sexual Nonconformity   190

Part III
The Era of Mandatory Marriage, 1850–1960   229

8. Better a Bad Husband Than No Husband at All: The Compulsion to Marry, 1850–1914   231

9. Love on the Dole: The Ritualization of Courtship in the Twentieth Century   260

10. The Lady Generally Likes White Weddings: Revival of the Big Wedding   285

Part IV
Conjugal Myths and Marital Realities, 1960 to the Present   305

11. Love and Marriage: The Unresolved Contradiction   307

Appendix   322

Notes   323

Bibliography   385

Index   409

Acknowledgments

I suppose this book could be regarded as the logical extension of my earlier work on youth, but, to tell the whole truth, it was the discovery of the rich archives of the Foundling Hospital in the Greater London Record Office that breathed life into the present project. I am greatly indebted to Mr. J. G. B. Swinley of the Thomas Coram Foundation for Children and Ms. A. L. Reeve of the Record Office for providing access to this remarkable source. I am no less grateful to Trefor Owen, Robin Gwyndaf, and William Linnard of the Welsh Folk Museum, John Widdowson of the University of Sheffield's Centre for English Cultural Tradition and Language, S. F. Sanderson of the University of Leed's Institute of Dialect and Folk Life Studies, and Dorothy Wainwright of the Mass Observation Archive for access to previously unpublished materials. Mr. L. E. Turner of Queen Charlotte's Hospital for Women and Mr. Brian Thornton of the National Children's Home were no less generous in providing working space for an interloping historian. The generosity of Dr. Elizabeth Roberts in sharing her Lancashire oral histories and Paul Thompson and Thea Vigne in providing access to The Family Life and Work Experience before 1918 Oral History Archive at the University of Essex is also gratefully remembered.

Lack of space prevents me from thanking all my correspondents at the County Record Offices of England and Wales. However, I must acknowledge the special assistance of the staffs of the British Library, Bodleian Library, National Library of Wales, Fawcett Library, Lambeth Palace Library, Alexander Library of Rutgers University, the Manchester Central Library, and the Firestone Library of Princeton University. I am especially indebted to the Folklore Society and The English Folk Dance and Song Society for use of their collections. The Institute of Historical Research and the library of the University of London also deserve special mention. Several persons, including Ms. Terry Toll, Jeffrey Looney, and Professors Andre Burguière, John Robson, Angus McLaren, Robin Fox, and the late David Glass, were kind enough to offer me parts of their own research. And there are those persons I have never had the pleasure of meeting, notably Reverend Roger L. Brown, J. H. Bettey, Hugh McLeod, and Rex Russell, who were also extraordinarily giving of their ideas and sources.

The research for this book was accomplished during two years in London supported by the Rutgers University Research Council and the National Endowment for the Humanities. Parts of it were first presented in the seminars of Eric Hobsbawm at the University of London and Dorothy Thompson at Birmingham University. I am no less indebted to Stephen and Eileen Yeo of Sussex University, James Obelkevich and Tony Mason of Warwick University, Leonore Davidoff and Paul Thompson of Essex University, and Peter Laslett and Richard Smith of the Cambridge Group for the Study of the History of Population and Social Structure for providing lively and critical forums. Thanks also go the organizers of the 1980 Past and Present Conference and the 1982 Anglo-American Conference of Historians for the opportunity to present my ideas. Numerous people on this side of the Atlantic have been no less hospitable and attentive to this wandering lecturer. I am thinking particularly of the organizers of the 1977 International Women's History Conference, Lawrence Stone of Shelby Collum Davis Seminar, Deborah Gorham of Carlton University, Bob Scally at New York University, Martha Verbrugge of Bucknell University, Burr Lichfield of Brown University, and Robert Moeller and Temma Kaplan of Columbia University and Barnard College.

Many of these listeners also read and discussed; I derived immense benefit from the comments of Christopher and Bridget Hill, John Bossy, Diana Leonard, Edward Shorter, Barbara Taylor, Steve Rappaport, Joan Scott, Raphael Samuel, Randolf Trumbach, Lance and Marjorie Farrar, Ellen Ross, Richard Andrews, Dorothy and Edward Thompson, Tony Wrigley, Jim Cronin, Polly Morris, Peter Laslett, David Levine, Mary Hartman, Peter Linebaugh, James Obelkevich, Susan Watkins, Lawrence Stone, and Anna Davin. No less deeply appreciated are my Rutgers colleagues, both faculty and students, who have seen me through all the phases of this work. Judith Walkowitz and Suzanne Lebsock provided the stimulation of the Women's History Seminar, where Anna Clark, Dina Copelman, Kelly Boyd, and Laura Tabili all provided useful suggestions. No less significant in the formulation of my ideas was the Social History Group and especially Traian Stoianovich. And there were those special people, Jim Reed and Al Howard, who make the teaching as well as the writing of history all that it ought to be.

Finally, I extend my thanks to Joan Bossert, a most able editor, and Nancy Lane, whose encouragement has been so essential.

New Brunswick, New Jersey   J.R.G.
June 1985

For Better, For Worse

Introduction

We live in a conjugal age, when the couple has become the standard for all intimate relationships, the unmarried and the married, the homosexual as well as the heterosexual. Commerce panders to the conjugal ideal and municipalities zone in its favor. Children play at it; teenagers practice it. Marriage has become a form of serial conjugality, a sequence of partnerships taken up and abandoned with bewildering rapidity, as men and women seek the perfect mate. Most of us will spend at least two-thirds of our lives as couples, much longer than any previous generation. Of course, there are moments when couplehood is broken by death or divorce, but these are perceived as intervals of loss and deprivation, when the sense of wholeness can best be restored by finding a new partner.

Sociologists have come to regard the couple as the basic unit of society; psychologists see it as the seat of our deepest feelings.[1] Not surprisingly, historians have also endowed the conjugal relationship with a life of its own. Abstracted from a fuller, more complex sociability, it becomes for them a thing of enormous power—the conjugal—that which drives history forward, whose triumph is the ultimate measure of human progress. That was the view of those great Victorian founding fathers of the history of marriage, G. E. Howard, Edward Westermarck, and Arthur Calhoun. It remains the perspective of recent grand treatments by Philippe Ariès, Edward Shorter, and Lawrence Stone.[2] While Ariès is notably ambivalent toward the progress of the conjugal, both Stone and Shorter celebrate it as our liberation from bondage to kin, peer group, and community, which they see as having for centuries limited the human capacity for real love and self-fulfillment. The conjugal is presented as the unique contribution of modern Western culture, setting us apart from, and superior to, other times and places.

For Stone and Shorter the conjugal is inherently progressive; all other social and emotional arrangements are archaic and regressive. They organize their histories around what they see as a set of distinctive stages, each more focused on the couple, each more liberated because of the independence from kin, peers, and the community at large. This, they insist, is *the* Western marriage pattern, singular and uncontested. They deny the historical plurality of heterosexuality and treat all alternative arrangements as mere survivals, whose fate it is to be swept away in the passage of time. In a view of the past so manifestly teleological, the triumph of the conjugal is predetermined.

When I began this study I too was searching for the origins of the conjugal, though at a social level below that which had been studied by most other historians. I had been led to expect that the emergence of the couple had been slow and painful among the peasants and artisans of the pre-industrial era, rapid and complete among the working classes of more recent times. When I discovered that working people had repeatedly experimented with forms of family life based exclusively on the conjugal bond only to reject these in favor of arrangements more broadly constructed, I was forced to rethink the basic premises of the conventional unilinear view of the history of marriage. Eventually, I came to see that as an organizing principle the idea of progress toward a conjugal ideal was deeply flawed. Not only did it not account for the real history of heterosexuality during the past four centuries, but it represented a very narrow class and a gender-bound view of the possibilities of just and amicable relationships between women and men.

If the past has any lesson to offer, it is that conjugal love by itself is rarely sufficient. There have always been lovers, but for most times and peoples the couple has proved too fragile a basis for establishing a home and family. Only the very privileged have ever believed in marriage based only on mutual affections; and, even among them, this romantic vision appealed more to men than to women. For ordinary people, and for virtually all women, marriage has never been just a private matter between individuals. That may have been the official position of church and state, as reflected in the law and the official marriage ceremony, but it was not the popular understanding of marriage, as expressed through the rites and festivities which people themselves brought to their nuptiality. They used their betrothals and weddings to construct a multitude of other relationships without which the existence of the couple would not be viable. In the sixteenth and seventeenth centuries there was no lack of tender passion in courtship, but people drew a sharp distinction between love and marriage, and took the precaution to strengthen the conjugal bond by enlisting the support of the entire community at the time of marriage. During the period of the Industrial Revolution, when the ideal of companionate marriage finally gained ascendance among the upper classes, ordinary people continued to value a broader set of relationships, even to the extent of rejecting monogamous marriage and the nuclear family in favor of nonconjugal arrangements that for them were more conducive to equitable, fulfilling heterosexual relationships. And, in our own century, when the couple has been more conspicuous among all classes, the construction of a home and family still requires more material and emotional resources than the couple can ordinarily provide. The way working-class people enlist the support of family and friends through elaborate betrothal and wedding rites is a measure of just how vulnerable the conjugal relationship, by itself, remains.

It is the central argument of this book that the conjugal has always been more an illusive dream than an attainable reality. In the seventeenth century, the idea that two people could find fulfillment in their mutual affection was so new as to be regarded as subversive; and, even when it became thoroughly respectable during the Victorian age, it was largely confined to the educated classes. Today, when the conjugal seems finally to have conquered popular culture, it still remains for many people, and especially for women, an ideal rather than lived reality. They are told they should find the ultimate happiness in their conjugality, and when this does not happen, the strain within marriage becomes even more pronounced.[3] Instead of being the source of liberation, the conjugal has become a new form of tyranny.

Historians who persist in seeing the conjugal as the exclusive requirement of satisfactory relationships between women and men distort the past and make the present unbearable. We would do well to put away mistaken teleologies and explore without the prejudices of ideology, class, or gender the immense variety of alternative arrangements people have chosen to deal with heterosexuality throughout history. In his brilliant comparative anthropology, *Friends and Lovers*, Robert Brain demonstrates the many ways human cultures have found to express and facilitate amity and justice among human beings of different and the same sex.[4] I am attempting to do something of the same with just one society, exploring within the limits of English and Welsh culture the immense variety of ways ordinary women and men have sought to bring mutually satisfactory order to their heterosexuality.[5] My historical anthropology may seem to some as bizarre and irrelevant as the exotic cultures Brain describes. Radical feminists will probably think my quest hopeless; believers in the myth of the conjugal will find it positively dangerous. Many may dismiss the courtship and marriage practices of the past as outdated, but I ask them to remember that history is our culture's repository of experience with the more problematic aspects of heterosexuality. If it can help us to understand our own ambivalences and cope more effectively with our present dilemmas, then the purpose of this book will be more than satisfied.

It is true that we can never be entirely free of the blinders that class culture, age, and gender impose, but we will more readily recognize our biases if we think of marriage not in legal, institutional terms, but as a social drama in which not just the couple but several parties play crucial roles. Only two persons stand before the priest or civil registrar, yet they are rarely on stage alone. Families, peers, even entire communities have a greater or lesser part in the making of any given marriage. Unfortunately, the way most historians have approached marriage has prevented them from seeing any actors other than the couple. They have concentrated solely on the legal or religious rite, not on the social activity leading up to and constituting the actual wedding. By coming in only at the official act of what is a much longer drama, they miss most of what ordinary people signify as the really important aspects of courtship and marriage. The festive behavior that has so fascinated anthropologists studying societies where there is no established church and state and therefore no official ceremony has been totally ignored by both historians and demographers of Western cultures. They confine their attention to the "facts" of marriage and birth as recorded by parish priest and census taker, defining all else as either illicit or irrelevant. It is not surprising that the standard historical sources, which are themselves ideologically constructed, should reinforce our tendency to consider only the conjugal, therefore wholly obscuring the complexity and multiplicity of meanings found in marriage both past and present.

The courtship and wedding are themselves forms of expression, not just "facts" to be recorded statistically but elements of the dramatic action that creates couples and transforms them into married persons. When history slavishly follows the social sciences in the direction of numerical abstraction, it violates not only its own canons, but the very nature of the historical subject. Because marriages are relationships, they have a dynamic quality that can only be expressed in a temporal way. The process of making a marriage is inevitably *eventful* because it involves such significant changes in the lives not only of the couple but their families, kin, friends, and neighbors. Together with birth and death it is usually the most important moment in the individual life cycle. For centuries it was also one of the most dramatic events in the life of the community as well. While there have also been times when wedding has been a perfunctory matter, even the most informal marriages have a certain dramatic form, expressing both the nature and the significance of the changes involved. This drama is not incidental. On the contrary, it is essential in creating the couple, but even more so in making a viable household and family. Therefore, to ignore it—as historians committed to a purely legal or formal interpretation of marriage have tended to do—is to overlook the very things that have meant most to people for centuries.

Church and state ceremonies are relatively recent additions, which have been grafted onto older popular rites whose legitimacy was dependent on no written law. Even today the amount of material and symbolic investment in rituals having no basis in law or scripture is immense. However much they may change over time, the rituals of courtship and marriage continue to meet the need to define, control, and otherwise cope with change, a need that is only partially met by the formal institutions of marriage. Although a largely unexplored mine of information, the history of popular rites can reveal the meaning of marriage to ordinary people. For some periods, when church and state were minimally involved, rituals of courtship, betrothal, and wedding constitute our only evidence of what matrimony meant. Today, when so much weight is placed on the legal, we have a tendency to think of ritual as "folklore," and thus insignificant. However, we would do well to reexamine this assumption in light of the extraordinary popularity and durability of the ceremonial in both courtship and marriage.[6]

The perception of ritual and symbol as somewhat less "real" and significant than the official acts of church and state is deeply ingrained in our culture. The seventeenth-century puritans denounced all wedding festivities that distracted attention from the couple; and later the Victorians invented the category of folklore to dispose of all those practices that did reinforce their notions of conjugality. Even in our own century, most historians have felt much more comfortable dealing with the official (i.e., conjugal) side of marriage, leaving the treatment of its "social" aspect to authors of less serious intentions. Recently, however, both anthropologists and sociologists have begun to show new interest in social ritual. They have discovered that it is by no means confined to exotic or archaic cultures, but, as Robert Bocock recently observed, "is more important in industrial societies than has been usually thought."[7] It is now generally agreed that ritual is particularly endemic in situations of change, at those times in the life of an individual, group, or society when there is the greatest uncertainty and when people have difficulty in expressing their ideas and feelings in a more direct way. In fact, ritual is dynamic and creative, because it allows people to handle situations that are otherwise troubling and disruptive. Ritual not only brings order out of chaos, but relieves people's fears about their personal and collective futures. "Ceremony can make it appear that there is no conflict, only harmony, no disorder, only order, that if danger threatens, safe solutions are at hand. . . . Ritual can assert that what is culturally created and man-made is as undoubtable as physical reality."[8]

Thus ritual makes (and unmakes) marriage just as surely and effectively as any legal proceeding. As late as the twelfth century it was the only way marriages were established; and until 1753 the Church of England ceremony had to compete with a variety of rites which, if done correctly, made marriages just as securely. Even after all self-marriage was abolished, ordinary people continued to arrange their heterosexuality in their own ways, and it was not until the end of the nineteenth century that illicit "little weddings" were finally discouraged. Even now the predominance of legal ceremony is again being challenged as cohabitation becomes ever more popular. In the past decade, courts have ruled that it confers a legitimacy comparable with official matrimony, thus restoring self-marriage to the quasi-legal standing it enjoyed before 1753.

This is partly a study of the long history of unofficial "little weddings," but it is also an exploration of the big wedding tradition. Even those people who have felt the need to establish their relationships by rites of their own making have usually resorted to the publicity of the church when it came to establishing a home and family. The big public wedding is not just an expression of the law-abiding character of the British or evidence of their religiosity. Instead, ordinary folk have been using the church as their stage on which to act out and thereby consecrate all those other social and emotional relationships they feel necessary to a proper marriage. Thus, by looking at the symbolism of both little and big weddings over the past four centuries we can "read" ideas and feelings that are never expressed in the official ceremony or found in the written record.

This is a history not of just the conjugal bonds but all those relationships that are a part of the marriage process. The multidimensionality of marriages accounts for their "politics"—that perpetual dissonance of class, age, and gender that is the source of the dramatic changes of the past four centuries. To construct a historical anthropology sensitive to all these facets, we must go beyond the legal and institutional to explore the larger context of heterosexuality as this affects not just the couple but families, peers, and community. We will pay careful attention to not only the more easily documented demographic and economic context, but to social and cultural factors such as age and gender. We will also need to understand the changing definition of family and household, popular notions of the life cycle, and, no less important, the prevailing norms of masculinity and femininity—all of which affect the marriage process.

A study of nuptiality concerned only with the couple is inadequate for a variety of reasons. The marriage process is simultaneously private and public; it is personal but also political. It belongs to that part of life which we, from our twentieth-century perspective, like to think of as voluntary, but which is actually subject to substantial constraints and obligations. While contemporary studies of marriages have given little attention to the public aspect, the perpetual conflicts in and about marriage remind us that the personal is also the political. The degree to which marriage is perceived as public or private is a function of time. Today we think of it as principally a personal matter, while in earlier periods it was the public side that was most emphasized. This change has to do with the transformation of the functions of marriage, but is also a reflection of shifts in the perceived boundaries of the public and private, and of the social and political. Together, changes in both behavior and ideas constitute the true history of marriages.

PART I

Courtship and Marriage in the Sixteenth and Seventeenth Centuries

CHAPTER 1

⟨ʃⁿ⟩ʃⁿ⟩ʃⁿ⟩ʃⁿ⟩ʃⁿ⟩ʃⁿ⟩ʃⁿ⟩ʃⁿ⟩ʃⁿ⟩ʃⁿ⟩ʃⁿ⟩ʃⁿ⟩ʃⁿ⟩ʃⁿ⟩ʃⁿ⟩

Neither Single nor Actually Married: Courtship and Betrothal in a Homosocial World

Couples were as exceptional in the sixteenth and seventeenth centuries as they are common today. Men married in their late twenties, women in their mid-twenties, and, because adult mortality was so high, the married couple's average duration was less than twenty years. Of the adult women in one seventeenth-century village, almost a third were either spinsters or widows; and, on average, ten percent of the population remained celibate during their entire lives, a condition that did not necessarily set them apart, for, if the entire population is taken into account, married persons constituted a little over a third of the whole at any given time. In our time, when nearly all adults either are or have been married, the proportion of couples is more like a half.[1]

Today we use the word "couple" to refer to almost any pair, unmarried or married, homosexual as well as heterosexual. In earlier times the term was reserved entirely for married people, who occupied a status sharply distinguished from that of single folk, whose world can best be described as homosocial.[2] After infancy, children were rarely alone in the company of the other sex. Work and leisure habits perpetuated the separation, so that throughout youth the strongest bonds were with persons of the same gender. There was some homosexuality, just as there was some premarital heterosexuality, but, even though youths of the sixteenth and seventeenth centuries were by no means chaste, they were steadfastly celibate, with their own life-styles and living arrangements separating them from the world of married folk.[3]

Marriage meant giving up one way of life to take on an entirely new existence. When the Welsh referred to the newlyweds as "starting their world," they were acknowledging the enormous gulf that separated the celibate from the married population. The formation of each new married pair was a strenuous, often conflicted social, psychological, and economic process. No wonder courtship was approached with considerable caution, even fear, and certainly with little of the romantic spontaneity that we expect of young lovers. This is not to say, as some historians have claimed, that sixteenth- and seventeenth-century people were incapable of love, but rather that affections were structured and communicated in a manner very different from our own time.[4] Direct and personal expressions of love were inhibited; and in their place we find highly ritualized forms of courtship, whose actions and symbols seem to us strangely impersonal. The process of getting married was an extended rite of passage, which began with formal betrothal and ended with the inauguration of a new household. What is for many today a simple legal act, taking only a few minutes and at most a few hours, was then a very public social drama with several distinctive acts—betrothal, posting of banns, a big wedding—stretching over several months. By our standards the people of the sixteenth and seventeenth centuries were awkward lovers, but not because they lacked the capacity for love, but because their personal relationships had always to be accommodated to other emotional attachments and social obligations to kin, peers, and the larger community.

Our understanding of self and society is so radically different that it is difficult for us to understand this past on its own terms. Those who believe the conjugal bond to be the only possible relationship capable of fulfilling the human need for companionship, intimacy, and love will find the homosocial world of the sixteenth and seventeenth century bizarre, even repelling. However, when we impose our own values on the past, we not only distort it but limit our ability to understand ourselves. As we turn to the sixteenth and seventeenth centuries it is well to keep in mind that it is not the capacity for love but the forms of affection that separates their world from ours.[5]

I

There has never been a time in recorded history when the relations between the sexes have not been highly problematic. Historians once assumed that the past was both static and uniform. Now we know better, for each new study of families and marriages seems to push back the time when variety and change were endemic features of British society.[6] While historical demographers have identified certain features—high age of marriage, considerable remarriage, unusually high levels of celibacy—as characteristic of much of northwestern Europe in the sixteenth and seventeenth centuries, they would be the first to admit great variations both over time and between social groups.[7] There were moments, such as the traumatic 1590s, when the demographic old regime threatened to collapse.[8] And we know that the behavior of the British nobility was very different from that of any other class, with eldest sons marrying much earlier than either their noninheriting siblings or the rest of the population.[9] The aristocracy also continued to give pride of place to kin and lineage, often treating marriage with supreme contempt. In sixteenth-century Lancashire, many lived in open adultery. They were shamed neither by their concubines nor by their bastards. When they did marry, they did so for convenience rather than affection, a principal reason why their wedlock was so frequently terminated by annulments.[10]

Lower down the social scale variety was no less evident. Among those still embedded in an essentially medieval economy of open field agriculture, where manor custom and communal norms were still in force, a distinctive peasant marriage pattern prevailed. Marriage was firmly linked to the formation of a separate household, and, because wedding had to wait on access to land by gift or inheritance, peasant men married in their late twenties, the women two or three years earlier. Although marriage was no longer subject to control by landlords, the couple's kin, age mates, and the larger community all still had a hand in regulating courtship and marriage. Because the household was the central unit of both production and reproduction, its formation was a major public event, subject to the politics of both family and community.[11] Much the same conception of marriage prevailed among that part of the urban population engaged in the guild economy. Artisans also married relatively late, for it was not until a man was a guild master that marriage was even conceivable. In sixteenth-century London, marriage was closely linked to the achievement of freeman status, both coming at about the age of twenty-eight. Once formed, the guildman's household was a highly stable institution, terminated only by death and usually reconstituted immediately by remarriage.[12]

If it is possible to talk of popular norm in the sixteenth and seventeenth centuries it was this peasant and artisan pattern. But then, as now, there were important exceptions, variations that were themselves the product of the advanced decomposition of both the peasant and artisan cultures in an already very dynamic Britain. By 1600 at least a third of the population no longer had any access to land or craft. Many among this burgeoning mass of migrant wage workers, squatters, expropriated peasants, and failed tradespeople were no longer subject to either church law or village custom. It was said in the mid-seventeenth century that "vagabonds be generally given to horrible uncleanness, they have not particular wives, neither do they range themselves into families, but consort together as beasts."[13] The little we know about Britain's first proletariat suggests that, while such accounts of their behavior were biased and exaggerated, their heterosexuality was often flexible and sometimes polygamous. No longer bound by the norms of village or guild, their behavior was individualistic, their values implicitly antinomian.[14]

But if peasant and artisan norms were being rapidly eroded from below, they were also losing strength among those groups who, having freed themselves from the constraints of village custom and guild regulation, were now transcending peasant and artisan culture and transforming the meaning of marriage to conform to their elevated economic and social standing. These included not only the prosperous yeomanry who had profitted, often at the expense of the poorer peasantry, from the enclosure of open fields, but also those who were now involved in varieties of production and commerce independent of the guild system. They were described by their contemporaries as the "middling sort," a term that distinguished them from both the well born and the poor. We can trace their roots, together with their distinctive attitude toward marriage, to earlier generations of town dwellers, but by the sixteenth and seventeenth centuries they were a significant strata of rural as well as urban society, constituting, as they did in the clothing districts of Essex, a village elite closely identified with the new puritanism.[15]

It was among this nascent middle class that heterosexuality came to have a form and meaning resembling that of our own conjugally organized society. The emerging capitalist economy encouraged the "middling sort" to mobilize the full productive capacity of the marital partnership. In pursuit of this end, the nuclear family cut itself loose from kin, peer group, and the community generally. Marriage came to be seen as a sanctified partnership, the relationship most conducive not only to productivity but to the fulfillment of all other spiritual and emotional needs. Especially in its radical puritan expression, this new conjugality came closest to the modern norm of companionate marriage, even to the extent of proclaiming the equality (albeit limited) of partners.[16]

Historians of such differing perspectives as Lawrence Stone and Christopher Hill have been correct in locating the origins of the conjugal ideal in the revolutionary 1640s and 1650s, but wrong in assuming a linear, continuous progression from that time to our own. In fact, the precocious conjugality of the 1640s and 1650s was utopian, a volatile ideal rather than a sustained reality. The idea of companionate marriage was subscribed to by only a very small number of people and, even among the puritans, was a controversial notion, which was not fully accepted, even among the new middle classes, until the Victorian period. It had little resonance at this time among the aristocracy and gentry, and its appeal was even less among the great mass of the population, who either remained steadfast in the ways of the peasant and artisan world or adopted the antinomianism of the dispossessed. It would be wrong, therefore, to concentrate too much on the new conjugality, even if it was to be one of the ideas that ultimately triumphed in subsequent centuries. We will gain a much richer understanding not only of the past but the present if we begin with peasant and artisan culture, for not only was this still the popular norm of the sixteenth and seventeenth centuries, but the standard of heterosexuality which, even if already eroded, shaped the new forms of popular behavior that were to emerge in parallel with and as an alternative to middle-class conjugality in the next two centuries.

II

Holders of small property made up fifty to seventy percent of the population in 1600, depending on the region and its economic structure.[17] Although they varied considerably among themselves with respect to wealth, peasants and artisans shared certain patterns of behavior and values that distinguished them sharply from the higher social orders as well as those propertyless people known simply as "labourers." This group married at a relatively late age because marriage meant establishing a separate, economically independent household. Designated heirs and heiresses were assured this by dowry or marriage portion, but, although inheritance was relatively egalitarian among smallholders, there was rarely enough to provide adequately for all those children who might wish to marry.[18] While those who expected land might stick close to home waiting the death or retirement of parents, children with lesser prospects had to earn and save in order to wed. Often this meant a long period as a servant in husbandry in another household or migration to a town where apprenticeships were available. For those whose inheritance was training in a craft or profession, the teens and early twenties were also celibate years, frequently spent in a series of places:

> Crake it had my infancye
> Yorke did my youth bringe up,
> Cambridge had my jollitie
> When I her brestes did sucke.
> London brought me into thraule
> And wed me to a wife
> Welcorne my carefull time had all
> Joyn'd with a troubled life.[19]

Marriage was a highly privileged status. As we have already seen, there were always at least a tenth of the population who never married, and the rates of mortality were such that the marrieds made up no more than about thirty percent of the population at any given time.[20] The lines between them and the rest of the population were very clearly marked. In the early sixteenth century, all single persons in Coventry, regardless of rank and age, were referred to as "lads" or "maids" and expected to show proper deference to the married "masters" and "dames" who were simultaneously their guardians, employers, and governors. A century later the same distinctions were still evident, perhaps even sharper because of the concentration of property into fewer and fewer hands. In Sheffield in 1615 only twelve percent of the population were classified as householders, mainly married men to whom the rest of the city was supposed to defer.[21]

In a society in which the boundaries between the single and married were delineated in everything from church seating to modes of address, the passages to marriage were necessarily as complicated as they were abrupt. It was a matter too critical to be left to individual whim or fancy, and thus was a matter of collective concern—a critical issue not only for family and immediate kin, but for peers and the larger community. The forms of courtship and marriage reflected this social reality. The very public, extremely formal nature of the preliminaries and the enormous publicity associated with the wedding itself testified to a complicated "politics," which over the course of previous centuries had found expression in a set of folk practices unique to this class of smallholders and their counterparts throughout northwestern Europe.[22]

There are many societies, including our own, in which marriages are often made very informally. The Trobrianders that Malinowski made famous announced their unions by sharing food. In the sixteenth and seventeenth centuries the very poor often established their conjugality by erecting a cabin or sleeping in the same bed. But this kind of informality was still exceptional. From the patricians down to the smallholders, three highly ritualized and successively more demanding steps constituted a proper marriage.[23] The first was the consent of the parties, publicly announced or at least symbolized by the exchange of rings or love tokens. This was followed, where required, by the public blessing by family and close kin. And finally there was the big church wedding, preceded by banns, at which the "politics" of peers and community was played out.

We can trace the nuptial process in the pages of a diary kept by William Whiteway, a Dorset man, beginning with his entry for April 6, 1620: "Was concluded the marriage betwixt me WM Whiteway and Eleanor Parkins, my best beloved which I pray God to bless and prosper." It might be thought Whiteway was referring to his wedding, but what we take to be the conclusion was only the beginning. On May 4, he recorded that the couple were "bewrothed in my father Parkins his hall about 9 of the clock at night, [by] Mr. John White in the presence of our parents." And on June 14 he records: "I William Whiteway was married to Eleanor Parkins by Mr. John White in the Church of the Holy Trinity in Dorchester, in the presence of the greatest part of the Town."[24]

It strikes us as very odd that anyone would call his betrothal a marriage, but then our perspective is the product of the relatively recent legalization of marriage, which has given the church and state almost the sole right to license nuptiality. Britain in the 1620s was just beginning to experience the process that would ultimately differentiate legal marriage from popular practice. People were still operating under much older rules according to which all forms of consent, when properly made and witnessed, constituted a valid marriage according to canon law. According to the leading authority of the day, Henry Swinburne, the validity of a union depended more on how it was done than where it was enacted or who officiated. As long as the vows were "done rite," they were as valid as a church wedding.[25]

Swinburne's use of the word "rite" is a reminder that the legal and the ritual were once identical. Words, symbols, and ritualized behavior, if freely given and in accordance with prevailing custom, had powers we now reserve for the legal authorities of church and state. In William and Eleanor's time, ordinary people were still conducting a very large part of the business of marriage themselves. Although the church had been trying to control marriage since the twelfth century, it had been only partially successful in doing so. No history of early modern marriage can therefore ignore those practices that, from our overly legalistic perspective, we tend to treat as mere social custom or folklore. So far as ordinary people were concerned, it was these and not the church service itself that constituted the real marriage. As William Whiteway's diary acknowledges, matrimony began with the ritual consents of the couple and proceeded through certain well-understood acts to culminate in the big public wedding. Marriage was not then, as it is now, an individualized legal procedure, a matter between the couple and the constituted authorities of church or state. Instead, it was a social drama involving family, peers, and neighbors in a collective process aimed at making things right economically, socially, and psychologically, as well as legally.

III

The origins of British marriage practice are lost in the obscurity of the early Middle Ages. The weddings of ordinary folk have left no trace because they were oral transactions, celebrated by the people themselves, whose witness and subsequent memory of the events constituted the sole basis for a marriage's legitimacy. Among the Anglo Saxons, the first step involved obtaining permission from the bride's kinsmen. Once this was accomplished, the groom and his people offered to the bride's guardians a series of sureties called *weds* that guaranteed that the bride would be maintained and protected. "If they then reach agreement about everything, then the kinsmen are to set about betrothing their kinswoman as wife and in lawful matrimony to him who has asked for her, and he who is leader of the betrothal is to receive the security."[26] The giving and taking of securities was thus the first stage of the wedding (*Beweddung*). Presided over by the father or some other relative of the bride, this was normally the occasion of public ceremony, featuring in Scotland and the north of England the joining of the couple's hands (the *handfast*) as well as an exchange of vows known as "plighting the troth." In Scotland both acts were done at certain ceremonial sites, where the couple would pass their hands through an opening in a stone, known locally as the "plighting-stone," "betrothal-stone," or "bridal-stone."[27]

Henceforth, the man would refer to the woman as "wyf," while the woman called him "husband." There remained only the giving away of the bride, which was also a secular ceremony presided over by her kinsmen. On the day appointed for the woman to leave her home, people would again gather to witness the transfer of guardianship, symbolized by the father or kinsman taking the woman by the neck and shoulders, and literally placing her in the hands of her new husband. A sword, hat, mantle, or shoe—all symbols of authority—were also offered to him. For his part, the husband pledged again his good faith and stepped on the bride's foot, a simple but definitive demonstration of his husbandhood.[28]

There also existed what were called "self-weddings," in which the woman gave herself to the groom in the absence of a guardian. Widows were apparently the first to do so, but other women who felt themselves free to marry also did so. Instead of the giving away ceremony, the partners exchanged *weds*, and, for the sword, mantle, hat, and shoe, they substituted more egalitarian symbols—rings, kisses, and the clasping of hands. This rite was presided over by an "orator," who, in the absence of a formal guardian, invited the witnesses, prompted the vows, and saw to it that the *weds* were given in a manner that ensured the legitimacy of the self-wedding.[29]

Neither kind of early medieval marriage involved religious or secular officials in anything but a private capacity. The lord of the manor might attempt to control the marriage choices of his bondspeople, but he had no formal role in their weddings. Similarly, the church made no concerted effort to associate itself with weddings until the twelfth century and even then was principally concerned with preventing persons from marrying who had violated the church's incest prohibitions. Initially, the couples came to church on the day after the giving away or self-wedding ceremony, and it was only gradually that these rites were brought to the church porch, henceforth called the "marriage porch" because of its new function. The priest was there largely to see that the parties were consenting and that there were no hindrances to the marriage. Troths were plighted a second time. By the twelfth century it seems to have been common for the groom also to pledge his endowment to the bride at this moment. Only after this business was completed did the parties enter the church to celebrate a bridal mass.[30]

Gradually the priesthood inserted itself into the process, first finding a role in the rites of the self-wedding, which required an orator, and later offering the church's porch and yard as ideal places to announce and witness rites that previously had been made at the market cross, in barns, on bridges, and at other conspicuous public places.[31] Only then did the clergy take over the role of the orator, asking the assembled whether there were any objections to the marriage and then having the couple repeat publicly their betrothal agreement.[32] This was symbolized by rings and coins placed on the priest's book. The priest then determined whether the parties consented to the marriage; each answered "I will" in what was essentially a repetition of their prior vows. Next came the question, "who gyes me this wyfe?" Either the father, kinsmen, or a special "chosen guardian," the latter a concession to the practice of self-wedding, was permitted to respond, which then led to the couple making their vows in the present tense:

> Here I take thee N. my wedded wyfe to haue and to holde, at bedded and at borde, for fayrer or fouler, for better for warse, in sekeness and in hele, tyl dethe us departe, and thereto I plyght thee my trouhte.

Once the couple had made their vows, the priest took the ring from his book and passed it to the groom, who then put it on the bride's middle finger, saying "With this rynge I wedde the and with this golde and silver I honoure the, and with this gyft I dowe the." The coins, symbolic of the dower, were then handed over to the bride. In some cases, the groom announced the dower explicitly, but in most cases, where manor custom determined the widow's portion, this was not necessary.[33] In the late Middle Ages, it was not uncommon for widows and heiresses bringing property to the marriage to indicate this by giving rings or other tokens to the groom, thus endowing him with what at the time was called "curtesy," the goods and lands that were for his use should his new bride die first.[34]

The assembled crowd might then move inside the church for a nuptial mass, but this was voluntary and was often dispensed with if the couple was too poor to afford its celebration. What appeal the mass did have seems to have derived largely from the popular rites that were grafted to it. It was not uncommon for medieval newlyweds to be joined at the altar by children born to them prior to the marriage. Manor custom held that the firstborn could become legal heir if it had joined its parents during the mass. This form of legitimation was widely practiced in the Middle Ages and continued in some places until the nineteenth century. Its publicity meant that it was accepted as evidence in both church and manor courts.[35] Another popular rite of the nuptial mass was the priest's kiss of peace, the *pax*, which was passed to all those present and guaranteed peace on an occasion when much emotion and social tension were present.[36] This was the last act of the formal service and a signal for the dancing, feasting, and gift giving to begin, which started in the church and ended perhaps in one of the "wedding houses" provided by the ecclesiastical authorities. The one at Braughing, Hertfordshire, was described as having a large room for feasting, together with a bed chamber "with bride bed and good linen."[37]

For reasons both spiritual and mundane, the clergy entered enthusiastically into their role as masters of ceremony, making as little distinction between the sacred and the profane as did most of their parishioners. They were later accused of tolerating all kinds of "heathenish toys" as part of the marriage service, of allowing "women to come bareheaded, with bagpipers and fidlers before them, to disturb the congregation."[38] All this, and more, was true. The pre-Reformation clergy had allowed the use of charms in the marriage service and even offered to bless the nuptial bed, a bit of magic that was still in demand in the seventeenth and eighteenth centuries.[39] By offering their services as notaries, caterers, and as magicians, the priesthood made themselves indispensable to those who wanted their wedding "done rite."

By the sixteenth century most people were bringing their vows to the church as the final step in the marriage process. Still, they reserved for themselves the right to make their own betrothals, as the first crucial step in matrimony. Although the church officially frowned on couples taking themselves as "man and wife" before it had ratified their vows, it had to acknowledge that vows "done rite" were the equivalent of a church wedding. It could penalize those couples found cohabiting before coming to church, but because its own canon law recognized mutual consent as the basis of holy matrimony, the church's own courts recognized that, in the absence of church rites, the various forms of betrothal—spousals, handfasts, trothplights, contracts—represented a valid marriage. As long as it could be proved that vows had been made voluntarily, in the present tense, or when in the future tense were followed by intercourse, these were upheld.[40] So it was that John and Marjory Beke were able to escape the heavy punishment mandated for those living casually or promiscuously together by calling witnesses who recalled with vivid detail their festive trothplight in 1371:

> John Beke, saddler, . . . called the said Marjory to him and said to her, "Sit with me." Acquiesing in this, she sat down. John said to her, "Marjory, do you wish to be my wife?" And she replied, "I will if you wish." And taking at once the said Marjory's right hand, John said, "Marjory, here I take you as my wife, for better or worse, to have and to hold until the end of my life; and of this I give you my faith." The said Marjory replied to him, "Here I take you John as my husband, to have and to hold until the end of my life, and of this I give you my faith." And then the said John kissed the said Marjory through a wreath of flowers, [called] in English, "Garland."[41]

Actions that would seem to us purely affectionate had a jural quality even the church was forced to recognize. By the sixteenth century, betrothal had taken on a ritual character which, though it varied greatly by region, universally rivaled church ceremony in scale, significance, and even in sanctity.[42] Writing in the 1540s, Bullinger acknowledged that "every man likewyse must esteme the person to whom he is handfasted, neon otherwyse than for his owne spouse, though as yet it be not done in the Church nor in the streate"; and, while he warned that the churchgoing should not be delayed too long, he noted there were many places "that at the handfastynge ther is made a great feaste and superfluous bancket [banquet], and even the same night are the two handfasted personnes brought and layed together, yea certain wkes afore they go to the Church."[43]

Such accounts make it clear that betrothal was not a quiet family affair, but a major public event rivaling the church wedding in social significance. By the sixteenth century the visit to the church was almost universally accepted as the final step in the marriage process, but the betrothal constituted the real beginning of marriage. In effect, it was a major rite of passage, not so much of the son or daughter from the family but from the homosocial to the heterosocial world. An extended period of service or apprenticeship had already transformed the child into a marriageable youth; what the betrothal and banns accomplished was the creation of the couple. Even the critics of popular practice, such as the puritan William Gouge, recognized this as the vital function of betrothal:

> contracted persons are in a middle degree betwixt single persons and married persons; they are neither simply single, nor actually married. Many make it a very marriage, and thereupon have a greater solemnity at their contract than at their marriage; yea many take liberty after a contract to know their spouse, as if they were married, an unwarrantable and dishonest practice.[44]

IV

Courtship belonged to the young. Its rites expressed their needs, its symbols their desires. While family consent was certainly considered appropriate in any marriage where property was involved and the parents were still living, the power of patriarchy was not nearly so great as many of the "conduct books," most of them puritan in origin, would have suggested. Because of high mortality rates, between two-fifths and two-thirds of all brides marrying in their mid-twenties would have already lost their fathers.[45] And, as the majority of the population fell into that category who, either because of class or birth order, could never expect to inherit, only a minority of young persons would have had reasons other than the sentimental to seek parental consent.[46] Those symbols of guardianship—the sword, hat, and mantle—had long since disappeared, child marriages were exceptional, and, apart from the highborn, few young people were married against their will under any circumstances. Young men were given considerable latitude in their courtships, and, although women were more closely controlled, there was, according to Keith Wrightson, nothing like the degree of parental dictation assumed by most historians:

> There is little evidence of cold-bloodedly "arranged" matches outside the very highest ranks of society. The likelihood of parents initiating or proposing a match was not uniform even at the highest social levels, while even when they did so, children usually seem to have enjoyed the right of refusal. Below the level of the aristocracy, upper gentry and urban plutocracy, the actual initiative seems to have lain with the young people, subject to the advice and consent of parents, friends, and even principal neighbours. The significance of that advice and consent would appear to have varied according to both sex and wealth, but on the whole it seems rare for it to have been withheld when a couple were determined to marry.[47]

The recession of the arranged marriage was perhaps inevitable in a society where first marriage occurred in the mid- to late twenties, and where women as well as men left home in the early teenage years to begin a period of service or apprenticeship which encouraged a certain degree of independence. Under these conditions, the family delegated much of its authority to other institutions, not only to the heads of other households, who were endowed by law with surrogate patriarchal authority, but to kin, neighbors, and especially to the peer group, which, in conjunction with communal norms, took the most direct and active role in regulating the heterosexuality of young people throughout this period. Peers, not parents, were the strongest influence not only for servants and apprentices, but also for those living at home in still relatively homogeneous rural or urban communities.[48] As long as the peer group reflected and reinforced shared values, parents were more than willing to cede to them those disciplinary functions that have always made relations between the generations so unpleasant for all concerned.

Parents worried about the misalliances of sons or daughters could consign their children to the homosocial world of the peer group with at least as much confidence as they showed when sending them off to celibate service, school, or apprenticeship. Young people did not begin to think of marriage until they were well into their twenties, and even then they made very awkward lovers. It was the rule of all but the dispossessed that there should be no marriage without the reasonable expectation of economic independence. "When thou art married, if it may be, live of thyself with thy wife, in a family of thine own," counselled William Whately.[49] This meant that young men, like the orphaned mercer's apprentice Roger Lowe, did not even begin to think of marriage until they were at or near the end of their apprenticeships.[50] William Whit promised marriage to Mary Gillett in the 1590s "as soon as he is out of service."[51] There was great reluctance on the part of both women and men to enter too early into monogamy. When a suitor brought Joan Wigg to church court in the early sixteenth century to enforce her promise to marry him, she subjected him to a vigorous cross examination:[52]

> John Newman, I marvel what you mean. . . . I cannot deny but I have made a promise to you to be my husband; but shall we marry so soon? It were better for us to forebear and [have] some household stuff to begin withal.

Traditions of live-in service and apprenticeship acted to limit access to the marriage market; and, among artisans and peasants, limited opportunities for ownership of land, employment, and housing regulated the number of weddings that could take place. Access to these vital conditions of marriage expanded and contracted in a most unpredictable manner. A sudden wave of deaths in a village was invariably followed by a spate of weddings. In the late sixteenth century, when high mortality rates were compounded by very uncertain economic conditions, contemporaries were convinced that the traditional restraints had broken down entirely and that the country was about to be overwhelmed by "over-hasty marriages and over-soon setting up of households by youth."[53] Similar anxieties were endemic throughout the early seventeenth century, when fears of "breeding beggars and multitudes of poor children" caused local authorities to impose their own controls over marriage.[54]

Yet, even in more tranquil times, there was much anxiety about courtship and marriage. People were less at ease with monogamous relationships, and even among courting couples the kinds of intimacy we expect of lovers were noticeably absent. Prior to a formal exchange of consents, young people were allowed little privacy. They practiced a form of innocent polygamy according to rules that prohibited the kind of pairing off that we would regard as normal. Their rambunctious round dances and kissing games seem to us quite juvenile, for, as a matter of fact, many of the activities that once belonged to young adults have become in our own time the province of children. The celebration of St. Valentine's Day was once a part of every young adult's calendar; and so too were the May and Midsummer games now practiced only by school children. In the seventeenth century, one of the most popular adult games was "Kiss-in-the-Ring," involving men and women chasing and saluting one another. Arthur Munby was clearly surprised when he found shop girls and servants still playing it at the Crystal Palace in London on a warm July evening in 1859:

[A] nice looking girl came up, & saying "Are you in the ring, Sir?" offered me her favour—a leaf. I acquiesed; I caught and led and kissed her: and stimulated by the feat we joined in the game;

The game ended as innocently as it had begun, causing Munby to remark:

Young men and women can do all this & be pure—can do it (the women at least) because they are pure. And so, the servant girl who rather enjoys being kissed in the hayfield or claspt round the waist behind the pantry door, is not therefore indelicate: the want of that "personal dignity," which makes young ladies revolt at this horseplay, is no shame to her.[55]

The fact that Munby felt compelled to defend the game's innocence suggests how much had changed by his time, and our own. Ritualized behavior permitted young people to show an interest without committing them to a more binding relationship. Just as horseplay allows young males in our own society to show affection that, if expressed in more positive form, might be taken for homosexual attachment, so these boisterous games expressed and at the same time controlled heterosexual interests that, if they had escaped the realm of play, would have threatened to disrupt the social order. In game, festival, and dance, young single persons were able to transcend, if only for a moment, those boundaries, social as well as sexual, that dominated ordinary life.[56]

Divisions between those with property and those without were widening rapidly in the late sixteenth and early seventeenth centuries, yet this was not yet reflected in the festive life of the young, who, with the

1. A sixteenth-century depiction of a courting couple. That the man is pulling the woman suggests that they may have been playing one of the fetching games that ritually tested a young female's preferences. (From the *Roxburghe Ballads*)

exception of the highborn, still mixed with one another on relatively equal terms. Children of yeoman farmers and small tradesmen had not yet withdrawn from the May and Midsummer dancing, from the horse-play of Easter Monday and Tuesday, or the ritualized familiarities of St. Valentine's Day. On the latter occasion, names were drawn by lot and the pairs exchanged gifts and kisses. Pepys was unperturbed when his wife drew a servant, Little Will Mercer, as her valentine, though there were others, like Dudley Lord North, who thought that a lady of quality should "never put herself to the chance of a Valentine, saying that she would never couple herself by chance." Puritans agreed with North that the whole thing was a "costly and idle" custom, though from numerous sources it seems clear that among rural folk and many city people the playful quality of St. Valentine's Day retained its appeal well into the nineteenth century.[57] By then it was common for lovers to exchange special valentines, but care was taken that no one was left out. In Derbyshire in the 1850s any girl who did not receive her own valentine was "bound to cast lots with other girls, and, if chance favours her, draws the name of her future husband out of an old top hat."[58] It was a day not just for lovers but for love itself, much like the modern Christmas, when everyone receives a greeting or gift of some kind or another. In Norwich the streets were said to swarm with young men carrying baskets of small gifts:

Bang, bang goes the knocker and away rushes the banger, after depositing upon the doorstep a package from the basket of stores. Anonymously, St. Valentine presents his gifts labelled only with "St. Valentine's Love" or "Good Morrow, Valentine." Sometimes of real value and otherwise simply fancy wrapping with a mocking note: "Persevere" or "Never Despair."[59]

Rank was similarly ignored in the "lifting" or "heaving" traditions associated with Easter Monday and Tuesday, which date from at least the thirteenth century. On the Monday groups of men went about seizing women, threatening to lift them in a chair unless bought off with a small gift. In some places, they stole the women's shoes, forcing them to buy them back with money or a kiss. The next day the tables were turned and the women did the lifting and ransoming, enjoying themselves so vigorously that in Coventry the traditional Easter Tuesday play featured "our English women" defeating the Danes in pitched battle.[60] The tradition was most entrenched in the Midlands, where one later witness reported he had seen "men run long distances, climb walls, etc. to escape organized bands of women on the look out for sport."[61] At Wednesbury it was said that as late as the 1860s it was not safe for men to appear on an Easter Tuesday: "A band of brawny women were generally lying in wait to 'have him' and mulct his pockets."[62] On that day not only sexual but social hierarchies were overturned. A Staffordshire servant remembered that she, with the other maids, summoned the nerve to knock at the door of their gentleman employer:

and I says, sheepish like: "If you please, Sir, it's Easter Tuesday and we've come to lift you."

"Aye, I know what you want wenches, but I am too weak. You go to Mrs. Smith and ax for five shillings: that's better till lifting o' me."[63]

Also in the 1880s, a Durham clergyman, "out of costume," reported paying a forfeit for his hat.[64] By that time, however, much of the old spontaneity was gone. Servants knew to knock before they approached their masters. In nearby Cheshire a William Pullen brought charges against some men who entered his house to "lift" his wife. Their defense that they were merely "endeavouring to carry out an old Cheshire custom" did not impress the magistrates, who made their leader apologize to Pullen and pay the court costs.[65]

No doubt there were people who objected in earlier centuries as well, yet for most young people there was nothing disreputable in this and other occasions of ritualized fun. They danced, sang, played, and feasted together at regular intervals beginning with New Year, at Shrove, May Day, Whitsun, the village feasts, hiring fairs and harvest festivals of late summer and fall, and during the Christmas season as well. Of these, it was "Maying" that was most directly associated with single persons. The actual celebrations began on May eve, an important "spirit night," when it was thought that divinations and love spells had the best chance of success. In Wales young women would lay a table: "The 4 women hideing themselves in ye corners of ye room. Their sweethearts will come in & eat, though a Hundred miles off."[66] After feasting, parties of young men and women would go caroling, staying late into the night to gather flowers and garlands, or to collect, as did Pepys' wife in 1669, the May dew, which was believed not only a marvelous cosmetic but an effective cure for innumerable diseases.[67] As Henry Bourne described it, the day began when:

> the juvenile Part of both Sexes, are wont to rise a little after Mid-night, and walk to some neighbouring Wood, accompany'd with Musick and the blowing of Horns; where they break down Branches from the Trees, and adorn them with Nose-gays and Crowns of Flowers. When this is done, they return with their Booty homewards, about the rising of the Sun, and make their Doors and Windows to Triumph in the Flowery Spoil.[68]

The "mayers" were no respectors of rank or status. In parts of the north, May eve was known as "mischief-neat," when "anyone having a grudge against a neighbour was at liberty to indulge in it, provided he kept his own counsel."[69] Of equal if not greater importance was the fact that "on this night all the young men turned out to pay a tribute of affection to their sweethearts, or mark their distain for girls who had jilted them."[70] May birching, as this was sometimes called, was still prevalent in Wales, the north, and the Midlands in the nineteenth century, but was also remembered in Essex where it was said that "the larger the branch that is placed at the door, the more honourable the house, or rather the servants, for if any of them should chance to have offended one of the mayers, a branch of elder with a bunch of nettles is fixed to the door, and that is considered a great disgrace."[71] Some such actions ended up in the church courts of the sixteenth and early seventeenth centuries when one party or another felt themselves defamed. On the other hand, a Bedfordshire apprentice was able to exonerate himself from the charge of theft by proving that he was engaged in sticking "May bushes" to people's doors at the exact time the crime was supposed to have occurred.[72]

Girls would wake up on May morning to find either well-known signs of love (hawthorn, wicken, or rowan) or equally powerful symbols of rejection (holly, briar, elder, or salt) stuck to their doors or placed under their windows. "The first thing on a May morning the house was quickly searched round before the old folk were astir," giving the women time to send their own compliment or rebuke to those who had placed the signs to be found.[73] Welsh bachelors also used May Day to settle scores between themselves. A jilted man would make a straw effigy of his rival and place it near his former sweetheart's house in what was called "hanging the straw man."[74]

Sometimes this would provoke fist fights or court actions, but in most cases the feelings involved were contained by the rules governing the festive occasion. Those who took the actions too seriously were considered poor sports and risked being left out of the games and dancing that followed. The flora not used in the birching were made into garlands and carried from house to house, as the youths asked for coins.[75] Young people often organized a Lord and Lady of the May, but the most universal custom was the May Pole itself, which to its critics was a source of great scandal:

> The daunce with disordinate gestures, and with monstrous thumping of feete, to pleasant soundes, to wanton songues, to dishonest verses. Maidens and matrones are groped and handled with unchaste hands, and kissed and dishonestly embraced: the things, which nature hath hidden, and moestie covered, are then oftimes by meanes of lasciviousnesses made naked, and ribaultdrie under the colour of pastime is dissembled.[76]

Yet, in reality, the promiscuity was more social than it was sexual. Country dances compelled the circulation of partners and prevented the pairing off that was to become the signature of the more genteel forms of dancing. Polite society eventually abandoned the rougher forms of popular dance because, as Sabine Baring-Gould observed, "it allows no opportunities for conversation and consequently of flirtation, as the partners stand opposite one each other, and in figures take part with other performers quite as much as with their own proper vis-a-vis."[77] As in games like "Kiss-in-the-ring," partners were made and unmade with such frequency that real intimacy beyond friendship was inhibited. The particular style of dancing prevalent at Cumberland hiring fairs seemed to one particularly acute observer to function much like the upper-class balls where the debutantes scrupulously avoided dancing with the same man twice:

> after a half-hours dancing, they return to the street again, and each party seeks a new adventure. This conduct, though it may seem rather light, particularly among the females, has nothing of criminality about it: it is a custom to which they have been long habituated, and its effects are tantamount to those of balls, assemblies, etc. among the higher orders of society.[78]

May dancing involved all the young people of the parish, who erected and defended their pole against the perambulating dancers from other villages. It was not uncommon for Glamorgan youth to attempt to steal one another's poles: "It was considered a great disgrace for ages to a parish that lost its birch, whilst on the other hand, the parish that succeeded in stealing a decked bough, and preserving its own, was held up in great esteem."[79] At such moments birth, age, even gender took second place to communal solidarity.

A similar kind of identity was displayed at the annual parish feasts and "wakes" that normally took place later in the summer. John Aubrey found these "much resorted unto by young people" in the seventeenth century; and things were no different in John Clare's time, almost two hundred years later:

> Where the fond swain delighteth in the chance
> To meet the sun tann'd lass he dearly loves
> And as he leads her down the giddy dance
> With many a token his fond passion proves
> Squeezing her hands or catching at her gloves
> And stealing kisses as chance prompts the while[80]

Here, too, roughhousing legitimated the expression of feelings that were otherwise forbidden. Young men engaged in wrestling, cudgeling, and other tests of strength that seem to us quite juvenile, but were for them an opportunity to demonstrate their prowess before an interested audience, which, as Sir Thomas Parkyns noted, was composed, mainly of young women:

> For the most Part our Country Rings for Wrestlings, at Wakes and other Festivals, consist of a small Party of young Women, who come not thither to choose a Coward, but the Daring, Healthy, and Robust Persons, fit to raise an Offspring from: I dare say, they sufficiently recommend themselves to their Sweethearts, when they demonstrate that they are of hail Constitutions, and enjoy a perfect state of Health, and like the Fatigue of that Day.[81]

Wakes, together with the annual hiring fairs that were a prominent part of the rural calendar, were known as a time for settling all manner of things: debts, indentures, quarrels, as well as courtships. The Oxfordshire Whit Hunt was a favorite time for rivals to fight over a woman, the winner take all.[82] In many places local youth would chase away the stranger, thus preserving the field to themselves. At Pudsey "he is looked upon as an interloper . . . and as a poacher on their preserves, and is often badly treated."[83] The girls were no less aggressive. They too resented outsiders, calling them names (Horsham girls were called "Hors-ham") and making up derogatory verses that later writers declared were "too coarse to quote, in which they imputed gross unchastity to each other."[84] The dancing and kissing games gave them opportunity to express their opinions in a most forceful way. Men they favored were handsomely rewarded, but those they loathed got quite another treatment. If a man had abused a girl, he was often tripped up, seized, and mounted on a stand or pole, and serenaded:

> Come on lads an' lasses an len' uz a han'
> Here's a wrong chap we've gitten astride o' this stang
> We dean't want him here
> Sike Ketment, this beast
> We're gatin' ti pin fou'd it,
> Good shuttance ti t' feast[85]

If it turned out he had gotten a girl in trouble, there was yet a worse fate: "if he didn't wed the one he'd made a drab of, why he'ed to flee the countryside, acoz folk made it too hot for him."[86]

At hiring fairs the business of finding places for the coming year was

usually completed in the morning hours. Young men and women lined
themselves up to be inspected by potential masters, who paid them
"earnest money" or "God's penny" to seal the employment contract.[87]
Once this was settled, the fun began: "fiddlers tuning their fiddles in
public houses, the girls begin to file off, and gently pace the streets,
with a view of gaining admirers; while the young men . . . follow after,
and having eyed the lasses, pick up each a sweetheart, whom they
conduct to a dancing room, and treat with punch and cake."[88] While
their elders made their bargains and paid their debts, the unmarried
went about their own business of courtship, an enterprise, which in its
rules and transactions, bore many resemblances to that which was going
on simultaneously in the marketplace. From the sixteenth through the
early nineteenth centuries, doing business invariably involved exchanging drinks or making token payments that, like the earnest money or
God's penny of the hiring, could be returned if the contracts were voided.
A similar kind of exchange went on among the young people, whose
main business was social rather than strictly economic:

> The lads get among the lasses, passing familiar jokes; some of them behave
> rather rudely, such may have been at the alehouse drinking during the
> day. If a young man prevails upon a young woman to accept a "tiding,"
> which means accepting a brandy snap and nuts, the ice is broken, and it
> is mostly looked upon by old and young as a kind of "god's penny," for
> the girl feels laid under some obligation to him; it is proof that they are
> making love to each other if not actually engaged. But if she consents to
> go with him to the public house, where there are a variety of attractions,
> mingled, we are sorry to say, with much drunkeness, it is considered a
> double proof that they are both in earnest and mean business.[89]

In places like Pudsey the first stages of courtship invariably went on,
as Joseph Lawson put it, "out of doors" and were thus subject to the
collective scrutiny and regulation of the peer group.[90] Relationships developed in a carefully prescribed order, starting with "talking," moving
to "walking," and, only much later, evolving to the most intimate stage
of "keeping company."[91] For most of their youth, both sexes shied away
from intimacy. It was acceptable to be seen together on festive occasions,
but only in groups. Even couples who were known to be courting studiously avoided daytime encounters, even going to great lengths to
avoid one another on the roads or in houses. Most of the serious courtship went on at night, out of sight of others.[92]

Nevertheless, there seems to have been strong pressure for those past
the age of confirmation to socialize. "There seems to be a sort of shame
in both sexes not to have either a 'young man' or a 'young woman,' "
noted one nineteenth-century Somerset observer. Yet, those who rural
people had traditionally called their "beau" or "sweetheart" were more
like friends than lovers. They changed very frequently; and, as Joseph
Lawson perceptively observed, these relationships consisted not so much
"in making each other's acquaintance, as in keeping each other's com-

pany as companions."[93] The joking and rough play that passed between them was all within the rules of the game; and they were both socially and psychologically different from those older youths who had moved onto the more serious stage of "keeping company." As the description of the Bradford Fair suggests, any relations resembling monogamy were strictly reserved to older youths:

> Would-be sweethearts, looked mischieviously askance at would-be swains, pairing off with them from time to time in a most mysterious manner; while full blown lovers walked about cracking nuts and nibbling brandyshap with all the assurance of matrimonially tied couples.[94]

V

As couples became more serious in their intentions, their meetings were no longer confined to feasts and fair days. They began to see one another more regularly, usually at the abode of the woman and often at night. An observation about nineteenth-century Wales could just as well apply to the earlier period:

> Everyone who knows the ways of country people is aware that courting throughout the night was the custom and that a young man going courting was terrified lest anyone should see him in "broad daylight."[95]

Night visiting allowed young people to become better acquainted without publicly committing themselves. To overcome their own inhibitions, suitors often took along a companion or what the Welsh called a *gwas caru*, courtship attendant.[96] This was the role that Roger Lowe performed for several of his friends, and they for him.[97] In Wales it was apparently common for farmers' sons and farm servants to go courting together, "the farmer's son to see the daughter of the house, and the servant to see the servant maid."[98] The presence of one or more companions gave both the man and woman a certain flexibility in deciding whether they wished to transform the initial visit into a more serious acquaintance. It also helped to have one's friends along should there be any trouble with the master of the house. The dogs might be loosed or chamber pots emptied on a visitor. In one case, a Welsh lad had his ear nailed to the kitchen table, but normally the courting parties gave as well as they took, threatening and cajoling until they gained access.[99]

In most cases it seems that parents simply retired to bed, leaving the young people to themselves. In areas of small farms in nineteenth-century Wales, it was said that "though the parties are generally careful not to disturb the household, still this kind of courting is done with the connivance of the employer, who excuses himself on the alleged ground that it would be difficult for him to keep any servants if he restricted them in these respects."[100] A farmer who would not let his daughter walk after dark with a young man would nevertheless allow him to court her under his own roof.[101] It gave him the opportunity to learn something about the fellow; and, because the courtship was clandestine, he had time to voice objections before things became too public and permanent.[102] At the same time, the ritual character of night visiting, which required the suitor to come tapping at the window, gave the daughter or servant girl an opportunity to turn away someone she objected to. She could always offer the excuse that her parents or master did not approve, thus saving herself and the young man a great deal of embarrassment.[103]

Night visiting was appropriately called "sitting up" in Cheshire and Cumberland, and "nights of watching" in Wales.[104] Roger Lowe must have had the tacit permission of the Naylor family when he spent "the first night I ever stayed up a wooing" with their daughter Mary in May 1663.[105] About a century later, Thomas Turner, a small shopkeeper in Sussex, spent two nights with a woman before deciding that she should be his wife.[106] In both these cases the couples seem to have confined their activities to conversing about the possibilities of marriage, though we know from other accounts of "bundling" practice that a certain degree of fondling and kissing was also permitted.[107] Because it was both more private and warmer, visits were allowed to the women's sleeping quarters. An early nineteenth-century doctor, who knew his Cardiganshire patients especially well, described their courting "on the beds . . . in the sight and with the approbation of their mutual friends and relations."[108] As with every other stage of courtship, strict rules controlled behavior. Naturally there were those who violated these, but they were held strictly accountable for their actions. When a woman became pregnant as a result of bundling, it was normal for her lover to marry her.[109]

While we cannot be sure just how extensive or elaborate night visiting in the sixteenth and seventeenth centuries was, it seems probable that it was widespread, perhaps reaching its peak in that period. There is no indication from Henry Best's very detailed account of Yorkshire yeoman's courtship in the 1640s whether the suitor's visits were in the day or night, but each was accompanied by a gift or love token:

> he perhaps giveth her a ten-shilling piece of gold, or a ring of that price; or perhaps a twenty shilling piece, or a ring of that price, then the next time, or the next time after that, each other time, some conceited toy or novelty of less value.[110]

It was not the value of the gift, but the giving and the acceptance that mattered. At less affluent levels of sixteenth-century society, stay busks (corset stays), hand carved and inscribed, were a favorite gift; the intricate Welsh "love spoons" made their appearance as love tokens in the seventeenth century and remained popular for the next two hundred years.[111]

A woman might encourage small gifts from several young men simply in recognition of their status as suitors. Attractive girls probably abused this on occasion, for it was not uncommon for them to have several

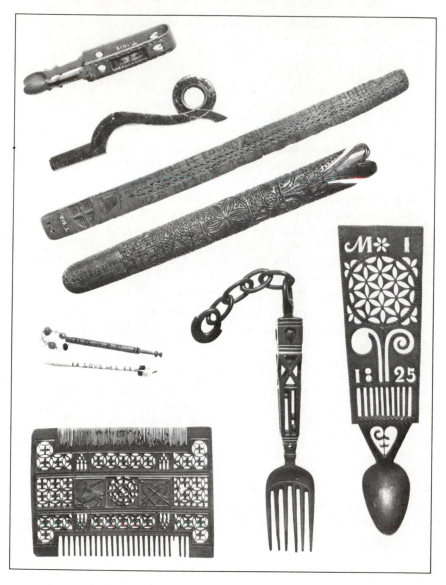

2. A variety of love tokens from the seventeenth and eighteenth centuries, including spoons, hair combs, stay busks, and knitting sheathes, all hand carved, some with love messages. (From the collections of the City of Birmingham Art Gallery)

ardent suitors. On the other hand, we find cases of sixteenth-century women suing men for the return of gifts that they had given.[112] Apparently even a series of gifts did not bind a couple so firmly that they could not extradite themselves by returning the items (often by means of a courtship attendant), and thus, like the ritual return of earnest money, free themselves from any obligation. As Lewis Davie remembered the custom:

> A young man and young woman who were courting used to break a three penny piece in two and each would take a piece as an oath of faithfulness to each other. If the courtship came to an end, the custom was to return the three penny piece as evidence of that. If this were not done awful consequences might overtake the unfaithful one of the two.[113]

Davie knew of a woman who had failed to return her gifts and for years could never look anyone in the face. Gifts were believed to have a magic power, so that to deliver a lock of hair, articles of clothing, even a kiss to another was to place oneself in that person's possession.[114] In North Yorkshire during the seventeenth and eighteenth centuries a favorite love gift was a garter, sometimes stitched with the initials of the man, "to be worn on the left leg aboon [above] the knee for to be yielded to her sweetheart after that she hath proved him true and it shall hold them both true unto each other." Verses spoke of garters as "witching, bewitching," and so were used as charms:

> Maidens used to bind about their left leg a garter made from wheat and oaten straws. These had to be drawn from a stook whilst the harvest moon was shining. Wheaten straws gave boys, oaten gave girls. As many children as they wished to have, so many straws they used. The plaiting and tying round the leg had to be done in secret. The fact that such a garter band was being worn had to be kept from the knowledge of the bridegroom. At least, he was on no account to see it whilst it graced his lady love's leg. . . . None but a true maiden dare wear such a band, the charm working evil on every child born out of wedlock if the wearer ever left the path of virtue.[115]

The intention of the giver had much to do with whether a gift had binding powers. Strong feelings were believed endowed with supernatural powers, a major reason why people were so careful and indirect in their modes of expression. Edmund Hodgson denied that he had made any commitment to Margery Wormely when he gave her "an olde grote, upon *frenship*, but as no token."[116] It seems that John Smith had given Christian Grimsdiche some money and had even received from her "silver and a handcheurchiefe," but he denied in the Chester church court that he had ever intended marriage:

> beynge askid, for what intent [he] gave so much money to the said Christian, beynge but a poor man, he sais, because he had, and wold have, to do with her, & knewe her Carnally; & not for that he would mary her. As for any other token, he sais ther was non sent from hym, or receyvid from her, by any messenger, as far as he remembres.[117]

The way a thing was given determined whether the parties were friends or lovers, whether a man was a vile seducer or true suitor, whether a woman was a potential wife or casual whore. So much depended on context that both men and women were insistent on the strictest formality, especially in the later, critical stages of courtship leading to betrothal. It was also why they employed intermediaries, so that every action should be witnessed. When a Somerset servant hid two friends nearby when her suitor came calling, she clearly intended them to notarize their dialogue:

> George, here you have come unto me often and made shows of great good will you bear me and do promise me fair but I cannot find . . . it to be good intent. . . . Many are the times . . . you have made vows and promises to me. If you mind well give me your hand upon [that] condition.[118]

Go-betweens and messengers often turn up as witnesses in church and civil court. Their testimony was vital in determining whether persons were just friends or true lovers, whether relationships were legitimate or illicit. Especially in small communities, where so much depended on hearsay and reputation, the resort to publicity was vital. Defamation suits in the late sixteenth and early seventeenth centuries suggest that both women and men were extremely sensitive to the question of sexual honor. In Yorkshire, defamation actions reached a peak in the 1590s and continued at high levels up to the 1720s. It seems that many people accused of whoredom and cuckoldry were concerned to clear their names and thus save themselves from prosecution for sexual irregularity, but at the same time there were others who were using the church courts to affirm their sexual respectability during a period when this was becoming a major test of social status.[119] That this degree of litigiousness should have resulted from the courtship practices of the period is not at all surprising. Young people who kept their relations on such a highly formal, almost legalistic basis found nothing strange in bringing one another to court to settle disputes that arose in the course of their courtships.

VI

Consent, witnessed or publicized, transformed friends into lovers and, by so doing, redefined much more than just the relationship between two persons. Homosocial relationships in this period had an intensity and volatility that is rarely encountered today, except among younger children.[120] Friendship was often as consuming as a love affair, and therefore a major psychological reason why both men and women approached marriage so late and so ambivalently, knowing full well that this meant an end to so many well-developed and emotionally sustaining associations of the very long years of bachelor and spinsterhood. Friendship overlapped with kinship and neighborliness, but differed from both in that it was chosen rather than given.[121] Its importance can be explained by the peculiar conditions of youth in the sixteenth and seventeenth centuries, a period when almost all young people, including women, left home by their mid-teens. Sometimes the cause was the death of one or another parent, but in most cases it was simply part of the normal course of life, connected with either training or employment. Poorer families could not support all their children at home and, because those higher up the economic scale required live-in labor, an exchange was facilitated. At any given time, at least fifteen percent of the population, most of them younger single men and women, were servants in the households of others, receiving room, board, and some small wages in return for their labor. Whether in formal apprenticeship or on annual hire, young people were accustomed not only to living away from home but moving about a great deal. Farm servants changed places with great frequency, usually yearly when their contracts were up, but sometimes even more often.[122] Most of the movement was within a relatively restricted area of contiguous parishes, but there were many servants who ventured on longer journeys, either out of a desire to better themselves or because necessity required it.[123] Towns fed on these migratory habits, but villages also exchanged populations at such a rapid rate that it was rare to find the same family in one place for more than two generations, especially if they were already at the lower end of the social scale where pressures to move in search of work were greatest.[124]

Women left home as early as men and experienced an equal if not greater degree of mobility as they moved from household to household. Young people ceased to be sons and daughters long before they even thought of becoming husbands and wives. In Terling, Essex, in the late sixteenth and early seventeenth centuries just over half of the grooms and over forty percent of the brides were fatherless at the time of their weddings.[125] Even those with living kin had spent little time with them, making their experience of youth strikingly different from that of the modern adolescent, who knows so little of life beyond home, school, and the immediate neighborhood, and, for whom, marriage is often the first separation from family.

It is evident then why friendship had a different meaning in their lives than it does in ours. That it carried much greater social and emotional weight is suggested by the fact that during the period the word "friend" could mean either a blood relation or a close companion.[126] Friendship involved obligations similar to those we would associate only with family. Friends were expected to stand by one another, come to one another's aid, provide bond, act as intermediaries and peacemakers, and, if need be, fight for their companions. This kind of homosocial solidarity is a little frightening to us, especially when it manifests itself among adults. We expect adolescents to gang together, but we encourage them to abandon these bonds as early as possible. In fact, we rely on interest in the opposite sex to pry the young loose from their earlier camaraderie. And we express relief when we see them settling into the kind of solitary courtship that in our day is an acceptable form of behavior for older youth.[127]

Sixteenth- and seventeenth-century courtship was neither as private nor as monogamous as our own. In its early stages, young people acted more like friends than lovers. As in their games and dances, they changed partners frequently, keeping open their options. Instead of separating the individual from his or her friends, courtship actually increased the strength of the prevailing camaraderie. Men rarely went "awooing" alone. When Thomas Smith wanted to know the intentions of Alice Leland he took along his friend Roger Lowe on the expedition. Thomas stayed discreetly out of sight while Roger did the talking. The result was a distinct success. Alice promised Roger that "she would then and there answer my desire either pro or con in the final engagement to Thomas."[128] Two years later, in 1665 Thomas was able to return the favor by assisting Roger at a difficult point in his courtship with Em Potter. He offered to talk with Em and "conclude a peace," one of the many truces that was necessary before that stormy courtship led to marriage.[129] Lancashire men of the 1660s appear to have preferred to use go-betweens when approaching both the women and the women's guardians. Roger Lowe acted for Henry Low on two occasions.[130] In another instance, Edmund Hayhurst, whom he had assisted earlier, "came an[d] enjoined me to go to Mr. Sorowcold to move hime to goe act the buisines for him for marriage."[131] In his own approaches to Ellen Marsh, Lowe used an equally complicated, though diplomatic method:

> I had before this time presented my service to Ellin Marsh of Ashton, who had a house and a liveinge, and kep a private mediator to intercede for me, from whom and by whome I received answer that she should give me the meeteinge ere long, onely I must be sacret [secret], to which I promised I would.[132]

Nothing came of this negotiation, but on other occasions Lowe used both James Naylor and Elizabeth Rosbothme as intermediaries.[133] James Jenkins volunteered his services as matchmaker, offering to introduce Lowe and Lowe's good friend, John Hasleden, to "a younge woman who is worth 11 li per Annum in house and ground."[134] Later, a Widow Jaxon suggested an even more attractive candidate, though nothing came of this either, perhaps because of the woman's reluctance.[135] As a mercer's apprentice, with no living parents or wealth of his own, Roger Lowe had good reason to be diplomatic in approaching women so obviously above his station. He had been burned once already when he became enamoured of Mary Naylor, a yeoman's daughter. She, like Ellen Marsh, suggested secrecy; and, although they were obviously fond of each other, they vowed "that we would not act soe publikely as others."[136] The reason for the clandestineness became obvious when the Naylors finally became aware of these affections. The match was broken up and Mary's brother James, previously a good friend to Roger, attempted to ruin his reputation with other eligible females.[137]

In a society of finely graded statuses, where growing differences in property and position were making courtship more complicated, young men and women often sought advice and assistance. Roger Lowe spent many an evening in the alehouse talking over the two things uppermost in his mind: "tradeing and how to gett wives."[138] The strategies devised had more the quality of a spy thriller than a love affair. Once, in order to get Ann Barrowe to meet him, Lowe "made also my self as if I ware John Naylor's man [servant] and was sent to town upon an occasion, and so had something to speake to Anne from her sister."[139] A similar furtiveness was taken for granted in all but the final stages of a courtship.

VII

While patrician families might control the marriages of their offspring, in no other part of seventeenth-century British society was parental authority nearly so absolute. Parents with some property to distribute had a strong influence on the choice of mates, but they did not often force their will on reluctant children.[140] In turn, young folk were careful not to be openly disrespectful and, whenever possible, sought to gain parental consent. This did not mean, however, that personal choice was unlimited. While peasant and artisan parents did not chaperone the young extensively, they could rely on the peer group to see that love play remained just that, innocent and polygamous. Despite the regular mingling of the sexes, illegitimacy remained infrequent and the sexual intercourse that did take place was largely confined to betrothed couples.[141] There were those, usually the "middling sort," a cut above the ordinary smallholder, who objected to peer control and insisted on internalizing the values of chastity, but for most ordinary folk the rites of youth still seemed sufficient bulwark against premature pairing.

It was one of the peculiarities of Britain (and northwestern Europe generally) that young people initially experienced love as a form of polygamous play, only gradually narrowing the field of choice as they approached marriageable age.[142] As long as village and town life remained relatively homogeneous, there was little danger in young persons making misalliances and so both women and men were allowed great freedom in the first stages of courtship. They spread their affections broadly, preferring to invest friendship with members of the same and opposite sex with the emotional intensity that we would reserve to our heterosexual relationships. Knowing that they would not have the chance to marry until their mid- or late twenties, it was understandable that they preferred rules that positively discouraged dyadic attachments and preserved friendship until the last possible moment. The rules of the game, as defined by peers, allowed Roger Lowe to shop around while at the same time permitting Mary Naylor and Ellen Marsh to entertain several suitors simultaneously. Men normally took the greater initiative, though women with property, especially widows, were often very active and few females were wholly passive. It was Ann Barrow who sent for

Roger Lowe, and Mary Naylor was by no means a shrinking violet.[143] When Mary insisted that Roger keep his attentions very private, she was ensuring a degree of latitude for herself. The intimacy that we regard as the culmination of a courtship, they viewed as an inconclusive beginning. Time and again, parties in breach of promise suits in church courts argued that private intimacy in and of itself was not proof of any commitment between two persons.[144] To go beyond friendship required the courtship be given a degree of publicity, and this was where the role of friends, acting as arbitrators and witnesses, assumed a crucial importance.

In Henry Best's account, the first stage of serious courtship, involving many visits and the exchange of gifts, lasted "halfe a yeare, or very neare." It was only then that the couple indicated their pledge to one another, which normally took the form of gifts, well-known love tokens such as rings, coins, and kerchiefs.[145] At what seems to us a very private moment, a measure of publicity and festivities was required. When Alice Wodfall and Thomas Torbock felt their courtship was entering a crucial stage in 1563, they "agreed that the said Alis suld take a daiseman [arbitrator] for her parte, & the said Thomas another for his parte. . . . " The first time they met, they "eate pigge and co[u]ld not agree." On a second try, however, they "agreed to certain Covenantes concerning marriage." This time they waited until the marriage business was complete before they "had good chere."[146]

The seriousness of a commitment was measured by the degree of publicity that attended it. Promises made in private were regarded as having little worth as compared with those before witnesses. Vows accompanied by tangible gifts had more weight than words alone. Even with regard to sexual relations, early modern people preferred a degree of publicity which seems to us, who tend to equate privacy with sincerity, a form of indecent exposure. We are shocked by the way John Cotgreve and Alice Gidlowe conducted themselves on a midsummer evening in 1549. It had apparently been a festive day and, as Cotgreve and his mates walked Alice to her home in Saltney, Cheshire, John asked her to make love with him in an empty house along the way. She had the good sense to demand a public promise of marriage and, as their friends stood by them, they made the appropriate vows, sealing these with a kiss. John then asked the witnesses "to goe a litill [little] before towarde Saltney," telling them without apparent embarrassment that he and Alice "wold shortlie come after."[147] That Cotgreve was himself a clergyman suggests just how different the sixteenth-century sense of propriety was from our own.

Most couples did not have to go quite this far to establish the seriousness of their relationship. Courtship was rarely out of sight of the community. We can infer from nineteenth-century evidence that "walking" couples were often shadowed by younger children, who reported back to their elders on what they had heard or saw. Peeping Toms were a common feature of country life, often encouraged by authorities concerned with detecting moral violations.[148] The peer group had its own ways of testing the seriousness of couples, at first mocking their affections, then physically snatching away the girl so that her young man would have to fight to get her back. The custom of "fetching and drawing" endured in Wales until very recently:

> The first few times a young man and a young woman appeared together at fairs, one of a group of young men was sent to "fetch" (*mofyn*) the young woman away on behalf of another member of the group. Her suitor had to buy her fairings in order to keep her, while the young man who tried to draw her away had to buy her fairings in order to entice her.[149]

But when friends were convinced that a relationship was serious, they showed their approval in a ritual manner. In the north of England, the ceremony was known as "pitchering," perhaps because a jug of water was held over the couple with the threat of a dowsing unless the man paid the "pitchering brass."[150] Similar hazing practices were known as "footings" in Lancashire, and, when a Cornish man was known to have "gone-a-courtin," his friends seized him, placed him in a wheel barrow, and dumped him in the nearest midden or pond. The treatment could be quite brutal if the suitor should be a stranger or refuse to pay the token fine. In the neighborhood of Kendal, the custom of asking a "footing" of a shilling of anyone courting a girl in another parish lasted well into the nineteenth century. Normally the money was spent toasting the couple, but, should the footing be resisted, what began amiably could end violently. This occurred in 1887 when four men accosted William Clarke and Jane Gibson. When Clarke refused to pay up, they grabbed him and attempted to truss him in a guano bag. Miss Gibson also complained that one of the men "put his arms around her waist and squeezed her, a proceeding which she objected to." Despite the perpetrators claim that it was all a joke, fines were levied against them.[151]

The hazing normally served to ritually express the intense feelings of jealousy and loss that were aroused any time a former friend became a lover. The hazings were all the more intense because of the high emotional value placed on friendship with both the same and opposite sexes. The endurance of the teasing and payment of the fine compensated the group symbolically and emotionally, while at the same time establishing the claim of the couple on one another. In Pudsey, couples paid "pitchering" once and were said to be "protected ever after."[152] It seemed a small price to pay as license for entering into the subsequent and more serious stages of courtship.

Peasants and artisans were perfectly capable of feeling those strong emotional attachments we call love, but their culture did not prepare them for the abrupt change from being a friend to becoming a lover.

The first encounter with passion for another individual could therefore be very upsetting. Roger Lowe was deeply shaken by his feelings for Mary Naylor:

> Att these times my effections ran out violently after her, so as that I was never contented one day to the end unless I had seen her, and cheefly my effections were sett upon her virtues and womenly quallities.[153]

Ballads of the period often dealt with the theme of unrequited love and there is no reason to believe that people then were any less capable of affection than we are, though they were undoubtedly more guarded about its expression. Lowe never allowed himself to fall in love with such intensity again. Even his relationship with Em Potter, the woman for whom he later developed a genuine affection and eventually married, was less intense. He and his contemporaries seem to have preferred it that way, for, if he was uneasy about his own strong feelings, he was even more fearful of the passions of others. He was constantly worried about the kind of ruinous betrayal of confidences he had experienced at the hands of James Naylor, Mary's brother, and, for a time, his best friend. The two had been very close during the time Roger courted Mary and James was wooing Roger's old flame, Ann Barrow. But the confidences Roger shared became a source of embarrassment when James began to question his finances:

> Nay, and above all he backebitt me, and said it would doe well if I could gett monys against my comeing out [ending apprenticeship], and said I durst never come in his father's sight, which was a lye. He said as soon as his sister angerd hime he would tell his father all—and this is the actinge of a seeminge pretended freind to me as can be, when in truth [he] is no better than a deivelish, malicious, dissembleing, knavish rascall.[154]

Roger's feelings on this occasion bear a striking resemblance to those he expressed when he finally broke with Mary six months later: "I spoke Roughly to Mary and shee seemed to be very effectionate, but I litle matered it. I cald [called] her a false dissemblinge harted person. She took it heinously."[155] In both instances, strong affection was almost ritually transformed into fierce enmity. In a small world, where gossip mattered a great deal, people let the world know who were their friends and who were their enemies. The dramatic public breaks with James and Mary Naylor were Roger Lowe's way of protecting his honor. This talk of a "knavish rascall" and "false dissemblinge harted" lover discharged whatever guilt he may have felt and cleared the way for new relationships. Other people were able to make and break relationships in a similar manner. When Gabriell Holt was rejected by his sweetheart, he not only spread it about the parish that "he did defile [her] body," but even moved to have her presented at church court as an immoral woman.[156] Her only recourse in such a situation would have been to sue him as a slanderer, an action which women were resorting to with

3. In the polygamous early stages of courtship, social conflict and emotional tension were frequent. Haynes King captured this in his *Jealousy and Frustration*, a Victorian rendering of an earlier age. (Courtesy of the Board of Trustees of the Victoria and Albert Museum)

increasing frequency in the late sixteenth and early seventeenth centuries.[157]

Like most people, Roger Lowe was perpetually concerned about his reputation. He was upset when he heard that a servant girl was telling tales about him; and, when he discovered that a William Morris had told Em Potter that he had been born a bastard, he confronted the man and, with the assistance of his friends, thrashed him.[158] Although Lowe never mentions witchcraft in his diary, his belief in the power of strong feelings, both positive and negative, is clear enough. By keeping things as public as possible, he sought to protect his reputation and prevent those rumors that, in a small community, could be so damaging to day-to-day social and economic relationships. While his dramatic breaks with friends and lovers were not without their cost, including deep depressions he went through after each episode, he was able to find in religion a comfort that made up for the sense of loss. We find him praying fervently, often in fields and sometimes in ditches, after each of his breakups with various women. And on the same day he broke with James Naylor, his diary reads:

And now it's best to gett and fear God for a friend, for we see man will faile us and world will be faile but God will not faile those that trust in hime.[159]

Soon the intense devotion would also ebb and Lowe would return to the alehouse to make new friends and talk, with renewed enthusiasm, about ways to get a wife. As a literate man, he made himself indispensable, scribing love letters, writing out wills and indentures, and serving as a notary to business both public and private. He was paid for such services either by a small fee or a few tankards of ale. For friends, however, he felt a special obligation and often involved himself as witness to their affairs. Richard Asmulle asked him and John Hasleden to go to Hindley where "a wench had laid a child on him. So we went, and in Mr. Lanckton's feilds she was, and she ardently manifested hime to be the father of the child in her wombe; so we parted." Presumably they testified against the woman, for on the way home Richard rewarded them with drinks at Hugh Platt's alehouse.[160] Thomas Tickle appears also to have had an equally compelling reason for inviting his friends to his wedding, for the day after he asked Roger and John Hasleden to accompany him and his new bride to Reinford:

The reason for our goeing was to avicee [evince] old Sepon the young couple's marriage. We came tither and the old man seemed displeased, but it was but a while.[161]

Friends were of great assistance when a marriage was opposed by parents or masters. Some months after Tickle's wedding, Lowe was again invited to play a part in a marriage, this time that of his fellow apprentice, John Chadocke. The groom lavished expensive favors (ribbons) on his guests, who loyally supported him by parading the couple through the town before giving them a splendid send-off. The fact that young Chadocke had "stoln his love away from Mr. Whitehead's" no doubt had much to do with this show of solidarity.[162] In any case, John Chadocke repaid Roger three years later when he went with him to Leigh to confront William Morris. Between them they "buffeted hime very mery."[163]

It was somewhat rare for a married man like Chadocke to remain involved in bachelor matters. Friendships were strongest between those in the single state. Married men rose to superior status and authority. They were likely to side with other married men whether it be in the village games or parish politics. In the sixteenth and seventeenth century, as the community became more economically divided, the boundary was further reinforced by considerations of property and status. The question of marriage invariably aroused those sensitivities. When James Naylor discovered that the impecunious Roger Lowe was serious about his sister, his sense of social superiority surfaced and friends became enemies. Even where there was nothing to separate old friends socially, the course of courtship and the approach of marriage meant a change in their relationship. Roger Lowe's most loyal friend was his fellow nonconformist, John Hasleden. They were often together, drinking, gaming, assisting one another when in trouble. When John got himself apprenticed by mistake when drunk, it was with Roger that he "contrived how to gett hime of [off]."[164] John thought it a great joke to inform Roger that he had been cited for dissent at the bishop's court, but only once did they allow themselves to be pitted against one another, and then only after considerable drink: "John and I begann to bett each with the other, which was contrarie to custome that we should act so against another."[165] While courtship in our time tends to separate young people from their friends, these bachelors' quests for wives (and we must assume spinsters' quests for husbands) brought them closer together as they seconded one another through the many twists and turns that led to marriage. So it was to be expected that Lowe's diary should record in March 1665: "I was envited and went to John Hasleden's mariage att Winwick; was his manne."[166] Thereafter, however, John virtually disappears from Roger's diary.

VIII

Betrothal normally marked withdrawal from the world of peers. It was the crucial rite of transition, involving separation from the homosocial world, the beginning of the liminal phase before final incorporation into the roles assigned to married folk. As Gouge suggested, the betrothed were "betwitx single persons and married persons," in a social category of their own, a status complete with liberties denied both the celibate and the married. Like all those who live outside the ordinary rules of behavior, the betrothed were the object of both attention and anxiety. They were under great pressure to complete their rite of passage, so much so that the time from formal betrothal to wedding seems to us almost indecently brief. Henry Best's model couple took only about six months "from the first goinge to the conclusion," while William Whiteway was betrothed and wed in a little over two months. "The longer you court, the shorter you'll live together," was the way the Welsh put it. In England the saying went: "Happy is the wooing that's not long in adoing."[167]

Today's couples often move toward marriage in a gradual, almost casual manner, but then the transition was very abrupt and highly formalized, consisting of betrothal vows always accompanied by tangible symbols such as rings, coins, locks of hair, trinkets, even pieces of lace or clothing. Bridget Rose was not unmindful of the aesthetic powers of her gifts when she gave as her pledge to Edward Arden a "sixpence and a cluster of nuttles [nettles]," explaining to him that "as close as these three stick together, so fast should her harte stick to him."[168] At the same time that these "privy contracts" drew on ancient pagan imagery, they also borrowed directly from the church's own ceremony, using words extracted directly from the Book of Common Prayer. There was an increased concern for literalism, but at the same time an evident faith in the magic power of the book itself. When John Brotherton, a Lancashire man, engaged himself to Alice Ince in the 1560s, he brought a book with him. His witness was unable to say which book it was, but "he thinkes hit was a Psalter-boke." While the witness held the book, John took Alice by the right hand and said, "I take the, Alice, to be my wief and non other woman, so God me helpe, and the Contentes of this boke." Alice was not satisfied, however, and declared that "those wordes were not well and sufficient," making John alter his vows to the following: "Here I take the, Alice Ince, to my wief, before all other women, so God me helpe, & Holidam! and bie [by] this boke." Satisfied, she then spoke the same words and they kissed. The ceremony, intended to impress both Alice and the witnesses, accomplished its ends. In court the latter were able to recall every vivid detail.[169]

Bystanders were also able to recall that Margery Pegge "took a shilling or xii[d] out of her purse and delivered the same unto the said Richard Thornton. . . . " He, in turn, took out a pair of gloves from his sleeve and "said in effect as foloweth, viz: I give you this (meaning the said gloves) on condition that I will marie you and be your wedded husband and thereupon I will plight, etc." Because the acceptance of such a gift laid the receiver under strong obligation to the giver, Margery, who later decided that she "would never marrye while she lived," had great difficulty in breaking her vows to Thornton. The clasping of hands, the contemporary way of striking any kind of bargain, had a similar binding power.[170]

Couples made their vows first in the presence of friends, not parents or kindred. There were of course those couples whose parents and guardians were deceased or who were making second marriages that required no dowry or portion. But, in addition to these, there were those matches where the couples feared some objection based on personal animosity or, what was becoming more common in a period of increasing social differentiation, status considerations. There had always been social gradations in both town and village, but now the number of propertyless Roger Lowes was multiplying as the gap between the propertied and propertyless widened in the late sixteenth and early seventeenth centuries.[171] Men like Lowe saw their best chance lay not with the parents but with the women themselves. By the late sixteenth century, the number of what contemporaries called "private spousals" were increasing at such a rate as to cause great concern among both parents and ecclesiastical authorities.[172]

"Private spousals" is something of a misnomer because most of those who betrothed themselves did so in a quite public manner. The scene was often the alehouse on a market or feast day, always an auspicious time for all kinds of business. It was at the Ashton alehouse that Roger Lowe spotted his future wife, Em Potter, and courted her by treating her to drinks. The alehouse provided a useful setting for publicizing a relationship in the making. Robert Peircy invited twelve friends to join with him and Agnes Davidson on the occasion of their trothplight. They drank and ate for more than an hour before the couple recited their vows, kissed, and Robert gave Agnes a ring and a piece of gold. Witnesses who later testified to the event also remembered that the "said Robert dranke to the said Agnes, and cauld hir his wyf, and she lyke manner dranke to the said Robert Peircy, and cauld him husband." The exchange was not dissimilar to that which took place a century later in the alehouse at Shipham, Somerset, during the village's annual fair. In this case, the man asked the woman for all to hear "what her intent was touching marriage between them, and whether she would go forward to the finishing thereof." At first she expressed reluctance because her aunt and uncle were opposed to the match, but finally agreed to marry him within the year if he would "keep it silent and not let my friends know of it." The couple then exchanged silver coins to complete the ceremony.[173] In a similar case of family opposition, Hugo Harold took Rosa Clarke by the hand, telling her:

> Rosa so it is that we have been in love together a long tyme and have stayed, thinking to have our frends goodwills but we see yt we cannot procure it therefore lett me know what you say to it. . . .

She then replied:

> You are the man that I do make choice of and therefore I do not care for their goodwills or consent I shall have never a grote the more than yt is my owe therefore I will look to myselfe.[174]

Hugo and Rosa then went and repeated their vows before witnesses, making sure there would be a record. It was necessary to get the form of the spousal, including the words, exactly right. Sometimes the couple trusted themselves to do this, but in other cases they called on a friend to act in the ancient role of "orator," leading them through the ceremony. In one such sixteenth-century betrothal a sixty-year-old weaver, John Patteson, joined the hands of William Richardson and Margaret Joyce, saying "now I have done asmoche as ther goostly father could doo, and I take recorde of theis wor[d]s of you that stands bye."[175] In the next century it was a blacksmith who performed the rite for a Somerset couple. According to those present, he directed them to speak the words "to have and to hold for better for worse, till death us do part," join hands, kiss, divide a silver piece, and then "acknowledge that they were man and wife."[176]

In many instances the couple went a step further and consummated their vows immediately. This is what Elizabeth Cawnt and Robert Hubbard did in 1598. They exchanged vows, coins, joined hands, kissed, and then went to bed in her house. "The next morning after the giving and receiving of the said piece of gold she the said Elizabeth did send for certeine of her frends to come to her house and there declared before them that they viz the said Robert and Elizabeth had concluded a marridge betwene them." When brought to court, their action was said to be "the comon use and custom within the countie of Leicester":

> anie man being suter to a woman in the way of mariadge is upon the daie apointed to make a final conclusion of the marridge before treated of: if the said marridge be concluded and contracted then the man doth most commonlie remaine in the house where the woman doth abide the night next folowing after such contracte otherwyse he doth departe without staying the night.[177]

George Johnson was following an ancient practice when he spent lavishly on the festivities celebrating his vows with Anne Yate, a victualler, and therefore a particularly good catch. The invited guests saw that Anne let George take money from her purse, which meant "that they were reputed and taken for man and wief amonge their neighbours." Witnesses noted that George moved in with Anne, "which thinges wold not have bene suffrid, but that the parish thought they were man and wief before God; for they did leye in one house and nothinge betwix them but a broken wall and a paintid clothe . . . neighbours thereabout did take them as man and wief, in so much that they have laine together in bed, and so used them selfes as man and wief."[178]

The 1590s were a time when vows in defiance of parental and parish authority were becoming so numerous as to provoke much public comment. Sixteenth-century ministers were repeatedly asked "whether they have exhorted yung folke to absteyn from privy contracts, & not to marry without the consent of such of their parents and fryends as have authority over them, or no." Puritans like Robert Cleaver were particularly insistent that all vows should be performed in the presence of parents, kinfolk, and "honest witnesses."[179] Most couples complied with the injunction of publicity, but they did not accept absolute parental power. In reality, this initial set of vows was a way of protecting themselves against patriarchy and legitimating their own choice of spouse. Because the church itself accepted as valid proper vows made between consenting parties, self-betrothal was a way of neutralizing parental and communal power. By the end of the sixteenth century it had become for those who stood in defiance of patriarchal authority a rite of great strategic significance in the "politics" of courtship and marriage. The next century saw an even further elaboration of these ancient forms of self-marriage, especially among the lower orders, who had less to lose from acts of filial disobedience.

Public opinion was still very much on the side of young lovers at the end of the seventeenth century. Richard Gough thought it outrageous that John Hussey should marry his ward, Elinor Butter, to his own son for the sake of her portion: "Hee might rather have taken notice of our old English proverbe, which sayes, that to marry children togeather, is the way to make whoremongers and whores." As it turned out, he was right. Elinor made life such hell for her husband that he ended up leaving her and giving her back the full amount of her portion just to get rid of her.[180] Still, by asking consent of their parents, young people perpetuated the fiction of the patriarchal veto. Ralph Josselin's daughters all brought their prospective suitors home to visit. This was largely a matter of courtesy, although Reverend Josselin regarded it his right to inspect the future sons-in-law, counseling against those he felt were unsuitable. Yet it seems unlikely that he would have opposed a daughter's choice had her heart been set on a particular man. Only one of his daughters married under the age of majority. Her sisters were in no rush to wed, but once they had set their minds to do so they, like their contemporaries, wasted no time. Jane's suitor asked consent in January 1670, in March the couple "testified to their agreement to marry," and at that point Josselin began to gather together Jane's portion. The wedding took place in August.[181]

By the time young people came to make their vows known to parents, there had already been a good deal of negotiating of an informal kind. The peer group had helped narrow the field and wholly unacceptable candidates had already been eliminated. The preliminary visiting usually resolved any lingering doubts, so that the patriarch was ready to move swiftly toward the next stage, agreement between families:

> See soone as the younge folkes are agreed and contracted, then the father of the mayd carryeth her over to the younge mans howse to see howe they like of all, and there doth the younge mans father meete them to treate of a dower, and likewise of a joynture or feeoffment for the woman; and then doe they allsoe appointe and sette downe the day of the marriage, which may perhapps bee aboute a fortnight or three weeks after. . . .[182]

In Wales this occasion was called "appointing the day." It was a time of hard bargaining and, if all went well, considerable festivity. Bullinger spoke of "a great feast & superfluous bancket." When Lancelott Ferry betrothed his granddaughter "after the contry [country]" manner in 1573, he did so in such a grand fashion that one of the invited guests, William Laborn, was moved to remark that the rite was carried out "as freely as ever this examinate [Laborn] hather done it at the church doore, which hath been twise maried."[183] Whether a "private spousal" or family affair, betrothal constituted the recognized rite of transition from friends to lovers, conferring on the couple the right to sexual as well as social intimacy. It was also what Victor Turner calls a liminal or unstructured moment, a time when the couple had the acknowledged right to break out of fixed roles and change their minds. Betrothal granted freedom to explore for any personal faults or incompatibilities that had remained hidden during the earlier, more inhibited phases of courtship and could be disastrous if carried into the indissoluable status of marriage. This ritual function was explicitly recognized by Robert Cleaver, who argued that sufficient time should be granted "for the learning of the triall of all lets and impediements, whereby promised marriage might be hind-ered . . ." and to consider the "troubles and afflictions that followe marriage."[184]

There was always tension involved in this rite of separation. Joking with peers or a festive meal with the new in-laws helped overcome the awkwardness. When Walter Woodward, accompanied by his elder sis-ter, paid his call on his future father-in-law, the first thing they did was feast:

> After a while they sat down at table and ate and drank together and in the process of talk . . . Walter told them that he did bear goodwill in the way of marriage to Christian and asked . . . whether he could have his goodwill to marry with her.[185]

Once the consent was granted, hard bargaining began. It appears that Walter asked Christian's father to support him for ten years, a price the old man found too high: "That is too much Walter. I have other children more to help so well as she, and if it be so that you like my daughter so well as you say you do, I will help her as far as my power will stretch." In the end, Walter settled for less.[186]

Women proved no less adept at striking a bargain, even taking the initiative, especially when they had some wealth of their own. Katherine Marshall and Christopher Robson had already exchanged rings when Katherine decided it was time to finalize the terms of the marriage set-tlement. As a young woman worth at least ten pounds, and possessing a house bringing in another four pounds annually, she must have felt herself in a strong position when she approached Robson's natural father, asking him to settle twenty marks on the marriage. When the man offered only five pounds, she felt justified in terminating the relation-ship. Robson subsequently brought suit in the Durham bishop's court on the grounds that he "had been as good a bargain then as she was, if the matter had gone forward."[187]

Not everyone made as direct an approach as Walter and Katherine, however. Many employed intermediaries—siblings, close friends, well-known matchmakers, who often included the parish priest—presumably to avoid embarrassment should they meet with rebuff or the negotiations fail. Ben Jonson's Parson Palate filled such a role:

> He is the prelate of the parish here
> And governs all the dames, appoints the cheer
> Writes down all the bills of fare, pricks all the guests
> Makes all the matches and the marriage feasts
> Within the ward; draws all the parish wills,
> Designs the legacies and strokes the gills
> Of the chief mourners[188]

Matchmakers sometimes had to enter into complicated transactions with the relatives of the couple in order to get their approval. Especially

4. *The Refusal* by David Wilkie, 1814. Based on a Robert Burns poem, Wilkie portrays the tension resulting from the young woman's rejection of her suitor. (Courtesy of the Board of Trustees of the Victoria and Albert Museum)

in second marriages, there could be many objections to be dealt with before the wedding could take place. Portions settled on the children were often a part of the betrothal agreement, but kinspeople also sometimes had to be satisfied with cash or goods before they would give consent to the marriage.[189] Once this was worked out, it was normal for the couple again to exchange vows and gifts before witnesses. When William Mead had gained Margaret Rome's mother's consent, he took her by the hand and, in front of her mother, pledged "I doe here take

you to my wief, and I doe give you here my faith and trothe." Margaret
pledged in similar words, but the mother, worried that there had been
no other family present, requested that they repeat the process before
her son-in-law "that there mighte be a daie a pointed for the marriage."[190]

IX

Those who had the support of family and kin found it easiest to marry
quickly and comfortably, but in the late sixteenth and early seventeenth
centuries there were more and more young people who had no farm to
inherit or guild membership to rely on. For many, perhaps the majority,
the liminality associated with betrothal, especially the right to a change
of mind without loss of status or honor, was its most essential feature.
Richard Lowe found himself in the uncomfortable position of having to
beg off marriage when the parents of his intended bride did not fulfill
their part of the bargain: "Her frendes promysed hym a pece of good
[portion] and would not performe it, so that [Lowe] was laoth to marie,
and not well able to kepe her, except he had had that marriage good."
As for Henry Smith, it was his apprenticeship that kept him from fulfilling his promise to Elizabeth Frysell.[191]

Migrant laborers, soldiers, and especially seamen, all had good reason
for valuing the liminal quality of betrothal. It seems that Roger Bybbye
had a flexible arrangement in mind when he approached the Mayor of
Liverpool in 1563 with a request that he betroth him to Eleanor Man-
waring. At first the Mayor was reluctant, but Roger explained: "I have
a voiage beyond the sea, toward Ireland, and wold have one in the
meane season to loke to thinges in myne house; and therefore, I pray
you, let her be made my wief, and then I trust you will suffer her to be
my housekeper without suspicion." At this "earnest request" the Mayor
consented, knowing that even if a church marriage never took place, a
proper betrothal would protect Eleanor's honor, Roger's property, and
his own responsibility to public morality.[192]

Although betrothal was considered binding as long as the conditions
were met, it was not an indissoluble contract. It protected both parties
in case it should be terminated. Betrothal placed the man under obligation to support or marry the woman should pregnancy result. On the
other hand, his liability in terms of property was strictly limited. In the
Lake District in the sixteenth century a handfast was supposed to last
no longer than a year and a day. If, at that time, either party wished to
end the relationship, they had a customary right to do so. Similar time
limits were in effect in Wales and on the Isle of Portland.[193] When Henry
Peddle of Somerton agreed to betrothal, he did so with the stipulation
that he should be free from all obligations by payment of a sum of 20
nobles to his betrothed.[194] To break a betrothal it was necessary to do
so publicly before either a priest, parents, or "other honest witnesses."[195]

This was apparently the meaning of a seventeenth-century entry found in the parish register of Clare, Sussex:

> I, Susan Ward of Clare, do resign all my right to John Manson to Susan Frrost, so that they may proceed to marriage.[196]

Intermediaries were often used to terminate a betrothal. Anthony Hourde asked Marion Martin to accept the arbitration of four persons, two of his choice and two of hers, to decide what penalty he should pay for breaking their contract.[197] Normally the return of gifts or the payment of an equivalent sum settled it if both consented, though sometimes a third party, usually a new suitor, would pay off the contract and thus free the woman to marry him. Edward Croxon promised Henry Marshall a ten-shilling piece if he would give up his claim to Joan Brewer. When the money was not forthcoming, Marshall forbid the banns of their wedding in an effort to get his money.[198] While on the surface of it this may seem like wife barter, the payment was more symbolic than substantial, similar to the return of earnest money that normally freed people from other kinds of conditional contracts. On the whole, the rules of betrothal seem to have favored the woman, perhaps the reason why we find so many of the early breach of contract suits in church and civil courts brought by them. *A Treatise of Feme Coverts or the Lady's Law*, published in 1732, established that if a man had a kiss from his betrothed he could recover at most half his gifts to her, but "the Female is more favoured, for whatsoever she gave, were there kissing or no kissing in the case, she may demand and have all again."[199] Perhaps Marion Martin was demanding more of Anthony Hourde than he wanted to give or perhaps she simply wanted to hold him to his original promises, but, in any case, she, and women like her, often went to the church courts, which were capable of stopping a marriage if it were proved that a prior contract existed unexpired.[200]

Because so much of the business of church courts in the sixteenth and seventeenth centuries were disputes over betrothals, we can assume that an even greater number were made and unmade without resorting to the judgment of outsiders.[201] Sometimes disputes were settled by arbitrators. The parish priest played a prominent role, but it was the popular recognition of the liminality of betrothal that allowed people to make and break relationships without unduly disrupting their own lives and the peace of the community. As a time set aside for establishing not only the economic but the social and psychological basis for marriage, betrothal rules took into account not only the complications that could arise in a society where marriage was only partially a matter of personal choice, but the difficulties of transforming friends into lovers. Like all such "liminal" situations, it suspended the normal determinancy of social relationships, giving the couple the time and the leverage to explore what, given the absence of divorce, was an irreversible decision.[202]

X

With betrothal began a short but very special period when, for the first time, the young people would act and feel like a couple. It marked their separation from the homosocial world, from those ties which were so strong that they could only be severed by a series of taboos against the usual forms of sociability. It was believed that the couple should not appear in church to hear their own banns read for otherwise their children would be born deaf and dumb.[203] Seclusion was regarded as vital, for, as Robert Cleaver put it, the couple needed time not only to gather together their material resources, but "to think on the causes why they are to be married and the duties of marriage."[204] Yet, as he and other puritan commentators were uncomfortably aware, the heterosocial also implied the heterosexual. The time between betrothal and wedding was normally conceived of as a moment of sexual license. By popular consent, the betrothed were allowed a degree of intimacy that in other circumstances would have been forbidden. Ellen Ricroft thought nothing wrong in intercourse after betrothal; and her neighbors refused to condemn her just because she "consented to his [her lover's] follye."[205] Like all similar rites of passage, betrothal placed the participants outside the usual rules of behavior.[206] And it was precisely this aspect of betrothal ritual that concerned puritans like Cleaver, who warned that "parties affianced are to be admonished, to abstaine from the use of marriage, and to behave themselves wisely, chastly, lovingly, and soberly, till the day apointed do come." But most people who were, as Gouge put it, "in a middle degree betwixt single persons and married persons," interpreted their duties differently. They felt impelled to become familiar with one another; and, as the high rates of prebridal pregnancy varying between ten and thirty percent during the period suggest, this included sexual intimacy.[207]

But even puritan parents winked at things they would not have tolerated under other circumstances; and Ann Winch's father allowed her to live for five weeks with her betrothed so she could make up her mind whether she was really in love with him.[208] Betrothal could obliterate differences in rank and alter the relationship between the sexes. It gave females a measure of choice and a degree of power more equal to that of men. For a brief moment they were the center of attention. Having been courted and fought over, they were in a position to make demands that were not possible for mere spinsters or wives. Betrothal was for them a magic moment, when they were the object of their lover's most ardent affections, their parent's sentimentality, and their rivals' envy. As such, it was also a moment of certain danger, one that should not be prolonged beyond a specified point.

Couples were encouraged to call their banns within just a few weeks of their betrothals. In most places the announcement of banns was a communal event, the last opportunity for those who objected to a wedding to make this known. In Montgomeryshire it was the custom for fathers wishing to stop a wedding to place a coin on the altar, thereby requesting a word with the parson. Others raised objections in a more direct manner by standing up in church. The parson was obligated to look into the matter. In other cases it was disappointed lovers who stepped forward to forbid, either by presenting evidence of prior betrothal or, as when Jane Sutton objected to Henry Robins marriage at Maidstone in 1655, by stating "she, the said Jane, is with child."[209] The banns books give few clues as to why marriages were cancelled, but it appears that banns provided the occasion for pressing claims—some just, but others vengeful. In 1657, during the period of civil marriage when the church courts were not adjudicating, Alice Webbe took her objections directly to the Wiltshire justices, declaring before them: "I forbid the publicat" on tell [until] hee White hath given mee satisfaction." The court called the parties involved together and decided that Webbe's claim of prior betrothal to White "was not lawful contract." The marriage, somewhat delayed, was allowed to proceed.[210]

Many objections, based on prior contract by one of the parties to a third person, ended up in church court for adjudication. Many were legitimate disputes, but sometimes an objection would be raised with blackmail in mind. Jeanette Williams admitted that she had stopped Charles Williams' wedding for the purpose of extorting money from him.[211] The possibility of such things happening was one of the reasons why increasing numbers of persons were avoiding banns by purchasing licenses to marry. These allowed them to marry without prior public notice and thus avoid embarrassing situations.[212]

But in the seventeenth century marriage by license was still largely confined to the superior orders, and most ordinary people would have felt vulnerable had they not gone through the "askings" or "spurrings," as the banns were called. This was their way of ensuring communal approval. In seventeenth-century Yorkshire, the congregation shouted in unison "God speed 'em well" after the third reading. In other places, the clerk spoke the blessing and the parish added its "Amen."[213] Banns were both an important social and "political" occasion. Women could rely on the church to compel marriage in cases where the banns had been asked and approved. Failure to follow through was called "mock of the church" and subject to fines, penance, and even excommunication.[214] Katherine Abbott was able to recover not only her honor but her goods by proving that, although Robert Dewgard "maketh a laughing stocke of the mater; and bragethe that he will not marry her," he had called their banns.[215] At Great Yarmouth in the early nineteenth century there was at least one fine a year for "mock of the church";[216] and, as late as the 1890s, a Norfolk clergyman was asked by an underage couple, whose banns had been twice refused, "What is to pay for mocking the church?"[217]

Banns were considered so binding that we sometimes find people calling them without their lover's knowledge so as to hold them to their promises.[218] Those who had second thoughts about marriage were said to be "hung in the bell ropes" and were taunted as being "rue bargains."[219] Even more effective was the public mockery known as rough music, which was used in Cold Aston, Derbyshire, as late as 1886 when a pair who had been "asked" in the local church fell out just before their wedding day. In an effort to compel the marriage, the villagers burned them in effigy.[220]

The banns were also a test, subjecting the couple to much teasing, practical jokes which served to clarify the couple's decision and confirm their removal from the homosocial world of single persons. Although puritans were horrified by the jokes and songs that accompanied the calling of banns, ordinary folk endured these with the same good humor that had helped them through the ritual "footings," which had accompanied the earlier stages of courtship. "Why, thoo's gotten one spur on thee" was a common jibe in northern England, directed at men who had undergone the first of the three Sunday "spurrings." Much of the joking was sexual, a reminder to the couple of the essential functions of marriage and, at the same time, an expression of envy. Joking also suggested the many well-known pitfalls of marriage, comparing it with a physical injury. "Vallen plumb out o' the pulpit lass Zunday," was a Wiltshire comment. In Lincolnshire it was said "He's gott broken ribbed today," while in Somerset people talked of the man breaking his knees. The man was invariably the one most exposed to these tests of resolve, and in Somerset it was also the custom for "expectant bridegrooms to have their knees rubbed or bandaged by their sympathizing friends."[221] The significance of the step for both women and men was further emphasized by the ringing of church bells. The so-called "spur peal" was said to ward off evil spirits and secure the fortunes of the marriage.[222]

By the end of the seventeenth century the joking and teasing that accompanied each calling of banns had become repugnant to a large segment of the upper classes. Some lesser folk were also adopting a quieter mode of marriage, though Richard Gough, a defender of the old ways, heaped scorn on those "proud, foolish Girles" of his native Myddle who refused to have their names read out before the parish.[223] To yeomen like Gough the ritual of the banns was as much a part of a proper marriage as the wedding itself. It assured that the couple had made a fair trial of their affections and that, despite all the teasing, were ready to take on the burdens as well as the pleasures of matrimony. In a society where marriage was the central economic and social institution such testing was essential. It was only when the pair had passed through this final segment of the extended rites of transition that they—and the community—were ready for the big wedding.

CHAPTER 2

∽⫝⌇⫝⌇⫝⌇⫝⌇⫝⌇⫝⌇⫝⌇⫝⌇⫝⌇⫝⌇⫝⌇⫝⌇⫝⌇⫝⌇∽

A Maie Game of Marriage:
The Politics of Big Weddings

Very little is known about weddings before and even during the six-teenth century. What can be found out comes often from observers who were not at all sympathetic to the rites inherited from the Middle Ages. The puritan element, who wanted to focus attention exclusively on the couple, were particularly critical of the public festivities that were a part of every big wedding. They scorned the popular practice of "carrying of wheate sheafess on their heads, and casting of corne," because, in their view, this made "a Maie game of marriage, [rather] than a holy institution of God."[1] In the late sixteenth century people were frequently brought before the church courts for what reformers described as heathen or papish practices. In 1584 some Oxfordshire men were forced to defend themselves for bell ringing. They denied "anie superstition nor [being] in anie contempt of the Queenes lawes," and said "they did yt because there was a brydalle the same daye."[2] Everywhere the old practice of parading the couple to church and home again was on trial. Henry Grey of Sowthrawelde, near London, was charged in 1604 with "making prep-arations with others, for to daunce the morice [morris] in the sermon while; and that they mett with the bridegroome and came dauncing the morris home with them."[3] No less suspect were the various forms of teasing and testing that were a part of the big wedding tradition. A West Ham man was said to have given "great offence to the congregation" when he "gott a bough hanged with rope endes and besett with nettles and other weedes, and conveyed the same in the streate and churchyard before the bryde."[4] And it was thought no laughing matter when in 1605 Edward Row put a pair of horns on the church gate while the wedding of Thomas Brocke and Rebecca Foster was in progress.[5]

Reformers believed that the medieval church had appropriated too many "heathenish toys" in an effort to popularize its own marriage ceremony. Milton blamed this on the avarice and ambition of the priest-hood, who "use many rites and ceremonies, especially judging it to be

profitable, and the increase of their authority."[6] The effort to purge the
big wedding, a movement which came closest to success during the brief
period of civil marriage 1653–60, encountered deep popular resistance
however. Some dissenting sects eliminated the publicity that gave offense to the purists, but the best the established church was able to do
was separate the feasting, music, dancing, and magic from the church
service itself. This did not put an end to the practices themselves, for
they took on a new life in unexpected ways. Denied the sanction of the
church, the big wedding moved to the tavern and the village green. The
processions to and from church became ever larger and more festive,
while the magical and social rites that had once been indistinguishable
from the church's own liturgy grew more rooted and resilient as they
became associated with a popular culture that during the sixteenth and
seventeenth centuries escaped the control of both religious and civil
authorities. When antiquarians and folklorists later recorded the details
of the big wedding, they were observing not the direct survival of a
medieval heritage, but forms unique to, and largely the product of,
developments since the Reformation.

The big wedding took its distinctive form during the early modern
period, but so too did those clandestine and irregular marriage practices
that also proliferated during the sixteenth and seventeenth centuries.
This fragmentation reflected not only the disintegration of ecclesiastical
marriage discipline, but differentiation by class. If there was no longer
a singular marriage custom, it was because there was no longer a common culture, even at the village level. The big wedding was being challenged from one side by puritan marriage practice, reflecting the habits
and values of groups intent on rising above what they regarded as vulgar
popular culture, and from the other side by a proletariat whose attitude
toward marriage was at odds with both the old peasant and artisan
traditions and the new puritan values.

I

Despite erosions at both ends of the social scale, the big wedding tradition remained dominant throughout the sixteenth and seventeenth
centuries. For a majority, wedding continued to be a collective event,
necessarily involving family, kin, age mates, and neighbors. We tend
to think of wedding as the legal act joining two individuals. However,
as we have already seen, the couple had already been created by betrothal. The wedding served a different, broader set of purposes. It
established the couple's relationship to the wider world through a series
of highly ritualized and dramatic events that began with the fetching of
the bride from her home and ended with the formal inauguration of a
new household. Because family and household were so much more than
private relationships and the newly created husband and wife so much

more than just a couple, the wedding was necessarily a public event, full of meaning and importance to the entire community.

Couples were normally allowed no more than six months to shed the polygamous egalitarian habits of youth and take their place in the monogamous hierarchies of adulthood. It should not surprise us that this rather abrupt transformation placed considerable strain not only on the couple but everyone connected with them. Betrothal allowed them time to consider themselves as a pair; now the wedding rites would clarify their broader responsibilities as heads of family and household. It focused on and completed their separation from family, from friends, and from the subordinate status of the unmarried. The couple would be ceremoniously removed from their old homes and installed in the new. The same rites would assuage parental loss and appease sibling envy, simultaneously inaugurating the couple into their permanent roles as masters and mistresses, reminding them in dramatic fashion of the public responsibilities of those who were privileged to head the crucial unit of social and economic life—namely, the household.

Each marriage was a political event in the life of the community, for it redistributed power as well as status and economic resources. In the seventeenth century the word "husband" was still the same as that for the small property owner (husbandman), a privileged, enfranchised position that only a part of the male population would ever attain.[7] Marriage invested a man with authority not only over his wife and children but his servants and, as an officer of manor or parish, over all those of subordinate status. The same was true to a lesser extent of the wife, who, as "dame" or "mistress" of her household, had considerable authority of her own, and who, as a widow, would come into even greater powers by virtue of her property and position.[8] For both man and woman wedding was a form of inauguration, both an investiture and an initial test of their authority as married persons.

Strict adherence to the rituals of the big wedding helped everyone get through this stressful and potentially dangerous moment. Once the banns were called and the congregation chorused "God speed 'em well," things went very quickly.[9] We know from Henry Best's account of yeoman weddings in the 1640s that, once the wedding day was set, the couple had about a month to make final preparations:

> and in that time do they get made the wedding clothes, and make provision against the wedding dinner, which is usually at the maid's father's. Their use [custom] is to buy gloves to give to each of their friends a pair on that day; the man shuld be at cost for them, but sometimes the man gives the gloves to the men and the women to the women, or else he to her friends and she to his. They give them that morning they are almost ready to go to be married.[10]

The distribution of favors was part of the homosocial leave-taking just before the wedding. Best's couple bid goodbye to their peers on the morning of the ceremony, but it was equally common for the groom to celebrate with his friends and the bride with hers on the night before. The wedding itself was trilocal, starting at the bride's house, proceeding to the church, and ending at the couple's new home. On the day itself, the groom accompanied by his male friends would arrive at the bride's home with great fanfare. Although Best does not elaborate, it seems that the fetching of the bride was of major importance, not only to the couple but to the bride's family. Ceremonially dressed, the woman waited with family and friends for the arrival of the groom, who entered the house and "takes her by the hand, and sayeth, 'Mistris, I hope you are willinge,' or else kisseth her before them, and then followeth her father out of doors."[11] Although Best's bride returned home for the wedding feast, an important separation was thereby accomplished, for she would come back not as a daughter but as a "Mistris," as wife.

A somewhat later account by Lewis Morris of Welsh weddings gives greater detail about this crucial moment. The groom's companions gathered at his place on the wedding morning to "have Bread & Cheese and a mug of ale each at his cost, and these they make their presents or pay *Pwython* [special wedding debts], and out of them pick about 8 or 10 or sometimes 20 of the best mounted to go to the Intended Bride's house to demand her in marriage."[12] These were designated "seekers" or "guiders," old friends who had probably assisted the groom at earlier stages in his courtship. Their progress to the bride's house was not unobstructed. Often they found their way barred by ropes, barricades, or the traditional quintain, "an upright post, on the top of which a spar turned freely. At the end of this spar hung a sand-bag, the other presented a flat side. The rider in passing struck the flat side, and if not dextrous in passing was overtaken and perhaps dismounted by the sandbag, and became a fair object of laughter."[13]

The quintain had been familiar in other parts of Britain for centuries. John Aubrey said it had been popular among "the ordinary sort" until the Civil War.[14] And while this aspect of the "riding wedding" lasted longer in Wales and parts of northern England, the contest between the groom's men and the bride's people was a standard feature of the big wedding in many places. In Wales it took a particularly ritualized form, for, on reaching the house, the groomsmen were "greeted by strong and sturdy men who have been appointed to prevent them from taking the girl away, and in the meantime, the girl would be guarded and the doors fastened." As Lewis Morris described it:

> The woman is there with her friends attending on her. Expecting the summons, and ready to be mounted as well as they can, sometimes there are 80 or 100 or 200 of them too, having paid their presents or *Pwython* there. But take notice, the woman is not to be got possession of without much trouble, and arguments in Welsh poetry sometimes for Hours together.

> I have seen papers containing some scores of what they call verses *pro & Con* on this occasion, and they have men who they call Poets, who make these verses Extempore. The Lord have mercy on such Poets.

In these they demand the Girl as a promised wife, and abuse another to all Intents and purposes, one party within the house and the other out of doors, to the great Diversion of the Company, Each Side Extolling the wit of their Poets.

Some of the Verses that are spoke at the Door of the intended Bride by the several Persons chosen to demand the Woman of her father, all on Horseback with their Hats off when they deliver their Orations and their answers are by the Persons appointed for that purpose.[15]

One of the scripts of such a contest was recorded in Cardiganshire during the nineteenth century:

BRIDEMEN	GROOMSMEN
Good day to you fair company What's your business to-day? Are you begging your way? Food is scarce this year	My business I will state In terms as plain as I can, But I have hastened on my journey and must get my breath first

Are you the people of oppression
Who come to sell the tithe?
Let me know if you come in
  peace,
As your countenances look so
  gloomy
	We are coming on an errand
	From a warm-hearted young man,
	To fetch your bright-eyed Annie
	To be his loving partner

If you intend promising marriage
You will get the answer from
  Annie
That there is certainly great
  trouble
In having a husband and family
	Quiet you silly fool
	The young woman is willing
	  enough
	And the only one that he will
	  have
	Is Annie of Dolebolion

Did you not suggest
To the young man this morning
That a man ought to be a pretty
  good scholar
To keep a wife and family
	The young man is an old scholar
	And makes heaps of money
	Drawing coal from the bowels of
	  the earth
	He can easily keep a wife

At this point the door is opened

Well, I had better say no more
  now
If they love one another faithfully
It is better you should take her
Than disappoint the lover's heart[12]

Ultimately, the "seekers" force entry to the house. Once inside they hunt about to find the bride, who was often hidden or disguised.[17] Finally, however, "the Father appears and welcomes his new Guests and they are desired to sit down to a cold Collation, and a Mug of ale is given to each." Then, just as it seems that the family is about to give up the bride, a new round of fighting, usually mock but sometimes real, erupts:

> This poetical dispute sometimes produces a quarrel, which is determined in their way to Church by Boxing or Cudgelling. In the Mean time while this dispute holds the Girl makes great moans & Lamentations, and if she can Counterfeit tears & Tearing of hair it is reckond a meritt. At last the man's poets having Carried the day, the Girl yields complaining of her hard fate, and up she is mounted behind her Father or Brother or some friend on the ablest swiftest horse that they can well procure.

> Here again the poor Intended Bridegroom runs a seeming hazard of losing his Intended Bride.

> Her friends as soon as she is mounted [try] to run away with her from the Company, and ride at all adventures like mad folks. They dont care whither, and it is very Common to have legs and arms broke on this Occasion. At last either the double horse is tired or the Bride thinks the time long aComing, she consents to go with them quietly, except a few starts of Endeavouring to turn out of the road now & then when a fair opportunity offers, until they get to church.[18]

The bride's separation from home was not everywhere quite so dramatic, but often equally ritualized. Women leaving for church were not supposed to look back. In some places water was poured over the steps to ensure that other marriages would "flow on"; and in Devon the threshold was thoroughly scrubbed as a sign of permanent leave-taking.[19] In Norfolk the throwing of shoes, a very old symbol of the renunciation of authority, was done every time a fisherman left for sea, servants changed places, or a bride went to church.[20]

Apart from the leave-taking, the wedding itself was left largely to the peer group. Fathers did not usually give away their daughters; it was brothers or friends who accompanied the bride to church. Among property holders, parental involvement was largely confined to the negotiations at the betrothal stage. As far as they were concerned, the marriage was complete once the portions and dowry had been arranged.[21] Those without property to settle on their children could offer only the proverbial wisdom: "Marry for love and work for siller (silver)."[22] The wedding day thus belonged entirely to the newlyweds. It focused on their ability to demonstrate their capacity to adapt to and maintain those broader social and psychological relationships the community regarded as vital to both the household and itself.

Friends were the ones who, with the melodious accompaniment of pipes and fiddles, paraded the couple to church. In many places the beat of drums and the firing of guns also called attention to the event and summoned crowds of onlookers.[23] It was a distinct honor to be accompanied to church by a vast throng, particularly if they were mounted, for in the north, the Midlands, and Wales a "horse wedding" was invariably saluted with bells and gunshots.[24] In return, the bride

5. Welsh newlyweds leaving the church. The wedding party, dressed in their traditional best clothes and sporting ribbons, consists entirely of young people. They are greeted by a throng, including a harpist, but the parents are absent. (Used by permission of the Welsh Folk Museum)

and groom were expected to demonstrate that measure of generosity and good humor that made life in this palpably unequal and hierarchical society tolerable for those who did not have access to the privileged status of marriage. The big wedding dramatized the ideal paternalistic relationship: on one side, respect and deference; on the other, tolerance and largesse. Unlike our own time, when the wedding is "given" by the parents, it was the bride and groom who were expected to play the role of benefactors. The participants were provided favors by the couple, sometimes gloves but more often ribbons. When John Chadocke organized his wedding in 1664, he spared no expense for his groomsmen, one of whom was Roger Lowe: "Each of us had a yard of ribbon of 12d per yard, and so rid through the towne." Ralph Josselin attended "a strange vaine wedding" of a poor man who gave "curious ribbands to all, gloves to the women and to the ringers."[25] And these were only the preliminaries. The generosity of the newlyweds would be put to much more severe tests as the big wedding progressed. In some places the ancient practice of distributing alms continued; in others the groom was still expected to provide "drink money" or a meal, an old manor custom.[26] While many of the formal obligations had lapsed by the sixteenth century, some, like the tradition of providing football or "bride ball" for the entertainment of the guests, continued in the north of England even as late as the nineteenth century.[27]

II

The church service, now at the altar rather than the porch, was the least important part of a big wedding. The groomsmen and bridesmaids could not wait for it to end and the clergy had great difficulty controlling the wedding party. The ceremony itself was anything but the quiet solemn formality we associate with church marriage. The throng was not much interested in the vows, which were merely a repetition in present tense of the words already spoken at the betrothal. Instead, they crowded in to see the rites popularly thought most essential to a wedding—namely, the blessing of the ring and the confirmation of the groom's dower to his bride, symbolized by the coins he placed on the priest's service book. Puritans objected that both these elements were pagan intrusions, but any effort to suppress them was met by popular resistance. Without a ring no peasant or artisan bride considered herself properly wed. Married women never removed their rings, and there were those who even avoided washing the ring finger. An Essex woman believed her husband was about to die because her ring broke: "I thought I should lose him . . . my sister lost her husband after breaking her ring. It's a sure sign."[28] Throughout the sixteenth and seventeenth centuries, the blessing of the ring by the priest was thought to give it magic so potent that it not only bound couples physically, but could cure a wide range of diseases, including epilepsy.[29] The vows themselves were apparently sufficient to endow the ring with supernatural strength. Even in the absence of a priest's blessing (as in betrothal), the ring was sufficient to confer permanence on a relationship.[30]

The fate of the coins, commonly called the "dow purse," was somewhat different. The upper classes gradually abandoned the practice, stigmatizing it as an archaic superstition and substituting for it the marriage settlement drawn up in lawyers' chambers.[31] By the eighteenth century it had disappeared from the marriage service in most of southern and eastern England, where common people, who had little or no property with which to endow, had little use for it either. It was kept alive mainly in those pastoral regions of the north and west where the marriage portion was still important. In Birkby it was still the habit of the groom to place a large coin on the parson's book. The priest would take his fee, turning over the silver to the bride.[32] A similar practice was observed in Cleveland until the 1870s, where it was "almost invariable practice for the man . . . to hand to the officiating minister, nominally in payment of fees, a handful, sometimes a very large handful, of money, taken without the slightest pretense of counting it from his trousers pocket, from which the said minister is expected to take the usual fees for parson and clerk; and, that done, to hand over the surplus to the bride."[33]

Southern clergy new to the custom sometimes mistook the coins for a generous gratuity, which outraged the bystanders, especially the women, for whom the coins were their symbol either of endowment or of the wife's right to her husband's wages. They were particularly vigilant on this point, sometimes correcting the clergy in the midst of the service:

> Oh, Sir, you should have put the siller into the bride's hand; the money's given to you that you might do so.[34]

The traditional kiss from the priest was also insisted on. What appeared to be a profanation to puritans was a blessing to ordinary people. The "kiss of peace" had once been passed through the entire congregation as a way of ensuring social peace at a potentially disruptive moment.[35] By the seventeenth century, the rite was limited to the parson kissing the bride, a signal for the wedding party to claim kisses from her. Among the unmarried it was thought very lucky to have the first kiss or at least to "rub shoulders" with the newlyweds, a privilege that smallholders in the north did not give up until the end of the nineteenth century. One new curate, not familiar with northern ways, had to be reminded:

VICAR   What are you waiting for?
BRIDEGROOM   Please, Sir, ye've no kissed Molly.[36]

No less important was the ritual of the garter, worn by betrothed persons and highly prized as a love token with magical qualities. In the sixteenth century, the bridal party could scarcely wait to seize the garters not just from the bride but from the groom as well. In 1635 several men were charged with assaulting a London groom named John Riggs, "pullinge of[f] his garters and behavinge themselves in a very irreverent and unciville manner."[37] That the name of one of the defendants was Edward Cumberland suggests that this may have been a case of mutual misunderstanding, a northerner acting in a customary manner, offending a southerner who did not understand his intentions. According to Pepys, Londoners did not try to take the garter in church, but waited until the couple were bedded to demand the love charm.[38] In the provinces, however, the scramble for the garter continued into the eighteenth century, until it was finally ousted from the church premises and assigned to a later stage of the festivities.[39] Kissing the bride, which in Northumberland was called "getting the garters" during the nineteenth century, became a substitute. The moment the service was over there would be a wild free-for-all, with the priest joining in the fun.[40] In addition, bystanders continued to throw grains and nuts, and in some places even the church hassocks flew.[41]

Purification of the church ceremony, initiated with the intention of purging the profane, often had the contradictory effect of extending and elaborating many of those rites the authorities objected to. The church ales, when terminated, took on new life in the local tavern. Toasting, feasting, and the distribution of favors and love charms, all of which had once been associated with the church, now evolved into a distinct set of secular festivities. Instead of seizing the bride's garter in church, Yorkshiremen raced from the church gates to the bride's house, the winner claiming the prize of removing the garter as the bride stepped across the threshold on her return home. Special verses were composed for the occasion:

> Good bride of thee I beg thou'lt lift
> Thy bridal goon, an' stand.
> I ask fra thou a lover's gift,
> 'Tis this, thy garter band
> Seea lift thy goon, fear now't fra me
> The race I won it fair,
> I call thy bridal bands to see
> An' claim yan o' thy pair,
> I claim to tak' it fra thy leg
> I claim it foor mah lass
> The race I wan, thy band I beg
> Yield it, an' thou s'all pan.[42]

Before the bride allowed the winner to remove the garter, she asked if there was anything "against this man's character? Hath he to your knowing brought shame upon a maiden?" Assured of his honor, the bride then lifted her gown, surrendered the garter, and was saluted with another round of song celebrating her qualities as wife and future mother:

> And bless the bride wheeas leg this graat
> An' bless the bridegroom too!
> May their love be trusty
> The'r bairns be lusty
>
> We wish ye bairs, an' graith and gear
> Long life, good health an' joy
> An from this nights embraces spring
> In good time a bouncy boy
>
> May you be free from t' stithe and o' foul disease
> May ye a'e luck to fick baith graith an' gear wi' ease
> Mayt' bairns' at come to ye from love's embrace
> Be bauf o' lim an' favoured well i' t' face

III

A similar process separating church from popular rites can be seen with respect to the various lifting and barring practices that the medieval

6. Weddings often involved a race from church to the new home of the bride and groom. In this early-nineteenth-century Welsh wedding, the newlyweds lead a wild chase, a test of their fortitude and compatibility. (Used by permission of the Welsh Folk Museum)

church had tolerated, but that were frowned on by puritan reformers and ultimately expelled from the ecclesiastical premises. Their terrain was once the church porch, the place where, before the marriage service was brought into the nave, they had been brought after first being part of the pre-Christian marriage ceremony. Often the couple would find themselves locked into the church by those waiting outside and released only when the groom passed money under the door.[44] This form of ransom, similar to a "footing," was prevalent in parts of Northumberland well into the nineteenth century, where it was said that village people "always lock the wedding party into the church till they have pushed gold under the church door."[45] In the Yorkshire Dales the same practice was preserved: "The idea being, the twain should meet and overcome their first trouble or obstacle in life, within the precincts of the church."[46]

Another common obstacle was a stone or wooden bench that during the service would be erected across the church door. In Northumberland, where the practice was most popular, it was called a "petting stone":

> It consisted of three upright stone flags set on edge, with one laid flat on the top like a step. When the bride appeared, two young fellows, one at each side of the bride, lifted her bodily over the barrier. The bridegroom

leaped lightly over after her, and dropped a coin into the hand of the "bride-lifters."[47]

The Northumbrian bride was supposed to show a certain reluctance: "it is 'etiquette' for the bride to appear to be unwilling to 'jump' and that the ordeal is made easier if she and the bridegroom have a coin ready to drop into the hand of one of the persons in charge of the 'Stone.' "[48] Resistance not only added to the fun of the occasion, but demonstrated a proper degree of modesty on the part of the new wife. It was said that most brides were only too pleased to jump, but that it was bad form to show too much alacrity, a sign of unbecoming independence. On the other hand, if a bride "pouted or hung back, or made a difficulty of observing the custom, she was said to have 'taken a pet,' " and "the poor husband was to be commiserated on the possession of a shrew."[49]

In places where the church objected to the use of its porch, the popular rites were moved to the church gates or to the road, where a long stick or rope was substituted for the petting stone.[50] Chaining and roping practices were probably as old as the quintain. When the West Ham man placed his "bough hanged with rope endes and nettles and other weedss" in the path of the couple in 1602, he probably meant only to test the temper of the groom, who was expected to pay a toll and thus assert himself in his new role as husband.[51] In North Devon it was customary for a couple to encounter several such roadblocks: "the bridegroom has again and again to pay his footing as a husband."[52] In the Flyde district all grooms taking a bride away from the parish were subject to "pennying."[53] It was said that in the Forest of Dean in Gloucestershire, where territorial rivalries were very intense, the roping of couples arose from the objection "to people, or especially brides, being taken from the parish, a form of some particular blood feud."[54] This may have been the origin, but by the early modern period the rite reflected not conflict between kin groups but tensions between the new groom and his peers. Rites such as these released in a harmless way the envy felt by the single for the married. Sometimes sods were thrown at the couple, but this, like the throwing of shoes, was a sign of recognition, not an intent to harm. In Wales, couples were actually seized and bound.[55]

Students of the King Edward VI School in Gigglesworth regularly barred the church door there, and in Burnley schoolboys were allowed a holiday until the 1870s for the purpose of extracting "fines," which were used to support the school library and cricket team.[56] By the end of the nineteenth century the scramble for coppers thrown by the groom had become child's play in Yorkshire, but this had not been the case a hundred years earlier when groups of young men, calling themselves "hustlers," did the honors. Richard Blakeborough described them as:

> gaily dressed, and with blackened faces. The captain of this band cried a halt, he declared that he and his merry men were in need of wives, and

7. In Coxwold, North Yorkshire, it is still the custom for children to "chain" the lychgate. Coins are tossed to them while the best man cuts through the twine. (Used by permission of Julia and Kenneth Monkman, Coxwold)

> unless the bridegroom paid them instantly 'bride guest money' his bride and every bonny bridesmaid would be kidnapped.[57]

The hustlers' declaration confirms that the jumping, chaining, and barring rites were a means of expressing and releasing the envy that surfaced on the occasion of every wedding. Those who barred the way were normally friends of the couple, for whom the marriage meant either the loss of a favorite companion or a former sweetheart, and sometimes both. By playing their parts with sufficient good humor, the newlyweds not only expressed the feelings of regret and guilt they may have felt, but clarified their new role as married people. The bride demonstrated the matronly qualities expected of a good wife; the groom, in his first act as husband, proved himself an adequate protector and provider.[58]

These were but the first of a series of teasings and testings that the couple would encounter on their wedding day, all part of a well-developed ritual tradition of "rough music" that was to remind the couple of their privileged position and paternalist responsibilities. Edward Row, with his horns, was probably acting out his role as a disappointed lover. Joan Swinyard of Bradford was doing the same thing when she mocked John Capt and his widow bride when they entered the church in 1600.[59] Normally these symbolic actions were sufficient to dissipate bad feeling.

We hear of them mainly when they were misinterpreted or carried to the point where they genuinely threatened the social peace. Apparently John Thompson's marriage in mid-seventeenth-century Froome, Somerset, had been strongly opposed by the greater part of that community. Everyone from the squire's wife to the mason's apprentice contributed horns, which were then mounted on a pole, decked with rosemary (a mockery of the bride's virginity), and placed across the path of the newlyweds. Thompson did not take the message placidly and brought them all into church court.[60]

For the most part, however, rough music at weddings promoted order by ritually expressing and containing the ambivalent feelings present on the occasion. In Devon, for example, particular attention was paid to couples when either the bride or groom were from "away." Some unpopular weddings were treated to a visit by a man with rams horns mounted on his head, a version of the traditional Devon "stag hunt," accompanied by the discordant music of a rough band.[61] In 1639, Ralph Brocke, a Sussex man, was charged in church court for "wearing a great payre of hornes uppon his head in the churchyard when Henry Hall and his wife were going to be married, shewing thereby that the said Hall was lyke to be a cuckold."[62] In other instances we find demonstration for rather than against weddings. As late as the 1880s, a Derbyshire couple who had backed away from their wedding were burnt in effigy by village lads.[63] When a Cambridgeshire man resisted fulfilling his promises to a Swaffam Prior widow, he was first confronted by her friends and then ceremoniously marched to church by a hundred people, all banging on tin pans and singing "Haste to the Wedding."[64]

Rough music had an ambivalent quality expressive of the mixed feelings of the participants. In Gloucestershire rough music or "tanging" was said to be the accompaniment of almost every wedding.[65] Drums, tin pans, and horns were the principal instruments of all rural rough bands, but in London butchers boys, armed with marrow bones and cleavers, claimed the privilege of serenading newlyweds up through the early eighteenth century. A group calling themselves "His Majesty's Royal Peal of Marrowbones and Cleavers" kept a schedule of fees and a register of its performances, which took place mostly under the windows of well-to-do patrons who could be expected to pay them off handsomely.[66] Elsewhere, things were not so organized, but the intentions were also less mercenary. At Bridestowe, Devon, it was always young people who beat the kettle drums.[67] In Cornwall the custom was for a "hal-lall" band to turn up under the newlyweds window later on the wedding night: "A judicious present of money was the only way to shorten a cacaphonous serenade which otherwise lasted for hours."[68] When the couple were of disparate ages they could expect a "regular ole shallal."[69] In Yorkshire turf was stuffed down the chimney if the groom did not pay "hendrinking" money.[70] In other places bushes were placed in the wedding bed, which was often shortsheeted. The Cornish bridal chamber was frequently broken into and the couple clouted with stockings filled with sand.[71] Pepys had invaded the bridal chamber in 1665 to kiss the bedded bride, and a century later Humphrey Clinker and his fictional wife were "bedded in an upper room, with the usual ceremony of throwing the stocking":

> This being performed, and the company withdrawn, a sort of catterwauling ensued, when Jack found means to introduce a real cat shod with walnut shells, which galloping along the boards, made such a dreadful noise as effectually discomposed our lovers.[72]

Puritans had long objected to these "bedding" practices, and Heinrich Bullinger was outraged that the newlyweds were allowed "no quietnesse. For a man shall fynd unmanerly and restlesse people, that will first go to theyr chambre dore, and there syng vycious and naughtie balates (ballads) that the deuell (devil) maye haue his triumphe now to the uttermost."[73] But long after the upper classes began to refuse entry to the bridal chamber, Yorkshire people still made it the practice for guests to enter "and standing with their backs to the foot of the bed, each throw a stocking over the left shoulder at the bride, who during this ceremony must sit up; the first to hit her is adjudged the next to be married."[74] In Cornwall the groom's ordeal was not over until the next day, when he was seized and, in a repeat of the local "footing" ceremony, ridden in a wheelbarrow through the village.[75]

Various crafts had their own ways of initiating their members to wedded life. In Coventry, weddings were compulsory events for the guildsmen; and in London the freeman's marriage was invariably a big affair, often extending over several days. Henry Machyn's sixteenth-century diary is filled with descriptions of big weddings, complete with grand processions ("the trumpettes blohyng"), lavish dinners, and much dancing.[76] Certain country trades, especially fisherfolk and miners, had similar corporate traditions. Mining people had a deserved reputation for rowdiness. Only fishing communities could match their hostility to outsiders, whose courtships and weddings were severely tested.[77] In Cornwall, when the mother of a bride was asked why she was crying, she replied: "Why, she's going to marry a furriner." "French?" "Aw dear, no Sir, it be worse than that—why he's a Curry man (someone from the neighboring village)."[78] Miners developed a powerful loyalty to the members of the gangs and crews with whom they worked. When one of their number married, he was expected to "pay aff" or "stand his hand," treating his mates in a manner similar to the footing expected of any workman entering into a new status.[79] In Northumberland, colliers insisted on mounting each new groom on a stang (pole) and carrying him to the public house, where, in recognition of his new status, he treated his workmates to a "blaw out," which was often also an excuse for a day away from work.[80] A similar practice was found among the quarrymen of the Isle of Portland, where the new groom treated his mates and then was "jumped":

> This ceremony was usually conducted by the oldest man amongst those celebrating the marriage. He appointed two tellers, whose duty it was to take the name of anyone who failed to observe the rites. Then, all hats having been removed, preparations were made for the "jump." The man last married held one end of the "jumper" (an iron rod used in the quarry for drilling holes) and the man who was supposed to be married next held the other end. All the married men lined up behind the former and all the single men behind the latter. Fines were imposed by the tellers for being out of place for wearing a hat and for talking. Then the M.C. recited the service:

> "Young men and bachelors, I bid you all adieu
> Old men and married men, I'm coming on to you."

> Over the rod went the victim, helped by two of his workmates with sticks and shovels. Then he jumped back again to the words,

> "Old men and married men, I bid you all adieu
> Young men and bachelors, I'm coming back to you."

> Finally he jumped for a third time, as the first verse was recited again. Thus the ceremony ended and the newly-wed joined the ranks of the married men. Fines were counted and the celebrations continued.[81]

While the wedding celebrations of most urban trades were considerably diminished by the eighteenth century, big wedding traditions were kept by certain strongly inbred occupations such as the London chimney sweeps, whose colorful processions attracted considerable public attention.[82] In Kent the path of the newlyweds was strewn not with grains or flowers but with symbols of the groom's trade—nails for carpenters, scraps of leather for cordwainers, wool for shepherds.[83]

IV

A marriage today may cause personal hurt or upset the equilibrium of particular families, but it does not threaten the social order in the way these weddings were bound to do. The medieval church had recognized the dangers, and parts of its nuptial mass, the "poison ordeal" and the kiss of peace, were explicitly designed to prevent social rupture.[84] The medieval church had also allowed its bells to be used to ward off evil spirits and, when the reforming clergy began to forbid their use for profane purposes, guns, drums, and rough bands were substituted. It was said of Upton St. Leonards in Gloucestershire that the beating of pots and pans was particularly prominent "at weddings if the bells were not rung."[85] But even though the reformed church preached solemnity and did its best to exclude unwanted guests, its public spaces remained a favorite place for settling old scores, and brawls were frequent at both weddings and funerals.[86] Therefore, couples attempted to ensure the happiness of their marriage by choosing the right month and day by a variety of means. The church provided one calendar of appropriate and inappropriate days, popular astrological calendars offered another.[87] Despite puritan objections to both kinds of "superstitions," they remained very powerful. Even though the church did not enforce its prohibitions with any vigor after the sixteenth century, York people consistently avoided Lent until the late eighteenth century.[88] Samuel Pepys assisted a servant couple in buying a license during Lent in 1668, even though they really did not need one to marry.[89] Others turned to wise men and professional astrologers to determine not only who but when they should marry. People were advised that a rising moon was propitious, but that the month of May, all Fridays, and certain holy days were to be avoided.[90] There were many things a couple could do to ward off malevolence on their wedding day. They could carry certain charms (garters and sigals [tokens]), take certain routes to and from church, wear the right clothing, and, since the priest was no longer likely to do it for them, perform their own exorcisms.[91] Yorkshire newlyweds did all these things and were especially careful when crossing bridges on their way from church: "The husband always took precedence, for was it not right that he, as master, and still more as protector of his bride, his wife, should go first and overcome all danger." Once the bride joined him on the bridge, the pair threw small objects into the water so that "it might carry with it every evil wish and ill spell wrought by wicked hearts that day."[92]

Spells and curses could best be prevented by keeping on the right side of friends and neighbors, by invoking their spirit of generosity, by inviting all to the wedding. Welsh people ensured the goodwill of their community by formally "bidding" all to the festivities. A local bard was hired to make sure that no person, even servants and strangers, was left out. Not only did bidding ensure the greatest number of wedding gifts, but it prevented anyone from taking offense. It was particularly important that all the young persons be in attendance, especially those couples who were "planning to be married very soon afterwards."[93] Although it added to the size and expense of the wedding, nothing was spared. For every groomsman there was a bridesmaid, and "to avoid jealousy it was said, the bride and her maids are dressed alike."[94] Not to invite someone was a major breach of neighborliness that could have serious repercussions. When Jane Milburne deliberately failed to ask one of her neighbors, Dorothy Strangers, to her wedding supper at Newcastle in 1663, she set off a chain of events that led to Strangers being accused of witchcraft. As Keith Thomas has reconstructed it, "the justly aggrieved Dorothy declared she would make her repent it; Jane was subsequently plagued by several mysterious cats, whom she knew at once to be Dorothy in supernatural disguise."[95] Something of the same kind may have been behind the cursing of a Yorkshire wedding some two hundred years later. An old woman stopped the bride and groom on the road:

> Ah've let tha be wedded
> But ah'll stop tha being bedded[96]

Malevolence that could be anticipated could be prevented, however. Several rites associated with weddings functioned to maintain harmony in a situation where bad feelings could have more than just momentary personal consequences. Parental loss was dealt with at the moment the bride left home. Parents saved themselves from further grief by staying away from the church service itself. In many parts of England and Wales it was regarded as unlucky for married persons to attend weddings.[97] One Staffordshire father politely refused a wedding invitation in writing: "We both hope you will please try to arrange for single people to go with them to [be] Married."[98] The practice seems to have been rooted in the belief that, as one Cumberland farmer explained, "the bridegroom runs away with the bride without the parents' consent."[99]

Tensions could also arise when a sibling married out of order. In this case teasing served to clarify and contain a potentially disruptive situation. The one passed over was sometimes made to carry a broom to the wedding.[100] More common, however, was the penance known variously as "dancing in green stockings," "dancing the hogs trough," or simply "dancing in stocking feet."[101] A woman who lived in the Vale of Clwyd in the early nineteenth century remembered that her brother had "undergone this penalty for permitting her, a junior, to get married before him."[102] In nearby Shropshire a young woman was confronted by her aunt:

> So I hear you didna dance barfut! I'm ashamed of you. If I'd bit there I'd made you do it. I've a good mind to pull yer boots for ye now this minute and make ye dance i' the street.[103]

The marriage of younger siblings cannot have been all that uncommon, especially in those places where inheritance practice provided incentive for doing so. In fact, the practice seems to have prevailed in those parts of the west and southwest where the eldest were expected to remain home longest, marrying only when the parents finally passed away or retired. Therefore, while the rite called attention to the plight of the eldest, it was also meant, as Brand noted, as something of a compensation, a means of changing the luck of the unfortunate one.[104] Francis Grose was also convinced of the benefits of the ritual, noting "it will counteract their ill luck and procure them husbands."[105]

Wedding day was also a time for humoring forsaken lovers, whose envy was much feared. Welsh brides could expect a ginger or hazel stick from their former sweethearts; and, if this was all that came, they felt themselves fortunate, for this was the polite symbol of disappointment.[106] One way to head off malevolence was to counter it by offering former suitors garlands of willow, a reference to their grief.[107] Throughout Wales, either a hazel stick or a piece of ginger was sent to a disappointed lover.[108] This was sometimes tied with black crepe and accompanied by "a verse or so of homespun poetry, setting forth the significance of the article transmitted, with also sundry complimentary references to the person addressed, on 'being on the shelf,' and other pointed pin-pricks calculated to open old sores and to wound the too susceptible feeling of a 'good-old-has-been!'"[109] At Cold Aston, Derbyshire, a former sweetheart found the wedding garland hung outside his house the morning after the wedding. Attached to it was a bottle of urine and an onion.[110] A Burnley man in a similar situation would have been "packsheeted," tossed in a blanket until he paid ransom, which "is immediately spent at the next public house." At Morley "socket money" was levied on former sweethearts of both sexes.[111]

While these rites may seem to us cruel, they are what Victor Turner calls "social dramas," involving the symbolization of the original breach in social relations as well as the effort at reconciliation, all aimed at preventing an escalation of the crisis.[112] Abandoned lovers were comforted in Cumberland by seizing and rubbing them with "pease straw." The girls did this for boys; and the males reciprocated:

> For Jock the young laird was new wedded
> His auld sweetheart Jennie luik'd ware
> While some were aw tittern and flyin
> The lads rubbed her down wi' peace strae.[113]

If the social dramatization of conflict did not bring appeasement, then there were various cures for "love sickness," dispensed by wise men and cunning women throughout the sixteenth and seventeenth centuries, that were still popular much later among the humbler classes, long after their social superiors had ceased to believe in such things. Nancy Clandwr of Cardiganshire apparently possessed a very effective remedy, involving the repetition of certain words, followed by a drink concocted of gin, beer, and saffron. Other early-nineteenth-century cures involved something more of an ordeal. The love sick were placed on their backs and a tub of water was placed on their chests, into which molten lead was then poured.[114] As with all the other rites associated with the big wedding, it worked best for those who believed in its effectiveness.

V

Love was regarded as something physiological as well as psychological. While natural enough to youth who "are hot and fiery by reason of the blood which boyles (boils) in their veines," it could be quite dangerous to the adult because "like a wild untamed beast it exceedes the bounds of reason [and] there is no misery which it brings not to the world, nor any disorder which it causeth not in our lives."[115] While we expect married couples to act like lovers, in peasant and artisan society the passions expected of a suitor were to be avoided by a spouse. The love conjured in courtship was exorcised at the time of the wedding. Although husbands and wives were supposed to show consideration and respect, conjugal love was a means to marriage not its end. Too much conjugal affection was perceived as unnatural and a threat to the broader social obligations that came with the establishment of a household. Thus, the power of love, symbolized by the bride's garter, was ceremonially transferred to single persons who would require it to make their own marriages.

The race for the garter took place on the return from the church as part of the final act of the big wedding, the installation of the new couple as master and mistress of their own household. From Henry Best's account it seems that this did not always take place immediately. The couple would return to the bride's home for the wedding feast and the young wife would stay on for a time until the new home was ready. The biggest celebrations of all were postponed until that day:

> hee perhapps fetcheth her hoame to his howse aboute a moneth after [the wedding], and the portion is paide that morninge that he goes away. When the younge man comes to fetch away his bride, some of his best friends, and younge men his neighbours, come along with him, and others perhapps meete them in the way, and then is there some jollity att his howse, for they perhapps have love [?] wine ready to give to the company when they light, then a dinner, supper, and breakfast the next day.[116]

It was apparently not at all uncommon for couples waiting for a tenancy or the delivery of marriage portions to put off living together until everything was ready.[117] This delay, which seems to us to deny the very purpose of marriage, was merely an extension of the well-established association of marriage with economic independence. Among those with property, whether substantial yeomen or smallholders, it was unthinkable that any marriage should start with less.

The timing of the setting up of the household varied, but the event itself was always ceremonious for publicity ensured the viability of the new household. In Cumberland it was the custom for farmers to convey their daughter's portion in a public procession, featuring a decorated wagon or "bride wain," loaded with goods and furniture.[118] Eighteenth-century Yorkshire brides also rode ox-drawn wagons, sitting with their spinning wheels in a matronly pose, stopping along the way to gather gifts from well-wishers.[119] In Glamorganshire the transfer was accomplished on horseback, "each matron in her appointed station, the nearest relations going first; all have their allotted basket or piece of small furniture, a horse and cart following afterwards with heavier articles."[120] In Cardiganshire weddings in the 1760s, the Friday before a Saturday wedding was set aside to "bring home the Stafell [or Chamber] of the woman if she is to reside at the man's house, or of the man if he is to reside at the house where the woman lives."[121] Threshold rites were reserved for the moment the couple first occupied a separate dwelling. Brides were sometimes lifted across, but the doorstep was also the place for the bride to receive a small cake on a plate:

> A little of this she would eat, throwing the remainder over her head, typical of the hope that the couple might always have plenty and something to spare. Then she handed the plate to her husband; this he threw over his head, their future happiness depending on its being broken.[122]

Breaking, cutting, and stepping over symbolized the new beginnings; and so too did the various objects—fire tongs, brooms, and keys—that were presented to the new bride inside the new home, thus establishing her claims as mistress of the household.[123] No less important, however, were the gifts that the newlyweds gave to their guests. These included not only the favors distributed to groomsmen and bridesmaids, but games, drinks, and especially the wedding dinner and its associated entertainments. The latter were provided not, as we would do, by the parents, but by the couple themselves, because in a peasant or artisan community a display of generosity was as essential as a demonstration of authority to the establishment of each new household. This would be put off until everything was ready, even if this meant postponing the wedding day until after a child was born.[124] Henry Best's groom clearly wanted to show off his new status as a householder when he served them "love wine" and gave them not only supper but breakfast the next day.[125] He probably served his guests as they sat at his table, for this too was the custom. Everywhere it was the new husband who was center stage during the wedding festivities, acting out his new status as Master of the household.[126]

Still, it might be some weeks before the public installation of the newlyweds was complete. In many places it was the couple's first visit to the parish church after their wedding that marked this moment. Some places even had a special "bride seat" reserved for the occasion. Taking her place among the adult members of the congregation meant that the bride "is ready to receive the visits and congratulations of her neighbors and friends."[127] This round of visiting normally marked the final incorporation of the couple into the hierarchies of age, gender, and social status, thus ending the transition that had begun several months earlier with the separation rites associated with betrothal. At that stage the focus of attention had been on both the young man and woman, but by the time of the wedding it was the male who played the central role in this highly publicized social drama of incorporation. While becoming a Mistress did mean a change in status, a woman was a dependent whether a daughter or a wife. Marriage made a much more abrupt change in a man's life. Suddenly he was Master, elevated above his peers, confronted with the privileges but also with the burdens of this ultimate status and authority. Wedding was *the* male rite of passage, and, as such, not only his moment of greatest glory but, as the rites themselves dramatized, of maximum vulnerability.

VI

As a dramatic rendering of the ideal relationship between the married elite and those who would be their subordinates in household and community, the rites of the big wedding were double-edged. They acknowledged the privileged status of the newlyweds, while at the same time reminding them of their duties toward those dependent on them. The big wedding anticipated and dealt with the tensions inherent in a highly stratified society. It also gave expression to the difficulties of married life, which were also the subject of endless proverbial wisdom. Chapbooks and almanacs were filled with dire marital predictions. The popular *Poor Robin* assumed "civil war between drunken husbands and scolding wives, mother-in-laws and daughters."[128] Ballads recited the trials of married life, particularly those first years when children were numerous and expenses high. Every union was a potential burden on the parish and therefore could not be considered a purely private matter. As a consequence, what began as a public event remained a focus of communal concern until dissolved by death or other misfortune. Formal jurisdiction over marriage was shared by church and manor courts for much of this period, but, as the big wedding itself gave indication of, popular intervention was also sanctioned by custom. When visitors to Rochester in 1602 asked what the large wooden beam extending out over a pond was used for, they were given the following explanation:

> They call it the wooden horse, and the bad wives are obliged to ride on it into the water. We were further told that in England every citizen is bound by oath to keep a sharp eye on his neighbor's house, as to whether the married people live in harmony, for though in this realm much liberty is granted to women, no licentiousness is allowed them. If by the neighbourhood any matrimonial differences are noticed, both parties are ordered to appear before the magistrates, who inquire on which side lies the cause of disharmony. If the husband is an unfriendly or obstinate fellow, he is condemned to pay a fine in money; if, however, the mischief is on the wife's side, the husband is likewise punished for not having been able to keep up his authority, but the wife is placed on the above-mentioned chair and ducked three times into the water up to the neck by the boys who roam about the streets. When she is well drenched and well shamed, she returns home to her husband, who after the custom of the country gives her comfort by getting her dried with warm clothes, especially in winter time.[129]

At Portsmouth men who beat their wives were bound over to keep the peace and fined when their violations became flagrant.[130] There, as at Rochester, the ducking or cucking stool had once been used mainly for violators of market regulations, but in the seventeenth century it was used as an instrument for punishing scolding women.[131] While men were sometimes ducked for quarreling, the stool was largely reserved for females. At the manor court of Stubbar and Middleton, Margaret Longfellowe was ordered in 1594 to be "dowckede on the Cockstoole before Maudlin daye or els forfait to the lord 6s 8d." Another woman was punished for using scandalous words and fined almost forty shillings. As a warning to husbands to keep their wives in check, her husband was ordered to bring her to court and pay her fine.[132] While ducking usually required the order of a manor court or one of its officers, it was quicker and cheaper than going through a long defamation hearing in a church court, perhaps one of the reasons why ducking seems to have increased while the church's matrimonial causes declined during the seventeenth century.[133]

Ducking began to lose popularity in the next century, and its decline coincided with that of the manor court itself. Husbands sued against having their wives publicly humiliated; and, while there was an official ducking as late as 1809 in Leominster, it ceased in most places much earlier.[134] But at Leicester, where the court ceased to function by the mid-eighteenth century, the stool itself was appropriated as part of an unofficial system of rough justice. In the 1770s a stool was "placed as a mark of disgrace in front of a house in Bond Street; the woman residing there had also, it appears, twice done penance in St. Margaret's Church, for slander."[135] The rough justice practiced in South Wales, known as the wooden horse (*y ceffyl pren*), seems to have been a popular adaptation of manor court practice. When domestic conflict became notorious "the neighbors step in with the *ceffyl pren* or wooden horse. An effigy of the offender is dressed up, seated on a chair, placed on a ladder, and carried on men's shoulders, a crowd in procession preceding and following the *ceffyl pren*, shouting, screaming, and beating tin saucepans, &e. Halting at intervals, the nature of the offense is thus described by the spokesman:

> Ran-dan-dan!
> Betty Morris has beat her man
> What was it with?
> Twas not with a rake, nor yet with a reel,
> But 'twas with a poker, that made him feel."[136]

The practice of this kind of rough music seems to have developed in parallel with and, increasingly, as a substitute for both church and manorial justice. Its moral objectives were quite similar to those of the church—namely, to uphold the lawful order of the household, seeing to it that wives did not complain too much or husbands exercise their authority too tyrannically. Church courts frequently ordered couples to reconcile and live together. In the Church of St. Ishmael in Ferryside, Wales, there was even a special two-seat bench designed specifically for the public penance of quarreling pairs. The 1655 inscription read:

8. A group of youth ride the stang for the quarreling couple seen just inside the door on the left. George Walker described this as an "ancient provincial custom" which was becoming less frequent in early-nineteenth-century Yorkshire. (From George Walker, *The Costume of Yorkshire*, 1814)

Husbands Love Your Wives
Let the Wife Reverence Your Husband[137]

In other places combative couples sat during the service with a sheet over their heads. If only one side was found guilty, he or she sat alone. Sometimes the secular power was used to reinforce the injunctions of the church courts, as was the case at Helmsley, Yorkshire, in 1657:

> Margery Watson of Whitby, being a scold [is] to be ducked by the Constable, unless she within a month do ask Jas Wilkonson and his wife of Sneaton foregiveness in Whitby Church publically and at the Cross in the market town there.[138]

The constable's right to intervene in marriage rested on the principle of the common law that "a scold in a legal sense is a troublesome and angry woman, who by her brawling and wrangling amongst her Neighbors, doth break the publick Peace, and beget, cherish and increase publick Discord."[139] Court leets were authorized not only to fine and punish unwed mothers, but to deal with all violations of heterosocial norms, including men and women living apart from their spouses.[140] But, like the church courts, they did not normally go out looking for offenders, and prosecuted mainly when irregularities were brought to their attention by other parties.[141] Adultery was usually tolerated if it were sufficiently discreet and caused no public scandal, for it was the publicity of marital breakdown that, according to both common law and public opinion, justified direct intervention.[142]

As manorial and church authority declined in the seventeenth century, there was a tendency for communities to apply their own unofficial sanctions to quarreling and scandalous couples. This was particularly true of waste and forest settlements where the power of established authority had never been strong and people developed their own means of social regulation. In places like the nonconformist Blackheath village of Woking, Surrey, it became the practice for members of the village to sit in judgment on their neighbors.[143] Licentious men and loose women were first subjected to the persuasive power of village gossip, but those who failed to respond were then visited with signs of their offenses—horns for cuckolded husbands; smelly bushes for unchaste women, hung on their doors or windows.[144] There were special times of the year—New Year's Day, St. Valentine's Day, Shrove, May Eve, and Guy Fawkes Night—when the uncomfortable truth could be told without the accusers risking retribution. On Plough Monday, it was the dancing Fool who, with his companion Bessy, made the rounds of the houses in the village, singing mocking songs about past misdeeds. In the West of England and in the Scilly Isles, Easter licensed what was called "guising" or "goose dancing," when "the maidens are dressed up for young men and young men for maidens: thus disguised they visit their neighbors in companies, where they dance, and make jokes upon what has happened on the island; when everyone is humorously told their own faults without offense being taken."[145]

Such rites of status reversal were possible in a world where heterosocial roles were obligatory only for the married and the personal identity of the young was not threatened by cross dressing. They did not upset the social order, for the intent was not to alter the relations between husbands and wives but to reinforce them.[146] In Ashton-under-Lyne, Shrove Tuesday was the time for shaming unfaithful spouses.[147] Elsewhere, Easter Monday and Tuesday had a special place in the calendar of marital order.[148] As far as extramarital sexuality was concerned, the strongest condemnation was reserved not for the single men and women but the married parties. Yet, even in this case, it was not the sexual but the social violation that was condemned. Public wrath was directed not against the adulterer, but the man who, in failing to uphold his authority over his wife, had shown himself to be unworthy of the office of husband. In the sixteenth century, "cuckold" was the worst a man could be called and the cause of most of the defamation suits brought by men to the church courts.[149] Next to the cuckolded husband it was the henpecked (often one and the same) who was most exposed to shame. While the insubordinate woman was also called to the bar of popular justice, the most painful forms of mockery were directed not at her but her husband.[150] It was he who bore the brunt of the most elaborate form of British rough music during the early modern period, known variously as the Skimmington, Riding the Stang, or, in Wales, the *ceffyl pren*. John Stowe was present on Shrove Monday, 1562, at Charing Cross in London when a husband who had allowed his wife to beat him was ritually humiliated. To shame the culprit, his neighbors induced the man next door to act as his stand in, riding a horse around the nearby streets with his face to the tail, while a crowd cried out the real offender's indiscretions.[151] A similar riding in another part of London was described by Andrew Marvell:

> From Greenwich . . .
> Comes News of pastime maritally and old:
> A Punishment invented first to awe
> Masculine Wives, transgressing Natures Law,
> Where, when the brawny Female disobeys,
> And beats the Husband till for peace he prays
> No concern'd Jury for him damage finds,
> Nor partially Justice ner Behavior binds,
> But the just Street does the next House invade
> Mounting the Neighbor Couple of lean Jade
> The Distaff knocks, the Grains from Kettle fly,
> And Boys and Girls in Troops run hooting by.
> Prudent Antiquity, then knew by Shame
> Better than law, domestick Crimes to tame
> And taught Youth by Spectacle innocent.[152]

London's way of humiliating henpecked husbands lasted to the end of the seventeenth century, but in time the custom tended to be confined to the countryside and smaller towns.[153] In West Country Skimmingtons the husband (or his stand in) was often joined by another figure representing the wife. She faced forward, he backward; she beating him with a large ladle, while the accompanying crowd set off a chorus of rough music, beating on pans, blowing horns, and hooting at the top of their lungs. In one such seventeenth-century Somerset "Skymerton," directed against a woman who had cuckolded her husband, more than a hundred persons paraded the village with effigies of the couple.[154] When it came to the notice of the parishioners of East Claydon that their parson, Hugh Hart, had been beaten by his wife in 1678, they took a similar course of action:

> Candlemasse Day last, the Men Servants of Bottle Claydon made a Riding about Mrs. Hart's beating her old Husband, who was so unadvised as to take notice of it yesterday in his Pulpit. They passed by my House yesterday & 'twas as foolish a thing as ever I saw. I suppose their Masters privately Egg'd on the Businesse, but appear'd not themselves nor their sonnes, only Will Holland my Miller's Sonn Ledd the Horse.[155]

It was apparently not uncommon for village elders to arrange the rough music, leaving it to the younger folk to carry out the sanctions. There is no evidence in Britain of formal youth groups such as the French

Abbeys of Misrule; nor were British charivari directed, as were those on the Continent, primarily against second marriages.[156] Nevertheless, the values underlying European rough music were generally the same. In the world of the peasant or artisan, marriage was a public institution, governed by certain well-understood rules enforced by the community. There was domestic violence, but it was not, as in our own time, thought of as a private matter. The husband ruled supreme, but he was not an absolute monarch. The wedding had not only established the standards by which a marriage was to be governed, but mandated a public to enforce them. A brutal or philandering husband was subject to the same sanctions as a scolding or adulterous wife.[157] And, while couples were urged to treat one another with kindness and respect, this was not a society so naive as to rely on affection as the sole guarantee of fair treatment.

VII

Courtship created a personal relationship; wedding made a public institution. As late as the mid-eighteenth century, family still meant to Samuel Johnson "those who live in the same house," whether or not they were related by blood or marriage.[158] In reality, the meaning of family was even more extended, for the term "friend" could still mean either a neighbor or blood relation. The heads of households were fathers not only to their own children but to all their apprentices and live-in servants. The married head of the house was "husband" to more than just his wife. In turn, the word "wife" referred to a woman's duties not her marital status. A "fishwife" or "housewife" need not be married. In certain circumstances, such as widowhood, a woman could "husband" a farm, just as a man could "wyfe" a house.[159]

When contemporaries distinguished between what they called the "little family" and the "great family," they were recognizing the difference between the conjugal relationship established at betrothal and the public roles inaugurated by wedding.[160] The contrast between the two was bound to create difficulties, for, even in our society, conjugal love and family duties do not always go together easily. Today's couples also find that the burden of keeping up a certain standard of living, together with the anxieties of childrearing, dampen the initial flush of marital happiness. In earlier times the strain was even greater because of scarce resources and more frequent childbearing. Young marrieds today enjoy a honeymoon, which gives them time to make the necessary personal adjustments. And, since they usually postpone having a family to a later stage of marriage, they also have more time to prepare for parenthood. For peasants and artisans, the entry into the full responsibilities of marriage was much more abrupt. Brides were often pregnant at marriage and, although marriage was postponed until economic independence was assured, the full burdens of a farm or business were upon the newlyweds before they had time to adjust to one another.

The rites of the big wedding recognized the abruptness of this transition and attempted to clarify and reconcile the contradictions between love and marriage. Betrothal emphasized the rights; wedding underlined the duties of marriage. Rough music during and after the event reminded married persons of their privileged position and the conduct appropriate to it. It acknowledged, as did the contemporary conduct books, that the man was "as a king in his owne house," the woman "the other married person, who being subject to her husband yieldeth obedience to him."[161] At the same time, marriage was described as communion, association, or, most commonly, as partnership. Husband and wives were encouraged to cooperate, respect one another, and provide "a mutual declaration of the signs and tokens of love and kindness."[162] In effect, peasant and artisan marriage was simultaneously patriarchal and companionate. It was both a public institution and a private relationship, in which the husband's formal authority was balanced and, at times, contradicted by the real power of wives and even children. There is no reason to think these couples quarreled less than their counterparts do today. It was in times of financial difficulty that Adam and Susan Eyre were at each other most. He needed money to keep the farm going; she refused to sign over her property. By 1647 things had come to such an impasse that Adam was thinking of separation, asking himself "whether I should live with my wife, or no, if she continued so wicked as she is." We have no record of Susan's thoughts, but it is certain that she gave as well as she took. Nevertheless, they managed to settle their differences eventually, Adam promising "her to become a good husband to her for ye tyme to come, and shee promised me likewise shee would doe what I wished her in anything, save in setting her hand to papers."[163]

Peasant and artisan culture recognized the contradictions between conjugal love and household responsibilities, and struck a ritual balance between them. It was a compromise that had existed for centuries, for even medieval conduct books counseled husbands to be responsive to the needs and feelings of other members of the household.[164] This equilibrium might well have endured if the smallholder society that had nurtured it had not been so badly eroded from both above and below in the course of the sixteenth and seventeenth centuries. On one hand, there was the growing mass of propertyless persons who could not sustain a "great family" in the traditional sense and no longer had any use for patriarchal duties. The poor were increasingly defying the laws of the church and the customs of the big wedding, asserting their right to conjugality and even carrying this to the antinomian extreme of advocating free love. At the same time, there were now the "middling sorts," who, in elevating themselves above the ordinary peasants and artisans, were rejecting the notion of marriage as a public institution imposing obligations that extended beyond the nuclear family. They also stressed the importance of the conjugal relationship but, instead of launching an all-out assault on patriarchy, they redefined it as a private matter, no longer subject to public control. The authority of priest and parish was reallocated to the father and the husband. Among this new middle class marriage became a family matter and the wedding a private affair. Big weddings were henceforth confined to a diminishing stock of smallholders, the only group for whom its publicity and the wider obligations this created still had meaning and function.

CHAPTER 3

∿∿∿∿∿∿∿∿∿∿∿∿∿∿∿∿∿∿∿∿∿∿∿∿∿∿∿

Neither Birth nor Portion Shall Hinder the Match: Clandestine Marriage and Sexual Nonconformity

The big wedding was far more demanding than anything the church required. Canon law was satisfied with mutual consents, but popular custom dictated an elaborate event, involving the huge expenditure of time and money. Without all the festivities, no smallholder could consider himself or herself properly married. But societies that demand so much of those entering matrimony also provide alternatives for those who cannot meet their exacting standards. The illicit necessarily coexists with the legal, the irregular with the conventional. "If two lovers want to get married against the wishes of their families, or against the rules of society which seem more or less useless or absurd to them, an accommodation is usually made," noted Arnold van Gennep. "Either the union is accepted as a *fait accompli*, or only a portion of the customary ceremonies is performed."[1] In Britain's case, the relationship between the big wedding and irregular marriage was not only structural, but dialectical. As access to the prerequisites of the big wedding diminished, the demand for illicit alternatives—clandestine marriage and common law arrangements—increased. It has been estimated that by the early eighteenth century the established church was losing at least a quarter and perhaps as many as a third of all marriages to irregular unions of one kind or another. If marriages by license are added, then "little weddings" were almost as numerous as big weddings.[2]

As long as the church did not attempt to close off these alternatives, its control over marriage was not directly challenged by either end of the social spectrum. The poor, no longer aspiring to a niche in either artisan or peasant society, were quite content to be "half married"; and, as long as it did not insist on too strict a definition of monogamy, the church was also able to maintain a comfortable (and lucrative) relationship with the well born. The generous provision of marriage licenses, together with the willingness of the church courts to provide annulments, guaranteed that the aristocracy and gentry, who played fast and loose with the marriage rules, were quite as contented as the wayward members of the proletariat.[3] It was only when the ecclesiastical authorities became too strict or grasping that either group was provoked into open defiance.

While it cannot be said that ecclesiastical discipline was very effective before the Hardwicke Act of 1753, which restricted legal marriage just to public ceremonies conducted in the church, there were pressures beginning in the sixteenth century for tighter control over secret betrothals and other forms of consent made in opposition to parents or parish. In some parts of the country, notably where capitalist agriculture and the cloth industry had made the greatest advances, the clergy were under pressure to close down the loopholes of "privy contracts" and clandestine marriage. Where smallholding remained more pervasive, mainly in the north and west, the church remained more accommodating to the traditional peasant and artisan marriage process. Local rather than national factors tended to determine the church's position. Everywhere the clergy remained sensitive to parish opinion, responding to change at the village and town level.

The changes in marriage discipline that were taking place were a reflection of a larger social process that witnessed the decomposition of the traditional orders of society and the emergence of two new groups, the nascent capitalist middle class and a huge body of rural wage workers, Britain's first proletariat. By the seventeenth century both had begun to develop their own distinctive cultures, the "middling sorts" with their distinctly puritanical values, and the "rascality," though less articulate, tending toward secular antinomian attitudes. They were not yet fully developed classes, and, in this period of decomposition, there were things that united as well as divided them. Both rejected the collective aspects of traditional courtship and wedding—the middling sort because they had deliberately removed themselves from the village community, the poor because they had been expelled from it. The behavior of both was individualistic and they tended to retain only those elements of peasant and artisan marriage practice suitable to their notion of marriage as personal choice. They tended to use the old betrothal rights and clandestine marriage when it suited them, though as these became less accessible, they developed their own distinctive marriage rules that ultimately brought them into direct conflict with the authorities.

I

But the initial challenge to the traditional wedding came from within the smallholder class itself. Resources were shrinking and families that, even in better times, had not been able to provide for all their children were now even more restricted. Conflicts among young people, parents, and parish increased to the point that even the ingenious reconciliatory mechanisms of traditional courtship and wedding were unable to prevent open rupture. Parents worried about premature marriages and misalliances that would drain resources from the family economy and cause ruin to all concerned. To the emerging "middling sort," matches not only with the propertyless proletariat, but with the smallholder class posed a threat to capital accumulation. Poor people had little to lose, but the nascent middle classes were now determined to reassert parental authority. They not only revived the commandment of filial obedience, but pressured the church to prohibit marriage of children under age. The puritan elements among them were particularly vigorous in pressing the claims of the family against peers and parish. In places where such groups were strong, it was said that any clergyman who dared wed children against parental wishes would find that "the Family which suffers, with all their Friends and Relations (who, perchance, may make the major part of the Parish) will be sure to fall upon him with their utmost Resentments."[4] Not satisfied with the existing canons, puritans were among the vanguard of those who were urging that the age of majority be raised to twenty-four.[5] Even those who were of age were "exhorted not to contract marriage, without first acquainting their parents with it (if with conveniency may be done), endeavoring to obtain their consent."[6] While it is impossible to know how many clergy complied with this, in at least one parish the register kept a careful record of the consent for all marriages made by license regardless of the bride's age.[7] We also know from banns books that marriages were forbidden by both parents and others. There is no way of determining the frequency of these prohibitions, but to judge from the numbers of contested marriages that came to the church courts they must have been considerable.[8] The practice continued into the eighteenth century, when Mrs. Boughton stood to forbid her daughter's marriage, telling the Reverend William Cole "tho' she had no Objection to Philip [the prospective husband] who is a sober industrious man; but only that she did not like to part with her [the daughter]."[9]

By the seventeenth century the prohibitions of individual parents evolved into what amounted to a class policy aimed at limiting access to marriage by the poor. In earlier times it had been a religious obligation of the prosperous to assist the unfortunate. Before the Reformation weddings normally took place on Sundays with all the parish present. The medieval practice of providing a "church ale" was considerable inducement to attendance, for the cup was passed and everyone was invited to the wedding feast, which was often held at a special "wedding house," also provided by the church.[10] Guests of any big wedding were under a certain degree of obligation. In sixteenth-century Coventry craftsmen were fined if they did not attend the weddings of their fellow guildsmen.[11] The presence of the squire at village weddings must have made attendance there equally mandatory. Traditionally he fulfilled his responsibility by giving a wedding dinner if the couple could not afford their own, sometimes inviting other gentry who could be expected to make a generous gift to the newlyweds.[12] In many places the church expected all those attending a wedding service to place contributions in a special plate provided for that purpose. In Wales, where "givings" (*cormortha*) had the force of local law behind them, all those wed in certain churches could expect to benefit from such a collection. So many outsiders took advantage of the *cormortha* at St. Peter's Church in Carmarthen by marrying there that the wealthier parishioners complained and the practice was suppressed in the sixteenth century. Henceforth, gifts were voluntary, given outside the church after the wedding service.[13]

In England the compulsory aspects of giving also came under criticism as the wealthy disengaged themselves from the life of the poor and denied any responsibility beyond that they owed to their personal employees. In the sixteenth and seventeenth centuries masters still gave wedding gifts to their servants, but privately and before the wedding itself, because they did not wish to encourage the festivities of those of a lower social station. In Coventry and other towns, guildsmen ceased to require attendance at weddings, while the church also withdrew its charitable functions. By the seventeenth century most of Essex's wedding houses had fallen into ruins. The ediface at Ansley had become a poor house in the 1630s; its counterpart at Great Yeldham was converted into a school. Bequests providing dowries to poor women lapsed and in many parts of England, especially in the south and east, it became rare for the clergy to take an active part in wedding festivities as they had once done.[14]

Town elites were no less assiduous about limiting the contributions that guests could make to a marriage. It was charged that big weddings encouraged drunkenness and tumult, and that the provision of ale and entertainment for a small charge violated local licensing law. The prohibitions were often justified in the name of economy, but when the officers of the Manchester Court Leet acted in the 1560s to limit the contribution of each wedding guest to four pence, they may well have been acting less to protect scarce resources than to prevent the poor from marrying on the proceeds of a big wedding.[15] The boroughreeve allowed the maximum charge to double over the next eighty years, but, in the meantime, imposed additional restrictions on the sumptuousness of the occasion, strengthened the monopoly of the municipal musicians (the waits) on the provision of entertainment, and limited the number of guests to twenty. In 1573 it was decreed that "Not servant or childe shall from henceforth Resort to any Weddinge howses or Ales w'hout they be sent by their fathers or masters," but this, like the other orders, were so often repeated that it is clear that compliance was far from complete. In 1606 the boroughreeve was again threatening people who "either privatelye or apptlye [on the sly] lay on a wedding feast above the fixed contribution of 6d." In the same year, the nearby Salford Portmote set a similar limit to prevent "extreame expenses and charges at wedding dynners." Shortly thereafter a man was fined by the same court for paying eleven pence; and a woman confessed that in addition to the legal contribution, she "gave a groate to the brid [bride]."[16]

These prohibitions were but part of the late sixteenth and early seventeenth century social reaction against so-called "beggar weddings" that also found expression in the enforcement settlement regulations, the tearing down of cottages, and outright prohibition of pauper marriages. William Harrison observed in 1577 that "a great number complain of the increase of poverty . . . very poor folks, often without all manner of occupying, sith (since) the ground of the parish is gotten up into a few men's hands, yet sometimes into the tenure of one, two, or three, whereby the rest are compelled either to be hired servants unto the other, or else to beg their bread in misery from door to door."[17] The attitude toward the poor among the village elites had so hardened that another Essex man, clergyman R. Younge, railed against "an uncircumcised generation, unbaptized, out of the church. . . . They have nothing in propriety but their licentious life and lawless condition. . . . They have no particular wives, neither do they range themselves into families, but consort together as beasts." The big farmers and clothiers who had once worried about labor shortage, now panicked at the glut. The alarm was sounded by Philip Stubbes in the 1580s:

> You have every saucy boy of ten, fourteen, or twenty years of age to catch up a woman and marry her . . . without any respect how they may hive together without sufficient maintenance. . . . Then they build up a cottage, though but of elder poles, in the very land end . . . , where they live as beggars all their life.[18]

Bunyan was no less insistent on the same point: "It is too much a custom of young people now to think themselves wise enough to make their own choice."[19] Although the effort to impose strict control over the marriage of minors was not to achieve complete success until the Hardwicke Marriage Act of 1753, generational tensions were evident throughout the entire seventeenth and early eighteenth centuries.[20] These were reinforced by social cleavages that tended to set the rate-paying elders of the community against the young, especially those who would make a "beggar wedding." Overseers of the poor were instructed not to provide houses to those young persons "as will marry before they have provided themselves with a settling."[21] Yarmouth aldermen ordered in 1625 that no poor persons could marry until they had proved they could support a family.[22] "If William Byfflett marry to Sarah Croslye contrary to the mynde of the townsemen, his collection [poor relief] should be detayned," was the decision handed down by the town meeting of Finchingfield, Essex, in the same period.[23] The first two decades of the seventeenth century were a critical turning point as far as poor law policy was concerned. Responding to economic crisis, the village notables of places like Terling became more conscious of the differences between themselves and the poor. The single paupers were left no alternative but to leave the village if they wished to marry, because, as happened to one Terling laborer who had his banns read in the Terling church, "the parish would not suffer them to marry. . . . " He and his sweetheart simply took up cohabitation.[24]

The parishioners of Stockton, Worcestershire, had forbidden the 1618 marriage of Anthony Addames because they were "not wiling he should bring her [a wife] into the parish, saying they would breed up a charge among them."[25] When Edward Morton, a farm servant to John Gadwin, announced his intention to marry Gadwin's daughter, Jane, in 1653, the villagers of Frampton, Lincolnshire, raised the question of whether Morton had been married previously. This seems to have been largely a pretext, for their real worry was not Morton's civil but economic status:

> they verily believed hee was a very poore man and yt hee had not then any house to live in, and therefore they did disgree that he might ere hee wur married gett some sufficient man to bee bound wth him to secur ye Towee from any charge by him or his.[26]

This kind of restrictive policy continued throughout the seventeenth century, relaxing and tightening according to how far the local oligarchies thought they could press their control of marriage. The 1650s seem to have been a particularly repressive decade. Frustrated by the church's inability to enforce its own canons, the puritans installed civil marriage as a more efficient means of discipline.[27] The experiment was brief but when it was over the young and the poor welcomed the return of a more lax ecclesiastical administration of marriage. Still, they were subject to a vigilant parish, which asked for securities when paupers announced their intention to marry. Money was speaking with increased authority, a fact that disturbed Carew Reynel, who thought it "is an ill custom in many country parishes, where they, as much as they can, hinder poor people from marrying."[28]

Caught between the poor and the rate-paying parishioners, seventeenth-century clergy found themselves in a difficult position. William Jackson, an Essex parson, may have thought he was currying favor with the right people when he urged his congregation to raise objections to the marriage of a pauper cripple, asking them "if they knewe lawful cause why they [the couple] might not doe so." However, apparently he misjudged the parish politics, for he "gave offense to parties then livinge and some others," and years later, when the churchwardens presented him for irregularities, they reminded him of his lack of charity.[29] Where a parish was tightly controlled by a major landowner or an oligarchy of rate payers, as in Terling, the story would have been different. The poor were forced to look to large, "open" parishes if they wished to marry and settle. In the next two centuries, much of the population growth would occur in those places, a reflection of the shrinking opportunities elsewhere.[30]

II

As country parishes and small towns became more restrictive, the opportunities offered by the larger cities became more inviting. Robert Johnson, an Essex laborer, had already been denied marriage once by his local parish. When he decided to try again, he avoided the publicity of banns by going to be wed in London, where he knew he could be married without difficulty.[31] He probably wed at one of the many "lawless churches," where parsons paid little attention to the residence or condition of those who paid the fees. A favorite resort of Essex people throughout the seventeenth century was St. Benets Paul's Wharf.[32] Many were under the mistaken impression that the chapel at the Tower of London was equally tolerant, for the minister there reported in the 1590s that he "refused to marry [fifty] coming w[i]th licence, and without parents consent w[i]thin the space of a half a yeare."[33] When several couples living in Marloe Magna, Oxfordshire, were interrogated in the 1660s about their marital credentials, it was discovered that one of them, William Hayward, a bargeman, had gone to great lengths to avoid the embarrassment of being refused marriage in his own parish. He too had sought the obliging clergyman at St. Benets Paul's Wharf in London and, although very poor, paid the fee for a special license to be married there.[34]

The alternative of marriage by license had originated in the fifteenth century as a special dispensation reserved for persons of high status willing to pay the bishop for the privilege of marrying at irregular times and without the publicity of banns. The church had not been able to limit the clientele, however, and during the next two centuries the sale of licenses increased enormously.[35] Although the well-to-do could better afford it, licenses were purchased by all manner of people. While the bishops retained nominal control over sale, they often issued blanks to surrogates among the parish clergy, who, for the sake of the lucrative fees, made mockery of the controls on age and parental consent they were supposed to administer. Both bishops and surrogates were supposed to administer oaths and demand securities, but these too were laxly attended to. The situation had already become a scandal by the late sixteenth century when the rector at the Weston Eve church allowed "a younge maide to be maried, knowinge that she was assured to another, and the banes forbidden by her mother." But the situation was even worse a century later when it was said that many surrogates were flogging cheap licenses: "some keep Markets weekly for this purpose, there exposing their blank Licence to Sale, as Tradesmen do their Wares."[36]

In seventeenth-century Somerset the parishes of Milverton and Putney, both in the Peculiar of Ilminister, drew many weddings away from other parishes.[37] Of Samuel Thompson, an East Anglican surrogate, it was said that "at his request, the wedding was performed in his church,

9. Elopement played an important part in the courtship process throughout the seventeenth and eighteenth centuries. Rowlandson made light of it in this 1812 print *Off She Goes*, even as church and state moved to reinforce parental authority. (Used by permission of the Trustees of the British Museum)

that he might recover additional fees."[38] This kind of parochial greed outraged the vicar of Almondbury, Yorkshire, who was losing many marriages in the same manner:

> I am prepared to name three several couples, all now living in this very Town; who (when I Refused to Proceed in ye Publication of Bans, because ye Fathers of ye several girls (women I canot call them) applied themselves to me, alledging a Lawful Impediment viz. nonage & want of Consent) all went away, in Contempt of their parents & were married by ye neighbouring surrogates.[39]

Although the license was not meant to encourage marriage against the will of parents or parish, it was used for this purpose, and apparently with increasing frequency. The vicar at Swinton Chapel in Doncaster was in trouble in the 1740s for marrying a couple who "both had Parish pay."[40] Already in the sixteenth century there were complaints that license undermined patriarchal authority. The bishops attempted to tighten their procedures in the face of criticism, but failed to do anything to reduce the problem. During the brief period of civil marriage in the 1650s, when licenses were abolished temporarily, the want of privacy was strongly felt. During the Restoration, the popularity of the marriage license increased still further to the point that in the early eighteenth century perhaps a third of all marriages were conducted in that manner.[41] Surrogates like Nottinghamshire's Amos Sweetaple and the Gloucestershire priest John Kelham attracted hundreds of couples from far and wide.[42] Their counterpart in Stratford-upon-Avon made his church a popular wedding place by offering attractive prices for wedding anyone who purchased a license there.[43] A particularly thriving business was done by the so-called Peculiars, places outside direct episcopal jurisdiction and therefore free from all regulation. The trade in marriages at Peak Forest Chapel in Derbyshire increased enormously from the 1720s through the 1750s, and was said to be worth a hundred pounds a year to the incumbent there.[44]

Most surrogates operated within the canon law, but there were other places where clergy took the liberty to conduct weddings without either banns or licenses. London had several dozen of these "Lawless churches" from the sixteenth century onwards, among them the Tower of London, Holy Trinity (Minories), St. James (Duke Place), and the chapels of the Mint and Newgate Prison.[45] Most infamous of all were the so-called "Rules" of Fleet Prison. Clandestine marriages had been conducted in the prison's chapel since 1613, but it did not become a major center until a hundred years later when its competitors were closed by parliamentary action. Holy Trinity probably conducted over thirty thousand irregular marriages in the period from 1644 to 1695.[46] From the 1690s, until it was suppressed in 1754, the Fleet is estimated to have conducted as many as 300,000 unions.[47]

The notoriety of the Fleet has obscured the existence of hundreds of other places where marriage without proper banns or license were performed. Clandestine practice was everywhere, in rural areas as well as in the larger towns.[48] While irregular forms of marriage had been a problem throughout the Middle Ages, the scale of clandestineness from the late sixteenth century onwards was unprecedented. We learn from the church court records that Thomas Clark was marrying persons from other parishes under the cover of darkness.[49] Moses Meacham, the curate of Honningham, Warwickshire, was brought before the magistrates for the same offense in the 1590s.[50] Candlelight was used by the Vicar of Elmton to conduct a wedding in 1601. Other illicit marriages were made in alehouses, barns, private houses, highways, meadows, and one was said to have been done "under a bushe."[51] Certain places soon gained a reputation for being lawless. Sandon Church attracted many from the surrounding Essex parishes in the early seventeenth century; later Reverend Henry Wooton made Little Pardon a kind of local Gretna Green for people from both Essex and Hertfordshire.[52] Sometimes a ruined church or chapel became popular because it no longer lay within episcopal jurisdiction. The lawless church at West Thurrock, Essex, stood alone in a marsh a half mile from the village and beyond a seawall.[53]

Similar places existed in virtually every part of England and Wales. Where there was no lawless church near, people would travel considerable distances to reach one. When seventeenth-century Somerset couples could not get a license in their own county, they "got themselves to Dorsetshire and procured themselves to be married there."[54] The people of Lyme Regis were accustomed to riding out into the countryside to find the cheapest fees and the greatest privacy; on the other hand, when an Essex girl "stole away from Mistress Elmeasure," she and her groom went to St. Botoloph's Church in London to be married.[55]

Many of the clergy involved in clandestine marriage were unbeneficed, ordained but without a salaried position. Others were regular clergy unable to get by on their meager earnings. In Glamorgan the trade was attributed to "a parcel of slotting curates," who "for a crown or at most a guinea, would marry anyone under a hedge."[56] The curate of Enderly in Leicestershire defended himself by saying his income was only eight pounds a year; at Wigston Magna the vicar was getting only thirteen pounds and had to petition for an increase in order to clothe himself. Many lived at a lower standard than their parishioners and were vulnerable to bribes from those in and outside their churches.[57] Stephen Sutton found a "lawless" curate ensconced in the parish next to his in Yorkshire and reported him to the bishop for "keeping a public Alehouse, his Marrying of Persons without any due Publication of Banns or Licence to do so, and likewise at uncanonical Hours." He did, however, urge leniency, for the miscreant had "a wife and a large Family of Children, [and] any great severity wou'd assuredly ruin both Him and Them."[58] One of the most successful Fleet "marriers," a man named Gaynam, pleaded for himself that "I am old and infirm and not able to get any Preferment."[59] When confronted by William Wynne with evidence of his clandestine practices in the 1730s, James Langford pleaded a similar, desperate poverty. Many parsons were so dependent on their parishioners that they felt themselves forced to violate the canon law:

> All our mean and unwarrantable compliances spring from this cause, *viz,* from our being but half Protestants, from our continueing still to receive money for obits and to accept their [the parishioners] oblations at funerals of their relations and friends. These perquisitions make us Welsh clergy very supple and obliging to a fault. We dare resist in nothing, especially if our benefices are small, or shou'd we but attempt to follow our own wills and inclinations in respects of christenings and the like, up starts some

supream rough coat, the *dux gregis*, and, with a stern, supercillious air, crys "we'l tame the sparks, we'll sink the offerings."[60]

Some of these obliging clergy not only provided marriage on demand, but catered to all wedding festivities. At Bedminster, Reverend Emuel Collins kept a public house, The Duke of Marlborough, where he conducted marriages and further supplemented his income by providing cakes and ale.[61] Elleanor Echersall of Winchcomb, Gloucestershire, was charged in 1616 with "suffering Mr. Jones, late Curate of Woolster, to marry people in her house."[62] Given the lucrative nature of the trade, it is not surprising to find a few enterprising laymen competing with the lawless clergy. William Thorndale was presented before the courts in 1677 "for marrying people being a lay man," though he may have been a member of a dissenting sect.[63] But there is no doubt about John Boroston, a Bristol barber, who was charged in Quarter Sessions in 1727 with "pretending to be in holy orders" and defrauding persons by marrying them for as little as eighteen pence.[64] In Berkshire a dairyman named Gabriell Ross used a public house as his place of celebration; and there were many others scattered over the face of England and Wales.[65] A Devon yeoman, Joseph Buckett, married a couple in 1725 at "a house commonly known by the name of smoking house within the parish of Marleton." And, when William Wynne investigated Breconshire in the 1730s, he found considerable irregularity:

> Evan Cadwalader, a layman, who, on conviction of having married 2 couples, was forc'd to fly the country, is now suffer'd to resettle in the town of Bala and violently suspected of doing the like jobs in secret. Its highly probable that he joins many and many hands, because few if none of the common sort have for these 3 months past had their banns publish'd without the visible marks of previous criminal conversation [sexual intercourse].[66]

The area known as the "Rules" of Fleet Prison provided perhaps the most complete accommodations. There the lawless parsons were on retainer to various well-advertised "marriage houses," whose "plyers" touted them in the streets around the Fleet: "Madam, you want a parson? . . . Sir, will you be pleased to walk in and be married."[67] Clients shopped for the best bargain, sometimes finding a "marrier" who would perform the service for as little as two shillings, six pence. Some of the Fleet parsons were totally unscrupulous, but many regarded themselves as operating just within the canon law (which until 1753 recognized all properly made vows as constituting marriage) and were careful to turn away couples they suspected of being grossly under age or harboring fraudulent intent. Most were themselves clerics, who donned vestments, followed the Book of Common Prayer, and saw to it that a ring was used, even going as far as renting these to the couple.[68] Special registrars were on hand to record the event and provide certificates, which were accepted by courts as evidence of marriage.[69] For a small additional fee the marriage houses provided bride cakes, ale, and even the marriage

10. A scene from the Fleet, 1747. The Fleet parsons compete for the wedding business of the young couple. The dwarf in the foreground is probably a tout for one of the marriage houses, the obese woman its owner. (Used by permission of the Trustees of the British Museum)

bed. John Floud recorded in his notebook that when Thomas Stringer and Ann Criswell came to him "it being pretty late, they lay ere, and paid me one shilling for bed."[70] In another instance the newlyweds did not even spend the night: "The couple were bedded about six minutes and paid only five shillings per total, being friends of Mary Hall."[71] Parents were rarely in attendance, but it seems that couples brought close friends to witness. They wanted their privacy, but not at the expense of that festivity which was commonly regarded as the essence of a proper wedding. Therefore, when Samuel Pickering attended a Fleet marriage in 1751, he gave the bride away, "saw the ring put on her hand, and broke the biscuit over her head."[72]

Court records, together with the notebooks of the Fleet parsons, provide a fascinating portrait of clandestine marriage, of the purveyors as well as the clients. Most of the latter were of the humbler classes, but not necessarily of the very lowest social order. Many were craftspersons and small traders, together with a fair number of soldiers, sailors, and travelers of all kinds. Fears that the Fleet encouraged the seduction of aristocratic heirs and heiresses appear to have been exaggerated, for there were relatively few wealthy patrons. Instead, it appears to have catered largely to the middle strata of the population who wished to marry "without loss of Time, Hindrance of Business, and Knowledge of Friends."[73] The fact that clandestine marriages were somewhat cheaper than wedding by banns, and a good deal less expensive than license, can explain only part of their appeal. Not all were as economical as the shilling weddings at the Dale Abbey Chapel. In London some went as cheaply as two shillings and sixpence, but most were seven or eight shillings with the cost of a certificate, a week's wages for ordinary crafts-men in the eighteenth century.[74] In reality, it was the privacy rather than the savings that made clandestine marriage so attractive. Widows and widowers making second marriages against the wishes of family preferred the secrecy. So too did couples disparate in age or social sta-tion, like old Thomas Ferris, who, when he wed young Mary Marshall from his death bed in 1638, wanted to keep it quiet because it was a marriage of convenience designed to maintain his family's claim on a valuable copyhold. Had it been known, his landlord might have at-tempted to stop it.[75] Sailors on short leave, persons marrying within the prohibited degrees, widows wanting to retain their jointures, and preg-nant women near to their time all found clandestine wedding advan-tageous.[76] Fortune hunters and bigamists also had obvious reasons for avoiding marriage in their home parish.[77]

By far the most common reason, however, was the desire to avoid "the Knowledge of Friends," meaning family. Like the secret betrothals of the earlier period, it was the young people's way of countering the power of patriarchy. When Gilbert Wright and Elizabeth Wheaton ran off to Formby Chapel to wed, she said "it was because of her frendes, that were against her, that she shuld not marry hym."[78] Most who resorted to clandestine marriages seem to have been persons of normal marrying age who had encountered parental or parish resistance. Typical was the Sussex couple who, when they first encountered objections, consulted with their parish priest, who advised them to see a Fleet parson because: "He would have done it himself but was apprehensive he might offend some Friends, he himself living in yt neighbor-hood. . . . " He offered instead to accompany the couple to London and "stand Father" to the bride.[79]

He was typical of the clergy who, while submissive to interests of parents and parish officers, had few scruples about assisting couples to marry outside their parishes, an act that did not endanger their position or add to the local rates.[80] When called to account in the church courts for their actions, clandestine "marriers" declared they had no intention of subverting authority. Invariably they rationalized their actions as sus-taining rather than subverting morality by facilitating matrimony.[81] As for their clients, John Pruett has noted that they were "marrying without their parents consent or in order to conceal a premarital pregnancy."[82] Most probably returned home after their "stoln" marriages, ultimately reconciling with their parents and local authorities. This was what the couples who patronized Thomas Morgan, the lawless vicar of St. Davids Church in Llanvaes, did. He testified that he wed people at midnight in his own house "in order to oblige the said parties to keep privately and conceal the said clandestine marriages till such tymes that banns should be published or licences obtained and be married again, and [he] saith that the said parties were afterwards married publically by banns."[83]

Those who came to Evan Cadwalader apparently wanted to protect themselves against the charge of premarital fornication, for most of them also subsequently married by banns even though at an advanced stage of pregnancy.[84] Should anyone have challenged their right to be lovers, they could simply have said they were already wed and innocent of any immorality. Almost sixty percent of the women who used the facilities of London's Savoy Chapel in the 1750s were said to be pregnant. In some cases women attempted to save their reputations and those of their families by backdating the Fleet marriage certificates. Mary Moore, who was about to have a child, applied in 1724 to Mrs. Hodgkinson, the keeper of the Hand and Pen, a marriage house in Fleet Lane, who told her that "for a half-a-guinea, it might be entered backwards in the book and would skreen her from the anger of her friends."[85] As the parish officers were also interested in her case, this entry was doubly valuable to Mary Moore, for it established simultaneously her social and legal claims to the rights of a married woman, including settlement in her husband's parish. She avoided removal, saved her reputation and perhaps that of her family, and, at the same time, made her child legitimate—and all for little more than the cost of a regular wedding.

Many couples seemed to have used the Fleet and other clandestine facilities as a way of satisfying their parents by removing some stigma, usually the imputation of bastardy. John Nelson and Mary Barnes, who were wed in 1729, asked the Fleet registrar to date "the wedding 5 November 1727 to please their parents."[86] Sometimes a couple would simply obtain a backdated certificate like the one noted in John Mottram's register: "Not married but obtained this private Register for fear of their parents."[87] In the Breconshire parish of Llancykil clandestine marriage had become a substitute for the betrothals, which had once legitimated a couple's right to one another's company, including intercourse. There couples used it as a kind of insurance. If the couple proved incompatible or barren, then they were free to pursue other mates. If they became a couple or a child resulted, a church wedding was facilitated:

> The country people, its to be imagin'd are first marry'd by either this layman [Cadwalader] or else by Langord [Langford] and, to screen themselves from publick reproach, and the parson that marries [them] from punishment, they some time after apply to the parish minister. When the females want but very few months, and sometimes but a few weeks, of lyeing in, their banns are in due and solemn form published, and, paying the parson and the clerk their respective fees, are all married without being ask'd any more questions than what the church form contains.[88]

Clandestine marriage functioned like the old betrothal rites in other ways as well. While it could protect the reputation of the couple, it was nevertheless something less binding than a big wedding, and thus more suitable to the fluid, unpredictable lives of these young people. It was clearly regarded as conditional, an intermediate status that could be terminated by consent of the parties. Many of the Fleet's clients went away "half-married" after completing only part of the ceremony or picking up only a registrar's certificate.[89] Like the betrothal, this meant they had some claim on one another short of indissolubility. The woman was protected should pregnancy result, but neither party was as yet completely committed to lifelong matrimony, which, in a formally divorceless society, was the accepted consequence of a big wedding.

III

The poor were not easily deterred from marrying, and, when the ways of the reformed church did not suit them, they fashioned their own rites out of the materials of the traditional betrothal and big wedding. Deprived of the church ale and the wedding house, they removed to the alehouse or the village green, where they set out signs called "bride stakes" or "bride bushes" to announce their wedding feast to friends, neighbors, and even passing strangers, all of whom were invited to contribute something for the food, drink, and entertainment, the profits going to the newlyweds. The village elites scorned what they called "penny weddings" or "beggar weddings," but they proliferated nevertheless.[90] While it had long since ceased to be the custom of persons of his class to solicit gifts or patronage for their own marriage, we find Reverend Ralph Josselin officiating at a friend's wedding in 1647 where "Frends offerd freely [and] he tooke above 56 pound."[91] Some decades later, in the same county of Essex, a similar wedding was recorded, where

> the people invited to it, like soldiers of a country train band, march up to the bride, present their money and wheel about. After the offering is over, there is a pair of gloves laid on the table, most monstrously bedaubed about with ribbon, which by way of auction is set to sale. And he who gives the most, and he whose lot it is for to have them, shall withal have a kiss of the bride.[92]

The larger the affair the better, for it was said that a successful "brideale" of this kind could earn a poor couple the equivalent of half a year's wages.[93] In places where the spirit of communal giving persisted, now mainly in the north and west, it was said that "each one brings such a Dish, or so manie with him, as his Wife and he doo consult upon, but alwaies with this consideration, that the lesser Friend shall have the better provision."[94]

The village elites did not encourage this form of charity and as early as 1608 it was said that "this Custome is only put to use amongst them that stand in need."[95] We know very little about the nuptial habits of the rural proletariat, largely because in order to avoid official censure they kept things very quiet. Many seem to have joined themselves together merely by consent, wishing a flexible arrangement that was compatible with the mobility demanded of a proletarianized labor force. The men often had to go off to other parishes in search of work and could not maintain a family in a way demanded by the rules of the big wedding. The churchwardens of Amstead Cherys presented Elizabeth Burridge and Grace Aviatts in 1662 as "(beyinge maryed women) for absentinge themselves and not living with theire husbands." Burridge told them her husband was a live-in servant; Aviatts' excuse was "that her husband worketh at Beckansfield for day wages and resorteth to her once or twic[e] a week at her father's house."[96] An increasing number of wage earning people must have been finding it difficult to live together. Of the indigent adult women living in Norwich in the 1570s, eight percent were said to be "deserted" wives.[97] This figure probably increased over the next two centuries as more couples found themselves forced to separate for reasons similar to those of the Burridges and the Aviatts.

It was apparently not unusual for a deserted woman to pick up with another man. A Wiltshire wife was arrested in Essex while on the road with a chapman, living "as if she were his own wife."[98] It is known that some nonconformist sects authorized divorces in the sixteenth and early seventeenth centuries, but there were probably many more "self-divorces," especially at the proletarian level. In 1575 a London man turned away his wife "sayinge that she is not his wief . . . for that she wold not be ruled." In another instance, John Brown refused to live with his spouse because "he thincketh she doth not love him."[99] Both men and women believed that they were free to remarry if their spouse was notoriously unfaithful, had left them for seven years, was reputed dead, or had themselves remarried. At Barking a man pleaded in 1579 that, because his wife had gone off with another man, "he thinketh that he might marry again." Churchwardens at Ravenstone did not know "upon what pretense of divorce" Anne Hannah had married a second husband when her first was still living, but she informed the church court that he had left her seven years earlier.[100] There was nothing casual about these self-divorces, which were often accompanied by financial agreements, sometimes written but mainly oral, made before witnesses.[101]

The proletarian practice of self-marriage and self-divorce clearly had its own rules. Like the contemporary betrothal, all that was needed was consent made in the presence of witnesses. It should not be surprising, given prevailing courtship patterns, that a certain amount of polygamy was also evident, especially among migrant workers. Essex authorities arrested one group in the 1590s that consisted of two men, four women, and twenty-six children. The leader of the band was a Yorkshire man, James Simson, who had apparently recruited his ménage during his wanderings through Lincolnshire, Cambridgeshire, and Norfolk.[102] Other such groups appeared with some frequency throughout the seventeenth century, apparently uninhibited by the stringent bigamy law of 1604 or the adultery act of 1650.[103]

IV

Resistance to ecclesiastical authority by the poor was far from new. Lollardy had expressed late medieval objections to marriage fees; and there was a renewal of popular anticlericalism when parish registration was introduced in the early sixteenth century. Because the reformed clergy were more dependent on fees than their Catholic predecessors, anticlericalism tended to take on new life in the sixteenth and seventeenth centuries. What made the sixteenth- and seventeenth-century rebellion against church fees so much more unsettling was the growing size of the population that could not afford them nor really needed the publicity of a big church wedding because they had no chance of ever attaining the status of a householder that made such a celebration useful or meaningful.

Even more disconcerting was the dissent of those who were now denying the authority of the church in matters matrimonial on the basis of principle. Gerrard Winstanley seethed at the idea that fees were charged for something that was supposed to be obligatory. "A man must not take a wife, but the priest must give him her . . . ," and all this was "but to get money."[104] Edmund Hall was no less upset with the church courts citing people "for working on holidays or marrying without license or upon a groundless suspicion of unchastity. Many such poor pretenses, merely to drain the people's purses, did their officers make."[105] Anything that stood in the way of matrimony—whether it be the mercenary church, tyrannical parents, or an uncaring community—was seen as detrimental to spiritual perfection and social well-being. "Everyman and woman shall have the free liberty to marry whom they love, if they can obtain the love and liking of that party whom they would marry," argued Winstanley, "Neither birth nor portion shall hinder the match, for we are all of one family, mankind."[106]

Today, when freedom and equality are so often defined in opposition to marriage, it is difficult if not impossible to appreciate the radical zeal and revolutionary consequences of this radical advocacy of the personal right to holy matrimony. For religious nonconformists it was a matter not only of material satisfaction but of personal salvation. To Jeremy Taylor, "marital love is a thing as pure as light, sacred as a temple, lasting as the world." Robert Crosse was convinced that conjugal relationship was an "earthly paradise of happiness."[107] Richard Greenham argued passionately that the well-ordered family was the only institution capable of generating a saintly social order: "If ever we would have the church of God to continue among us we must bring it into our households, and nourish it in our families."[108] These were people who had lost confidence in other social and economic institutions, including the village and the guild, and for whom the couple was now the true repository of all "healthful pleasures and profitable commodities."[109] A sound marriage, based on a unique emotional bond William Baxter designated "Conjugal Love," was in the view of other puritans "a business of greatest consequence, and that whereon the maine comfort or discomfort of a mans life doth depend; that which may make thine house to bee as an heaven or an hell here upon earth."[110] Even friendship, which had previously been seen as essential to well-being (at least for men), was now subordinated to that unique bond that could exist only between husband and wife.[111] Conjugal love was the model and the guarantee of a stable, consensual society that these early capitalists hoped would replace the old order of privilege and birth. In the context of the sixteenth and seventeenth centuries, the puritan insistence on its supremacy, which seems to us so conservative, was in fact revolutionary.

To make sure that neither "birth nor portion" would infringe on a man or woman's right to marry, Winstanley proposed a community fund for marriage portions, an idea that found resonance a hundred and fifty years later in Tom Paine's advocacy of marriage and maternal benefits.[112] But Winstanley and the more radical Ranter sects were isolated from the moderate puritan elements in their concern for the plight of the poor. Most of the latter were of the "middling sort" and were much more concerned with their own individual right to material and spiritual salvation than any collective solution. On the village level it was precisely these puritan elites who were withdrawing their support from the traditional marriage charities and closing down the old bride ales. They wished to promote holy matrimony, but only for those who could afford to establish economic independence. Their advice to the poor was to work hard and be chaste, for there was no reward on earth or in heaven for those who "hive together without sufficient maintenance."

This class division was partly obscured by the generational tensions that cut across the divisions between the propertied and the poor. Whether rich or poor, young people often encountered parental opposition and thus were drawn to the alternative forms of marriage that thwarted patriarchal authority. Gender conflict also tended to unite women of different social origin against the existing marriage law. The decomposition of peasant and artisan society had affected women as much and perhaps even more than men. As we have seen, women had enjoyed a good deal of freedom in courtship. They were bound to resent any restriction imposed by parents or parish; and so it is not surprising to find the daughters of the middling sort as well as the poor pressing for their right, as junior partners, to elect their future spouses.[113]

Many young women and men turned to nonconformist religious sects for the approval and support denied them by parents or parish. Separatist religious congregations attracted many young single persons precisely because they were supportive both spiritually and materially of marriages made by their converts, even when these were in defiance of parents or kinfolk. Younger sons and daughters, the persons least likely to get parental support, were prominent among the early Quakers.[114] They, together with Baptists, Grindletonians, and other sects, carried on the sixteenth-century Familist practice of marrying without a priest before the assembled body of believers. While this was illegal, they justified it by the idea that these unions were witnessed by godly elders, who, by virtue of their own sainted marriages, were the spiritual equals of the clergy. Using the same logic, radical puritans also justified self-divorce when it was properly adjudicated and witnessed by the congregation.[115]

This radical nonconformity remained somewhat hidden until the revolutionary 1640s and 1650s, when both clerical and secular authority collapsed and there occurred what can justifiably be called the first modern sexual revolution, a broadly based revolt against traditional marriage discipline in which the strands of puritanism and antinomianism seemed at times to reinforce one another. The puritans' notion of marriage as a spiritual and material partnership was carried to its logical conclusions. Not only was patriarchy challenged by children claiming their right to marry, but wives, no longer content with spiritual equality, claimed social parity with their husbands. The Quakers dispensed with the vow of obedience in their marriage ceremony, and their leader George Fox acknowledged his spouse's right not only to her conscience but her property.[116] Other sectarians took the opportunity to press for a single moral standard (a strict one, of course), and there were even those who promoted the idea of equal grounds for divorce for both men and women.[117] While puritans did not wish to abandon marriage as such, some believed a bad marriage was ungodly and should be terminated. The same revolutionary decades produced an intense discussion of ways to perfect that "earthly paradise," including varieties of polygamy and marriage by annual contract, renewable by the parties involved.[118]

In their insistence on the privileged status of conjugal love, the moderate puritans tended to ignore all other social and emotional relationships. It was the Ranters who, being more reflective of the values and needs of the poor, offered alternatives to monogamy and the nuclear family more in line with the polygamous courtship and big wedding traditions of the peasants and artisans. The disinherited listened more attentively to antinomians like Thomas Webbe, the Wiltshire parson, who declared "it was lawful for him to lie with any woman," for "there is no heaven but women, nor no hell save marriage."[119] Abiezer Coppe, an Oxford scholar who asserted that "community of wives is lawful," also taught that monogamy was the true source of wickedness. "Give over thy stinking family duties," he proclaimed, "for under them lies snapping, snarling, biting besides covetness, horrid hypocrisy, envy, malice, and evil-surmising."[120] Here, in the divisions between the moderates and the radicals, we can detect the long-standing tension between the rights of conjugal love and the duties of household and family. Those who followed Winstanley saw in the public provision of marriage portions their last chance to establish the prerequisites of an independent household. Coppe's disciples had given up that hope and now saw monogamy and the nuclear household more as a burden than an advantage.

To the substantial householder monogamy was heaven; for the men and women without the resources to maintain the economic independence this required, the nuclear family could be hell. The latter were appealed to by John Holland, who wrote: "The way that for one man to be tied to one woman, or one woman to one man, is the fruit of the curse; but, they say, we are freed from the curse, therefore it is our liberty to make use of whom we please."[121] This antinomian position was a favorite of itinerant preachers—some crisscrossing the country with their common-law wives, others loving and leaving women as they went. The men's holiness was apparently highly seductive, especially to women who knew no other way to salvation but through the masculine godhead. When Mary Gadbury attached herself to William Franklin, a ropemaker who said he was Christ incarnate, she thought of herself as the "Spouse of Christ" until her holyman betrayed himself and their union to the authorities.[122]

The preachings of Ranters like Coppe and Holland, together with the behavior of William Franklin and Mary Gadbury, would seem to anticipate the critique of the nuclear family launched by socialists and feminists two centuries later, but in reality they had little in common with these modern movements, for they either looked back to older antinomian traditions or served up polygamist utopias no less patriarchal than the monogamy they criticized. The antinomians offered no social vision and, while the polygamists might promise women security, they said nothing about equality. Not surprisingly many women preferred the traditional role of virgin brides of Christ to the very risky union with the carnal godhead tried by Mary Gadbury. A strong ascetic element was intertwined with seventeenth-century radicalism; not only women but also men, like the Quaker leader George Fox, were uncomfortable with the physical aspects of marriage.[123] This pious asceticism anticipated not only eighteenth-century Methodist behavior but the renunciation of earthly marriage by the latter-day prophetesses, Mother Ann Lee and Joanna Southcutt. It seems that seventeenth-century women were aware that sexual freedom without birth control might be heaven for men, but meant hell for women. And if they needed any further warning, there was Gerrard Winstanley's timely admonition: "Therefore you women beware, for this ranting practice is not the restoring but the destroying power of creation. . . . By seeking their [men's] own freedom, they embondage others [women and children]."[124]

The Ranters offered no real alternative to holy matrimony. They might rebel against convention, but they could not transform it. When secular and religious authority was restored in the 1660s, they were either hounded out of Britain or forced to return to the silence that had been their lot in previous centuries. The stronger historical movement was represented by those who wished to perfect rather than destroy the patriarchal nuclear family. They were Britain's premier middle class, the successful farmers and businessmen who, while they championed freedom for other people's wives and children, took a much harder line when it came to their own. They acknowledged that young persons should not be coerced into marriage against their will, but they insisted on parental consent. The nonconformist congregations they founded and supported had a much stricter marriage discipline than did the established church. Members were expelled not only for premarital fornication, but failure to obtain the consent of their elders. Ironically, many young Quakers were forced to turn to the Church of England to find a form of clandestine marriage when their matches were forbidden by their own Meetings.[125] A major reason why puritans had been advocates of civil marriage since the late sixteenth century was not a libertarian one, but rather their perception that the Church of England was too lax and that civil magistrates, as heads of households, would be much more severe against both adultery and elopement. When civil marriage was introduced during the Civil War, it effectively closed those loopholes in the canon law that had for so long frustrated patriarchal authority.[126]

The attitude held by the middling sort toward women was no less patriarchal despite its new emphasis on conjugal affection. What appears to us as an obvious contradiction between the puritan advocacy of the spiritual equality of men and women and the insistence that the female be the subordinate partner in marriage did not bother them unduly, except during the radical 1640s and 1650s, when so much else was in dispute. Once the revolutionary crisis was over, what William Gouge called the "little commonwealth" regained its equilibrium. Women of the new middle class had no choice but to accept the patriarchal nuclear family. As Christopher Hill has pointed out: "As long as the family farm and the small family business predominated, the patriarchal attitudes corresponded to economic realities; it became nauseating only when transformed into the impersonal relations of developed industrial capitalism, dominated by the blind working of the market."[127] Marriage remained a matter of property, and fathers and husbands, who controlled that precious commodity, remained the masters. Richardson's Clarissa Harlow might object "the world is but one great family. Originally it was so. What then is this narrow selfishness that reigns in us, but relationship remembered against relationship forgot?"[128] But her critique, so much like that offered by Gerrard Winstanley in the seventeenth century, provoked (as far as we know) no radical action among the novel readers of the eighteenth century. The vision of the world as one great family might appeal to dispossessed peasants and artisans, but it had no place in the ambitions of the new middle class.

It is true that none of the puritans' favorite projects for reinforcing the patriarchal nuclear family were immediately successful. Civil marriage was repealed after only seven years, and was not reintroduced until 1836. Another of the nonconformists' plans for perfecting the conjugal—namely, the provision for divorce for couples who could no longer abide one another—never went beyond sectarian practice and was not introduced into law until 1857. In the first phase of its struggle for social power, the new middle class did not achieve any permanent legal breakthroughs. The canons of the church were restored; the traditional tolerances continued. The radical perfectionism that came suddenly to the surface in the 1640s and 1650s retreated once again into the domestic sphere, where, in the course of the next two hundred years, it focused the bourgeois sense of social and moral obligation even more firmly on the nuclear family and monogamous marriage. By the end of the eighteenth century, the conjugal ideal was no longer a threat to the established order but its bulwark, for by that time the aristocracy had also been converted. But, concurrently, the sense of broader obligation, previously dramatized in the big wedding tradition, had also gained new strength among some elements of the rapidly expanding rural and urban proletariat. When family and marriage again became public issues in the 1790s, the sides were different, but the contest no less intense.

PART II

Conflict and Change in
the Age of Agrarian and
Industrial Revolution,
1750–1850

CHAPTER 4

∿∿∿∿∿∿∿∿∿∿∿∿∿∿∿∿∿∿∿∿∿∿∿∿

The Better Man of the Two: Changing Relations between the Sexes, 1750–1850

Wherever communities of smallholders and artisans persisted, old habits of courtship and marriage were slow to pass away. When Thomas Turner, a Sussex shopkeeper, courted his second wife during the 1760s, he scrupulously followed the traditional proprieties, twice staying up all night with her, but, as far as we know, never going beyond polite conversation. Bundling was sustained by Welsh smallholders well into the nineteenth century and has even survived among a tiny minority of rural folk into our own time.[1] The big wedding also flourished in those parts of Wales and Yorkshire where small farms persisted, but, in areas where the effects of the agricultural and industrial revolutions of the late eighteenth and early nineteenth centuries were felt, courtship and marriage practices were irreversibly altered. For the greater part of the British people, work and leisure ceased to be so segregated by age and gender, and, when young women and men became more accustomed to one another's company, courtship became more precocious and less inhibited. Rituals that previously served to regulate sexual relations gave way to more direct, spontaneous forms of intimacy.

By the late eighteenth century the changing relations between men and women had been translated into a demographic revolution. The heterosexuality typical of the preindustrial era—late age of marriage, substantial celibacy, considerable remarriage—disintegrated and population began to rise rapidly. England and Wales had experienced periods of demographic growth before, but in this case the change was sustained and apparently irreversible. By the 1870s hardly a trace of the old demographic regime could be found, except in those few rural areas where small farms or shops still held out against the advance of the agricultural and industrial revolutions. Those were also the only places where big weddings persisted. Elsewhere courtship and marriage had been wholly transformed.

While declining mortality may have played some part in this great surge of population, it is now established that the decline in the age of marriage was the single most important factor. In the first half of the eighteenth century the mean age of first marriage for males and females was 27.5 and 26.2 years, respectively. During the next fifty years these figures dropped to 26.4 and 24.9, and in the first half of the nineteenth century they were 25.3 and 23.4.[2] A greater percentage of marriages were now first time nuptials. In the sixteenth century remarriages constituted as much as thirty percent of all marriages; by the mid-nineteenth century they made up just over eleven percent.[3] This may have resulted from fewer marriages being interrupted by death, but, whatever the cause, the change meant that a greater proportion of brides and grooms were of fertile age.

There is also evidence that access to marriage was becoming easier in the course of the eighteenth century. The proportion never marrying had reached a high point in the late seventeenth century and then plummeted to a low level of only five percent in the 1750s.[4] While the numbers of those who cannot be found in marriage registers recovered somewhat in the early nineteenth century, this return to celibacy is probably more apparent than real. Marriage figures are based on those formally wed and do not include common-law unions, which were increasing in the late eighteenth and early nineteenth centuries.[5] In reality, most of the old obstacles to heterosociability had been cleared and the age of precocious heterosexuality had arrived. The Hardwicke Marriage Act of 1753 terminated the old rights of betrothal and clandestine marriage, but their disappearance did not deter a large part of the population from making marriages in their own way, regardless of the laws of church and state. There is solid evidence that people were entering into courtship and sexual intercourse earlier.

The incidence of prenuptial pregnancy rose rapidly from the 1750s onward; and so too did illegitimacy, which accelerated at a rate unprecedented in the known history of the British population. While a certain part of the increase can be attributed to seduction and abandonment, recent studies suggest that a very large part of the rise was the result of the simultaneous increase in the numbers of common-law unions, whose offspring were recorded as bastards. At Culcheth in South Lancashire the illegitimacy rate rose to thirty percent in the early nineteenth century. At Ceiriog in North Wales the percentage was even higher, but in neither place was abandonment the major cause of recorded bastardy, for each had its conjugal conventions that, though viewed as a form of "domestic republicanism" by church and state, represented a functioning alternative to formal marriage.[6]

The temporal relationships among a decreasing age at time of marriage, rising rates of prenuptial pregnancy, and illegitimacy are easily demonstrated. The actual rate of common-law marriage is a dark area that cannot be easily determined from the parish records, but it, too,

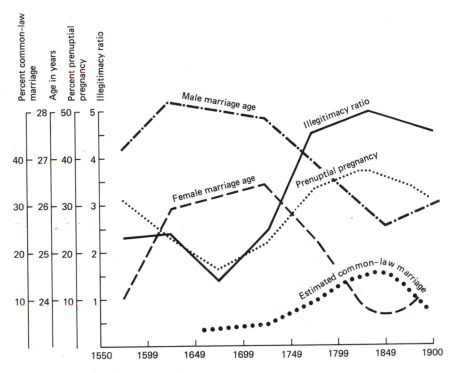

11. Age of marriage, prenuptial pregnancy, illegitimacy, and common-law marriage in Britain, 1550–1900. (From Laslett, p. 24, and Newman, Gandy, and Jones; the estimates of common-law marriage are mine.)

seems to have increased markedly in the late eighteenth century, receding, as did the other indicators, about a century later.

I

Behind the startling figures lay radical changes in the way ordinary men and women constructed their relations. We can begin with the rural poor of the south and east, where, as a result of the advances of capitalist agriculture, the typical laboring family was no longer an owner of the means of production capable of providing a livelihood to all its members.[7] Instead, it was now largely a supplier of the labor force, producing the children who would be employed by others. Having no inheritance to pass on, parents propelled their offspring into the labor market at an early age, hoping thereby to provide them with the means to make their own marriages:

> The children of these cottagers, brought up under an industrious father and mother, are sent to yearly service amongst farmers, etc, and if in the

course of a few years service the young man can scrape up £20 or £30 and finds a young woman that he likes, possessed with nearly an equal sum, they strike a bargain and agree to marry as soon as they can find a cottage near the common; they then stock their cottage with cows, calves, sheep, hogs, poultry, etc, as much as their little fortunes will admit of. He then hires himself as a day labourer to a neighbouring farmer, and the wife stays home to look after the livestock.[8]

On smaller farms the unmarried servants still lived cheek and jowl with the family, eating at the same table, sharing work, leisure, and social custom, complicitous in all things, including sexual relations. If a farmer's son did not join the servant lads in sport or night visiting, there was thought to be something wrong with his masculinity.[9] In larger households relations between masters and men, mistresses and maids, were not so intimate, but nevertheless members of the household mixed a good deal more than they would later in the nineteenth century. Looking back from the 1830s, one laborer remembered:

> When I was a boy I used to visit a large Farmhouse, where the Farmer sat in a room with a Door opening to the Servants' Hall, and everything was carried from one Table to the other. Now they will rarely permit a Man to live in their Houses; and it is in consequence a total Bargain and Sale for Money, and all Idea of Affection is destroyed.[10]

As prices rose from the 1770s onward, farmers found it a good deal cheaper to let labor fend for itself, paying for its own food and lodgings out of wages or poor relief. "Why do not farmers now feed and lodge their workpeople, as they did formerly?" asked William Cobbett. And he answered his own question: "Because they cannot keep them upon so little as they give them in wages."[11] On one hand, the termination of the old living arrangements offered unprecedented freedom to court and marry at earlier ages, a liberty that was reflected in the declining age at time of marriage among the daughters of the agrarian proletariat in the later eighteenth century. The marriage age for men remained more stable, however, suggesting that more was involved than just the opportunity to wed.[12]

The decision to marry was influenced by a variety of factors, not the least of which was the cost of bringing up a family. Paid weekly and even hourly wages, the agricultural proletariat of the south and east found itself tyrannized by price fluctuations in food and housing. In places like Terling, Essex, marriage was particularly sensitive to the price of bread: many wed when the cost was cheap, few when it was dear. Not surprisingly, illegitimacy increased in times of high prices, receding again when things improved.[13] The rural proletariat was so vulnerable during the disastrous harvests of the 1790s that justices in the south and east were impelled to provide a permanent kind of poor relief to supplement starvation wages. The community itself also imposed its own sanctions, trying to limit the number of marriages. At one wedding in

1800 a voice from the back of the church asked whether the "young fool knew that a pound of bread costs a shilling."[14]

But the system of poor relief prevailing until 1834 discriminated most against single men and women, and thus encouraged the trend toward early marriage already evident in arable regions before the 1790s. The live-in system, which still prevailed in the more pastoral parts of Britain, had favored celibacy; now everything, including the law, was on the side of heterosexuality. An elderly Devonshire laborer, who had experienced the radical reversal, vividly recalled that when he was young "farmers preferred a man who was single to a married worker, and that he used to live in the house with them; that they didn't use to marry till they had got a character as good workmen and had put by some of their earnings."[15] But from the late eighteenth century onward, employers and overseers in the south and east favored marriage as a source of cheap, docile labor. They could have the toil of the husband at a pittance and, when it was needed, that of the wife and children as well. C. P. Villiers was told by a Gloucestershire bachelor, already thirty, that:

> if he was a married man, and had a parcel of children, he would be better off, as he should either have work given to him by the piece or receive allowances for his children.[16]

The man's work mate added: "Yes, Sir, that is how it is, a man has no chance unless he is a family man."[17]

For the agricultural laborer the choice was often between migration and marriage. "Go away and work, you foolish boy," one man was told by his parish overseers. "Ah, but sir," he replied, "I married yesterday, and I expect the parish to find me a place to live."[18] Women were under even greater pressures to marry, for if they got pregnant and ran away they would be sent back to their home parish by vigilant officials determined not to have another child dependent on their rates. If they stayed, they would probably be forced to marry by their home parish, whose interest it was to see that every woman and child had a man to maintain them. There was little work or outrelief for single women. Women were being excluded from harvest work in the areas of capitalist farming as early as the 1750s. Their wages began a steady fall a decade later, and the absence of alternative employments meant that marriage was their only option if they did not take the overseer's advice to emigrate.[19] Young women from Tysoe in Warwickshire were given six pence to get themselves to the Kington Mop (the local hiring fair) to find a place in domestic service. A widow was given four shillings "to take her to Birmingham to a place in service."[20] From the 1790s onward, large numbers of women were moving from Essex to London in a similar exodus because their previous source of employment, the textile trade, had collapsed. The story was much the same in the South West and East Anglia, where work for single women was becoming less available.[21]

Those who stayed behind married and gained work through their husbands, usually at the harvest times when the demand for labor exceeded the supply of men. The typical proletarian couple were the Bettesworths. They had no land and depended entirely on wages. The wife, Lucy, was born to field work, and, as George Bourne noted, her marriage made no real difference to her life.[22] She continued to do stoop labor when she could get it. Her home would never have been mistaken for one of the old-time peasant households, not only because it was only she and her husband who resided there, but because it was not an independent unit of production. Even motherhood made no great demands on Lucy, for her two children died. According to Bourne, the marriage was a "kind of dogged comradeship—I can find no better word for it—[which] is what commonly unites the labouring man and his wife; they are partners and equals running their impecunious affairs by mutual help." After years of marriage, Lucy Bettesworth had acquired none of those characteristics that Victorians thought of as naturally feminine. Even to her friend Bourne "she seemed too unlovely to love."[23]

II

Laboring people, dependent themselves on wages, had no way to endow their children. Once it ceased to be a unit of production and became simply a reproducer of labor for others, the rural proletarian family became ever more nuclear, without extended kin ties or the continuity of generations. It was now in the interests of parents to encourage the independence of their children, sending the girls into service in their early teens, encouraging the boys to migrate or to marry as soon as they could earn their own bread. Instead of restraining precocious heterosexuality, parents began to encourage it. In Cambridgeshire, poor folk facilitated night visiting by offering prospective suitors a hot meal before obligingly leaving the couple to make themselves a bed before the fire. In Littleport, a fen village, the practice of bundling was eagerly appropriated from migrant Irish laborers who brought it to the area. The socially superior denounced it, but it served the interests of impoverished parents and children too well to be rooted out. As Enid Porter remarked: "many a Fen youth must have been forced to marry."[24]

Young people were courting more freely, and, if the evidence of increasing premarital pregnancy is any indication, initiating sexual relations earlier and more frequently. There is also an indication that the rural proletariat was now taking advantage of the old betrothal license to cohabit before marriage. As one observor in the 1850s described it:

> young people come to a distinct understanding with each other to cohabit illicitly, until the woman becomes pregnant, the man promising to 'make an honest woman of her' as soon as that takes place. This they find more convenient than marrying at once, in as much as the girl may be in service for herself, and the man elsewhere employed all the time. They meet occasionally and are thus relieved at least of the responsibilities and duties

of housekeeping, living better on their separate earnings than they could do in a house of their own.[25]

In early nineteenth century Ash-next-Sandwich, in East Kent, at least fifteen percent of the couples there seem to have omitted marriage altogether.[26] The situation was no better in John Monkhouse's Hampshire parish during the 1820s. He used the parish register to denounce both pregnant brides and common-law couples. "Those who gain husbands are more fortunate than those who bear bastards, but not more virtuous," he noted, inscribing Maria Tidcomb as "whore" and Mary Burchett as "kept mistress."[27]

In rural Berkshire, "When a marriage did not take place, the child is generally consigned to the care of the mother of the girl, whilst she herself, when she can, goes out in the capacity of a wetnurse."[28] But when the child was a burden it was in everyone's interest to see that a marriage took place sooner or later. A pregnancy, previously something to be kept quiet, now became an instrument for securing either marriage or parish maintenance. Women used it to gain husbands and, when they would not press the matter, the parish did it for them. The rising premarital pregnancy rates reflected all these various pressures. Courtship became more precocious. Couples were less likely to abstain from intercourse, in part because this was one of the ways a woman could be sure of enticing and, if pregnant, holding a man. It is significant that in places like Terling, Tysoe, and throughout the arable counties, it was said "there has been no increase in chargeable bastards, but a great increase of marriages to prevent it."[29]

Bastardy in the arable regions did not rise to the levels typical of the pastoral areas of the north and west, but instead there was a rapid increase of cover-up marriages from the 1760s onward, many voluntary but others coerced. Parson Woodforde's diary is filled with instances of such unions, which he abhorred but was compelled by the parish to perform. Most of the men were from other parishes, dragged back in irons and kept under close guard until a combination of threats and bribes brought them to Woodforde's altar. In January 1789, he was called on to marry Robert Astick to Elizabeth Howlett, who was pregnant with his child:

> The Man was a long time before he could be prevailed on to marry her when in the Church Yard; and at the Altar behaved in a very unbecoming way. It is a cruel thing that any Person be complled by Law to marry. . . . It is very disagreeable to me to marry such Persons.[30]

His colleague, Reverend Skinner, had fewer scruples about such things and often involved himself in the negotiations with putative fathers. One case dragged on while the girl sat in the church weeping, berated by her mother, who seemed to be as eager as the parish officers to get rid of her:

MRS. BRIMBLE   If thou doesn't ha [have] him, I will put a whittle [knife] in thy troat [throat].

MISS BRIMBLE   I'll ha he, but he doesn't want ha I.[31]

Parents and clergy in the south and east could congratulate themselves that marriage was increasing. Those who felt somewhat uncomfortable with the coercive aspects of the system found it convenient at times to blame the women themselves, who they claimed were using their right to swear their babies as a means to gain marriage and, in its absence, child support. There is some evidence that women in the eighteenth century did use the 1733 law to provide for themselves and their children, and their claims, especially against upper-class males, had strong popular assent.[32] Next to despotic fathers the most frequent target of satire was the aristocratic rake and the promiscuous parson. In the "Frolicsome Parson," a girl gets her revenge on the clergyman, who had first seduced and then abandoned her, by presenting him with his child in the midst of his Sunday sermon:

> T'was then a court was called in town, for to invest
> the case
>
> There was the parson, cook, and parlour maid
> they met face to face
>
> And many more in court appeared, to hear the sport and fun
>
> This damsel swore the parson was the father of her son.[33]

III

The precocious heterosexuality of the agricultural regions of the south and east found expression in early cover-up marriages. In the north and west, where rural industrialization had been taking place from the mid-eighteenth century onward, the old patterns of courtship were also breaking down, but in a quite different social and economic context. There the family remained an economic unit and parents were not so eager to have their children off their hands. Kinship, particularly that formed along matrilineal lines, became a prominent feature of these proto-industrial areas. The young, particularly women, tended to stay at home longer and marry locally. The notion of family extended beyond the single household to include those related by blood or marriage. Unlike the agricultural proletariat, where a narrower conjugality built on "dogged comradship" was becoming a way of life, the new industrial proletariat expanded the notion of legitimate love relationships to include those outside as well as inside marriage. Their definition of family also expanded, as did their idea of parenthood. The definition of mutual obligation burst the boundaries of monogamous marriage and the nuclear family to create radically new forms of heterosexuality.

Close kin ties, something virtually unobtainable among the rural proletariat of the south and east, became a prominent feature of the proto-industrial areas. Community took on a new stability and identity, reinforced by either religious nonconformity or some more secular form of plebeian culture, which contrasted sharply with that imposed by the church or gentry in the arable regions. A village of miners, weavers, or framework knitters was much more likely to show an independent spirit, yet to be no less strict in its own distinctive forms of social and moral discipline. These were places known for their clannishness and independence of established authority. The miners of the Forest of Dean, where there was no church until 1803, were reputed to be "a sort of robustic, wild people," who kept their own morality.[34] It was the kind of place that would have been a hotbed of religious nonconformity in the seventeenth century and, while the taste for dissent had since diminished, the miners continued to savor their social and cultural independence.[35] In places like this the family remained the main unit of production, though in a way different from earlier forms of household labor. These were not the patriarchically organized households of peasants or artisans, nor were they exactly like the "little commonwealths" of the nascent bourgeoisie of the previous century. The rural industrial or mining household was no longer in control of the means of production as the latter had been. It did not master the sources of raw materials and did not command the distribution of the finished product, which were now managed by capitalist merchants in what was commonly called the "putting out system." The demand for the household's labor was now determined by factors outside its control, but it nevertheless continued to control the actual labor process, a crucial distinction between these petty producers, who I have chosen to call the plebeians, and the wage-earning agricultural proletariat, who were by now wholly at the command of their employers.[36]

Plebeian parents were more dependent on the labor of their children, who, in turn, were more dependent on them.[37] Relations between men and women were characterized by a similar interdependence; and marriage was more likely to take the form of a partnership between persons participating in some common task, like the Northhamptonshire shoemakers, of whom it was said:

> No single-handed man can live; he must have a whole family at work, because a single-handed man is so badly paid he can scarce provide the necessaries of life. . . . As soon as they [the children] are big enough to handle an awl, they are obliged to come downstairs and work.[38]

At Shepshed, in Leicestershire, emigration slowed with the introduction of framework knitting as a cottage industry there in the late seventeenth century. The young people of Shepshed were able to gain access to employment and marriage at a younger age, thus ensuring the continuity as well as interdependence of generations.[39] The same tendency toward endogamy was evident everywhere domestic industry, mining, or fishing prevailed. Of handloom weavers in the valleys of

Lancashire, it was said "a weaver would scorn to marry a servant girl, but chooses a weaver, who earns as much or half as much as himself."[40] In a contemporary song, "Weaver in Love," a father warns his son, who has taken a liking to a servant, not to marry her:

> And if her favour I should win
> Then I would wave and she should spin
> My Father scornfully to me said
> How could I fancy a servant-maid.[41]

This young man defied parental edict, but on the whole weaving communities were notoriously inbred. This was also true of mining, quarrying, and metal working villages. When miners' wives were excluded from pit work in 1842, many disguised themselves as men so they could work alongside their husbands as they had previously done.[42] In the thousands of small forges in the Black Country, men normally operated the "oliver," the spring-loaded hammer, assisted by women and children. But at Cradley Heath, a Mrs. Hadley ran a chainmaking shop with four hearths while her husband worked as a collier. She would not let her daughters go into service, but trained them in the smithing trade.[43] It was said that "the effects of early work, particularly in the forges, render these girls perfectly independent. They often enter beer shops, call for their pints and smoke their pipes like men."[44]

The interdependence of such family operations produced their own peculiar tensions. There was little parents could do to prevent early courtship and marriage, however much they wished to retain their children's labor. In the smithing community some unique arrangements evolved as a result of this situation:

> There is a general custom in the district for boys and girls of seventeen or so to marry, and each to continue at work, living in the home of their respective parents. . . . This tendency has been sufficiently strong to overcome the usual English practice of making a home first.[45]

In the weaving village of Culcheth in Lancashire, women also showed a preference for staying at home longer, delaying formal marriage even after their love affairs had resulted in one or more children. And in the Ceiriog Valley of North Wales, where the men quarried while the women prepared wool, the formation of new households was similarly postponed.[46]

Where marriage was no longer associated with setting up a separate home, the old definition of the wife as the Mistress became obsolete. A woman could be a spouse without being a housewife. At Cradley Heath, many women were also mothers before they became wives, another innovation that middle-class observers could neither comprehend nor condone. Still other women dispensed with formal marriage altogether, maintaining themselves and their children under their parents' roof "without a murmur."[47] In these places love was redefined to mean something that could exist outside as well as inside matrimony.

IV

Everywhere proto-industrialization developed, age and gender distinctions tended to be reoriented. Young people able to earn adult wages at earlier ages ceased to be dependent on their parents for marriage portions and began to accumulate their own out of their own earnings. In these industrial settings young women and men worked, ate, and drank together, ignoring the usual traditional homosocial divisions.[48] The parson of Aston Clinton, Buckinghamshire, where the straw plaiting trade provided employment to both sexes, said the work contributed to early independence, "leading to very early marriages, and worse." His colleague at Irvinghoe reported: "It makes parents afraid of offending their children, who thus become hardened and intractable," though it is apparent that young folks took quite a different view of the matter.[49] They pursued their plaiting even as they courted by hearthside or in the country lanes. When they were ready to wed, they announced it in a matter-of-fact way, without obtaining parental consent or going through a formal betrothal. One young strawplaiter simply declared she was ready to draw her money from the bank. "So am I, too," added her young man. "We're both a goin' to draw out, and we're goin' to be married on the plait money. Ain't we, Mary."[50]

Everywhere cottage manufacturing was introduced, the propertied classes complained that it tempted the young away from domestic service, led to loose habits, illegitimacy, and worse still, prostitution. When factory employment became available in Lancashire in the early nineteenth century, the same dire consequences were predicted. But, on close inspection, it was found that even those who had left the rural handloom for daily factory employment were usually living at or near home. The new employments sustained the continuity of generations, while at the same time changing parent-child relations:

> A young woman, prudent and careful, and living with her parents, from the age of sixteen to twenty-five, may, in that time, by factory employment save £100 as a wedding portion. She is not then driven into an early marriage by the necessity of seeking a home; and the consciousness of independence in being able to earn her own living is favorable to the development of her best moral energies.[51]

Although living at home, young people had money of their own and a voice in family affairs. The old patriarchy, while still in place, was modified. Of female textile workers it was said "they had their father to keep, and they would not be dictated to by him."[52]

Mining communities were also targets of the moralists, but there too family loyalties were not incompatible with the new independence. Reverend John Skinner found it virtually impossible to discipline the colliers of Camerton, whose habit of marrying just before the birth of the child he scornfully called the "Camerton mode":

12. In Wensley Dale, Yorkshire, stocking knitting was a family employment well into the nineteenth century. Family members knit as they walked to town to sell their product and purchase new materials. (From George Walker, *The Costume of Yorkshire*, 1814)

June 27, 1830	The bride was round as a barrel, and according to custom, I suppose there will be a christening in the course of the honeymoon.[53]

Early-nineteenth-century mining revolved around the "family pit," with the father employing his children and even his wife.[54] A man without a family was doomed to perpetual dependence, a reason why young marriage and high fertility were commonplace among miners and quarrymen.[55] It was said that Cornish pit workers "kept company" in the manner of the Welsh, the women encouraging the bundling (including intercourse) in order to gain husbands.[56] While the social context of their courtship was very different from that of the agrarian proletariat, the results were superficially the same:

> Being pregnant at marriage is very common. Subsequent marriage so as to legitimize the child is the rule. Some few cases of desertion occur, not one in three of these in agricultural [mining] districts. The public opinion of the miners would be strong against it, so as probably to drive a man away from the neighborhood.[57]

The difference lay in the fact that most marriages were not forced; and when they were, it was community pressure and not the law that provided the coercive powers.

Changes in the culture and economy of family life had an immediate and visible effect on the pattern of courtship wherever industry came to the countryside. Where young women stayed at home or lived in, the old practice of night visiting expanded enormously. Masters had to make concessions in order to keep female servants. In Wales even the Methodists despaired of discouraging bundling:

> So powerful is the custom [bundling] that many gentlemen state that they must either overlook the fact of their female servants giving into it, or make up their minds to employ only men servants, or old women.[58]

In Cheshire the situation in the dairy region was the same, for masters knew if they did not allow their employees visitors "without enquiry or reproof" they would be shorthanded in the summer months.[59] In mining areas few women could be attracted to service and those who were had the upper hand. Reverend Skinner lost his cook after he chased her lover from the kitchen; and a maid quit when refused permission to attend the Timsbury Revel.[60] Efforts in the 1840s to form a society for the suppression of bundling in Dolgelly failed when only a few old bachelors could be induced to sign the pledge. Women would have nothing to do with it.[61]

In the pastoral and industrial regions it was not uncommon to find widows and unmarried women living in small cottages, renting or owning small plots of land, supporting themselves and their children by selling eggs and milk, brewing, laundering, or working in the handicrafts.[62] Conditions conducive to female independence endured in such places well into the nineteenth century, long after these had vanished in the agrarian areas of the south and east. The fact that communities in the north and west also tended to be more socially homogeneous meant that both men and women had a wider choice in the search for a mate, though this advantage was somewhat mitigated by the fact that families reliant on the earnings of their children often put obstacles in the way of courtship. Therefore, there was a tendency for the traditions of clandestine courtship and marriage to continue there.[63] Northumberland miners courted "under hidlings."[64] When Joseph Gutteridge, a Coventry ribbon weaver's apprentice, encountered difficulty from his stepparents, he and his bride took their banns to a church in another part of town where they were not so likely to be forbidden.[65] Sam Bamford encountered similar problems when he first began courting in the 1820s.[66]

The competition between parents and suitors was often intense; and, because young male immigrants so heavily outnumbered women in the newly industrializing and mining regions, males did all they could to monopolize local girls. The old traditions of "fining" strangers, customs which had fallen away in other parts of the country, were intensified and elaborated in the north and west. The interloper would first be warned to keep his distance and then, if he persisted, subjected to savage hazing. The lads of Graveley, Hertfordshire, had a particularly ferocious reputation. They were known as the "Grinders" for their habit of exposing the backside of trespassers to a whirling grind stone.[67] In Morley, Yorkshire, strangers were "packsheeted," placed in a blanket and tossed about before being run out of the neighborhood.[68] If a suitor could not be frightened off, local lads then turned their attention to the girl herself. In Sheffield those who had accepted the attentions of strangers had their chastity impugned.[69] In the Ceiriog Valley of North Wales the young men took any woman's interest in an outsider as "an insult, which made them believe that she did not regard them as perfect men. Her movements were closely observed, and her courtship with the stranger was subject to gossip. She was criticized by the young men's mothers for her arrogance and ostentation by leaving her home town to look for a lover elsewhere, and they predicted misfortune and shame on her."[70] If the pressure of local opinion did not work, the boys themselves took more drastic action:

> When a handsome and loveable girl refused to stop and talk with us, boys, or would pass us on the road without taking any notice of us, we decided that she was seeking a lover elsewhere. We came to the conclusion too that her people did not consider one of us good enough to become the husband of their daughter. We would therefore make up our mind to *rhythu* her. It would come to our ears that she would be on the road in her best clothes on a particular afternoon. Then we would arrange to hide ourselves in the hedge on the roadside to await her coming. When she would come by, we would jump into the road, and would surround her closely. Each of us would grip the brim of her hat firmly with our teeth, and then, regardless of her screams and cries, each one of us would take out his *membrum virile* and make water on her until her clothes would be dripping wet. In this condition she would be compelled to return home for very shame, but not before she had proof that we were equal in virility to lads from far away places.[71]

Competition for brides was also fierce in the Durham area: "Round about Ferney Hill, Hey for Hell; There's many a bonny lass, but few to get."[72] It took real courage for any stranger to walk through one of these places, and for a stranger to marry in was a test not only of strength but determination.[73] But there could be no such thing as a completely closed community, especially in those expanding "open" parishes where so much of the industrial and population growth of the late eighteenth and early nineteenth centuries was taking place. The tramping artisans, roving miners, migrant farm servants—these wanderers were incorporated, as were strangers in earlier centuries, through a series of ritual ordeals, extensions of the old tradition of the "footing," known variously as "pitchering," "packsheeting," or "socket."[74] The nineteenth-century Sheffield term "cockwalk" suggests even more vividly the courting privileges earned by those who had passed through the ritual hazing.[75] And should the "cock of the walk" become a bridegroom, he could normally expect to pay another footing at the time of the wedding.[76]

V

The competition among males enhanced the power of eligible women. In pit villages it was said that widows were pressed with proposals of marriage even at their husbands' funerals, not because they had any inheritance but for their housekeeping and their children.[77] When Charles Warren, a Dorset smallholder advertized for a wife early in the nineteenth century, he specified that he was looking for a woman between thirty and forty because he already had three children and "I do not want a second family."[78] But miners, weavers, and fisher folk sought not only women who could assist them in their work but could provide them with large families. A collier needed sons to assist him; weavers were equally dependent on their children, and no fisherman could survive without sons to man his boat, daughters to bait, and a "fishwife" to mend his nets and sell his catch. A maxim current in fishing communities aptly described a woman's qualifications:

> A woman suld na wed
> Till she can win her man's bread[79]

The fact that marriage depended so much on both the fertility and earning power of women meant that the priorities and, to some extent, the character of courtship shifted. Men looking for wives now sought them out where they worked. In Yorkshire women gathered to knit in what came to be known as "sittings." Their suitors joined them there, with the result that "going-a-sitting" acquired the dual meaning of work and courtship.[80] In Wales, the "knitting assembly" (*nason weu*) also became a major occasion for courtship.[81] Instead of visiting girls at home and giving gloves and coins, suitors began to present practical gifts like sheathes for the knitting needles and bobbins for lace making, both elaborately carved and initialed.[82] In such places young folk organized their own work bees and dances without, it was said, "any supervision by elder folk."[83] In the straw plaiting districts courtship came out of doors in good weather. The same roads that the rich used on Sunday mornings to display their wealth and piety in horse-drawn "church parades" were used in the afternoons by the working classes for a different purpose:

> quite a different set of promenaders these, to those of the morning, neither so decorous, nor so correct in speech and manner as they, but still quite their natural selves, more out for the enjoyment, and so it was among these happy promenades "cupid's arrow" then as now, found its mark.[84]

The traditional calendar of courtship was being changed and augmented. While Valentine's Day, Easter Monday and Tuesday, the First of May, and Midsummers Eve still retained much of their popularity even in the early industrial towns, the proliferation of village wakes and hiring fairs in the eighteenth century added many new occasions that were no longer under the control of either the civil or religious authorities. These were times for men to show off their strength in a variety of sports: "Tom Short behaved himself so well that most People seemed to agree it was impossible that he should remain a Batchelour till the next Wake."[85]

Women's new interest and participation in physical, sometimes violent, sport reflected a premium that was now placed on a female's strength and health.[86] In the poem, "The Colliers' Pay Week," it is evident that plebeian dancing had broken free of the traditional country forms and had become a competition for attention by both sexes:

> The damsel displays all her graces,
> The collier exerts all his power;
> They caper in circling paces
> And set at each end of the floor.
> He jumps, and his heels knack and rattle,
> At turns of the music so sweet
> He makes such a thundering battle
> The floor seems afraid of his feet.[87]

The violent exertions on the dance floor are followed by a brawl between the two village youth groups, ending when one of the combatants is shorn of his breeches and, by implication, his virility. As late as the 1850s, young men were still risking breaking their pates in order to win female attention. In Thomas Hughes' *Tom Brown's School Days*, Willum Smith enters the ring at the annual "Veast" to win the prize for his sweetheart Rachel:

> Now doan't 'ee, Rachel! I wouldn't ha' done it, I only wanted summut to buy'ee a fairing wi' [by you a fairing with], and I be as vlush o' money as a twod o' veathers.[88]

All this strenuous display, together with undeniable signs of increasing male aggressiveness toward rival suitors and uncooperative sweethearts, suggests that men were becoming anxious about the increase in female independence evident in the late eighteenth century. "If a girl fancies a man and can't get to know him," it was noted, "she'll send him a message with her proposal or advertise."[89] In Middleton women were taking over the Valentine Eve custom of slipping messages under the door. Samuel Bamford was sitting down to a meal at his uncle's table when one such bold missive was delivered. His aunt exploded: "it's come to summit [something], at any rate, 'at one canno' sit deawrn to one's meat 't one's own hoawse, but we munbi haunted we young snickets comin' after thee, an' snickin' ther letters under th' dur." Middleton women were no less aggressive one May morning, when they traded insult for insult with any man who threatened their honor:

> If a young man wished to cast a slur on a lass, he would hang a rag containing salt at her parent's door, or he would cast some of the same material on her doorstep, as indicative of gross inclinations. If he remained unknown he escaped punishment, but if he were detected, or his secret became divulged, he generally got thrashed, as he deserved, by a brother or some favoured swain, or he might get his face channelled by the fair one's nails the next time she met him, or a mop slopped against his cheek, or a vessel of odorous liquid poured on his clothes as he passed the desecrated threshold; all or any of which retaliations would earn him but small sympathy with his neighbours—the men chuckling or laughing and saying nothing; and all the women agreeing, "Aye, it sarves him quite reet, th' wastril."[90]

Female initiative, previously confined to those special occasions when such behavior was licensed, had broken free of calendrical restrictions. In South Wales women were known to be violent combatants. In one village three collier women took revenge on a grocer by tarring him and then throwing dirt. When the court ordered them to pay for his ruined clothes, they refused and were saved from going to jail by their husbands. This was the same place that women were active in administering the Welsh form of rough music, the *ceffyl pren*, to adulterers and wife beaters.[91] Women were active in bread riots, enclosure disturbances, and all manner of trade disputes throughout the late eighteenth and early nineteenth centuries, but in the sphere of sexual relations their weapons were more subtle.[92] The female tongue was particularly feared in those close-knit communities where reputation among one's peers counted more than the opinion of the squire or parson. This was true not only of pastoral places, but of the Ceiriog Valley and the Isle of Portland, where small farming coexisted with industrial pursuits.

In addition to gossip, women were able to use the lingering belief in their supernatural powers to good advantage. The image of the woman as witch figured in the popular imagination of the north and west longer than it did in other parts of Britain. In early-nineteenth-century Wales it was said that "unfaithful young men would soon fulfill their promise when they found out that the girl they had slighted was consulting a witch."[93] It was a common notion that a new mother possessed extraordinary powers, a potent belief that unwed mothers were able to exploit to their advantage when all else failed them. Sexual relations were believed to establish a physical sympathy between partners, such that the father shared the sufferings of the woman during both pregnancy and birth. In late-nineteenth-century Yorkshire "when an illegitimate child is born, it is a point of honour with the girl not to reveal the father; but the mother of the girl forthwith goes out to look for him, and the first man she finds keeping to his bed is he."[94]

VI

The power of women, supernatural or otherwise, was bound up with their fertility, a connection that had a firm basis in the economic as well as the cultural conditions of rural industrialization. While children had always been valued in agricultural communities, the status of motherhood seems to have been further enhanced by the growth of cottage manufacturing. Children were even more valuable to a weaver or framework knitter than to a farmer. They could begin to work earlier, and girls were no less capable than boys at all the small tasks associated with a cottage economy.[95] The desire for children was no less strong in mining and quarrying communities like the Ceiriog Valley of North Wales, where men worked the slate while women were engaged in wool production. Even adolescent girls were said to "talk about sex as if they were experienced women, and their love for babies is so strong and profound that they draw the attention of any man (or stranger)."[96] It was considered a personal tragedy if a couple proved barren, and in the Ceiriog and similar places opinion sanctioned a trial of fertility, allowing the parties to separate without shame if pregnancy did not occur.[97] Virility was equally esteemed and, to "prove" himself, a man would ask his sweetheart "to walk with him, and if she agreed, he would take her to a lonely desolate place, and ask her 'Do you wish to . . . (*rhythu*).' If she said 'yes,' he would hold the brim of her hat between his teeth, then open the front part of his trousers and urinate on her dress. By exposing himself, he was proving his virility to the woman."[98]

On the Isle of Portland, a clannish place where the men worked the stone and the women did dressmaking, it was "the custom, from time immemorial, that they never marry till the woman is pregnant." Here the true disgrace was "having no child," something the prevailing courtship practice was meant to avoid:

> The mode of courtship here is, that a young woman never admits of the serious addresses of a young man but on the supposition of a thorough probation. When she becomes with child, she tells her mother; the mother tells her father; her father tells his father, and he tells his son, that it is then proper time to be married. . . . If the woman does not prove with child, after a competent time of courtship, they conclude they are not destined by Providence for each other; they therefore separate, and as it is an established maxim which Portland women observe with great strictness, never to admit a plurality of lovers at one time, their honour is in no ways tarnished, she just as soon (after the affair is declared to be broken off) gets another suitor as if she had been left a widow, or that nothing had ever happened but she had remained an immaculate virgin.

Just how strictly the custom was kept is reflected by the very low illegitimacy rate in Portland. Sometime in the 1750s London masons working the quarry violated local custom by refusing to marry their pregnant sweethearts. "On their refusal, the Portland women arose to stone them out of the island; in so much that those few who did not choose to take their sweethearts for better or worse, after so fair a trial, were in reality obliged to decamp. On this occasion one bastard only was born, but since then matters have gone according to ancient custom."[99]

Throughout Devon and Dorset it was said to be "a gross breach of a man's honour to refuse to marry a woman with whom he has been 'keeping company' and has caused to become *enceinte*."[100] In the 1770s Jonas Hanway was writing of similar practices: "if a woman *proves*, as they term becoming pregnant, then the parties marry by a kind of honour and decency."[101] He was convinced that it was a rural practice and the evidence would seem to support him. In nineteenth-century Norfolk it was said that "no labourer entered into the bonds of wedlock until he was assured that his future wife would be fruitful."[102] One quite respectable mother explained: "What was the poor girls to do; the chaps say that they won't marry 'em first, and then the girls give way. I did the same myself with my husband."[103] In Cornwall the practice of premarital intercourse seems to have been most rooted in the mining population, though fisher folk had a similar tradition. As soon as a young man began to earn full wages at seventeen or eighteen, he "immediately thereupon . . . gets a new set of clothes and a watch; after which he fancies himself sufficiently set up in the world to commence a courtship, which generally leads to an early marriage by the course [premarital sex] mentioned. In some parts of Cornwall the immorality of the females *at work* is notorious and proverbial."[104] Although betrothal had ceased to have legal force after 1753, its rules were still being adhered to by the working classes. Women entered into sex with the knowledge that they would be protected in case of pregnancy; and, even should the marriage fail to materialize, they had their own labor and family to fall back on.

The practice of "proving" was reflected in both the rising rates of prebridal pregnancy and in the increases in illegitimacy recorded from the 1770s onward.[105] These rose everywhere in Britain, but their regional variation reflected differing economic and social conditions. We have seen that in areas of capitalist agriculture like Terling (Essex) bastardy was kept low by cover-up marriage. This was generally true of the south and east, where there was strong pressure to marry because unwed motherhood was severely stigmatized. Recorded illegitimacy was higher in the pastoral and industrial north and west, though there was a great deal of local variation everywhere.[106] Levels of unwed motherhood were extremely high in the Ceiriog Valley and Culcheth in South Lancashire, places where employment for women at or near home was most abundant.[107] These were also areas where the proportion of women registered as married was low. Women were becoming mothers before they became wives. Some were giving birth to several children and never marrying at all. While the old betrothal tradition sanctioned having the first child out of wedlock, the increase of the number of women with multiple bastard births in the late eighteenth century was something new.[108] Some were daughters of families with previous histories of unwed motherhood, but changes in social and cultural conditions also had much to do with the extension of the practice.[109] At the same time, there is no reason to think that the children recorded as bastards were without fathers, socially if not legally. Men were also becoming accustomed to separating paternity from husbandhood, making arrangements to support their children outside conventional marriage. In places like Ceiriog, Culcheth, and the Kent parish of Ash-next-Sandwich, high recorded bastardy went hand in hand with a tolerance of such arrangements.[110]

Moralizers were convinced that rising bastardy rates were a sign of social and moral disintegration. This may have been so in some instances, but, where rural industrialization had made headway, it seems that the ability and willingness of women to have children outside of wedlock was a product of familial and communal cohesion rather than breakdown. In Shepshed unmarried mothers were more likely to be found living with kin, contributing to the family economy while being assisted with the upbringing of their children.[111] Whereas in agricultural areas unwed mothers went out to service, their counterparts in industrial communities tended to stay home. Their labor was welcome and their bastards were often "adopted" by grandparents or other relatives.[112] The official treatment of bastardy also varied enormously. In the zone of capitalist agriculture, where there was little work for single women, a great effort was made to marry off the unwed mother. Shotgun weddings were less prevalent in the north and west where unwed mothers stayed home or supported themselves with the help of maintenance extracted from the father. Parish officials there recognized that to force marriage on young couples who could not easily get a home of their own would be disastrous for everyone and ultimately an even greater burden on the rates. Couples were encouraged to remain apart until they could afford a household. Often men entered into agreements to maintain their children in the manner that Evan Jones did in 1778. He agreed to pay Elizabeth Williams of Ceiriog four shillings each week until she was delivered and then five shillings a month thereafter. If the child lived, then he would pay three pounds and ten shillings each subsequent year.[113] From a Cheshire account book of the 1870s we learn that Pege Benet had "loved not wisely but too well" and that Thomas Hansel agreed to pay as follows:

First general expenses	£1	6s	6d
to ye midwife		10	6
when the Crisning		2	6
to 2½ [yards?] of Flanel		2	10
Agreed with Nele Spark for			
Pege Bene Child for [year?]		5	50[114]

Cardiganshire officials operated in a similar manner, the men paying the women through them. This kind of relief amounted to a fifth of all their welfare expenditures in the 1830s, and, although it was administered parsimoniously, it was done without the reforming zeal that was typical of poor relief in those places where squire and parson used the vestry as an extension of their authority.[115] In Tysoe, Warwickshire, the maintenance per child (2s6d per week) was so meager that few mothers could afford to remain unmarried for long.[116] In Wales and the north, however, the intention was not to force marriage, but to give the parties some choice:

> the general practice was for the overseers first to obtain the money from the putative father before they gave any relief to the woman. It was, in fact, treated through the district as a system not of administering relief, but of providing redress to the woman under the grievance sustained, or rather of forcing the two parties to combine in the maintenance of the child, and not as an indemnity to the parish, for the number of cases before the parish were not cases of destitution, the parish being applied to by the woman to set her right as regards the contribution on the part of the man to the maintenance of the child.[117]

The system in eighteenth-century Merioneth has been described as a "rough and ready system of outdoor relief, bolstered by charitable donations and neighborly assistance"; and throughout the north and west it was normal for bastardy to be treated in a pragmatic way, allowing women to do with the maintenance payments what they wished as long as they did not become a further burden to the rate payers.[118] At Aberdare, Wales, young girls working the mines "were frequently with child before marriage," and in Shepshed, where there was also plenty of work to supplement the maintenance payments, there was no rush to marriage among pregnant women.[119] Many of the Shepshed women married later on but the choice was theirs, as it was for those living in places where female employment other than domestic service was available at or near home. Rural traditions of female independence transferred quite easily to the towns of the north and west, where it was said that female workers in the early factories made it a practice of separating motherhood from wifehood:

> many of the most respectable looking women refused to take upon themselves the responsibility of husbands; not at all, however, from Malthusian principles, as I have understood that they had not in all cases the same objection to a family. I was told, also, that matrimony was not considered a very permanent institution, and that many young couples, from jealousy or other causes of quarrel, frequently separated and took up with the original causes of jealousy or others, as it suited either inclination or convenience.[120]

The plebeian culture of the region did not make so much of the distinction between the married and unmarried mother, or between legitimate and illegitimate children. Popular language was dissembling on this point. Bastards were referred to as "chance children" or "chanclings" in Yorkshire. The same tolerance was extended to the mother, who was described as a "grass widow" or "grace widow," and sometimes recorded as such in the register.[121] In North Wales it was said she had either been "taken through the bush" or "jumped o'er t' besom before she went to t' church," a reference to some prior betrothal that legitimized the child in the eyes of the local people if not the law.[122] A Lincolnshire woman who expected a bastard was said to have "found 'm under a goose-berry bush," while in Cleveland they said: "Ah, poor gell, she's had a misfortin; but she's none the worse for 't."[123] These were the same places where the women retained their maiden names after marriage, so it was not easy to tell which children were legitimate and which were not. In most cases the bastard took his or her mother's surname and was thus "adopted" by her family. In Wales as well as in Yorkshire there were many who grew up regarding their own mothers as sisters or aunts, for they were, in effect, their grandparents' children.[124]

VII

The contrast was evidently one of class as well as region, illegitimacy being only a little better than prostitution in the eyes of the educated elites. By the early nineteenth century even the slightest degree of independence in sexual matters could render a middle-class woman unfit for marriage or society. The sexuality of a wife or daughter was presumed to belong to the husband or father. They could sue those who tampered with their "property," and even rape was treated as an offense not just against the woman but against patriarchy. As Dr. Johnson put it so crudely: "We hang a thief for stealing sheep, but the unchastity of a woman transfers sheep and farm and all from the right owner."[125]

Among the working classes, however, whatever the desire of men might be, women were not ready to relinquish control of their sexuality. Instead, they used it boldly, even aggressively, when circumstances required. Sexual attractiveness was becoming increasingly important, but it was women's virtues as workers and mothers that was the greatest source of pride and allure. Samuel Bamford had good reason to be grateful for the sturdy independence of a Yorkshire woman whom he had been involved with. He had made her pregnant, but could not bring himself to "become the husband of one I had thus injured. I was relieved, however, by learning that she took the affair less to heart than many would have done, and that the obtainment of a handsome weekly allowance was with her as much a subject of consideration as any other."[126]

Bamford was happy to pay maintenance, but had he not he would have been visited not only by the parish officials (which he was) but also by communal indignation. In Wales the wooden horse (*ceffyl pren*) was often on the side of the women in the early nineteenth century.[127] During the Rebecca Riots of the 1840s a quiet schoolmaster at Narbeth was arrested for writing a threatening letter to a local gentleman, who had seduced a local girl. When asked why he did it, the schoolmaster replied that "he thought it would do good; here was a poor woman starving, and there was this Mr. . . . , who was very well off, and he ought to give something to the poor girl to help her nurse her child."[128] Much later another Welshman remembered the customary way of dealing with a man who did not own up to his duties:

> A few neighbors came together, took the child from the young girl and took it down to the reputed father to bring up—and to show they meant business they had brought their guns with them. If he did not want to bring up the child himself—and that was usually the case—the girl could make a better bargain for taking it back than she could otherwise have done.[129]

Unwed mothers were very rarely subject to rough music. A woman was "tinged" in the Cambridgeshire Fenlands, not because she had two illegitimate children, but because she was suspected of spreading venereal disease.[130] The clergy were less likely to be so tolerant of women, but there were many ways of offsetting their censure, especially when the community thought no wrong had been committed. In Pickering, Yorkshire, popular pressure during the 1820s finally put to an end the practice of making pregnant girls do penance. The upper classes had long since ceased to stand before the church in the white robes of shame, and now villagers decided the penalty outmoded:

> So strong a feeling against this way of judging our daughters for a fault of this kind that they [the villagers] have set their faces against any lass ever being so judged, and though our clergy be to a man but a desperate, reckless lot, I hear that mostly they are of the same mind as their flock.

When one father refused to have his daughter made to stand, he was supported by local opinion and the clergy gave way:

> and the whole thereabout siding with the lass, it was held by the parson and his fox-chasing, wine-bibbing crew for to pull in their tongues a piece which they most wisely did, or, for truth they would have found themselves astride the wrong horse.[131]

The horse the diarist referred to was the Yorkshire version of "riding the stang." During the course of the eighteenth century the targets of rough music had changed considerably. The old instruments of misrule, previously directed largely against violators of the rules of household government, especially cuckolded or henpecked husbands, were now deployed against anyone who had severely offended local standards of decency, whether they be ill-tempered school masters, agents of the press gang, engrossers, scabs, or enclosers of the common lands.[132] By the end of the nineteenth century, child abusers and homosexuals had been added to the list of those who could expect a riotous tin panning or worse.[133] Still, the main focus of rough music were moral offenders— the notorious seducer, loose women, and adulterers of both sexes whose exploits were too public or disruptive. Scolds and termagant wives still came in for some ritual condemnation, but the frequent attention that in the seventeenth century had been paid to the henpecked or cuckolded husband now shifted to the wife beater. As Edward Thompson has shown, there was a significant increase in the rough music for violent husbands in the course of the eighteenth and nineteenth centuries.[134] In the north and west they were treated to the Skimmington, the riding the stang, and the *ceffyl pren*; in the south and east, "a sort of first warning was given by strewing a lot of chaff from a threshing-floor before the man's door in the dead of the night." If he did not desist from his abuse, then a different, more violent means was employed:

> As soon as it was dark a procession was formed. First came two men with huge cow horns; then another with a large old fish-kettle around his neck, to represent the trumpeters and the big drum of a serious procession. Then came the orator of the party and then a motely assembly of hand-bells, gongs, cow horns, whistles, tin kettles, rattles, bones, fying pans, everything in short from which more and rougher noise than ordinary could be extracted. At a given signal they halted, and the orator began to recite a lot of doggerel verses, of which I can remember on the beginning:
>
> > There is a man in this place.
> > Has beat his wife!!   *(forte. A Pause)*
> > Has beat his wife!!   *(fortissimo)*
> > It is a very great shame and disgrace
> > To all who in this place
> > It is indeed upon my life!!
>
> After some score or more lines of such "sweet poesy" another signal was given, and the orchestra burst out "in transport and rude harmony," aided by the howling and hooting of those breath was not otherwise engaged in giving wind to the horns and whistles. A bonfire was then lighted, round which the whole party danced as if they were crazy. I was told the noise was heard two miles off. After keeping this up for near half an hour, silence was proclaimed, and the orator advancing hoped he should not be obliged to come again, and recommended better conduct for the future. This rough music was secretly encouraged by the neighbours, who clubbed for beer for the band, and it was believed to have the best moral effect on all parties. The husband was certain to be ashamed of his position; and if the wife by her ill-conduct had brought this on herself, she could not avoid the suggestions of her own conscience thereupon. I believe it to have been a more effectual remedy than appeals to police-magistrates, or Sir Crewell Cresswel, or even to the cat-o'-ninetails threatened by Lord Palmerston.[135]

Evidence from various parts of Britain suggests that rough music was initiated once behavior had become so notorious that it could no longer be ignored. In the Blackheath community of Woking, the church choir was said to have constituted itself as the court of public opinion; in other places the informal jury convened in public houses like Hardy's fictionalized Peter's Finger, a plebeian version of the manor court which had once presided over moral offenses. Our only account of such a session comes from Wales, where such "courts" were said to have existed until the 1860s.[136] One such, called a "Coolstrin Court," was encountered by Charles Redwood in Glamorganshire sometime in the early nineteenth century. There it had become public knowledge that a tailor had been beaten by his wife. Discussion began among the men at the public house, but "further debate was adjourned to a meeting at the church porch, that there might be no room for the women to impugn the sobriety of their proceedings." One man, "uncommonly knowing in old adages and customs, and something of a humorist to boot . . . ," was chosen as judge; and a prosecutor and defender were also appointed. On the agreed day, the judge, with a collar bone of a horse on his head and dressed in a long robe, led a procession into the church yard, seating himself on the church wall. The facts of the case were presented. It seems that the angry wife had invaded the forbidden precincts of the alehouse; and, failing to get her husband to come with her, waited for him to return home, where she bloodied him. She refused to defend herself at the Coolstrin, as women had previously done, and this gave the judge the opportunity to enter into a long discourse on how:

> all the danger is from the WOMEN. For we all know well enough that if we give them but an inch, they will be for taking an ell [a unit of measure].

Then he passed judgment, ordering that a "riding" be held for both the tailor and his wife:

> that these hectoring wenches may see what a pretty figure they cut, and learn what it is we think of them; and that all men may be put in mind to keep the reigns tight, and not part with the breeches, nor ever knock under the henpecking.

On the appointed day, the judge, followed by various "musicians," led an all-male procession, carrying two poles, one with a petticoat on top, the other with a pair of breeches hung upside-down. Two men impersonated the offenders, the female with a ladle and the male with a broom, following the procession as it toured the neighboring villages, picking up an increasingly large and antic crowd of men and boys. When the circuit had been completed, the pole with the petticoat was planted opposite the tailor's house and pelted with eggs and mud until it fell to the ground. In its place was hoisted the breeches, which was left afixed to the offenders' roof as a "standard of masculine government."

This would seem to have represented a very old-fashioned charivari, if it were not for the fact that both the verdict and the riding itself roused a response very different from that of the traditional peasant or artisan community. While the men in the surrounding villages had pealed the church bells to welcome the procession, women remained indoors and "mocked at them through the windows." Female opposition was even more evident at the tailor's house, where they had "collected to scoff . . . , and poured out a din of hoots and yells, that could not be drowned even by the Coolstrin band."[137] While the female opposition had not been able to halt the proceedings, their protest called into question the "masculine government" the men were attempting to uphold. In South Wales the sexual balance of power had shifted considerably. Women had become considerably more independent since the beginnings of mining and industry there; and this, in turn, was reflected in the sexual politics of both courtship and marriage. It was one of the things Wirt Sykes found most remarkable when he visited the area early in the nineteenth century: "It happens in matrimonial partnerships that she bears the reputation of being the 'better man of the two' with a frequency that is quite wonderful."[138]

CHAPTER 5

~~~~~~

Time Changes Fau'k an' Manners: Private Marriages versus Public Bridals

By 1850 the marriage customs that had once been common practice were confined to a dwindling minority of small farmers and provincial artisans. In the place of a single betrothal and wedding tradition there now existed several competing practices, each reflecting a different notion of correct courtship and proper marriage. In the course of the previous hundred years both betrothal and wedding had become the subject of passionate controversy, an issue not so much of religion but of class. People in different parts of Britain now married in quite different ways; the distance between the mores of ordinary people and those of the educated elites had never been greater. The ideal of the nuclear family and companionate marriage, something that had divided the middle class from the aristocracy in the seventeenth century, now united them in common opposition to the less strictly monogamous behavior of their social inferiors. From the mid-eighteenth century onward sexual politics became increasingly bitter as the propertied classes attempted to impose their standards on the rest of society.

The convergence and tightening of upper-class views on marriage were evident early in the eighteenth century. While there were still a few aristocratic holdouts, the monogamous standards that had once been associated previously with the puritan "middling sort" now provided a basis for consensus among people of property regardless of sectarian persuasion. For most of the eighteenth century and until the rise of the joint stock company in the nineteenth century, the family was a crucial means of capital accumulation and economic enterprise. Marriage played a central role in mobilizing wealth and power, and the control of courtship, particularly that of heirs and heiresses, remained essential. While young people were told they must marry for love and were given a certain latitude in the choice of mates, the courtship process was carefully constructed to prevent misalliances.[1]

If young people were still given a certain degree of freedom in their choice of mates, this was largely due to the development of a set of institutions on both the local and national levels that ensured against disagreeable results. From the late seventeenth century onward the important provincial market towns provided balls and assemblies whose social exclusivity was a guarantee against misalliance. Various watering places like Bath also offered safe opportunities for courtship; and, in London itself, the emergence of the Season, established a national meeting place which by the nineteenth century had assimilated not only the landed elites but a good part of the wealthy bourgeoisie.[2] "The English have much more opportunity for getting to know each other before marriage, for young folk are in society from an early age; they go with their parents everywhere. Young girls mix with the company and talk and enjoy themselves with as much freedom as if they were married," noted the Duc de la Rochfoucauld in the 1780s. He was surprised to find so many marriages based on affection; and attributed this to the longer courtship typical of the upper classes: "Accordingly the Englishman makes more effort to get to know his bride before marriage; she has the same desire."[3]

"Those marriages generally abound most with love and constancy that are proceeded by a long courtship," advised Joseph Addison; "The passion should strike root and gather strength before marriage is grafted on to it."[4] Among the upper classes courtship became more extended and the age of marriage rose. Among the wealthy, betrothal became a family affair. It lost its public, jural character and became known as "engagement," a prelude to nuptuality that was never to be confused with marriage itself. A fiancé would never have dared to call his fiancée wife, just as she could not think of him as husband until the wedding. Just as the words changed, so did the meaning of betrothal. It no longer bestowed access to the full conjugal rights, including sexuality.[5] Even before the Hardwicke Act of 1753 deprived betrothal of its legal status, chastity was the norm among the propertied classes.

Among the patricians betrothal had lost its ritual importance even before the mid-eighteenth century. Serious negotiations over the marriage settlement took place in lawyers chambers; and, because strict settlement was increasingly popular among merchants and big landowners, the actual terms of agreement were often out of the hands of both parents and children.[6] The worth of the bride was prearranged in many cases; and, while it was still fashionable before 1800 to announce the value of the match in the local press, this was the only glimpse the public was permitted of the business of marriage itself.[7] As for the social side of betrothal, it was usually celebrated within the social circle of the families involved. A clergyman might be present, but only if he had the social credentials equal to the other guests, and then only in a private capacity.

The patrician wedding was also changing, in the direction of greater privacy. Henri Misson found that nearly all wealthy Londoners married by license in the early eighteenth century.

> To proclaim Banns is a Thing no Body now dares to have done; very few are willing to have their Affairs declar'd to all the World in a publick Place, when for a Guinea they may do it *snug* and without Noise; and my good friends the Clergy, who find their Accounts in it, are not very Zealous to prevent it. Thus then, they by what they call *Licence* are marry'd in their Closets, in the Presence of a couple of Friends that serve as Witnesses.[8]

After witnessing a "mob" waiting at the church door when an alderman's daughter wed in 1770, Fanny Burney expressed horror at all forms of the big wedding: "I don't suppose anything can be so dreadful as a public wedding—my stars! I should never be able to support it."[9] She would have approved of arrival and departure by closed carriage, an eighteenth-century innovation, which served to protect the privacy of the couple and exemplify social distance. Misson described London gentle folk marrying "incognito," arranging to arrive at church early in the morning, to be "marry'd with a low voice, and the Doors shut."[10] As for the actual ceremony, the bare minimum was preferred. The business of marriage, traditionally symbolized by the dow purse and ring, fell into disuse. The dow purse was completely neglected and much less was made of the ring, whose appeal was purely aesthetic and no longer magical.[11]

Patrician nuptials were arranged to give the family almost total control over the events of the day. Some of the features of the traditional big wedding remained, but they functioned in a very different manner. Peers and neighbors might play a supporting role, but they were no longer the central actors. In the account of the marriage of a Gloucestershire gentlewoman, Dorothea Trotman, wed on a Thursday in 1712, there was no fetching of the bride or petting stone. The preliminaries were apparently too insignificant to mention, for the description begins with the arrival of the bride and groom at church, conveyed there separately by carriages, accompanied only by their parents and household servants. The hasty exit after the service provided no opportunity for the usual postnuptial rituals. The wedding party returned immediately to the Trotman home, where they were joined by close friends in performing the only popular custom—breaking cake over the newlyweds—that was permitted to intrude on the otherwise very decorous celebrations. We are told that the day was spent in "dancing, card playing, and bell ringing until the couple retired." Nothing is said about the bridal chamber, and the only music performed was that of hired players, who sweetly roused the household the next morning when more gentry arrived to celebrate. On Saturday, employees of the Trotman estate were permitted a holiday in honor of the wedding: "the poor labourers feasted that day with us, which made up our number at dinner at 115, besides

50 poor served at ye door." On Sunday six coachfuls of house guests heard Reverend Loveryhome preach a wedding sermon on Proverbs 18 & 19 before they began to depart. Even then the celebrations were not quite over, for we hear that "the dromers" were still saluting the new couple on the evening of the next Tuesday, almost six days after the wedding.[12]

Weddings of urban gentry were even more private. It was said that London's bourgeoisie stole away to church as "quietly as lambs," though it was still the case that "if the Drums and Fiddlers have Notice of it, they will sure to be with them by Day-break, making a horrible Racket, till they have got the pence."[13] The desire to emphasize conjugality was also the reason why the upper classes began to take honeymoons. While the former Miss Trotman surrounded herself with friends and relatives at her home, others took their closest companions with them on their wedding trip. As Lawrence Stone notes, "the premarital habits of single-sex bonding and association thus continued as before, and the newly married pair had apparently no privacy at all for the first two weeks of their marriage except at night in their bedroom, to which they only retired very late after cards, dancing, and singing until midnight or after."[14] It apparently took an extended period of celebrating and visiting before the newlyweds were quite sure of themselves as a married couple, though, by the early nineteenth century, it was becoming the fashion for middle-class couples to begin their honeymoon trips immediately after the wedding and to go unaccompanied. While the completely private honeymoon did not become wholly fashionable until the Victorian age, the idea of a time for seclusion, a substitute for the kind of intimacy denied them during their engagement period, must have been attractive to many couples.[15]

Still, the patricians dispensed with many of the older forms of publicity for class as well as personal reasons. Miss Trotman's wedding served not to incorporate her and her husband into the communal order, but to emphasize the social distance between persons of their class and the rest of the community. Everything that violated social hierarchy, even the kiss by the parson, was discouraged. The footings, firing of guns, the race for the garter—all were regarded as vulgar and unnecessary. Misson found that bridesmaids and groomsmen still accompanied high-born newlyweds into the bridal chamber to pull off the bride's garter and drink the posset, but this too was dispensed with by the end of the eighteenth century.[16] The upper classes signaled their contempt for popular practice by withdrawing themselves from village wedding celebrations. They sent their good wishes and contributed impressive gifts when one of the couple was a faithful employee or the child of an old retainer, but stopped short of actually attending what they viewed as indecorous festivities. The clergy, particularly in the south of England, followed their example. They too no longer felt comfortable kissing or toasting the common bride, and thus came to restrict themselves to the most perfunctory performance of their official duties.[17]

Of course, the upper classes expected the poor to celebrate their marriages in a prescribed, deferential manner. The largesse distributed at gentry weddings encouraged rural laborers to drop their more boisterous salutes in favor of rituals invented by their patrons. At Felton Park in 1792, Sir Walter Blount distributed food and coin to the poor, rewarding handsomely those who unhitched his wedding carriage and yoked themselves to it.[18] In Radnorshire, the people of Presteigne showed the pleasure at their squire's wedding in 1845 by getting up a subscription and funding a fete that lasted an entire week.[19] By the nineteenth century this kind of self-conscious ostentation had spread to the urban bourgeoisie, who had previously confined their marriage festivities to family and close friends. Even Quakers, who had previously struggled so valiantly against luxurious display, were giving into the impulse, not so much because they had come to value popular custom, but because like other members of the middle classes they now felt it was their social and civic duty to exercise some form of paternalist ritual.[20] The wedding rites of nineteenth-century factory magnates were perfected to an extent that they ultimately rivaled even the elaborate productions of the landowning classes. When the children of the great Preston and Bradford textile families were united, there was invariably a great turnout. Loyal employees were treated to feasts and railway trips to Morecombe. In return, they dressed themselves and their dwellings, paraded and presented their congratulations, all in the most orderly and respectful fashion.[21]

The style set by the wealthy was appropriated by all those wishing to associate themselves with higher social status. Clara Alcock's description of a mid-Victorian middle-class wedding in Manchester dwells largely on what the bride and bridesmaids wore. There is no mention of any public celebration, except that "the church was not very full." The marriage service was followed by a "grand breakfast," after which the couple left for Paris by way of London.[22] Weddings of substantial farmers followed the same pattern, and even rural artisans tended to follow fashion by the end of the nineteenth century. A Herefordshire blacksmith's daughter, married around 1910, had the latest style gown, "a reception in a marque," and a seaside honeymoon. Only the fact that the groom's father gave as his gift a pig identified this as a rural wedding.[23]

I

The one thing that had prevented the patricians from abolishing public betrothal and turning the wedding into a completely private act much sooner was the law of the Church of England that for centuries had attempted to balance the rights of parents with those of children, while at the same time insisting on the communal character of the marriage rites. In the seventeenth century, puritan sectarians had fought in the name of the patriarchal family against both the church's acceptance of betrothal as self-marriage and the publicity of banns, attempting to replace these with a civil marriage act that emphasized parental discipline and the priority of private over communal interest. They had failed, but now the conjugal ideal for which they had struggled was accepted by the propertied classes at large. United in their vision of a nuclear family based on conjugal affections, the patricians were in a position by the mid-eighteenth century to impose their will on the established church. They were now convinced that the legality of betrothal together with the church's toleration of clandestine marriage were, as Daniel Defoe was so fond of pointing out, crimes against both property and patriarchy: "a Gentleman might have the satisfaction of hanging a Thief that stole an old Horse from him, but could have no Justice against a rogue for stealing his Daughter."[24] Their clamor for stricter control was seconded by both civil lawyers, frustrated by the confusions arising from contradictory canons that allowed betrothal and clandestine marriage to stand as equal to church weddings, and those clergy who, seeing their incomes diminished by marital entrepreneurs, were likewise eager for reform. Stephen Sutton, the Yorkshire clergyman, may have understood why the curate in the neighboring parish was forced by poverty to perform clandestine ceremonies, but he nevertheless felt he must report him to the episcopal authorities. An earlier mood of toleration was evaporating as many clergymen sought closer alignment with the interests and views of the propertied classes, thereby gradually dissociating themselves not only from the practices but from the interests of ordinary people.[25]

Although the pressure for reform of the marriage laws had been building for some time, Lord Hardwicke's "Act for the better preventing of Clandestine Marriages," introduced in the 1753 parliamentary session, took many, including the dissenting community, quite by surprise. Only the Quakers and Jews managed to have their marriage rites exempted from its provisions, which stipulated that after Lady Day 1754 no marriage other than one performed by an ordained Anglican clergyman in the premises of the Church of England after either thrice-called banns or purchase of license from a bishop or one of his surrogates was valid. In the case of both banns and license, at least one party had to be resident for at least three weeks in the parish where the marriage was to be celebrated. Parental consent for those under twenty-one was strictly enforced. All other kinds of marriages were henceforth invalid; and, while the act did not propose to make these a felony, it did make it a criminal offense, punishable by fourteen years transportation, for any Anglican priest to conduct any but the prescribed Church of England service during legal hours. Tampering with the registers became a capital offense. But of even greater importance was the provision that betrothals were no longer sufficient either to sanction or obstruct marriage. They ceased to have any validity in the church courts, leaving civil action for breach of promise the only means open to a party who believed a promise had been broken. After 1754 no vow other than that made in the Church of England, Quaker Meetings, or a Jewish Synagogue had any legal standing as marriage.[26]

In Parliament, the Hardwicke bill, which was to apply only to England and Wales, occasioned one of the most impassioned debates of the century. Opponents, led by the flamboyant Henry Fox, accepted the sponsors' argument that something needed to be done to halt the fraudulent seduction of heirs and heiresses, but condemned the law as altering the very fabric of British society. Fox declared it would enhance the power of a few aristocratic and wealthy families, which was "of more danger to our constitution than ever the military power was, which they in former times separately possessed."[27] Absolute parental control of children under age would contribute to a castelike social order. "Our quality and rich families will daily accumulate riches by marrying only one another," argued Robert Nugent, who was also convinced that the law would obstruct the marriage of the poor and create a particular hardship for women. From his experience as a rural magistrate, Nugent understood clandestine marriage to be the people's equivalent of marriage by license. A man "does not like to be exposed so long beforehand to the jeers of all his companions; and to be married by license cost more money than poor people can well spare. How fond our people are of private marriages and saving a little money."[28] Especially hard put would be seamen, soldiers, transport and other itinerant workers, who were constantly changing abodes, but it was women who were especially at risk by virtue of the abolition of the binding power of precontracts or betrothals:

> A young woman is but too apt by nature to trust to the honour of the man she loves, and to admit him to her bed upon a solemn promise to marry her. Surely the moral obligation is as binding as if they had been actually married: but you are by this Bill to declare it null and void, even though it be in writing.[29]

Without recourse to the courts, women would be vulnerable legally and thus more easily abandoned when pregnant. They would find it difficult to bring men to the altar when the only option was marriage by banns. "Now, if he can't afford licence, this [the pregnancy] cannot be concealed, and shame will be on both, which may cause him to decide not to marry at all."[30] Illegitimacy would increase and worse still "you will be the cause of the murder of many infants, either after they are born, or by abortion." Nugent's warnings were seconded by Charles Townshend, for whom the bill was "one of the most cruel enterprises against the fair sex that ever entered into the heart of man."[31]

Other critics attacked the inconsistency of allowing the rich their privacy by license, while condemning the poor to publicity by banns. A whiff of anticlericalism was introduced by Colonel George Haldane, for whom license was a way of "putting money into the pockets of our clergymen and some of their officers."[32] He predicted that "by taxing and throwing obstacles in the way of marriage, you of course introduce clandestine marriage, and if you prevent these by severer laws, you will force the poor to make the best shift they can without marriage."[33]

Despite vigorous opposition in and outside Westminster, the Hardwicke Act passed by a large majority. As Lady Day 1754 approached, the business at the marriage houses of the Fleet and elsewhere boomed. Walpole wrote that "the Duchess of Argyle harrangues against the Marriage Bill not taking place immediately, and is persuaded that all the girls will go off before next Lady-Day."[34] When the Fleet closed its registers for the last time, some of the veteran "marriers" hurried north to Scotland where the new law did not apply.[35] Two clergy of the Savoy Chapel, who foolishly stayed behind to test the law, were promptly prosecuted and transported, thus making the determination of church and state abundantly clear.[36] The parson of Great Houghton grumbled in the privacy of his register that this was a "punishment little inferior to ye gallows and inflicted generally on ye most profligate and abandoned part of mankind," but neither he nor many of his fellow clerics dared open defiance of the new law.[37]

Most parsons were only too happy to find their flock returning to their altars and their own incomes rising accordingly. Even those who had previously opposed tight discipline saw the advantages of obedience, as did most of their dissenting counterparts, Protestant and Catholic, who counseled their members to obey the law and go through a Church of England ceremony in spite of whatever other private rites they might wish to have. The religious resistance that might have been expected never materialized, in part because dissenters were equally concerned as parents and elders about runaway marriages. The discipline of the Quakers and Jews was exceptionally strong already, a major reason why these denominations were exempted from the law.[38] Intellectual opposition was kept alive by those like Blackstone, for whom Hardwicke's legislation was "an innovation on our antient laws and constitution." Later unsuccessful efforts to repeal used his argument that:

> Restraints upon marriages, especially among the lower class, are evidently detrimental to the public, by hindering the increase of the people; and to religion and morality, by encouraging licentiousness and debauchery among the single of both sexes.[39]

II

Having defined marriage as an essentially private legal act, the upper classes were determined to eliminate those elements of the big wedding that symbolized the collective interest in nuptiality. The practice of the clerk and congregation shouting "God speed 'em well" was frowned on and the vicar in one Yorkshire parish did away with it because it "frequently excited some rather unseasonable mirth among the younger portion of the congregation."[40] By the mid-Victorian periòd the old rituals of "askings" and "spurrings" lost their appeal even to ordinary people. The cost of bell ringing was too much for the Rutland poor and it was discontinued in the 1870s.[41] As these preliminaries became attenuated, so did the big wedding itself. Everywhere, behavior in church was becoming more decorous. At Donington-on-Bain, Lincolnshire, the old practice of pelting the newlyweds with hassocks ended in the 1780s when a new parson was struck by one of the missiles.[42] Northern clergy eventually abandoned the custom of kissing the bride; and by the end of the Victorian age even the dow purse, a practice dear to the smallholders of Yorkshire and elsewhere, had fallen into disuse.[43] Parsons were not only refusing to tolerate that which did not conform to the Book of Common Prayer, but were increasingly censorious of popular uses of church property. In the village of Ford, Northumberland, grooms of all social stations had always been given the choice of jumping a local stream called the "Gaudy Loup" or paying a fine. In 1803, Lord Deleval was said to have chosen the latter, paying a handsome tribute to the assembled crowd. Later, when the Loup was filled in, festivities moved to the church yard, where "it was customary at a village wedding for the young men of the place to take a long pole, known as the 'petting-stick' and hold it across the principal exit from the church yard, thus barring the bride's exit unless she chose to jump." When the parson of Ford tried to ban the practice, the villagers "not wishing to give up old 'rights' abandoned the church yard for the outside of the church yard gates," substituting a long rope for the stick.[44] Elsewhere as well, jumping and chaining managed to survive largely on the support received from small farmers, miners, and cottage workers.[45] One old parson at Whittingham, Northumberland, R. W. Goodenough, was said to have enjoyed jumping the petting stone in his own church yard, but he was a dying breed, out of step with the attitudes of his class.[46] At Brampton, Cumberland, Reverend W. Dacre took two farm laborers to court in 1893 when they barred the door of his church during the wedding of the daughter of a local farmer. He knew it to be "the custom," but was determined to end it once and for all. The justices agreed with him, using the incident to announce that "in the future [they] should deal severely with offenders brought before them."[47]

According to those who knew the chaining custom best, it was the unremitting pressure of the local gentry that eventually eliminated it. "Unsympathetic vicars are shocked at the merriment so near the church, when it is done at the door of the building," W. Crooke reported.[48] While the lower classes still looked forward to it, "just above the common folk the custom is considered 'vulgar,' and the throwing of rice, etc is indulged in, in imitation of the customs of the upper classes."[49] Among those persons whose memories of weddings are on record in the Essex

oral history collections, only one, the son of a quarryman from somewhere in the southwest of England remembered the practice lasting into
the early twentieth century:

> Bride has to step over, she had a long gown on, draggingly she'd pull up
> and step over the bridesmaid used to pull up the back and people laughing.
> Oh, always a crowd on—for a wedding.[50]

Respectability threw its full weight against the old wedding practices.
The Reverend Jones of St. Peter's, Llanelly, was admonishing his congregation for throwing rice in church and decreeing that no one should
tie the church gates shut without first obtaining the permission of the
couple.[51] Apparently, his congregation supported him in this; and, in
other Welsh parishes, newlyweds were putting up resistance to "roping," pressing charges of their own against those who kept the custom.[52]
At Middlewich, men laid a rope across the path of a bridal carriage. The
driver refused to stop and a serious accident occurred. Thomas Lowe
defended himself in court by claiming "it was customary in the district
to 'rope' a wedding party. They acted in fun, and were desirous of
drinking the health of the newly married couple (much laughter)."[53] He
got a sympathetic hearing, for the magistrate treated it as a simple case
of highway obstruction and refused to order damages. But by 1900 toleration had dissipated and "it was agreed that 'roping the road' was an
old custom, but fines were imposed, so it seems probable that this long
established practice will soon be a thing of the past."[54]

Roping and chaining did not die out entirely even in the twentieth
century, but instead passed, like so many other customs, into the cus-
tody of children, who even today tie the church gates in the Forest of
Dean and other isolated places.[55] A Welsh woman, who married in 1922,
remembered throwing money to children. The rope was "in our street,
see, right across the street—you couldn't—they wouldn't let you pass.
No, have money first. That was—tradition you know."[56] In parts of
Somerset children were already in charge in the 1850s, but in the north
of England older youth were not displaced until somewhat later.[57] The
boys at the King Edward VII school in Gigglesworth kept the custom
until the 1850s. At Burnley it lasted somewhat longer, but the head-
master there remembered that in the 1870s he had been asked "on several
occasions to resuscitate the practice, but it seemed to me hardly in accordance with the dignity of a grammar school."[58] David Dippe Dixon
recalled that "in those happy days when there was no 'time table' hanging on the walls of the village school . . . the kindly master always allowed
the scholars an hour's play whenever it was known there was going to
be a wedding."[59] Thus, the custom descended to preschool children,
where it is kept today.[60]

Especially in the south and east, the big wedding was succumbing to
a combination of official pressure and Victorian notions of respectability,
but even in Yorkshire the helter skelter of the riding wedding passed

into folk memory by the 1880s.[61] Magistrates put down the practice of firing guns on the grounds it was a public nuisance. Rice had long since replaced shoes and sods in polite circles, though one unskilled worker recalled that at his wedding some of his friends managed to tie "a couple of old boots on the back of me coat. Yet, I was only laughing. I didn't mind."[62] But even this vestige of the traditional teasing was considered offensive by many Victorians. "At a time when the young bride is looking her last at sorrowful parents and an old home, [shoe throwing] is annoying and ill-timed," noted one critic of the rough music tradition.[63] In a more temperate age, the wedding party was not so likely to be offered toasts by well-wishers. Instead, "as the little procession passed along the road one might have heard women's voices here and there, calling out from doorways of the roadside cottages, expressing best wishes for good luck and happiness . . ." but not presenting alcoholic "hot pots" as had been the previous custom.[64] Even in Wales the magistrates were refusing in the 1890s to issue temporary licenses to sell drink.[65]

III

The erosion of the traditional big wedding proceeded more quickly in the agricultural south and east, in part because the power of the parson and squire was stronger there, but also because the rural proletariat no longer had any reason to celebrate its weddings collectively. For those with no property, marriage had become a personal rather than collective matter; and, one by one, the rites of the old big wedding—the fetching of the bride, the treating of peers, and the inauguration of the new household—all came to be regarded as meaningless luxuries. There was no mock battle for the bride in places where parents and parish encouraged, even forced, early marriage. The couple simply walked to church on their wedding morning accompanied by a handful of friends, and then returned to work in the afternoon. Baring-Gould noted with regret that "village weddings are now quiet enough, no feasting, no dancing."[66] In most places the wage worker did not have the time or the money. A Lincolnshire woman remembered that "labourers, etc all got wed in meal breaks, many at 8 A.M. in the morning. The girl then went back to the kitchen and the man to the field."[67] As Edwin Grey remembered it:

> Cottage weddings in my boyhood days [the 1870s] were simple, homely affairs, though often pretty and picturesque in their rural surroundings. The dresses of the bride to be and her attendant maiden (for only one girl friend accompanied her) were very generally made of some serviceable material of a pretty shade, with a bonnet or hat to correspond, the young women no doubt having in mind that these same dresses would, as a matter of course, come in afterwards as best, that is for Sunday wear, holidays and so on. Maybe the best man was a relative, but, however, he would

13. *Happy Is the Bride*, by James Hayllar, 1890. One of quiet weddings typical of country churches of the later nineteenth century. The father, in his smock, brings the bride, dressed in her Sunday best. (Courtesy of the Atkinson Art Gallery, Southport, England)

give the bride away, for very very rarely did the father conduct his daughter to church, in many cases he would have to be at his work on the farm, for he could ill afford any reduction of his small wage owing to loss of time; however, he would be in at the evening' merriment. All weddings that I can remember at this early period of my life were what are now alluded to as walking weddings; carriages, retinue of bridesmaids, veils, wreathes of orange blossoms, etc were not then in vogue at the weddings of farm workers' daughters.[68]

The poor now married as quickly and as quietly as they could, sneaking off to church "to avoid spending the sum of money that they could ill afford treating their fellow workmen." A big wedding was simply out of the question: "those days they didn't do it; they didn't have the money you see."[69] Any celebration was limited to the immediate family and pushed ahead to the evening, "so that any members of either family who have been at work on the farm would have by this time arrived home, and having washed and spruced up a bit, would now be able to be present at this pleasant tea-time meal." There was a wedding cake; and presents were received, "but they would be, as a rule, from their own respective families, near neighbors, and more intimate friends, and mainly in the form of food or useful household items."[70] The couple usually provided the bulk of their own start in married life, the man supplying his wife with rolling pins, bowls, and other small household utensils. In Pudsey "it is considered a famous affair if her 'dowry' should be a 'Kist' or a bedstead. Wedding presents (if any) consist of small, but useful articles, and what more can be expected from a people possessing such scanty means."[71] In rural Oxfordshire "it had become the custom for the bride to buy the bulk of the furniture with her savings in service, while the bridegroom redecorated the interior of the house, planted the vegetable garden and put a pig, or a couple of pigs, in the sty."[72]

Because so many proletarian couples began their married lives doubling up with parents or other relatives, there was no elaborate inauguration of a new household, no threshold ceremonies or nights of rough music. In the evening of the marriage it was common to gather in the bride's parents' house, push aside the furniture, listen to songs or step dance.[73] The wedding night was quiet enough, and those postnuptial rites of inauguration, such as taking the "bride seat," had long since lost their appeal.[74] Many proletarian couples never went anywhere near the church after they had been wed there. And there was no honeymoon either, for as Edwin Grey pointed out, "the young couple would not be able to afford it, and again in most cases, the young man would have to be up and about his work on the farm the next morning at the usual early hour."[75] A Derbyshire man who married in 1904 could not remember anyone of his class ever going away. "Never heard of any as had honeymoons," he said, "It took 'em all their time to get money to get married."[76]

IV

The big wedding was also changing in the north and west, but there the plebeian population did not submit easily to the pressures from the local elites. In the 1780s, the parson of Bedale in Yorkshire threatened to boycott local weddings if the old "nominys" (songs) with explicit sexual references were not dropped. It seems that the clergyman won the first round, for the brides of Bedale asked their men not to sing the verses "because they didn't not like to have the parson come."[77] The clergy then turned their attention to the garter, threatening to forbid it also. About 1812 the vicar at Pickering demanded it be ended; and at Bedale, the wife of a new clergyman took it upon herself to reform the practice. When she heard that Dora Lumley was stitching a garter in preparation for her wedding, she stormed into her family's cottage without knocking, lecturing the Lumley women on the immodesty of the custom. In turn, Dora's mother informed her in no uncertain terms of the antiquity and seemliness of the practice, which had been kept by Bedale women for generations: "Ah allus kept mahsel respectable, an mah mother war reckoned to yan o't maist respectablest women 'at anybody ivver clapped 'e's on, an' her garter was raced for." She then showed the parson's wife the door.[78]

The battle was joined by the craftsmen and smallholders who made up the Bedale population, most of whom regarded the race for the garter as an "old and much loved custom, their fathers and mothers had indulged in the rite, they saw no harm, and truly there was none."[79] Dora Lumley and her mother became local heroines, whose resistance was remembered to the end of the nineteenth century when Richard Blakeborough first heard of the original incident. As one resident remembered it: "when ivver't [the old parsons] and standards died, an' new parsons cam' in the'r place, they all tried for t'deea away wiv oor au'd customs."[80] Verses composed at the time of the struggle expressed the same feelings:

> Different days
> A's different ways...
> Time changes fau'k an' manners[81]

In Bedale the new parson and his wife became the focus of intense hostility, expressed in rough music:

> He [the old parson] prayed and preached and sang
> And in a bridal race and bard
> He never seed ought wrong
> At many a bridal door he stood
> When t' winner claimed his prize
> And monny a bridal leg he seed

> But now [the old parson] hes deedd [dead]
> God rest his head
> And t' new com'd's ta'en his place
> We're teeched its wrang [wrong]
> Fer t'bride to shew
> Her led at t' bridal race

> His old dame she
> says it maint be
> Shas shamm'd what a bride'll stand
> In front o'folk and lift her goon
> While she yiels up her bridal band

> To sikan [such] a farse
> I say my harse [arse]
> Our mother sticked and ware ther band
> And wi' lifted goon ivvery yan did stand
> An war all true Maids at Heart.[82]

Dales women found themselves the focus of a bitter contest between class cultures. Masters and ministers demanded they give up the custom; mothers and sweethearts insisted they keep the old ways. The daughters of cottagers, small farmers, and tradesmen remained most loyal, but those slightly higher on the social scale had already deserted custom and the culture that sustained it. The daughters of the big farmers, whose social pretensions were reflected in their boarding-school refinements and their fondness for low-cut Empire dresses, were the subject of mocking verses:

To blush she's forgotten, it's true 'at she'll dance
As no prudent lass would dream on or dare
Wi' her goon all uplifted an' bubbies all bare

Of our lasses are wrong wother that way or this
But the worst of all Bitches is a Boarding School Miss.[83]

The Bedale schoolmaster, David Naitby, railed in his diary against the hypocrisy of those

who in their stinking mock mollishness would fain make us believe that a Bride does demean herself who lifts her gown; and these very prudes who cry shame upon all who dare for to do what they mothers did afore' 'em, will show their paps [breasts] as brazened as an old cow in milking time. Psha, I cry a pox on all those misses, who would not lift their gown to yield their garter band, but who would not stop to doing the same deed in one of our bawdy dances.[84]

His contemporary, George Calvert, who was no less contemptuous of those "scaumpy calfed [scrauny legged] lasses [as] have catched at the whisper of some straight-laced parson dame or mayhap some methodraudy [methodist] preacher that it be a fault and immodest for our brides to lift their gouns as their mothers did afore 'em."[85]

As an alternative to the garter, some brides began to offer ribbons or handkerchiefs as the racers' prize. But the garter had become so central to the conflict that this was unacceptable to the defenders of tradition. They composed verses to girls who did it the old way:

Neea prude is Nance; they saay sha's maade,
Her brahdal bands ov gowden braad [golden braid]
Noo fer a ribbon Ah weean't run
It gi'es neea luck, an' stops wer fun
Sike ninny nammy waays ez sum
Cum drink ti t' bridal garter O.[86]

If she were a member of the upper classes, then the honor paid to her was all the greater. One "Lady" was praised for defying the conventions of her class by offering her garter to one of her own stable hands when he won the race. "I intended to be properly married and have the luck I am entitled to," she declared at the threshold, "Take it off, Tom, and give it to your sweetheart, and may it bring luck to both of you."[87]

Martha Sheppard earned her popularity in a similar way. "Since Martha's brave deed she has been a town's favorite," noted Naitby.[88] On the other hand, those girls who betrayed their peers became, like Martha Muscrop, an object lesson:

At Martha Muscrop's wedding there was nowther bite or sup
She didn't don the garter band, she could not ho' yan up
So she loosely tied a ribbon, aboon her sandal
But not a lad wad run for it, so there it had to hing

So lasses take warning, from every yan we beg

> To stich and wear a bridal band, and show a bridal leg
> For if you sport a ribbon, we lads and lasses know
> You've gotten bowed and scraggy legs, which you do shame
> to show[89]

Young dalesmen were ready to take by force what was denied them by false modesty. Brawls resulted, which only reinforced the determination of the clergy and those who valued the new respectability to abolish the garter race entirely. By the 1830s this had been largely accomplished. The garter was by then a collector's item and the new generations grew up ignorant of the old verses and the controversy that had inspired them. They were content to race for a ribbon or other favor, though, as Richard Blakeborough discovered, something of the garter's old magic still lingered. "I doubt," he noted, "if the bride and bridegroom would consider themselves properly wedded if there were no race for the ribbon or handkerchief."[90] But, at the time of his writing, the 1880s, even this remnant of earlier big weddings was largely a thing of the past.

V

The events in Bedale suggest that the politics of marriage had shifted from issues internal to the family and community to questions of class. Henceforth the big wedding was itself at issue, with the plebeians acting as the champions of that venerable institution. They adapted it to their own changed circumstances, playing down the role of the patriarchal household and emphasizing the expanded place of kinship and community. Less was made of the prenuptial formalities, and fathers seemed to have been much less involved at every stage of the marriage process. Because it was no longer the dowry or portion that made the wedding but rather the earnings of the couple and gifts from friends, the timing also changed. In newly industrialized South Wales the last Saturday of the month, the day the miners were paid, became a favorite: "Yes, the day for weddings was normally pay day, and that pay, you may be sure, was given to the young wife, every penny of it."[91]

The role of the patriarchal household was played down. The bride was not fetched from home, but now met the groom at the church where the festivities began. "The knight errant Cavalcade on horseback, the Carrying off the Bride, the Rescue, the wordy War in rhyme between the parties, etc which formally formed a singular Spectacle of mock contest at the celebration of Nuptials, I believe to be now almost, if not altogether, laid aside everywhere . . . ," noted the *Cambrian Register*'s correspondent in 1796.[92] The relatively smaller role played by the patriarchal household did not reduce the wedding's size, however. Northumberland colliers normally made a holiday of the marriages of their mates, trooping in their hundreds to Newcastle to celebrate:

mostly double mounted, or a man and a woman up a horse, [which] made a very grotesque appearance in their parade through the streets. The women and horses were literally covered with ribbon.[93]

To one unsympathetic observer of Cornish miners, "the wedding was then little better than a drunken spree for the bridegroom and his companions, continuing their orgies for three or four days, or until their little savings were expended."[94] No one seemed much concerned about calling banns, especially where the relationship had already been announced by the pregnancy of the bride or the existence of one or more natural children. Miners and other plebeian folk were not great church attenders, and from the 1780s onward there was growing tension over church fees, which in the Newcastle area resulted in public demonstrations. William Fowler, a self-described publican-carver-schoolmaster-tailor-farmer, had circulated a broadside in the spring of 1823 denouncing the Reverend Mark of Tynemouth Church for raising the fees as set in 1789. By summer two hundred parishioners were joined in a court suit against their parson and the movement had spread to Houghton-Le-Spring, where the clergyman was the subject of a particularly bitter broadside:

> It may perhaps be urged on behalf of this Reverend Oppressor of the Poor, that being striken in years, he took to himself a Wife much younger than himself by whom he has had many children, in addition to the old stock, who must all like the Wives and Children of Gentlemen Clergymen be maintained at the Public Expense. But why should not this Gentleman Parson betake himself to honest gainful labour, and make his children also *useful* members of Society in preference to throwing them on the Parish for support.[95]

Popular anticlericalism was not new to the Newcastle region. Edward Chicken, the local poet, knew that eighteenth-century colliers "came to church but very rare," and usually only for a big wedding:

> Some shout the bride and some the groom,
> Till just as mad to church they come;
> Knock, swear and rattle at the gate,
> And vow to break the beadle's pate,
> And call his wife a bitch and whore;
> They will be in or break the door!
> The church is full of folks and in,
> And all the crew, both great and small,
> Behave as in a common hall;
> For some perhaps that were three score
> Were never in a church before.[96]

The clergy found it difficult to keep control even of the marriage ceremony itself. Women were no more obedient than the men. In Yorkshire they endeavored to keep a thumb free when the hands were clasped, a sign that they meant not to be dominated.[97] And then there were the brides who, intending to omit the word "obey," raced through the vows, hoping the parson would not notice, but clearly intending that the wedding party would be aware of their revisions.[98] In earlier centuries couples were sometimes presented to the courts for not adhering to the liturgy. In the nineteenth century the clergyman was more likely to warn the woman: "You must say it or go home again."[99] In other instances couples cross-examined one another about the meaning of their promises:

GROOM: Will you get up in the morning and clean my boots?
BRIDE: I dunno about that. If we went to the Work House they'd part us.[100]

Clergy could do little to prevent such repartee, especially when the witnesses were accomplices to these deviations. In fact, by purging the marriage service of its original contractual and magical content, the church had actually encouraged many of the irregular practices that now seemed to threaten those same ceremonies. When people found that they could not make their marriages in the way they wanted, they tended to take them elsewhere, before 1753 to renegade clergy within England and Wales or, later, over the border to Scotland, where a wider range of ceremonies constituted marriage. A wedding could be completed there by a simple formula: "Put on the ring, the thing is done, the marriage complete." When one such Scottish border wedding came to the matter of obedience, the groom interrupted: "Say no more about that, Sir, if this hand remains upon my body, I will make her obey me." At this point the bride turned to the priest and asked if the marriage was yet complete. When she was told it was not, she left the groom standing.[101]

In Chicken's "Collier's Wedding," the crowd takes over as soon as the vows are complete:

> Our couple now kneel down to pray,
> Much unacquainted with the way
> Whole troops of colliers swarm round
> And seize poor Jenny on the ground
> Put up their hands to loose her garters,
> And work for pluck about her quarters,
> Till ribbons from her legs are torn
> And round the church in triumph borne.[102]

Once outside the church, friends would rope or chain the couple, but there was now less emphasis on the ritual expression of precedence and hierarchy than in the traditional big wedding. Bridesmaids challenged the groomsmen in the race for the garter; and the post-church festivities shifted from the household to the nearest tavern or village green.[103] In Chicken poetic rendering, it is the bride's mother who presides at the dinner, but a more common plebeian practice was a "public bridal" in which the assistance of the community made the wedding possible.[104]

VI

The public bridals that proliferated in the industrializing areas in the late eighteenth century were new variations of the "beggar weddings" of an earlier period, now adopted not just by the very poor but people contemporaries described as having "respectability and slender means." While the patricians trimmed their guest lists, the plebeians expanded theirs, simultaneously constructing a system of mutual giving that enabled many to marry who would otherwise not be able to do so. In South and West Wales this took the name "bidding wedding," a popular institution that revived and extended the old traditions of giving (*cormortha*), while at the same time secularizing the practice and removing its original paternalist flavor. Persons without dowry or marriage portion would engage a local bard known as a "bidder" (*Gwahoddwr*) to go about the local farms announcing their wedding.[105] The more who knew of the event, the more would attend, "so it was the advantage of the bride and bride-groom elect to make their wedding as public as possible, as the greater the number of guests, the greater the donation."[106] Tom the Bidder, the last of a line of Devil's Bridge bards, was remembered performing his duties in the 1850s in a swallowtail coat, breeches, and a top hat, carrying a long staff decorated with ribbons, the symbol of his office.[107] His speech or *rammas*, delivered at each house, was probably much like that of John Williams, a Carmarthenshire bidder whose oration was recorded in the 1840s:

> I was desired to call here as a messenger and a bidder. David J.... and Ann W.... in this parish of Laugharne, the hundred of Derllys, County Carmarthen, encouraged by their friends to make a wedding on Tuesday next; the two young people made their residence in Gosport, No. 11, then to St. Michael's church to be married. The two young people return back to the young woman's father and mother's house to dinner. They shall have good beef and cabbage, mutton and turnips, pork and potatoes, roast goose or gant, perhaps both if they are in season, a quart of drink for fourpence, a cake for a penny, clean chairs to sit down upon, clean pipes and tobacco, and attendance of the best; a good song, but if no one can sing, then I'll sing as well as I can; and if no one will attend, I'll attend as well as I can. As a usual custom with us, in Laugharne, is to hold a "sending gloves" before the wedding, if you'll please to come, or send a waggon or a cart, a horse and a colt, a heifer, cow and calf, or an ox and a half, or pigs, cocks, hens, geese, goslings, ducks, turkeys, a saddle or bridle, or a child's cradle, or what the house can afford. *A great many can help one, but one cannot help a great many*, or send a waggon full of potatoes, a cartload of turnips, a hundred or two of cheeses, a cask of butter, a sack of flour, a winchester of barley, or what you please, for anything will be acceptable; jugs, basins, saucepans, pots and pans, or what you can; throw in £5 if you like; gridirons, frying-pans, tea-kettles, plates and dishes, a lootch (a wooden spoon) and dish, spoons, knives and forks, pepper boxes, salt-cellars, mustard-pots, or even a penny whistle or a child's cradle.

Invariably the bidder also reminded his listeners:

> Ladies and gentlemen, I was desired to speak this way that all *pwython* (payments) due to the young woman's father and mother, grandfather and grandmother, aunts, brothers and sisters, and the same due to the young man's father and mother, etc etc must be returned to the young people on

14. A bidder, equipped with his staff of office, arrives at a Welsh farmhouse to invite all those present, master and mistress as well as the farm servants, to an upcoming wedding. The bidder was a familiar figure in the Welsh countryside until the middle of the nineteenth century. (Used by permission of the National Museum of Wales)

the above day. So no more at present. If you please to order your butler, or underservant, to give a quart of drink to the bidder.[108]

Although few could afford an expensive gift, none could refuse the invitation. In many places the gifts were delivered on the night before the wedding in what was called *Pwrs a Gwregys* (Purse and Girdle). Careful note was taken of each gift, for, as the bidder's oration stated, these were repayments for gifts previously given at other weddings by the groom or bride's relations. In time it would be the newlyweds' turn to give, so that such records were vital to the system of reciprocity that knit together very large numbers of people, mainly family members, who would pay off one another's *pwython* in the course of attending the dozens of weddings that made up such a large part of the Welsh social calendar.[109]

Most of the gifts were small, but multiplied by two hundred guests, this amounted to a tidy sum. According to Lewis Morris, an ordinary bidding wedding in the 1760s brought in "a round sum of money, sometimes £30 or £40 is Collected this way in Money, cheese & butter to the great benefit of a Young Couple who had not otherwise scarce a penny

CARMARTHEN, MAY 5TH, 1847.

As we intend to enter the MATRIMONIAL STATE on TUESDAY, the 25th day of MAY inst., we are encouraged by our Friends to make a BIDDING on the occasion the same day, at the Young Woman's Father's House, called PENROSE COTTAGE; when and where the favour of your good and agreeable company is humbly solicited, and whatever donation you may be pleased to confer on us then will be thankfully received, warmly acknowledged, and cheerfully repaid whenever called for on a similar occasion,

By your most obedient servants,

PHILIP REYNOLDS LEWIS,
BUTCHER,

ELIZABETH DAVIES.

The Young Man's Father (David Lewis), his Brother and Sister-in-law (John and Anne Lewis), his Nephew (John Lewis), his Brothers (David and Thomas Lewis), and his Brother-in-law and Sister (John and Jane Evans), desire that all gifts of the above nature, due to them, be returned to the Young Man on the above day, and will be thankful for additional favours granted.

The Young Woman's Father and Mother (Thomas and Anne Davies), her Brothers (John, David, and Henry Davies), and her Brothers-in-law and Sisters (John and Mary Harries, and David and Anne James), desire that all gifts of the above nature, due to them, be returned to the Young Woman on the above day, and will be thankful for all favours conferred on her.

W. SPURRELL, PRINTER, CARMARTHEN.

15. This 1847 example of a printed bidding letter from Carmarthen asks that all those who have received gifts from the families of either the bride or the groom reciprocate in the customary manner. Philip Lewis and Elizabeth Davies could expect a generous start in married life if all complied. (Used by permission of the Welsh Folk Museum)

to begin the world with." In South Wales the bidding popular among "servants, tradesfolk, and small farmers" was described in 1784 as follows:

> Before the Wedding an Entertainment is provided, to which all the Friends of each party are *bid* or invited, and to which none fail to bring or send some Contribution, from a Cow or Calf down to a Half-a-crown or a Shilling. An account of each is kept; and, if the young Couple do well, it is expected that they should give as much at any future bidding of their generous Guests. I have frequently known fifty pounds being thus collected, and have heard of a *bidding* which produced even a hundred.[110]

It was no different in the early nineteenth century, when it was said that "such collecting sets a deserving young couple at once in a state of comparative wealth and independence."[111] In the north of Wales, where most couples did their own bidding, the sense of mutual obligation was apparently less family oriented. In Denbighshire it was said that everyone "having the slightest acquaintance with either of the happy couple, considers it their duty to call upon them, nor does anyone go empty handed, presents of all description from a chest of drawers to a packet of tea or a pound of sugar being made."[112] Cards were sometimes sent to wealthy people to solicit additional contributions, but it was not charity but the idea that "a great many can help one" that the plebeians principally relied on until the 1850s, when the bidding tradition began to wane.[113]

Parallel practices in the northern parts of England drew on a similar culture and constituency. In Cumberland the counterpart to the Welsh bidding wedding was the plebeian "bridewain."[114] The term had originally applied to the wagon that carried the bride's portion to her home, picking up additional gifts of furniture and stock along the way. Some wealthy farmers still transported their gifts in this way, but for the smallholder and the laborer the bridewain now meant the collection made at the wedding feast itself, during which the bride herself collected the gifts by "holding a pewter dish on her knee, half covered with a napkin. Into this dish every person present makes it a point to put something."[115] Similar collections, called "penny weddings," were reported in Northumberland in the 1820s and in Durham villages in the 1830s and 1840s.[116]

The concept of mutual assistance also extended to childbirth. We have already seen that a notion of collective mothering was present where grandparents looked after children born out of wedlock, but the sense of shared responsibility often transcended individual families.[117] Frederick Eden reported at the end of the eighteenth century that "it would be deemed ominous, if not impious to be married or to have a Child born, without something of a Feast," which invariably meant contributions. Maternity, like marriage, was regarded as a social rather than individual event, eliciting the support of the entire community:

> A deserving young Couple are thus, by a public and unequivocal Testimony of good will of those who best know them, encouraged to persevere in the

16. Guests at a Welsh bidding wedding present their gifts to the newlyweds. Some come with goods, others give coins, but the total collection was often enough to establish a small farm or workshop. (Used by permission of the Welsh Folk Museum)

paths of Propriety, and are also enabled to begin the world with some advantage. The birth of a Child also, instead of being thought or spoken of as bringing on the parents new and heavy burthens, is thus rendered, as it no doubt always ought to be, a Comfort and a Blessing: and in every sense, an occasion for rejoicing. . . . I own [remarked Eden] I cannot figure to myself a more pleasing, or more rational way of rendering sociableness and mirth subservient to prudence and virtue.[118]

Even where the old traditions of mutual aid had broken down, plebeians proved ingenious in making money from their weddings. In some parts of Wales bidding had taken on a strong entrepreneurial aspect by the beginning of the nineteenth century. When John Jones and Mary Evans invited people to gather at the Butcher's Arms in 1827 to celebrate their wedding, they offered them "bread, cheese, and kisses," the latter auctioned off to the highest bidder. A special point was made of the fact that John and Mary had "the privilege (by paying the duty) of selling ale to the persons assembled." So successful were their efforts that it was said they raised between fifty and a hundred pounds.[119] To attract the largest possible number, Cumberland couples placed invitations in the local newspaper:

17. *Penny Wedding*, an early-nineteenth-century painting by David Wilkie in 1819, provides a rare glimpse of plebeian festivities, in this case in Scotland. The whole community is present, some sitting down to a meal while others dance. (Reproduced by Gracious Permission of Her Majesty the Queen)

> Suspend for one day your care and your labours
> And come to this wedding, kind friends and good neighbors
>
> You'll please observe that day
> Of this grand bridal pomp in the thirteenth of May
> When 'tis hop'd that the sun, to enliven the sight
> Like a flambeau of Hymen, will deign to burn bright.[120]

In 1803 the *Cumberland Pacquet* announced ''A Public Bridal'':

> Jonathan and Grace Musgrove propose having a Public Bridal, at Low London Bridge End, near Cockermouth, on Thursday, the 16th of June, 1803; when they will be glad to see their Friends, and all who may please to favour them with their Company; . . . for whose Amusement there will be various Races for Prizes of different kinds; and amongst others, a Saddle, and Bridle; and a Silver-tipt Hunting Horn for Hounds to run for. There will also be Leaping, Wrestling, etc, etc.[121]

The idea of the public bridal was not new, but the nineteenth-century versions rivaled anything staged in previous periods. In addition to the games and races, Joseph Rawlings and Mary Dixon announced that their wedding would feature a ''Pantomime Exhibition.''[122] George and Ann Collins offered as prizes a saddle, two bridles, a pair of gloves, and ''a girdle (*Ceinture de Venus*) possessing qualities not to be described, and many other articles, sports, and pastimes, too numerous to mention.''[123]

In addition to the money contributions, guests were often expected to help in erecting so-called "one-night houses," squatters' cottages made of wood or sod, which, if they could be built undetected on waste or forest lands, gave the couple the "right" to settle there. In Cumberland, Cornwall, Lancashire, and North Wales what was called a "clay daubing" or "clay biggin' was particularly frequent in the period from 1790 to 1840. It was usually young people, who "always ready to help one another . . . would assemble about dawn at the appointed spot, and labouring with good will, each at an allotted task, would erect, long ere sunset, the clay walls of a dwelling for some young couple who would rely on the bride wain for means to finish and furnish it."[124] In many places the settler would still establish claim to the land by paying a "fine" for entry at the local manor court, henceforth paying a rent like any other copyholder. In North Wales, where such settlements were very common in the late eighteenth and early nineteenth centuries, the right to the *Ty un nos* (one-night house) was jealously guarded:

> This custom in modern time presumed the right of any newly married resident to a cottage which he had himself, with the help of friends, built upon waste land in the township in a single night (smoke seen issuing from the chimney in the morning being claimed to be sufficient evidence of completion), and also a certain area of land round the cottage.[125]

VII

As for the bedding and rough music traditions, some of these persisted in the proto-industrial areas. What did not survive were those inauguration rites that established hierarchy within and between families. Threshold rites disappeared, and plebeian couples no longer bothered to take their seats in church. For women, becoming a mother was more important than becoming mistress of a house, with the result that the rites of childbirth came to rival the wedding itself.[126] As for the men, fatherhood was sometimes experienced as *couvade*, though it would seem that, as the traditional forms of patriarchy eroded, young children belonged increasingly to the mother and her side of the family. In the Ceiriog and elsewhere they took the matriarchal surname. Should the couple separate, they stayed with the mother.[127]

The plebeian big wedding created a union very different from its peasant or artisan prototype. It established a partnership based on mutual obligations, more egalitarian and less hierarchical. Such marriages no longer created the social and economic distinctions that invited envy and required symbolic compensation. Instead, the plebeian big wedding emphasized horizontal rather than hierarchical relationships, thus underlining the importance of kinship and the need for communal support, creating a network of obligations that were sustained throughout the lifetime of the couple. Community pressure, expressed through gossip and charivari, now functioned not as reinforcement of patriarchy, but as a guarantor of equity. Marriage was for the plebeians a form of partnership, but, unlike the upper classes, their sense of mutual obligation was not confined to the nuclear unit. While they too valued affection, they did not limit this to conjugal love. They acknowledged the legitimacy of sexual relations outside marriage and extended the concept of mutual obligation well beyond the nuclear family.

The plebeian variant of the big wedding reflected not only changed material circumstances, but a distinctive world view. Unlike the smallholders, whose work did not necessarily expand their property, inheritance, or marriage chances, the male and female cottage worker could perceive a positive relationship between labor and resources. The plebeian population no longer regarded their world as finite. Neither subsistence nor affection were in such limited supply that each new union was viewed as a zero-sum game in which the winners must compensate the losers.[128] On the contrary, plebeian practices reflected the belief that the pleasures and necessities of life were a common inheritance. Marriage and parenthood were seen as rights rather than as privileges. And the big wedding, with its underlying assumption that "a great many can help one, but one cannot help a great many," thus became part of the intense struggle between patrician individualism and plebeian collectivism.

CHAPTER 6

The Last Stage of Their Hope:
From the Celibate to the Conjugal City

We think of the city as being always in the vanguard, yet during the seventeenth and eighteenth centuries the marital habits of the country-side were probably changing more rapidly. City people continued to marry at a later age, and more remained celibate. According to John Graunt, seventeenth-century London produced fewer "Breeders" be-cause men left their wives in the country when they came to town for business or for pleasure. He also noted that "many Sea-men of London leave their Wives behind them, who are more subject to die in the absence of their Husbands, then (sic) to breed either without them, or with the use of many promiscuously"; and the "Apprentices of London, who are bound seven, or nine years from Marriage, do often stay longer voluntarily."[1] A century later, William Brakenridge was saying much the same thing: "in London and Westminster the one-half of the people at least live single, that are above twenty-one years of age."[2] The image of the celibate city was already deeply rooted when Cowper wrote his famous lines:

> God made the country, and man made the town
> What wonder then, that health and virtue . . .
> Should most abound.
> And least be threatened in the fields and groves?[3]

Graunt and the others were wrong in thinking that the marital fertility of the town was lower than the countryside, but they were correct about the overall lower nuptiality of the city.[4] During the sixteenth and sev-enteenth centuries, the rate of marriage was retarded by a variety of factors, probably the most important being the craft economy of the city, which produced two distinct marriage patterns—one typical of the native population, the other of the immigrants, both conducive to high levels of celibacy. The courtship of the natives, whether master artisans or merchants, was not unlike that of the propertied classes of the countryside. Sons and daughters who could expect some share in the family patrimony were subject to control. For a native son, marriage waited on the establishment of both a business and a household. Only a few months separated the act of becoming a guild master (and a Freeman) from becoming a husband. In the sixteenth century the average marriage age for London men was twenty-eight.[5] Nuptiality at younger ages was discouraged not only by the rules of apprenticeship, but by the accepted wisdom that "until a man grows unto the age of twenty-four years, he (for the most part though not always) is wild, without judgement, & not of sufficient experience to govern himself . . . and therefore has more need to remain under government, as a servant and learner, than to become a ruler, as a master or instructor."[6] As for native daughters, they lived at home, dependent on their parents until marriage, which for them took place when they had just reached their twenties. They were wed from home after the matter of dowry and marriage portion had been settled by negotiation between families. Normally, they would marry a city man; and, while these matches were not imposed against the will of the couple, the strong hand of patriarchy was often evident. Women married early because it was their fate to be governed but, as for men, "over-hasty marriages and over-soon setting up of households . . ." were forbidden by ordinance.[7] A short, formal betrothal was usually followed by a big wedding in much the same way as in the country.

Of course, it was not always possible to enforce this marital discipline, and we find sixteenth-century London aldermen bemoaning the premature nuptiality of those "so poor that they scantly have of their proper goods where with to buy their marriage apparel and to furnish their houses with implements and other things necessary for the exercise of their families."[8] Urban authorities attempted to prevent beggar weddings, but, when obstacles were put in their way, couples made use of license and clandestine marriage in the same way as country folk. Resorting to irregular marriage was evident in the sixteenth century and was believed to have increased during the next hundred years, but it did not displace the conventional practices of resident propertied classes.[9]

The marriage practice of immigrants constituted a distinctly different pattern. They often arrived orphaned, propertyless, and unskilled, seeking apprenticeships or places in service, and a chance to acquire the resources necessary to both an occupation and marriage. Newcomers to seventeenth-century London married later than the natives because they had to fashion their own futures. Women brought with them no dowry apart from savings painfully accumulated through years of hard work. The men had to wait out their apprenticeships. Normally they did not compete in the same marriage market as the natives. They did not marry as well or as often, thus contributing to the high rates of urban celibacy.[10] London's leading astrologers, Simon Forman and William Lilly, owed a large part of their business to the anxieties of those who feared they would die single. Young female servants were prominent among their clients, but they were also consulted by men concerned about marital matters.[11]

For the immigrants the celibate life was both an opportunity and a necessity. While some spent their youth in riotous living, most used the time to accumulate those skills and savings necessary to establish an independent existence. Men ambitious to attain freeman status delayed marriage into their late twenties, often choosing an imigrant servant near to themselves in age. Because few could expect the assistance of family, they were freer to select their own mates. They betrothed themselves, stretching out the period of courtship well beyond that of native Londoners. Dorothy Ireland, a domestic servant, met an oastler who was to become her husband when she was twenty-eight, but did not marry until eight years later, having been "sure together" the entire time.[12] Sybil Powell, the daughter of a rural widow, who "not able to bestow any portion upon her and therefore has left her to her own disposition," spent seven years in London service before meeting Richard Lackeland. When leaving her master, she went directly to live in Richard's brother's household, where her future husband maintained "her at his own cost until such time as they shall be married conveniently."[13] Under such circumstances a certain amount of premarital pregnancy was bound to occur, but these couples normally married before a child was born. Illegitimacy rates remained low, lower than in the countryside.[14]

There were those, especially among the very poor natives as well as unfortunate immigrants, who never married. We know that large numbers of impoverished women fell into prostitution, an urban occupation that was already immense in the seventeenth century. Their clients included the multitudinous males who, for a variety of reasons, could or would not form more permanent relationships.[15] There were also those who formed irregular, if temporary, unions. Women like Frances Palmer, "a vagrant . . . , having two children begotten and born in whoredom . . . ," were already beginning to worry city officials by the end of the sixteenth century. Her children, fathered by a servant named William Wood and delivered in the street, did not survive.[16] Nor did many of those born into poverty. To the high level of infant mortality due to disease was added a certain amount of infanticide, the recourse mainly of unwed mothers. Low levels of urban illegitimacy also reflected the practice of abortion, also a result of the very severe marital discipline of this, the celibate city.[17]

I

Some features of the celibate city persisted into the eighteenth and even the nineteenth centuries, but after 1700 urban nuptiality was transfigured by changes that virtually reversed the prior relationship between town and country. These came slowly and often imperceptibly, but by the early Victorian era the cities had surpassed the countryside in the rate of marriage. Except for artisan towns like York, the age of marriage and the proportions never marrying fell simultaneously.[18] In both the northern manufacturing centers and in London precocious heterosexuality became characteristic among the common people. Conjugality was replacing celibacy, but most of the urban poor found it impossible to construct their relationships strictly according to the rules of monogamous marriage and the nuclear family laid down by the ruling classes. Thus they began to construct a variation of conjugal love more compatible with the realities of their urban experience.

The wealthy of the city continued to postpone marriage until the man could attain full economic independence. This meant a late age of nuptiality and considerable celibacy. Many upper-class females remained spinsters throughout their lives. For all women of this group virginity was obligatory. Their class had broken with the older tradition of betrothal that had offered the couple some measure of premarital conjugality and had substituted for it a highly ritualized courtship that for women began with the "coming out" party and ended with the elaborate white wedding, symbolizing their purity and status. Couples did not really come to know one another until marriage, a condition that was compensated for by the honeymoon, another of the innovations peculiar to the Victorian upper middle class.[19]

Only one other group held so stubbornly to the traditions of the celibate city. For master artisans and respectable tradespeople, marriage was still associated with the establishment of economic independence. In London and towns like York skilled craftsmen married late, usually to women of their own class who brought a dowry to the marriage. Wives did not normally work except to assist their husbands, and the children of the petty bourgeoisie were equally dependent. Here the patriarchal household survived almost intact, though the decomposition of the artisan and shopkeeping class as a whole exacted its price, producing tensions between parents and children as well as between husbands and wives.[20] Instead of easing, patriarchal control became ever more stringent. Francis Place could remember the freedoms enjoyed by the sons and daughters of London artisans in the late eighteenth century when that class was at the peak of its prosperity. By the 1820s and 1830s the position of the city's petty bourgeoisie had become precarious and their tolerance limited. In an effort to distance themselves from the impoverished, they tended to adopt a rigidly puritanical standard of sexual respectability, insisting on chastity for their daughters and celibacy for their sons.[21]

Vestiges of the celibate city could also be found among certain segments of urban immigrants, especially apprentices to the skilled trades and domestic servants. Both tended to marry late, and sometimes not at all. Although a rapidly diminishing group by 1800, apprentices still had to wait until their time was out before settling down. As for servants, both male and female, they normally came to the city without any inheritance beyond their labor power. It took years before they accumulated sufficient savings to marry. Thus, as in the seventeenth century, their courtships tended to be extended and even those with the most promising liaison often failed to consummate their marriages. Of all the groups in Victorian London's female population, it was servants who were most at risk of unwed motherhood, largely because there were so many obstacles to their nuptiality. Together with the upper middle class and the privileged artisans and shopkeepers, they constituted a remnant of the celibate city, now confined in London's case largely to the West End, where these groups were heavily concentrated.[22]

Once outside these privileged precincts, celibacy was no longer the norm, however. Henry Mayhew was struck by the fact that "in passing from the skilled operatives of the West End to the unskilled workmen of the Eastern quarter of London, the moral and intellectual change is so great that it seems as if we were in a new land, and among another race."[23] Similar observations were made about the geography of northern manufacturing towns, where the contrasts between middle-class life and the proletarian culture were even more strongly drawn.[24] Virtually, everyone agreed on the precociousness of urban working-class courtship. Young women as well as men enjoyed great personal freedom and showed little of the awkwardness of earlier generations when it came to pairing off. Mayhew said of London's costermongers that they made no distinction between married and unmarried couples: "There is no honour attached to the marriage state and no shame to concubinage."[25] Of factory workers it was remarked that "the chastity of marriage is but little known among them."[26] Observers were prone to exaggeration, but, nevertheless, there was a distinct tendency for marriage too lose its privileged status among the urban working classes. What Mayhew and other urban explorers of the 1830s and 1840s were discovering were the consequences of more than a century of change in plebeian habits and values. The transition had been long in coming and there was still much about the new proletarian culture that was consistent with the traditions of the old artisanate. Yet, theirs was a conjugal rather than a celibate city.

II

This epochal transformation was largely the product of the undermining of the traditional urban economy, and especially the guilds. In 1600 a full fifteen percent of the London population at any given time were apprentices in one of the city's skilled trades. By 1700 only four percent of Londoners were young men obligated to remain in celibate training until their mid- or late twenties.[27] A century later the place of the guilds was even further diminished. The independent craftsman or woman of old, capable of controlling not only the means of production but the distribution of the product, constituted no more than ten percent of any of the London trades by the early nineteenth century. Economic independence and the status that went with it were still aspired to by many, but now achieved by only a few.[28]

The situation in the northern and midland factory towns represented an even more dramatic departure from the traditional craft economy. Guild production was not only less developed there, but, in the course of the early nineteenth century, it had been swamped by the growth of factory production. In places like Birmingham and Wolverhampton, there was still a mixed economy of small workshops coexisting with larger capitalist enterprises, but in Lancashire the mill had come to dominate by the 1830s and 1840s. Factory employment offered wage work not only to men but to women, and, while the acceptance of the dependence that was a consequence of the wage economy came slowly and grudgingly, especially for men, working people were beginning now to accept the family wage economy. It had become the habit in Preston, Oldham, and other mill towns for the earnings of all family members to be pooled and for each to receive back an allowance. Wives took what they needed for housekeeping; children over fourteen were said to "contract with their parents for board and lodging, and put the rest in their pockets."[29] Family roles were no longer dictated by status. "Sometimes, when the husband is unemployed, while his family are at work, the normal structure of the family is reversed," noted Engels.[30] Under these circumstances children learned to bargain with their parents, establishing relationships based on reciprocity at an early age. According to one observer, "parents found themselves dependent, to some measure, for support upon their children's earnings. How these were to be appropriated became a new source of contest and bickering; for the parents would appropriate the greater share for domestic purposes, the children would spend it in enjoyments."[31]

But despite these tensions the interdependence of family members remained strong. Most children remained home until marriage, and it was said that "a young woman, prudent and careful, and living with her parents, from the age of sixteen to twenty-five, may, in that time, by factory employment, save £100 as a wedding portion."[32] It was not at all unusual in Preston for young marrieds in the 1840s also to live with parents (usually the bride's), contributing to the family fund until such time as a growing family forced them to find a separate residence. An independent household was now characteristic not of the beginning but of the midpoint of married life, and, even then, married persons with small children would often take in elderly kin, exchanging room and board for their services as housekeepers or babysitters, so that the wife could continue in factory work.[33]

In dispensing with the traditional equation of marriage with economic independence, the factory proletariat made marriage more accessible, at least for those in steady employment and good wages. The result was a lower age of marriage for factory workers, lower than that of the middle classes, artisans, and even self-employed persons like the handloom weavers.[34] Fewer factory people remained celibate (fewer men than women) than the population of the surrounding countryside or artisan towns like York.[35] While there was some illegitimacy, it was not of a very high level and did not seem to indicate abandonment, as was the case in other places where factory employment was less usual.[36] On the contrary, factory towns seem to have been marrying places. When couples lived together without matrimony, this appears to have been the result mainly of a failed previous marriage rather than any reluctance to wed in the first place.[37] For the male factory operative with good wages, who was willing to share housing and accept the interdependence that this invariably involved, there were few real or imagined barriers to nuptiality. Marriage presented no particular difficulty to women either. They expected to continue working and, although middle-class observers were scandalized by the ubiquity of working mothers in the factory districts, the northern proletariat found nothing dishonorable in a woman's contribution to the family welfare. Lancashire women were far less concerned with domesticity as an end in itself, though they felt the burden of their dual role as workers and housekeepers, and agitated throughout the nineteenth century for both the equal pay and family allowances that could alleviate some of the contradictions in their position.[38]

The transition from the celibate to conjugal city was also evident in London, though the shift to earlier, more universal marriage was retarded somewhat by the artisanal legacy of the metropolis. There was very little factory employment in the metropolis. Production in the major trades—garment making, shoe manufacture, furniture making, and so on—expanded within the labyrinthine context of the subcontracting system, employing the labor of thousands of men and women who worked either in their own lodgings or in very small workshops. Although essentially wage workers, the metropolitan productive force did not experience proletarianization in the same way as the factory operatives of the north, who early on had to accept their total dependence on a few capitalist employers. Often working on their own, though no longer really in control of either the means of production or distribution, Londoners clung to an artisan identity, even as the basis of their economic independence was being eroded by forces outside their control.

By the early nineteenth century the type of craftsperson capable of controlling the means of production and distribution constituted no more than ten percent of any of the London trades.[39] While many aspired to independence, a diminishing few ever attained it. Most tradespeople were assigned to some degree of dependence: subcontractors (the "sweaters"), piece workers, or home workers, most fortunate if they owned their own tools or were capable of posting security for materials or renting a work place. At the bottom of every trade there now clustered masses of journeymen and apprentices who would never attain the masterships that their sixteenth-century predecessors had been virtually assured of. Journeymen were now organized separately from the more privileged masters, defending as best they could their pathetic wages and worsening working conditions.[40] Still, many clung to the dubious honor of being called a "chamber master" or "garret master," a title appropriated by those with enough capital to rent work space and employ a few persons even more unfortunate than themselves. Distinguished from the proletariat more by their aspirations than by their earnings or working conditions, most of these little masters endured a precarious existence.[41]

The metropolitan version of the subcontracting system promoted a family economy that was dependent on the labor of wives, children, as well as hired hands. At this stage of the city's economic development some form of conjugal arrangement was one of the few means open to an aspiring little master who had only a slight chance of making it on his own. In the eighteenth century, marriage had become a "business partnership . . . [in which] the wife's portion was the means of setting her husband up as a master."[42] For the journeyman, celibacy was no longer a guarantee of eventual success. He was better off taking a wife or, if that seemed impossible, living with a woman whose savings or skills would allow him his one chance of establishing a foothold in the trade. "My wife and family help me or I couldn't survive," a typical garret master told Mayhew.[43] It was said of young weavers that their best opportunity lay in joining "with a woman capable of earning perhaps nearly as much as himself, and performing for him various offices involving an actual pecuniary saving."[44] In garment making, shoemaking, or any of the other trades where the capitalist subcontracting system predominated, the imperative of precocious conjugality was reflected in the low age at time of marriage and high levels of cohabitation. Throughout the nineteenth century tailors and shoemakers had one of the lowest marriage ages of any occupational group.[45] It was said of London weavers during the 1830s that "many of them, instead of having lawful married wives, keep women whom they call tacks."[46] Little masters found various ways to extend their family workforce, often bringing into the home sons-in-law or daughters-in-law to add to the wage fund.[47] Because the traditional female crafts, such as millinery, had also undergone proletarianization, it was advantageous for women to enter into conjugal arrangements. From the middle of the eighteenth century they had been warned: "You cannot expect to marry in such a manner as neither of you shall have occasion to work, and none but a fool will take a wife whose bread must be earned solely by his labour and who will contribute nothing towards it herself."[48] In most of these arrangements, the little master was male, but there were some traditionally female occupations such as shopkeeping, streetselling, and laundry in which it was not unknown for the man to become the woman's assistant.[49]

III

For most of the eighteenth century and until the end of the Napoleonic Wars, this urban version of cottage industry produced an acceptable standard of living for many, and, for some, even a modest but enviable affluence. It was said of the ordinary tradesman in 1705 that they "live better in England than the masters and employers in foreign countries can, and you have a class of topping workmen in England, who, being only journeymen under manufacturers, are yet very substantial fellows, maintain their families very well."[50] Literacy was high, club life flourished, and working people were known for their cultural achievements as well as their well-kept homes and pretty gardens.[51] A silk-weaver remembered fondly his "good little house. . . . Then I'd had a nice little garden and some nice tulips for my hobby, when my work was done."[52] It was this kind of life that attracted and held country people who in earlier centuries would have turned their backs on the celibate city after apprenticing or educating themselves there.[53] From the mid-eighteenth century onward, London and the expanding industrial towns of the north seemed to offer the better future:

> Young men and women in the country fix their eye on London as the last stage of their hope; they enter into service in the country for little else but to raise money enough to go to London. . . . [T]he numbers who have seen London are increased tenfold and of course ten times the boasts are sounded in the ears of country fools to induce them to quit their healthy clean fields for a region of dirt, stink, and noise. And the number of young women that fly thither is almost incredible.[54]

By the 1820s and 1830s the competition of urban industrial production was also driving the young from the cottages to the factory towns. Often it was the women who were the first to migrate:

> Where are the girls? I tell you plain
> The girls have gone to weave by steam;[55]

In the south and east the exodus was the result of the pressures of capitalist agriculture as well as the pull of urban opportunities. We have seen how the rural proletariat was forced to choose between marriage and migration. Increasingly there was pressure on the smallholder class to follow their example of leaving home. Reverend William Cole, a Buckinghamshire vicar, was particularly struck by the plight of Will Wood, who wanted to marry but whose family "can't afford to settle him":

> The Times are so hard, small farms so difficult to be met with, the Spirit of Inclosing, & accumulating Farms together, making it very difficult for

young people to Marry, as was used; as I know by Experience in this Parish, where several Farmers' Sons are forced to live at Home with their Fathers, tho' much wanting to marry & settle, for Want of proper Place to settle at. Which sufficiently shews the baneful Practice of Inclosures, & that the putting any the least Restraints upon Matrimony (as the last Marriage Act did, contrived by Lord Chancellor Hardwicke on selfish Family Motives, as it was common said), is a great Disservice to the Nation.[56]

A farmer's son would lose status should he take up the position of a common laborer. Many were turning to service in the houses of the local gentry, where "the allurements of greater gain and better fare draw them from the plough and flail." Once conditioned to "laced livery, high wages, and card money . . . away he flies to London, or some other seat of opulence."[57] It was said that young women "all want to be housemaids or mantua makers, or something of that sort. They object to such work as the dairy; they are too delicate for that."[58]

The children of small farmers and rural tradespeople were conspicuous among the rural exodus, but they were joined by those of the rural proletariat unwilling to settle for forced marriage and a life of drudgery on the land. Women often left home before their brothers and sweethearts, drawing them in their wake.[59] George Turner was an example of those who followed their betrothed to London. Bridget Conner, a twenty-year-old servant, was already planning to leave Ireland to look for work in England when she met John Scally, a farm laborer. He followed her to London despite the fact that he, as an unskilled man, had no certain prospects there.[60]

Flight to the conjugal city reflected the struggle not just of individuals but of whole families and even communities to survive the devastating changes taking place in rural Britain from the 1770s onward. In those regions of the south where massive proletarianization was taking place, each son or daughter who went off to the city relieved a hard-pressed family of the expense of room and board, and the rate payers of an additional dole. Migration served the functions once provided by live-in service. In the north, where the economy of small farms and the cottage industry continued into the early nineteenth century, the children of the poor continued to provide labor, but, where the family economy no longer survived, each migrant not only improved his or her own future, but provided additional chances for those who stayed behind.[61]

Migration was selective, determined as much by the economics of the rural family as by the opportunities of the city. The prevailing high rates of mortality meant that by the age of twenty-one as many as a half of all children would have lost at least one parent.[62] Orphans were common among migrant Londoners. Often the loss of a parent meant that, while some of the children went off to the city, others were compelled to remain at home, sometimes with disastrous results. Eldest sons and daughters, who in earlier times might have benefitted through inheritance, were increasingly at a disadvantage with respect to younger children who were freer to leave home. At Langley in Buckinghamshire, Mary Toms, who was the eldest of seven children, automatically took over the role of mother in her widowed father's household. He was a small farmer who kept no other female servants, leaving Mary with the yard as well as housework. She had to clean and cook for the male servants in husbandry and thus was thrown together with William Silvester, one of her father's live-in hands. There was apparently something between them, although Mary was repelled when William took advantage of her one morning while they were alone in a bedroom. He said he was sorry and proposed marriage, but Mary refused it, saying she had "lost all affection for him." Her father did his best to conceal the matter and, because Mary's younger sister was by then eighteen and ready to take over the role of mistress of the household, he made plans for Mary to go to London to give birth and have the child adopted by the London Foundling Hospital. Among his neighbors it was widely believed that Mr. Toms had as much to answer for as did Silvester. It was said that he had given Mary "few opportunities of mixing with society" and thus was to blame for her humiliating involvement with a man beneath her station.[63]

The experience of other rural women who brought their children to the London Foundling Hospital between 1800 and 1850 reflects the declension of suitable local marriage prospects and the resulting tensions between parents, determined to maintain family respectability, and children, eager for marriage on their own terms. The growing social distance between "middling sort" like the Toms and the proletarians like William Silvester exacerbated tensions already apparent in the patriarchal family. Mary Toms may have encouraged William as a way of getting out from under her father's domination. One suspects that the daughter of a Deptford shipwright, Elizabeth Johns, was also tilting against patriarchy when she became pregnant by John Dunn, a worker in the same trade. She might have been expected to win approval for such a match, but her mother had just walked out on her father and he, left with nine other children, could not afford to lose the services of his eldest daughter and so forbid the wedding. Elopement was a possibility, but in the end Elizabeth remained a dutiful daughter and decided to give up both John Dunn and the child in order to remain with her father. Mary Hurst, a Sussex woman, found herself in a parallel predicament when her mother died when she was eighteen. Her father was then sixty-five and poor, so she hid her relationship with a local grocer. Her pregnancy may have been part of their plan to provide a reason for marriage, but unfortunately the grocer died and she was left with the baby. Mr. Hurst reacted angrily to what he regarded as filial betrayal, but, when he had time to consider his daughter's desperate situation, he agreed to send her to her brother in London on the condition that, once the child was taken off her hands, she would return to keep house for him.[64]

It is easy enough to understand why those who left home considered themselves most fortunate. Mary Harcourt, the eldest daughter of a minor Wiltshire farmer, developed a taste for freedom when apprenticed in dressmaking in Bath in the 1820s. Times were hard after the Napoleonic Wars and her father found it easier to afford the lower premiums required in the provinces. His daughter would probably have preferred the more prestigious London training, but she was being courted with considerable energy by a local schoolmaster, George Turner, and therefore was content to move in respectable if somewhat parochial Wiltshire circles. However, all that changed when Turner began pressing his case too strongly; and Harcourt, doubtful whether he could afford to marry his daughter to an impecunious man, decided that it was finally time that Mary "improve" herself in London. This would be far less expensive than the marriage portion Turner was asking for and, besides, Harcourt had seven other children and a deranged wife to think about, so it seemed better that Mary be put out of her suitor's way.

If all had gone as planned, Mary would have spent two or three years in the metropolis, perhaps living in at one of the fashionable dressmakers there, an arrangement that would have allowed her to save something out of her wages. Should she impress her employers and earn a longer stay, she might even earn as much as fifty pounds a year, plus room and board, more than enough to justify the expense of a premium and sufficient to set up a small business on her return to Wiltshire. By that time she would be in her late twenties, Turner would have lost hope, and farming might be on its feet again.

Unfortunately, Harcourt did not reckon on Turner's tenacity. He followed Mary to London, seduced and abandoned her there. Still, she was able to find adoption for the child, thus saving her family from acute embarrassment while restoring herself to employment and respectability.[65] In doing so, she followed the precedent of those seventeenth- and eighteenth-century mothers who had traveled long distances to give birth in a clandestine manner.[66] Advertisements in early-nineteenth-century provincial newspapers often gave notice of London "apartments to lie in":

> The utmost consolation has resulted from this undertaking to many respectable families in the Kingdom, by securing peace and concord amongst relations and friends. Honour and secrecy have been the basis of this concern for forty years, may be relied on.
>
> Mrs. Symonds, Midwife
> St. Paul's Churchyard

Saving social status and restoring family peace were perhaps not of such great concern to those who were not a part of the patriarchal culture of the smallholder and master artisan. Nevertheless, the rural poor also found comfort in migration. Mary Palmer was one of those who had lost her father when a child; and, because her mother was poor, she had begun work early without the opportunities for training available to Miss Harcourt. Widow Palmer's only income came from washing and she could not afford to keep Mary beyond the age of twelve or thirteen. Thus, after a series of rural places, she went to London to seek work in service there. When she failed to establish herself in the highly competitive upper ranks, Mary took up the needle trade, work that could be done in lodgings and therefore did not require fine clothes and cultivated manner. She had no choice but to stay on in London, for her mother had remarried to a man who was an impoverished cripple. Susan Ward's mother was also a widow, but she could not even afford to keep the family cottage in Hampshire and had taken a position of live-in housekeeper, which meant that all her children had to depend on themselves or on relatives. Susan followed her mother's example, but instead of seeking rural service, she came to lodge with a brother in London, a jobbing shoemaker, who supported her while she sought a metropolitan position.[68]

IV

Whether they left home by choice or necessity, the exodus forced both women and men to establish a personal independence and alternative social relationships. In factory towns the young of both sexes became accustomed to having their own wages, which enabled them to bargain with both parents and masters, and caused them to regard all relationships, including the conjugal, as products of a certain give-and-take, not as something bestowed and unalterable.[69] The conditions in London, while somewhat different, were conducive to a similar result. There, too, migrants arrived with the intention of making a life for theselves, different from that which they had left behind. Many came with the hope of making the marriage that had eluded them in the countryside or small town. Mary Whitlock and John Butler had already been cohabiting for nine months when they walked together to London from Devon in 1816. He was a bricklayer and she had been in country service. They had apparently been putting off the legalization of the relationship until both could find steady work, and it was with the intention of seeking employment that they tramped from Exeter with little more than the clothes on their backs. Mary and John separated at Hyde Park because they did not want to inhibit one another's search for work. Mary's chances as a servant depended on presenting herself as single; and John must have known that he would have to move from work site to work site if he were to gain London wages. With some luck they would meet again and marry.[70]

Men and women who arrived alone were often assisted in finding their first job by a relative or former neighbor; and this network served them socially as well as economically throughout the urban sojourn.[71] In earlier centuries many men returned to their native towns or villages to find a mate, but, as the urban sex ratio swung in their favor, there was no reason to look further than the city suburbs for a suitable partner.[72] The city was not nearly so anonymous as it appeared. Extended lines of kinship and community brought together people like Margaret Williams and James Griffith, who had known each other as children in Wales, but had lost contact until reintroduced by a fellow villager.[73] John Grosse and Ann Humber probably met because both were from Staffordshire and working for the same London master.[74] It was reassuring to converse in a similar dialect and share memories of a world left behind, as Ann Pyrock and George Sylvester must have done when they met while working in the china trade.[75] Another couple had known each other since childhood in Coventry, where both had been trained as ribbon weavers. Lucy Davies was the first to migrate when the trade went flat in the 1820s and she tried her luck in Spitalfields. Apparently, she found nobody more to her liking than her old sweetheart, who followed her there three years later.[76]

Like was attracted to like in town as well as in countryside. Servant girls in London's West End rarely overreached there station in forming liaisons with men above their social class. They knew better than to take up with masters or married men, and encouraged instead the attentions of the young journeymen and shop assistants with whom they came into contact and who were close to them in terms of age and class.[77] Women engaged in one of the manufacturing trades tended to meet men of similar status through their work. This was how Betty Turnbull became involved with George Croom, a man who had picked up tailoring while working as an errand boy for one of the warehousemen in the garment trade. He had taken to calling himself a journeyman by the time she met him. At the time she began living with him he was a "little master," hiring several women to work for him.[78]

Previously marriage had depended on attaining economic independence; now the situation was almost reversed. Without marriage or similar conjugal arrangements, men like George Croom could never hope to fulfill their dream of becoming their own masters. As apprentices, servants, or journeymen, they could not, on their own, save enough to establish themselves in even the lowest levels of their respective trades. Thus the three to four pounds saved by a housemaid were just enough to set up a petty cabinetmaker; a tailor could begin with as little as a single pound; and there were a host of other occupations equally dependent on another's contribution in order to realize even modest success.[79] It was not only what a woman brought to the arrangement, but her labor and housekeeping that made the difference between survival and destitution. In London, where the prosperity of most trades was seasonal, it was not at all unusual for families to be entirely dependent on women's work when the man's trade was slack. When gas workers were laid off during the summers, their wives did laundry. The rhythm in builders' families was just the oppposite. The men earned the bread in summer, the women took on that responsibility in winter.[80]

Women with savings or skills found themselves the special object of male attention. When Henry Kirby lost his job with a painting firm, he saw this not as a defeat but a chance to become his own master. He struck out on his own in the Kilburn area, searching simultaneously for work and a bride. There he found Joan Cressey, whose savings from service made her extremely attractive.[81] John Butler, a jobbing bricklayer and active suitor, probably reckoned he could set himself up with as little as a pound or two for tools, plus a little more as security for materials.[82] London's skilled woodworkers might pay as much as twenty times that amount to outfit themselves, but this sum was not beyond the reach of those lucky enough to find the right partner. A member of the honourable society of carpenters, John Sharp, saw just such an opportunity in Susan Thane, a Hatton Garden housemaid, who had put away most of the 150 pounds left her at her father's death.[83] Elizabeth Dunn's contribution was of a different kind. She met Joe Bradley when she was an apprentice in his small staymaking business. He found her handy and proposed marriage after only two months. The trade was already in trouble and he probably knew he would not have to give Elizabeth as a wife what he had paid her as an apprentice.[84]

In the trades that required little capital to become a little master, the boundary between employer and employee was very fluid. The rise and fall of masters and mistresses was extremely rapid, and relations quite unstable. Jane Whitby's suitor, Henry Browne, was a tailor who hoped to set up his own shop in Pimlico. Their marriage depended on this and, when Browe failed and emigrated to America, Jane turned back to her old landlady and former employer, Widow Frye, to maintain herself and the child that had resulted from the liaison.[85] The records of the London Foundling Hospital and other public insitutions suggest that women like Jane Whitby who had some marketable skills to fall back on were far less vulnerable to this kind of abandonment than were the domestic servants for whom a pregnancy meant a spoiled "character" and the impossibility of continued employment in that celibate profession. Before fierce price cutting in the garment and other trades during the 1820s and 1830s finally undermined their position, women in the subcontracting sector were less likely found among those who had to seek charitable assistance when their conjugal relationships broke down or they were left with a child.[86] They still had something to bargain with and could fall back on their skills to support themselves until the man reappeared or another suitable situation presented itself.

V

The imperative of finding a partner capable of assisting in the creation of the conditions of economic independence dominated the emerging courtship patterns of the early-nineteenth-century metropolis. As in the countryside, where a woman's skills were also highly valued, men tended to seek brides among women in the same trade. Much courting went on in the garrets and slop shops where male and female garment makers toiled their long hours. Elizabeth Thomas, a maid-of-all-work with an Upper Thames Street timber merchant, met Thomas Pullen, a weekly jobbing carpenter, because, as her employer put it, "they necessarily mixed their employment." Similarly, Mary George, servant to a Lambeth baker, was much in the company of Horace Coville, the baker's journeyman.[87] Even in the most strictly governed domestic situations, there was ample opportunity for the kind of day-to-day intimacy that was so rare in a more homosocial era. Cooks got to know shop assistants; maids became intimate with painters and carpenters working in or about their places of employment.[88]

Urban lovers were both more precocious and less awkward. They were accustomed to the opposite sex and more casual in their presence. In 1840 the Mayor of Coventry remembered that previous generations had been much more inhibited:

> The young men of those days with their habits of activity [games, etc] did not make sexual attachments so early as they do now. The instances of youth marrying before his time was out were very rare, and they were seldom out of their time until twenty-one, sometimes not till later. There were no such things as children's marriages. The only one of his father's apprentices he remembers to have married before he was out of his time was at the age of twenty-three. The age of marriage has become much earlier with the increase of indoor habits.[89]

These "indoor habits" included the taverns, theatres, and bagnio, where urban couples could meet with greater anonymity.[90] Even the backsteps of an urban residence provided more privacy than did the country lane; and urban courtship was less constrained by time as well as space. Its calendar became both more secular and generous, organized around numerous holidays and days off that allowed young people to come together. Easter and Whitsun had traditionally licensed London courtships. On Palm Sunday troops of young persons hiked in the early morning from inner London to the Surrey Hills to gather willow branches ("palms"), drink milk-and-rum, and return, somewhat fuddled, in time for parish church services. Francis Place remembered that in the late eighteenth century "the sons and daughters of multitudes of tradesmen and others were then under comparatively little restraint; and the boys used to knock on the doors of the parents to get the girls to go with them, as had been previously agreed, and out they went."[91]

Elizabeth Duggan, a servant in Leadhall Street, met her sweetheart, a Spitalfields painter, at St. Bartholomew's Fair in 1807. Janes Miles was courted at the great Easter Greenwich Fair in the 1820s, the same occasion where Place had previously seen "lads and lasses making their way to the Hill hand in hand playing at thread-the-needle. Other groups were intensely occupied at Kiss-in-the-ring. Others playing at leapfrog in a long train of twenty or more."[92] At Mill Bank on Easter Sunday it was common in the 1790s to see "youths with 'pipes stuck in their faces,' " together with "tradesmen's daughters dressed up by their foolish mothers to go blackguarding with the boys."[93] Although Place claimed that these forms of courtship were in disrepute among respectable artisans by the 1820s, Arthur Munby found masses of youth playing Kiss-in-the-ring at Crystal Palace in July 1861; and Place himself observed the dancing of the "pully-hauley" kind (similar apparently to the Welsh practice of "drawing and fetching") in the 1840s.[94]

Whitsun provided another setting for "billing and cooing" at London's numerous tea gardens, coffee houses, and beer shops.[95] Such places also provided accommodations for love making when the weather prevented outdoor excursions.[96] Coster boys and girls frequented raffles and gaffs until they decided to pair off, while the Apollo Gardens, the Dog and Duck, and Merlins Cave were the favorites of "flash men" and "fancy women" seeking sex outside the formal boundaries of courtship. The numerous "Cock-and-Hen Clubs" of the early nineteenth century, meeting in rooms rented in public houses, were the trysting place for those who, for one reason or another, were not ready to marry, yet wanted the company of the opposite sex:

> This club was held in a large long room, the table being laid nearly the whole length of it. *Upon* one end of the table was a chair filled by a youth, *upon* the other end another chair filled by a Girl. The amusements were drinking,—smoking—swearing—and singing flash songs. The chairs were taken at 8 P.M., and the boys and girls paired off by degrees 'till by 12 o'clock none remained.[97]

The Hens were women who earned their living partly by prostitution. The Cocks were young tradesmen, most of whom also had a "sweetheart who was the daughter of some tradesman" and were simply waiting until their time was out to marry respectably.[98] London apprentices had been bending the rules of celibacy for centuries. What was different now was that many were intimate not just with the Hens, but with the women they intended to marry.

Getting down to serious courtship at age nineteen meant Francis Place gave up his former associates and favorite haunts. His betrothed, Elizabeth Chadd, was then in service, a mature seventeen but from an impoverished family with no dowry of her own. Place feared that his father, who was then in one of his periodic bankruptcies, would object to the match; but when, to his surprise, the paternal consent was forthcoming, he and Elizabeth went ahead with the preparations, giving over all their youthful vices, scrimping and saving as they had never done before;

> As my intended had a good stock of cloaths and I hoped that I should be able by working hard to increase my very scanty quantity, I thought we would go on well in this respect. I had now no acquaintance with any one

out of my own and my wife's family. I ate bread and bread only for my breakfast and drank nothing.[99]

Similarly, Joseph Gutteridge, the Coventry ribbon weaver's apprentice, was careful in selecting a bride with the skills necessary to assist him in this work. He did not get his family's approval, for they resented losing his labor, and was forced to wed secretly in another part of town. Marrying in a friendless and impoverished condition constituted a great risk, but together the newlyweds struggled to overcome this disadvantage.[100] Others were not so fortunate as Place and Gutteridge. Ruth Gell's father, a carpenter living near the London docks, apparently wanted to keep her near home so that she could help her mother run a small meat shop. When she became involved with a widowed docker, James Bromwich, she pretended she was in service so that she could live with him. It was only when he failed to pay the rent that she was turned out and the affair became known.[101] Catherine Kitchen was still contributing to her family's income at age twenty-five and was therefore afraid to tell her father, a journeyman tailor, about Harry Staybridge "lest he should disapprove of the match."[102] A quarrel with her mother caused Ann Croyden to leave her Barbican home and live with William White, a journeyman tailor from the nearby Bunhill district. They pretended to be married until White was called to the Hereford militia in 1809. He urged Ann, who was by then pregnant, to return to her mother "that you shall Friends will bee in union and Love one with each other."[103]

Winning parental consent was easier for some than others. Mayhew reported that a London coster girl simply told her parents " 'she's going to keep company with so-and-so,' packs up what things she has, and goes at once without word of remonstrance from either father or mother. A furnished room at about four shillings a week is taken, and the young couple begin life."[104] Parents too poor to contribute a marriage portion had less say in their children's decisions. And because only about a third of Londoners at this time were native born, many others were just too far away to be involved. In the sixteenth century, Joan Dowell, the child of a Herefordshire innkeeper, had come to the city to relieve her parents, explaining "her said father doth not as yet knowe of this intended marriage but when he shall understand thereof he will be verie gladd of it because yt is for her pferment [preferment], her father bing but a poore man and having more children is not able to give much at marriage with her."[105] Two centuries later young people were still flocking to the city to save their parents from expense and embarrassment, and many parents still preferred "not to know" about their children's relationships. They probably first learned of it when they received a letter painstakingly modeled on the following taken from a collection intended for the newly literate. In it a maid servant tells her parents in the country about her prospects with the young Mr. Jones, a printer:

I have fairly told him how little he has to expect from me. However, I could not conclude on anything till I had acquainted you with his proposals and asked your blessing and consent.

A reply is provided for the parents:

Our distance from you must make us leave everything to your discretion; and as you are so well satisfied with Mr. Jones' character, as well as are all friends, and your master and mistress, we give you our blessing and consent with all our hearts. We are only sorry that we can do no more for you. Let us know when it is done, and we will assist, as far as we are able, towards housekeeping.[106]

VI

When betrothal was a purely personal affair, there was less need for formality. The length of the plebeian "engagement" was determined mainly by the vicissitudes of the couple's economic situation. In the seventeenth century, William Whiteway had betrothed and wed in less than three months. It took Francis Place and Elizabeth Chadd a year to come to the point they felt they could establish a household, and then Elizabeth's mother, who depended on her, began to raise objections and they had to marry secretly.[107] The earnings of both men and women had become so uncertain by the early nineteenth century that it was virtually impossible to set a wedding date in the traditional manner. In London, marriages tended to bunch at the end of the Season, in midsummer, when earnings and savings were highest and servants normally left their places. There was another bulge at Christmas, the other major moment of prosperity in the proletarian year. Yet, on the whole, urban marriage showed less marked seasonal change than its rural counterpart, the reason being that city people married when they could, stretching the traditional betrothal to suit the new economic circumstances.[108]

The London Foundling Hospital records show that relations were direct and open. Sexual intimacy was normal once marriage had been promised.[109] Couples might set a date and then, for no fault of their own, see it pass, with the woman pregnant or the child already born. This is what happened to the majority of those women, mainly domestic servants, who gave up their illegitimate children to the Hospital. Most of their relationships had begun in a very conventional way. Alexander Hay and Jane Mitton shopped together for a ring and bought linen in preparation for their wedding. When Jane found herself pregnant, she left service and lodged as a married woman, expecting that it would be only a matter of time before James legalized the arrangement. They had kept the engagement to themselves in order not to inform Jane's mistress; and it may have been the same desire for secrecy that impelled Alexander to promise Jane in a letter, which she no doubt kept tucked away with the linens and the ring in her servant's box:

Dear Jane Mitton

I solemnly promise to marry you my dear girl.

18 December 1840

Yours affec.

Alex Hay[110]

Women rarely entered into sexual relations without first obtaining such a promise. Rural betrothal customs carried over to the city, and in some instances couples seem to have been "proving" fertility in the same way as country folk. Some men refused to marry until there was positive proof of pregnancy, though there were also a few who, when they found out about the child, suggested abortion and threatened to desert if it were not carried out.[111] No doubt there was much voluntary abortion on the part of women both in the metropolis and in the northern factory towns, but often the women, valuing motherhood more than marriage, insisted on bearing the children even when they knew the father would abscond. It was not uncommon for these "chance children" to be adopted by the woman's family, especially in the northern towns. In London, where family support was rarely so close to hand, women struggled to keep their children and only in the last resort gave them up to the workhouse or the Foundling Hospital.[112]

There was little shame attached to premarital pregnancy and couples tended to put off the marriage ceremony until a time economically convenient for both parties. Often this meant the child was already born, a condition that did not seem to concern them unduly. The Foundling Hospital cases suggest that men took their promise of marriage seriously, providing support during the pregnancy, making preparations for marriage or, in its absence, acting as a proper husband would. Sarah Pinchbeck and William Hodge took furnished rooms and lived as a married couple during her pregnancy.[113] John Windham came to Westminster, took lodgings, and told the neighbors that his "wife" was coming to town. He and Sarah Watley lived together until two weeks after the delivery, when they quarreled and he enlisted as a soldier.[114] Esther Hanley also lived "as Man and Wife" with her lover until he took sick and died.[115] They appear to have been quite content to live outside legal marriage, as were an Irish couple who came to London in the same period. The latter's arrangement broke up only when the man failed to find work.[116]

It was not uncommon for couples to set up housekeeping in anticipation of marriage. Camilla Bonds and David Lodge did so in Kentish Town in 1822, but they postponed the wedding so many times that the child was born illegitimate.[117] John Marsh, an exciseman in Bramley, told Ann Sims in 1838 that "his Circumstances would not allow him to marry but when they were better he would." He supported her in lodgings at five shillings per week, but unfortunately was dismissed from his post just before their child was born and was never able to fulfill his original intentions.[118] When Margaret Williams became pregnant, James Griffiths acted as any honorable Welshman would; he asked her to leave service and live with him until a marriage could be arranged. They apparently quarreled and, even though he continued to offer support, she would not have him. The child was born a bastard.[119]

The probability that a couple would live together before marriage seems to have been determined largely by occupation. Women in service preferred to remain there even when pregnant because it was so much cheaper that way. They could conceal their condition until the very last minute, thus saving the cost of room and board and adding to their chances of a successful marriage.[120] Women in the trades were in a very different position. They were often approached by a co-worker, anxious to get a partner, who proposed that they could live together more cheaply than singly until it was time to marry. Women with dependents found such offers especially attractive. A needle worker who lived with her widowed mother readily accepted a young tin worker as a means of gaining for them some measure of security. It did not matter to her that he said they could not wed immediately, for she was happy enough to contribute her earnings toward their joint future:

> He told me that if I came to live with him he'd take care I shouldn't want, and both mother and me had been very bad off before. He said, too, he'd make me his lawful wife, but I hardly cared as long as I could get food for myself and mother.[121]

Other women interviewed by Mayhew talked of their relations with men in the same manner. A garment worker, who lived with a dock laborer, said she did so "only to get a living and save myself from doing worse," but added that "if I could get a living otherwise, I can't say I would leave him. . . . He's willing to marry me the first day he can afford. . . ." A widow with two children, whose relations with a man were her only maintenance, believed he would marry her "if ever it was in his power." To another shop worker, the arrangement was a matter of necessity: "It's not in his power to marry me, his work won't allow it; and he's not able to support me in the manner he wishes and keep himself."[122]

These women were desperate, but they were not deluded. They were acting on assumptions consistent with traditional betrothal practice. Most recognized their relationships were outside the law; many felt the pangs of conscience; all knew they were taking a risk. Nevertheless, they regarded the arrangements as justified under the circumstances. They insisted on a promise of marriage before allowing intimacy; and, as had been the case for centuries, intercourse was for them not just sex but a symbol of commitment. London women had no difficulty distinguishing between relations to which they gave their consent and those in which force or deception had been used. And they used their sexuality to bargain with men they hoped to marry. Although Emma Stokes' intimacy with Charles Walkin began with his assaulting her, she decided to sleep with him again, "this in the hope that he would marry her." A Marylebone general servant, Priscilla Perk, also continued to encourage her lover: "Fearing I should be in the family way, I kept up the acquaintance."[123]

There were women making the best of a bad situation, but they were acting on the old and still widely held notion that sexuality endowed a relationship with certain mutual obligations. For this reason they made sure that others knew about their intimacies. The cook at Ellen Handock's Hyde Park household knew that she had slept there with her lover seven or eight times over a three-month period, but "did not think [it] was wrong as she expected they would have been married."[124] Women suspecting that men were about to abscond felt no shame in telling their friends of their situation. It was more difficult to inform a master or mistress, whose attitude might be more punitive than sympathetic, but many servants took that risk and often pressure was put on the man to marry. Sometimes it was successful, in other instances tempers flared and the man fled, but the fact that women still resorted to public opinion suggests the persistence of the ancient notion of betrothal rights even in the great cities.[125] Whether living together or intimate only on occasion, these couples acted as the betrothed had traditionally done, except that they were on their own in gathering the resources necessary to sustain a household and family. Most could not expect their families to provide anything, and, because the woman's contribution was as important as the man's, she had a real bargaining power, which most were not afraid to use. There was nothing passive about the way London women used their sexuality, savings, and labor power in this situation. Martha Emery lived with Francis Parkins for three weeks, but, when he mistreated her, she had no hesitancy about leaving him, even though she was pregnant at the time. He even promised to support her and the child, but she preferred to make a go of it on her own.[126]

This was a time of testing and, while few working women could afford too resort to court for breach of promise, they could (until 1834) use the threat of swearing the paternity of the child should a lover threaten to desert. Even in the relative anonymity of the metropolis, this was often sufficient to bring a quick settlement, either a renewed promise to marry or, what was more common, the promise of child maintenance. As Samuel Bamford found to his great relief, Lancashire women often preferred to have the payment rather than marriage, enough to keep both the child and their autonomy.[127] Much the same thing seems to have motivated the young petitioners to the Foundling Hospital, who, like Martha Emery, had chosen not to marry. Sarah Smitherton's Bishopgate master considered her "one of the family" and had been instrumental in objecting to her relationship with a sailor, who was described as not "being of any trade." Although an immigrant whose parents were dead, she trusted enough in her adopted "family" to reject the man's repeated offers of marriage.[128] As in the north, it was often the support of family or friends that permitted women to reject marriage with men they had grown to dislike. A mother insisted on taking her pregnant daughter back to Wales, where she was needed; a brother objected to a suitor, turning his sister against marriage; a stepfather warned against a man "who appeared to be frequently out of situation and much given to drink."[129]

A woman's freedom of choice and her bargaining power were much greater under the old customs of betrothal than under the new law of marriage. She remained in possession of her property and, while all her contributions to the marriage were recoverable, only a portion of the man's were. She might claim maintenance for many children conceived during the betrothal, but he had no corresponding right of paternity. In effect, while she could claim the full rights of motherhood, he had no similar claims to fatherhood. In addition, she was protected against violence and theft in a way a wife was not. Whereas a married woman was *feme covert*, without legal identity or rights apart from her husband, the betrothed had a legal and social position more favorable in some ways than that of daughter or wife. She was liberated from the paternal control of her own family, but not yet subject to the patriarchy of marriage. She was something of an anomaly but, as such, in an advantageous position, the realization of which caused many women to prefer a man's promise of marriage to the thing itself. One, who had been living with the same man for forty years, asserted that "he would have married me again and again, but I could never see the good of it." Another explained that she "didn't chose to be knocked about, nor see her children treated bad, neither." A third preferred to keep a strong bargaining position, for, as she asserted, "once they were married she had no hold over him."[130]

Men also knew the benefits of keeping things open; and there were those who argued that it was better to live with a woman than marry her, because "if I married her I should never be sure of my tea."[131] Nevertheless, without making some commitment, a young journeyman could never hope of achieving even a semblance of his ambitions. In the London economy, more so than in a northern factory town, to remain celibate was to forfeit all chance of adult status and the manliness that was associated with economic independence. Time was against a man, especially where skill and strength were involved. Younger, healthier males were constantly pressing forward; the competition for jobs and patronage was intense, and becoming more so. If a man had not accumulated sufficient capital or standing on his own by his mid-twenties, his only real chance was to find an able woman who could help him achieve what he had failed to do on his own.

At the same time, men of high ambition and great pride would not think of setting up a family that they could not support. Thus, the masculine identity of provider and protector often worked against marriage. Pride turned to anger when men were confronted by parents or masters. Harry Crown, a coachman, was willing to admit paternity and even make a settlement with Annie Balham's parents, but he would be pressed no further. "Fellows of my breed won't stand that kind of pressure and you seldom find them a coward," he told Mr. Balham just before breaking off all relations.[132] Henry Mayhew encountered the same stubbornness in a garment worker who was living with one of the women who worked with him. When Mayhew offered to pay half the expense of marriage by banns, the man still demurred, saying he had been forced to pawn his coat and "he could not go to be married in his shirtsleeves."[133]

Unlike the factory operatives, who readily accepted the possibility that their wives would work after marriage, London's tradesmen would not hear of such a thing. While they might live with a woman, and accept her assistance in making a marriage, they refused to contemplate any arrangement that would violate the traditional artisan notion of husbandhood, the ideal of the protector or provider. Martha Brighton's parents thought they had found "a protector for their daughter" in James Thames. He was considerably older and well established, but the relationship between the pair was not a happy one, and, while he promised to support the child, he ran off when the Brightons became too insistent on marriage.[134] Thomas Lyons, a clerk, promised Harriet Wolfolk that he would marry her as soon as he could "place himself in business"; James McLachlan told his fiancée that he would do all he could to "protect her"; others also used similar patriarchal language in explaining why they could not marry before they had attained full economic independence.[135] Since women they courted shared the similar expectations, nobody was unduly troubled by premarital intimacy as long as a man's promises were reinforced by his eventual prospects for economic independence. Much was tolerated as long as the man had the potential of becoming a provider, but when Margaret Harmon became pregnant and Thomas Slaughter insisted on honoring his promises, her family intervened on the grounds of his "being without a trade."[136]

VII

In northern industrial towns couples could often share the costs of housing and the duties of childrearing with their kin. In London, with its greater fluidity and instability, the nuclear family was more on its own. Housing was scarce and expensive; two could live almost as cheaply as one, but this tended to encourage illicit conjugality rather than legal marriage. Setting up a household and establishing a family commensurate with the tradesmen's standard of living were daunting prospects:

> A young couple live very happily, till the woman is confined to her first lying-in. The cessation of her employment then produces a deficiency in their income, at a time when expenses unavoidably increase. She therefore wants many comforts, and even the indulgences necessary to her situation: she becomes sickly, droops, and at last is laid up by a fever, or pneumonic

complaint; the child dwindles, and frequently dies. The husband, unable to hire a nurse, gives up most of his time to attendance on his wife and child; his wages are reduced to a trifle; vexation and want render him at least diseased, and the whole family sometimes perishes.[137]

Establishing a legally indissoluable marriage also meant acceptance of roles that, if not properly fulfilled, could bring shame to all concerned. Family violence in nineteenth-century London was usually occasioned by the failure of either spouse to live up to his or her prescribed duties. A wife was beaten when she did not keep the rooms clean or failed to have a meal ready. Husbands were nagged, taunted, and even physically assaulted when they failed to keep a steady job or provide sufficient earnings. Mary Ann Ford considered that her husband was holding back on her and she took his whole pay packet. "I have treated you kindly all day and you have robbed me of my week's hard earnings," he responded. They began to quarrel and he beat her to death. "I never meant to kill her," he told the court, "She should have kept her hand out of my pocket."[138] The more rigid the marital roles, the greater the chance of dispute and violence. Just as today, married couples found themselves faced with demands and tensions they had not encountered during betrothal when roles are less structured.[139] The term for those living outside marriage—"tally couples"—suggests a degree of give-and-take ("they tally well together") that was not easily reproduced in a legal marriage, where the roles of husband and wife, father and mother, were so much more clearly defined by law and custom. Coster couples "living tally" were said to act like lovers, showing a degree of jealousy that was rare among those formally married.[140] If wedded persons were less emotionally possessive, they were nevertheless more demanding in other ways. They had to contend with the equally strong emotions of duty and guilt, honor and shame.

It is not surprising then that men should have preferred the less socially and financially demanding role of putative father rather than assume the full duties of husbandhood. It was also easier psychologically for women to be mothers rather than wives, as long as they could find alternative provision for themselves and their children. In the rural and urban manufacturing areas of the north, unwed mothers often fell back on their families. This was more difficult in London, but there too single parenthood was thought preferable to a bad marriage. When there were no parents, sisters and aunts provided assistance.[141] Although women could rarely make it on their own, many had access to female networks that could provide shelter and employment. When John Dunn disappeared on another of his frequent sea voyages, Hannah Potter and the woman she had worked with at silk winding in Spitalfields were ready to bring up the child who was about to be born. They would have done so, but depression hit the trade in the early 1820s and there was no alternative but the Foundling Hospital. "Work is slack or she would maintain the child," she told its inspectors.[142]

Early-nineteenth-century masters were often quite supportive in assisting pregnant employees with tickets to the city's various lying-in charities. Their motives were not entirely altruistic, for experienced employees were hard to come by and they hoped by having the child nursed or adopted to retain the woman in their employ.[143] Servants and others without marketable skills were very vulnerable when left with a child to support. They were the ones most likely to end up in the workhouse or at the gates of the Foundling Hospital. And it was their illegitimacy that was most certain to be noticed, stigmatized, and recorded. If recorded illegitimacy in the metropolis was lower than that of the countryside, one of the reasons was the ability of unwed women in other trades, who did not have to seek public assistance or private charity, to register their infants as legitimate. Sarah Kent did not bother to have her children registered at all; and Ann Thoms, living as Mrs. Barchester, seems to have falsely registered hers. Before the 1880s, at least a third of all London's illegitimate children were never properly recorded.[144]

Thus the modest recorded level of illegitimate births was only the tip of a vast iceberg of unsanctioned heterosexuality that developed in the course of the eighteenth century and reached its full mass sometime after the Napoleonic Wars. The celibate had become the conjugal but not yet the marital city. The consistently higher recorded age of marriage of Londoners was deceptive, for this hid the vast numbers of people living together, enjoying flexible relationships, and postponing marriages. Patrick Colquhoun noted in the 1790s the "prodigious number among the lower classes who cohabit together without marriage."[145] Mayhew's contemporary, J. F. McQueen, claimed that, if those living together were added to the couples married by license, the two together would outnumber those married by banns.[146] Many simply pleaded poverty, telling the clergymen who urged them to marry that "it wasn't convenient to get a bit of money together, and so we took each other's word for it."[147] Some rejected church weddings out of principle: "They had got it into their heads that marriage was instigated only by the clergy, for the purpose of drawing money out of the public." But in one Westminster neighborhood, where only two-sevenths of the couples were believed to be legally wed, the reasons were not so much ideological as social: "We don't see any need of such a thing: we have agreed between ourselves and that is enough." When pressed to marry, many indicated a willingness to do so at some future time, but on their own terms. In the meantime, they preferred the flexibility which the essentially liminal state of betrothal provided them.[148]

VIII

Few couples who had made their vows to one another thought of their cohabitation as a permanent condition, but they saw no more shame in their liminal status than did those peasants and artisans who used the betrothal rite to legitimize premarital intimacy during earlier centuries. On the other hand, when it came to establishing their conjugality on a permanent legal footing, the urban poor no longer did so in the ritualized manner of a big wedding. If and when urban couples married, they normally did so by the cheapest and quickest means they could find. The most popular days, in addition to Saturdays, were Christmas, Easter, Whitsun, and, later in the nineteenth century, the August Bank Holiday, times when working classes had a little time off and some extra money to spend. Manchester Cathedral's low fees attracted hundreds, especially on Christmas and Whitsun, when the applicants had to be married in batches.[149] The same was true of London's "marrying churches," located mainly in the East End, where the fees were reduced and couples also lined up to be wed. A London cabinetmaker, who married in 1904, remembered standing in line with five other couples before the altar:

> And the old padre came along you know—wilt thou—and you know, the usual marriage ceremony, individually. Oh yes. Then we filed into the vestry and signed our names you know, and—one after the other and then—out—out we came. Had to rush because of the morning service you see, Christmas morning, about half past ten.[150]

The festivities, and thus the expenses, were kept to a minimum. Couples going to be married were described as being "cool and business like, as though, having paid a deposit on the purchase of a donkey or a handsome barrow, they were just going in with their witnesses to settle the bargain."[151] Many came to church without the required attendants, and the pew openers had to be enlisted as witnesses. The only extravagance the London working people of the 1850s allowed themselves were white gloves, and these were rented for the occasion. "Sometimes the whole dress is hired, and the poor seamstress flaunts in an old white satin and dirty veil of the West End, or rather, of the sold-off wardrobe of some minor theatre. There is something painful, as well as ludicrous, in such an appearance," noted one observer.[152] For the most part, however, urban workers wed in their ordinary clothes, often returning to their jobs immediately after the service. The contrast between this and the fashionable West End white wedding with honeymoon did not go unnoticed: "In no European town can a marriage be celebrated at less cost and with less 'fuss' than in London, or with more pomp, and, from a pecuniary point of view, more extravagant splendor."[153]

The patrician white wedding, with its giving away of the virgin bride in white, was an expression of the kind of patriarchy that had very little resonance among the urban plebeians. Working women were neither so subject to their fathers nor so subservient to their husbands, a condition reflected in their preference for wedding ceremonies that were restricted to the exchange of consents, with vows of obedience mumbled or left out entirely. Nor did the other function of a big wedding—namely,

18. Rowlandson's *The Tailor's Wedding* of 1814 suggests the boisterous, secular character of plebeian nuptials at the time. Tailors were among the groups most likely to flaunt the marriage law. (Used by permission of the Trustees of the British Museum)

the establishment of proper relations among the couple, their families, peers, and the community—seem so necessary as far as the urban working class was concerned. The old customs of teasing and treating, once so central to realigning social relations, were now a nuisance, hardly more than a form of begging. The rural plebeian form of big weddings found its way to the northern factory towns, although even there the scale of festivities was much diminished. The closest thing to a "public bridal" was breakfast at the local beer shop, where it was customary to take up a collection to help the couple furnish their rented room.[154] Traditions of mutual assistance would eventually develop in the mills, but, because newlyweds so often moved in with parents, the traditional fetching of the bride and the rites of the threshold had lost their meaning. Working people were supportive of each other's marriages, but weddings were now family affairs, and rather subdued. Anything more elaborate added to the burden of founding a family, something that was studiously avoided. By the time the couple came to the church (or, after 1837, the civil registrar), they were already socially and psychologically a couple and, often enough, also parents. They did not feel the need to have their status validated by public celebration; and there was therefore no felt need for the elaborate rites of passage that in the celibate city had transformed single into married couples and, among the propertied classes, still continued to serve that purpose.

The sharp transition from daughter to wife, son to husband, characteristic of persons of property was absent among the urban working classes. They had already worked out the heterosexuality that would be the pattern for their married lives. No honeymoon was needed, and most were back at work the next day, or, if it was not a holiday, the same afternoon. And even the most critical observers had to concede that they were "industrious folks, who have no time for idle amusement and do not make a holiday even of their marriage morning. In these cases the wooing had probably been longer, and the chances of domestic happiness were generally greater."[155] Whether working people faced with such precarious economic conditions found greater happiness in marriage is, of course, doubtful. Their problem was not one of personal adjustment, but of coping with the respective roles of husband/provider and housewife/mother under conditions of extreme uncertainty and great privation. This uncomfortable prospect, so often emphasized in both folk ballad and music hall song, was the major reason why so many delayed and even rejected formal marriage. In the conjugal city it was easier to live together in a flexible, conditional way than face the social and financial strains of a legally indissoluable marriage. Yet, in a time when there were no sure means of contraception, conjugality was not without its own risks and dire consequences. However tenaciously propertyless women and men might struggle to control their destiny, the independence so many aspired to was always just beyond their grasp.

CHAPTER 7

∾∾∾∾∾∾∾∾∾∾∾∾∾∾∾∾∾∾∾∾∾∾∾∾∾∾∾∾

Married but not Churched:
Common-Law Marriage and the
Renewal of Sexual Nonconformity

By the late eighteenth century sexual nonconformity had become so widespread that a direct challenge to the marriage law was inevitable. Opponents of the Hardwicke Act had predicted that the abolition of betrothal rights and clandestine marriage would force a great part of the populous "to make the best shift they can without marriage." When Lewis Morris visited pit villages in Wales during the 1760s he found "the late Act of Parlamt [sic] is look[e]d upon only as a Cruel and wicked restraint upon the liberties of the Mine Country." A decade later it was reported that marriage law was "looked upon as no more than a Ballad," and openly defied.[1] During the era of the French Revolution there was hysterical talk of Painite radicalism toppling the authority of husbands over wives, parents over children, and ultimately bringing down the whole social order. By 1840 the editors of *The Christian Lady's Magazine* were convinced that the apocalypse had indeed arrived in form of socialism and feminism:

> The main plan . . . is, first, to wholly abolish marriage . . . secondly, to take every child from its mother at the time of its birth . . . and to commit the infants to persons appointed for the charge, who shall nourish them like a promiscuous litter of pigs. . . . Thirdly, to do away with that sacred and endearing thing—home. . . . There is to be no separate dwelling, no husband, no wife, no parent, no child, no brother, no sister, no neighbour, no friend, no pastor, NO GOD.[2]

This kind of rhetoric had been heard before in Britain. During the 1640s and 1650s similar fears had been expressed about the advocates of religious nonconformity. Now, however, it was often members of the old puritan denominations who felt most threatened by the new sexual radicalism. The major bodies of eighteenth-century dissent chafed at the laws that, with the exception of the Quakers, prevented their members from marrying in their own churches, but they did not counsel disobedience. Only some minor sectarians, whose lineage can be traced to the religious radicalism of the 1640s and before, kept alive a belief in self-marriage and divorce. The Camisard prophets who came to London in the first decades of the century caused marriages to break up and new unions to form. Later, when some of their followers became associated with the Manchester Quakers, they caused further marital upheavals. One young convert, Ann Lee, was so moved by their doctrine of the evils of the flesh that she renounced her marriage and committed herself to the radical asceticism that became the basis of the later Shaker movement.[3] And when John Wesley encountered a member of a Birmingham antinomian sect in 1746 and asked him "Have you also a right to all the women in the world?," the considered reply was: "Yes, if they consent."[4] A decade later Wesley was confronted by another challenge, this time by the Nicolaitans, latter-day Familists, who were strong in and around Wednesbury in Staffordshire. He wrote that "they lived in promiscuous immorality not believing in marriage, and were plunderers and robbers." He was most shocked by one of their female members, who declared that "If I am a lair, God Himself is a lair."[5]

Wednesbury was one of those centers of early industrialization where social and religious nonconformity blended together to produce an especially robust antinomian ethos.[6] The district's population of colliers, male and female nail makers, and petty tradespeople were famous for cockfighting, bull baiting, and "wife selling," habits that set them apart from both the established church and the chapel culture of the old dissent and the new Methodism.[7] And there were hundreds of similarly booming, unruly places that, with the great population increases of the late eighteenth century, became centers of opposition to organized religion. The new anticlericalism built on the traditional hostilities to tithes and fees. The tax on marriage enacted in the 1690s had been called a "fine on the marriage bed"; and an additional three pence added in 1784 was so resented that even the clergy complained that the new tax would be "most unproductive to the State."[8] Political tensions in the 1790s further intensified class divisions, so that by the end of the Napoleonic Wars people were refusing the services of the church in unprecedented numbers. Reverend Wilmot, the parson of two plebeian parishes of Morley and Smalley in Derbyshire, worried that baptisms had not kept up with the rapid growth in population. He attributed this in part to the resurgence of Baptists in the district, but also noted in his register that "I believe we are indebted to the works of the infamous Paine, which have eradicated the principles of religion from the minds of the lower orders of the people."[9] By this time conventional marriage had less to fear from religious dissent, which tended almost everywhere to uphold the norms of respectability, than from a volatile skepticism, which alternated between total indifference and militant secularism.[10] The cleric of another Derbyshire industrial community, Edale, described his parishioners as a "singularly barbarous people":

You know that in that rude uncivilized district the lord of misrule has erected his most despotic throne: that in that place are found all the practical blessings of perfect equality; that subordination is totally unknown, that scarcely anyone possesses influence of controul even over those whom "the laws of God, the laws of their country, and of reason" have placed under their jurisdiction; that everyone does just "that which is right in his own eyes," and nothing else; that, in short, liberty had degenerated into perfect licentiousness, and general independence into universal impudence.[11]

A similar secular nonconformity was rising everywhere that the squire and parson were not firmly in control. At Kingswood, Gloucestershire, where there was no church until the 1750s, the colliers were described as not being "responsible to any Civil Officer or Minister for their behavior or Religion."[12] Even in the south and east, where things were relatively subdued, disputes over tithes caused a particularly violent resurgence of anticlericalism in the 1830s. Not surprisingly, militant secularism also turned up in cities during the early nineteenth century. In the 1840s London City Missionaries found a multitude of "avowed Infidels" living among the shoemakers, tailors, and petty tradespeople, who, as in the countryside, constituted some of the groups most likely to live outside legal marriage.[13] In the cities the inchoate anticlericalism of the late eighteenth century had taken on a definite radical and even socialist form. Shaped by Painite freethinkers, early feminists, and socialists, the debate over marriage took a new, distinctly secular direction, articulating what a large part of the rural and urban working classes had already been expressing in action for several decades.

I

Like Britain's first sexual revolution, the sexual radicalism that ultimately found expression in the 1830s and 1840s was only the most visible and articulate aspect of fundamental shifts in conjugal habits that had been occurring among the plebeian strata during the late eighteenth and early nineteenth centuries.[14] As they had done before, Britain's "ungovernable people" gave the appearance of conforming to the official marriage discipline, while seeking every means to turn the system to their advantage. One immediate effect of Hardwicke's legislation was that many turned to marriage by license as a substitute for the lost right of clandestine marriage.[15] For the next one hundred and fifty years license remained immensely popular. Among the aristocracy it was universal; the gentry and urban middle classes tended to follow their lead, for both groups could easily afford the costs, which mounted by the mid-Victorian period to over four guineas, nearly four times the cost of marriage by banns and a month's wages for a skilled worker.[16]

But surprising numbers of working people also scraped together the money. In parts of Wales, the Midlands, and the north of England (especially Cumberland) the proportion of those marrying by license was as high as twenty-eight percent in the 1840s.[17] In some places like Holy Trinity, Stratford on Avon, these high numbers can be accounted for by the presence of a bishop's surrogate, but in others convenience alone will not explain the large numbers of working people who sought by this means to avoid the publicity of banns.[18] In the Carlisle area easy access to Scotland had accustomed people to being able to avoid wedding in their own parishes by simply crossing the border to places like Gretna Green. When that option was terminated by law in 1857, many resorted to license despite the cost.[19]

The Registrar General remarked at the time that in the south and east license marked a distinct class boundary: "nearly all the people of the middle class and some artisans marry by licence, while all the laboring population marry by banns, or its equivalent certificate." The agricultural laborers apparently either could not afford or, what is more likely, did not feel the need for privacy. But in the north and west, where working people purchased license in large numbers, there was still a felt desire for the kind of "little wedding" that the outlawed clandestine marriage had previously provided. It was in this same region that civil marriage, available for the first time in 1837, would have the largest clientele, and for many of the same reasons.[20] The north and west were the places that also clung most stubbornly to the traditions of the big wedding, so it seems that license was functioning there as a way of relieving the heavy social obligations attendant on marriage, while in the south and east, where marriage was now regarded as a purely personal matter, there was much less need for an alternative.

In the big cities people could marry by banns and still have their privacy. Residence and age requirements were virtually impossible to enforce in densely populated urban parishes where the priest and his clerk were too busy to check on each and every couple. Reverend Coke of St. James the Great was especially burdened thanks to the parish's marriage fund that provided virtually free weddings. Because he performed over fourteen hundred weddings a year in the 1860s, Coke's efforts to restrict access were constantly frustrated:

> I kept a man to enquire but the inhabitants threatened to throw water over him if he came to search after the girls. He positively refused to perform the duty.[21]

In London and in other large cities like Manchester, people moved as freely across parish boundaries as they did in the days when renegade clergy conducted clandestine marriage. Residents of Highgate journeyed south to St. Pancras to wed; the people of Westminster crossed the bridge to Lambeth. "Many seem to think London is one great parish," complained the vicar of St. Mary's, Spitalfields, at one point during the 1850s.[22] It was said at the time that the people of Bethnal Green "have very strong objection to be married in their own Church, desiring to avoid their neighbors."[23] Forty years later the feeling had not abated.

Moorfields folk were said to resent the "chaffing of neighbours"; in Spitalfields "they try to escape the risk of jeering and rude banter"; while in Stepney "poor people have a great desire to marry secretly," which they satisfied, when intent on having a church wedding, by going to the next parish.[24]

In cities it was easy enough to find a lodging housekeeper who would testify falsely to residence. If no one could be found who would perjure him or herself, the couple would set up housekeeping in anticipation of the wedding, an obvious extension of the old betrothal practice, except insofar as many who began this way kept postponing the formalities until a point was reached that solemnization no longer seemed to matter.[25] Because working people moved around a great deal within the city, they often claimed, as a "liberty," marriage in a parish where they had been baptized or where their parents had been wed. "Sentiment runs deep when relations have been married in a certain church," reported a Shoreditch parson, who found it virtually impossible to prevent extraparochial marriages.[26] He understood that the poor greatly resented the ability of the rich to marry anywhere with only minimal residence (two weeks' residence was required for purchasers of license at that time), a grievance the justice of which many of his fellow clergymen had come to recognize by the mid-nineteenth century. "We must," declared one, "make it easy for the poor to do the same."[27]

Some clergy had long conceded the right of the poor to marry in the so-called Mother Church of a large district, even when they did not attend it regularly. In the 1790s people were going from Harwich to Dovercote "for privacy and because it is the Mother Church where they could take the liberty."[28] This continued throughout the next century, especially where "the view prevails that the inhabitants of all the district parishes have the right to be married in it [the Mother Church]."[29] The Manchester Cathedral was the scene of mass weddings because, as Reverend J. Rushton admitted, "the parishioners have the general common-law right of resorting to the Mother Church, and it is therefore impossible for me to know whether they are the parties they represent themselves to be."[30] The pastor of Havering, Essex, John Wiseman, was one to honor old customs and the numbers married in his church rose precipitously when he took over in the 1820s. Wiseman was an old-fashioned parson who farmed his own land and once boasted that the could preach a sermon, plough an acre, and drink a bottle with any man in England. But he was also an exception as far as the newly "improved" countryside of agricultural capitalism was concerned; and, when he died, the Havering marriage figures receded to their former levels.[31] Should country people want privacy, they would have to seek it in the city.

II

The desire for privacy varied by class and region. The upper classes had created the socially exclusive wedding. The poor of the south and east, for whom the big wedding no longer served any real purpose, married as quickly and cheaply as they could. It was in the north and west, where family and community interdependence remained strongest, that people who could not fulfill all the obligations of a big wedding still had the greatest need for a clandestine alternative. Unless they were fortunate to have a large city or a John Wiseman nearby, those who could not afford a license were placed in a difficult position. If they lived close enough to the border of Scotland, they enjoyed (before 1857) the singular advantage of access to quick, private Scots marriage ceremonies without any residence requirements. Under Scottish law any vow made before witnesses constituted legal marriage. As in England and Wales before 1754, people could just as well have done this for themselves, but they preferred to pay a few shillings to have it witnessed and registered by one of the motley collection of "priests" who set up shop at places like Coldstream Bridge, Lamberton Toll, and, of course, Gretna Green. Before 1754 movement across the border had been two way. The parson of Gretna itself had been much agitated in the 1730s by clandestine marriages notarized by John Murray, a Cumberland clog maker who accommodated Scottish as well as English couples. It was not until late in the same decade that the first of the famous "marriers" started practice in Gretna itself. With the passage of the Hardwicke Act, his business boomed and many others established rival places of solemnization. Most were poor men seeking to supplement their meager earnings; most were of local origin, although they were eventually joined by Englishmen whose trade in marriages was now illegal in their homeland.[32]

The principal clients of Gretna Green and other border marriage shops were not the few rich runaways enshrined in legend, but thousands of quite ordinary folk who, for a variety of reasons, wished a cheap, quick, and private union. People from the Carlisle region flocked to Gretna Green during the annual hiring fairs, those interludes in the calendar of rural labor when there was time and money enough for at least a "little wedding." Like the Fleet parsons, the border priests offered a variety of accommodations for feasting and consummation. One even built an inn on the English side of the border to satisfy the popular belief that a Scots wedding should be consummated on English soil.[33] Local people crossed the border at all times of the year, however, indicating that convenience was not the only motive. There was the Cumberland man who, when pressed to marry a woman of inferior social station whom he had made pregnant, preferred the privacy Gretna Green offered. He lived with her on that basis from 1823 to 1835, and then married her in the local Church of England.[34] In many cases young couples who eloped across the border returned to marry in their parish church, suggesting that the border weddings, like the clandestine marriages before them, were a part of complicated intrafamilial and intracommunal relations.[35] Around Ford, Northumberland, miners and other workers courted in such secrecy that the vicar there called it an obsession. "Courtship is not carried on openly as it is in the South, and even parents are kept in ignorance of an engagement until the banns are published," he noted, "you heard it stated that a certain couple are engaged, but from experience you hesitate to congratulate either part lest you should give offense."[36] Because Ford and other places in Northumberland were also famous for their big weddings, it seems likely that it was those who had encountered some obstacle who arranged to walk the seven or eight miles to Coldstream under the cover of darkness, locally called "under hidlings," to be married there.[37] One young miner who was intending to wed a gypsy girl named Nan Allen was said to have been intercepted by friends, who, despite Nan's objections, contrived to convince him that, if he returned to Ford to go through a church wedding by banns, he would be rewarded five guineas by the vicar. While the miner ultimately discovered the trick, by that time he had lost interest in Nan and called the banns for another, more acceptable bride.[38]

After both civil marriage and nonconformist marriage became available in 1837, resort to the border declined appreciably. In 1857 it became impossible for anyone to marry in Scotland without twenty-one days' residence, thus effectively terminating the appeal of border crossing to those who were seeking a quick, private alternative. The Presbyterians could now go to their own chapels. Those without religious preferences, who could tolerate the stark, sometimes humiliating, conditions of the registry office, turned there for privacy. "So it is evident that the class of people who formerly married in Scotland now marry in the registry office in Carlisle," the Registrar General noted in 1866.[39] The border traffic slowed to a trickle and Gretna Green became the historical curiosity it is still today.

III

The number of marriages lost to the border "marriers" was small compared with the volume of self-marriages that took place in the period from 1750 to 1850. The extent of common-law marriage cannot be determined exactly, in part because few outside the plebeian communities were privy to its existence. The clergy were often quite oblivious. Typical of their innocence was one nonconformist minister, who had worked for decades among the people of South Wales before his "great discovery" at the time of World War I that many members of that community, including some of the most respected, were living outside legal marriage or, as they called it, "living tally." It was a member of his own chapel, a tolerant fellow but one with definite views on the subject of church and marriage, who first enlightened him:

> You have married a lot in your time . . . but I'm thinking whether couples are as happy as Tom and Mary Jones who have never married. It strikes me that ceremony and flowers and rice and parson do not make marriage, but something else. What this is I do not know. I am no scholar.

That same evening the minister went to find out for himself. Mary Jones seemed embarrassed when he appeared at the door, but when it

19. Nineteenth-century naive painting of Gretna Green by unknown artist. An eloped couple is wed by the legendary smithy while the groom and carriage wait. (Used by permission of Mr. and Mrs. Andras Kalman, from their collection)

became apparent that the visit was a friendly one she relaxed sufficiently to explain the cause of her initial apprehension:

> What will the neighbors think of you Sir, calling on the likes of us? Tom and I have never been properly married Sir. We are living tally, Sir, but we are very happy. I does my duty to him and he—well there is not a better man on earth than my Tom.[40]

The encounter reveals the enormous gulf between clergy and people that had developed since the eighteenth century. After 1754 few clergy

wanted to know anything about illicit marital relations except to condemn them. An exception was David Jones, whose register the folklorist
Gwenith Gwyn discovered when he was checking births in the Llansantffraid parish of the Ceiriog Valley of North Wales. The baptism
register contained a number of puzzling entries that seemed to indicate
that some kind of irregular marriage had been practiced there in the
period from 1769 to 1799. Sixty percent of all births were attributed by
Jones to conjugal arrangements which, while not yet formally solem-
nized in church, were nevertheless sufficiently stable to be recorded as
separate from those births in which no father was declared.

On further investigation Gwyn found that the irregular unions notarized by Jones were known locally as "besom weddings," a form of
public, secular rite that provided both self-marriage and self-divorce to
the people of the Ceiriog. A seventy-three-year-old woman, born about
the middle of the nineteenth century, was able to provide Gwyn with
a considerable amount of fascinating detail:

> It was a real marriage in the estimation of the public, and I would think
> that women thought much of it. It was the women that spoke about it
> when I was young. Only when speaking about very, very old people would
> men refer to it. The besom wedding was a wedding after this manner: A
> birch besom was placed aslant in the open doorway of a house, with the
> head of the besom on the doorstone, and the top of the handle on the
> doorpost. Then the young man jumped over it first into the house, and
> afterward the young woman in the same way. The jumping was not rec-
> ognized a marriage if either of the two touched the besom in jumping or,
> by accident, removed it from its place. I should think this form of marriage
> was very common in this part of the country at one time, but I never saw
> one.[41]

It was apparently common to invite witnesses to watch the jumping.
In the Ceiriog there is a hint that an old woman presided over the rites,
but in Caernarvonshire, another place where besom weddings existed,
"when parents consented to a marriage the oldest man of the district
was called, and the young couple were asked to leap over the broom,
made of oak branches. . . . " In any case, the publicity was essential and
a successful jumping was greeted with loud cheers.[42]

If a couple proved barren or found themselves incompatible within a
year of the ceremony, divorce was possible as long as both partners
consented. In this case, "the one who had made the decision of separating would call all members of both families to witness the act."[43] An
old man explained to Gwyn the exact nature of the divorce rites:

> By jumping backwards over the besom the marriage was broken. The wife
> had the right to jump back, too. But this step had to be taken by either
> within the first year. Both of them, afterward, were free to marry again. If
> there was a child the father was responsible for its upkeep. In jumping
> backwards to break a marriage, as well as in jumping forward to make a

marriage, if any part of the body touched the besom or the door post the effort was in vain. There were witnesses there to watch.[44]

At the time Gwyn recorded the custom in the 1920s, it was ambivalently remembered by the old people of Ceiriog. Doubtful husbands told their wives, half in jest, "If I had only married you 'over the broom,' I could jump back."[45] But it was the women who were most eager to talk about it. They were the ones who "thought much of it," and the reasons for their nostalgia were obvious:

> It was unusual for a besom marriage to fail. When it did happen, it was not regarded as a disgrace or a hindrance for either party to marry again. If there was a child from the marriage, the father would acknowledge his obligations for the support of the child, and the mother could take possession of her personal endowment [her original dowry or household belongings].[46]

Even after the ritual itself had died out in the 1840s and the people of the valley returned to conventional church or chapel marriage, it was not a disgrace for a child to be born out of wedlock as long as there was a father to contribute to its upbringing. "It is not unusual to see a woman who had a child from a married man being on friendly terms with his wife," Gwyn noted. Furthermore, "it is customary for wives to keep their property separately from that of their husbands, from generation to generation." Even to the end of the nineteenth century, women kept their maiden names for their entire lives. Children normally took their mothers' surnames; and the illegitimate were treated no differently from the other offspring.[47]

Because the marriage register of Llansantffraid parish was not available to Gwyn, he was unable to determine how many of the besom unions were later celebrated in church, though it seems likely that some, like the earlier Welsh clandestine marriages, were.[48] It is known that elopements were common in the Ceiriog in the later nineteenth century. It being a place where small farms mixed with rural industry—slate quarrying for men; cottage wool production for women—the valley was a place where both sexes stayed at home and were subject to strong familial authority. Courting strangers was strongly, even violently, discouraged, and parental intervention was frequent:

> If the girl is not acceptable to the family of the young man, the family opposes the marriage, even when she is pregnant. In the same manner, if the young man is not accepted by the girl's family, they oppose the marriage, even if she is already expecting his child.[49]

In this situation running away "over the mountain" was not unusual. Couples would usually return "to the home of the bride, and she would show her wedding ring to her mother. This was, usually, followed by weeping, scolding, and forgiving."[50] After 1837 it was the register office twelve miles away at Corwen that beckoned the runaways; a century before, various lawless churches probably provided similar facilities. It seems likely that during the period from the 1750s through the 1840s the besom ceremony became the substitute for older betrothal rituals, establishing the conjugal relationship without the necessity of founding a nuclear family. Apparently many of the besom brides continued to live at home, contributing to the family economy and postponing until a future time the establishment of a home of their own. During that time the besom bride was treated much like a "spouse" in the old tradition of the betrothal, neither simply single nor actually married. In time, the lovers might marry. If not, "a girl, who has had a child out of wedlock, is not regarded with disrespect by other young men. In fact, she is admired, and is more likely to find a husband before any girl who considers that purity is the most important thing she possesses."[51]

When time came to set up a household, the people of the Ceiriog kept the custom of the big wedding. Although some couples went to nearby Llangollen to avoid the expense of a really lavish wedding, the local celebration, known as a "feasting," always started off by the fetching of the bride:

> It was customary for the bride, on the morning of her wedding day, to pretend running away, or hiding. Then it was up to the groom and his friends to find her and make believe she was taken by force to the church, thus, showing the groom's conquest.[52]

Gifts were given, old shoes thrown, and the groom's quarry mates fired off blasting charges as their particular salute.[53] But the fact that there were no elaborate rites installing the bride and groom as master and mistress, and thus investing them with special privileges, suggests that Ceiriog marriages were egalitarian in many respects.

IV

There were other parts of North Wales and Anglesey where besom weddings are known to have existed in the late eighteenth and early nineteenth centuries. Further south there developed what were commonly referred to as "little weddings," rites that were similar to the besom weddings but more obviously adapted to the conditions of early industrialization. John Evans recorded that "in the little weddings persons cohabit together; and if, after trial they have reason to be satisfied with each other, the friends are invited to witness the intentions of the parties; they are considered as man and wife. If the parties, prior to this, are dissatisfied the woman is dismissed; and such repudiation is not considered a hindrance to future marriage."[54] Lewis Morris gives still further detail about the plebeian practices he found prevalent in South Wales:

> Some Couples (especially among the miners) either having no friends, or seeing this kind of public marriage too troublesome and Impracticable,

procure a man to wed them privately which will not cost above two or 3 mugs of ale. Sometimes half a dozen Couple[s] will agree at a merry meeting, and are thus wedded and bedded together. This they call *Priodas vach* (i.e., the Little wedding) and is frequently made use of among miners and others to make sure of a woman. . . . The little wedding doth not bind them so Effectually, but that after a months trial they may part by Consent, when the Miner leaves his Mistress, and removes to a Minework in some distant Country, and the Girl is not worse look'd upon among the miners than if she had been an unspotted virgin, so Prevalent & Arbitrary is Custom.[55]

A similar practice has been noted in nineteenth-century Yorkshire, where it was said that miners sometimes "exchanged" wives. An agreement to part and remarry would be made and witnessed in a public house; there would be a feast and the men would make token gifts to their new brides, "whom they now maintain together with the 'childers' of the former union." In the Midlands miners were also known to have engaged in "swappin' " or " 'sellin' " of wives. While this practice seems to have been in decline after mid-century, "those engaging in the transactions never seem to doubt about their right to do so."[56]

Sailors were another group to which common-law arrangements appealed. In the eighteenth century they had been patrons of the Fleet, but now had to make their own marriages. John Carmichael, who was already married to one woman, wrote out a special contract in taking Sarah Stubbins as his common-law wife. Both were said to have taken their vows according to what Carmichael called "the customs of Devon."[57] In Southhampton many women established a temporary arrangement with a mariner, drawing his half-pay while he was at sea and looking after him while in port. Some of these "wives" had engaged in part-time prostitution, but it was assumed that a woman drawing a man's allotment by his consent was no longer in the trade. In the 1870s it was said that the arrangement "is looked upon as nearly as good as marriage among that class." When asked if she were still a prostitute, Harriet Hicks replied, "No, only to one man." The magistrate pressed her further: "You mean that you are not a prostitute, other than as living with one man without marriage? . . . Yes, that's what I mean."[58]

Common-law arrangements were most useful to itinerant workers, especially canal and railway navvies. At Woodhead in Cheshire, where a thousand navvies were camped in 1845, it was reported that:

the couple jumped over a broomstick in the presence of a roomful of men assembled to drink on the occasion, and were put to bed at once, in the same room.[59]

These were people constantly on the move and their relationships were necessarily temporary, without being casual. The arrangements allowed the men to tramp in search of work while the women stayed behind to make other arrangements for themselves.[60] The practice continued into the 1880s when the heroic age of railway construction came to an end.

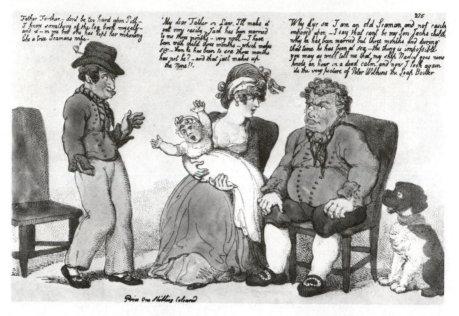

20. Rowlandson's *A Seamans Wifes Reckoning*. A young wife explains to her father-in-law how it could be that she has borne a child while her husband has been away at sea. Mariners were among the groups most likely to resort to self-marriage and self-divorce. (Used by permission of the Trustees of the British Museum)

Similar forms appear to have been typical to Britain's other eighteenth- and nineteenth-century "frontier" regions, where mining and other new industries produced a sudden surge in numbers of a highly mobile population.[61] Practices that had previously been introduced to the South Wales coal fields were found in the northeast of England when the mining boom shifted there in the 1860s and 1870s. In all probability they were carried there by roving workers in much the same way that court-ship customs such as bundling were transferred from one part of Britain to another by migrant workers.[62] As the besom practice spread from Wales to other regions it inevitably lost some of its floral symbolism. In the north of England it became known as "jumping brush and steel," indicating a substitution of symbols more appropriate to the new in-dustrial era.[63]

Long after the besom wedding itself had disappeared from the Ceiriog Valley, the phrase "they had jumped over the besom" was still a way of announcing a pregnancy outside marriage.[64] Sidney O. Addy found that Sheffield people believe that:

> If a girl strides over a besom-handle she will be a mother before she is a wife. If an unmarried woman has a child they say "She's jumped o'er t' besom" or "she jumped o'er t' besom before she went to t' church." Mothers

used to be particularly anxious that their daughters should not stride over the broom, and mischievous boys have been known to leave brooms on door-steps, and such like places, so that girls might accidentally stride over them.[65]

The lingering powers of the broom were known in Somerset's Quantocks region, where it was said until quite recently, "Never step over a broom if you are unmarried. You will bear a bastard child."[66] In the working-class neighborhoods of Salford people were tolerant of those they knew to be "livin' tally" or "over t' brush," a phrase also current among South Yorkshire miners even in our own time.[67] In Warwickshire around 1900 a "hasty, or at any rate irregular marriage is spoken of as a 'marriage over the broomstick.' " And the fact that by the 1870s a registry office marriage was often spoken of as a "broomstick coupling" suggests that civil marriage came to serve as a substitute for common-law ceremony in the mid-Victorian period.[68]

Jumping the broom seems to have been the most elaborate and there-fore most visible of the common-law rites, but there is evidence of other ingenious rituals, elements of which were clearly borrowed from earlier betrothal and marriage practices. When a farmer near Sheffield decided he wanted to formalize his relationship with his "housekeeper," he invited two friends to witness while he presented her with the keys to the house, instructing her to enter, lock the door, and then, on his request, open it to him. Once the farmer and his friends were inside, he "called upon the two men that he took the woman for his wife."[69] More common, however, was the use of the ring, still a powerful symbol of union whose magic transcended the church service. The fact that parish officials invariably paid for a ring as inducement for couples to marry gave official endorsement to the popular feeling about the powers of the wedding band. Without it no union could possibly be enduring. If a proper ring could not be had, a twist of tobacco, a curtain ring, or the church key would do. A leather thong was used in one "stolen match."[70] One of the major objections to marriage in the register office after 1836 was that the ring was not a part of the official ceremony. London poor-law guardians were willing to pay George Stiffell to marry Ellen Barrett in 1844, but he balked at the idea of a marriage without a ring. "I said at the office that it would not do without the ring, and they said I could put that [the cost of the ring] into my pocket," noted Stiffell. His best man, a silk weaver named Thomas Green, was no less incre-dulous: "Never saw such a marriage in my life. . . . There was no ring put on."[71]

Many found themselves in the position of the couple who told Rev-erend Edward Coke that "it wasn't convenient to get a bit of money together, so we took each others word for it."[72] But if they could not have a church ceremony, they usually managed a form of vows and at least a brass ring. Women were most insistent on this point. It was believed unlucky to drop, break, or even take off a ring; and in Shropshire and Wales the belief prevailed among the lower classes that, "if a husband failed to maintain his wife, she might give him back the wedding ring, and then she would be free to marry again."[73] Such women were known in many parts of Britain as "grass widows" or "grace widows," whose divorce from their husbands, once established by witness and reputation, was valid in the eyes of the community. Unwed mothers were also known as "grass widows," as long as they had established their relationship with the man who was the father of their child.[74] Failing to get civil protection from a brutal husband, one working woman at the end of the Victorian period finally resorted to the device of showing her marriage certificate to her neighbors, then publicly removing her ring, thus gaining the common-law right to live apart in peace.[75]

London's poorest class of shoemakers called their common-law wives "tacks" and would send their coats out to pawn in order to have a drunken celebration of their unions.[76] In Yorkshire it was apparently sufficient to exchange the words "If thee tak, I tak thee."[77] South London people saved wedding fees by attending a church where large numbers of couples were married at one time. They did so "with the intent that they shall themselves be married—by silently following the responses and exchanging vows—they become united as the parties joined before the clergyman."[78] In the 1840s Henry Mayhew found the English-born London costermongers to be positively hostile to church marriage, which they said only served to put money in the "parson's pocket." They married in church only when this could be had free of charge.[79] The costers married young, encouraged by parents "as a convenient means of shifting the support of their child [the daughter] to another's exertion, and so thoroughly do they believe this to be the end and aim of matrimony, that the expense of a church ceremony is considered a useless waste of money and the new pair are received by their companions as if every form of law and religion had been complied with."[80] An exchange of handkerchiefs appears to have been the way young costers sealed their partnerships, which involved the woman helping her mate to establish himself in the street trade. Once children had begun to arrive, the woman's place was more confined to the home, a dependence which many coster wives, used to trading on their own, clearly resented.[81]

Among sweeps and dust collectors, also largely hereditary occupations, there were similar common-law traditions.[82] Women often assisted their husbands and even carried on businesses of their own, something that as legally married women or *feme covert* they would have had trouble doing. Mary Vinson, a London sweep with a business of her own, was well aware of the advantage of remaining single (or at least retaining the appearance of single status) when she placed the following notice in a London newspaper in 1787:

> Many in the same Business have reported I am married again, which is totally false and without Foundation, it being calculated to mislead my Customers.[83]

Although Mayhew found that street traders of Irish origin were more likely to seek church marriage than were English-born costers, among the Irish immigrants to large cities another kind of union was common. While vows before a Catholic priest were not illegal, they had no civil standing before 1837 and therefore the Roman hierarchy instructed the faithful to go through the Anglican service in addition to private vows made before their local priest. But many immigrant Irish were apparently disobedient, in part out of hatred of the established church but also for financial reasons. Common-law unions were widespread among them; and it was only after living together for fifteen years and having three children that John and Sara Sullivan decided to wed.[84] Other Irish said their vows only before a Catholic priest:

> These marriages satisfy the conscience of the wife, and while the parish requires no relief, their invalidity is unknown or unattended to. But as soon as the man becomes chargeable and the parish proceeds to remove him and his family, he shows that he is not legally married, and his children claim settlement in the parishes in which they are born.[85]

Women who did not want to follow their spouses to the workhouse found it equally convenient to dispense with formal marriage. This became a particularly pressing consideration after 1834, when outrelief became more difficult to obtain. It was said that many were avoiding marriage because of the horror of being forced into the "Bastilles" and being separated there.[86] Resentment at the policy of separating wives from husbands, and children from parents, ran deep. One man interrupted his own marriage service at the point the vicar invoked the indissoluability of marriage to remark: "We mustn't go to the workhouse, or they'd part us." In Merthyr, Wales, a local bard named Blind Dick composed a song of protest in the 1830s in which a groom responds to the vicar's words "Till death do us part" with the bitter comment, "No vicar, damt it, only until the new workhouse is built."[87]

There were many who out of contempt for both church and state simply refused to use their facilities. When Francis Fulford took an informal census of the inhabitants of his Cambridgeshire parish in 1843, he noted a man named Nash, living with Mary Newman:

> These parties are not married. He is a very free spoken man, and justifies his life by quoting scripture, and the examples of David and Solomon. I have warned and rebuked and presented them at the Visitation. The woman would marry gladly.[88]

It is probable that Nash had been involved in the violent threshing machine riots a few years earlier and that Mary Newman was the wife of a man who had been sentenced to prison for his part in the disturbances. Like so many others living in common-law marriages, they would have been unable to marry because Mary's husband was still living. Earlier in the century, Lincolnshire parsons found many "people living together as Man and Wife without Marrying at all, and, who according to the laws of God and Man cannot be married." Some of these people had husbands or wives still living and did not want to be prosecuted for bigamy, a felony. Others had relationships that violated the prohibited degrees; still others were adulterous arrangements, like the "woman who left the Bed of her husband, and was united in the same morning to her Servant."[89]

In Yorkshire, Lancashire, and Cheshire those who had gone through some kind of common-law rite were said to be "married on the carpet and the banns up the chimney" or "married but not churched," while in almost every part of Britain the term "living tally" established itself:

> They're livin' tally
> They've made a tally bargain
> They're noant wed, they'r nobit livin' tally.[90]

The origin of the term *tally* is obscure. It may have come from the Welsh word for love token, *tali*, or it may refer to the tally stick that miners used to mark the amount of coal dug. But, whatever the origins, the term itself first became widespread in the nineteenth century, indicating the growth of a practice that was clearly distinct from both casual cohabitation and formal marriage. It conveyed a notion of definite, if conditional, contract or "bargain," based on the consent of both parties and protecting the woman in case of motherhood. Furthermore, it suggested a partnership based on some degree of affection. When any couple quarreled it was said "they doan't tally well together," implying that, as in the case of Mary and Tom Jones, tally couples were regarded as particularly well matched, there being nothing but their mutual agreement to keep them together.[91]

V

Although common-law practice seems to have been most frequent in industrializing areas, it has also been discovered in other places like the Kent parish of Ash-next-Sandwich, where an estimated fifteen percent of the couples living together between 1740 and 1834 leave no evidence that they were married in church.[92] We have seen that in earlier centuries a disregard for marriage law was by no means absent, but what is striking is that those who now defied both church and chapel were by no means just the vagabonds and the disinherited. Common-law practices were now found embedded in whole communities, often places where petty farming mixed with new manufacturing pursuits. In the Ceiriog farming was no longer the main occupation. Men were involved in slate quarrying and the women in wool production, with the work located in the valley itself. At Culcheth in South Lancashire, another of the places where a heavy concentration of tally couples has been found, a similar situation prevailed. There cottage handloom weaving had been a major occupation from the 1770s onward and, as in Ceiriog, its rise coincided with the beginnings of common-law marriage, which prevailed until the 1840s, when weaving was removed from the cottages and became a factory employment.

In both Ceiriog and Culcheth marriage was no longer tied to access to land, even though many still owned or rented small properties. The family economy of domestic production worked to break down the old division of labor between parents and children, as well as between men and women. The role of the master of the household was transformed. In the Welsh valley, women took over men's work around the house while they were at the quarries; this led to what Gwenith Gwyn described as "an independency of character" on the women's part.[93] He also noted that "the mothers [were] the more predominant partners in the home." Children took their mothers' surnames and both "boys and girls [were] more attached to their mothers than their fathers." Thus the family was more matrifocal than patrifocal. The esteem that had attached to the role of mistress now shifted to the role of mother. "The strength of the maternal instinct in very young girls [is] abnormal," with the result that Ceiriog women had a "stronger feeling of motherhood, than being a wife."[94]

Gwyn was convinced that the high value placed on maternity, together with the crowded conditions of the typical valley cottage, encouraged this precocious desire for children.[95] Young people were no longer so inhibited about acting in an adult manner. They apparently felt no shame about being seen in public together. Their courtships were conducted more openly than was the case in purely pastoral communities. "As regards sexual matters boys and girls mature young. Girls on the whole [are] more rapid in development than boys. Boys and girls consider that taking liberties is natural."[96]

Where there was abundant domestic work, courtship tended to begin earlier. In Shepshed, Leicestershire, conjugality began earlier when framework knitting was introduced there in the late seventeenth century.[97] This may also have occurred in the Ceiriog, when industrial development began in the late eighteenth century, but apparently it was more difficult to set up a new household, and so young lovers preferred to remain with their families, even after children were born. This also suited their parents, who valued their children's labor and now could even anticipate additional help when their grandchildren reached the ages of eight or nine. Ceiriog families seem to have been particularly possessive, discouraging matches that threatened to take members away from either the village or the immediate kin group. Gwyn found that "it is undignified for a man to marry a woman, or a woman marry a man, without the consent of both families. Feelings of revenge remained when the teachings of families regarding marriage were ignored."[98] Here, as in other proto-industrial communities, the family was expanding rather than contracting as kin ties came to have new significance.

In Culcheth the rise of both illegitimacy and common-law cohabitation coincided precisely with the growth of cottage weaving. As G. N. Gandy has shown, the unwed mothers were simply staying home, shifting the costs of housing and nursing their children to their parents, who were compensated by the additional labor. Eventually, most of the women would marry either the father of the children or some other eligible male, but in the short term the arrangements outside marriage proved satisfactory to everyone involved, including the parish, which did not have to support either the mothers or their children. As in Ceiriog, local opinion attached little or no stigma to those relationships, and even the parson felt obliged to register many of the children as legitimate.[99] Like his colleague in Llanssantffraid parish, Culcheth's Reverend Joseph Jones knew the habits of his flock well enough to realize that, if they were not prematurely shamed, many would eventually married in the church. He complained of what he called the prevalent "domestic republicanism" and lamented the decline of parental authority, but made no concerted effort to challenge the practice itself.

Common-law practice, especially among young people, seems to have been most prevalent in those places where there was enough work to occupy the whole family, where neither sons nor daughters had to be sent away in their teen years to seek employment. Where there was no family economy, as in the Oxfordshire villages that Flora Thompson knew so well, there was occasional illegitimacy, but no common-law tradition. Local girls would sometimes return from domestic service pregnant, but every effort would be made to marry them off.[100] This was generally true of the south and east, except in heath or fenland communities like Woking, an isolated place on Surrey's Blackheath. The inhabitants there had long been at war with authority, first in their struggles against the king's forest laws in the 1630s and later as militant Parliamentarians. Woking people had also taken up the cause of the radical dissenters called Brownists, and nearby Walton-on-Thames was a hotbed of Ranter and Digger sentiment, much of it directed against the authority of the church and the marriage laws.[101] The enthusiasm for dissent had waned in the eighteenth century, though the heath dwellers had not lost their taste for rebellion. They were active in the corn riots of 1830 and were rumored to be very free about marriage and divorce.[102] It was said that the cottagers even exchanged wives on a regular basis:

> The custom was spoken about among the villagers so freely that I see no reason to doubt it subsisting well into the last century [the nineteenth century], nor did those who spoke of it seem either to think it shameful or immoral. As morality is commonly understood the district was a particularly good one, erring, if anything, on the side of narrow-mindedness.[103]

A similar combination of social nonconformity and moral self-discipline is found in smithing villages in the Midlands, mining and navvy camps in Cheshire, Northumberland, and South Wales, weavers' settlements in the valleys of Lancashire and Cumberland, and the out-of-the-way fenland, heath, and forest settlements of the south and east. At Long Framlingham, a poaching village on the Rimside Moor, the marital nonconfirmists believed as firmly as any puritan in the righteousness of their habits:

> The folk of Framlingham say that none but Whores and Blackguards Marry; Honest Folk take each other's words for it.[104]

Liberties with respect to the making of marriages seem to have gone hand in hand with stern condemnation of notorious seducers, loose women, and adulterers. Woking, for example, subjected the offenders to a particularly comprehensive form of rough music:

> The person who has been "rough-musiced" was practically boycotted, and I could give instances where persons once occupying positions of village importance never, after being rough musiced, were again able to hold up their heads. In more than one case the culprit was refused regular employment, and it was not unusual for shopkeepers and others to decline their business.[105]

In Ceiriog it was also noted that "after marriage, the morality is blameless."[106] Elsewhere, people living in "open cohabitation" did their utmost to act like a loving couple. Those who had to rely on the world as their witness were naturally most conventional in their behavior. Even the clergy admitted that they were "married in every sense but one" and "in God's sight man and wife."[107] We know so little about tally couples precisely because with the approval of family and community they were so successful in establishing their credentials.

VI

In addition to young persons who postponed or omitted church marriage, the other major constituency of common-law practice included those already married, who, separated from their spouses for one reason or another, wanted to remarry but had no access to legal divorce. In earlier generations they might have turned to the Fleet or another renegade facility to notarize a second marriage without fear of recognition and prosecution for bigamy. The Hardwicke Act ended all that and forced those who wished to remarry to find new ways of establishing their union for the world, if not the law, to know. The result was a set of secular divorce rites that, while they drew on the symbolism of an earlier period, were apparently unique to the eighteenth and nineteenth centuries. In Wales and the regions bordering it, it became established that "if a husband failed to maintain his wife, she might give him back his wedding ring, and then she would be free to marry again."[108] When a Welsh woman, whose husband was an inmate of the workhouse, wanted to separate from him, she "carried out the whole programme" by formally returning the ring in the presence of the entire workhouse.[109]

As we have already seen, reversing the besom ceremony was another means of self-divorce, though presumably valid only for those who had gone through a broomstick marriage in the first place.

Self-divorce was not done lightly, nor were witnesses likely to assent to the rite if a woman did not show good cause why she should be granted the status of a "grass widow." The beaten or deserted wife had the most public sympathy, but a proper "divorce" had to be very carefully managed.[110] "For a husband to free himself from his wife was a degree more difficult, as it would require some sort of consent on the part of the wife," noted Charlotte Burne.[111] Husbands were required by custom to obtain a verbal or written release from their wives. A Plymouth man who remarried when his first wife was still living said "that it is all right, as his first wife is remarried, and wrote a letter to give him leave to follow her example."[112] In Shropshire, Staffordshire, and parts of Westmoreland, the agreement was called being "leased." Of a couple who had spouses still living it was said "they are not married, they are only *leased* to one another." An old woman, testifying in a Staffordshire court in the 1880s, said "No, I'm not married, I'm *on a lease*. I suppose that's all the same." In the area, people excused a woman who had left her husband by saying that he "had leased her out."[113]

Previously married men and women did not feel entirely free to begin cohabitation until they had received formal release from their former spouse, had been separated for seven years, or knew that the old partner had begun cohabiting with someone else. The latter fact was frequently cited in bigamy trials and seems to have been popularly considered the final stage of a common-law divorce.[114] The rules of separation and divorce seem to have been relatively egalitarian. Either man or woman could begin the process and both had certain rights, which they had to consent to relinquish before the thing became final. Wives had to signify they no longer insisted on being maintained; husbands had to relinquish their right both to the woman's earnings and her obedience. When both sides kept their pledges nothing further was recorded. However, on occasion, when some party reneged, the case might end up in court. This happened in Birmingham in 1853. It seems that Elizabeth Capras had agreed sometime previously to "lease" her husband William to Emily Hickson. To put the new union on a firm footing the couple consulted Mr. Campbell, a Birmingham lawyer, who drew up a marriage agreement that, while not correct by canon law, he said would protect the new Mrs. Capras against the old if the latter "gave her any annoyance."[115] Apparently, this did not provide the necessary deterrence, for the first Mrs. Capras continued to bother the couple. William assaulted her and was brought into court, where the whole affair became public. In the course of the trial, the common-law agreement between William Capras and Emily Hickson was introduced as evidence:

> it is hereby mutually agreed upon, by and between said William Charles Capras and Emily Hickson, that they the said shall live and reside together during the remainder of their lives, and that they shall mutually exert

themselves by work and labour, and by following all their business pursuits, to the best of their abilities, skill, and understanding, and by advising and assisting each other, for their mutual benefit and advantage, and also to provide for themselves and each other the best supports and comforts of life which their means and income can afford.[116]

Normally, bigamy charges were brought only when the original spouse decided to make trouble. In this case there had been no second wedding so the charge was simple assault. No doubt many preferred to keep their union on a common-law basis to avoid the possibility of a bigamy conviction, which could bring several years of imprisonment, though juries were usually quite lenient.[117] Nevertheless, William Capras might have been better off if he had made a more formal "lease" with his former wife. William Sergeant made certain that he had a written release from Mary Osborne's first husband before he made her his wife in 1815:

[John Osborne] does agree to part with my wife, Mary Osborne and child, to William Sergeant, for the sum of one pound, consideration of giving up all claim whatever.[118]

The notion that something "done rite" was made legal was also evident in the words and actions of those who participated in what was the eighteenth and nineteenth centuries' most visible form of self-divorce, the so-called "wife sale." The precedent for it probably lies with the old rules of betrothal that permitted men to release themselves from a premarital contract by accepting a token sum of money from a rival suitor. The first recorded instance of an exchange of money for releasing a husband (as opposed to a fiancé) from the obligations of his marriage comes from Bilston, in the 1690s, when "John ye son of Nathan Whitehouse, of Tipton, sold his wife to Mr. Bracegirdle."[119] Not long afterward a man was presented in the Thame church court for cohabitation with another's wife. During the proceedings it came out that he had "bought her of[f] her husband at 2 1/4 pence the pound."[120] By the early eighteenth century references to wife sales were finding their way into the press. The *Annual Register* carried the following account in August 1733:

Three men, and three women, went to the Bell Inn in Edgbaston-street, Birmingham, and made the following entry in the toll book which is kept there:

Samuel Whitehouse, of the parish of Willenhall, in the county of Stafford, sold his wife, Mary Whitehouse, in the open market, to Thomas Griffiths, of Birmingham. Value, one guinea. To take her with all her faults.

Signed Samuel Whitehouse, Sarah Whitehouse

Voucher: T. Buckely, Birmingham.[121]

In 1760 Gloucestershire magistrates heard the case of a woman who had married in the 1740s. She and her husband did not take long to part by means of wife sale. Her new husband was a coal miner, Nicholas Read, who took her to Bath, where they were married "by one parson

21. This depiction of a wife sale appeared in broadside form in about 1832. The old husband holds the wife by a halter, while the new husband makes his "offer." The scene is a cattle market, with a good crowd in attendance. (Used with permission of British Library, Pressmark LR 271,A.2, Vol. 4, No. 290)

Crey, a lawless minister there." Later, when Read died, his wife became impoverished and applied to the court for support from her first husband, who was still living.[122] After the Hardwicke Act it would have been much more difficult for such a couple to make a second marriage. Those who wished to split up and remarry could still do so, but they would have second thoughts about going to a church where they were known. Many must have migrated to the cities, for there no one would have known or much cared about a former marriage. But in smaller places, where the population was not migratory, a second marriage was virtually impossible once the access to clandestine marriage had been closed in 1754. People who wished to certify that one union was ended and another begun had to find ways like the besom divorce to notarize their action. It was in these circumstances, mainly in small towns and rural communities, that the practice of wife sales, a public rite of divorce, came to enjoy such enormous popularity.

By the 1790s the practice had become so widespread that it was the subject of editorial comment. "As instances of the sale of wives have of late frequently occurred among the lower classes of people who consider such sale lawful, we think it right to inform that, by determination of the courts of law in a former reign, they were declared illegal and void, and considered (the light in which religion must view them) a mere pretense to sanction the crime of adultery."[123] The end of the Napoleonic Wars was also a particularly busy time:

> In the manufacturing districts in 1815 and 1816 hardly a market-day passed without such sales month after month. The authorities shut their eyes at

the time and people were confirmed in the perfect legality of the proceedings, as they had already been satisfied of its justice.[124]

A man was prosecuted in 1837, but this seems to have had no deterrent effect on George Hitchinson of Burntwood, Staffordshire, who brought his wife to the Walsall Market in November of the same year:

> They came into the market between ten and eleven o'clock in the morning, the woman being led by a halter, which was fastened round her neck and the middle of her body. In a few minutes after their arrival she was sold to a man of the name of Thomas Snape, a nailer, also from Burntwood. There were not many people in the market at the time. The purchase money was 2s 6d, and all the parties seemed satisfied with the bargain. The husband was glad to get rid of his frail rib, who, it seems had been living with Snape three years, at any time erroneously imagining that because he had brought her through a turnpike gate in a halter, and had publicly sold her in the market before witnesses, that he is thereby freed from all responsibility and liability with regard to her future maintenance and support.[125]

The transaction between the Hitchinsons and Thomas Snape appears to have been typical. The "sale" served to notarize what had already been arranged beforehand. Earlier, at Chesterfield, Cambridgeshire, a stocking weaver

> being desirous of getting rid of his wife, and she, equally as willing to leave him, he made a proposal of selling her. . . . A purchaser being accordingly found (with the consent of all parties) a writing was drawn up, and the husband agreed for the sum of £15 (guineas) to resign all right and pretensions to his wife whatever; but to make the above transaction (as the parties supposed) more firm and valid, she was formally delivered up by the husband to the purchaser, on Wednesday morning, with a halter about her neck, in the public market place, the husband saying on delivery, he did it as his act and deed, and the purchaser replying he received her as such. All went away pleased.[126]

Eighty years later, in nearby Oakington, a man refused to deliver his wife when the new husband did not pay him a promised ten pounds. The "sale" never did take place because the wife became impatient and made it known that she would go to the new husband, "as she liked him the best, and he [the old husband] might help himself how he could, and no more of this nonsense. So she packed up her cloathes, and followed her purchaser to his house, whither she was escorted by a large train of boys beating the kettles."[127]

Enormous care was taken "carrying out the formula which custom had sanctioned as to give a sort of legal force to the proceedings."[128] In 1784 a Bristol man who had been away for several years returned to find his wife had taken up with a chimney sweep. They agreed to "a legal transfer by purchase," but took the precaution of consulting a lawyer. It was he who "advised the parties, as a mutual security, to have the woman taken by her husband, with a halter round her neck, to a public market, and there exposed for sale."[129] The first step was to give notice. Often a cryer was hired, announcing the appropriate market day and exact time. A Devonshire stonecutter satisfied the same requirement by putting up a sign that read:

NOTICE

This here be to hindform the publick as how James Cole be disposed to sell his wife by Auction. Her be a decent, cleanly woman, and be of age twenty-five years. The sale be to take place in the New Inn, Thursday next at seven o'clock.[130]

Next, a halter and rope were procured, new ones if possible. On the appointed day, the wife would be outfitted and led from her old home to the market, often several miles distance. Care was taken to pass through the toll barrier and receive a receipt for the charges. "In some instances the husband had been known to drive the unfortunate wife through three toll-gates and pay toll at each instance, to make the proceedings more binding."[131] Arriving at the announced time, the couple would expect a large crowd to be waiting and an auction table or overturned barrel to be supplied. The husband mounted this and began to recount the wife's virtues and faults, a process that involved much repartee with the boisterous crowd. In early-nineteenth-century Wednesbury, Moses Maggs, a collier known locally as "Rough Moey," put on a memorable performance:

Now, my lads, roll up, and bid spirited. It's all right, accordin' to law. I brought her through the turn-pike, and paid the man the toll for her. I brought her wi' a halter, and had her cried; so everythin's right accordin' to law, and there's nothin' to pay. Come on wi' yer bids, and if yer gies me a good price for the ooman, I'll gie yer the young kid in the bargain. Now, gentlemin, who bids? Goin', gooin', gooin'!![132]

The bidding itself was part of the ritual, done entirely in fun, for the taker had been prearranged. At a Hereford sale the bidding ended at one shilling, with the buyer then conducting his own marriage ceremony on the spot:

Be you willing, Missus, to have me and take me for better,
for worse?
I be willing
And be you willing to seel her for what I bid, Maister?
I be, and will give you the rope into the bargain.[133]

According to Lawley, "in nineteen cases out of twenty the purchaser was a former lover, or a secret paramour, whose readiness to relieve the husband of his wife was known to him."[134] The price was in reality "luck money," something always given when a bargain was struck, usually no more than a few shillings, which, once it had been turned over, was spent on drinks at the local inn. Any more substantial exchange of goods or money had been agreed and acted upon ahead of time.[135] The "sale" itself was only a form of notarization, concluded under conditions of maximum publicity:

> The end of the halter was transferred from the husband's to the purchaser's hand, the paper drawn up by a "learned clerk" making the transfer duly signed, the halter was duly removed, and then the purchase money was spent in spirits and beer, the party drinking together as good humordly as though no such thing as divorce had ever been heard of.[136]

All this was meant to symbolize the transference of the husband's responsibility. The woman's part was, as noted earlier, somewhat simpler. Since it was assumed that she had no responsibility for things of a material nature, but only the obligation to obey, the simple act of taking off her wedding ring, a rite that sometimes accompanied a wife sale, was sufficient.[137] In addition, the woman sometimes signed the separation agreement. Papers, obtained either at the toll or drawn up at the alehouse afterward, were treated by the women involved as their "lease." One such, from Hereford, read: "We agree to part wholly and solely for life, and not trouble one another for life."[138] Challenged to prove she was married, a Yorkshire woman who called herself Mrs. Dunn admitted in court in 1881 that "Yes, I was married to another man, but he sold me to Dunn for twenty-five shillings . . . and I have it to show in black and white, with a receipt stamp on it, as I did not want people to say I was living in adultery."[139]

The final step was for the new husband to lead the woman home in halter, only removing it once they had crossed the threshold to their new life together. This was what Henry Frise did when he "purchased" his wife at Oakehampton, Devon. He "led her home with him a distance of twelve miles, by the halter, he holding it in his hand, she placidly, contentedly wearing the loop about her neck. The report Henry Frise was leading home his half-crown bride preceded the arrival of the couple, and when they entered the village all the inhabitants turned out to see the spectacle." The news had also reached the Squire and parson, both Baring-Goulds, who called Frise on the carpet:

> Henry Frise maintained that Anne was his legitimate wife, for he had not only bought her in the market, but had led her home, with the halter in his hand, and he'd take his Bible oath that he never took the halter off her till she had crossed his doorstep and he had shut the door.

> The parson took down the Bible, the squire opened Burns' *Justice of the Peace*, and strove to convince Henry that his conduct was warranted by neither Scripture nor the law of the land. "I don't care," he said, "her's my wife, as sure as if she was spliced at the altar, for and because I paid half a crown, and I never took off the halter till her was in my house; lor' bless your honours, you may ask any one if that ain't marriage, good, sound, and Christian, and everyone will tell you it is.[140]

There was also no doubt in the mind of a Yorkshire laborer who was contemplating a similar transaction in 1860. He said calmly that "I've thought of it, and I'm right sure I can buy her, by law." When told that a gentleman had declared the contrary, he showed some irritation: "Ah, your master's not seen much law lately; maybe he's never read the new Divorce Act [of 1857]!" Thinking that this legislation was meant to provide easier access to divorce for the poor as well as the rich, he followed through on his original intention.[141]

It seems clear that divorce by "wife sale" or other less conspicuous means was supposed to take place only under certain well-defined conditions. The marriage itself had to have broken down to the point that both parties acknowledged it was hopeless to continue. In the case of one Furness couple, the match had been doomed to failure, forced on the woman by her parents. Only a few weeks after the wedding, Mrs. Stable, "preferring Huddleston, a maker of Slate Pencils in Scaleback . . . she and Huddleston ran off to Whitehaven." The husband found them there "but she was unwilling to return with him Home; so after taking Advice on the Subject Stable bought a Halter which he put around the Neck of his Wife and led her into the Marketplace and exposed her to Sale, where she was purchased by Huddleston, the [price] being something less than one shilling."[142] In other cases the sale was simply ratifying a break already known to the community. Moses Maggs was twice the age of his wife Sal, a former pit-brow lass. He had convinced her with a "new gown and other articles of dress, with a fortnight's treat, to marry him." When she turned her affections to a younger man, he had beaten her and she had retaliated in kind when he was drunk enough to be defenseless. At their parting, the crowd, and particularly the women present, gave her and her lover great support and sympathy, urging Maggs to get on with it. "The bargain being thus concluded, the halter was placed in the young man's hand, and the young woman received the congratulations of the numerous dingy matrons."[143]

Not every wife agreed to be divorced, however, and when there was no consent the "sale" was voided. A North Bovey man made a "private agreement" to transfer his wife in 1868. "When he returned home with the purchaser, the woman repudiated the transaction, and, taking her two children with her, she went off at once to Exeter, and only came back to attend her husband's funeral."[144] At Bewcastle, Cumberland, in 1810 another woman was remembered for having refused to be divorced on her husband's terms. She managed "to get her husband pressed for service with the Royal Navy and soon he found himself on board a frigate for distant waters. Instead of selling his wife, she sold him."[145]

The enormous publicity attending this form of divorce suggests that the consent of the community was highly desirable, if not actually required. There were instances where crowds intervened to thwart a sale.[146] And the Yorkshire laborer who had so confidently arranged to sell his wife in 1860 found himself burnt in effigy on the village green.[147] On the other hand, the inhabitants of Oakington were ready to resort to tin kettles when an expected sale did not transpire.[148] There is evidence that in the late eighteenth and early nineteenth centuries local authorities tolerated and even instigated divorces where it was in the rate payers interest to do so.[149] In 1819 the Parish of Spalding, Lincolnshire, argued that John Forman, who held a settlement in Spalding, had sold his wife Prudence seventeen years before to a Skirbeck man by the name of Joseph Holmes and thus it had no responsibility for the three children subsequently born to Prudence. Skirbeck's attorney countered that "the sale of the wife by the husband was a scandalous action, detrimental to the morals of society" and won the case.[150] About the same time, Sussex parish officers were actually conniving with a man to sell his wife. The wife of Henry Cook, a resident of Effingham, had become a burden on the workhouse there. He agreed to have the master of the workhouse take her to Croyden Market, where she was "sold" to a Dorking man by the name of John Earl. The Effingham officials were so delighted to be rid of Mrs. Cook that they gave the couple a leg of mutton for a wedding feast. After several years, and numerous children, the marriage broke up and Earl deserted. The former Mrs. Cook was returned by Dorking Parish to Effingham, whose officials took the original husband to court to get him to support his former wife. The judge ruled against them.[151]

Although parish officials no longer conspired to sell wives later in the nineteenth century, the notion that the wife sale constituted a just and legal termination of mutual obligations remained deeply rooted in popular consciousness. As late as 1881 the *Leeds Mercury* reported a Sheffield case in which a man refused to pay his "former" wife's medical bills on the grounds they had been divorced by sale.[152] Women divorced in this way also asserted their rights. A well-dressed woman came to the Exeter police court in 1872 to try to get a man to maintain what she said were his children. She was not ashamed to argue that when they had separated by wife sale he had agreed to keep the two children. "Since, however, he had followed her about and annoyed her in various ways, and now he turned the children out of doors, and told her to keep the lot." The court thought her conduct disgraceful and told her she must keep the children as part of her duties as a wife.[153]

Clearly, magistrates were no longer willing to listen to arguments based on custom. By the 1860s and 1870s most communities were no longer happy about having their markets and toll houses used for what were now regarded by both the police and the respectable public as a disgrace. The Plymouth constables intervened to halt a sale as early as the 1820s; in 1837 a Yorkshire man was prosecuted, even though local opinion thought he was acting within his rights.[154] The participants in a sale at Spilsby, Lincolnshire, in 1848 were arrested. The woman was discharged, but the men were brought to trial and received a strong rebuke.[155] The rites survived longest in those same small relatively homogeneous communities of miners, cottage workers, and smallholders where common-law marriage also flourished. Both common-law marriage and divorce became popular in the mid-eighteenth century; both were in eclipse a century later, when the economic, social, and legal circumstances that had accounted for their rise began to disappear. Accounts of wife sale suggest a plebeian constituency of people below the rank of respectable artisans but above that of wholly pauperized workers. Weavers, miners, smiths, quarrymen, watermen, navvies, and semi-skilled workers are mentioned far more often than either small farmers or farm laborers. Although a few sales involving smallholders have come to light, the rite itself was not meant to deal with marriages in which property was involved. Nor was it particularly attractive to those working people who, in migrating to the large cities, had ceased to be part of communities where name and reputation still counted. Wife sales were much less frequent in large cities, where people could separate and remarry without anyone knowing or caring. In plebeian communities of a smaller scale, where a "public" had to be satisfied, ritual forms of marriage and divorce were still in some sense obligatory.

Occasionally, such as after the Napoleonic Wars, the practice could become almost epidemic. Returning soldiers and sailors found their wives had taken up with other men out of necessity. Rather than break up these arrangements and accept the burden of children who were not their own, they were willing to part amicably by ritual auction.[156] They acted like the convicted embezzler who, having been in jail for five years, was not surprised to find his wife living with another man. He inquired whether she wished to continue that way and, when she said yes, he undertook to confirm the new relationship by selling her for a quart of beer.[157] For the most part, however, the public rites of self-divorce were occasioned by much less dramatic circumstances. Like common-law marriage, they were a normal part of the regulation of marriage among a class of people who, while they possessed little in the way of property, wished to keep their legal and social relations free of embarrassing or burdensome complications. Just as common-law marriage served to sustain an honest reputation and certify mutual obligations, so too did the various rites of divorce.

Before the mid-eighteenth century, separations (both legal and informal) were the only way open to ordinary people of terminating a violent or bankrupt household. Popular opinion was on the side of the cruelly abused wife or cuckolded husband not so much because people were concerned with personal relationships, but because an essential social and economic institution was in danger. Now the household as such was pushed to the background—but a sense of social responsibility remained. Most wife sales took place when the original partnership had broken down, and the woman has already formed a relationship with another man.[158] The focus of the rite was the couple, but it is clear that an individual's right to divorce was conditioned by family and communal considerations. Like common-law marriage, self-divorce reflected not the breakdown of a sense of social obligation, but its endurance. We see here not the triumph of individualism, but the recognition of collective responsibilities.

VII

Although there is no way the actual extent of either common-law marriage or divorce can be measured, studies of rural areas have found that as many as one in seven couples may have been "living tally" at any given time. In Gloucestershire ten percent of marriages known to have existed cannot be located anywhere in the official record.[159] While many may have married out of the county, Anthea Newman's careful reconstitution of the parish of Ash-next-Sandwich in Kent showed that at least fifteen percent of the couples living there in the period from 1750 to 1834 were not legally married.[160] We have seen that the proportions in parts of Lancashire and North Wales were even higher, and, thus, it would not be exaggeration to suggest that as much as a fifth of the population may, at one time or another in their lives, lived in an illicit relationship, most no doubt as a prelude to legal marriage, but also some as a substitute for it.[161]

Resistance to the marriage laws had been building throughout the late eighteenth and early nineteenth centuries, but a public movement for reform did not command national attention until the 1830s. In May 1834 Charles Bradley stood at the end of the regular service of the Laurence Street Chapel in Birmingham to read out the following:

> Before this congregation, I, Charles Bradley, jun, give you, Emma Harris, this ring to wear as a memorial of our marriage, and this written pledge stamped with the impressions of the United Rights of Man and Woman, declaring I will be your faithful husband from this time forward.

Once Emma Harris had made an identical vow, another couple went through the same ceremony, "after which the papers were signed by several witnesses, and thus the marriage contract was made without the intervention of either priest or clerk."[162] Their actions were hailed by the radical as well as the dissenting press as a major act of civil disobedience in a campaign that was finally gaining headway in the wake of other reforms.[163] Legalization of chapel and civil marriage would be achieved just two years later, but the struggle was not without its martyrs. The fate of two sisters sentenced by an ecclesiastical court in 1787 to twelve years in prison for defying the marriage laws was still remembered in Nottingham.[164]

Established dissent reaped the benefits of the 1836 Marriage Act, but it appears that the burden of the struggle had been carried by the more marginal nonconformist sects. The Laurence Street Chapel was itself associated with the Southcottians and would later be a center for socialist activity. It was the more plebeian sects that had consistently defied the law, reviving the sexual radicalism of the 1640s and 1650s, whose traditions had run underground for much of the eighteenth century, cropping up occasionally in Methodist ranks, but finding more visible expression in a variety of millenarian movements, ranging from the highly ascetic Shakers to the polygamist Mormons.

Both asceticism and antinomianism reflected the ambivalence toward conventional matrimony felt by that very large part of the population experiencing the first stages of industrialization and urbanization. Many, especially women, no longer had reason to seek material comfort or social satisfaction in the forms of patriarchal relations mandated by the official marriage discipline. This ambivalence was reflected even in Methodism, whose ascetic tendency had considerable difficulty subduing the sexual radicalism of its early adherents. John Wesley, like George Fox before him, preferred spiritual to carnal relations with the opposite sex. He married very late and seems to have found no great comfort in marriage.[165] The founders of several of the major eighteenth-century millenialist movements also found the flesh a source of evil and disorder.

There was a strong ascetic element among the "simple and low in the world" who were attracted to the Swedenborgian movement. It may have had a strong influence on the Bolton "Shaking" Quakers, who in the 1750s were joined by a young woman, Ann Lee, who was soon to become their spiritual leader.[166] Lee, who was of plebeian background, had experienced not only the loss of her mother, but an unhappy marriage and tragic motherhood (all four of her children died in infancy) when it was revealed to her that "marriage of the flesh is a covenant with death and an agreement with Hell." While she continued to live with her husband, she henceforth regarded herself as "married to the Lord Jesus Christ. He is my head and my husband, and I have no other."[167] The Shaker movement which she founded and relocated to America in the 1770s constituted an extended holy family, Mother Ann sharing with Christ the position of supreme authority. Once established as settled communities, the Shakers practiced strict celibacy, depending entirely on external recruitment to reproduce themselves. From the late eighteenth throughout much of the nineteenth centuries, they were highly successful in attracting those who rejected holy matrimony. As John Harrison has noted, "membership in a Shaker family was likely to appeal to the uncompetitive, unadventurous, or socially inadequate elements of the population. Women in particular—single, widowed or unhappily married—were likely to find a refuge in Shakerism."[168]

A similar hostility to conventional marriage pervaded the teachings of the most important female prophet of the 1790s, Johanna Southcott. She too had lost her mother and had seen a great aunt to whom she was very devoted die of a broken heart resulting from a forbidden love match. The daughter of a quite ordinary Devonshire farmer, and handy in dairy and field, Johanna had had more than her share of marriage offers, but had rejected all in favor of spiritual union in which Christ became her dream lover:

> She felt herself laying as if were in heaven, in the hand of the Lord, and was afraid to move, fearing he would remove his heavenly hand, which she felt as perfect as ever woman felt the hand of her husband.[169]

Southcott subsequently declared herself the second Eve, determined that this time woman should redeem the world through a successful confrontation with the temptations of the flesh. Ultimately, she would fantasize herself pregnant with Shiloh, whose birth was confidently predicted for the autumn of 1814. In order to make him legitimate, she consented to go through a private marriage ceremony with one of her disciples. All the preparations were in vain, however, for Johanna, age sixty-four at the time, died that December. An autopsy found no pregnancy, though her followers continued to believe that a birth had occurred and Shiloh had risen directly to heaven.[170] During the next few years Southcottians fervently prepared themselves for his coming. Hundreds of female faithful allowed themselves to be "married" to the Lord following Johanna's example.[171]

Shakers and Southcottians bear a striking resemblance to certain seventeenth-century sects. Their holy fellowship provided them with the same spiritual and material support, and lifted from their shoulders all the worries and burdens of marriage. For women there was the additional advantage of being relieved of the terrors of maternity. The liberty and equality that Quaker women had found in the Society of Friends Shaker females now found in Mother Ann Lee's earthly version of the holy family. Recruits to Southcottianism were also attracted by a similar religious feminism, which elevated the status of women spiritually as well as materially.

However, the same unfortunate experiences with marriage that moved many plebeian men and women to celibacy also propelled others in search of new forms of heterosexuality that promised to overcome the contradictions of the nuclear family. After separating from her potter husband in 1782, Luckie Buchan, a Banff woman, declared herself "Friend Mother," the third person of the Godhead. Having predicted the second coming of Christ, whom she regarded as her brother, she gathered around herself a small band of followers, who, taking as their example the early apostles, "had all things in common," including marriage. Mrs. Buchan took up with a married man, Hugh White; all the married women reverted to their maiden names; and the resulting children were brought up by the community. Robert Burns, who was personally acquainted with the Buchanites, reported that "they lodge & lye all together, & hold likewise a community of women, as it is another of their tenents that they can commit no moral sin." According to their leader, the millenium made obsolete the laws of church and state, or what she called "carnal marriage":

> Where the Holy Spirit of God occupies all the person, and reigns throughout the flesh, it matters not much whether they marry or not.[172]

The antinomian tradition found further expression in several northern plebeian sects, the most important of which were the Christian Israelites, founded by a Bradford woolcomber, John Wroe, in the 1820s. Inheritors of the Southcottian tradition in the Yorkshire region, the Wroeites demonstrated the ambivalence toward heterosexuality that was so evident during this period. Their leader seems to have thought himself above sin. Wroe adopted the role of an Old Testament prophet, whose mission was to purify the world. He advocated circumcision, prohibited tobacco and spirits, and taught sexual moderation. The wayward were punished physically by the women of the sect, who were commanded to beat the men with one hand while holding the male genitals with the other.[173] Wroe surrounded himself with "Virgins," who were devoted to him carnally as well as spiritually. His Old Testament patriarchy was not unlike that which was to be instituted by John Smith, whose Mormon missionaries were later to recruit a number of Wroe's former followers. In their version of holy polygamy, the Mormons offered a solution to those who found conventional marriage and the nuclear family unworkable. Their strongest appeal was in the proto-industrial districts and in London, where men and women of plebeian occupation were prominent among the British converts.[174]

The sexual radicalism of the plebeian sects was paralleled by, and often indistinguishable from, the more secular libertarian currents of eighteenth-century rationalism. Tom Paine's Quaker background had influenced his anticlericalism and probably his views on marriage, which were very egalitarian. Just before leaving for America in 1774, he had formally separated from his wife, returning to her the property that she had brought to the marriage. Later he was to praise the fact the American Indian marriage had "no other ceremony than mutual affection, and last no longer than they bestow mutual affection."[175] Paine, like Gerrard Winstanley, regarded marriage as a fundamental right and proposed in Part II of his *Rights of Man* that marriage allowances and maternity benefits be provided to enable everyone to enjoy matrimony.[176] William Blake also hoped to see the day when "A Religion of Chastity, forming a Commerce to sell Loves" would be overthrown; and Shelley advocated full freedom to marry and divorce, arguing that "love withers under constraint."[177] Similar beliefs were shared by other freethinkers like William Godwin, Robert Burns, Mary Wollstonecraft, Thomas Spence, Richard Carlile, and Elizabeth Sharples. The latter two formed a free union consistent with their belief in sexual equality. "I do not like the doctrine of women keeping at home, and minding the house and family," Carlile wrote in 1832, "It is as much the proper business of the man as the woman's, and the woman who is confined is not the proper companion of the public useful man."[178] Thomas Spence, who had asked "what signifies Reforms of Government or Redress of Public Grievances, if people cannot have their domestic grievances redressed?," advocated making divorce accessible to ordinary folk, who he knew had long chaffed under the existing system:

> This subject is so feelingly understood in this country, that it is supposed the Chains of Hymen would be among the first that would be broken . . . in case of a Revolution, and the family business of life turned over to Cupid, who though he may be a little whimsical, is not so stern a jailor-like Deity.[179]

Wollstonecraft, who had repeatedly defied the laws of Hymen herself, did not at all approve of turning things over to the whimsy of Cupid, and instead advocated putting marriage on a rational basis that would secure women against being treated as the toys of men. A republican age demanded a republican conjugality. "The *divine right* of husbands, like the divine right of kings, may, it is hoped, in this enlighted age, be contested without danger."[180] Her illegitimate child by Imlay and her common-law arrangement with Godwin made her a target of the wrath of the evangelical movement. "A woman who had broken through all religious restraints, will commonly be found ripe for every species of licentious indecorum," howled her detractors, who made no effort to distinguish between the libertarian and the libertine.[181]

Most of the rationalists had great difficulty getting beyond the point Winstanley had reached in the seventeenth century. Their ideal society was composed of petty producers, happy nuclear families, each with sufficient property to live free and independent lives. Godwin, Shelley, and most of the radical intellectuals were unaware of the needs of the propertyless proletariat; and even Mary Wollstonecraft's feminism was not adequate enough to understand the circumstances of plebeian women.[182] Paine and Spence were aware that the poor could not even enter matrimony without some material assistance, but they could see no reason why, if assisted with marriage portions and fees, the poor could not attain conjugal happiness. There was a residue of puritanism and not a little patriarchalism among male radicals, who regarded the nuclear family as the basis of the social and political order. Their fear of libertinism was forcefully expressed during the Queen Caroline affair; and the defense of the family remained a constant theme of male radical thought throughout the early nineteenth century.[183]

The freethinkers were the tribunes of that part of the plebeian class who could still rely on the family economy for their well-being. Those who had some hope of establishing a small business or farm remained firm advocates of conjugal love and the nuclear family, though, as we have seen, they were ready to bend the rules of matrimony to achieve that end. These plebeians, who could no longer expect to survive on the basis of the nuclear family and conjugal affections alone, had already begun to explore alternatives, however. When eighteenth-century religious and secular radicalism faltered, the torch was passed to a new

socialist-feminist movement, whose views on marriage were more responsive to the realities of nineteenth-century proletarian existence.

VIII

The socialist-feminist movement that emerged in the 1820s was convinced that the future lay not in perfecting the nuclear family but in
replacing it with a broader definition of love and justice. Even the most
perfectly liberated love match could not overcome the contradictions
that property introduced into the heterosexual relationship. The husband's possession of the wife's property, earnings, and even her children, mandated by law, nullified all true companionship, even that
founded on the most passionate love. It automatically made the male
senior partner and produced that "narrow selfishness" that Clarissa
Harlowe had cried out against a century earlier. It was the myth of
companionate marriage that William Thompson challenged in his *Appeal
of One-Half the Human Race, Women, against the Pretension of the Other Half,
Men* in 1825:

> Each man yokes a woman to his establishment, and calls it a *contract.* . . .
> Audacious falsehood! Contract! Where are any of the attributes of contracts,
> of equal and just contracts, to be found in this transaction? . . . Have women
> been consulted as to the terms of this pretended contract? . . . Men enacted,
> that is to say, *willed* the terms, let women like them or not; man to be the
> owner, master, and ruler of every thing, even to the minutest action, and
> most trifling article of property brought into the common stock by the
> woman; woman to be the moveable property, and ever-obedient servant,
> to the bidding of man.[184]

Thompson's ideas owed much to the inspiration of Robert Owen, who
considered the nuclear family, religion, and private property to be the
main obstacles to human happiness. To Owen, legal marriage was an
"artificial union of sexes, as devised by the priesthood, requiring single-
family arrangements and generating single-family interests."[185] The nuclear family reproduced class divisions and generated the selfish individualism that to Owen and other early socialists were the curse of the
world:

> The children within these dens of selfishness and hypocrisy are taught to
> consider their own individual family their own world, and that it is the
> duty and interest of all within this little orb to do whatever they can to
> promote the advantages of all the legitimate members of it. With these
> persons it is *my* house, *my* wife, *my* estate, *my* children, or *my* husband;
> *our* estate; and *our* children . . . *our* house and property. . . . No arrangement
> could be better calculated to produce division and disunion in society.[186]

Beginning with his American New Harmony experiment in the 1820s,
Owen began to devise ways to overcome affective individualism, so
that, as one of his followers put it, "the instinct of the family would,

for the first time in human history, become productive of individual felicity and public benefit."[187] He shared with the rationalist and the romantic radicals of the 1790s their abhorrence of involuntary chastity and celibacy, and regarded sexual attraction one of the primary social bonds. His plan for the "enlargement of the home" included projects for collective housekeeping and childrearing. Property was to be shared equally, and women were to have access to the education and employment that would finally allow them to be full citizens. William Thompson wrote to Anna Wheeler in 1825 of "a better state of society, where the principle of benevolence shall supersede that of fear; where restless and anxious individual competition shall give place to mutual co-operation and joint possession; where individuals, in large numbers male and female, forming voluntary associations, shall become the mutual guarantee to each other for the supply of all useful wants."[188]

The home was to be socialized, brought into the realm of the public, to avoid the creation of invidious distinctions of age, gender, or class. "Our females are not considered by the males . . . as their inferiors . . . mere creatures made for their sexual pleasure and indulgence; but . . . as their equals, confidential companions . . . in their moral and intellectual improvements and enjoyment" wrote another Owenite.[189] The wedding itself was to be a fully public, collectivized event, acknowledging the responsibility of the community as well as that of the individuals. The marriage ceremony Owen devised bore a striking resemblance not only to Quaker ritual but to secular plebeian practice, much like the besom wedding. The couple were required to make their intentions known to the community at least three months before final vows. During the interval sexual intimacy was permitted; and there was no priest at the wedding. Divorce was allowed, but never without mutual consent and prior publicity. It could not take place until the marriage had endured at least twelve months and, once the couple had declared their intent to separate, they were to wait another six months to give the community time to deliberate and, if possible, to effect a reconciliation.[190]

Owenite women were particularly insistent on these formalities and were instrumental in seeing to it that not only marriage but motherhood was socialized, with the community sharing in the responsibility for childrearing. Reproduction itself was collectivized; and, while prepared to support unwed parenthood, socialists like William Thompson believed that "no unmarried mother could add a child to the infants of the schools without the knowledge of the whole community, nor of course without being liable to the influence of the public opinion of the whole community." Implied was the use of some form of birth control— a revolutionary idea that never did gain universal acceptance among the early socialists, in part because it smacked of a hated Malthusianism.[191]

Much of Owen's ideal of social marriage was realized in the various Owenite communities that proliferated in Britain during the 1830s and 1840s. At Queenswood and Orbiston there were attempts at collective housekeeping, but it was at Menea Fen, where the leader William Hodson lived in free union with his dead wife's sister, that the most radical implications of plebeian collectivism were realized. Many of the recruits supported Hodson's abolition of private property and legal marriage. When challenged, the community's newspaper remained defiant: "As to being very lax on the subject of marriage, we have the pleasure to . . . plead guilty."[192] Owenites living outside the established communes also experimented with a variety of ménage. Four cloth workers set up a house together in Failsworth; and other socialists advertised for like-minded persons, regardless of sex, to join them in collective house-keeping.[193] When one man, describing himself as a middle-aged father of two adult children, advertised in the socialist press for a wife of similar age who could bring 50 pounds a year to the union, the editors felt impelled to comment:

> Some may think it unsocial to make a money bargain of a match; but it is done upon the true principles of liberty and equality. He wants his partner to be independent of himself that she may be "free." There are only three conditions: forty years, fifty pounds, and womanhood; virginity, we suppose, is not necessary—no Socialist could insist on it.[194]

IX

It was the female socialists who were most keen on the full realization of collective housekeeping and childrearing. They were the ones who insisted that the conditions of equality be laid down before any changes in the marriage discipline were initiated. "Let not the change be attempted at the expense of women's tears, of women's sorrow" one pleaded.[195] Frances Morrison insisted that the present society was not ready for total freedom. Margaret Chappelsmith agreed that love unions would have to wait until socialism had achieved a material and social basis for equality, and even then sexuality would have to be regulated by "public opinion."[196] A single needlewoman wrote to the *New Moral World* of the necessity of a firmer social foundation for marriage:

> I am no man-hater—no enemy of matrimony—and far from me is removed any desire to deprecate a tie which if contracted wisely and virtuously must have beneficial influence: but I have the fullest conviction that love with men rarely exists as a sentiment, and with women, as seldom sinks to a passion.[197]

Socialist women were more insistent than their male comrades on creating rites of marriage that would provide support beyond that which the couple themselves could afford. Like the plebeian brides who insisted on a "public bridal" as the social and material basis of their marriages, Margaret Chappelsmith knew the values of a big wedding and therefore urged that both marriage and divorce be performed publicly because "under such circumstance, infidelity and jealousy are not likely to arise."[198] For similar reasons, Owenite women remained skeptical of birth control and insisted on the socialization of childrearing. Without it, noted Frances Morrison, women would never feel free to divorce.[199]

Under these pressures, Owen himself began to retreat from his early libertarian positions. While still advocating divorce reform, the Owenite convention of 1840 ruled out further disobedience to the existing marriage law, pending the arrival of the New Moral World. They began registering their Halls of Science and branch meeting places as locations where marriages could be performed under the Marriage Act of 1836. The Laurence Street Chapel was one such place, the Carpenter's Hall in Manchester another.[200] The vows were not very different from those of the dissenters and middle-class radicals.[201] The real point of departure was the publicity of the ceremony and the collective celebration that followed. Weddings were normally scheduled for a Sunday morning meeting when the largest attendance could be expected. Choirs sang, congratulations were extended, and "an excellent breakfast was provided."[202] Apart from the absence of drink, there was nothing sober about the socialist version of the big wedding. "Make a new ceremonial for yourselves—a rival ceremonial—which shall win the people to your side." James Morrison had counseled, "Theirs was the tyrant's ceremony—let yours be the people's."[203] In carrying out that project, socialists drew heavily on the traditions of the public bridal with its emphasis on mutual support beyond the conjugal pair.

Women were very active in creating the socialist version of the big wedding, and one suspects that it was they who insisted that the Owenite version of divorce also take a public form. Although explicitly rejecting the patriarchal elements of the wife sale, socialist divorce rites bore a striking resemblance to the plebeian "leases" described earlier. When Amelia and James Vaughan separated in 1842 so that Amelia could join her lover William Stanbury, the couple drew up an agreement that was witnessed by their fellow members of the Communist Church of Cheltenham:

> This is to certify that I, James Vaughan, and I, Amelia Vaughan, do mutually and peaceably propose, consent, and agree to separate and live apart; and especially I, James Vaughan, hereby do agree that Amelia Vaughan, my wife, may live where she likes and with whom she pleases, so long as she does not contract any debt, or cause any debt to be contracted, or trouble James Vaughan, her husband, or refuse to give up her son George when required after two years of age; and I, James Vaughan, do agree and consent that the said Amelia Vaughan, should be as free, as regards the disposal of her person and property (should she hereafter possess any) as though she had never been married.[204]

However, socialist men were less enthusiastic about the full implementation of the new heterosexuality. They held a narrower view of family responsibilities. William Lovett was typical of those who found Robert Owen's ideas on marriage to be too radical. He declared that if the full program were carried through he could "never consent to it."[205] As with the plebeian practices which were its prototypes, the new marriage discipline stirred not only class but gender antagonism. The old patriarchalism did not die easily, even among those proletarian males that in the late eighteenth and early nineteenth centuries had been most sexually nonconformist; and by the 1850s even the most radical elements were abandoning their public opposition to the nuclear family and the monogamous marriage.[206] The combined forces of economic, social, and political change had begun to alter the conditions of working-class life in such a way that the alternatives to legal matrimony no longer seemed feasible or attractive. Almost a century of sexual nonconformity was ending; a new, more conservative period was about to begin.

PART III

The Era of Mandatory Marriage, 1850–1960

CHAPTER 8

∽↶

Better a Bad Husband Than No Husband at All: The Compulsion to Marry, 1850–1914

By the mid-nineteenth century there were sure signs that Britain's second great wave of sexual nonconformity was receding. The mid-Victorian period saw a mass return to legal marriage, albeit in ways consistent with the secular culture of an advanced industrial society. Common-law marriage and divorce retreated, holding out in the poorest neighborhoods, but no longer publicized. In Salford, "livin' tally" or "over t' brush" was tolerated as something better than unwed motherhood, but distinctly inferior to regular marriage.[1] When it came to a matter of who was better than whom in the back streets of Lancashire or South Wales, the issue was now settled by a woman producing a "clean" rent book or, better yet, a marriage certificate:

> When I have a quarrel with the woman next door, and she begins to call me names I just ask her to come to my house and see what she hasn't got though she lives with a man.[2]

The advance of "domestic republicanism" had been halted as early as the 1840s. Illegitimacy ratios were beginning to decline by that time and would not again reach early-nineteenth-century levels until the 1960s.[3] Premarital pregnancy was slower to recede, but it too would eventually retreat. We will never know the exact figures on common-law marriage, but its eclipse seems to have begun at mid-century. Besom weddings disappeared from the Ceiriog sometime in the 1840s, and the people of Culcheth returned to conventional marriage during the same decade. Simultaneously, London couples who had previously defied the law were accepting the assistance of the church in returning to marital conformity. When City Missionaries approached known tally couples, they found that the women in particular were most receptive to the idea of legal marriage.[4]

Irregular marriage persisted in some of the boom areas of mining and railway construction as late as the 1880s, but everywhere else there was a pronounced tendency for couples to return to legal matrimony. When Charles Booth investigated the marital habits of the London East End in the 1890s, he found that even among the poorest inhabitants "young men and women court and keep company and marry in a proper and orderly manner. If there are slips occasionally they are felt a serious disgrace and hidden up."[5] The only element of the old sexual nonconformity to persist in a major way was self-divorce. Wife sale ceased to exist, but, for the great mass of the population who could not afford an expensive civil divorce, more informal procedures remained popular. Booth found that most of those living tally in London were older, formerly married persons: "More license is granted by public opinion to the evasion of the laws of marriage by those who have found it a failure, than is allowed to those whose relations to each other have not yet assumed a permanent form."[6]

By the turn of the century the clergy could congratulate themselves on the return of the people to their altars. The rapid advance of civil marriage subsequent to its legalization in 1837 had been slowed, and now banns were regaining their old popularity. Even the upper classes were beginning to return to the practice of posting banns; and the working classes were following suit.[7] People were not only marrying more conventionally, but earlier and more often. The age at which people were marrying had risen slightly during the last third of the nineteenth century, only to begin a steady decline after 1910. This trend accelerated in the late 1930s, and by the 1950s the British were marrying younger and more frequently than at any time in their history. The proportion of single folk fell between 1871 and 1961 from 61 percent to 44 percent, but it was among the younger age groups that the new surge of matrimony was most noticeable. In 1931 only a fifth of the age group from 20 to 24 were married; by 1950 this had reached a third.[8]

To many commentators the new conformity to the marriage law was proof that the long predicted triumph of the conjugal ideal had finally been achieved. In 1869 John Stuart Mill was able to assure the public that the "association of men with women in daily life is much closer and more complete than it ever was before." He wrote of the "progress of civilization" that had "thrown the man very much more upon home and its inmates, for his personal and social pleasures," a change that Tennyson greeted as the salvation of both sexes:

> seeing either sex alone
> Is half itself, and true marriage lies
> Nor equal, nor unequal. Each fulfills
> Defect in each.[9]

However, the popularity of marriage should not be taken as a sign that conjugal love had finally conquered the working classes. As one particularly well-informed observer pointed out, while women felt compelled "to be legally married to the man they live with, and where no obstacle exists to a legal union will, as a rule, insist on marriage before commencing cohabition," this preference was "due mainly to the legal hold over her husband which marriage gives a woman rather than to any sense of sanctity of marriage or to the recognition of the immorality of irregular union."[10] The same unromantic attitude was evident even as late as the 1950s. By then there were even fewer women who would have dared live outside legal marriage, but they still did not regard it as their only, or even primary, source of personal fulfillment. On the contrary, heterosexual intimacy remained a source of awkwardness and anxiety for most working-class young people. Mill's ideal of companionship was rarely achieved in married life, for most found their relations with family and friends far more personally satisfying than those with their spouses. While they might subscribe to the ideal of conjugal love, they did not necessarily live it.

In many respects, the period from 1850 to 1960 saw a retreat from marriage as partnership. Even as the heterosexual possibilities narrowed and monogamous marriage became virtually mandatory, the conditions for satisfactory conjugal relations became ever more problematic. Not only the changing legal situation, but the economy and social structure made it very difficult for working-class people to sustain a satisfactory home and family life on the resources available to the couple alone. Invariably they turned to family, friends, and community to provide what law and social respectability mandated but the couple by themselves could not supply. This need was ultimately reflected in both a reritualization of the courtship process and the renaissance of the big wedding—both of which mediated the contradictions between the impossible ideal of companionate marriage and the realities of working-class existence. This chapter will explore the narrowing definition of marriage and family in the period from 1850 to 1914; subsequent chapters will show how women and men came to deal with the strains that this imposed.

I

The compulsion to marry was increasingly evident from the 1850s onward. When young Flora Thompson declared that she had no intention of becoming anyone's wife, her brave declaration was met with knowing smiles by the village matrons: "All right, my girl, I've heard that tale before. You wait until Mr. Right comes along. When he says 'skip' you'll say 'snap' fast enough, I'll warrant. . . . Better a bad husband than no husband at all."[11] Music hall lyrics of the turn of the century expressed the view that, whatever its disadvantages, there was no real alternative to marriage:

> When first they come courting,
> How nice they behave

> For a smile and a kiss
>> how humbly they crave
> But when once a girl's wed,
>> she's a drudge and a slave
> I think we would all prefer
>> marriage with strife
> Then to be on the shelf
>> and be nobody's wife.[12]

Growing anxiety about being "left on the shelf" is partially to be explained by the surplus of unmarried women in the period from 1870 to 1950. A higher death rate among males and their greater emigration meant there were considerably more single women of marriageable age.[13] Yet the pressures to marry were not just numerical. Practical considerations were pushing both women and men toward proper marriage and away from common-law arrangements. Illicit unions were increasingly confined to older people. In Uxbridge, just outside London, bricklayers and laundry women were still living tally in the early years of the twentieth century, though it was said that this was much less common than earlier.[14] The vicar of another rural parish in Enfield reported that when he first came there in 1895 there were several unmarried couples, but a decade later all but two had been persuaded to marry.[15] At Whitton in Middlesex it was the market gardeners, a shifting, seasonal people, who showed a "laxity as to marriage and cohabitation."[16] But once the boundary to London itself was crossed, evidence of open cohabitation was much more difficult to come by. There were no doubt many like Tom and Mary Jones of South Wales, who kept their common-law situation very quiet and led ultra-respectable lives to avoid the censure of neighbors, but they were primarily older people, the last generation to keep the old common-law traditions.[17]

There were still some occupational groups that relied on the old practices. With their men away on long voyages, Plymouth women often took up with male lodgers as a way of making ends meet. The chief constable there found the "Jack Tars . . . are generally very forgiving, and they frequently forgive where I am afraid I should not."[18] In London, too, mariners had a reputation for common-law arrangements; and it was said that their "wives" indulged in part-time prostitution when they needed the money.[19] Among Cornish miners, who were sometimes away in America or South Africa for years at a time, a similar pragmatism persisted. The roving miners sent money home, but when this was not sufficient the lodger often took the position of the husband. In turn, Cornishmen felt justified in living with other women while abroad, "but they keep it very close, and they do not tell on each other when they come home."[20] Depressed conditions in Cornwall itself perpetuated common-law practice longer than in other more prosperous and settled mining areas, where by 1900 church marriage was becoming the norm.

The end of the great era of railway construction in the 1880s also meant that navvies were no longer "jumping brush and steel."[21]

Almost everywhere marriage was assuming a more conventional form. Allen Clark found in Lancashire that "though there is a good deal of sexual intercourse between young persons this is not promiscuous, but between courting couples, before marriage."[22] In commercial cities like London, tally couples were confined more and more to rough districts like Bow and Poplar. Booth drew a sharp distinction between them and the rest of the East End working class: "Among the upper working class there is no reason to suppose that any such latitude exists."[23] These were the kind of people who would keep their "marriage lines" above the mantle to remind themselves and others of their respectability. Booth found in the 1890s that ordinary working people "think it unlucky to be without support of the church"; in the north, civil weddings were also considered second best and associated with hasty, cover-up affairs that invariably carried a stigma.[24] At the level of the unskilled there might still be a certain amount of cohabitation before marriage, but not nearly so much as earlier. Marriage fees were no longer a real obstacle, and for those who did not wish to have to treat their neighbors there was civil marriage as an inexpensive way of avoiding the publicity of wedding in a local church.[25] It was mainly artisans, the carriers of London's secularist tradition, who resorted to the register office out of principle. One such man, a printer, told the widow he was living with that, while he would make a home for her and her two sons, he could not go through a church wedding because it was "a bit of priestcraft" and only put money in the clergyman's pocket. Yet this couple lived very respectably in a good neighborhood, and it was only after the printer's death in 1897 that their relationship became known.[26]

For the most part, however, civil marriage was now used by pregnant brides and runaway couples who found the register office a haven of privacy. After the 1840s the people of Ceiriog resorted to the nearest register office when they encountered any obstacle to their marriages. With church marriage reasserting itself in so many places, the civil wedding began to function like the early modern clandestine marriage, providing an alternative for those who wanted a bit of privacy or who could not meet the standards of masculine self-sufficiency and feminine innocence demanded by contemporary standards. When Stella Davies suggested a civil ceremony, she was told by her family that "hardly anybody went to a register office unless they were pregnant."[27] A civil wedding was regarded as a kind of penalty, an acknowledgment of indiscretion, that placated those neighborhood gossips who reserved the full measure of their contempt for those brides who attempted to hide their shame. Jane Williams' family thought it "awful" that the girl next door went through with a big wedding, concealing her pregnancy by tight lacing: "she was showing you see too. That's why they pulled her in you see." The child, born mentally deficient, was to be a perpetual reminder of her disgrace, placing her only a little above those who could offer no "marriage lines" at all.[28]

It was not just a respect for law that was causing people to choose to live monogamously in nuclear families. This is shown by the fact that even those whose marriages had broken down and who lived in common-law arrangements in order to avoid the possibility of bigamy prosecution tended to do so in a very conventional manner. The earlier practice of lovers remaining with their respective kin even after the birth of one or more children lost all popularity. It became unthinkable for a woman to become a mother without first becoming a wife; and men too came to feel that a home of their own was necessary to their social and material well-being. The 1912 Commission on Divorce found that even those who had been unhappy in one marriage invariably set up marriagelike arrangements soon after they separated. Women left with young children found it necessary to form "an irregular union with a lodger," while "a working man, whose wife leaves him to live with another man, is practically compelled to take a housekeeper to look after his children and his home."[29] Booth's investigators reported that in Poplar there were not all that many living tally, but of those that were "most are widows [who] begin as housekeepers—and then cohabit or a 'rearrangement'—divorce—is made."[30] Many of these women were probably "grass widows," women who had separated themselves from their husbands. One of these recounted how, after failing to get protection from a brutal husband by appealing to the civil authorities, she finally resorted to the device of showing her marriage certificate to her neighbors, then publicly removing her ring, thus gaining the common right to live apart from her husband. Still, she felt uncomfortable with this arrangement and told the Divorce Commission: "I cordially long to regain that freedom which will relieve me of the necessity of passing myself off as a widow."[31]

Few women with children could afford even this kind of independence; nor could men in a similar position. They usually found themselves cohabiting with another person and, after a decent interval, marrying them, even though their legal spouses were still alive. This was a long-standing practice in northern rural areas, where in one case neighbors of a deserted husband "openly advised him to commit bigamy."[32] William Good, an elderly resident of London, married Isabella Vickery, his servant, in 1876, having lived with her for two years after separating from his legal wife. At Good's bigamy trial, Isabella testified that he had told her he did not think "he had done wrong in marrying me, in the sight of God, [though] he might have in the sight of man." The jury was sufficiently impressed with Good's forthrightness that they refused to convict him.[33] Similar leniency was shown to Robert Brown, a former sea captain, then in the humbler circumstances of a cooper, who believed his former wife dead when he remarried in 1857. He had already lived with his new "wife" for six years and his only aim in marrying again "arose from her sense of the disgraceful way in which they were living."[34]

By 1914 the desirability of marriage was evident to virtually everyone. At the beginning of the Great War common-law wives and unwed mothers found to their dismay that they were often excluded from the benefits extended to those dependents of soldiers who could produce proper marriage and baptismal certificates. Women who had lived quietly and respectably were told by unsympathetic relief workers that "you went into this with your eyes open. You will just have to suffer." One sixty-year-old mother, whose son had never known of his illegitimacy, found herself unable to pay the rent: "I have a comfortable home but how I am to keep it I do not know and, as you say, I would rather die before I would let anyone know that my children are illegitimate." One son was so perturbed at the situation that he wrote to his mother: "You can write to the War Office and let them know your son will desert if they don't help their mother." Common-law husbands, equally desperate, went on leave without permission to marry and ensure that their wives receive the proper benefits. Other women were forced to take their case to the authorities more directly:

> Dear Sir
>
> I beg to ask you if you will kindly be kind enough to let me know where my Husbin is—though he is not my legible husbin as he as a wife though he ses she is dead, but I dont think he nos for sure. . . . I have not had any money from him since he joined though he told Mrs. Harris that lives on the ground floor that he was a pretty officer for 6 shillings a week and lots of warm underclothing for the winter and cold weather. I have three children what is being the father of them though he ses it was my fault.[35]

II

It was women who felt the strongest compulsion to marry. By 1900 it was no longer possible to separate motherhood and matrimony. The child conceived outside marriage that in earlier generations had been accepted as a "chancling" was now regarded as a mistake that could and should have been avoided. This change was already apparent during the middle decades of the nineteenth century. Illegitimate fertility had begun to decline in the 1840s, a full two decades before the birth rate of married couples showed any declension. Whereas early-nineteenth-century couples had been unconcerned with birth control as long as they were reasonably sure of one another's intentions, caution was quite apparent in the histories of premarital sexual relations collected by the Foundling Hospital inspectors in the second half of the nineteenth century. Charles Wrexham had been practicing some form of birth control when Ellen Emingford became pregnant, for he wrote to her of his embarrassment "at the thought of loosing [sic] self-control," adding that there was "no cause to trouble about that," referring to an abortifacient. He told Ellen he had the "long wished for article and hope we may prove to each other in the future what we have anticipated in the past," but the child was born nevertheless, and with disastrous consequences for the mother, who was forced to give it up to the Foundling Hospital.[36]

The Foundling Hospital records tell us only of those efforts at birth control that were refused or failed, but the growing incidence of attempted abortion after 1850 suggests a growing anxiety about the consequences of sexual intercourse, the burden of which fell mainly to the women involved. Mary Baines was deserted by her lover when she refused to abort, he telling her "he would do nothing for me because I would not take the drugs."[37] Because effective birth control was not available, men and women were now reluctant to risk the kind of premarital relationships that earlier had accounted for such a large part of recorded illegitimacy. As the difficulties of unwed motherhood were realized, many resorted to abandonment and infanticide. Increasing numbers of women were impelled to reassess their own sexuality in relation to men. Many found safe haven in premarital virginity; others, somewhat bolder, risked physical intimacy with the intention of a hasty, cover-up marriage if anything went wrong. Winifred Foley fortified her particular decision by repeating the cautionary verses she learned as an adolescent:

> There was a young lady so wild
> She kept herself pure undefiled
> By thinking of Jesus
> Venereal diseases
> And the danger of having a child.[38]

A century of Christian evangelism, reinforced by medical campaigns against venereal disease, contributed greatly to fears about all forms of extramarital sexuality. Respectability and chastity were firmly linked in the minds of those who aspired to higher social status; and even Welsh farm women, who in the early nineteenth century had been so uninhibited, were now reassessing the consequences of premarital intimacy in light of the changing balance of sexual power:

> Ah, Sir, it is a fine time for the boys now. . . . It's a
> bad time for the girls, Sir, the boys have their own
> way.[39]

The single woman's loss was to some degree the married woman's gain. The celebration of married motherhood, growing ever more pronounced from the mid-century onward, reflected and reinforced a change in the very nature of girlhood, now defined as a period of dependence, a preparation for adult life, the access to which was identified entirely with marriage. A boy's sense of himself was less bound up with home and children, but by 1900 an increasing awareness of and hostility to homosexuality had made men wary of persisting in their bachelorhood much beyond the permissible limits of youth.[40] The gradual fall in the age at time of marriage after 1910 reflected the increasingly close association of "normality" with the marriage, even among the poorest elements of the population.

Those who defied the authorized code of sexual relations found themselves at an increasing disadvantage from the 1840s onward. The resistance that had sustained common-law practice under the Hardwicke Act was becoming more difficult in an era of Benthamite efficiency, when, in exchange for a wider choice of official forms of marriage, the enforcement of existing law became more rigorous. The reforms of 1836 permitted both civil and nonconformist marriage, but at the same time transferred control of vital registration from church to state. The change came immediately on the heels of the poor law reform of 1834 and was part of a more general effort by a triumphant bourgeoisie to improve the machinery of the state and, through it, to control the lives of the poor. The New Poor Law mandated the elimination of all outrelief to individuals and families, substituting for it the unpalatable conditions of the workhouse. To obtain her share of her husband's dole, the wife had to enter the workhouse with him, there to be separated both from him and any older children. Women's rights to welfare were defined in a vigorously patriarchal manner. Wives had to prove that their husbands had deserted them for twelve months before they could gain relief on their own. Even landladies with male tenants were sometimes denied relief because it was suspected they were being supported. Only the unwed mother was treated as independent and she was forced to bear the entire burden of the bastard child.[41]

The clauses with respect to bastardy were among the harshest of the entire 1834 code. Unwed mothers were stripped of their right to outrelief, even that provided by the putative father under an affiliation order from the magistrates. The affiliation procedure of 1733 was virtually eliminated, and, while a woman could still apply to Quarter Sessions, the chances of her getting an order were slight because she was obligated to provide corroborative evidence of the man's involvement. In order to obtain ordinary assistance, she now had no choice but the workhouse, a provision which was introduced with deterrence in mind. In the words of Lord Broughham, "For common sense dictated that though want of chastity was a crime, a sin in a man, it was still greater in a woman, whose error corrupted society at its very root."[42]

There was considerable initial opposition to the bastardy clauses, but there is no question that the long-term effect of the New Poor Law was to discourage motherhood outside marriage. The law's proponents noted with satisfaction that "one constantly hears the females of the lower classes complaining of the new law, and proving they understand it."[43] In Ash-next-Sandwich, where bastardy and common-law arrangements had been frequent before 1834, there was now a rush to marry.[44] At

Terling, Essex, bastardy actually increased after 1834, probably because the parish no longer had the power to force marriages, but now the failure to marry was not so much a matter of deliberate postponement but the consequence of other factors not under the control of the individuals involved. The group most victimized by the New Poor Law was made up of young male agricultural laborers. They were forced to spend the unemployed winter months in the workhouse, while married men were allowed relief at home. However, because there was very little female work in this region of developed capitalist agriculture, marriage was a risky business. When the parish ceased to force and fund the marriages of the poor after 1834, their situation became even more precarious. Whereas in earlier centuries the unwed mothers in Terling had once been older than the wedded, clearly a result of the postponement of nuptiality, now they were more than a year younger, a measure of the increasing vulnerability of young love generally.[45]

Throughout the proletarianized regions of the south and east shotgun weddings were commonplace.[46] This was also true of London, especially in the East End where many of the inhabitants were migrants from the surrounding rural areas. In the neighborhoods of Stepney and Bethnal Green forced marriages were frequent. Premarital intercourse was tolerated, but once pregnancy occurred a wedding of one kind or another was sure to follow.[47] When a marriage failed to materialize it was usually because the pair were very young and did not have the resources or the permission to marry. Whereas the unwed mothers who had come to the Foundling Hospital had previously been roughly the same age as the metropolitan brides of roughly the same background and prospects, now they were increasingly younger. The age of applicants to the Foundling Hospital fell from the 1840s onward, a reflection not only of the greater vulnerability of younger women but also the fact that older females, who were in a better position to marry, were doing so rather than attempting some more irregular arrangement as earlier generations had been prone to do.[48]

Even in the north there was a sense that things had been better in "grandfather's days":

> If a young man went a-courting a damsel meek and mild
> And if she from misfortune should hap to have a child
> By going to a magistrate, a recompense to seek,
> They'd make the man marry her, or pay a crown a week.

> But now by the New Poor Law he nothing has to pay
> Nor would he, even if he got twenty children every day.[49]

Henceforth women had to weigh the possible harm publicity might do them against the pittance they might receive by winning their court case. Among men as well, Victorian standards of respectability worked against common-law arrangements. Herbert Walker, a traveling photographer, had begged Bessie Clark and her father to allow him more time to marry: "I assure you my attentions are honourable and we wish to be married as soon as possible. . . . I am always travelling and what has been the principal thing, I have had scarcely any money having had such severe weather." He pleaded against a court case: "Of course it matters little to you as you were not brought up in this place, but to me it means complete disgrace and I'm unable to help myself." He disappeared rather than face the magistrates and the public.[50]

Abandonments were increasing and the numbers applying to the Foundling Hospital and other such institutions rose sharply after 1834. Despite the horror they provoked, workhouses were used with greater frequency as a place where children could be both born and abandoned.[52] Leaving a child to nurse there represented an indirect form of infanticide, a fact acknowledged by those complicitous in the practice: "Ah! it's *sure* to die—they all die here: we feed them on our workhouse bread and that's enough."[53] Private nursing of infants had no less deadly effects. In the manufacturing districts, mothers could rely on grandparents, neighbors, and other kin to take care of infants while they went back to the mills, whereas women in service found it much more difficult to combine work and motherhood. They were the chief patrons of urban "baby farmers," to whom they paid up to five shillings a week for a miserable standard of dry feeding. Anytime women were unable to breast feed, death was virtually certain, a situation that was probably worsening in the period of the 1860s and 1870s when service was claiming a larger share of female employment. Both the wed and the unwed were forced to resort to mercenary nurses, but bastards fared worst of all. In the manufacturing districts their survival rate was reckoned at about forty percent; in London it was as low as one in ten.[54] According to one metropolitan medical officer who knew the situation well, "illegitimate children of the poorer classes are almost always killed, either intentionally or unintentionally."[55] They were much more likely to be victims of child murder, an event so widespread in the cities that authorities chose to ignore it or, when it came to trial, treat with extreme leniency.[56] The fact that no one could ignore, however, was that the life of the child depended directly on the mother's employment. In this, as in everything else, it was a "bad time for the girls."

III

The law by itself is not sufficient explanation of the new compulsion to marry. In earlier periods the working classes had not been afraid to defy church and state as long as economic and social conditions offered viable alternatives to the nuclear family and monogamous heterosexuality. While the unremitting pressures of a century of moral vigilance campaigns may have been partly responsible for the new conformity evident by 1900, the single greatest factor was the evolution of industrial capitalism, which undermined the independence of the family economy and consigned to men the role of principal breadwinner and to women the destiny of dependent wife and mother. From the 1840s onward, women were losing their place in that part of the economy that had offered them the highest wages and greatest independence. In 1851 that part of the female work force employed in textiles was 22 percent; by 1911 it was only 16 percent. The share of manufacturing in women's paid employment dropped from 43 percent to 37 percent in the same period.[57] Women in retailing increased, but the greatest shift was to domestic service, which reached a peak of 46 percent of the female work force in 1871 and was still the largest single employer of women in 1911. Even as late as 1931 almost a third of all female wage earners were still in domestic employment.[58] Equally significant was the fact that participation of adult women in paid employment declined in the late nineteenth century, remained steady until World War II, and only began to rise rapidly in the 1960s. Married women's work remained low during the first three decades of the twentieth century, much lower than it had been a century earlier. In 1911 only a tenth of all married women had a paid job. By 1951 this had risen to twenty percent, but the greatest changes came after 1960 when the proportion rose to over one-half.[59]

Young women employed in industrial work now seemed all the more exceptional because of the independence their wages allowed them. "That's the worst of factory work for girls," critics said, "They can earn so much when work is plenty, that they can maintain themselves."[60] In London the few women who enjoyed decent factory wages were also distinguished by their freedoms, their spending money, and the "bracelets and other finery in which [they] appeared on Easter Monday at Greenwich Fair."[61] Their numbers were dwindling, however. Faced with industrial competition, most of the trades that had previously employed skilled women declined. Female apprenticeship, never very widespread to begin with, became even more uncommon; wages fell and work conditions deteriorated. In London's vast garment industry both men and women were occupied principally in "slop work" that became organized in an increasingly competitive way, a form of the subcontracting system dominated by capitalist entrepreneurs. Tailoring had enjoyed a certain prosperity earlier in the century. Little masters, called "Dungs," employing large numbers of apprentices and women, had entered the trade alongside the more privileged and entirely male "Flints," the guild tailors.[62] In 1824 there were four Flints for every one Dung; twenty years later the ratio was reversed. At first there was no overt tension between the two sectors, but by the 1830s wage cutting by the merchant entrepreneurs produced a crisis:

> since the increase of the puffing and the sweating system, masters and sweaters have sought everywhere for such hands as would do work below the regular ones. Hence the wife has been made to compete with the husband, and the daughter with the wife; . . . If the man will not reduce the price of his labour to that of the female, why he must remain unem-

ployed; and if the full-grown woman will not take the work at the same price as the young girl, why she must remain without any.[63]

In 1834 the Flints attempted to drive women from the trade by strike action. The females responded by reminding them of the right and necessity of women's labor: "What is to become of the numerous women now working at the business, many of whom are tailors' widows, who have no other means of providing for themselves and families?" But the men of this and other hard-pressed trades would not listen. Instead, they preferred to lecture female labor on its domestic responsibilities:

> your places are in your homes: your labours are your domestic duties: your interests in the welfare of your families, and not in slaving thus for the accumulation of the wealth of others, whose slaves you seem willing to be: for shame on you! Go seek husbands those of you who have them not, and make them toil for you; and those of you who have husbands and families, go home and minister to their domestic comforts.[64]

The tensions latent in the more flexible marital and familial arangements of the early nineteenth century now surfaced when the prosperity of the family economy was undermined by the rapid development of capitalist factory production. Where home work persisted, it became ever more exploitive and exclusively female. On the other hand, where productive processes were removed to a factory setting, the work became male dominated. Even in the textile districts, where women's work outside the home was most available, the male came to be defined as the principal breadwinner, the female as the supplementary wage earner. In the long run, male workers were able to convert the earlier notion of a collective family wage into the notion of a minimum necessary for the husband to support a wife and children, but in the short term many were prevented from marrying as they might have wished. "I am now living with a young man," a needlewoman told Henry Mayhew, "I am compelled to do so, because I could not support myself. I know he would marry me if he could. . . . He has earned nothing for the last three weeks. If he had money, I know he would marry me." For another, cohabitation with a docker was clearly a makeshift situation: "I can state solemnly in the presence of my Maker that I live with him only to get a living and save myself from doing worse. . . . He's willing to marry me the first day he can afford, but he hasn't the money to pay the fees."[65]

During the 1850s conditions improved sufficiently so that such men could fulfill their promises, and, by the end of the century, there were very few men who by their mid-twenties could not afford to pay the costs of legal marriage, though they might not have the additional funds to put on a big wedding. Many would have to move in with parents because they could not afford to establish a separate home, but the ideal was nevertheless the nuclear family and the separate household. Had more been able to afford it, the age at the time of marriage would probably have begun to fall even earlier than it did. During the Great

Depression of the last third of the nineteenth century, many were having difficulty attaining the level of male wages thought necessary to support a family.[66] The upper working class would not have their wives work, and their reasons for delaying marriage were much like those of this London boatbuilder:

> I don't think I could very well afford to keep a wife, though it's very lonesome having nobody to care about one. No doubt I could get a wife, but to keep her is another thing. I shouldn't like two to be in poverty instead of one, and I wouldn't like a decent girl I might marry to have to work for the sweaters to make ends meet when work's scarce. Some have to do it, though, to my knowing; and don't the girls find out the difference between that and being in good service, as some of them have been![67]

The marriage age was also kept high by the fact that at least a third of all working-class women were in domestic service at some point in their lives. It took a servant longer to save her contribution to a marriage; and her lack of experience in other areas of work made it likely that, once married, the family would be mainly, if not entirely, maintained by the husband's wage. Thus this very common form of female work confirmed the prevailing view of females as dependent creatures. Service had once encompassed a very wide range of male and female employment in and outside the household, but in the second half of the century it had become domesticated, routinized, and feminized. Male indoor servants had been largely dispensed with, in part because the Victorian middle class looked for a set of qualities—deference, humility, and sweet temper—that was associated exclusively with females.[68] As I have shown elsewhere, service inhibited heterosexuality and diminished the bargaining power that women in other employments were able to exercise. The domestic servant faced dire consequences should her liaisons be discovered or a pregnancy be known. As the Foundling Hospital records demonstrate, this was the group of women most at risk with respect to illegitimacy.[69] It is not surprising therefore that servants should also be the ones most obsessed with sexual propriety. Employers demanded it; mothers implored it. Surrounded by middle- and upper-class symbols of decorum, servants had either to adapt to these conventions or lose their chances of employment. By the 1840s they were already wearing the distinctive uniform—dress in "decent black," white apron, and cap—which set them apart from other working women. The rule was, as Mayhew put it, "no ringlets, followers, or scandals."[70] Once a woman was suspected of looseness, "no lady will take them after and would think it quite shocking to have such a person in the house."[71] The Oxfordshire mothers who Flora Thompson knew in the 1880s were also full of anxiety about propriety: "I allus tells my gals that if they goes getting themselves into trouble they'll have to go to the work 'us [workhouse], for I won't have 'em at home."[72] Forty years later Winifred Foley went off to London with her father's warning running through her mind:

"We know thee'lt be a good little wench and not do anything to let thee old Mam and Dad down."[73]

It was true that "service is not inheritance," but the cultivated manners a woman picked up in service were not immaterial to her marriage chances. A wife who could offer a little refinement was often preferred by men who considered themselves a cut above the common lot. There was much discussion as to whether former servants made better house-wives and mothers than factory girls, but there was no question as to which were the more practiced at dissembling men, whether masters or husbands.[74] A servant's long conditioning to subservience must have made her attractive to many men who were, by their own experience, used to thinking of women as subordinates.

IV

The domesticization of the female was reinforced still further by the fact that increasing numbers of young women were going out to neither service nor factory work, but staying at home.[75] Earlier this meant a productive role in farming or domestic industry, but with the mature stages of urbanization the meaning of living home changed entirely. The first generation of urban women, often single migrants, had experienced considerable autonomy, but those who were born to the city found themselves yoked to their families in subordinate roles, first as daughters and then as wives.[76] In a wage economy in which at least a third of the population was at any given time at or below the poverty line, a house-hold's margin of survival depended on the earnings of women and children. In the factory districts, wives worked until their children were old enough to contribute to the family purse. Only then did they "re-tire."[77] Food, clothing, and other necessities were no longer produced by the household, and purchasing power was especially dependent on teenagers, who were now kept at home for longer periods than ever before.[78] Except for the very highest ranks of working-class families, amounting to no more than fifteen percent of the whole, further training in the form of secondary schooling or apprenticeship was beyond reach. On leaving school, boys were encouraged to take whatever job paid the best, regardless of the future it offered. Most of the "boy labour" of the late nineteenth and early twentieth centuries involved minimal skills and led nowhere.[79] The situation for girls was even worse, for they always came second to the sons when further training was at issue. They were even more likely to be taken out of school early to act as "little mothers" to younger children, assist with the housework, or scrounge the neighborhood for whatever daily work it had to offer.[80]

From the 1870s onward, the percentage of women listed as employed in the census began to fall.[81] Of course, the listings of "unoccupied" wives and daughters failed totally to comprehend the true extent of work within the home and merely reflected official assumptions about the sexual division of labor, which assigned to men the public role of breadwinner and to women the obscurity of domestic work. Similarly, statistics showing rising wages and shorter working hours hid the unevenness in the way these benefits were distributed by sex and age. The wages and hours of the female home workers did not keep pace; women did not share in the new prosperity of late Victorian male workers.[82] They were the ones to bear the burden of high fertility, with the attendant high rates of infant and maternal mortality. After 1870, when compulsory schooling removed younger children from the labor market, the full weight of meeting the family budget fell to the mother and the older children. Should a husband become disabled, unemployed, desert, or die, there was virtually no way that a woman, who normally earned less than half a man's wage, could support herself and children without resorting to private or public charity.[83]

The expansion of orphanages in the later nineteenth century was a response not only to parental death but familial destitution. Very few of the National Children's Home admissions were total orphans, but instead were children of widows, deserted wives, and, to a lesser extent, widowers.[84] Mary Cogan was fortunate to have only one child when her husband, a printer, died in 1892. She rented a room in Hoxton for two shillings and six pence a week, and managed to get by on the eight shillings she made at box making, a form of home work that allowed her to look after her son. As the boy grew older, the burdens increased and she was finally forced to accept the offer of marriage of a man who, having gotten her with another child, went off to become a soldier in the Boer War. Once again, she was plunged into the single woman's world of low-paid, uncertain employment. She feared more for her children than for herself when she finally applied to the Children's Home: "It [the baby] is almost starving and above all he [the older boy] gets so saucy as he gets older that it is more than I can bear. I have been a widow for years and I find the older he gets it is more a struggle to fund his clothes and boots."[85]

Deserted or separated wives found themselves in a similar dilemma. The court had ordered Reuben White to make regular payments to his estranged wife, but in the course of six years he was jailed eleven times for failing to do so. Meanwhile, he had taken care of his own comforts by establishing himself in a distant part of Bethnal Green with another woman, while his wife tried to make do in her rented house by taking in lodgers. When her daughter and son-in-law moved out, she could find nobody to replace them. Falling behind in the rent, she began to pawn her belongings, including two of the three beds by which she made her living. It was at this point that she too was forced to part with her youngest child.[86] Even a resourceful women like Margaret Nelson, former mistress of a gentleman who had accumulated enough savings to buy her own house in Ealing and a small shop besides, found she could not make ends meet when her eldest son, on whose earnings the family budget depended, died suddenly. Left with a younger, equally delicate child, she found she could not continue in business. And, as her relatives had cast her off when she was sixteen, she had nowhere to turn.[87]

Only women who were securely atop the working class, the fifteen percent who were blessed with a high-paid, regularly employed man as breadwinner, could expect to avoid these kinds of situations; and even they were constantly reminded of the presence of poverty by those just below them. In an effort to distance themselves from that which they feared, the aristocracy of labor tended to segregate themselves residentially. Their withdrawal from the slums to the suburbs accentuated existing divisions within the working class. In Greenwich and Woolwich, the highly paid engineering and shipbuilding workers separated themselves from the casually employed of the dockside. London's building workers sorted themselves out in a similar manner from the 1850s onward: plumbers and stone masons at the top, sawyers and painters at the bottom, and bricklayers, plasterers, and other woodworkers somewhere in the middle.[88] As the gap in wages between skilled and unskilled increased, status divisions became so rigid that a bricklayer's daughter felt justified in rejecting "with scorn" the proposal of a man who was "only a labourer."[89] Caroline Lane's father, who was a docker, had refused to press her seducer, a common laborer, for the practical reason that "there was no good to be got out of him." Rachel Lofting's father rejected her suitor on the pretense that he was a drinker, but it is likely that the Loftings' superior social position had much to do with his hostility to William Ross, who was a miner. When Rachel became pregnant, he would no longer allow her in the house because he was so concerned with the reputation of his other daughters. They had to think of their position and "how people would talk."[90]

The skilled were cutting themselves off from the rest of the working classes by recruiting exclusively from their own ranks and by intermarrying more with one another.[91] Their sons went on to apprenticeships and further education. They would live at home until this was completed and were certain of the steady work and good wages that were the rewards of extended training. By then in their mid-twenties, these young men would settle down and marry a woman of similar age and background. As for the sons of unskilled workers, they were normally pressed into some form of unskilled "boy labor" as soon as they could leave the elementary school. This would last until they were "turned off at 16 or 17 when they want more money. Then they do nothing or trust to odd jobs or work as scavengers on the dust shoot. The home is therefore supported by women and children in most instances. . . ." After two or three years of conditioning to casual employment, the unskilled would marry, normally at a younger age than the skilled men and to a very different class of women.[92]

V

Although the division between the skilled and the rest of the working class was not new, the kind of status distinctions that were evident from the 1850s onward had a distinctive Victorian dimension. As important as the skills and earnings were the life-styles associated with them. Wives and daughters played a particularly important role in distinguishing between the respectable working class and those below that level. This was one more attribute of the pronounced sexual divisions of the period, which assigned to males the role of wage earner and to women the family manager. Margaret Loane noted that women "kept the purse under their pillow and regulated the expenditure of the household. Men are so well aware that they cannot 'make the money go round' that they would hand their wages over to a sixteen-year-old daughter 'who knows what her mother used to do' rather than make the attempt."[93] A widower or deserted husband could simply not do without a woman's labor at home. He had to hire a housekeeper or, because this was too expensive for most working men, take another wife or mistress.[94]

Children belonged to the female sphere, and their care and discipline were entirely the mother's responsibility. That burden became ever more demanding in the course of the century, especially among those who wanted their children to appear respectable. London's artisan elite had begun to limit the freedom of their offspring as early as the 1820s, when Francis Place began to notice that they no longer allowed their daughters to go "palming" or attend the Easter and Whitsun fairs. The Cock and Hen clubs disappeared about the same time; and the bawdy ballads, once sung by both girls and boys, were said to be "unknown to youths of the rising generation." Place was probably speaking for only a small minority when he said the respectable working man could not even look at a pornographic book "without disgust and would very generally be ashamed to own it," but this kind of prudery was far more common a half-century later, having become by that time a part of the system of social stratification within the working class itself.[95]

Those ranking lower on the labor scale simply could not keep up the appearances of respectability even when they held the same moral values. The rented room of a sweated tailor or struggling cabinetmaker did not lend itself to conjugal contentment. Francis Place knew well that domestic peace was impossible when a woman had "to eat and drink and cook and wash and iron and transact all her domestic concerns in a room in which her husband works, and in which they sleep."[96] The burden of maintaining a modicum of respectability fell largely to the woman, who labored, scrimped, went sleepless and hungry, and even prostituted herself in order to meet the standards of a happy home life. Toward the end of the century it was common for couples to go into debt in order to furnish their dwellings; and it was the bride who had to satisfy the hire-purchase man. If she could not, then the marriage was endangered because "the husband finds he is not getting as many luxuries as he did when he was living at home with his parents, and he becomes dissatisfied."[97]

The effort to keep up appearances also took a toll on a woman's relationship with the community. The wives of London artisans liked to hire "step girls" to do the less desirable outdoor work. In Salford, those who felt themselves superior closed their doors to the disorder of the street and made for themselves what was a very lonely existence.[98] Even in small country places, the "best" housekeepers had a reputation for being "arid ground for borrowers and cadgers. They kept to themselves in their prim little dwellings. They didn't laugh a lot."[99]

Prior to World War I, those who could make a decent home on the wage of a husband alone were still a minority. A third of the population was below the poverty line at any given point in time; and all but a minority of working-class people would experience real scarcity at some point in their lives, usually at the point in the marriage when the children were numerous, yet too young to be contributing to the family budget.[100] For wives there was no alternative but to take in work or in very hard times turn to relatives, friends, and neighbors. Age-old traditions of female sharing found new life in the "urban villages" of the late nineteenth century, where women exchanged services—cooking, nursing, clothing, and housing—and would even supervise or sometimes "adopt" one another's children, erect neighborhood defenses against drunken husbands, rent collectors, and school board inspectors, and provide a vital "safety net" in times of death or separation that neither the state nor the nuclear family could provide.[101] Mother-daughter relationships were particularly crucial, and the tendency of married couples to settle near the wife's family was noted from the mid-nineteenth century onward. But the bond was not strictly familial, and women were known to support other women as women, particularly in conflicts with men. "You stick to it," "Go on wiv' it," "Get your separation," women called out when one of their own sought a separation order in a London magistrate's court.[102] By and large, a wife's most intimate relations were not with her husband, but with her children (especially the girls) or with the other women.

The male was the provider who gave his wife her "wage" and left her to manage on that and whatever other supplementary income she or the children might produce.[103] In return for support, men normally kept back (or, in the north, were given back) a part of their earnings to spend on tobacco, drink, and other masculine pleasures. Men had a life outside the home they did not usually share with their wives. The pub was a male preserve in most working-class neighborhoods, a place safe from women and children of "warmth, bright lights, music, song, comradship," where the husband renewed his bonds with his pals, where he reaffirmed his masculinity.[104] When women went out it was usually to their own locales where their presence would not embarrass their

22. The segregated world of women and children in the late-nineteenth-century city. Moss Alley, Bankside, London. (Used by permission of Guildhall Library, London)

men.[105] In turn, husbands left the house to the women and children, and

> displayed virility by never performing any task in or about the home which was considered by tradition to be women's work. Some wives encouraged their partners in this and proudly boasted that they would never allow the "man of the house" to do a "hand's turn." Derisive names like "mop rag" and "diddy man" were used for those who did help.... One quiet street in the village [Salford] where several husbands dared help their wives

regularly became known in the pubs as "Dolly Lane" or "Bloody-good-husband street."[106]

This is not to say there were no companionate marriages, but these were few even among the highly paid workers for whom the home was already by the late nineteenth century a "sanctuary of married life."[107] In the textile districts, where the employment of wives was most common, there was actually more sharing than in those places where women rarely went out to work. "I think when you work they [husbands] should pull their weight with the housework because they are benefitting from your money," said a Preston mill worker.[108] But even in the two-earner households, the conjugal by itself was a fragile arrangement. The man invariably earned more than the woman. Should he get sick, go on strike, or die, she was hard put to maintain the family at their previous standard of living. Even under normal conditions, many men had great difficulty in providing; and when a husband did not bring home a wage for an extended period of time, a woman was allowed by popular opinion to call herself a "grass widow" and take up with another man who could support her and the children.[109]

Nobody expected marriage to go smoothly and domestic dispute was a major theme of music hall comedy at the turn of the century. The tensions over wages and housekeeping that were joked about on stage were acted out with great violence on the typical London weekend:

> From Saturday afternoon, when wages had been paid, till Monday morning the court was often a field of battle and bloodshed, and Sunday was a pitiful day . . . men kicking their wives round the court like footballs, and women fighting like wild tigers![110]

That which was most likely to irritate a man was evidence of a wife's poor housekeeping or money management. A wife's unwillingness to acknowledge a man's "conjugal rights" could also lead to the sexual insults and open violence that were so frequent in nineteenth-century working-class neighborhoods.[111] At the same time, it was taken for granted that neither party would make emotional demands. Observers were struck by the absence of conjugal jealousy among the laboring poor. Wives allowed their husbands their nights out, while men accepted the bond between women, especially the mother-daughter relationship which, despite the deluge of mother-in-law jokes in the late nineteenth century, was recognized as central to the survival of the working-class family. Women were constantly exchanging vital services and it was said that the poor "ignore all relationships but those on the mother's side."[112] In some cases, the ties were so close that they amounted to a kind of extended household and the "young wife neglects her own house to go to her mother's."[113]

A great amount of tolerance was also extended to extramarital relationships, as long as these did not upset the institutional arrangements of a marriage. Hull wives said "they do not mind the husband having a certain woman in the house—much younger and more attractive—but they cannot stand being abused by them." Plymouth sailors returning from long voyages often found their wives living (from necessity) with other men, but "they frequently forgive," arranging a mutual separation only with great reluctance.[114] Among London men "the necessity for a mate of the opposite sex is felt very urgently," and few could afford to live alone. Those who left their wives soon began cohabiting "largely through the pressures caused by the increased cost of living separately," which in 1912 was estimated as a half to three-quarters greater than living together with a woman.[115]

VI

Companionship was not something working men and women expected to find in marriage. Fathers and sons sought their gratifications outside the home, at work, in the pub, or on the football ground. While the music hall and new cinema catered to young people of both sexes with money to spend, the lives of married women were confined largely to the home, which by 1900 had become uniquely matrifocal. The woman's strongest emotional bonds were with her children, especially her daughters. Among the better class of working people, motherhood had become a full-time occupation and domesticity a symbol of status: "a married man whose wife worked, well, you turned your nose up at him." A cabinetmaker, who married during World War I, lived with his in-laws for two years to save money and, even though it was a struggle, never allowed his wife to go out to work: "if she did go out to work you never told anybody. In any case, it would be housework she'd had to do—there was nothing else for a woman."[116]

Of course, there were many who had to do much more than housework. Although they went out to work only when the family budget required it, it was not uncommon for wives to take in a bit of home work when this was available.[117] In contrast to the men, their world was much more interior, though there was no question who was boss within the house itself. A Lancashire man aptly compared the urban working-class family to a ship at sea: "it is the wife that is captain, and right nobly does she discharge her part."[118] Henry Hammon became aware of just how dependent a man with children could be when his wife died in 1901. Although a bootmaker with good earnings, he was plagued by bouts of rheumatism and had to rely on his eldest daughter, aged sixteen, who he called "little mother" to the other six children. "I cannot give the attention to them as a mother could"; and living in an undesirable neighborhood, "I fear the results will be disastrous." Periodic unemployment sapped his savings and his will. "Sick and tired of walking about," he complained, "there is nothing doing anywhere and people seem today to be offended even when you ask for work." When his daughter's health began to break, he was at wits end: "It is easy enough to get down in the world, no one seems to care."[119] George Mansfield, described as an "ordinary case of the difficulties of a working man widower," was in an almost identical situation. He too relied on a daughter to keep the house and a large family. Since his relatives also had many children of their own, there was no possibility of their adopting and the only solution seemed to be remarriage, which he and Henry Hammon did, with good results in both cases.[120]

The indispensability of the housewife and full-time mother was reflected in the pre-1914 adulation of the maternal "instinct," which assumed the character of patriotic crusade among the upper classes. They were concerned with the falling birth rate and the threat this supposedly posed to Britain's strength in an increasingly competitive international situation. No less terrifying to them was the latest surge of militant feminism, which affronted not only John Bull's military but sexual superiority. To the horrifying image of the suffragette was counterposed the figure of true womanhood, the "kindly figure in a white apron." "The tendency of the times is too much in favor of girls being educated in the accomplishments in which only a few can excel," warned the 1903 *Imperial Review*. "What is wanted for the comfort of their husbands and the proper raising of their children is the knowledge of duties of everyday life. To darn a pair of socks and to make an appetizing meal is far better than to strum a piano."[121]

By 1913 England had its counterpart to the American Mother's Day, inspired by a Nottingham evangelical, C. Penswick Smith, who resuscitated the ancient celebration of mid-Lent Mothering Sunday as a means of attracting people back to the churches. Before the Reformation the day had nothing to do with actual mothers, but was a pilgrimage to the mother churches of large parishes. Detached from its ecclesiastical origins, it later became an excuse for sons and daughters, away from home, to return for a brief reunion. In the north and west, where the tradition was strongest, Mothering Sunday was for most of the nineteenth century a strictly plebeian holiday. In Warwickshire and Shropshire mid-Lent was a time of family get-togethers, while in London, where employers did not recognize it as a holiday, it existed largely as a day of remembrance for distant or deceased mothers.[122]

Penswick Smith's revival, which was enthusiastically supported by the Mothers Union, the Girl Guides, as well as various religious bodies, sought to appropriate the "divine instinct" of motherhood for the interests of church and state. The notion that "every woman comes into the world with an inherent gift of motherhood" even inspired a book of hymns:

> We find no Second Mother
> We find no Place like Home[123]

Working people scarcely needed reminding of the importance of Mum, however. They had long been honoring her in their own ways, keeping the secular version of Mothering Sunday, trying to christen and marry in her parish church, honoring her in death as well as in life.[124] As rural customs declined, the celebration of mother was brought more and more into the sanctuaries of urban culture, the theater and music hall. Songs like "Home, Sweet Home," "Violet from Mother's Grave," "Kiss Me Mother, Kiss Your Darling," and "Be Kind to Thy Father" circulated massively in broadside form.[125] The lad who went courting in Lisson Grove encountered sentiments as powerful as any that had existed in bygone eras. He asks the girl to marry him, but she puts him off:

> How wicked 'twould be to pa and ma
> And home to sacrifice.[126]

Male attachment to Mother was no less powerful:

> I never found another I could love like my mother,
> Except my own sweet temper'd wife.[127]

These were the expression of new forms of family life in which children were at home for a much longer part of their lives and their relations with parents, especially with mothers, were more intense. Although women were having fewer children by 1900, there was no diminution of the responsibilities of motherhood. Mothers were more likely than fathers to be involved in the formal eduation of children, for it was the mother who faced down the bullying schoolmaster and prying "skuel board man."[128] She was the family disciplinarian in all but the most serious cases, as well as its doctor, nurse, and funeral director. She served as all-purpose adviser on a wide range of subjects and accepted the responsibility when something went wrong. While fathers in regular employment might be able to put in a word for sons, helping them to get a place in their factory, men who were in more casual kinds of employment were not in much of a position to help boys in getting their first job. Below the rank of artisans, placement of both boys and girls fell to mother, who was in a position to hear of possibilities in her daily round of the neighborhood shops or in street corner gossip. It was through her that girls started as babysitters at the age of twelve and boys gained their first job immediately after leaving school. The wages of girls were delivered directly to mother; and sons were no less eager to show her similar gratitude. The day Joseph Marklin went to seek his first job he wore long trousers for the first time: "But the proudest moment of my life was the first Saturday when I took home my first week's wages."[129]

Children were intensely aware that the well-being of the entire family depended on the time and effort that mother put into cultivating relationships not only with potential employers, but with kin and neighbors. It was she who kept in touch with her former mistresses, thus providing places for daughters in service; it was she who corresponded with distant kin, nursed neighbors, and cared for ailing grandparents, always in the knowledge of the importance of reciprocity.[130] These were precisely the kinds of services that bachelors and widowers missed so sorely. Practical experience lent weight to the very widespread notion that "a mother is more likely to do right to her children than a man, because a man may provide for them, but he cannot look after them."[131]

Married daughters tried to settle as near to mother as possible. They had always preferred to wed at home and give birth there, but now there was much more opportunity to do so once migration had slowed and the cities attained a more settled pattern. Late-nineteenth-century Salford, Preston, and Bethnal Green all sustained a much greater generational continuity than most rural villages.[132] Children lived with their parents until marriage and, if money was tight, even after. To establish a separate household was the ideal, but invariably the new couple set up their first home somewhere near their parents, usually the bride's. Martha Wrigley forfeited marriage when George Haines asked her to go with him to America because she could not bear to leave her mother. When it turned out that she was pregnant and George was gone, the full wrath of her father fell upon her. But her mother repaid her loyalty by secretly assisting her through the pregnancy.[133]

To the same degree that the peasant or artisan household had once been patrifocal, the working-class home was now matrifocal. Mothers controlled key economic resources within families, shaped their internal relationships, and were their chief representatives to the outside world:

> The care and management of the house is so much in the mother's hands that it is really more her home than his. The man rarely brings in a friend to sit by the fire and chat. Such social delights are tasted elsewhere. The neighbours who do come in are, as a rule, the wife's friends. It is she who entertains and makes the laws of hospitality. . . . If a stranger calls he [the husband] will leave it to his wife to represent the family interests. Though still maintaining his headship of the family, and asserting it on occasions with ruthless force, the wife on ordinary days reigns as ruler of the home.[134]

A mother's power over her children was more than just emotional, as sons-in-law discovered. Male mother-in-law jokes of the Edwardian period reflected mothers' pervasive influence; and daughters-in-law also had reason to complain of matrifocal husbands. Because Mary Tamworth's family was large and poor, she had no alternative but to move in with her husband's family when married in 1912. The couple had no savings and they put off having children three years, perhaps because relations between Mary and her mother-in-law were so strained. She got on well with her husband's father, but his mother was another matter:

> Oh, she was a monkey she was honestly. . . . She didn't think I ought to have him, he was her only son. . . . She'd give him a good meal but wouldn't give me—that kind of person. She'd mark—she'd mark the front step and

let it look as though someone had been in and she'd distinctly say to him, she's [Mary] had men in the house.[135]

Powerful bonds, which had previously been mitigated by high death rates and frequent migration, were a factor of increasing importance in the more settled city of the late nineteenth and early twentieth centuries. Not surprisingly, urban parents were much more likely to be deeply involved in their children's courtship. Even the best matched couples could come to grief when parental sentiments came into play. Alfred Wigan, a farrier who had been a lodger at Mrs. Streatham's Richmond Hill house and had been accepted as her daughter's suitor, saw his prospects dissolve when the mother began to take a dislike to him. She sent her daughter into service to get her out of his way and asked him to move out, not knowing that a pregnancy had already occurred.[136] The whole Winston family so disliked Max Hermann that the brothers set on him in his hairdresser's shop and were brought to court as a result. Only the fear that their sister's reputation would be ruined ultimately led them to settle with Hermann, but the match was destroyed.[137] Violence had become more common by 1900 and, at times, other than kin were involved. The men who worked with Walter Ranger as porters said that if they "had only known what had happened they would have given him a good hiding, for he was not at all liked." But this did not necessarily help Ada Jones, for she had already been turned out of her own home for her relationship with Ranger.[138] Male violence reflected the renewal of patriarchalism. Mothers, on the other hand, were more conciliatory, conspiring with daughters to keep the news of an indiscretion from the father. Emily Ryder's mother sent her pregnant daughter to relatives, writing ahead to say "she must not come home under the present circumstances. What would the neighbors say. Her father must not know about it. He would go out of his mind."[139]

VII

Families were taking a much more active role in their daughters' courtships, though not always with the results that were intended. In most working-class communities pressure could still be brought on a suitor to make an "honest" woman of his pregnant sweetheart. "Most young men are bounced into marriage," noted an East End doctor; "the man if a decent fellow willingly and if not [he] is warned into marriage. Then they make the best of it."[140] The Edwardian norm of masculinity was such that too much pressure could have undesirable effects. Rosa Camley's father was willing to pay for the wedding ring, provide the church fees, furnish a room, and even support the couple until George Hargrove found a place in the tailoring trade. George's own mother urged him to marry, as the Camleys were in her eyes a highly respectable family, but he bravely objected that "he intended to marry, but could not do so by charity. When he could find work he would fulfill his promise, not until then." For the Camley family the waiting became unbearable and eventually they went to the police with the information that Hargrove was an army deserter. "I did this to revenge myself because he would not marry me," was the way Rosa explained her part in this ruinous action.[141]

Families were often no more sensitive to their daughters' feelings, especially when their collective sense of honor or status was threatened. The Ryman family had always been extremely close, constantly lending assistance to one another. Ellen had met Allen Creighton, a carpenter, through her brother; and because she was already thirty, the brother encouraged the relationship even to point of offering Creighton furniture to start a household. It was Ellen who broke off the engagement when Allen seduced her against her will in the kitchen where she worked. "We never walked again as I declined to," she said, demonstrating an independence that was as incomprehensible to her family as it was to her fiancé.[142] "A fall from the paths of virtue is a very serious matter for their families and themselves," noted Charles Booth about the kind of upper working class of which the Rymans were a part.[143] A woman's disgrace was felt by all her family, one of the reasons that unwed mothers were so much more likely to be ostracized in the second half of the century.[144] Sarah Roberts was powerfully aware of the "stigma resting upon the family through her," even though she had been the victim of what was clearly a rape by a dentist who used chloroform to seduce her.[145]

Relationships that, with time, might have developed successfully were now more likely to be terminated abruptly. When Harriet Monkton's master discovered her pregnancy, he first pressured his foreman, Herbert Hendrick, and then, when Hendrick prevaricated, ruined him by withdrawing all his recommendations.[146] Raphael Florence met a similar fate, thus precluding any chance of her lover supporting his child. Knowing this, both parties put a high premium on secrecy. James Wilkie wrote to Clara Tarboy's mother:

> It is my intention to do the best I can for your daughter so far as my means (which are very limited) will permit. At the same time, the quieter the matter is kept the better for all parties concerned.[147]

Above all, it was exposure in court that was most feared. This was Herbert Walker's greatest anxiety, for he knew it would ruin his photography business and all chances of a married life.[148] When Sarah Dillon's father approached William Thring through a mutual friend, he made the mistake of threatening court action and Thring absconded immediately.[149] Elizabeth Symonds was typical of those who had the most to fear from publicity. She lived with her parents in respectable Camberwell, nursing an invalid mother and going out only to teach Sunday School. When she became involved with Roger Staley, an apprentice draftsman who lodged with her parents, she may well have been trying to escape the fate of a dutiful daughter. Staley was not ready for marriage, however, and suggested abortion when Elizabeth found herself pregnant. This she could not bring herself to do and, when the parents found out, they were so horrified they moved from Camberwell, cutting themselves off from all acquaintances. A court action was considered, but the "dread of exposure, which an application to a police court would bring upon the . . . parents constrains them to keep the case secret." Instead, the child was adopted by the Foundling Hospital.[150] The reasons Jane Pear's father sent her away to her sister in Bristol were even more basic. He was an elderly carpenter on an estate in Kent and would have lost his position had his daughter's condition been known to his employer.[151]

Previously, publicity had been vital to securing the pressure that forced a man to maintain his child or marry. Fairs, public houses, and country lanes served as witness to the sexual relations of earlier generations, but in the vastness of the city, proof was harder to come by. The best evidence that Judy Spilkey could provide of her intimacy with James Timberlake was the timetable of the inner-London railway, which showed that the train had stopped at a darkened siding at the time she claimed they made their regular rendezvous. Even so, she lost the case, as did Jane Pear, who could not find local witnesses when her case against George Butcher was heard in Bristol.[152] While increasing numbers of women were turning to the courts from the 1870s onward, aided by the poor law guardians who were allowed after 1868 to assist in affiliation suits, they found it a frustrating, often humiliating, experience. Because corroborative evidence was still required, only a quarter of unwed mothers applied and, of these, only a tenth were successful, obtaining only a maximum of five shillings a week child support, inadequate to meet costs in a period of rising prices.[153]

VIII

The patterns of working-class life established in the closing years of the last century were to endure for a surprisingly long time. The sharp division of roles between the male breadwinner and the female homemaker, the matrifocality of family life, the gulf between youth and adulthood, and the ambiguous relations between adolescent children and their parents—all of these were still very evident in the Bethnal Green of the 1950s. As long as the law defined women as dependent creatures and the economy favored the adult male worker, things would remain the same. Over the course of the twentieth century, this mode of family and married life took on a peculiarly stylized character, which lent an aura of seeming permanence to relationships that had come into being only fifty or sixty years earlier. Richard Hoggart grew up thinking that monogamous marriage and the nuclear family were eternally sacred. In his working-class world an illegitimate child or a broken marriage was regarded with genuine horror:

> "Sin" is any act against the idea of home and family, against the sense of importance of "keeping the home together." . . . Where almost everything else is ruled from outside, is chancy and likely to knock you down when you least expect it, the home is yours and real: the warmest welcome is still "Mek y'self at home."[155]

But for all its outward appearance of conformity to the norms of the nuclear family and monogamous marriage, the working-class conjugal relationship itself lacked the prescribed element of companionate intimacy. While a century of adherence to a marriage law, which prohibited extramarital relations and mandated the dependency of the wife on the husband, had lowered the illegitimacy rate substantially, greatly reduced the incidence of common-law arrangements, and even silenced the public debate on alternative forms of heterosexuality, this long era of mandatory matrimony had utterly failed to transform the myth of conjugal love into lived reality as far as ordinary people were concerned. On the contrary, working-class marriage remained highly segmented, with both husband and wife relying on the material and emotional support of others. Especially for women, the ties to the maternal family remained vital. Just in order to survive the fissional pressures that at every point threatened to explode it, the compulsory form of monogamous marriage and nuclear family required not only material assistance but powerful symbolic reinforcement to give it the stability that the conjugal bond by itself did not provide. The direct give-and-take of nineteenth-century proletarian partnership had given way to a family life described by Hoggart "as formal and stylized as any that is attributed to, say, the upper classes."[156] Nowhere was this more apparent than in the courtship and wedding rituals that had come to maturity by the 1950s. They remind us in many ways of the rites of the sixteenth and seventeenth centuries, and, in a period when the gulf between single and married life had once again become so pronounced, they served many of the same functions.

CHAPTER 9

∽∾∽∾∽∾∽∾∽∾∽∾∽∾∽∾∽∾∽∾∽∾∽∾∽∾∽∾∽∾∽∾∽∾

Love on the Dole: The Ritualization of Courtship in the Twentieth Century

When people lose control over vital aspects of their lives, they seek ways to compensate symbolically, thereby gaining a measure of subjective satisfaction by interpreting and expressing events in their own idiom. This is not to say that gesture and symbol have no power of their own, but, even when the effect is only psychological, any activity that proves satisfying will be repeated, thus becoming ritual. We can see this in the phenomenal growth of new courtship and marriage rites that has taken place in our own century. The early-nineteenth-century city was relatively barren of ritual activity, in part because the first generations of urban immigrants felt relatively free to determine their own personal relationships and required little symbolic mediation. It was not until almost the end of the Victorian era, when working-class matrimony again became a complicated, contradictory process, that the forest of symbols thickened appreciably. By the 1950s reritualization had gone so far that both courtship and marriage rites rivaled in scale and expressiveness even the elaborate betrothals and big weddings of the sixteenth and seventeenth centuries. In part the new ceremonialism expressed the affluence and respectability of the twentieth-century working classes, but ritualization also reflected those problems that adherence to the approved norms of monogamous marriage and the nuclear family had created for both sexes.

We think of ritual as archaic, belonging to the village not the city, to the past rather than to the present. Yet the impulse to create order through repetitive, symbolic behavior is evident everywhere we look. The desire to exorcise conflict and to clarify ambiguity did not vanish just because some areas of modern life became more regimented. Ritual receded from some realms, such as work, but found new life in other areas, like sport. It shifted across class and space, reemerging wherever there was a need to cope with the anxieties aroused by the capricious aspects of human experience. As Jonathan Raban suggests, it is now the city

> where superstition thrives, and where people often have to live by reading the signs and surfaces of their environment and interpreting them in terms of private, near magical codes. It seems worthwhile—at least as a corrective measure—to stress and explore some of the magical properties of city life at the expense of the customary rational ones, and to treat the evidence on this issue not as a vestige of some inferior, pre-city stage of human development, but as a possibly organic constituent of urban experience.[1]

Ritual crops up at those times and places in modern life where chance plays the greatest role—on the playing field, at moments of birth and death, and, most frequently, in the affairs of the heart. It is at those moments of ambiguity and tension that we reach for symbols to communicate that which cannot be said directly.[2] And it is among those groups which have the least control over events that we find the most highly ritualized, symbolic behavior. Superstition is rife among gamblers, athletes, and those employed in mining, seafaring, and other occupations where there is great personal risk. But it is most pervavise among the young and especially women, who, as marginal groups, have a perpetual need to interpret and express symbolically what they cannot control directly. During the first sixty years of this century, these needs again manifested themselves. New forms of ritual sprouted and established themselves so much so that, by the 1950s their luxuriance rivaled even that of the sixteenth and seventeenth centuries.

I

The reritualization of courtship was not something imposed from above; instead it was an indigenous response to the changing age and gender conditions. Working-class young people borrowed something of the customs prevalent among the upper classes, but for the most part these were rites of their own creation, reflecting the sharp age and gender divisions that added complications to the marriage process so great that to transform the single man and woman into a married couple required an extended rite of passage rivaling that of the pre-industrial period. By 1900 the homosocial world of youth and the heterosexuality of adulthood were once again highly segregated. The labor market was increasingly age structured. Compulsory education and enactment of new sumptuary legislation, such as the minimum drinking age, further underscored age differences. Young people were once again subject to adult authority both in and outside the family. As rural-urban migration slowed and the working-class neighborhood took on a more settled character, teenagers stayed at home longer, leaving it only to be married. In the early nineteenth century, many a young man and woman had already as-

sumed the responsiblities of adulthood in their teen years. In this century, those same years came to be defined as a distinct phase of
adolescence, a perpetual state of becoming, a preparation for "real life,"
which did not begin until marriage.[3] Not until the 1960s did youth begin
to regain a measure of independence, but then it was the middle-class
rather than working-class youngsters who enjoyed the greatest autonomy. For virtually all young people, but especially women, the period
from 1890 to 1960 was one of lost status and diminished independence,
greater uncertainty and perpetual anxiety, a situation reflected in the
growth of distinctive male and female subcultures, each with their own
distinctive styles and ritual practices.

The age group that in the nineteenth century had been largely on
their own became homebodies in the twentieth century. The result was
an intensified and ambivalent emotional relationship between parents
and children that wholly transformed the process of courtship and marriage. Until the greater affluence of the post-World War II era, parents
had very strong reasons to desire to control their adolescent children.
The earning power of younger siblings had been severely restricted by
child labor laws in the late nineteenth century, while compulsory schooling added costs while diminishing income. And even though there were
many who left school early, in a period when large families were still
very common, especially among the lower social strata, the family income, dependent heavily on the male wage earner, was severely
squeezed.[4] It was with the idea of helping parents rather than becoming
independent that one York lad interrupted his teacher:

> Half past ten, my lad; but what's the matter? Please sir, then may I go, sir?
> My mother said I should be fourteen at half past ten this morning, and I
> could leave school when I was fourteen, sir.[5]

When an Essex boy went to look for his first job he had the additional
privilege of wearing his first pair of long trousers.[6] For an apprentice
cooper, work "meant the end of childhood and the beginning of manhood, the first wage packet to be taken home heralding the new independence from parents, the chance to smoke openly and (I thought) the
chance to swear like a man."[7] Such expectations were bound to be
somewhat disappointed, for, while the lad was freer outside the home,
he was still subject to parental authority. Most apprentices got little or
nothing and had scant pocket money. The less skilled might earn more,
but they were expected to turn their wages straight over to mother, just
as their sisters were required to do. "I was only earning about twelve
shillings a week, and I had to give mother eight so I didn't have so very
much," explained a woman born in 1891, who had labored as a cardboard
box maker.[8] A Derbyshire shop assistant of the same age remembered
being better off than his peers: "My mother used to let me off fairly
cheaply you see for board, so long as I put some in the Post Office you
see." Normally, his keep would have cost him twelve to fourteen shill-

ings a week, but she charged him only ten out of his one-pound earnings. "I got off lightly."[9] In Preston, girls had to give up all their wages until they were close to marriage. Then they would be allowed to go on what was called "board," paying their mothers for their keep and saving the rest as their "bottom drawer."[10] Throughout the industrial north "when a man or woman became engaged they paid to the home not all their earnings. Women chiefly paid ten shillings a week, and men twelve or fourteen shillings, and of course also began to buy their own clothes. They tried to save out of what was left, ready for setting up a home of their own."[11]

Families could not afford to give up their wage earners too early, especially in those cases where the father was ill or absent. Phyl Hall, a Southwark girl born in 1910, courted a year before getting engaged, "but it took five years to get married on, just about in 1936. My mother did not exactly encourage us as she could see an end to my weekly contribution to the family expenses."[12] Parents expected and usually received deference in addition to support. When Phyl and her "young man" spent a weekend at Margate, they booked at a respectable boarding house: "A letter had to be shown to my parents as proof we did indeed have two separate rooms."[13] Eldest daughters felt obligated to look after younger siblings and, if a mother died, would automatically become mistresses of the house, even to the extent of becoming surrogate wife and mother.[14] The daughter of an East Anglican farm worker "walked out" with her future husband for twelve years, in part because he had no money, but also because her parents were dependent on her.[15]

Psychological dependence was often indistinguishable from the economic. A Cornish woman's parents "put-off" several young men and she was ultimately forced to marry secretly by license.[16] In the case of a shipwright's daughter, attachment was reciprocal. She did not begin to court until seventeen and then married the boy next door: "I never wanted to go very far . . . far from mother."[17] Feelings for sons could be just as strong, and there were men who kept their marriage plans secret so as not to hurt mother's feelings.[18] Nevertheless, right through the 1950s, the strongest bonds were between mothers and daughters. In Bethnal Green, as in other working-class neighborhoods, daughters settled as near as possible, if not in the same building then in nearby streets: "If you're living in these buildings it just goes on and on. If you've got any daughters getting married, they get a flat. Outsiders don't get it. It's all in the family."[19] Sons were also "spoken for" with landlords, but, as the proverbial wisdom suggested, they were expected to be more independent: "A son married is a son lost . . . . A daughter's a daughter all her life."[20]

Parents of daughters could expect to gain from marriage: "You're not losing a daughter, you're winning a son."[21] They took their rights of control and supervision very seriously, cajoling, threatening, even bribing their girls to give up sweethearts they objected to for reasons of age, religion, or status. Mary Manchester's mother told her, "Now look! If you will only pack him up, I will buy you a dance frock?" Mary accepted the offer.[22] In large families it was not uncommon for brothers to be equally protective. "I think boys were very sensitive about their sisters," explained a Welsh woman who had several brothers, "They wanted them to have the best."[23] Both boys and girls had curfews, strongly enforced by fathers. Alexander Pease remembered his sisters had to be in by 10 P.M.: "My dad used to be behind the door too if they were later than that."[24] One of his neighbors, who met her boyfriend in church, could recall being confronted by her father in the street late one evening: "He tapped me on the shoulder and said 'in,' at twenty-two years old."[25] Other girls fared much worse, however. Parents without the material resources to threaten or entice often used violence. Some daughters were beaten, others physically confined.[26] Boys were freer, but only relatively so. A young man, a mule spinner in good wages, argued with his parents about their 9:30 curfew— "It was like being in jail and you were working hard"—and as a result left home. But he eventually returned, finding, as most did, that home was cheaper and life more comfortable there.[27]

Middle-class families had long exercised tight control over their adolescent children and, while such Victorian restrictions as chaperonage were lifting by 1900, parents continued to influence courtship by the institutions they selected for their children's education and social life. Paternal influence did not stop there, however. One father was so outraged that his daughter was buying furniture for her marriage on hire purchase that he rang the firm to tell them (falsely) that the groom was under age. His patriarchalism was extended a step further by the new husband. When he decided that his wife should no longer work for the Air Ministry, he sent in her resignation without her knowledge. She was furious, but, because he held a high position in the Ministry, there was nothing she could do.[28]

If this kind of authority was not available to most working-class fathers and mothers, they were nevertheless quite capable of imposing their wills. Throughout the first half of the twentieth century, working-class children were extraordinarily accepting of parental decisions. One woman, devoted to her widowed mother, did not marry until she was forty and then because the mother pressured her suitor: "She was the one that—made me—start marriage; get—save up, she said, nearly time you married this girl."[29] On the other hand, problems at home were often the cause of early marriage. When eighteen-year-old Ada Bennett's father died in 1919, her stepmother "put ten shillings on the table and told me to get out." Within a year she was engaged to the only boy she had ever gone out with; and, after twelve months, they were married.[30]

II

Working-class parents were asserting a degree of authority they had not claimed since the eighteenth century. While they were not always successful, the augmentation of parental influence is undeniable and should warn us against assuming the historical declension of parental power. Economic, social, and psychological conditions of working-class life in the early twentieth century were in fact quite conducive to the revival of both patriarchy and matriarchy. In the newly stabilized "urban villages" family life found new vigor; kin ties reasserted themselves; and young people were subject to both greater vigilance and stronger social pressure. When Sarah Bennett came to marry a local boy from a family poorer than her own, it was her uncle who "gave him an excellent character."[31] While men were the ultimate source of authority, their absence during the day shifted much of the responsibility to women. More often than not it was the "old queens," grandmothers and older wives, who had the time to exercise real power in family matters. They were the assigned guardians of family morality and delegates to the court of public opinion meeting daily at doorstep and corner shop, passing perpetual judgment on everyone in a manner reminiscent of the Coolstrin Courts of earlier periods. "Over a period the health, honesty, conduct, history and connections of everyone in the neighborhood would be examined," noted Robert Roberts. "Each would be criticized, praised, censured openly or by hint and finally allotted by tacit consent a position on the social scale."[32] Sanctions at the disposal of such women ranged from "the matronly snub to the smashing of the guilty party's windows, or even a public beating."[33] By the twentieth century the powers of rough justice had clearly passed to the matriarchs. In matters moral and social (usually one and the same) their authority was undeniable. Offenses like incest or rape that might otherwise have been handled by the police were often punished informally.[34] Outsiders, including school teachers and social workers, met especially strong resistance when they attempted to substitute their power for that which already existed.[35]

Salford's matriarchs took a special interest in young folk. "Mothers round washing lines or going to the shop half a dozen times a day would inevitably hear of the peccadillos of their offspring."[36] Once boys were at work their behavior was subject to the authority of foremen and workmates, so the full force of gossip necessarily fell on the girls, whose lives were a good deal more local and who, as women, were viewed as being more morally responsible. In Preston it was women who were invariably blamed for lapses, social and sexual. People could remember distinctly a wedding in which a pregnant bride was actually stoned on her way to church, with the women hurling both the insults and the missiles.[37] The more common punishment, however, was more subtle and devastating. "If a single girl had a baby she lowered of course not only the social standing of her family but, in some degree, that of all her relations, in a chain reaction of shame."[38]

Young women were particularly vulnerable, for, while a married woman and even a common-law wife had certain fixed status, anything a daughter did affected herself and her family. The parental concern and the interest brothers took in their sisters' courtships were not wholly altruistic. An Oxfordshire girl remembered her courtship as a "very nerve wracking business"; and others also reported anxiety and even depression at the time of their entry, at age seventeen or eighteen, into serious heterosexual relations.[39] This was reflected not only in young women's reliance on fortune tellers and love potions, both of which remained surprisingly popular well into the twentieth century, but also in their resorting to ritualized modes of courtship more like those of the sixteenth and seventeenth centuries than the open, direct heterosexuality of the early industrial period.

Anxious to prevent rupture within the family, young people adopted a clandestine style of courtship that bore strong resemblance to the old rural practices. Knowing that her father would object to a musician as son-in-law, one Welsh woman kept her engagement secret until the last moment.[40] Mary Swan, who met her future spouse at church, kept him away from the house for a year.[41] Young men were brought to the house only when the relationship had reached a very serious stage. "There appears to be a deep seated idea that two sexes cannot mix in their dwellings with any degree of friendship, or with the knowledge of their parents, without the ulterior motive of marriage," it was said.[42] The home was a place for family, not for friends or mere acquaintances. The suitor knew his intentions were welcomed when he was invited for a meal; and only when "courting strong" would the couple be left alone in the parlor, always with someone else in the house: "You was never left alone with a young man in the house . . . that was sacred you see."[43] Courting on the couch was regulated by rules no less strict than those that governed bundling practices of the past; and only engaged couples felt free to engage in sexual intimacies.

As long as their authority was not directly challenged, parents were quite ready to grant a certain license to the young. They were even willing to put up with some ritualized rebellion, especially on the part of boys. As long as they were not too overt, generational tensions actually reaffirmed authority while, on the symbolic level, satisfying youth's desire for status and independence.[44] A degree of rebelliousness was expected, even encouraged, in boys; and mothers were ready to acknowledge the right of daughters to have their "fling":

> "Let them have it now!" my mother used to say. "Let girls go dancing, all dolled up. It's the only happiness a lot of 'em will ever get! Before long they'll be stuck down some warren with two kids and expecting again. That'll be 'romance' for the rest of it." Many girls knew this well enough. "All dressed up in glad rags," they sang, "Tomarrow they'll turn into sad rags"—a few happy heydays of freedom now before the clamps of marriage. Our *mores* required them to get a man, romantically, if possible, but get one—a tradesman's son at best, though, in the end, almost any youth would do who had a job and could work. But don't be left on the shelf![45]

In the twentieth century, adolescence itself had become a kind of collective rite of passage. Both boys and girls knew, however, that as a liminal phase it had to end sometime. "You have your fling, then settle down," observed one Bethnal Green boy during the 1950s; "You expect to get married." "You can't be a teenager all your life," said another.[46]

III

The expulsion of adolescents from the world of adults had been accompanied and reinforced by the simultaneous segregation of the sexes. Physically separated at school and work, boys and girls had fewer opportunities for the kind of everyday, casual mixing so characteristic of the early industrial period, which had diminished abruptly at the end of the nineteenth century. Not only were male and female roles more strictly defined by 1900, but the world of youth had once again become predominantly homosocial.

The sex and age segregation of the modern adolescent was the invention of the late Victorian era. The middle classes were the first to insist on excluding the teenagers from the adult world of work and leisure, segregating them in same-sex schools and erecting elaborate social barriers reinforced by rigid rules of etiquette.[47] The working classes were slower to adopt the new norms of sexual segregation, in part because crowded housing conditions and overlapping spheres of boy and girl labor made this impracticable. However, as the century progressed, they too began to adopt views on gender similar, if not identical, to those current among the upper classes. A certain amount of heterosociability was acceptable among children, but adolescence now became a phase of compulsory feminization for girls and viralization for boys. Flora Thompson thought it was only in the country where "a girl who showed any disposition to make friends of, or play games with, the boys was a 'tomboy' at best, or at worst, 'a fast forward young hussy,'" but, in fact, in towns like Preston the same stigma fell on young ladies who stepped across the gender boundaries.[48] Inhibitions that had previously been upper class became part of the working-class code of respectability. Any adolescent who dared show too much interest in the opposite sex felt the displeasure not only of parents but peers.

In the course of the early-twentieth-century sexual taboos multiplied. Among females the onset of menses came to mean withdrawal from all contact with the opposite sex. A Preston woman born just after World War I remembered running to tell her mother, who ordered her to "go home and in my bottom drawer you'll find some cloths. Put them up against you and keep warm, and keep away from lads." Her sense of vulnerability was further heightened when girl friends warned her "Don't let a lad touch you."[49] Almost total ignorance of anatomy, shared by women of this particular period regardless of class, fostered a fear of all forms of contact, apart from kissing. Sexuality was almost never discussed at home and there was an abhorrence of nakedness, even in the presence of other women. Women could remember learning nothing from their mothers about reproduction: "Everything was kept hidden from us. We couldn't talk like the ... mothers and daughters to-day. ... Everything was hushed up. You didn't know life as we ... know it now."[50]

As for boys, the beginning of adolescence also marked a significant turning point. Until the end of their schooling boys were, like their sisters, the object of what one contemporary called "ferocious affection."[51] Little distinction was made between male and female children; and at the beginning of the century it was still the habit to keep little boys in long curls and gowns until the age of three or four before "breeching" them. Even then, they spent their school years in the short trousers known as knickerbockers.[52] When it came, the break with childhood was even sharper for boys than for girls. It usually coincided with leaving school and entering work at fourteen, a point at which the son was also relieved of all household duties and, like his father and older brothers, became a privileged person in the household. One father, who had four daughters but only one son, always took the boy for a walk when there were domestic chores to be done, declaring "I'm not having him growing up a cissy with all these females."[53] As part of his viralization, the boy ceased to attend church, except for social purposes, and gained the freedom of the streets. Gradually, he would acquire masculine dress, language, and that certain swagger that would make him a regular in the local public house: "The act of 'going out with the boys' on Friday night, for the first time, was an initiation into manhood."[54]

Entry into the exclusive fraternity of manhood was far from automatic however. Because most juveniles lived at home, still beholden to if not actually wholly subject to their mothers, boys were under constant pressure to prove their masculinity. The felt ambiguity of their situation resulted in exaggerated behavior designed to demonstrate an independence of women. Coarse language, employed at work, on the street, and in the pub, underlined this separation. Younger lads were often as ignorant of sex as their sisters and could believe the story of the girl who became pregnant "through having a bath after the lodger," but no male could risk appearing not to know all about it:

> In the lavatories at the end of our fitting shop every cubicle partition, from skirting board to ceiling, carried a mass of graffiti which, in form and content, outfaced the walls of Pompeii. There, in sketch, rhyme, and apothegm, man's sexual activities, normal and deviant, lay fully exposed; a true "Open Sexame" as one wit had scrawled. Seated behind a bolted door, suspended, as they say, between "time and eternity," we absorbed it all, wondering, and later, with many a snigger, asked questions of one another on this or that aspect, each one seeking self-adjustment to the new knowledge according to temperament and upbringing.[55]

All association with women's work was studiously avoided. Men who helped with the cleaning or cooking when their wives were not fit to do the work were called "mop rags" and "diddy men." Boys who were too domestic were labeled effeminate, and, unless they also showed a certain toughness, they would be marked for life. As Robert Roberts remembered:

> The male weakling in certain households, often known even through manhood as "Sonny," would be a subject of whispered concern among neighbours. . . . One "mother-bound" youth among us, son of a widow and clerk in a city warehouse, strolled out on Sundays wearing of all things gloves, "low quarters," and carrying an umbrella! The virile damned him at once—an incipient "nancy" beyond all doubt, especially since he was known to be learning to play the violin.[56]

Too much concern with girls at too early an age could also stigmatize a boy as "soft" or "cissified," and often it was the most spoiled and dependent youths who acted most aggressively toward women, denying all interest in girls and sneering at those who did. Before age seventeen or eighteen no he-man was supposed to show any concern for girls, just sex. "Copulation, with the preliminaries leading to it, was a major topic of conversation" in the mills of turn-of-the-century Salford.[57] A half-century later the banter in northern mining towns was no different. To treat girls as anything but sex objects was to risk the scorn of one's mates.[58] To adolescent boys, girls were invariably known as "tarts," "pushers," or "bits of skirt"; to the girls, the smart lads were "knuts" and "bhoys." Females gave as much as they took. When a boy asked "does your mother know you're out?," the girl would reply, "Yes, she gave me a farthing to buy a monkey with—are you for sale?"[59]

By ganging together, adopting distinctive dress and hair styles, adolescent males further emphasized—and exaggerated—their masculinity. Loosely associated with certain streets and neighborhoods, gangs of males adopted a particular costume, "the union short, bell-bottomed trousers, the heavy leather belt, picked out in fancy designs with the large steel buckle and the thick, iron-shod clogs," in order to establish their identity and territorial dominance.[60] Aggressive-sounding names—Redskins, Hell Hounds, Black Hand League—were preferred for similar reasons. In Manchester the frequent encounters between rival groups, known as "scuttles," evolved into a gamelike pattern, reminiscent of those preindustrial brawls in which the combatants, once bloodied, withdrew without further damage. As Robert Roberts recalled it, "all the warring gangs were known by street names and fought, usually by appointment—Next Friday 8 P.M. Hope Street v. Adelphi."[61]

The violence was verbal, highly ritualized, and normally symbolic rather than real, a homosocial drama designed more to reassure the young warriors of their masculinity than to do harm to the opponents. One Manchester veteran recalled:

> We'd sort of glare at one another at first and wait for the first one to start. . . . They used to have sticks and all that, not big hefty sticks, small sticks. 'Course, if they came, we'd sort out something ourselves. It was more or

less brandishing them to frighten one another, more or less it was with fists. . . . We rarely used belts. It wasn't too serious; every party was more or less satisfied with a black eye or a nose bleed."[62]

By the 1950s the homosocial rites of youth had become an accepted part of working-class life. It was only when ritual battles, like those between the Mods and Rockers, disrupted their everyday existence that adults took much notice, and then the attention given to the more violent aspects of male ritual tended to obscure its more benign, essentially conservative, features.

Antagonism between male youths, and between them and adolescent girls, was normally quite restrained, but could take quite bizarre forms on occasion. During World War I, boys from the Ancoats area of Manchester, known as the Napoo gang, roamed the streets with razor blades stuck conspicuously in their cloth caps:

They'd creep behind girls and women in the street, grab the long plaited hair which hung down the back (that was the style of the day) and with a sharp pair of scissors cut off the plaited hair and run off with it as a souvenir. They got bolder and bolder hunting the women with plaited hair. Some used to go upstairs on the trams late at night, and if a woman was sitting on her own, they'd cut off her hair, then, like lightening, dash off without being caught. The idea was probably hatched from the films of Red Indians scalping the whites. The toughs would take the plaits to the public house to show how clever he was at hunting.[63]

These incidents, and others like them in later decades, were the subject of great public outrage, but what moralists missed was the essentially ritual character of the antagonism between young men and women.[64] Working-class girls were no less rough in their behavior and gave as much as they took on occasions like the St. Giles Fair at Oxford, where it had become a tradition for girls to parade about "dressed in jockey-caps . . . imitation open jackets and waistcoats, and smoking cigars or cigarettes."[65] Young females went around the streets in groups, and when they met a gang of boys, did not wait for introductions: "Why, if we wants to talk to a chap, we just knocks off 'is cap."[66] Mills in Lancashire initiated the Christmas holidays with "wholesale kissing between the sexes. If a female (after a struggle) was able to kiss a male, he was obligated to pay a 'footing' of one shilling, which helped pay for the meat pies and other eatables."[67] Those who confused these "rites of reversal" with sexual promiscuity would have done well to remember Charles Booth's observation about the rough behavior of Bromley working girls: "Their gregarious nature prevents them from harm."[68]

IV

Society had little to fear from these and similar formalized encounters between the sexes. By 1900 courtship was already circumscribed by rules of time and place as elaborate as any of those that had prevailed in preindustrial society. These served to ease youth's own anxieties about heterosexuality by postponing intimacy, for courtship had acquired a new calendar, which severely limited the contacts between the sexes. At the turn of the century, the weekend was already taking on a recognizable modern structure, with most weekdays rigidly segregated by sex. On Fridays women stayed home to pretty themselves and the house; for males, "finglin neet" or "jinglin neet," as it was known in the northern industrial districts, was "almost a permanent stag night. In a way it was sacred—a recurring feast dedicated to the holy celebration of masculinity."[69] Should a man be found courting Friday night he would be treated to rough music by his mates. For a girl to neglect her cleaning caused no less offense; and suitors would be sent away with the comment "he awt to know better."[70]

Saturday and Sunday nights were now youth's moment of license, but not without definite rules limiting courtship to certain fixed times and places. From the 1890s until World War II, everyone obeyed the codes of the "Monkey rank," gathering at locales like Manchester's Oldham Street.[71]

> From Hulme, from Ardwick, and from Ancoats they come, in the main well dressed, and frequently sporting a flower in the buttonholes of their jacket. But the motive is not so much that of meeting their friends, as of forming an acquaintanceship with some young girl. Girls resort to Oldham Street on a Sunday night in nearly as large numbers as the boys... The boys exchange rough salutations with the girls, who seem in no way less vigorous than the boys themselves, and whose chief desire, one would think, was to pluck from the lads' buttonholes, the flowers which many of them wear.[71]

Boys and girls began "skylarking," "getting off," or "stagging" in their early teens.[72] In Preston, Saturday night "clicking" commenced when the youth left school. Until they were seventeen or eighteen, both sexes would "click" with several different partners each month, making and breaking relationships with relentless regularity.[73] Each of the promenades had its own age and social geography. The Fishergate topped Preston's status hierarchy. It attracted the better class of older apprentices and shop assistants:

> It was one mass of boys and girls that used to walk up and down, and kind of meet girl friends... Aye, they all used t' walk about an' if they saw anybody they fancied, they'd whistle, you know, er say "ello" and try and pick up a conversation.

> That were the idea of finding a mate, in Fishergate, when I were very young like. Shall we say sixteen. From about sixteen onwards like. But I personally, I had no new suit. They used to put their new suits on, you know, and

walk up and down Fishergate. . . . very rarely did I walk up, walk up and down Fishergate, because I 'ad no decent clo'es ta walk up an' down.[74]

Avenham and Miller Parks were less demanding; and down at Tram Bridge, known as "Swaddie's Corner," the soldiers hung about. But the least selective of all was Moor Park, where the unemployed in their shabby clothes went through the motions in sad isolation.[75] Everywhere, similar gradations were evident. At Chorley, "The Drag" featured a "Tuppence-ha'penny side" for factory workers and a "Tanner side" for clerks and office girls.[76] In London young people sorted themselves out in a similar manner.[77]

> After tea, the bright boys wash, clean their boots, and change into their "second-best" attire, and stroll forth, either to the picture palace or to the second house of the Balham Hippodrome; perhance, if the gods be favourable, to an assignation on South Side Clapham Common; sometimes to saunter, in company with others, up and down that parade until they "click" with one of the "birds." The girls are out on much the same programme. They, too, promenade until they "click" with someone, and are escorted to a picture palace or hall or chocolate shop. Usually it is a picture palace, for, in Acacia Grove, mothers are very strict as to the hours at which their young daughters shall be in. Half-past ten is the general rule . . .
>
> As the boys pass the likely girls they glance, and, if not rebuffed, offer wide smiles. But they do not stop. At the second meeting, however, they smile again and touch hands in passing, or cry over the shoulder some current witticism, as: " 'Snice night, Ethel!' or "I should shay sho!"
>
> And Ethel and Lucy will swing around, challengingly, with scaping feet, and cry, "Oooh!" The boys linger at the corner, looking back, and the girls, too, look back. Ethel asks Lucy, "Shall we?" and Lucy says, "Ooh—I d'no," and by the time the boys have come down level with them . . . "Well—shall we stroll 'cross the Common?" "I don't mind." Then boys and girls move forward together . . . They have "got off."[77]

By the 1920s, dance palaces and cinemas were bringing adolescent courtship indoors, though, as Ada Iles, a Bristol bus conductress remembered, the basic ritual was unaltered: "I went out with literally hundreds of boys before I started walking out seriously with one of 'em."[78] Worsley's "rabbit run" lasted until World War II, though by that time most of the traditional promenades had been abandoned by the better-off members of the working classes.[79]

For those not allowed to join the monkey ranks for reasons religious or social, the Sunday School youth class or cycling club served a similar purpose. Walking home from chapel or choir served many of the same purposes as the promenade, permitting acquaintance without commitment, imparting experience while certifying innocence. Booth had noticed that, in London's Bromley district, some went to church in hopes of charity, others to show off their new clothes or "to do a bit of courting.[80] Among Preston's closely knit Catholic community, young people "both-

23. Hampstead Heath on the August Bank Holiday, 1896. The photograph by Paul Martin shows girls dancing with one another while the boys look on. (Used by permission of the Gernsheim Collection, Harry Ransom Humanities Research Center, The University of Texas at Austin)

ered together in a crowd. It was a Church crowd. And we all went to Benediction first, and then we all used to come back and play cards at our house. Some of them, two or three of them, married to one another."[81] The rites of the streets were no less selective and innocent, however. Ada Iles' multitude of flirtations had not forfeited her virtue.[82] A Preston man remembered: "We weren't sex mad or anything like that. I mean, a girl could trust herself with us; we might have had thoughts and ideas but we certainly kept them to ourselves."[83]

In Edwardian London the music hall had become a favorite venue of courtship.[84] And, after the ordeals of World War I, people no longer objected to young women in pubs, so that they, together with the cinemas and dance palaces, took over when the halls faded in popularity.[85] Preston's dance halls were, like the churches, clubs, and promenades, socially differentiated and closely supervised. One woman remembered that the Regent was the place to meet "nice" boys: "There were very few tatty people. They weren't allowed in the Regent. Some used to be scruffier. They used to be at Delaware Street, up New Hall Lane, and Magestic... Park Ballroom was fairly decent, but the Regent was, if you went to the Regent... They were all better-class people that went."[86]

Modern dance was a favorite target of contemporary moralists, but in reality it served many of the same functions as traditional country dancing. Young people went to places like the Regent in groups, more to be seen than to pair off. Young girls danced with their "mates," who, more often than not, were of their own sex, while the boys watched from the sidelines. The dance was more homosocial than heterosocial, maintaining rather than subverting the distance between boys and girls. Despite the fears that the dancing craze aroused, neither the venues nor the dances themselves promoted precocity. When, after 1910, dancing broke with the traditions of the waltz and the polka to become faster paced, more individualistic, and athletic, the frantic style and frequent changes of partner gave very little encouragement to premature monogamy.[87] As late as the 1950s, putting on a dance record still produced what seems to us a very peculiar effect:

> The adolescent girls at once all got up and started dancing together. The interesting thing is that many of them had their boy friends there, but not one of them danced. They sat tightly with their girl friends, but as soon as each record started the girls got up and danced while the men watched. . . . Each girl danced with her "mate," they knew each other's step perfectly, they were experts together. For instance, I noticed one young girl who did not at first join in the dancing. Half-way through the evening her "mate" came in from work. The two girls danced together non-stop for the rest of the evening. Sometimes it appeared they were showing off to their boys.[88]

V

The homosocial character of the adolescent subculture preserved innocence as effectively as any form of adult supervision. Working-class youngsters chaffed at rules laid down by the authorities, but slavishly obeyed their own very strict rules of etiquette. Among middle-class youth chivalry prevented undue intimacy, but in places like Ancoats and Bethnal Green it was rough rather than genteel behavior that served this purpose. Liza of Lambeth was courted by blows in a manner that would have been familiar to any peasant couple:

> He looked at her for a moment, and she, ceasing to thump his hand, looked up at him with half-opened mouth. Suddenly he shook himself, and closing his fist gave her a violent, swinging blow in the stomach.
>
> "Come on," he said.
>
> And together they slid down into the darkness of the passage.[89]

The norms of viralization and feminization prohibited direct intimacy, thus leaving joking and teasing as the only acceptable way of expressing affection. The fifteen-and sixteen-year-old boys who kept diaries for Peter Willmott in the 1950s never went anywhere without their best friends: "Went to the Regal with three of my mates. We sat behind some birds and tried to start talking to them. They kept on giggling and telling us to shut up."[90] The lads were still feigning indifference to the girls they liked to save face with their peers: "I don't want to get caught with a girl. I still like going out with the boys," Peter Willmott was told.[91] In northern working-class neighborhoods, the same rules governed sexual relations as late as the 1960s:

> Courting is done in groups. You'll see a group of girls in mid-evening pass a group of boys, exchange a few words and carry on. Yet at the very end of the evening the groups will meet again, break down into couples and the apparently casual exchange of words earlier turns out to be between boys and girls who have already fixed their wedding day.[92]

Despite all the sexual boasting and aggression, most of these boys had no real experience of sex until their late teens or early twenties. If they had intercourse, it was usually with prostitutes, the "harpies" who often hung about the margins of the monkey ranks.[93] It cannot be said that they had any real knowledge of women as women; and their notions of females were almost as idealized as the views that adolescent girls had about men.

> The young apprentice retained an innocence, dreaming romantically still of some schoolteacher perhaps, a near-asexual goddess of childhood, "mystic, pure, clothed in white samite," or worshipping a film star, remote and inexpressibly lovely. All this, however, in no wise prevented our having designs, unattainable but vile, lustful and guilt-ridden, on the plump young "pusher" at the greengrocer's, in which fantasy our graffiti could provide some peculiar data.[94]

This combination of fear and attraction produced a peculiar awkwardness that prevented intimacy beyond sex play with women of the same age and status. Early encounters were limited to symbolic gestures, and even later on boys found themselves unable to express their feelings. "We hadn't the vocabulary they have today, you know," was the admission of one former Preston dandy, who always made it a point to carry a raincoat as ground cover should a girl prove unexpectedly willing. "We had to do it in a more round about way. Sometimes it would take you about a month, four Saturday nights and four Sunday nights to pluck up courage even to speak to her."[95]

Otherwise very rough men often behaved quite childishly in private or domestic settings when their mothers, sweethearts, or wives were present. The public sexual bravado compensated for feelings of weakness men experienced in the domestic setting. The swagger and obscenity of street and shop floor were signs not of sexual confidence but the lack of it. Such behavior was a bond among men and a barrier between them and women. At home, while courting, and even in bed neither men nor women felt comfortable with their own sexuality. The lovemaking was as inhibited as their conversation, accompanied, as Robert Roberts so perceptively observed, by an undeniable tendency toward regression on the part of the man:

Respectability sank deep through working-class womanhood; in the naming of sexual parts and actions a wife might have known all the terms on the tongue of the prostitute, but her husband, if he talked on the pillow at all, was permitted only euphemisms—private, infantile and dialectical. And that was how he wanted it, for the wife he so often called "mother" was a "good" woman and in her presence no sexually obscene words ever escaped his lips.[96]

This reticence might be thought to have resulted from those official campaigns for sexual purity launched late in the Victorian period by church, school, and various private vigilance bodies. A Bath schoolboy remembered vividly the four cuts with the cane he had gotten for "kissin' a girl through the railings" in the sex-segregated playground.[97] In Plymouth, Oxford, and other places where feasts and fairs were said to contribute to the "bearishness" of girls and boys, there was strong pressure to limit these activities.[98] Church and choir had normally been coeducational, but the new youth organizations, beginning with the Church Lads and Boys' Brigades, and culminating with the Boy Scouts and Girl Guides, were now segregated. But when labor and socialist youth groups—notably the Kibbo Kift Kindred, Cooperative Youth Movement, and Woodcraft Folk—self-consciously created integrated activities, no adolescent orgies resulted.[99] Working-class boys and girls hiked and camped together, but the result was not, as the middle-class purity reformers feared, premature promiscuity. Quite the contrary, Preston Scouts and Guides shared tents with the innocence of small children. "You were younger then," recalled a former Guide. "Boys and girls all used to be together. You would play out in a gang, not in one's [pairs] like they are now from being kids."[100]

It was not as if adult authorities were responsible for the sexual inhibition evident throughout the first sixty years of this century. Even when thrown together, adolescents exhibited no natural instinct for conjugality. They were deeply troubled by relationships with the opposite sex and thus found the ritual formalities very reassuring. Ada Isles, who described herself as having been a "real she-cat" during the 1920s, always played by the rules of the game:

> We'd either go promenading or get them to take us to the pictures an' get 'em to pay as well. . . . We'd give 'em a kiss an' let 'em do a bit of smooching but we wouldn' let 'em get far. There was never any sex. . . . We didn't know anythin' about it, an' in any case we'd be scared of getting caught. There wasn't much chance for that 'cos most of us 'ad to be in by ten o'clock every night till we was married.[101]

A Preston man of the same generation remembered that what pairing off there was always occurred in the company of peers: "We didn't sit round hugging and kissing in front of the neighbors. . . . And Still, we didn't go round dark corners for it! You had to book your seats [in the park] at 6 o'clock, you know. There was one couple on one end and

24. A scene photographed by Paul Martin on Yarmouth Beach in 1892. The young couples may have shocked some observors, but their courtship was as innocent as it was public. Courting in groups was perfectly acceptable among the working classes. (Courtesy of Gernsheim Collection, Harry Ransom Humanities Research Center, The University of Texas at Austin)

one couple on the other, and six foot of space."[102] These same older people tend to pity rather than envy the precocious monogamy of young people today. They clearly enjoyed their protracted adolescence: "I don't weigh these young 'uns up. They want to end their lives before they've started."[103]

If the low rates of illegitimacy and premarital pregnancy are any indication, the generations from 1890 to 1960 were perhaps the most severely restrained in modern times. The ratio of illegitimate to legitimate births, which had begun to fall from the mid-nineteenth century onward, reached a low at the turn of the century and showed only slight increases (except in war times) before turning sharply upward in the 1960s. Prebridal pregnancy followed the same downward trend until it was only sixteen percent of all births just after World War II.[104] While something of this low rate might be attributable to the use of birth control, it is very unlikely that the young, who have been the last to adopt contraception, were escaping pregnancy by this method. A more likely explanation is the chastity of the sort practiced by Bethnal Green adolescents in the 1950s. Few girls had intercourse before marriage; and the boys who had had done so with prostitutes or with the few girls known as "bangers."[105] The lads were obsessed with sex, but wary of girls. Masturbation was very widespread among them; and, while there is also some evidence of homosexuality among young working-class men, this was usually a passing phase, also associated with adolescence.[106] If the males gave almost no thought to marital relations at this time in their lives, girls were almost totally absorbed in reading, talking, and dreaming about such things. Having had no real experience, they tended to idealize men, conjuring up dream lovers modeled on fictional and cinematic heroes. Male fantasy worked in another way, dividing women into those good girls, who were fit to marry, and the "harpies," who were good for nothing but sex. "Among the 'improvers,' older apprentices, there was much serious talk about the dangers of taking 'damaged goods' into wedlock and the need to marry a virgin," recalled Robert Roberts. "Out of this welter of talk the young male formulated a marriage ideal—his bride-to-be had to combine all the virgin purity of the school miss with the lubricity of that girl at the greengrocer's. He usually settled for less!"[107] By contrast, the girls' images of men tended to be more unified and more thoroughly romantic. They imagined their lovers to be tall, dark, and handsome heroes, who would sweep them into marital bliss. "Simple natures all," Walter Greenwood called them, "prey to romantic notions whose potent toxin was to become part of the fabric of their brains."[108] Throughout the twentieth century, sixpenny novels and romantic films claimed a massive female audience, who found their vision of ideal love affairs, devoid of sex or realistic relationships, wholly compelling.[109] "Many women, married or not, didn't buy photographs of stars like Valentino for nothing; they purchased fantasy too."[110] For most, any real heterosexual intimacy, before or after marriage, would remain just that—fantasy.

Girls fell in love earlier and more often than the boys, not because they were more fickle, but because there was great pressure to fall in love with *a* man, whether or not it was *the* man.[111] They wrote love notes, while the boys sent those obscene, sadistic comic valentines that had become so popular since the end of the nineteenth century.[112] Girls were much more practiced at love, if only in their imaginations, and were often the eager initiators when, at seventeen or eighteen, serious courtship became possible. For boys the transition was more abrupt. While females were prepared to have several suitors, males usually married the first eligible woman they felt strongly attracted to.[113]

If women were better prepared for love, it was because they had to be. Encouraged to be in love with men from an early age, they were thus psychologically prepared for a marriage market in which men were the choosers. In the twentieth century the jilted man was once again the object of great solicitude, for rejection threatened his very masculinity. Permanent bachelors were to be pitied, but old maids despised. For men celibacy was assumed to be a matter of choice. Single men who lived together sometimes aroused suspicion and even violence, but the lonely bachelor was left alone. But for women celibacy was a sign of failure, something unnatural, which subjected them to the taunts of local children and the scorn of married neighbors.[114]

Thus women were under great compulsion to enter the courtship process early and to make themselves as attractive as possible. They often took the initiative in the early stages, and when men spoke of "getting hooked," this was a tribute to their initiative. However, a man did not like to admit any romantic inclinations that might suggest a feminine trait in his nature. If a boy began to court too early he was called a "cissy" by mates who exercised a powerful control over the timing of courtship. A young man's confession that he had gotten "caught" was the only acceptable excuse for his withdrawal from his peers, and even then they would insist that he spend Friday ("fingling") night in their company.[115] When a young man did fall, it was usually sudden and unexpected, proof of love's mysterious powers and (next to sex) the best excuse to abandon his mates during that period of serious courtship leading to engagement and then to marriage.

VI

As the end of adolescence drew near, courtship evolved from "walking out" to "keeping company." The change might be marked by whispered vows or the exchange of small love tokens, but it was usually kept secret from parents and peers until the couple judged the time right for a more public announcement.[116] A proper engagement meant a ring, usually costing about a week's wages.[117] Early in the century only the most affluent of the working class had a formal engagement party and placed an announcement in the local newspapers, but the ring was virtually obligatory.[118] It had special meaning for those couples who encountered real or imagined obstacles. For some, like the Welsh woman who kept hers hidden until her family had given permission, the ring worked as a bargaining chip in much the same way that the old "private spousals" had served.[119] Something of the old ring magic had also returned. Harry Mallory exchanged rings with Sally Ringrose just before he went away as a soldier. He worried when his broke because he believed she would think it intentional and would say "we're parted, we're parting, you've broken your ring." Women seem to have taken such signs much more seriously than men, however; and it was they who usually insisted that the engagement be done just right, an expression of their greater anxiety about the whole process. When Trixie Packe and Jack Baker formalized their engagement in the 1920s, it was she who went into the jeweler's. Jack waited outside.[120]

Engagements appear to have become progressively longer and more ritualized over the course of the century. Married couples surveyed in 1947 had a minimum engagement of a year, but by the 1950s two years seemed to have become the norm.[121] At the beginning of the century, the poorest strata had been used to short courtships and informal engagements for reasons that were social as well as financial. Unskilled workers married younger and, because of the greater uncertainty of

25. *The Proposal* found a place in many turn-of-the-century homes. It reflected the growing ritual importance of engagement. (Courtesy of the Board of Trustees of the Victoria and Albert Museum)

employment and housing, more precipitously. One seventeen-year-old had not had time to save because of his low factory wages. "To get married they used to sub it you know—sub[scribe] the money. I know I subbed a couple of pound. Well that did all the lot of us. Wedding ring, barrel of beer." Five shillings each had gone for the ring and the bride's dress; the marriage lines had cost a little over seven shillings; the rest went for beer and whisky.[122] The daughter of a Darlington boilerman knew her husband only a year and did not have time to save before she married in 1913: "I didn't think I was going to be married so soon you see because—there was a vacancy, that's how we were married soon."[123] A miner who had no formal engagement—"we just used to walk out"—led an equally hand-to-mouth existence. When he married in 1912, he had just enough to buy a license and the couple was forced to move in with his parents, though they would have preferred to have a home of their own.[124]

By the 1940s the length and formality of engagement had grown in tandem. The war caused many couples to be somewhat more hasty, but by the 1950s courtship was again an extended process, with less than a third of all couples marrying within a year of first meeting.[125] Two to four years' acquaintance was now considered vital to the success of a marriage. "Half the broken marriages of today are caused through marrying without getting to know each other thoroughly," observed one upper-working-class woman.[126] It was Stella Davies' impression that the time needed to "furnish a house in the manner suitable to their station in life" was the major reason that couples had long engagements.[127] Hire purchase may have truncated this process somewhat, but credit was not available to the vast majority of working people until after World War II and, therefore, engagement remained the crucial preliminary to most marriages.

Couples did not expect to marry until the groom was earning a "man's wage." Bank clerks were required to obtain special permission if they married before achieving a minimum salary set by the firm, but it would appear that working people had their own, no less rigorous standards, which were applied to grooms by parents at the time they gave consent.[128] However, a bride's savings were no less vital than the man's wage. One woman of quite humble background, who had known her fiancé for six years, used the time profitably to construct the resources for a big wedding. "Oh yes, you didn't get married as soon as you met anybody those days you know," she later observed, also remembering that her parents helped out by giving the couple second-hand furniture.[129] In the 1930s it took Phyl Hall and her fiancé five years to save for the appropriate "three piece [bedroom] suite"; it took Trixie and Jack Baker a little less time because his mother was in the furniture trade and let them have their suite at cost.[130]

By far the greater burden of establishing the new house fell to the bride's kin. There was no longer formal dowry (or even the word "dowry") as such, but her parents felt under much greater obligation. In Sussex it was the habit of the bride to have all necessary dental work done during the engagement to save future expenses. Premarital extractions were also common in the north of England as late as the 1940s.[131] Among middle-class people "a bride was often given enough to make her at least partially independent of her husband," but the contributions at lower social levels were, by necessity, less substantial.[132] Parents and close kin normally gave linen and useful household items that made up the proletarian "bottom drawer." Men were not supposed to bother themselves with domestic matters. "It would be terrible . . . if a young man bought your—clothes or—provided anything, that wouldn't be the thing at all," noted a Cornish matron.[133] While a man might use the engagement period to accumulate an independent bank account for his own use, all the bride's earnings went directly into the future home. It was acceptable for a man to keep something back, but odd for a woman to do so, even though some did put something aside for their first maternities.[134] Thus women not only mortgaged themselves to marriage, but became habituated to the role of domestic managers and consumers.

Twentieth-century engagement had become, like the pre-industrial betrothal, a major rite of separation and transition. It separated the couple from the homosocial world of adolescence, allowing them to concentrate not only on one another but on the complicated negotiations with family (especially her family) that were so vital to the establishment of a new household. It was also one of those transitional liminal periods, replete with new freedom but also with special dangers. Both men and women were supposed to show sexual as well as material restraint as they approached marriage. Surveys done in the 1940s found that it was the young who were most insistent on premarital chastity. Even males who might have had other sexual experiences were often chaste with their fiancées because they believed that marriage should be a "new experience, a new thrill."[135] The most common metaphor for the non-virgin was not so much moral as mercantile—"second hand," "shop soiled"—not fresh and desirable.[136] Women were even more insistent than men on making marriage a unique sexual experience, but it is worth noting that men more often favored a single sexual standard, emphasizing restraint for both sexes.[137] "It was joy on my wedding night to know this was my first experience," one working man told Geoffrey Gorer; "If he [the male] has ideas of finding a virgin he should do likewise," stated another.[138]

It is estimated that in the 1950s only a third of women under twenty had had intercourse, a very low figure compared with both nineteenth-century figures and the eighty-percent levels common today. What is more, almost all the sexual intimacy was occurring during betrothal. There was very little premarital cohabitation and illegitimacy remained very low, but, as in the pre-industrial period, some couples were exercising the liberties allowed them during this liminal moment to become sexually intimate.[139] Nevertheless, most women were still kept from temptation by the vision of a white wedding, for "as virgins they had cherished a solitary dream, the expectation of the climax of their wedding day. Wedding day, when, clad in the appropriate—afterwards utterly useless—finery, they appeared for a glorious moment the cynosure of a crowd of envious females."[140] For men it was the notion of the "good" woman and the fear of "damaged goods" that was the major deterrent.[141] Even the Preston dandy, who was always prepared with a ground sheet in case a girl was willing, did not really expect to use it. "You heard about the odd girl having a baby before she was married," he noted, "but not as many as today."[142]

In a society in which the homosocial world of youth had become so radically dissociated from the heterosexual realm of adulthood, a ritualized transition was absolutely vital to the success of a marriage. Families no longer negotiated—in fact, families often did not meet before the wedding day—but it was the time for the couple to try their new relationship before the court of peers and kin. The posting of banns had ceased to be the occasion for the public test of a couple's commitment, but the betrothal was still a crucial probation period, especially for the man. Engagement was a rite of separation for both sexes, but, because the working class woman would remain so closely attached to her family, it was more significant for the male. If a man ever gave up his rough, homosocial habits, it was during engagement. He spent a great deal of time at the bride's home, proving himself a worthy husband but also adjusting to the family that would become as important, if not more important, than his own. In Bethnal Green in the 1940s and 1950s future sons-in-law were subject to intense scrutiny. In addition to the father's consent, they had to pass mother's inspection. It was said that "any mother wants to have a look at her daughter's young man. . . . She wants to see the goods laid out on the table." One suitor, whose social credentials were initially suspect, remembered it felt as if he were before a "Judge and Jury." Visits served not only to screen young men for possible social or moral flaws, but to adjust them to a new social situation. Willmott and Young aptly called it "courting mother-in-law," a time when "he rehearses while a suitor his future role of son-in-law as well as husband."[143] Earlier, suitors had felt obligated to obtain parental approval only when a bride was under age, but by the 1950s asking father's consent had become a moment of real significance and occasional high drama.[144] Joseph Molder had been privately engaged for five years when he finally summoned the nerve to approach Elizabeth Chambers' father. He acted with the deference and diplomacy of a seventeenth-century suitor, the only difference being that instead of being queried about what lands he possessed he was asked for his Post-Office savings book.[145] This practice had become so common by the 1940s that it was described as a "ritual," the male's principal rite of passage, separating him from his family and incorporating him into hers.[146]

The formal dowry had long since disappeared, but the prospective bride's family had once again taken on the responsibility for endowing the marriage by helping to set up the new home and by providing the wedding itself. In pre-industrial society it had been more his marriage than hers, the man being the one responsible for the household and providing the big wedding. For most of the nineteenth century, arranging the marriage and setting up house (what there was of it) were more often a joint venture, but now, with the separation of home and work along lines of sex, the domestic responsibilities were hers—with the assistance of her family. At the beginning of the century, it was understood that the woman was to provide the linen and cooking utensils, the man the first month's rent and some of the furniture, but as time went on women and their families bore the greater burden. We are told both parties saved, but it was the men who came up short on the wedding day. In one case, the mother and sister helped the bride with basic things and her workmates bought her a tea service.[147] In another instance, the parents of the bride made the marriage possible at the last minute by taking the couple into their crowded home, though not before having a "thorough talk" with the errant groom.[148] In any case, it was the woman who was responsible for the home. When newlyweds moved in with parents, it was more often with the bride's than the groom's. Women remained much more dependent on their families, particularly their mothers, a major reason for the matrifocality of the whole courtship process.[149]

Even in courtship the full resources of the bride's family were at the suitor's disposal. At the same time he was coming to be accepted by the father and brothers, he was being fed, waited on, and catered to by the women of the family. After the wedding he would have the right to call his in-laws "Mum" and "Dad."[150] On the other hand, girls rarely visited their future in-laws. One bride's family was so poor that her fiancé felt obligated to feed her, "otherwise she'd have faded away," but normally it was the male who was the beneficiary of parental attention.[151] Even before a girl was wed, she was practicing the role prescribed for her in marriage: giving, serving, attending to all the domestic details.

Engagement served to confirm the female dependency on marriage and identify her with domesticity, but it also reaffirmed in innumerable small ways the extended character of working-class family life by reinforcing female bonds. One woman, who had lost her own mother in childhood, was eternally grateful to her stepmother, who found houses for all her children in the neighborhood. "They had to go where she said, you see. They couldn't please themselves."[152] Another told Madeline Kerr: "I couldn't get on without me mother. I could get on without me husband, I don't notice him."[153] In some cases the family of the bride even found employment for the groom.[154]

The extended engagement process incorporated the groom into the bride's family circle, but he was drawn into a conjugal relationship only to the extent that the prevailing norm of the male as provider would permit. Men put away boyish things and modified their relations with their mates, but only temporarily. In the course of the engagement, they also transferred their familial attachments to the required degree, yet socially and emotionally engaged men had entered into conjugality about as far as they would ever go. Never again would a man be so careful with his language and appearance, or be so chivalrous or romantic. Early in the century, "courtship was a time when one assumed the airs of a class superior to one's own," observed Robert Roberts, for, after marriage, and sometimes even before, a man would lapse back into his old homosocial ways, knowing that, apart from financial support, less was expected of a husband than a suitor.[155] Even in the 1950s, the intimacy was no easier to sustain. So fragile was the conjugal relationship that "after the first few months of intensive wooing the love-affair either breaks off or becomes more pedestrian, with the prospect of permanence."[156] The closer the wedding day, the more the groom would retreat to the safety of the homosocial world of the pub and football grounds. Betrothal was his rite of both separation and incorporation. As far as he was concerned, the marriage was complete even before he arrived at the church. The wedding was her day, her rite of passage.

CHAPTER 10

꧁꧂꧁꧂꧁꧂꧁꧂꧁꧂꧁꧂꧁꧂꧁꧂꧁꧂꧁꧂꧁꧂꧁꧂꧁꧂

The Lady Generally Likes White Weddings: Revival of the Big Wedding

Traditions are hallowed not by the realities of the past, but the felt needs of the present. In the late nineteenth century the veneration of everything old and "truly" British became an obsession with the educated classes. Their preservationist instincts were reflected in the Gothic revival, the garden city movement, and multiple resurrections of civic, military, and academic pageantry.[1] The same desire for continuity was evident in the folklore and folksong renaissance, whose genteel adherents searched village and small town for evidence of an uncorrupted cultural lineage. The revival of courtship and marriage ritual was an integral part of this preservationist program, but the folklorists did more than restore, they invented. One enthusiastic Lincolnshire parson had taken to knotting his stole loosely around the hands of the couple after the blessing of the ring, a pretty practice that was much admired until a colleague tactfully pointed out that it was pure invention, there being no historical precedent in any prior marriage service.[2] Other revivals, such as the marriage at the church door performed at Thaxted, Essex, were more authentic, but it was not the genuinely historical that captured the popular imagination.[3] The big white wedding had come to epitomize tradition, even though not one of its major elements—the gown and veil, giving away the bride, the rice, the honeymoon—predated the nineteenth century. Thiselton Dyer, one of the few folklorists concerned with historical authenticity, was moved to point out that the veil was probably "nothing more than a milliner's substitute."[4] Others were forced to admit that until Indian rice became a part of the mid-Victorian upperclass diet it had never been associated with weddings. It too proved to be a substitute for the "vulgar custom" of throwing shoes and clods of earth, still practiced in some northern places almost to the end of the Victorian era.[5]

The popularizing of the big white wedding as *the* British nuptial tradition was, as were the other revivals of the period, an act of self-veneration by those seeking to legitimate and impose their own social standards. The original was the creation of the Victorian upper classes and—through the symbolism of giving away the bride in white, the family reception, and the honeymoon—emphasized their ideal of conjugal love and the nuclear family. The big wedding remained principally theirs in the early part of this century. A few working people had big weddings, but not many:

> You couldn't afford to invite any Tom, Dick, and Harry in those days. It was a bit of an effort... to get married and have a decent wedding—everybody tried to get married, I mean to say—they always gave their daughters a good white wedding if they could, if it was a white wedding occasion. But then—then—sometimes that didn't always happen like that, but still if you got your daughters a white wedding you was very pleased and you'd do it, if it was your last penny.[6]

It was not really until mid-century that the big wedding became universal. By the 1950s, fifty-seven percent of all weddings were big church affairs. The highest percentage was still among the middle classes (66%), but fifty-eight percent of skilled workers and forty-five percent of unskilled couples now also wed in a grand manner.[7]

On the surface it seemed that the conjugal ideal had finally conquered, but the meaning of the big wedding varied by class. The popular version borrowed selectively, emphasizing some but not all of the elements of the fashionable white wedding. It had evolved in its own way, reflecting the importance now attached to legal marriage but also revealing the tensions between the conjugal ideal and the realities of working-class existence. By and large, working-class weddings placed less emphasis on the separation of the bride from her family, celebrated the extended rather than the nuclear family, and played down the conjugal as opposed to kin and peer group relationships. The official ceremony declared the man and woman a couple, but the social festivities told a different story. The big wedding was not so much a confirmation of the conjugal as an acknowledgment, particularly on the part of women, of its inadequacies.

I

Big weddings divided rather than united men and women. Surveys taken in the late 1940s showed women (68%) preferred big weddings much more than did men (46%). Many males were simply indifferent, but some had very strong opinions. "Any kind of wedding is dreadful," said one. "Got to go through with it, that's the way I look at it." "They're always terrifying to a man," replied another. Regardless of class, women attached greater importance to the publicity and ceremony. "I think of a church wedding and a white bride because there's no doubt about it but this is *the* time of her life" was the response of a middle-class woman who had married late in life. The wife of an unskilled laborer agreed that "every girl likes to get married in white." Neither of these women had had a big wedding—the first because she thought herself too old, the other because hers was a religiously mixed marriage. Nevertheless, they had a very firm notion of what a "proper" wedding should be. "If you've the money you should have as nice a wedding as possible, after all it only happens once" was the current sentiment.[8]

As we have seen, betrothal was a man's rite of passage. The difference between male and female views of the big white wedding reflected the fact that a woman's transition to adulthood was not complete until her new status had received further ritual confirmation. Novels, films, and women's magazines all urged girls to identify womanhood not just with conjugal love but with a home and family.[9] Men's adult identity continued to be associated with work and leisure activities outside the home, but a woman's self-image was dependent on her success as mother and homemaker. Men tended to marry the first woman they were seriously attracted to. They were able to associate love with personal independence, but for women love meant home and family, a dependency reinforced by the economic realities of low female wage rates and poor career prospects. Women were more cautious and pragmatic, for they (and their families) had the greater burden of making and maintaining the institutional aspects of marriage. Though supposedly the more romantic sex, the female actually had the more practical view of marriage. Her symbolic statements—especially the rites of the big wedding—expressed the view that conjugal love was by itself not enough to sustain a marriage.

When asked why they wished to marry, a common answer among working-class women was the desire to "have a home." For one woman who had married at eighteen, the major incentive had been "to get out of my Mum's house. . . . I wanted to get married and have a home of my own and a bit of peace." Few surveyed mentioned the desire for children as a major motive, though a marriage without children was virtually as unthinkable as children without marriage. "It's the children who make the home," remarked one of those questioned; "I think they count a lot in married life. The husband gets attached to the home. Otherwise he finds every excuse for going out in the evenings." Indeed, in this and later surveys, it was found that parenthood appealed at least as much to men as it did to women.[10]

Men had become progressively more child oriented by the 1950s, but it was not as father or companion but as breadwinner that men were most appreciated by women. In turn, what husbands looked for most was good housekeeping. Women still looked to the man as the chief provider, and many continued to tolerate the system by which the husband gave the wife an "allowance," keeping the rest of his wages to himself. "I give her enough to run the house and keep the kids" was the way one young Bethnal Green husband put it.[11] There was still a tendency for men in his neighborhood to regard the home as female territory and to spend most of their time in the pub. "I'm the man of the house," said one; "Here's my money. And if anyone wants me, you know where I am,"[12] With the expansion of domestic space that went with post war suburbanization, the strict division of spheres was moderated somewhat, but even in the 1950s it was still his work and her home, his duty to beget the children and hers to bring them up. While the birth rate among working-class couples had fallen drastically, it was invariably the male who initiated sex and controlled the method of birth control. Things had not changed all that much, except that couples now agreed that large numbers of children were undesirable.[13]

A man's reputation for being a good husband and father still depended on being hardworking, reliable, and, in the view of women, above all "understanding," by which they meant consideration rather than intimacy. The trait wives disliked most was selfishness, especially if a man's inconsideration made her housekeeping more difficult. Yet they did not mind that a husband did not understand them, as long as he understood their role. For their part, men ranked "give-and-take" as the most important attribute of a good marriage. "Each to his own task, the man for wages, the woman for 'exchequer' work," declared one satisfied Salford husband.[14] With them as with the women, personal fulfillment was not something they expected to find in marriage. Men looked for this outside the home, in work or leisure activities shared with their mates. Self-realization was more closely identified with the home in the women's case, but it was not with their husbands but with their children or with other women that they found the greatest personal satisfaction.

II

Over the course of the late nineteenth and early twentieth century, marriage had become virtually the only means of achieving the satisfaction and status of adulthood. Unlike the upper classes, the working class measured maturity not

> by "coming-out" parties or "coming of age" dinners, but by more tangible displays of the beginnings of a new life. They get married; they attempt to live in a house of their own; or if that proves too ambitious . . . they get one or perhaps two rooms of their own. In working class circles this is a distinct sign of courage and a bid for independence.[15]

The reasons for having a big wedding were still the same in the 1950s, when Richard Hoggart observed: "real life . . . is marriage; for both sexes the main dividing-line in working class life is this, not a change of job or going to a university or qualifying for a profession."[16]

Nevertheless, marriage made more of a difference to a woman's life than to a man's. If the marriage rate for women remained lower than men, this was more the result of the adverse sex ratio than any aversion to matrimony.[17] Laws continued to discriminate against mothers without proper nuptial credentials and, with each additional extension of the welfare state, there came more pressure to conform to the rules of matrimony.[18] Female employment possibilities were highly restricted during the first half of the twentieth century, hovering at a little less than thirty percent of the female population and rising rapidly only after World War II. In 1911 only one in ten married women were in recognized paid employment; by 1951 this had become one in five, but the most rapid rise was still in the future.[19] There were some shifts in the kind of work women did—more secretaries and fewer live-in servants; fewer women in textiles and more in retailing—but women's work remained low prestige, subordinate, and poorly paid. Although several factors were involved in a woman's desire to marry, it can be shown that women in low-wage employment were often under stronger pressure to become brides.[20] A man's occupation also had an effect on his nuptial inclinations. Because some men began to receive their maximum adult wages in their early twenties, the case with the vast majority of unskilled laborers, there was no incentive to postpone matrimony. The unskilled continued to marry two or three years younger than the skilled, whose earnings tended to begin somewhat lower but improved with experience.[21] When H. Seebohm Rowntree first studied the city of York before World War I, he found a third of that city's unskilled workers married by age twenty-two, whereas only a fifth of the skilled had taken a similar step. When York was resurveyed in the early 1930s, the same pattern was evident. Not until after the second of the great wars were these differences finally obliterated.[22]

The age at which couples married was largely determined by the man's earning ability, together with the availability of housing. Once he was in receipt of his adult wages, courtship became more serious and the wedding followed. Couples did not always wait until they could establish a home of their own and often lived for a time with parents, but the housing shortages of the interwar period had some effect on nuptiality. During the interwar period the age at time of marriage remained relatively high, and only with the return of prosperity in the early 1950s did access to marriage become much easier. The marriage age, which had already begun to fall in the late 1930s, dropped significantly. Men, who had been marrying at an average age of 26 in 1930, were wed at an average age of 24 in 1950. The decrease in women's average age was from 24 to 22. The compulsion to marry had become progressively more intense. Now that they could afford it, more couples were marrying earlier than ever before.[23] Never before had so many married, and with such elaborate ceremony.

Yet, if the men had had their way, the whole process would have been quick and informal. It was the women who insisted on the symbolic as well as material consecration of the marriage. It was they who invested most in building those social and economic relationships on which the success of the marriage depended. The greater the publicity of the engagement, the stronger the material base of the marriage. In the 1950s, when engagement parties and newspaper announcements had become much more common, the circle of contributors was quite extended. Working-class engagement parties remained small by middle-class standards, but they usually initiated several rounds of gift-giving that would culminate in the wedding presents themselves. Brides could now expect generosity not only from close kin, but neighbors and work-mates.[24] The subscriptions and showers of these years represent some-thing of a return to the "biddings" of an earlier age, except that they were organized by family and friends rather than by the couple them-selves, and were meant only for the bride. The groom did not concern himself at this stage. Even if he saved up for the first month's rent, it was often the bride's mother who found the flat.[25] Dorothy Scannell was the one who saved all the money for the furniture; and, while it became increasingly common for grooms to provide the consumer durables, their contributions were still seen as a form of voluntary "gift" rather than as a customary obligation, as was the case for the bride and her family.[26]

A man spent less time with his peers during the engagement period, but his ties with them were never completely severed. The stag parties which became increasingly popular in the twentieth century were a recognition of the approach of marriage, but they were not so much a final farewell as a ritualized adjustment among mates who would con-tinue to enjoy one another's company. This was a time for intense teas-ing, when the groom was supposed to appease his pals by "treating" them.[27] There were those who would try to keep their marriage secret, but, as railwayman Alfred Williams remembered, the word had a way of getting out:

> As soon as it is known that the banns are published—and this is certain to leak out and news of it be brought into the shed—he [the husband-to-be] becomes the object of very special attention. The men come to him from all quarters and offer him their congratulations, sincere and otherwise, very often accompanying them with advice of different kinds, sometimes of a highly sarcastic nature. Many insist upon shaking hands with him, and with mock ceremony, compliment him on his decision to join the "Big Firm," as they call it, assuring him, at the same time, that they shall expect him to "stand his footing." Occasionally, if their mate is poor, the men of a gang will make a small collection and buy him a present—a pair of pictures, a piece of furniture, or a set of ornaments. Perhaps this may be carried out ridiculously, and the whole thing turned into a joke, whereupon the prospective bridegroom loses his temper and soundly lashes his mates for their unsolicited patronage.[28]

Jack Devonshire, a miner, was "skin broke" on his wedding day after paying for all the drinks the night before. A man had to "buy drinks for everybody, 'til he go—blindo himself and broke and—carried home." His bride was in considerably better condition, having only homemade wine at her hen party.[29] Stag parties were most prevalent where a man's workmates were also his social companions, but everywhere the bachelor night was associated with heavy drinking and sexual joking. In the 1950s, grooms were dressed in cardboard top hat and tails; a finishing touch, a ball and chain, served to symbolize the groom's future status.[30] Joking recognized the groom's new status, but also served to solidify the bond between mates, which, while altered by marriage, did not necessarily dissolve.

The female counterpart of the bachelor night, the "hen party," was much slower to develop and did not become common until the 1940s and 1950s. Even then it was confined to those women who worked in offices and factories, and symbolized a break with rather than a continuation of the peer group. In Bolton, a girl leaving the factory for the last time would be "dressed up by workmates and paraded around town. Sometimes she was tied to a post and left there, "a symbol of the impending loss of freedom."[31] At a Romford sweets factory the bride was decked out with a crude veil, while at a Gosport solicitor's office she was subject to mild pranks, some with a sexual reference.[32] In many places there would be a subscription to buy a present for those leaving; everyone was obliged to pay even though they would probably not attend the wedding itself.[33] But even the most boisterous hen party was somewhat different from the male stag party. It had little of the bachelors' wild public drunkenness and there was something more final about the leave-taking, which often meant the end of a working relationship.[34]

The greatest changes in a woman's life were still ahead of her. While a man had attained a degree of adulthood through work, a female's transition to adult status was much less complete at the time of engagement. Women's work, a low-wage, deadend proposition, did not confer adulthood but, instead, perpetuated girlhood. As long as she remained single, a woman who valued her reputation was also cut off from adult sexuality. Only wedding could bridge the chasm of status and identity that separated a daughter from a mother. Marriage was her great opportunity, but also her major anxiety.

Men also had their fears, but, because they had the initiative, they worried less about the choice of mate and could afford to be more romantically impulsive. They tended to marry their first love and, once engaged, think everything settled.[35] When they worried, it was about the cost of establishing a home and having children. James Dawkins had heard too often of "love going out the window when poverty came in at the door" not to be somewhat anxious about his impending wedding during the Depression. Although women also worried about finances, their fears were more personal.[36] Anna Thomas, who had already encountered a certain amount of parental resistance, had won the support of her mother, but nevertheless found the days before her 1924 wedding unnerving. She, like most women of this generation, knew very little about sexuality; and the joking of the young men in the shop where she worked became unbearable: "they made your life agony for the last week before you were getting married, telling you terrible things—

to upset you, to put you right off. . . . Oh, the thought of going to—sleep with a man, they were telling me shocking things. Oh, oh, they were dreadful. I was really scared stiff when I got married."[37]

Women had also to fear childbirth, still a major cause of female mortality during the early twentieth century. And there was the question of whether she could measure up to the demanding standards of wifehood. Given the high value placed on marriage, these were not the kind of reservations that could be expressed directly. Instead, the ambivalence found expression in popular song, in joking, and in the festive rites of the wedding itself. But what sustained women like Anna Thomas and overcame their very real fears was not only their idealized vision of marriage, but the prospect of the "glorious moment" itself, the drama of a wedding in white, confirming as much to herself as to family and friends her new status. In earlier centuries marriage had been as much his day as hers. Now men had come to believe the wedding should "suit the girl" and its details should be left "for the girl to decide." While many would have preferred something a little quieter and less costly, they were still willing to accept the fact that "the lady generally likes white weddings" and go along because, as one put it, "it do show that everything really matters."[38]

III

The bride and her family took charge of the wedding itself. It was a time when mothers and daughters renewed bonds that had become tenuous during the latter's adolescent years. Daughters drew close, not just because they would probably share a neighborhood and even a house with their mothers, but because they knew they would be responsible for the older woman, especially if the latter were widowed. As one elderly Bethnal Green woman put it: "When you grow old you've someone to support you. You get the benefit of children when you grow old. . . . They're a comfort to you, and your little grandchildren come round to see you."[39] The assistance given at marriage was meant to be repaid by the daughter at a later point in time. In many places these reciprocal female obligations extended well beyond the immediate family, to all those who had given to a bride. Something of the old "bidding wedding" is visible here, but the mutuality was now entirely female.

Women chose the site of the ceremony, showing a preference for church weddings more than men not necessarily because they were more religious, but out of a desire to find a place that would add a special meaning to marriage. This desire was responsible for the twentieth century return to church marriages in places like South Wales, a region where civil marriage had been especially popular in the previous century.[40] Marriage by banns also regained popularity. Often it was the bride who put up the banns, for it was usually her church or chapel, or, if she were not a regular attender, the nearest Church of England

that was chosen for the wedding.[41] A domestic servant chose the Ard-
leigh church in 1916 because it was her mother's place of worship: "Mother
always felt that the Church was the proper place to be married. I don't
think it makes so much difference, but Mother was brought up to the
Church that they went to."[42] As the century went on, such sentimentality
became even more pronounced. The church or chapel was chosen because it was old or quaint, even if it had no family connections. Modern
church architecture repelled the bride as much as the Gothic attracted
her. It was fortunate for contemporary vicars that their livings did not
depend on fees, for the pastors of modern churches in Birmingham
performed almost no weddings.[43]

The upper classes had led the return to the church wedding by banns,
and they were responsible for such fashions as morning suits for men
and, beginning in the 1930s, white gowns for the bride.[44] But, on the
whole, the working-class white wedding, while bearing certain resemblances to the upper-class version, was its own original creation, a ritual
expression of the actual circumstances of the people themselves. There
were also links to the past, yet here again the twentieth-century big
wedding was selective in its borrowings and current in its symbolic
meanings. Big weddings in the seventeenth and eighteenth centuries
had been patrifocal, starting with the separation of the bride from her
family and ending with the inauguration of a new household. Now there
was no fetching of the bride for she was not to be separated from her
family. It was thought unlucky for the couple to see one another before
church, and the bride in white would never permit her appearance to
be sullied by any prenuptial festivities.[45] Both parties proceeded separately by carriage or, later, by motor car. And it was now the groom
who played the role of the reluctant participant, always the one to be
late, fetched from the pub and escorted up the church steps by the best
man as if going to the gallows.[46]

In upper-class weddings, the father of the bride was an important
figure, but he was far less prominent in working-class festivities. One
Preston man refused to give away his daughter early in the century
because it was reported that he was jealous of the groom "taking one
of his best lasses. He said he couldn't give her away." And instead her
sister did the honors. Dorothy Scannell's father went off to a cricket
match "as it upset him too much" to see her married.[47] By the 1950s
fathers were doing their duty, but nevertheless giving away the bride
was one aspect of the upper-class white wedding which was played
down in popular practice. The working-class wedding was distinctly
matrifocal, centering on the bride's home and family. It celebrated not
the loss of a daughter but the gain of a son, a situation that caused one
canny Welsh miner to observe:

> I've always thought the wedding ceremony in church was all wrong myself.
> Don't they say "Who giveth this woman in marriage?" And the father of
> the bride hops forward and says "I do." But he doesn't at all, at least if he

does he's not speaking for the wife, now is he? I say it should be altered. "Who giveth this man in marriage"—th's the proper question, lad. And make the mother of the bridegroom say "I do." Most fathers don't give a damn either way in my experience.[48]

The wedding was very much a female event. Sam Fitten remembered that it was mainly women who were the spectators at Lancashire weddings, gossiping about the bride's dress and passing judgment on the costs.[49] The size of the crowd was proportional to "how much they respected you and how much they thought about you," and it was invariably the bride who got most of the attention. In Preston, where an errant woman could still attract rough music early in the century, it was now the "good girls" who could expect the most boisterous treatment. "When I got married all the street came out and they all got confetti," remembered a woman married in the 1930s; "You got your character, she was a nice lass or she wasn't. At a funeral or a wedding, you got your character."[50]

But the most spectacular innovation of all was the appearance of the bride. In the nineteenth century she wore her "best" dress and was indistinguishable from the rest of the wedding party. By the 1930s, however, virtually all women who could afford it were marrying in lustrous white, by then the universal symbol of feminine purity and virtuous womanhood.[51] Grooms were renting morning suits, but their dark tones in no way competed for attention. His sober attire highlighted her ceremonial presence. The attention was not on the couple, but on the bride. He could be himself; she could not, for this was the day when she ceased to be herself and become his wife.

Despite the many references to conjugal bliss in the official ceremony, the deeper structures of the wedding reveal not closeness but distance. There was no symbolic reference to sexuality; and the stereotypical bridal gown, while desexualizing the bride, did more to emphasize her femininity and bonds with other women than her heterosexuality. It was not unusual for brides to wear their mothers' or sisters' dresses, thus reinforcing a familial rather than conjugal identity.[52] To men such borrowings were a threat to their individuality, but for a woman it was a welcome opportunity to express continuing family attachment.

Postmarital festivities served a similar purpose. Instead of following the upper-class practice of proceeding from the church to a hotel or club, the wedding party normally returned to the bride's home. Early in the century the postnuptial reception was a smallish affair, limited by the size of the house and usually restricted to the families.[53] Martha Whitten, whose mother was very poor, brought her party of four back to the house. A midday meal was served, but, as she recollected it, her mother never sat down with them.[54] A London couple, who had lived in the same street, had "just a little party that was all—well you—one couldn't afford it."[55] On the other hand, when a pair of Prestonians married from one of the poorest streets during the 1920s, they received over sixty gifts

26. David Cartwright and Ivy Ann Darlow were married in All Saints Church, Bedford, on July 29, 1961. On leaving the church the new bride was presented with a wooden spoon and lucky horseshoe, contemporary symbols of a happy marriage. (My thanks to David and Ann for permission to reproduce this photograph)

from their neighbors.[56] It was not until the 1920s and 1930s that receptions were beginning to be held in places other than the bride's home. A Preston cabinetmaker, married during the Depression, remembered going to the photographer's studio after the ceremony and then proceeding to the White Horse Cafe where a "do" for thirty guests had been laid on.[57] Even as late as the 1950s, however, people in Bethnal Green were still holding a family party at home and then going out later to the local pub to receive the congratulations of neighbors and workmates.[58]

The reception was a time for drinking, dancing, and the obligatory toasts. If the parson were invited, he might make a brief speech. Otherwise, the toastmaster was the best man or, as in rural Lincolnshire, a local wit, who "almost always perpetuates a few jokes of a rather crude type."[59] Gifts were given by the guests and, before they left, the non-relations had a chance to kiss the bride. Once the couple had changed clothes, it was then their turn to leave. This was the major moment of farewell, the point of greatest tensions, when tears flowed and envy was expressed through the modern equivalents of rough music. In a few rural places there was still in the 1920s a tradition of nighttime charivari, with "ran-tan weddings" reserved for unpopular couples.[60] In North Wales this had fallen away by the 1950s, made obsolete by the fact that couples now spent their wedding night away from the village. The result was a compromise in which the old rough music became a part of the leave-taking.[61] Everywhere teasing and pranks had become a standard part of the send-off. The carriage or car was decorated with ribbons and signs, and, where old shoes were not thrown, they were tied on as well.[62] Elsewhere it became the practice to "see the couple off down the train or somewhere. And they used to put—if they was going away by train—detonators all along the line, bang, bang, bang."[63] In Wales "the extent of such roistering is a measure of the popularity of the couple and their families."[64] Women took it with good humor: "that was nice you know, it was considered to be—an honour then."[65] Jimmy Johnson did not take it amiss when friends tied boots to the back of his coat and then afixed bells to the springs of his wedding bed, but he was somewhat upset by the artificial worm, which "frightened the life out of the wife."[66]

Yet, until the 1940s, an extended honeymoon was largely confined to skilled workers. A Derbyshire bleacher, who married in 1907, had "never heard of any as had a honeymoon. It took 'em all their time to get money to get married."[67] Not until after the Great War did Preston people get away to Blackpool, and then for only a half-day.[68] Among the greater part of the working class the honeymoon remained exceptional until after World War II. It was rare in Bethnal Green even in the 1950s, not because couples could not afford a night away, but because they hated to leave the family party and therefore delayed departure for Clacton until the following morning.[69] On the whole, it was the men who were most keen on getting away. Fifty years after his wedding, John Patterson could still recall the excitement of climbing the stairs to the Blackpool bedroom where he and his bride had their first moments of real intimacy.[70] Working-class brides approached the honeymoon with much greater anxiety. In most cases it was their first sexual experience. They expected to be expertly initiated, but unfortunately most husbands were scarcely more knowledgable than themselves. Middle-class couples who wrote to Marie Stopes seeking sexual advice during the 1920s were plagued with difficulties arising mainly from ignorance, and her working-class correspondents complained of many of the same problems, for it was even more rare for them to discuss sexual matters before marriage.[71] Though birth control was supposed to be the male responsibility, most working-class men knew very little about contraception or, even if they did, wished not to use it. John Patterson had only with great difficulty prepared himself for his wedding night:

> I stood outside [the chemist's shop] for ages waiting while a male assistant was free. Then I dashed in and asked for my requirements. I was answered, I thought, in a very cultured "We don't sell them." I dashed out of the shop with my face red. I had another long wait outside another chemists. This time I wrote my requirements on a piece of paper. The male assistant laughed and asked what size was required. I was stunned and muttered "average." He was joking and put me at ease.[72]

Dorothy Scannell was another who left it to her husband "to arrange the nonarrival of a family." He had done his duty, but on the wedding night the sheath proved too small. When she returned from her honeymoon, her mother listened to her account of all that had happened and curtly observed: "I could have told you it was overrated."[73]

But the major reason the middle-class honeymoon did not catch on easily was the fact that the conjugal ideal it represented was not central to what marriage meant to a very large part of the British population. Until well after World War II, many still began their married lives doubling up with parents. To them the emphasis on separation and the establishment of a nuclear family made no sense whatsoever. After his wedding in 1919 Jimmy Johnson spent a week away at Watford, but at his sister's place. He could not remember carrying the new Mrs. Johnson across any threshold: "that's only something new ain't it. . . . I never thought of anything like that."[74] For most working-class couples marriage meant not increased closeness, but the intensification of the division of roles. Their version of the big white wedding anticipated and confirmed the limits of the conjugal ideal, while at the same time establishing those social and emotional relationships with kin and peers vital to the success of the marriage.

IV

The "politics" of the twentieth-century version of the big church wedding suggests a parallel with the sixteenth and seventeenth centuries when considerations of kinship and community were also dominant. Naturally, not everyone could meet the demands made by family and friends and, therefore, the desire for privacy was directly proportional to the renewed emphasis on publicity. In the 1950s over forty percent of all marriages were "quiet" affairs, all quite legal, the larger part (23.5% of all marriages) being civil weddings. The percentage partaking in civil marriage had increased even as big weddings multiplied, suggesting a relationship between the two not unlike the dialectic that had prevailed in earlier periods when the social and financial demands of a proper marriage were also such that a wedding was "done rite" or not done at all.[75]

There were those who objected to church marriages on principle. John Hargrave and his wife were socialists and married in a civil ceremony: "I've thought often how different it has been for some folk who have had quite a lot of fuss and show and so forth at a wedding and it hasn't turned out as well as our very ordinary weddings." Another man, an atheist, also rejected religious ceremony, but said he would go through with it "for the girl's sake."[76] However, the great majority of quiet weddings were the product not of principle but of necessity. During the two world wars haste was the major factor; and as late as the 1940s cost was still a deterrent for many working people.[77] But civil marriages were also likely to occur when the couple had encountered some kind of obstacle, real or imagined. When an Oxfordshire farmer's son married a lowly servant, the entire village boycotted the wedding, drawing down their blinds, a gesture usually reserved for funerals.[78] A Yorkshire mill girl never quite got over the resistance of her husband's family, who thought their son had married too low. This couple married quietly and even their golden wedding anniversary was celebrated in a very subdued fashion.[79] Because Elizabeth Browlow was a strong Methodist, a civil marriage was impossible, but, because she was encountering objections from her parents, she arranged to be married by license in a distant chapel, a tactic that eventually brought her family around so that she was able to make up for it by having a lavish golden wedding celebration.[80]

Often social mixed with religious objections. Monica Oxnard married in the Register Office because she was church and her husband was chapel, and she thought it "would save a lot of trouble."[81] Another common cause was a mixed Catholic-Protestant marriage. These were frequent in Preston, where there was a large Irish population. The Catholic priests would not perform them, and parents on both sides raised objections.[82] Mary Deptford knew of a Protestant girl who had been flogged and expelled from home when she revealed she was pregnant by a Catholic lad.[83] When great rifts appeared, the normal recourse was to the Register Office or a quiet wedding in a nearby Church of England. "They didn't make it like a wedding," it was said, "they had to go in a side door."[84] When Elizabeth Thomkins married a Catholic milkman, she did not dare tell her mother directly: "We were married at the Register Office and I sent him home with the marriage lines. I never came. And—then we were received in the church."[85] It was commonly believed that many Catholic girls got pregnant to receive dispensation from the church, but it is also possible that it was their way of getting parents to agree to their choice of partners, a tactic reminiscent of the sixteenth and seventeenth centuries, when clandestine marriage was also followed by reconciliation and a regular church marriage.[86]

The "politics" of marriage had become enormously complicated in the course of the century. A couple had to conform to requirements of the model bride and groom, otherwise they had no right to a big wedding. The visibly pregnant bride was regarded as highly offensive. "She wasn't supposed to wear white. No, no one would ever—wear white in their right mind if they were going to have a child."[87] A Barrow woman remembered that "you were generally having a baby if you went to the Register Office."[88] One desperate woman wanted a big wedding so badly that she laced herself so tightly that the child was born brain damaged.[89] In the 1950s pregnant brides, especially the teenagers whose premarital pregnancy rates were twice that of women in their twenties, routinely used civil marriage as a form of clandestine marriage.[90]

The same was true of those older than average and persons marrying for a second time. "If you're young, a bit of show is nice. If you marry late, a quiet one" was the conventional wisdom.[91] Widows and widowers married without much ceremony, as did divorced persons. Many clergy refused to marry those divorced and so they were forced to turn to the Register Office, through this was not their only reason for privacy.[92] The big wedding's rites of passage were wholly inappropriate for anyone who had already attained adult status through marriage. Early in the century, M. E. Loane had noted that working people thought one church wedding enough: "They seem to think that one marriage consecrates all subsequent connections—at any rate it entitles them to be 'respectable.' "[93] One of the major reasons why civil marriage continued at such a high rate in the 1940s and 1950s was the rising divorce rate of the period.[94]

The shame associated with divorce affected women more than it did men, however, and when couples chose a quiet wedding, it was normally for the sake of the bride rather than the groom. For the minority of women who planned to work a white wedding made no sense either. Dorothy Wrightson, who could certainly have afforded a big wedding in the 1920s, had rejected it "because I was going back to work and I thought that was silly, a big wedding and going back to work."[95] Civil marrige was invariably more common with widows than widowers, and with women who had been divorced rather than divorced men.[96] It was the woman by far who carried the greater social and symbolic burden in maintaining the proprieties that society expected of matrimony. Her status dictated the kind of wedding that was appropriate.

V

The white wedding was not so much challenged as complemented by the modern version of clandestine marriage. The shame of a premarital pregnancy or failed marriage was proportional to the honor accorded the virgin bride and the two-parent home. At no time since the eighteenth century had the institution of matrimony made such powerful demands on the individual and the community, and now these focused much more on the woman than the man. Earlier it had been his house; now it was her home. The removal of economic functions had disengaged the male, thus creating an asymmetrical relationship that assigned to women virtually all the major domestic functions. "As long as she was working in a man's world the daughter behaved in many ways like a man, clocking into a factory like her brother and earning her own money to spend as she chose. But when she marries, and even more when she leaves work to have children, she returns to the woman's world, and to her mother" was the conclusion of those who studied Bethnal Green in the 1950s.[97] Early in the century, the boundaries of the female world were sharply defined by dress, language, and demeanor. In the north of England it was the shawl that was the "badge of marriage." Wives were expected to give up girlish dress, makeup, even their natural gaiety no matter what their age. "The vivacity of their virgin days was with their virgin days, gone; a married woman could be distinguished from a single by a glance at her facial expression. Marriage scored on their faces a kind of preoccupied, faded, lack-lustre air as though they were constantly being plagued by some problem. As they were."[98] The toll of frequent childbearing and money worries were only a part of the cause; the rest must be attributed to the subservient role marriage assigned to women. "The contrast between the factory girl and her mother is perhaps the very saddest spectacle that the labour world presents," remarked another observer of marriage's remarkable transformation.[99]

By World War II the shawl was gone, but the contrast between the attractive single girl and the wholly sexless mother had not disappeared. A Preston woman, born in 1919, recalled that she never went out when she was pregnant: "I used to feel ashamed, because I knew they would think what I'd been doing and I used to think it was terrible."[100] Even in the 1950s, mothers in London's East End were still insisting that their daughters "church" themselves after birth. While the younger women regarded this as "superstition," they nevertheless went along with the general assumption that sexuality was somehow polluting. In many respects the domesticization of married women had already become more pronounced. Standards of housekeeping and childrearing had risen steadily, adding to the women's responsibilities:

> Working-class women have grown more refined; they desire better homes, better clothes for themselves and their children, and are far more self-respecting and less humble than their predecessors. But the strain to keep up to anything like a decent standard of housing, clothing, diet, and general appearance, is enough to upset the mental balance of a Chancellor of the Exchequer. How much more so a struggling pregnant mother![101]

Among that part of the working class whose income remained precarious throughout the interwar period, the ideal home remained an elusive dream. A decent standard could only be maintained through the support of female kin and neighbors. The matrifocality of working-class families at that level remained intense.[102] "Since we've had the children I've got no more friends—outside the family I mean," observed one Bethnal Green wife. Another agreed: "I don't see my best friend much. She's married too, and she's always round *her* Mum's like I'm always round mine."[103] Every effort was made to stay in touch with mothers, and those women without maternal assistance felt it keenly. Most brides knew almost nothing about the practical aspects of childbearing and rearing. Anna Parsons, who suffered a nervous breakdown when her husband left her near the time their first child was born, became completely dependent on her mother even though the two had been at odds over her marriage. Although she continued to resent her mother, she had no place to turn. Later she remembered the whole thing as an extended nightmare, a refutation of all the romances she was so fond of reading.[104]

Women who left the old neighborhood tried to keep in touch with their mothers and other female networks, but they felt even more isolated. "You lose contact with parents and relations once you move out here," observed one former resident of Bethnal Green who had moved his family to suburban Greenleigh. "You seem to centre yourself more on the home. Everybody lives in a little world of their own."[105] Women felt this far more keenly than the men, however. Many wives came to resent the isolation, the constant competition with other women for who could keep up the best home, the boredom of a life without even the interest of street-corner gossip or a good old-fashioned public row. While they shared their husband's pride in having the house, which was now the definition of a "good home," they would have appreciated it more if they had also had time away from the squalling babies and dirty dishes. 'When we first came [to suburban Greenleigh] I'd just had the baby and it was all a misery, not knowing anyone. I sat down on the stairs and cried my eyes out,"recounted Mrs. Haddon. "For the first two years we were swaying whether to go back. I wanted to and my husband didn't. We used to have terrible arguments about it. I used to say 'It's all right for you. I have to sit here all day. You do get a break.' "[106]

VI

Life in the new working-class suburbs revealed the real limits of the conjugal ideal.[107] When married people were asked what they had most in common, shared hobbies, children, and home were mentioned in that order of priority. A couple may have been doing more things together, but few talked about shared intimacy or a social life together away from the home and children. Mutual activity centered mainly on playing with the children and keeping up the house. Few couples went out much together after they married; and, while over a third thought "companionship" the best thing in marriage, less than ten percent associated this with mutual attention or the sharing of personal problems. Even fewer (less than one percent of all men) mentioned sexual intimacy as adding to the happiness of marriage.[108]

Working men persisted in viewing marriage as an institution rather than a personal relationship. First and foremost it was a convenience. "A single feller comes home and his people may be out or something, but for the married feller his wife is always there" was a typical masculine comment. Most could appreciate their wives, but principally as mothers of their children or as "someone to do the domestic offices." Women judged a husband mainly on how well he lived up to his institutional obligations. They were most concerned with security and disliked drinking or gambling men. "It's all right when you've got a good husband, but if you've got a husband who is selfish it's worse being married than single," observed a middle-aged wife in the late 1940s. To a husband of the same generation, the worse thing that could happen was "when the woman tries to be the guvnor, if you get my meaning. When the woman wears the trousers."[109]

The stability of marriage was dependent on how well a husband and wife performed their respective duties, not on how well they got along as a couple. With the liberalization of the divorce codes in the 1930s and 1940s, many more working people could afford to terminate a bad marriage legally, but the decision to do so was based on essentially the same view of matrimony that had been the grounds for the illicit forms of marital separation fifty years earlier. Geoffrey Gorer found that tension over money and allocation of authority within the home were the major causes of discontent in the 1950s.[110] Most people held firmly to the view that a bad husband or a bad wife was better than no spouse at all. Only forty-two percent of the people polled in the 1940s approved of divorce, with women considerably more disapproving than men.[111] Yet two-thirds of all married persons (more men than women) had considered divorce and rejected it as a solution to their marital problems.[112] It seems that children were a major consideration in the decision not to separate. "I know there'd be a lot of marriages broken up if there wasn't any children," noted one woman, an observation confirmed by the greater tendency of young, childless couples seeking divorce.[113]

There was an equally pronounced propensity to keep the matrimonial institution alive, despite personal unhappiness. Martha Howell, born in Manchester in 1891, remembered the troubles a drunken, spendthrift father could cause. Her mother initially wanted to move out, but ultimately resigned herself to the situation. Martha recalled that "only just occasionally would she say, well, you live your own life, but don't get married."[114] Martha never did marry, but few others seem to have been deterred by the bad relationships of their parents. Indeed, the desire to escape a fractious household seems to have been a major reason for early marriage throughout the first half of the twentieth century. People stuck with marriage as an institution even when they had lost all hope in their particular partners. Many were like Mary Foxon, who had wed at nineteen to the second man who courted her. He proved so shiftless that her mother advised her to leave him, but she endured the rocky first years, bore three children, and proved her mother wrong. "I said, 'I'd stick to my marriage vows,' and she knew I would."[115] Surveys found that both husbands and wives responded to marital difficulties by blaming themselves and attempting to repair the damage. Women's first impulse was invariably to improve their housekeeping and appearance, while men were in agreement with the worker who said he would first "consider whether or not he is free from blame. Consider (well) if they have kiddies."[116]

There was surprisingly little sexual jealousy, and even adultery was treated in a matter-of-fact way. Few took the romantic position that it was "morally wrong to keep bound to one partner who prefers another."[117] The affairs of a wife could provoke violent reactions among men, but even brutal tiffs were regarded as insufficient grounds for termination, especially if there were children. Women had less violent ways of punishing wayward husbands and, when Harriet Parker discovered her mate with another woman during World War I, she refused to share a bed with him for the next twenty-five years.[118] However, probably more common was the case that Robert Roberts knew of, where a wife had not spoken to her husband for months, but nevertheless allowed him to continue to exercise his "conjugal rights."[119]

Similar attitudes prevailed right through the 1950s, and it strikes us as very odd that sexual relations should continue even when everything else had broken down. But sex, like everything else, was seen in highly impersonal terms, as a duty or a right that transcended personal sentiment. The days when husbands and wives hurled sexual insults at one another in public places were long over, but, within the "little world," marital conflict, accompanied by considerable violence, continued unabated. The perpetual battles within the Howell house contributed to that family's isolation from neighbors, who were reluctant to intervene in any domestic circumstance. Mrs. Howell feared to leave because her husband might sell the furniture and make them all homeless.[120] Women simply could not afford to live alone and it was regarded as "an awful thing to happen to anybody . . . everybody turns away from a divorced woman."[121]

For men as well, a failed marriage meant a precipitous drop in comfort and status. In Salford, they could lose their place among the men at the pub and be reassigned to the "boys" on the corner, where they, "because of age and experience enjoyed some esteem there, though their stock stood low in adult circles."[122] In the earlier part of the century, married men separated from their wives found it almost impossible to get along on their own, because they could not afford to buy prepared food or rent bachelor lodgings. They were forced either to hire a female housekeeper or, if that was too expensive, find a woman who would live with them outside marriage.[123] Two could still live cheaper together even in the much more affluent postwar period; and the greater tendency for men to remarry when widowed or divorced suggests that no institutional alternative to marriage had yet presented itself.[124]

Love and marriage were inseparable as far as the vast majority were concerned. When asked in 1947 how they felt about unmarried persons living together, eight-six percent disapproved or gave only conditional acceptance, with men and women giving almost identical responses.[125] Another study found that only ten percent gave unconditional approval to extramarital sexuality. Women were more intolerant than men, but both sexes clearly valued marriage as the only institution capable of serving their material and social needs. Now the working classes were the most critical of alternative forms of heterosexuality. Earlier class positions were reversed, and by the 1950s the middle classes were the more accepting of conjugality outside marriage. Only when it came to failed marriages were popular attitudes less stringent. Working-class opinion of divorce was relatively tolerant, but this did not mean that marriage itself was held in any lower esteem than earlier. On the contrary, its stock had risen, reflected not only in the celebration of big weddings but evident in the fact that the younger generation was consistently the age group most favorable to matrimonial institutions.[126] It could be argued that this was because they had yet to experience the trials of nuptiality, but, in any case, the conventionality of the young was one of the striking features of the 1950s.

When Geoffrey Gorer investigated the state of British marriage early in that same decade, he concluded that "there seems every reason to believe that the sexual morals of the English have changed very little in the present century."[127] Indeed, the continuity of this period is striking. Courtship had become progressively more ritualized and big weddings were now regarded as virtually obligatory. Not since the eighteenth century had institutional imperatives of nuptiality been felt so strongly and universally. Marriage meant family; and family meant marriage. The rates of illegitimacy and cohabitation were at the lowest points in more than a century. Gorer, himself an anthropologist familiar with the variety of sexual relationships present in other cultures, did not even bother to explore any other possibilities apart from marriage. They were to him, as they were to other observers of the postwar period, simply unthinkable.

PART IV

Conjugal Myths and Marital Realities, 1960 to the Present

CHAPTER 11

᠕ᡕ᠕ᡕ᠕ᡕ᠕ᡕ᠕ᡕ᠕ᡕ᠕ᡕ᠕ᡕ᠕ᡕ᠕ᡕ᠕ᡕ᠕ᡕ᠕ᡕ᠕ᡕ᠕ᡕ᠕ᡕ᠕ᡕ

Love and Marriage:
The Unresolved Contradiction

Love and marriage, love and marriage
Just go together like horse and carriage
This I tell you, brother
You can't have one without the other.[1]

Popular Song, 1950s

Love and marriage were regarded as inseparable until the 1960s. Then, with apparent suddenness, they came apart. Living together outside marriage, something that had previously been shameful and secretive, became public and acceptable. In the 1950s only one percent of women marrying for the first time lived with the man for an extended period before wedding him; by the early 1980s this had risen to twenty-one percent and showed no sign of decreasing. Among women marrying for the second time the rate was already thirty percent in the mid-1970s, and sixty-seven percent today.[2] It seemed that the idea of conjugal love was finally powerful enough to legitimate all relationships. There were those, including some historians, who were ready to announce that marriage had been replaced "by the free floating couple, a marital dyad subject to dramatic fissions and fusions, and without the orbiting satellites of pubertal children, close friends, or neighbors . . . just the relatives, hovering in the background, friendly smiles on their faces."[3]

Such proclamations now seem somewhat naive, and certainly premature. Large numbers of young people might live together, but most would ultimately marry when it came time for having a home and family.[4] The delay in marriage was evident in the rising age at time of nuptiality, but the marriage rate itself remained fairly steady.[5] The new cohabitation had many of the features of the old betrothal. It was an extended rite of transition—a liminal period—which was brought to a ritual conclusion when the couple decided it was time to incorporate themselves into the adult world of mothers and fathers. The mode of marriage itself did not change all that much. The big church wedding held its ground, especially among the working classes. It was mainly the educated middle classes who turned their backs on elaborate ceremony and opted for the informal, even casual, marriage that attracted so much press attention in those decades. There were some small changes in wedding fashions during the 1970s, but in the present decade all the elements of the formal betrothal and big wedding—the ring, a bride in white, lavish reception, and the honeymoon—were back in place, apparently more popular than ever before.[6]

To be sure, there has been some movement toward the conjugal ideal. Marriages today certainly involve more sharing and intimacy than in the preceding generation. Many different forces, but especially the influence of the women's liberation movement, have been felt within the family, promoting an updated version of perfect conjugality. Today, both men and women say they believe in equal relationships, both in and outside marriage, but, as we have seen throughout history, the ideal is not always the reality. And, as in the past, this contradiction summons forth its own particular set of rituals to clarify and mediate the difficult transition from the relatively egalitarian status of lovers to the much more complicated condition of a married couple with a home and children.

I

Heterosexuality today would appear to be moving in contrary directions. On one hand, many of the earlier inhibitions to conjugality, external and internal, have diminished considerably. Youth now are much more comfortable with adult sexuality. Because young people have gained greater access to well-paid work, sexual segregation has been relaxed in the schools and universities, and some parental control has been forfeited, youth have regained a measure of the status and independence that they had lost at the beginning of the century.[7] More young people, especially the highly educated, now live apart from their parents.[8] Their world became much less homosocial as women began to gain access to the training and careers that had been previously reserved for young men. The increasing numbers of women intent on making employment a life-long career probably did more than anything else to transform the whole process of courtship and marriage.[9]

Young men and women feel more comfortable with one another, with the result that the early stages of courtship have become more casual and less ritualized.[10] Promenading in the "monkey ranks" is only a memory now, and both working- and middle-class teenagers are more likely to go about as couples, a habit that has contributed to earlier sexual intimacy which now begins in the mid-teens rather than late teens.[11] Sexual activity is not only more precocious but more tolerated, though, as Geoffrey Gorer discovered, sex and betrothal are still closely associated. Most couples do not begin intercourse until engaged and, if that is taken to be the start of serious monogamy, then forty-six percent of men and eighty-eight percent of women are still "technical virgins" at marriage.[12] "I don't think sex before marriage is wrong," remarks Janice, Jeremy Seabrook's composite of the contemporary woman, "Anybody who has had sex before marriage, I wouldn't say anything against them. It's just their personal belief. I don't think I'd have sex before marriage unless I loved the person."[13]

Youth are, if anything, more monogamous now than twenty or thirty years ago. Parents appear to be more relaxed and today's peer pressure seems to encourage rather than discourage early conjugality. As one woman put it:

> "You know yourself, you go around with a crowd and everybody gets engaged, everybody gets married, and then people start to have a family and you think 'What's happened to me?' "[14]

The early stages of courtship may have become more casual in recent years, but engagement has assumed an even greater significance. It not only legitimates sexual intimacy and initiates the couple's withdrawal from the company of peers, but now legitimates living together. Working-class people may cohabit less frequently than their middle-class counterparts, but they clearly recognize betrothal as a distinctive transition phase.[15] As a Swansea bride put it:

> Well, when you're courting there's no ties—you can finish when you like. When you're engaged you're more or less married—got a ring on—halfway there. You know you're going to get married. You can't go with anyone else. If you're only courting you can't start saving or making plans.[16]

Young people today begin to act like married couples when they are only in their teens, something members of earlier generations find very disconcerting: "They're savin' up fer an 'ouse afore they've left school," observed one older Preston man, 'Why don't they just have their fun first like we did?'[17] Those who choose to live together have convinced themselves they are in love and that their pooling of resources—a form of mutual gift exchange—legitimates their behavior to the wider world. They are like Gouge's betrothed, neither single nor actually married. In their own terms, they are "half-way there." While Britain has not gone as far as Sweden, where *sammenboende* (living together) has been put on a legal and social status equal to that of conventional marriage, a series of laws, administrative rulings, and court decisions since 1960 has restored to *de facto* couples that legality denied them by the Hardwicke Act of 1753. This is clearly a case of the law catching up to social change, for most of those who live together consider themselves to have rights and duties similar to those the old betrothals and besom weddings once bestowed. They feel free to terminate the relationship, but at the same time they feel obligated to one another in certain fundamental ways.

The law now provides that dependents in such a relationship can claim reasonable maintenance. The so-called "mistress charter" gives protection to the woman who can prove she lived as a wife, though outside legal marriage. Children born to the couple are also considered legal offspring and can claim virtually the same rights as those born in wedlock.[18]

Together law and society appear to have reinstated a situation very much like that which existed before 1753, when betrothal licensed premarital conjugality. It is also like the situation that existed in the late eighteenth and early nineteenth centuries when so many people made their own private "little weddings," postponing the public, official event until such time as they could gather the resources necessary to a proper household. That was a period when age and gender distinctions were rapidly eroding and there were fewer barriers to heterosociability. But if men and women today have become less anxious about their conjugal relations and feel less need to regulate these by the laws of church and state, they still feel a need to legitimate their relationship when it comes to establishing a home and family. In most respects, then, the contemporary situation is much like the pre-industrial period, when the household, with its highly institutionalized roles, was so prominent. The difference lies in the fact that the household is now more a female than male domain, and the big wedding the culmination of her rather than his rite of passage.

Two-thirds of women who had married the man they cohabited with during the 1970s had done so within a year.[19] No doubt, there were many more who lived briefly with a man and then broke up, but, whatever the actual numbers may be, one thing is clear: virtually everyone regarded this as a transitional not a final arrangement, for, when it came to setting up a home and having children, most couples preferred a big wedding to a more private ceremony. For this reason British marriage, while postponed, did not diminish in the manner of other Western countries like West Germany, Sweden, and the United States.[20] Legal wedlock held its own even in the face of what appeared to be a sexual revolution. Love and marriage may no longer go together, but the latter normally follows the former, especially when the couple decides to become a family.

Even more significant is the fact that the mode of solemnization has not changed radically. There were more civil weddings in the 1970s, caused largely by the rising divorce rate and the preference of those marrying for a second time for a quiet wedding.[21] There were somewhat more bachelor-spinster civil marriages after 1976, but, while it had become "trendy" among educated people to talk about the white wedding as an "outdated charade," Diana Leonard found no declension in the symbolic and ceremonial meaning working-class people attached to marriage even when their weddings were held in a Register Office.[22] Certain aspects of the popular ceremony had changed since the 1950s—even royal brides no longer vow obedience—but the scale of the festivities is still very impressive. The language of the official ceremony may be more egalitarian, but the symbolism of the popular rites suggests that the social content and meaning of marriage have not changed all that much since the 1960s. Couples still prefer Gothic over modern churches because these seem to convey greater solemnity; and Register Offices have had to accede to the popular demand for a more "sacred" setting, redecorating to disguise their bureaucratic character. Even in a civil setting the big wedding retains its popularity, particularly in the northeast and Wales, and especially among the working classes.[23] The feeling is strong, however, that there is only one proper wedding: "I don't think it seems right in the Register Office—just in and out. It don't seem real."[24]

The white wedding has never been more popular, especially among working-class people, though there have been some significant changes in elements of the celebration over the past two decades. It has become more like the middle-class celebration, focused less on the bonds between the bride and her family and more on the couple as such. Fathers now give away their daughters, a symbol of separation that was played down earlier. The reception is less likely to be at home, less frequently catered by the bride's mother. Working-class people now spend as much if not more than the upper classes on the commercial provision of the festivities.[25] The biggest change of all, however, has been the enthusiastic adoption of the honeymoon. Few couples today miss the opportunity to get away for an extended period, thereby confirming their separation from both family and peers. When they return it will be to a separate house or apartment, and thus the opportunity for a final series of threshold ceremonies which, while already a part of middle-class ritual from the beginning of the century, were not taken up by the working classes until the massive proliferation of single-unit housing during the recent decades.[26]

But other things have remained much the same. The bride dresses in lustrous white, while the groom remains inconspicuous in his conservative lounge suit. During the 1960s there was a brief effort to brighten up the man's appearance by introducing more colorful wedding outfits, but the new fashions did not last long. The experiments with new bridal colors also failed, and by the 1980s white and ivory had re-established themselves.[27] The big wedding still means different things to men than it does to women. It is still her day, her moment, still clearly her major rite of passage, even though today's bride may be older and more sexually experienced. It does not really matter that today's brides are not virgins, for, as one youth explained it:

> There's virgins and virgins. There's girls who've lost their virginity to lots of fellows, and others who lost it only to the one they're marrying.[28]

A woman who is older or expecting may select a different shade, but the first-time bride will invariably wear white and surround herself with

27. The big white wedding remains an intrical part of working-class culture. John Allin, one of the best known of London's East End artists, suggests the element of performance by juxtaposing the church and the cinema. (Allin's *The Wedding*, 1970, courtesy of Portal Gallery, London)

bridesmaids dressed in different colors to emphasize her special role in the ceremony. The groom dresses formally, but not differently from the other men in the wedding party. We may tell his class position by whether he wears tails and a tophat or simply a dark suit, but it is the bride who is still singled out as the person who is about to undergo a major change in status from independent woman to the stereotypical wife and mother. Thus, the big wedding's symbolism confirms the existence of separate and unequal roles within marriage, even as it celebrates companionship.

II

The tension between love and marriage, between the myth of the conjugal and the fact that the woman's marriage is still very different from the man's marriage, is by no means resolved. In the sixteenth and seventeenth centuries people took the incompatibility of love and marriage for granted and, through various ritual means, put aside intimacy and equality when they founded a household and family. The conjugal myth is so dominant today that many would deny there is anything fundamentally irreconcilable between the egalitarian dimension of conjugal love and the roles women and men assume when they set up homes and have children. Even the marriage law now pretends there is no difference between husbands and wives as far as their respective rights are concerned.[29]

But what the law dictates and what people actually do are two very different things. Ideologically, the society is committed to an egalitarian conjugal ideal, but in practice it is very far from achieving it. By their symbolic behavior people show they are aware of this discrepancy. The big wedding itself is a statement (largely a woman's statement) that our contemporaries do not believe that the real conditions that could make equality possible in marriage have been achieved. By their presentation of themselves as dependent domestic creatures even those brides in white who will work after marriage give symbolic expression to the special role assigned to women within the family. They recognize what too many glib observers have overlooked—namely, the striking inequalities that arise when a couple cease to be just lovers and become parents and homeowners.

Basic to this glaring contradiction is the current legal status of parenthood. While the legal situation of the woman as wife has improved dramatically over the past eighty years, her role as mother has been more sharply defined and reinforced. She can be equal as a wife but not as a mother. As R. H. Graveson has pointed out, "the absolute or individual status of a married woman, as distinct from the relational status of wife, has almost ceased to exist."[30] Today, it is not the husband and wife, but the mother and father, that the law is most concerned with: "The trend seems toward the recognition of the status of the parent as opposed to that of the married man or married woman. Where there are children, but no marriage, certain duties of mutual support and maintaining children are imposed on the parents."[31] It makes no difference whether the couple is married or not. The law treats them as mother and father for the sake of the child.[32]

At the same time marriage has been "deregulated," there has been even greater intervention in parenthood. Beginning with the initiation of compulsory schooling in the 1870s and followed by various health and welfare standards over the next century, the demands on parents have increased substantially.[33] Despite the introduction after World War II of family income supplements, national health services, and some day-care facilities, the burden of childrearing still falls principally on the parents and especially on the mother.[34] The early-nineteenth-century radical vision of the socialization of parenthood, a demand that was put forward intermittently over the next hundred years, has not been realized. Today, the nuclear family is still the mandated arrangement for bringing up children. Single fathers, keeping their own house and children, are still very few in number; and single mothers find it extremely difficult to maintain the standards that the conventional couple—the male breadwinner with wife as supplementary earner—can provide. Despite improved maintenance by the welfare state, the single parent, especially the female parent, is likely to live in poverty and isolation. In our time it is not the married woman but the single woman who is likely to face the greatest legal discrimination, particularly if she dares become a mother.[35]

Contemporary society defines the nuclear family as the preferred unit of reproduction, but does little to ease the burdens of childraising. Other collective living arrangements are made difficult, if not impossible, by tax laws and housing policies.[36] Present conditions favor childless couples, for, if two do not live cheaper, they are still more affluent than either singles or parents. A teacher in his mid-thirties remarked that "one thing I've noticed is how much better off I've been over the past couple of years. My wife's a teacher and there's only the two of us. It's not bad, really: you can buy what you want and you can go on holiday, go abroad, and that sort of thing."[37] Couples experience a decline in living standards when children arrive and the mother leaves her employment or works only part-time. Worst off are single parents, especially unmarried mothers of working-class backgrounds. They not only suffer from the inferior wages of women generally, but face discrimination in terms of housing.[38]

Thus, the current conditions encourage the postponement of marriage and childbearing, but nevertheless reinforce the link between the two. Studies made during the 1960s found that ninety-four percent of female teenagers believed they would marry. For them this meant principally settling down and rearing a family.[39] When the surveys were repeated in the 1970s, the results were virtually the same.[40] The majority of those

interviewed thought that parenthood was essential to marriage and believed, in fact, it was children that made a marriage.[41] The association
of nuptiality with children was particularly strong among women, who,
in their projections of their own futures, often thought of themselves
more as mothers than as wives. Joyce Joseph found that in stories about
their imagined futures "large numbers of girls reported the deaths of
their husbands when husbands had performed the limited function of
providing them with children."[42] For women, children provided a major
incentive for marriage. "It's given me something in life; I feel that I've
achieved something now," one wife told Ann Oakley. Another spoke
of her children as if there was no other parent: "I look at her and think
you're *mine*, you're nobody else's."[43] For women, married motherhood
still provides the only unambiguous access to adult status. In Britain the
illegitimacy rate, while up, has fluctuated uncertainly, reflecting the
intensely popular feeling that marriage means children, and children
marriage. As one woman put it:

> I would never have got married, and I don't think he would've either if
> we hadn't wanted children. Well, what's the sense in getting married if
> you're not gonna have children really.[44]

Although couples delay pregnancy for two or three years, it is clear
that parenthood remains the ultimate objective. Without it, marriage can
become a personal tragedy, as it was with a woman who had tried for
more than three tortuous years: "I can see that what has made the last
few years so difficult is that I accepted, along with society, that child-
lessness within marriage is not only abnormal but socially unacceptable."[45] Men are even keener than women on parenthood and are the
ones that urge the start of childbearing, even when wives want to continue working.[46] They are eager to assume the full role of fatherhood,
which for them means becoming the chief breadwinner. The teacher,
who had enjoyed such affluence in the first childless years of his marriage, thought graduation rather than his wedding was the most important day of his life. His wife attached a great deal more importance
to the ceremony than he did: "she would think it was great. But I've
never really . . . it sounds awful to say it . . . " For him, as for other men
(regardless of class) among this younger generation, "a mortgage for a
house marked the real transition from youth to adult status. It had no
connotation of debt and disgrace: it was a mark of dignity and honour."[47]

In our relatively affluent society, the measure of manhood is more
often consumption than work. Career is still very important to middle-
class men's image of themselves as adults, but for all men the principal
goal is to be a good provider. Steady employment and good earnings,
as expressed through home, car, and the good life for wives and children,
make a man today.[48] However, the male still likes to think of himself as
being "caught" or "dragged" into matrimony; and it is women who are
most involved in the preparation for a wedding.[49] Working-class women

begin to think of marriage earlier than do their middle-class counterparts, who are more involved in school and career, more likely to have left home for the university or their own apartment, and thus less subject to parental control. Living at home, working-class women are more likely to have experienced tensions with their parents. For them, early marriage and motherhood are the means to independence. "Quite frankly I got fed up not being married, I was jolly pleased to do so and have children" was the story told by a woman married at seventeen.[50] Hannah Gavron observed in the 1960s that "flight into marriage by those young working class girls is perhaps their only way of acquiring the outward signs of adulthood and a limited and temporary limelight."[51] Today, the white wedding remains for most women a moment of great importance, not because it enhances the conjugal relationship, but because it legitimates motherhood. "I was pleased," remembered one woman; "I felt I was somebody important." Another remarked: "I don't think a woman is a woman until she has had children."[52]

III

Most of today's young marrieds do not face a real test of their conjugal relationship until the first child arrives. It is only then, usually two or three years after marriage, that the honeymoon really ends. The newlyweds continue to act like lovers while the bride works and there is plenty of income.[53] The real turning point comes when the couple decides to begin a family. At a propitious time in the pregnancy, the woman withdraws from work; often, if she is of the working class, she leaves full-time employment permanently. Even the men, who had experienced little or no personal change at marriage, begin to find their lives radically tranformed: "a first child deeply modified social relations, marked a major change of social state, and transformed the whole life."[54]

It is then that many couples face their first marital crisis because their relationship, however egalitarian, is overwhelmed by a stereotyped division of parental roles.[55] They may persist in the "ideal of equality, of husband and wife doing everything together, of minimal separation of interests and pursuits outside working hours," but the reality of their lives as parents bears little resemblance to the "symmetrical marriage" that so many observers thought they saw emerging in the 1960s.[56] Young fathers mean to be more helpful, but studies show that in reality the woman's burden in homemaking and childbearing has not been substantially alleviated. In fact, Geoffrey Gorer found that "today's young husbands put *far more* emphasis than the earlier generation did on a wife's skills as mother and housekeeper." When asked what they wished to see in a wife, they were explicit about just those qualities. A clerk talked about the importance of "being a good mother and being able to be thrifty"; a plumber presented his ideal as "good cook; good manager; good mother"; while an electrical engineer valued a woman who could be a "good cook; keep good clean house; stimulate exciting sexual relations."[57]

The arrival of children also reinforces men's tendency to see themselves as principal breadwinners and to view women's work and careers as secondary. The dual income which had previously been a source of mutual enjoyment, now becomes a source of dispute and, for men, a threat to their masculinity. Very few British couples (especially of the working class) pool their incomes. The husband either gives the wife his own pay packet and takes back pocket money, or gives her an allowance on which to manage house and family. Even when a woman is providing supplementary income, she has no money that she can call her own and is accountable for everything she spends out of their joint earnings.[58] The main responsibility for home life falls on her shoulders. Couples begin their marriages sharing household tasks, but the novelty soon wears off and by the time the first child has arrived a division of labor is firmly in place. "While I'm working he'll help," remarked one Swansea bride. "But once I stop he won't do anything—he believes it's women's work."[59]

Recent research shows that young husbands do take a greater interest in cooking, child care, and housework than their fathers did, but the wife is still regarded as principally responsible for both home and children. He "helps" her, but does not venture into full responsibility for the still highly feminized tasks of mothering and housekeeping. In reality, the increased standards of both mean that the wife normally does much more than forty hours of work per week, even when she has a job outside the home.[60] The fifty percent of married women who continue to work find themselves on a double shift, making their days longer and harder than those of their mothers who did not go out to work.[61] Hannah Gavron observed in the 1960s that "it may be that the mother today spends more time with her children than did her mother as she has no one to leave the children with."[62] Middle-class women can afford the domestic services and day care that allows them to get away from home and children, but the mutual assistance that was common in working-class urban neighborhoods as late as the 1950s had all but disappeared when Gavron made her study of London. By then, the city streets were regarded as unsafe for children, and the new suburbs were felt to be cold and unneighborly.[63] Those female bonds that had been so supportive earlier had vanished. The old matrifocality was much diminished even when daughters lived near their former homes.[64] Daughters were still attached to their mothers, but the bond was a sentimental one rather than a practical relationship involving day-to-day exchange of services.[65]

The homosocial world of men has not been unaffected by changes in work and leisure in the 1960s and 1970s. The younger generation is more home and family oriented, less likely to go out to the pub alone in the manner of their fathers. "The tellie keeps the family together," remarked one Greenleigh man. "None of us ever have to go out now."[66] However, men do get out of the house during the day; they have more evenings out and more holidays than do their wives. While the half of married women who work are able to get away from home and children for short periods, the situation for the working-class, full-time mother appears to be more homebound and isolated today than it was in the 1950s. She is less likely than her middle-class sister to be neighborly, and she has remarkably few friends.[67] "To my mind the only friends you really have is your own Mum and Dad, and your husband if you are lucky," remarked a young London mother.[68] Although women today generally feel on a more equal standing with their husbands, what is meant by equality differs by class. Among the middle-class women it means getting out of the house and having a life of their own; for the working-class wife it means drawing the man into the domestic sphere, something that does not so much change her routine as reinforce it:

> When you're first married you can go out together; well, when you've got a child that stops all that doesn't it.[69]

It is certainly true that couples try hard to live up to the conjugal idea. Wives expect husbands to talk with them, share their feelings as well as their beds. "We talk to each other you know—my parents never really talked, what you might say closely, to each other."[70] People expect more of the conjugal relationship. It is made to bear the full weight of needs for intimacy, companionship, and love, needs which were previously met in other ways. Couples expect more of one another. The wife of a press operator takes it for granted that wives "still need courting after marriage."[71] Husbands are also more prone to jealousy than their fathers ever were.[72]

The problem arises when this conjugal ideal is confronted with the realities of parenthood and the nuclear household. In our day there has been a "tendency to oversell marriage as a kind of unending affair, in which the partners are expected to remain at the high point of infatuation for the rest of their lives."[73] The women's magazines, movies, and television all seem to conspire in offering this as the perfect form of matrimony.[74] However, those who plunge into marriage on romantic impulse alone, without going through the series of ritual steps from betrothal to the big wedding, have been shown to be the most vulnerable to marital problems and early divorce.[75] Even women who have taken the greatest care in ritually constructing relationships beyond the conjugal find themselves under great strain when the first child is born.[76] For many, motherhood is a major crisis. It is not just that they are poorly prepared for the personal changes that motherhood brings, but they now find themselves socially isolated and helpless to deal with the many demands placed on them.[77] Children diminish marital happiness, more so for women than men. Sexual relations deteriorate and couples draw apart. Mothers are more subject to poor health and mental depression, conditions that necessarily affect the marriage.[78]

Most couples ride out this and subsequent crises, but the arrival of the first child is quite often the occasion for separation and divorce.[79] Husbands who were so keen on parenthood take flight when presented with its reality. Despite the ideal of shared parental obligations, the burden of childrearing invariably falls to the woman. In most divorce settlements the easily evaded task of child support is assigned to the male, the unavoidable responsibilities of child care to the woman.[80] Under these circumstances their only real option is that of remarriage, a cycle of dependency from which there is no escape.

The divorce rate quadrupled in the 1970s, but remarriage continued at a high level and the nuclear family remained the preferred form of parenting and domesticity. It must not be forgotten, however, that most marriages are not broken; and there is firm evidence that the proverbial wisdom "Marry in haste, repent in leisure" still holds true, because those with the longest engagements also have the most enduring marriages. A recent study concluded that "those who do experience a more ritualized transition from the single to the married state (and in particular women who do so) are better equipped to allow their marital relationships to develop at a slower pace, since they enter marriage with a stronger sense of their own new marital identity and are more likely to see confirmation of this from their partners, especially in the earlier stages of marriage."[81] But the same rituals that assist couples coping with marriage also reinforce the sexual divisions that are the root cause of many a problem. The white wedding expresses and at the same time reinforces the relative vulnerability and dependency of women. Feminists may want to treat it as an ephemeral vestige of patriarchalism, but the social and economic realities which it reflects are not so easily exorcised. Even in this conjugal age, when both men and women more readily accept the notion of companionship based on liberty and equality, the tension between ideal and reality remains an intractable one.

IV

For most of the twentieth century both sexes have been torn between the potent force of modern individualism and the equally strong desire to have a home and family. Women have been the ones who have had to subordinate themselves most completely to the institutional imperatives of marriage; and it is not surprising that in the marriage reform movements of the 1960s and 1970s they have taken the leading role. There is no question that with respect to values both men and women are more libertarian and egalitarian than twenty years ago. Today, there is a tendency for younger women to postpone marriage and older women to abandon it. Men have also found an advantage in putting off family commitments in favor of personal freedom. But couples who postpone establishing a home and having children also put off some of life's hardest decisions. Their individualism and egalitarianism are invariably tested when they take on family responsibilities, and, as we have seen, ideals are not easily transformed into practice. The money matters that were so easily dealt with when each paid an equal share become more complicated when there is a mortgage. The decision of who shall parent and who shall work is an additional source of difficulty. Even sex becomes problematic.[82] The transition was not easy even in those earlier times when marital roles were so much more fixed and at the time of the big wedding the whole community gathered to confirm the passage from the status of young lovers to that of married adults. Today, when family life is so much more private, a great deal more is left to the couple to work out for themselves. Conjugal love is now the excuse to leave the family alone and isolate its members, particularly women and children, from the world of work and the real sources of power. Couples are told that through sensitivity training and sex therapy they can work out their problems, but, as Robert Brain has recently reminded us, love is rarely enough:

> More and more often, romantic love ends not in acceptance and adaptation to the harsh realities of marriage, but in boredom, disillusion, and open infidelity—and a search for a new passion and a new bout with hopefulness. Romantic love is still alone in producing the wonderful sense of wellbeing, the ecstatic feelings which transfigure both lover and beloved, but we are finding that it disregards all the important realities when two people decide to live together in marriage for a lifetime.[83]

The harsh reality we all must face is that the solutions to this contemporary dilemma are social rather than individual. The most obvious problems are the result of social and economic conditions that cause women's educational and employment opportunities to remain inferior to those of men and that produce massive inequalities in income and real power. As long as women's earnings remain so much below those of men, the assignment of the breadwinner role to the male will continue to be virtually automatic. Until there is a radical reorganization of both housekeeping and child care, inequalities arising from the division of labor within the family will also continue. Equal pay, affirmative action in employment, subsidization of household work, and the provision of full child-support services offer obvious solutions to this dilemma. None of these ideas are new, nor are the problems they are addressed to, but we would do well to get on with the long delayed project that William Thompson outlined at the beginning of the modern industrial era— namely, the task of constructing a social and economic order "which will complete and for ever ensure the perfect equality and entire reciprocity of happiness between women and men."[84]

This will not happen as long as we continue to understand marriage as a private issue, either too sacred or too emotionally sensitive to be treated as a matter of collective concern and public interest. Living together as adult couples is properly a matter of individual discretion, but the founding of a family is not. It was precisely this truth that was affirmed by the big wedding in the early modern period and sustained by public bridals until the nineteenth century when the privatization of marriage and family finally prevailed. Today's conjugal myth perpetuates the illusion that each family is essentially on its own and that love between two people is sufficient to produce just and amicable relationships. Even some feminist critics seem to assume that, when women are given the same rights and opportunities as men, affective individualism will solve all the remaining problems. They would do well to remember Mary Wollstonecraft's warning that "love from its very nature must be transitory. To seek for a secret that would render it constant would be a wild search for the philosopher's stone or the great panacea: and the discovery would be equally useless, or rather, pernicious to mankind. The most holy bond of society is friendship."[85]

Law prefers to sanction only conjugal relationships, even to the extent of now conferring the legitimacy once reserved for married couples on the unmarried as well. No similar privileges are assigned to friendship. Yet, what the law does not provide, people legislate for themselves through gesture and symbol. Even in our modern era, having something "done rite" still establishes powerful obligations. The big wedding, so often the subject of the sophisticate's scorn and the historian's neglect, is a testament to ritual's legislative authority. Through all the various forms it has taken, one theme runs deep and strong: "A great many can help one, but one cannot help a great many." The bidder's phrase is a reminder that marriage has been and always will be a public as well as a private matter, whose history is not just that of lovers but of all those who are in any way touched by their relationship.

Appendix

Age and Occupations of Unwed Mothers Whose Children Were Admitted to the London Foundling Hospital, 1801–1900

		Professions and Teaching	Retail and Distribution	Personal Service	Clothing Trades	Other Manufactures	Listed as Helping at Home	Not Employed or Unemployed	Not Stated
1801–1810	—	0	0	69.2	10.0	4.2	3.3	10.8	2.5
1811–1820	22.3	1.7	0.8	64.7	7.6	5.0	3.4	16.0	0.8
1821–1830	23.5	2.5	1.7	68.3	10.8	0.8	4.2	10.8	0.8
1831–1840	23.1	0	0.8	59.2	20.0	1.7	2.5	15.0	0.8
1841–1850	22.9	0.8	0.8	65.0	13.3	1.7	5.0	13.3	0
1851–1860	22.3	0.8	0.8	65.0	7.5	1.7	11.7	12.5	0
1861–1870	21.7	1.7	2.5	64.5	10.7	3.3	5.8	11.6	0
1871–1880	21.4	1.7	1.7	69.7	6.7	4.2	3.4	12.6	0
1881–1890	21.1	—	4.2	70.0	10.0	1.7	5.0	9.2	0
1891–1900	21.5	0.8	5.0	60.5	7.6	5.0	6.7	12.6	1.7
Average for century	22.2	1.0	1.8	65.6	10.4	2.9	5.1	12.5	0.7

Source: Compiled from records of successful admission to the London Foundling Hospital.

Notes

Introduction

1. For the most recent sociological treatment, see Philip Blumstein and Pepper Schwartz, *American Couples*, New York, 1983; psychological approaches to the family are thoughtfully assessed by Mark Poster, *Critical Theory of the Family*, New York, 1978.
2. G. E. Howard, *The History of Matrimonial Institutions*, 4 vols., London, 1904; Arthur W. Calhoun, *A Social History of the American Family*, 3 vols., Cleveland, 1917–19; Edward A. Westermarck, *The History of Human Marriage*, 3 vols., New York, 1922. Philippe Ariès, *Centuries of Childhood: A Social History of Family Life*, New York, 1965; Edward Shorter, *The Making of the Modern Family*, New York, 1975; Lawrence Stone, *The Family, Sex and Marriage in England, 1500–1800*, New York, 1977.
3. The classic argument for looking at marriage from the perspective of "his marriage" versus "her marriage" was made by Jessie Bernard, *The Future of Marriage*, New York, 1973, pp. 5–9.
4. Robert Brain, *Friends and Lovers*, New York, 1976.
5. I have excluded Scotland from consideration because its marriage laws were not the same as those of England and Wales. Those who wish to explore the Scottish experience should consult T. C. Smout, "Scottish Marriage, Regular and Irregular, 1500–1940," *Marriage and Society*, ed. R. B. Outhwaite, New York, 1981, pp. 204–36; Norah Smith, "Sexual Mores and Attitudes in Enlightenment Scotland," *Sexuality in Eighteenth-Century Britain*, ed. Paul-Gabriel Boucé, Manchester, 1982, pp. 47–73; Kenneth M. Boyd, *Scottish Church Attitudes to Sex, Marriage and the Family, 1850–1914*, Edinburgh, 1980.
6. The utility of this approach was suggested to me by Diana Leonard's *Sex and Generation: A Study of Courtship and Weddings*, London, 1980, pp. 1–3. See also Charles Phythian-Adams, *Local History and Folklore*, London, 1975. A similar approach to ritual events is to be found in Victor Turner's concept of "social drama." See Victor Turner, *Dramas, Fields, and Metaphors: Symbolic Action in Human Society*, Ithaca, 1974, pp. 23–59.

7. Robert Bocock, *Ritual in Industrial Society: A Sociological Analysis of Ritualism in Modern England*, London, 1974, p. 16.
8. Sally F. Moore and Barbara Myerhoff, "Introduction: Secular Ritual: Forms and Meanings," *Secular Ritual*, eds. S. F. Moore and B. G. Myerhoff, Assen/Amsterdam, 1977, p. 24; Turner, p. 124.

Chapter 1

1. A general introduction to early modern demography is provided by Lawrence Stone, *The Family, Sex and Marriage in England, 1500–1800*, New York, 1977, pp. 42–60. For recent trends in marriage, see Joan Busfield and Michael Paddon, *Thinking about Children: Sociology and Fertility in Post-war England*, Cambridge, 1977, pp. 8–11. The changing proportion of the population married is very difficult to calculate because most statistics for the early modern period come from household composition rather than actual civil status. However, useful comparative information is provided by Richard Wall, "The Household: Demographic and Economic Change in England, 1650–1970," *Family Forms in Historic Europe*, eds. Richard Wall, Jean Robin, and Peter Laslett, Cambridge, 1983, p. 498.
2. According to the Oxford English Dictionary, it was not until the seventeenth and eighteenth centuries that the term "couple" was generalized.
3. I do not deal with homosexuality directly. For those interested in the subject, there is Jeffrey Weeks, *Sex, Politics and Society: The Regulation of Sexuality since 1800*, London, 1981, pp. 96–121; Weeks, *Coming Out: Homosexual Politics in Britain, from the Nineteenth Century to the Present*, London, 1977, part one; and Randolf Trumbach, "London's Sodomites: Homosexual Behavior and Western Culture in the Eighteenth Century," *Journal of Social History*, XI (Fall 1977), pp. 1–33.
4. A devastating critique of the view that the past was affectionless is provided by Linda A. Pollack's *Forgotten Children: Parent-Child Relations from 1500–1900*, Cambridge, 1983, passim; and Michael MacDonald, *Mystical Bedlam: Madness, Anxiety and Healing in Seventeenth-Century England*, Cambridge, 1981, especially chapter iii. Similar revisions are to be found in Martine Segalen, *Love and Power in the Peasant Family*, Oxford, 1983.
5. A similar point is made by Robert Brain, *Friends and Lovers*, New York, 1976.
6. See Alan Macfarlane, *The Origins of English Individualism: The Family, Property and Social Transition*, Oxford, 1978; Richard M. Smith, "Population and Its Geography in England, 1500–1730," *An Historical Geography of England and Wales*, eds. R. A. Dodgshon and R. A. Butlin, London, 1978, pp. 199–238; Keith Wrightson, *English Society, 1580–1680*, New Brunswick, 1982; Angus McLaren, "Reproductive Rituals: The Patterning of Human Fertility in England, 1500–1800," unpublished manuscript; and E. A. Wrigley and R. S. Schofield, *The Population History of England, 1541–1871*, Cambridge, 1981, passim.
7. John Hajnal, "European Marriage Patterns in Perspective," *Population in History*, eds. D. V. Glass and D. E. C. Eversley, Chicago, 1965, pp. 101–43; Richard M. Smith, "Some Reflections on the Evidence for the Origins of the European Marriage Pattern," *The Sociology of the Family*, ed. C. Harris, Monograph Series of *The Sociological Review*, 28 (1980), pp. 74–112.

ine and Keith Wrightson, "The Social Context of Illegitimacy in
lern England," *Bastardy and its Comparative History*, eds. Peter
rla Oosterveen, and Richard M. Smith, Cambridge, 1980, pp. 158–

    ....., pp. 44–49.

10. Christopher Haigh, *Reformation and Resistance in Tudor Lancashire*, Cambridge, 1975, pp. 46–48; Stone, pp. 85–90.

11. Wrightson, *English Society*, chapter iii.

12. Steve Rappaport, "Social Structure and Mobility in Sixteenth-Century London," unpublished Ph.D. dissertation, Columbia University, 1982, chapter V.

13. R. Younge, *The Poores Advocate* (1654), quoted in C. Hill, *The World Turned Upside Down: Radical Ideas during the English Revolution*, Harmondsworth, 1975, p. 320. This subject is dealt with at length in David Levine's "Production, Reproduction and the Proletarian Family in England," *Proletarianization and Family Life*, ed. D. Levine, forthcoming.

14. Hill, pp. 314–23.

15. Keith Wrightson and David Levine, *Poverty and Piety in an English Village: Terling, 1525–1700*, New York, 1979, chapter vii; K. Davies, " 'The Sacred Condition of Equality'—How Original Were Puritan Doctrines of Marriage?," *Social History*, no. 5 (1977), pp. 563–80; W. Hunt, *The Puritan Moment*, Cambridge, 1983, pp. 74–76; Stone, pp. 142–50.

16. Hill, pp. 306–14; C. Hill, *Society and Puritanism in Pre-Revolutionary England*, 2nd ed., London, 1967, chapter xviii; Hunt, pp. 140–55; Stone, pp. 129–40.

17. Smallholders were concentrated in the north and west. In the south and east, where capitalist agriculture was making its greatest strides, the percentage was already below a half. See Hunt, pp. 10–23; and Wrightson, *English Society*, pp. 23–38.

18. J. P. Cooper, "Patterns of Inheritance and Settlement by Great Landowners from the Fifteenth to the Eighteenth Centuries," *Family and Inheritance: Rural Society in Western Europe, 1200–1800*, eds. Jack Goody, Joan Thirsk, and E. P. Thompson, Cambridge, 1978, pp. 192–327; Cicely Howell, "Peasant Inheritance Customs in the Midlands, 1280–1700," ibid., pp. 112–55; Margaret Spufford, "Peasant Inheritance Customs and Land Distribution in Cambridgeshire from the Sixteenth to the Eighteenth Centuries," ibid., pp. 156–76; J. A. Johnston, "The Probate Inventories and Wills of a Worcestershire Parish, 1676–1775," *Midland History*, I, no. 1 (Spring 1971), pp. 20–33.

19. The author is Sir John Gibson, quoted in Alan Macfarlane, *The Family Life of Ralph Josselin: A Seventeenth Century Clergyman*, New York, 1977, p. 210; also John R. Gillis, *Youth and History: Tradition and Change in European Age Relations, 1770 to Present*, New York, 1975, pp. 14–18.

20. Wall, p. 498.

21. See Charles Phythian-Adams, *Desolation of a City: Coventry and the Urban Crisis of the Late Middle Ages*, Cambridge, 1979, pp. 83, 89; figures from Sheffield provided by Keith Thomas, "Women and the Civil War Sects," *Crisis in Europe, 1560–1660*, ed. T. Aston, Garden City, New York, 1965, p. 333; on age relations generally, see Thomas, "Age and Authority in Early Modern Britain," *Proceedings of the British Academy*, LXII (1976), pp. 209–45.

22. For other parts of Europe, see Edward Shorter, *The Making of the Modern Family*, New York, 1975, chapter I; Jean-Louis Flandrin, *Families in Former Times: Kinship, Household and Sexuality*, Cambridge, 1979, pp. 4–22; Matti Sarmela, *Reciprocity Systems of the Rural Society in the Finnish Karelian Culture Area*, Folklore Fellows Communications, no. 207, Helsinki, 1969, especially chapter ii.

23. Nicole Belmont, "The Symbolic Function of the Wedding Procession in Popular Rituals of Marriage," *Ritual, Religion, and the Sacred*, eds. R. Forster and O. Ranum, Baltimore, 1982, pp. 2–6; Beatrice Gottlieb, "The Meaning of Clandestine Marriage," *Family and Sexuality in French History*, eds. R. Wheaton and Tamara Hareven, Philadelphia, 1980, pp. 49–83.

24. W. Barnes, "The Diary of William Whiteway," *Proceedings of the Dorset Natural History and Archeological Field Club*, XIII (1892), p. 59.

25. Henry Swinburne, *A Treatise of Spousals or Matrimonial Contracts*, London, 1686, p. 5.

26. Description of betrothal, dated between 975 and 1030, in *English Historical Documents, c. 500–1042*, ed. D. Whitelock, New York, 1955, p. 431.

27. A. E. Anton, " 'Handfasting' in Scotland," *The Scottish Historical Review*, XXVII, no. 124 (October 1958), pp. 90–91.

28. G. E. Howard, *The History of Matrimonial Institutions*, I, London, 1904, p. 270; also John Thrupp, *The Anglo-Saxon Home*, London, 1862, pp. 49–70.

29. Howard, pp. 280–83.

30. Anton, pp. 92–93.

31. Howard, pp. 282–83.

32. Ibid., p. 304.

33. George C. Homans, *English Villagers in the Thirteenth Century*, New York, 1975, pp. 170–71; Howard, pp. 306–8.

34. Homans, p. 184.

35. Ibid., p. 172. For a nineteenth-century instance, see Ruth Tongue, *Somerset Folklore*, London, 1965, pp. 148–49; and *Notes and Queries*, 1st Series, VI (December 11, 1852), p. 561.

36. John Bossy, "Blood and Baptism: Kinship, Community and Christianity in Western Europe from the 14th to the 17th Centuries," *Sanctity and Secularity: The Church and the World*, ed. D. Baker, Oxford, 1973, pp. 138–40.

37. *Notes and Queries*, 8th Series, IX (February 29, 1896), p. 171.

38. Quoted from *Admonition to Parliament of 1572*, eds. W. H. Frere and C. E. Douglas, London, 1907, p. 27.

39. Homans, pp. 172–73.

40. Stone, pp. 31–33; Homans, pp. 164–65.

41. R. H. Helmholtz, *Marriage Litigation in Medieval England*, Cambridge, 1974, p. 28.

42. The changes on the continent are discussed by Andre Burguière, "The Marriage Ritual in France: Ecclesiastical Practices and Popular Practices," *Ritual, Religion, and the Sacred*, Baltimore, 1982, pp. 9–21.

43. Quoted in Anton, p. 97.

44. Peter Laslett, *The World We Have Lost*, New York, 1965, pp. 143–44.

45. Peter Laslett, "Parental Deprivation in the Past: A Note on Orphans and Stepparenthood in English History," in Laslett's *Family Life and Illicit Love in Earlier Generations*, Cambridge, 1977, p. 164.

46. I concentrate here on first marriages, which constituted seventy to seventy-

five percent of all nuptiality at this time. For second marriages, see *Marriage and Remarriage in Populations of the Past*, ed. J. Dupâquier, et al., London, 1981.

47. Wrightson, *English Society*, pp. 78–79; also A. Macfarlane, "The Informal Social Control of Marriage in Seventeenth Century England," in V. Fox and M. Quitt, *Loving, Parenting and Dying*, New York, 1980, p. 113.

48. Wrightson, *English Society*, pp. 79–80; Gillis, pp. 21–35.

49. Wrightson, *English Society*, p. 69.

50. *The Diary of Roger Lowe*, ed. William L. Sachse, New Haven, 1938, passim.

51. Laslett, *The World We Have Lost*, 2nd ed., New York, 1971, p. 151.

52. Ibid.

53. Stone, p. 50.

54. From a Westmoreland prohibition on marriages by poor persons, dated 1614, cited in *Byegones*, 2nd Series, III (June 28, 1983), p. 106.

55. *Munby: Man of Two Worlds*, ed. Derek Hudson, London, 1974, pp. 103–4. See also Iona and Peter Opie, *Children's Games in Street and Playground*, Oxford, 1969, pp. 198–203.

56. On the element of play in courtship, see Johann Huizinga, *Homo Ludens: A Study of the Play-Element in Culture*, Boston, 1950, p. 43.

57. John W. Wales, "St. Valentine's Day," *The Antiquary*, V (February 1882), pp. 46–49; A. R. Wright, *British Calendar Customs*, II, London, 1938, pp. 140–43.

58. Wright, p. 145.

59. *Notes and Queries*, X (July 1, 1854), p. 5.

60. W. Crooke, "Lifting of the Bride," *Folk-Lore*, XIII (1902), pp. 247–51; Phythian-Adams, *Desolation of a City*, p. 91.

61. *Notes and Queries*, 6th Series, VIII (September 22, 1883), p. 234.

62. F. W. Hackwood, *The Wednesbury Papers*, Wednesbury, 1884, p. 60.

63. *Notes and Queries*, 6th Series, VII (September 22, 1883), p. 234.

64. Ibid., December 11, 1883, p. 883.

65. *Yorkshire Gazette*, April 7, 1883; *Folklore Journal*, I (1883), p. 270.

66. Lewis Morris, cited in Trefor M. Owen, *Welsh Folk Customs*, Cardiff, 1978, p. 98.

67. Christina Hole, *A Dictionary of British Folk Customs*, London, 1976, p. 193.

68. Cited in Robert W. Malcolmson, *Popular Recreations in English Society, 1700–1850*, Cambridge, 1973, p. 30.

69. Samuel Bamford, *Passages in the Life of a Radical and Early Days*, I, London, 1905, pp. 144–45.

70. W. S. Weeks, "Further Legendary Stories and Folklore of the Clitheroe District," *Transactions of Lancashire and Cheshire Antiquarian Society*, XXXVIII (1920), p. 68.

71. Hole, pp. 191–2; U. B. Chisenhale-Marsh, "Folk Lore in Essex and Herts," *Essex Review*, V (1896), p. 147.

72. Malcolmson, p. 30.

73. W. S. Weeks, p. 67.

74. Owen, pp. 98–99.

75. Hole, pp. 195–96.

76. Ibid., pp. 203–4; Malcolmson, p. 9.

77. Sabine Baring-Gould, *Old Country Life*, London, 1890, p. 192.

78. H. Jollie, *Sketch of Cumberland Manners and Customs*, Carlisle, 1811, p. 40.

79. Owen, p. 109.
80. Malcolmson, pp. 53–54.
81. Ibid., p. 55.
82. Percy Manning Collection, Scrapbooks and Notes, MS Top Oxon d 199, fols. 166, 186–88, 258, Bodleian Library.
83. Joseph Lawson, *Letters to the Young on Progress in Pudsey during the Last Sixty Years*, Stanninglen, 1887, p. 11.
84. Joan J. Scott, "A Description and preliminary Discussion of the Rhymed Blason Populaire Tradition in England," *Lore and Language*, II, no. 2 (January 1975), p. 20.
85. Richard Blakeborough, Volume of Cuttings: Legends of North Riding, p. 63, Blakeborough Manuscript Collection, Sheffield University.
86. Ibid., p. 35. This was collected in the early nineteenth century.
87. Earnest money is discussed in *Nottinghamshire and Derbyshire Notes and Queries*, IV (1896), p. 31.
88. Malcolmson, p. 54.
89. Lawson, pp. 13–14.
90. Ibid.
91. Edwin Grey, *Cottage Life in a Hertfordshire Village*, Harpenden, 1977, p. 147.
92. A complete discussion of this is found in Robert K. Wikman, *Die Einleitung der Ehe*, Abo, 1937, pp. 255–57.
93. Lawson, p. 10; also T. F. Elworthy, *West Somerset Word Book*, London, 1886. Further materials on courtship are to be found in the Folk Lore Society archive, University of London, Box 121.
94. J. Burnley, *Phases of Bradford Life*, London, 1889, p. 83.
95. Trefor Owen, "West Glamorgan Customs," *Folk-Life*, III (1965), p. 47.
96. T. Gwynn Jones, *Welsh Folklore and Folk Custom*, London, 1930, p. 187.
97. *The Diary of Roger Lowe*, pp. 20, 43, 49.
98. J. C. Davies, *Folk-Lore of West and Mid-Wales*, Aberystwyth, 1911, p. 2.
99. Incidents recorded in Katrin Stevens notes on courtship and marriage customs made available to me by the Welsh Folk Museum. This particular incident apparently happened in the 1860s. See also the David Thomas Collection, B39, National Library of Wales.
100. "General Report on the Agricultural Labourer: Wales," *Parliamentary Papers* (1893–94), XXXVI, pp. 33, 63; also E. S. Turner, *History of Courting*, London, 1974, p. 169.
101. From Katrin Stevens' notes, Welsh Folk Museum.
102. Enid Porter, *Cambridgeshire Customs and Folklore*, London, 1969, pp. 1–5.
103. D. Parry Jones, *My Own Folks*, Llandysul, 1972, p. 175.
104. Christina Hole, *Traditions and Customs of Cheshire*, Cambridge, London, 1937, pp. 3–4.
105. *Diary of Roger Lowe*, p. 20.
106. Stone, p. 606.
107. Henry Stiles, *Bundling: Its origins, progress and decline in America*, Mount Vernon, 1937, pp. 22–27.
108. E. W. Jones, "Medical Glimpses of Early 19th Century Cardiganshire," *National Library of Wales Journal*, XIV (1965–66), pp. 260–75.
109. Turner, *History of Courting*, p. 169.
110. Henry Best's account of Yorkshire weddings, from *Rural Economy in York-*

shire in 1641, being the Farming and Account Books of Henry Best of Elmswell in East Riding, Surtees Society, no. 33, 1857, pp. 116–17.

111. Owen, *Welsh Folk Customs*, pp. 147–51.
112. See S. R. Bird, "Some Early Breach of Promise Cases," *The Antiquary*, VI (November 1881), pp. 185–86. This was also evident in Finland. See Sarmela, pp. 64–68, 88–89.
113. Owen, "West Glamorgan Custom," p. 50.
114. John C. Jeaffreson, *Brides and Bridals*, I, London, 1872, p. 66; on the magic of hair, see *Byegones*, 2nd Series (April 1, 1896), p. 213, and *Bygones*, 2nd Series (May 6, 1896), p. 332.
115. Quoted from an unpublished manuscript memoir of George Calvert, fol. 9, Institute of Dialect and Folk Life Studies, Archive Acc. 2218, Leeds University. The memoir seems to have been composed in the 1820s at Kirby Moorside, North Riding, Yorkshire. For additional references to the magic power of the garter, see *Notes and Queries*, 13th Series (February 16, 1924), p. 114; R. Blakeborough, *Wit, Character, Folklore and Custom of North Riding of Yorkshire*, Salburn-by-the-Sea, 1911, pp. 94–95; E. Gutch, *Country Folklore: North Riding of Yorkshire, York and the Ainsty*, London, 1901, p. 289.
116. F. J. Furnivall, *Child-marriages, divorces, and ratifications in the diocese of Chester*, London, 1897, p. xlix.
117. Ibid., p. 57.
118. Cited in G. R. Quaife, *Wanton Wenches and Wayward Wives: Peasants and Illicit Sex in Early Seventeenth Century England*, New Brunswick, 1979, p. 44.
119. J. A. Sharp, *Defamation and Sexual Slander in Early Modern England: The Church Courts at York*, Borthwick Papers, no. 58, York, 1980, passim.
120. Iona and Peter Opie, *Lore and Language of School Children*, Oxford, 1959, pp. 325–27; Brain, pp. 40–42.
121. On the difference between friendship and neighborliness, see A. Macfarlane, *The Family Life of Ralph Josselin*, pp. 149–50.
122. On farm servants, see Ann Kussmaul-Cooper, "The Mobility of English Farm Servants in the 17th and 18th Centuries," unpublished paper, Library of the Cambridge Group for the History of Population and Social Structure, 0 1281. See also Ann Kussmaul, *Servants in husbandry in early Modern England*, Cambridge, 1981, pp. 31–38, 51–68.
123. Peter Clark, "The Migrant in Kentish Towns, 1580–1640," eds. P. Clark and P. Slack, *Crisis and Order in English Towns, 1500–1700*, London, 1972, pp. 134–36.
124. Peter Laslett, *The World We Have Lost*, chapter iii.
125. Wrightson and Levine, *Poverty and Piety*, p. 131.
126. Wrightson, *English Society*, p. 55.
127. For an illuminating discussion of the various forms of friendship, see Brain, passim. Also Benjamin Nelson, *The Idea of Usury: From Tribal Brotherhood to Universal Otherhood*, Princeton, 1949, pp. 141–51.
128. *Diary of Roger Lowe*, p. 20.
129. Ibid., p. 91.
130. Ibid., pp. 43, 49.
131. Ibid., p. 89.
132. Ibid., p. 27.
133. Ibid., p. 37, 72.

134. Ibid., p. 73.

135. Ibid., p. 87.

136. Ibid., p. 20.

137. Ibid., pp. 28, 47.

138. Ibid., p. 37.

139. Ibid., p. 34.

140. Wrightson, *English Society*, pp. 72–77.

141. Peter Laslett, "Introduction: Comparing Illegitimacy over Time and between Cultures," *Bastardy and its Comparative History*, eds. P. Laslett, K. Oosterveen, and R. M. Smith, Cambridge, 1980, pp. 12–26.

142. William J. Goode, "The Theoretical Importance of Love," *American Sociological Review*, XXIV, no. 1 (February 1959), pp. 44–45.

143. *Diary of Roger Lowe*, p. 14.

144. Ralph Houlbrooke, *Church Courts and the People during the English Reformation*, Oxford, 1979, pp. 57–66; J. Ingram, "Ecclesiastical Justice in Wiltshire, 1600–1660," unpublished D.Phil dissertation, Oxford University, 1976, pp. 114–28.

145. Best, p. 116.

146. Furnivall, p. 197.

147. Ibid., p. li.

148. Lawson, p. 14.

149. David Jenkins, *The Agricultural Community in South-West Wales at the Turn of the Twentieth Century*, Cardiff, 1971, p. 127.

150. Lawson, p. 15.

151. From *The Banner*, August 19, 1887. Found in Archive Box 12, Folklore Society, University of London. A similar case reported in *Yorkshire Gazette*, November 4, 1882, cited in *Folklore Journal* I (1883), p. 59. Also see M. A. Courtney, *Cornish Feasts and Folk-Lore*, Penzance, 1890, p. 166.

152. Lawson, p. 15; B. A. Neale, "A New Look at an Old Manuscript and Its Author," postgraduate diploma thesis, Leeds University, 1975, on deposit at the Institute of Dialect and Folk-Life Studies, Leeds.

153. *Diary of Roger Lowe*, p. 24.

154. Ibid., p. 47.

155. Ibid., p. 61.

156. From church court case of 1591, cited in William H. Hale, *A Series of Presentments and Proceedings in Criminal Causes, 1475–1640, from Act-Books of the Ecclesiastical Courts of Diocese of London*, London, 1947, p. 205.

157. On the use of defamation causes by women, see Sharp, pp. 17, 18.

158. *Diary of Roger Lowe*, pp. 84, 105.

159. Ibid., p. 47.

160. Ibid., p. 67. For a similar sixteenth-century case, see James Raine, ed., *Depositions and other Ecclesiastical Proceedings from the Courts of Durham*, Surtees Society, XXI (1845), p. 283.

161. *Diary of Roger Lowe*, p. 13.

162. Ibid., p. 50.

163. Ibid., p. 105.

164. Ibid., p. 53.

165. Ibid., pp. 36, 38, 58.

166. Ibid., p. 82.

167. From Evan Jones' Notebooks, Welsh Folk Museum.

168. Cited in J. D. Chambers, *Nottinghamshire in the Eighteenth Century*, London, 1932, p. 311.
169. Furnivall, pp. xlvii, 68–69.
170. A. Percival Moore, "Marriage Contracts or Espousals in the Reign of Queen Elizabeth," *Reports and Papers of the Associated Architectural Societies for 1909*, XXX, part one, p. 273, 287–89; Furnivall, pp. 57, 194. On the binding power of the hand clasp, see John Aubry, *Remaines of Gentilisme and Judaisme*, London, 1881, p. 56; also J. S. Burn, "Sponsalia," *Collectanea Topographica Genealogica*, III (1836), pp. 322–25.
171. Wrightson, *English Society*, pp. 31–38.
172. *Diary of Roger Lowe*, pp. 37, 68.
173. Quaife, p. 44; Clarke, p. 63; *Notes and Queries*, 11th Series, I (January 22, 1910), p. 66.
174. Moore, pp. 295–97.
175. Richardson/Joyce case is from 1563, Raine, pp. 79, 241.
176. Quaife, p. 44.
177. Moore, pp. 290–91.
178. Furnivall, pp. 57–59.
179. From Robert Cleaver, *Godly Form of Household Government*, cited in Furnivall, pp. xlv, xlviii.
180. Richard Gough, *The History of Myddle*, Harmondsworth, 1981, p. 124.
181. Macfarlane, *The Family Life of Ralph Josselin*, p. 96.
182. Best, pp. 116–17.
183. Raine, p. 241.
184. Furnivall, p. xlviii; Victor Turner, *Dramas, Fields, and Metaphors*, Ithaca, 1974, chapter VI.
185. Quaife, p. 46; Wrightson, *English Society*, p. 77.
186. Quaife, p. 46.
187. Raine, pp. 227–28.
188. Moore, p. 276.
189. Moore, pp. 280–83; also 1561 case quoted in *Depositions taken before the Mayor and Aldermen of Norwich, 1549–1563*, ed. W. Rye, Norwich, 1905, p. 68.
190. For the 1577 case of *Meade v. Rome*, see Hale, p. 170.
191. Raine, p. 79; Furnivall, p. 56; *Notes and Queries*, 11th Series, I (February 20, 1910), p. 177.
192. Furnivall, pp. 67–68.
193. John Brand, *Observations on Popular Antiquities*, London, 1977, p. 346; John Hutchins, *The History and Antiquities of the County of Dorset*, II, London, 1863, p. 820.
194. Quaife, p. 47.
195. Burn, p. 325.
196. *Notes and Queries*, 3rd Series, VI (June 17, 1865), p. 477.
197. The 1535 case is cited in Raine, p. 52.
198. F. G. Emmison, *Elizabethan Life: Morals and Church Courts*, Chelmsford, 1973, pp. 49, 144.
199. *A Treatise of Feme Coverts or the Lady's Law*, London, 1732, p. 30.
200. Bird, pp. 185–88; W. S. Holdsworth, *History of English Law*, VI, London, 1924, p. 631.
201. Ingram, pp. 112–28; Houlbrooke, p. 67.
202. For further discussion of ritual, see Arnold van Gennep, *The Rites of Passage*,

Chicago, 1960. Also Victor Turner, *The Ritual Process: Structure and Anti-structure*, Chicago, 1969.

203. Elizabeth M. Wright, *Rustic Speech and Folk-Lore*, London, 1913, p. 272.

204. Furnivall, p. xlviii.

205. The 1563 case is cited in Furnivall, pp. 59–61.

206. Turner describes this as a "liminal" condition in which those who are in transition from one state to another are exempted from the rules applicable in normal conditions. Turner, *The Ritual Process*, passim.

207. Furnivall, p. xlvii; on prebridal pregnancy, see Laslett, "Introduction: Comparing Bastardy over time and between cultures," p. 23.

208. MacDonald, p. 90.

209. J. S. Burn, *History of the Parish Registers in England*, 2nd ed., London, 1862, p. 168; R. W. Muncy, *The Romance of the Parish Registers*, London, 1933, p. 75; Hale, p. 255.

210. T. F. Thiselton Dyer, *Old English Social Life as told by the Parish Registers*, London, 1898, p. 130.

211. This 1732 case is found in the records of the Diocese of Landaff, National Library of Wales, LL/CC/G.

212. D. J. Steel, *National Index of Parish Registers*, I, London, 1968, p. 54.

213. J. Vaux, *Church Folklore*, London, 1894, pp. 91–93; E. and M. A. Radford, *Encyclopaedia of Superstition*, London, 1961, p. 27.

214. Punishments in cases from 1584 and 1599, cited in Hale, pp. 182, 218.

215. Ibid., p. 195.

216. *Church Times*, February 4, 1898.

217. Ibid., December 17, 1897.

218. *Cupid's Pupils*, London, 1899, pp. 55ff; also see Radford, p. 27; Vaux, p. 94.

219. Wright, p. 272.

220. I. and M. A. Radford, p. 27.

221. G. E. Howard, I, p. 457; Wright, p. 271; *Church Times*, June 24 and 29, 1898; *Reports and Transactions of the Devonshire Association*, 57 (1925), p. 128.

222. E. and M. A. Radford, p. 27.

223. Gough, p. 112.

Chapter 2

1. *Admonition to Parliament of 1572*, eds. W. H. Frere and C. E. Douglas, London, 1927, p. 27; D. Giesen, *Grundlagen und Entwicklung des englischen Eherechts in der Neuzeit bis zum Beginn des 19. Jahr-hunderts*, Bielefeld, Gieseking, 1973, p. 385.

2. E. R. C. Brinkworth, *The Archdeacon's Court: Liber Actorum, 1585*, II, Oxfordshire Record Society, 1946, p. 155.

3. William H. Hale, *A Series of Precedents and Proceedings in Criminal Causes 1475–1640, from the Act-Books of the Ecclesiastical Courts of Diocese of London*, London, 1847, p. 227.

4. Ibid., p. 226.

5. Ibid., p. 229.

6. Quoted in Giesen, p. 385.

7. See *Oxford English Dictionary*; and also George C. Homans, *English Villagers of the Thirteenth Century*, New York, 1975, pp. 72–74.

8. Charles Phythian-Adams, *Desolation of a City: Coventry and the Urban Crisis of the Late Middle Ages*, Cambridge, 1979, p. 89.
9. For the importance of banns, see above p.   –   .
10. *Rural Economy in Yorkshire in 1641, Being the Farming and Account Books of Henry Best*, Surtees Society Publications, no. 33, 1857, pp. 116–17.
11. Ibid.
12. Trefor Owen, "West Glamorgan Customs," *Folk Life*, III (1965), pp. 50–51; Dayffd Ifans, "Lewis Morris ac Afrerion Priodi yng Ngheredigion," *Ceredigion*, VIII, no. 2 (1972), p. 194.
13. Trefor Owen, *Welsh Folk Customs*, Cardiff, 1978, p. 163.
14. John Aubrey, *Remaines of Gentilisme and Judaism*, London, 1881, pp. 171–72.
15. Owen, "West Glamorgan Customs," p. 52; Ifans, p. 194.
16. Owen, *Welsh Folk Customs*, pp. 164–65.
17. *Notes and Queries*, 8th Series, III (April 29, 1893), p. 325.
18. Ifans, p. 200.
19. Sabine Baring-Gould, *A Book of Folklore*, London, n.d., p. 256.
20. *Choice Notes from "Notes and Queries,"* London, 1859, p. 265; also *Notes and Queries*, 4th Series, II (October 10, 1868), p. 434; and *Notes and Queries*, 4th Series, II (November 7, 1868), p. 450.
21. Keith Wrightson, *English Society, 1580–1680*, New Brunswick, 1982, pp. 71–86.
22. Quoted in Ivy Pinchbeck, *Women Workers and the Industrial Revolution, 1750–1850*, New York, 1930, p. 179.
23. From *Admonition to Parliament of 1572*, p. 27; Eileen Power, *Medieval People*, New York, 1963, pp. 165–66. On continental practices, see Nicole Belmont, "The Symbolic Function of the Wedding Procession in Popular Rituals of Marriage," *Ritual, Religion, and the Sacred*, eds. R. Foster and O. Ranum, Baltimore, 1982, pp. 3–4.
24. M. C. Balfour and N. W. Thomas, *Examples of Printed Folklore Concerning Northumberland*, London, 1904, pp. 92–93.
25. *The Diary of Roger Lowe*, ed. William L. Sachse, New Haven, 1938, p. 50; Wrightson, p. 89.
26. Homans, p. 173; G. G. Coulton, *Medieval Village, Manor and Monastery*, New York, 1960, p. 53.
27. Homans, p. 173; Lydia Fish, *The Folklore of the Coal Mines of the North of England*, Norwood, Pennsylvania, 1975, p. 115.
28. W. Jones, *Finger-ring Lore*, London, 1898, p. 169.
29. Ibid., pp. 154–55; *Notes and Queries*, 4th Series, I (June 13, 1868), p. 561.
30. J. S. Burn, *History of the Parish Registers in England*, 2nd ed., London, 1862, p. 154.
31. Lawrence Stone, *The Family, Sex and Marriage in England, 1500–1800*, New York, 1977, p. 244.
32. *Notes and Queries*, 5th Series, XII (August 16, 1879), p. 125.
33. J. C. Atkinson, *Forty Years in a Moorland Parish: Reminiscences and Researches in Danby in Cleveland*, London, 1891, pp. 206–7.
34. James Vaux, *Church Folklore*, 2nd ed., London, 1902, p. 101.
35. John Bossy, "Blood and Baptism: Kinship, Community and Christianity in Western Europe from the 14th to the 17th Centuries," *Sanctity and Secularity:*

The Church and the World, ed. D. Baker, Oxford, 1973, pp. 131–43; *Cupid's Pupils*, p. 329.

36. Keith Thomas, *Religion and the Decline of Magic*, New York, 1971, pp. 526–27.
37. Hale, p. 258.
38. Samuel Pepys, *Diary of Samuel Pepys*, ed. H. B. Wheatley, New York, 1896, I, p. 28; V, p. 30.
39. Margaret Baker, *The Folklore and Customs of Love and Marriage*, Aylesbury, 1974, pp. 38, 45; the custom was defended in *Gentleman's Magazine*, 1748, p. 462.
40. David D. Dixon, *Whittingham Vale, Northumberland: Its History, Traditions and Folklore*, Newcastle, 1895, p. 54.
41. The new curate of a Swansea church used force to end the throwing of nuts and apples in the eighteenth century; see *Notes and Queries*, 9th Series, XII (December 19, 1903), p. 469.
42. Richard Blakeborough, "A Country Wedding a Century Ago," fol. 13, unpublished article, Blakeborough MSS, Sheffield University.
43. Ibid. The second and third verses are from a nominy sung in the honor of Martha Sheppard, ca. 1762, recorded in David Naitby's unpublished diary, fol. 30, Sheffield University.
44. Richard Blakeborough, *Wit, Character, Folklife and Customs of the North Riding of Yorkshire*, Salburn-by-the-Sea, 1911, p. 92; Baker, p. 38.
45. W. Crooke, "Lifting the Bride," *Folk-Lore*, XII (1902), pp. 228–29.
46. R. Blakeborough, "A Country Wedding a Century Ago," Blakeborough MSS, Sheffield University.
47. Crooke, p. 227.
48. Ibid., p. 229.
49. Ibid., pp. 230–31.
50. This occurred at the church at Ford, Northumberland, sometime in the nineteenth century; see Crooke, p. 230; also Balfour and Thomas, p. 94.
51. James Raine, ed., *Depositions and other Ecclesiastical Proceedings from the Courts of Durham*, Surtees Society, XXI (1845), p. 226.
52. Sarah Hewitt, *Nummits and Crummits: Devonshire Customs, Characteristics and Folklore*, London, 1900, p. 101.
53. A note on pennying can be found in the box marked "Marriage Customs," Folk Lore Society Archive, University of London.
54. Noted in *Folk-Lore*, XXII (1911), p. 237.
55. Sods were thrown at Pudsey couples in the early nineteenth century. Joseph Lawson, *Letters to the Young on Progress in Pudsey during the Last Sixty Years*, Stanninglen, 1887, p. 20; also S. O. Addy, *Household Tales with Other Traditional Remains*, London, 1895, pp. 121–22; Crooke, p. 232.
56. *Notes and Queries*, 9th Series, VII (March 16 and April 6, 1901), pp. 208, 273.
57. Richard Blakeborough, "A Country Wedding a Century Ago," fol. 11; Similar customs are still found in Ireland, where groups of masked men, called "straw boys," appear at weddings.
58. On wedding as a rite of separation, see Arnold van Gennep, *The Rites of Passage*, Chicago, 1960, chapter vii.
59. F. G. Emmison, *Elizabethan Life: Morals and Church Courts*, Chelmsford, 1973, p. 155.

60. Cited in G. R. Quaife, *Wanton Wenches and Wayward Wives: Peasants and Illicit Sex in Early Seventeenth Century England*, New Brunswick, 1979, p. 199.

61. Theo Brown, "The 'Stag-Hunt' in Devon," *Folk-Lore*, 63 (1952), p. 106.

62. Walter C. Renshaw, "Notes from the Act Book of the Archdeaconry Court of Lewes," *Sussex Archeological Collection*, XLIX (1906), p. 64.

63. S. O. Addy, p. 76.

64. *Cambridgeshire Chronicle*, July 15, 1852, p. 4.

65. *Folk-Lore*, 22 (1911), p. 237.

66. R. E. Chambers, *The Book of Days*, I, London, 1864, p. 361; Edward Walford, *Old and New London*, IV, London, n.d., p. 322; also the printed advertisement for "His Majesty's Royal Peel of Marrowbones and Cleavers," in the Noble Collection C22/85, Guildhall Library, London.

67. *Reports and Transactions of the Devonshire Association*, 60 (1928), p. 126.

68. Tom Minors, "Quaint Marriage Customs in Old Cornwall," *Old Cornwall*, I, n.d., pp. 23–24.

69. M. A. Courtney, *Cornish Feasts and Folk-Lore*, Penzance, 1890, p. 167.

70. *Notes and Queries*, 2nd Series, VIII (September 17, 1859), p. 239.

71. Minors, p. 24; similar things happened in Montgomeryshire in 1940s, see Alwyn Rees, *Life in a Welsh Countryside*, Cardiff, 1975, p. 90.

72. Tobias Smollett, *The Expedition of Humphrey Clinker*, New York, 1968, pp. 332–33; also *Diary of Samuel Pepys*, V, ed. H. B. Wheatley, New York, 1896, p. 30.

73. Cited in Power, p. 166; also F. W. Hackwood, *Staffordshire Customs, Superstitions, and Folklore*, 2nd ed., Wakefield, 1974, p. 62.

74. William Henderson, *Notes on the Folk-Lore of the Northern Counties and the Borders*, London, 1879, p. 42; *Notes and Queries*, 2nd Series, VIII (September 17, 1859), p. 239.

75. Minors, p. 24.

76. Henry Machyn, *The Diary of a Resident of London*, London, 1847, pp. 243–44, 288. I am indebted to Steve Rappaport for this reference.

77. Fish, p. 10; T. S. Ashton, "Coal Miners in the 18th Century," *Economic History*, I (1928), pp. 307–34.

78. Quoted in *Old Cornwall*, April 26, 1926.

79. David Rovie, "Mining Folk of Fife," *County Folklore*, VIII, London, 1914, p. 393; John Raven, *The Folklore of Staffordshire*, London, 1978, p. 61.

80. Balfour and Thomas, pp. 98–99.

81. R. Douch, "Customs and Traditions of the Isle of Portland, Dorset," *Antiquity*, XXIII (1949), pp. 149–50.

82. The chimney sweeps' weddings remained big even into the early nineteenth century, see John Ashton, *Social England under the Regency*, II, London, 1890, p. 101.

83. *Notes and Queries*, 1st Series, X (September 2, 1854), p. 181.

84. On the poison ordeal of the mass, see Keith Thomas, *Religion and the Decline of Magic*, pp. 39, 45.

85. *Folk-Lore*, 22 (1911), p. 237.

86. Glanmore Williams, *The Welsh Church from Conquest to Reformation*, Cardiff, 1962, pp. 510–11; Geraint H. Jenkins, *Literature, Religion and Society in Wales, 1660–1730*, Cardiff, 1978, p. 92; Homans, p. 173; E. R. C. Brinkworth, *The Archdeacon's Court: Liber Actorum, 1584*, Oxfordshire Record Society Publications, XXII (1942), pp. 124–25.

87. Bernard Capp, *Astrology and the Popular Press: English Almanacs, 1500–1800*, London, 1979, pp. 127–28.
88. Thomas, pp. 620–21.
89. *Diary of Samuel Pepys*, VII, p. 254.
90. Thomas, p. 297; Capp, p. 123; A. Baily Williams, "Courtship and Marriage in Late Nineteenth Century Montgomeryshire," *Montgomeryshire Collections*, LI, part 1 (1950), pp. 123–24.
91. Capp, pp. 117–22; Atkinson, p. 59.
92. Richard Blakeborough, "A Country Wedding a Century Ago," fol. 12.
93. Enid Porter, *The Folklore of East Anglia*, London, 1974, p. 27.
94. Balfour and Thomas, pp. 96–97.
95. Thomas, p. 556.
96. Blakeborough, *Wit, Character, Folk Lore*, p. 179.
97. Porter, p. 27; Hackwood, p. 61; W. Henderson, *Notes on the Folk-Lore of the Northern Counties of England and the Borders*, London, 1879, p. 35.
98. *Byegones*, 2nd Series, V (April 21, 1897), p. 80.
99. Vaux, p. 103.
100. This was the custom in Gloucestershire. *Notes and Queries*, 6th Series, VIII (August 23, 1883), p. 147.
101. *Reports and Transactions of the Devonshire Association*, 57 (1925), p. 128.
102. Elias Owen, *Some Old Stone Crosses of the Vale of Clwyd*, London, 1886, p. 92.
103. C. S. Burne, *Shropshire Folklore: A Sheaf of Gleanings*, London, 1883–86, p. 291; a similar practice was reported in Sussex, *Notes and Queries*, 6th Series, IX (April 19, 1884), p. 315.
104. Burne, p. 290; Elias Owen, *Some Old Stone Crosses in the Vale of Clwyd*, pp. 290–91.
105. Francis Grose, *A Provincial Glossary*, rev. ed., London, 1811, p. 293.
106. *Notes and Queries*, 4th Series, VII (April 1, 1871), p. 285.
107. A. McCauley, *History and Antiquities of Claybrook*, n.p., 1791, pp. 127–31.
108. *Byegones*, 2nd Series, VI (1899), p. 37.
109. T. Owen, *Welsh Folk Customs*, p. 158.
110. Addy, p. 127; *Notes and Queries*, 8th Series, IV (July 1, 1893), p. 9.
111. J. Harland and T. T. Wilkinson, *Lancashire Legends*, London, 1873, p. 175.
112. Victor Turner, *Dramas, Fields, and Metaphors: Symbolic Action in Human Society*, Ithaca, 1974, pp. 33–44.
113. *Old Yorkshire*, I, ed. W. Smith, London, 1881, p. 135; also Henderson, p. 41; *Notes and Queries*, 8th Series, II (August 6, 1892), p. 117.
114. T. F. Thiselton Dyer, *Old English Social Life as Told by the Parish Registers*, London, 1898, p. 75; *Cymru Fu*, June 2, 1882, p. 192; Thomas, pp. 233–34; T. Gwynn Jones, *Welsh Folklore and Folk Custom*, London, 1930, p. 131; Angus McLaren, "Reproductive Rituals: The Patterning of Human Fertility in England, 1500–1800," forthcoming book, especially chapters i–iii.
115. Quoted in Lawrence Babb, "The Physiological Conception of Love in the Elizabethan and Early Stuart Drama," *Proceedings of the Modern Language Association*, LVI, no. 4 (December 1941), p. 1025.
116. *Rural Economy in Yorkshire in 1641, being the Farming and account Books of Henry Best of Elmswell in East Riding*, Surtees Society, no. 33, 1857, p. 117.
117. *Byegones*, 2nd Series, VI (January 1883), p. 182.
118. A. Craig Gibson, "Ancient Customs and Superstitions in Cumberland, *Transactions of Historic Society of Lancashire and Cheshire*, X (1857–58), pp. 100ff.; also *Folk-Lore* 40 (1929), pp. 279–80.

119. Baker, p. 47.
120. Ibid., p. 49.
121. Ifans, p. 194.
122. Baker, pp. 25, 50; R. Blakeborough, *Wit, Character, Folklore*, p. 93.
123. Baker, p. 50.
124. Homans, pp. 164–65.
125. *Rural Economy of Yorkshire*, p. 117.
126. The notion of the master and mistress of the household lasted in the regions of small farms in Wales well into the twentieth century. See David Jenkins, *The Agricultural Community in South-West Wales at the Turn of the Twentieth Century*, Cardiff, 1971, pp. 74–75, 138–39.
127. Dixon, p. 290; *Notes and Queries*, 1st Series, VI (September 11, 1852), p. 246; *Notes and Queries*, 1st Series, VI (October 30, 1852), p. 424.
128. Capp, pp. 122–24.
129. "Diary of the Journey of the Most Illustrious Philip Julius, Duke of Stettin-Pomerania through England, 1602," *Transactions of the Royal Historical Society*, VI (1892), p. 65.
130. *Portsmouth Record Series: Borough Sessions Papers, 1653–1688*, London, 1971, pp. 23, 94, 142; also *Warwick County Records*, VIII, Warwick, 1953, p. 8.
131. J. W. Spargo, *Juridical Folklore in England, Illustrated by the Cucking-stool*, Durham, North Carolina, 1944, pp. 14–46, 110–149; S. Meeson Morris, "The Obsolete Punishments of Shropshire," *Shropshire Archeological and Natural History Society*, IX (1885), pp. 84–113; and T. N. Brushfield, "On Obsolete Punishments," *Journal of the Architectural, Archeological and Historic Society of Cheshire*, part vi, 1857–59, pp. 203–34.
132. R. Collyer and J. H. Turner, *Ilkly, ancient and modern*, Otley, 1885, p. 126; W. Nicholls, *History and Tradition of Ravenstonedale*, Westmoreland, Manchester, 1877, p. 31; Emmison, p. 235.
133. Court leets were often used to settle petty disputes and were popular because, unlike the church and regular courts, there was little or no fee. F. J. C. Hearnshaw, *Leet Jurisdiction in England*, Southhampton, 1908, p. 219; also John M. Ingram, "Ecclesiastical Justice in Wiltshire, 1600–1660," unpublished D.Phil. dissertation, Oxford University, 1976, chapter iv.
134. Morris, p. 104; Brushfield, p. 229; F. A. Carrington, "On Certain Ancient Wiltshire Customs," *Wiltshire Archeological and Natural History Magazine*, I (1854), p. 78.
135. Brushfield, p. 231.
136. Quotation is from Owen, *Welsh Folk Customs*, p. 168.
137. From the penance seat at St. Ishmael's, Ferryside, cited in *Cymru Fu*, March 2, 1889.
138. Spargo, p. 83.
139. William Sheppeard, *A Grand Abridgment of the Common and Statute Law of England* (1675), cited in Spargo, p. 121.
140. Nicholls, p. 32; Hearnshaw, p. 220.
141. Ingram, pp. 144, 215–21; Emmison, pp. 161–64.
142. Morris, p. 85.
143. A. C. Bickley, "Some Notes on a Custom at Woking, Surrey," *Home Counties Magazine*, IV (1902), pp. 25–29.
144. Quaife, p. 199; Emmison, pp. 54, 62, 105, 108, 127, 212.
145. Natalie Zemon Davis, "Women on Top," *Society and Culture in Early Modern France*, Stanford, 1975, pp. 138–39.

146. Ibid., p. 131; Burne, pp. 147–50.
147. Winifred M. Bowman, *England in Ashton-under-Lyne*, Atricham, 1960, p. 551.
148. Charles Phythian-Adams, *Local History and Folklore*, London, 1975, p. 28.
149. J. A. Sharpe, *Defamation and Sexual Slander in Early Modern England: The Church Courts at York*, Borthwick Papers, no. 58 (1980), passim.
150. Martin Ingram, "Le Charivari dans L'Angleterre du XVIᵉ et du XVIIᵉ siècle," in J. Le Goff and J.-C. Schmitt, *Le Charivari*, Paris, 1981, pp. 251–64; Keith Thomas, "The Place of Laughter in Tudor and Stuart England," *Times Literary Supplement*, January 21, 1977, pp. 77–81.
151. Violet Alford, "Rough Music or Charivari," *Folk-Lore*, 70 (December 1959), p. 510. For a sixteenth-century example, see Machyn, p. 301.
152. Quoted in Natalie Zemon Davis, "The Reasons of Misrule," *Society and Culture in Early Modern France*, Stanford, 1975, p. 303.
153. Peter Burke, "Popular Culture in Seventeenth Century London," *The London Journal*, III, no. 2 (1977), p. 144.
154. Quaife, p. 200.
155. E. C. Cawte, "Parsons Who Rode the Stang," *Folk-Lore* 74 (1963), p. 400.
156. Davis, "Reasons of Misrule," pp. 105ff.
157. Wrightson, pp. 98–100.
158. Jean-Louis Flandrin, *Families in Former Times: Kinship, Household and Sexuality*, Cambridge, 1979, pp. 4–5.
159. *Oxford English Dictionary*.
160. Randolf Trumbach, "Kinship and Marriage in Early Modern France and England: Four Books," *Annals of Scholarship*, II, no. 4 (1981), p. 116.
161. Wrightson, p. 90.
162. Ibid., p. 91; also James T. Johnson, *A Society Ordained by God: English Puritan Marriage Doctrine in the First Half of the Seventeenth Century*, Nashville, 1970, passim.
163. Wrightson, pp. 96–97.
164. Edmund Leites, "The Duty to Desire: Love, Friendship, and Sexuality in Some Puritan Theories of Marriage," *Journal of Social History*, XV no. 3 (Spring 1982), pp. 383–408; also M. Todd, "Humanists, Puritans and the Spiritual Household," *Church History* 49 (1980), pp. 18–34; K. Davies, " 'The Sacred Condition of Equality'—How Original Were Puritan Doctrines of Marriage?" *Social History*, no. 5 (1977), pp. 563–80.

Chapter 3

1. Arnold van Gennep, *The Rites of Passage*, Chicago, 1969, p. 123.
2. This estimate is provided by Lawrence Stone, *The Family, Sex and Marriage in England, 1500–1800*, New York, 1977, pp. 34–35. For additional evidence, see *The Parish Registers and Parochial Documents of the Archdeaconry of Winchester*, eds. W. A. Fearon and J. F. William, London, 1909, pp. 9–10; John H. Pruett, *Clergy under the Later Stuarts: The Leicestershire Experience*, Chicago, 1978, pp. 131–41; D. J. Steel, *National Index of Parish Registers*, I, London, 1978, p. 299; E. A. Wrigley, "Clandestine Marriage in Tetbury in the Late Seventeenth Century," *Local Population Studies*, no. 10 (Spring 1973), pp. 15–21.
3. The church had little success with aristocratic morality in sixteenth century

Lancashire. See Christopher Haigh, *Reformation and Resistance in Tudor Lancashire*, Cambridge, 1975, pp. 46–47.

4. Evan Jones Notebooks, 1793/414, Cardiff, Welsh Folk Museum.

5. Keith Thomas, "Age and Authority in Early Modern England," *Proceedings of the British Academy*, LXII (1976), pp. 227ff.

6. Presbyterian Ordinance of 1645, quoted in G. R. Quaife, *Wanton Wenches and Wayward Wives: Peasants and Illicit Sex in Early Seventeenth Century England*, New Brunswick, 1979, p. 40.

7. T. F. Thiselton Dyer, *Old English Social Life as told by the Parish Registers*, London, 1898, p. 143. The parish was Serbergham.

8. J. Ingram, "Ecclesiastical Justice in Wiltshire, 1600–1660," unpublished D.Phil. dissertation, Oxford University, pp. 114–22; Ralph Houlbrooke, *Church Courts and the People during the English Reformation*, Oxford, 1979, pp. 57–84; Ingram, "Spousals Litigation in the English Ecclesiastical Courts, c. 1350–1640," *Marriage and Society*, ed. R. B. Outhwaite, New York, 1981, pp. 44–57.

9. *The Bletchley Diary of Rev. William Cole, 1765–67*, ed. F. G. Stokes, London, 1931, p. 87.

10. *Notes and Queries*, 8th Series, IX (February 29, 1896), p. 164; U. Chisenhale–Marsh, "Folk Lore in Essex and Herts," *Essex Review*, V (1896), p. 155.

11. Charles Phythian-Adams, *Desolation of a City: Coventry and the Urban Crisis of the Late Middle Ages*, Cambridge, 1979, p. 86.

12. J. C. Jeaffreson, *Brides and Bridals*, I, London, 1872, pp. 228–29.

13. M. Ashley, *The Stuarts in Love*, London, 1963, p. 54; G. Dynallt Owen, *Elizabethan Wales: The Social Scene*, Cardiff, 1962, p. 49.

14. Jeaffreson, p. 229; *Notes and Queries*, 10th Series, I (January 9, 1904), p. 15; *Notes and Queries*, 8th Series, IX (February 29, 1896), p. 164; H. Edwards, *A Collection of Old English Customs and Curious Bequests and Charities*, London, 1842, pp. 208–19.

15. *The Court Leet Records of the Manor of Manchester*, I, Manchester, 1884, pp. 103, 162, 220; II, Manchester, 1885, p. 193; III, Manchester, 1886, p. 86. Also Arthur Redford, *The History of Local Government in Manchester*, I, London, 1939, pp. 48, 71, 78, 132.

16. *The Portmote or Court Leet Records of Salford, 1597–1669*, ed. J. G. de T. Mandley, Cheatham Society Publications, no. 46, I, Manchester, 1902, pp. 51–60. For European patterns, see Hugo Soly and Catherine Lis, "Policing the European Proletariat, 1500–1850," paper delivered at Rutgers University, New Brunswick, New Jersey, May 1983.

17. William Hunt, *The Puritan Moment: The Coming of Revolution in an English County*, Cambridge, 1983, pp. 41–42, 52–53, 74–75. Also Keith Wrightson and David Levine, *Poverty and Piety in an English Village: Terling, 1525–1700*, New York, 1979, passim. On the repression of the public brideales, see *Byegones*, 2nd Series, III (June 28, 1896); and T. Gwynn Jones, *Welsh Folklore and Folk Customs*, London, 1930, p. 189.

18. Stubbes, *Anatomie of Abuses* (1593), quoted in D. Giesen, *Grundlagen und Entwicklung des englischen Ehrerchts in der Neuzeit bis zum Begin des 19. Jahrhunderts*, Bielefeld, 1973, p. 565.

19. Roger Thompson, *Women in Stuart England and America*, London, 1974, p. 121.

20. Quaife, pp. 40, 95; Thompson, pp. 119–25; Joan Thirsk, "Younger Sons in

the Seventeenth Century," *History*, LIV (1969), pp. 358–70; Keith Thomas, pp. 217–44.

21. Ashley, p. 60.
22. *Notes and Queries*, 8th Series, VII (January 19, 1895), p. 56.
23. *Early Essex Town Meetings*, ed. F. G. Emmison, London and Colchester, 1970, p. 117.
24. Wrightson and Levine, pp. 80, 133.
25. Keith Wrightson, *English Society, 1580–1680*, New Brunswick, 1982, p. 78.
26. *Lincolnshire Notes and Queries*, I (1889), pp. 109–10.
27. This critical period is dealt with by Keith Wrightson, "The Nadir of English Illegitimacy in the Seventeenth Century," *Bastardy and its Comparative History*, eds. Peter Laslett, Karla Oosterveen, and Richard M. Smith, Cambridge, 1980, pp. 176–91; J. C. Cox, *The Parish Registers of England*, London, 1910, p. 83.
28. C. Reynel, *The True English Intent* (1674), reprinted in *Seventeenth Century Economic Documents*, eds. Joan Thirsk and J. P. Cooper, Oxford, 1972, p. 759.
29. William H. Hale, *A Series of Precedents and Proceedings in Criminal Causes, 1475–1640, from the Act-Books of the Ecclesiastical Courts of Diocese of London*, London, 1847, p. 259.
30. Wrightson and Levine, pp. 4–7, 19–42.
31. Ibid., p. 80.
32. *Essex Review*, XXIV (1915), pp. 46–47.
33. From "A Note of Diverse Incestuous and Unlawfull Marriages Made by Licences by Vagrant Ministers in Lawlesse Peculiars," Geisen, ca. 1597, p. 674.
34. E. R. C. Brinkworth, *The Archdeacon's Court: Liber Actorum, 1584*, II, Oxfordshire Record Society, 1946, p. 18.
35. Patrick McGrath, "Notes on the History of Marriage Licences," *Gloucestershire Marriage Allegations, 1637–1680*, ed. B. Frith, Publication of Bristol and Gloucestershire Archeological Society, n.p., n.d., pp. xxi–xxx.
36. For a 1584 violation, see Hale, p. 178; and for later criticism of the practice, see "The Case of Clandestine Marriage Stated," *Harleian Miscellany*, I, 1744, p. 364.
37. Quaife, p. 97.
38. *The East Anglian*, New Sevies, VIII (1899–1900), p. 223.
39. *Archbishop Herring's Visitation Returns, 1743*, 4 vols., Yorkshire Archeological Society Record Series, I, 1929, p. 18.
40. Ibid., III, pp. 87–88.
41. Steel, I, p. 299; Stone, pp. 34–35.
42. Steel, I, p. 315; J. D. Chambers, "The Vale of Trent, 1670–1800," *Economic History Review Supplement*, III, 1957, p. 50; Wrigley, pp. 15–21; Pruett, pp. 20, 74–75, 131–41; Quaife, pp. 96–97; Cox, pp. 95–96.
43. Steel, I, p. 228; also L. Stone, "Literacy and Education in England, 1640–1900," *Past & Present* 42 (February 1969), pp. 106–7.
44. Steel, I, p. 134; *Marriage Allegations in the Diocese of Gloucester, 1681–1700*, Publications of the Bristol and Gloucestershire Archeological Society, IX (1960), p. xi.
45. Stone, p. 33; Steel, I, p. 299; Roger Lee Brown, "Clandestine Marriages in London, especially within the Fleet Prison, and the Effect in Hardwicke's

Act, 1753," unpublished M.A. thesis, London University, 1972, pp. 32–38, 180ff.

46. Brown, pp. 32–38; Steel, I, pp. 298–99.
47. Brown, p. 4.
48. Leslie Bradley, "Common Law Marriage: A Possible Case of Under-registration," *Local Population Studies*, no. 11 (Autumn 1973), p. 43; *The Churchwarden's Presentments of Oxfordshire Peculiars*, ed. S. A. Peyton, Oxfordshire Record Society, X (1928), pp. 133, 164, 184, 202.
49. James Raine, ed., *Depositions and other Ecclesiastical Proceedings from the Courts of Durham*, Surtees Society, XXI (1845) p. 223; also J. Purvis, *Tudor Parish Documents of the Diocese of York*, Cambridge, 1948, p. 72.
50. *Warwick County Records*, IX, Warwick, 1964, p. xl.
51. Cited in *Local Population Studies*, no. 2 (Spring, 1969), p. 56; see also Hale, p. 222.
52. Harold Smith, "Marriages from Outside," *The Essex Review*, LXII (1933), p. 204.
53. Emmison, p. 158.
54. Quaife, p. 96.
55. G. Roberts, *The History and Antiquities of the Borough of Lyme Regis and Charnworth*, London, 1934, p. 256.
56. *Glamorgan County History*, IV, Cardiff, 1974, p. 441; F. Furnivall, *Child-Marriages, divorces, and ratifications in the diocese of Chester*, London, 1897, p. lxii.
57. Pruett, pp. 131–32, 141.
58. *Archbishop Herring's Visitation Returns*, II, p. 100.
59. Brown, p. 75.
60. "A Report on the Deanry of Penllyn and Edeirnion by Rev. John Wynne, 1730," *The Merioneth Miscellany*, no. 3 (1955), p. 8.
61. John Latimer, *The Annals of Bristol*, 2 vols., Bristol, 1893, I, p. 158.
62. *Marriage Allegations in Diocese of Gloucester*, II, p. xii.
63. Ibid., p. xi.
64. Latimer, pp. 158–59.
65. Steel, I, p. 314; another case can be found in Clywd Record Office, DD/DM/128/21; also M. E. Richards, *Gloucestershire Family History*, Gloucester, 1979, p. 14.
66. *Devon and Cornwall Notes and Queries*, XI, n.d., p. 365; quotation from "A Report on the Deanry of Penllyn . . . ," p. 41.
67. Brown, p. 116; Stone, p. 33.
68. Brown, pp. 120–21.
69. Ibid., pp. 151–60.
70. J. S. Burn, *The Fleet Registers*, London, 1831, p. 55.
71. Ibid., p. 55.
72. Brown, pp. 122–31; Burn, *Fleet Registers*, p. 58.
73. Brown, pp. 132–41.
74. *Marriage Allegations in Diocese of Gloucester*, p. xii; Brown, p. 140; Burn, *Fleet Registers*, p. 100.
75. J. H. Bettey, "Marriages of Convenience by Copyholders in Dorset in the Seventeenth Century," *Dorset Natural History and Antiquarian Field Club*, 98 (1978), pp. 1–5.

76. Brown, p. 140; Burn, *Fleet Registers*, p. 100; for a discussion of clandestine marriage and prohibited degrees, see Jack Goody, *The Development of the Family and Marriage in Europe*, Cambridge, 1983, pp. 173–74. On marriage discipline in other parts of Europe, see S. Ozment, *When Fathers Ruled: Family Life in Reformation Europe*, Cambridge, 1983, pp. 25–49.

77. Burn, *Fleet Registers*, pp. 49, 53–54, 61; W. T. McIntire, "Gretna Green Marriages," *The Genealogists' Magazine*, IX, no. 3 (September 1940), p. 82; Brown, pp. 167–69.

78. This occurred in 1563. Furnivall, p. lxxxviii; R. Tudor Jones, "Religion in Post-Restoration Brecknockshire, 1660–68," *Brycheiniog*, VIII (1962), p. 37.

79. Burn, *Fleet Registers*, p. 64.

80. Smith, p. 204.

81. Brown, p. 120.

82. Pruett, p. 131.

83. Consistory Court Records, Archdeaconry of Brecon, SD/CCB (G) 268, 268a, National Library of Wales.

84. "A Report of the Deanry of Penllyn . . . ," p. 8; on the Savoy, see Brown, pp. 96ff.

85. Burn, *Fleet Registers*, p. 38.

86. Steel, I, p. 304; J. S. Burn, *History of the Parish Registers in England*, London, 1862, p. 153.

87. Burn, *Fleet Registers*, p. 11.

88. "A Report on the Deanry of Penllyn . . . ," p. 8.

89. Some who came to the Fleet did not complete the ceremony and were recorded in the parsons' notebooks as "half-married." See Brown, p. 155.

90. Hunt, p. 131–32.

91. Diary entry of 8.7.1647. *The Diary of Ralph Josselin*, ed. Alan Macfarlane, London, 1976, p. 98.

92. "The Famous History of Sir Billy of Billericay" (1687), cited in George Monger, "A Note on the Similarities between Some Wedding Customs in England and France," *Lore and Language*, II, no. 1 (July 1974), pp. 36–37; also *Essex Review*, V (1896), pp. 154–5.

93. Jeaffreson, pp. 225–26.

94. John Brand, *Observations on Popular Antiquities*, London, 1877, p. 382.

95. Ibid., p. 387.

96. Brinkworth, VII, p. 10.

97. Stone, pp. 38–39.

98. Hunt, p. 52.

99. Hale, pp. 157, 161.

100. Emmison, p. 170; Brinkworth, pp. 62–63; Hale, p. 103.

101. Thompson, pp. 170–72.

102. Hunt, p. 52.

103. Keith Thomas, "The Puritans and Adultery: The Act of 1650 Reconsidered," *Puritans and Revolutionaries: Essays in Seventeenth Century History Presented to Christopher Hill*, eds. D. Pennington and K. Thomas, Oxford, 1978, pp. 257–82; Hunt, pp. 53–54.

104. Christopher Hill, *Economic Problems of the Church*, Oxford, 1956, p. 161.

105. Christopher Hill, *The World Turned Upside Down*, Harmondsworth, 1975, p. 31.

106. Ibid., p. 312.

107. Stone, p. 137.

108. C. Hill, *Society and Puritanism in Pre-Revolutionary England*, 2nd ed., New York, 1967, p. 443.

109. Michael Walzer, *The Revolution of the Saints: A Study in the Origins of Radical Politics*, New York, 1969, p. 193.

110. Baxter and Gataker quoted in E. Leites, "The Duty to Desire: Love, Friendship, and Sexuality in Some Puritan Theories of Marriage," *Journal of Social History*, XV, no. 3 (Spring 1982), p. 388.

111. Ibid., pp. 293–94; Benjamin Nelson, *The Idea of Usury: From Trival Brotherhood to Universal Otherhood*, Princeton, 1949, pp. 141–64.

112. Hill, *World Turned Upside Down*, p. 312; Thomas Paine, *The Rights of Man*, ed. H. Collins, Harmondsworth, 1983, pp. 269–70.

113. Hill, *World Turned Upside Down*, pp. 310ff.

114. Joan Thirsk, "Younger Sons in the Seventeenth Century," *History*, 54 (1969), pp. 367–71; Richard T. Vann, "Nurture and Conversion in the Early Quaker Family," *Journal of Marriage and the Family*, XXI, no. 4 (1969), pp. 639–43; Richard T. Vann, *The Social Development of English Quakerism, 1655–1755*, Cambridge, 1969, pp. 183–87.

115. Hill, *World Turned Upside Down*, p. 310.

116. Ibid., p. 312.

117. Ibid., pp. 308–9.

118. Ibid., pp. 313–14. On Petty's speculations on "California Marriage," in which "six men were conjugated to six women," see John Cairncross, *After Polygamy Was Made a Sin: The Social History of Christian Polygamy*, London, 1974, pp. 138–39.

119. Stone, p. 627.

120. Hill, *Society and Puritanism*, pp. 479–80.

121. Hill, *World Turned Upside Down*, p. 318.

122. Ibid., p. 316.

123. Ibid., pp. 318–19.

124. Ibid., p. 319.

125. Vann, *The Social Development of English Quakerism*, p. 187, R. S. Mortimer, "Marriage Discipline of Early Friends," *Journal of Friends Historical Society*, 48, no. 4 (1957), pp. 175–95.

126. On the other hand, the civil marriage procedure was often violated. See Wrightson, "The nadir of English illegitimacy in the Seventeenth century," p. 184.

127. Hill, *Society and Puritanism*, p. 453.

128. From Samuel Richardson's *Clarissa* (1748), quoted in Christopher Hill, "Clarissa Harlowe and Her Times," in Hill, *Puritanism and Revolution*, London, 1958, p. 372.

Chapter 4

1. On Turner's courtship, see Lawrence Stone, *The Family, Sex and Marriage in England, 1500–1800*, New York, 1977, p. 606; on Wales, see Alwyn D. Rees, *Life in a Welsh Countryside: A Social Study of Llanfihangel yng Ngwynfa*, Cardiff, 1975, pp. 85–87.

2. E. A. Wrigley and R. S. Schofield, *The Population History of England, 1541–1871*, Cambridge, 1981, p. 255.

3. Ibid., pp. 258–59.
4. Ibid., pp. 259–65.
5. Anthea Newman, "An evaluation of bastardy recordings in an East Kent Parish," *Bastardy and its Comparative History*, eds. Peter Laslett, Karla Oosterveen, and Richard M. Smith, Cambridge, 1980, pp. 141–57.
6. Peter Laslett, "Introduction," *Bastardy and its Comparative Hisotry*, pp. 17–41. G. N. Gandy, "Illegitimacy in a Handloom Weaving Community: Fertility Patterns in Culcheth, Lancashire, 1781–1860," unpublished D.Phil. dissertation, Oxford University, 1978, chapter ii; William Rhys Jones, "A Besom Wedding in the Ceiriog Valley," *Folk-Lore*, 29 (1928), pp. 150–51.
7. Robert Malcolmson, *Life and Labour in England, 1700–1780*, New York, 1981, chapters i and ii.
8. *A Political Enquiry into the Consequences of Enclosing Waste Lands*, 1785, cited in Malcolmson, p. 68.
9. J. C. Davies, *The Folk-Lore of West and Mid-Wales*, Aberystwyth, 1911, p. 2.
10. Eric Hobsbawm and George Rudé, *Captain Swing*, New York, 1968, pp. 43–44.
11. Ibid., p. 45.
12. J. M. Martin, "Marriage and Economic Stress in the Felden of Warwickshire during the Eighteenth Century," *Population Studies*, XXXI (1977), pp. 528–30. On age patterns of marriage, see David Levine, *Family Formation in an Age of Nascent Capitalism*, New York, 1977, chapters vi and viii; E. A. Wrigley and R. S. Schofield, *The Population History of England, 1541–1871*, Cambridge, 1981, pp. 255–56.
13. Levine, p. 133.
14. John Watts, *The Facts of the Cotton Famine*, London, 1866, p. 348.
15 . *Report of His Majesty's Commission to Inquire into the Poor Laws*, 1834, appendix A, part II, p. 19.
16. Ibid.
17. Ibid.
18. Ibid., p. 29.
19. Keith Snell, "Agricultural Seasonal Unemployment, the Standard of Living and Women's Work in the South and East, 1690–1860," unpublished paper, Cambridge Group for the History of Population and Social Structure, C 672; also Ann Kussmaul, *Servants in Husbandry in Early Modern England*, Cambridge, 1981, pp. 84–85, 110–14.
20. A. W. Ashby, "One Hundred Years of Poor Law Administration in a Warwickshire," *Oxford Studies in Social and Legal History*, III, Oxford, 1912, p. 67.
21. Snell, pp. 9–33; Kussmaul, pp. 22–1, 82–3, 114–17.
22. George Bourne, *Lucy Bettesworth*, London, 1913, passim.
23. Ibid.
24. A. J. Peacock, *Bread or Blood: A Study of the Agrarian Riots in East Anglia in 1816*, London, 1965, p. 61; Enid Porter, *Cambridgeshire Customs and Folklore*, London, 1969, p. 4.
25. Jennie Kitteringham, "Country work girls in nineteenth-century England," *Village Life and Labour*, ed. R. Samuel, London, 1975, p. 130.
26. A. Newman, p. 151.
27. R. C. Newman, *A Hampshire Parish: Bramshott and Liphook*, Petersfield, England, 1976, pp. 97–98.

28. *Victorian Working Class*, pp. 33–34; *The Rector and His Flock: Francis Fulford*, ed. David Ellison, Bassingbourne, 1980, p. 59.

29. *Report of His Majesty's Commission to Inquire into the Poor Laws*, 1834, p. 96; Levine, chapter ix; Martin, pp. 522–30, Ashby, pp. 67–78.

30. James Woodforde, *The Diary of a Country Parson*, II, London, 1924–31, entry for January 25, 1789.

31. John Skinner, *Diary of a Somerset Rector 1803–34: John Skinner*, eds. H. and P. Coombs, Bath, 1971, pp. 63–64; Ashby, p. 94.

32. U. R. Q. Henriques, "Bastardy and the New Poor Law," *Past and Present*, no. 37 (July 1967), pp. 104–7; E. Hampson, *The Treatment of Poverty in Cambridgeshire 1597–1834*, Cambridge, 1934, pp. 168–71.

33. "The Frolicsome Parson Outwitted," *The Common Muse: An Anthology of Popular British Ballad Poetry, 15th to 20 Century*, eds. V. de Sola Pinto and A. E. Rodway, Harmondsworth, 1956, p. 488.

34. H. B. Nicholls, *Nicholl's Forest of Dran*, Whitstable, 1966, p. 145.

35. Alan Everitt, pp. 411–12; Christopher Hill, "Pottage for Freeborn Englishmen: Attitudes to Wage Labour," *Change and Continuity in Seventeenth Century England*, London, 1974, pp. 219–22.

36. Hans Medick, "The proto-industrial family economy: The structural function of household and family during the transition from peasant society to industrial capitalism," *Social History*, III (1976), pp. 291–315.

37. Medick, pp. 297–98.

38. Ibid., p. 305.

39. Levine, chapter vi.

40. Ivy Pinchbeck, *Women Workers and the Industrial Revolution, 1750–1850*, New York, 1925, p. 179.

41. Song to be found in Cecil Sharp's *Book of Broadsides*, Cecil Sharp House, London.

42. Pinchbeck, p. 264.

43. E. Orme, "Conditions of Work in the Nail, Chain, and Bolt Making Industries in the Black Country," Royal Commission on Labour, *Parliamentary Papers*, XXVI (1892), p. 573.

44. Pinchbeck, p. 273.

45. Orme, p. 573.

46. Gandy, pp. 186–200; William Rhys Jones (Gwenith Gwyn), "Lore of Courtship and Marriage," translation from the William Rhys Jones papers, National Library of Wales, fols. 88, 92–96; Jones "Besom Wedding in the Ceiriog Valley," pp. 149–60.

47. Pinchbeck, p. 273.

48. Edwin Grey, *Cottage Life in a Hertfordshire Village*, Harpenden, 1977, pp. 69–711.

49. Pamela Horn, "The Bucks Straw Plait Trade in Victorian England," *Records of Buckinghamshire*, XIX (1971–74), pp. 48–49.

50. Kitteringham, p. 127.

51. Pinchbeck, p. 314.

52. W. F. Neff, *Victorian Working Women*, New York, 1929, p. 53.

53. Skinner, p. 409.

54. Christopher Storm-Clark, "The Miners, 1870–1970: A Test Case for Oral History," *Victorian Studies*, XV, no. 1 (September 1971), pp. 49–74; T. S.

Ashton, "Coal Miners of the Eighteenth Century, "*Economic History Review*, I (1929), pp. 307–34.

55. Michael Haines, *Fertility and Occupation: Population Patterns in Industrialization*, New York, 1979, pp. 23–27, 54–54. Lydia Fish, *The Folklore of the Coal Mines of the Northeast of of England*, Norwood, Pennsylvania, 1975, pp. 113–14.

56. *First Report of the Commissioners (Mines), Parliamentary Papers*, XVI (1842), pp. 806, 841.

57. Ibid., p. 850.

58. *Report of his Majesty's Commissions to Inquire into the Poor Law*, , II (1834), Appendix A, p. 180.

59. R. B. Walker, "Religious Change in Cheshire, 1750–1850," *Journal of Ecclesiastical History*, XVII, no. 1 (1966), p. 83.

60. Skinner, p. 14.

61. Elfyn Scourfield, "Fact Finding in a Welsh Rural Community," *Folk-Life*, X (1972), p. 64.

62. H. M. Neville, *A Corner in the North*, Newcastle, 1909, p. 87.

64. Ibid., p. 107.

65. *Master and Artisan in Victorian England: The Diary of William Andrews and the Autobiography of Joseph Gutteridge*, ed. V. Chancellor, London, 1969, p. 113.

66. Samuel Bamford, *Passages in the Life of a Radical and Early Days*, London, 1853, pp. 128–131, 149–57.

67. Doris Jones-Baker, *The Folklore of Hertfordshire*, London, 1977, p. 65.

68. *Old Yorkshire*,I, ed. W. Smith, London, 1881, p. 135.

69. S. O. Addy, *Household Tales*, p. 131.

70. William Rhys Jones, "Lore or Courtship and Marriage," fol. 85.

71. William Rhys Jones Papers, 2593/63, Welsh Folk Museum. *Old Cornwall*, I, p. 36; Tom Miners, "Quaint Marriage Customs in Old Cornwall," *Old Cornwall*, I, pp. 23–24.

72. John J. Scott, "A Description and preliminary discussion of the rhymed blason populaire tradition in England," *Lore and Language*, II, no. 2 (January 1975), pp. 9–22; also Lawson, p. 11.

73. Addy, p. 130; E. Gutch, *Country Folklore: North Riding of Yorkshire York, and the Ainsty*, London, 1901, p. 289; Richard Blakeborough, *Wit, Character, Folklore and Customs of the North Riding of Yorkshire*, Salburn-by-the-Sea, 1911, p. 90.

74. W. S. Weeks, *The Clithero District*, Clithero, n.d., p. 40; *Notes and Queries*, 2nd Series, VIII (September 17, 1859), p. 239.

75. Addy, pp. 132–33; S. O. Addy, "Garland Day in Castleton," *Folk-Lore* 12 (1901), pp. 406–7.

76. William Smith, *Morley: Ancient and Modern*, London, 1886, p. 149.

77. Fish, pp. 10, 113–14.

78. *Notes and Queries for Somerset and Dorset*, XXI (1935), p. 140.

79. Peter Anson, *Fisher Folklore*, London, 1965, pp. 55–67.

80. W. Howitt, *The Rural Life of England*, London, 1862, p. 238.

81. S. M. Tibbutt, "Knitting Stockings in Wales—A Domestic Craft," *Folk-Life*, XVI (1978), p. 66; David Thomas Collection B39, National Library of Wales.

82. Information gleaned from an exhibition of love tokens, Birmingham Museum, February 1980.

83. H. Jollie, *Sketch of Cumberland Manners and Customs*, Carlisle, 1811, pp. 39–42; W. Howitt, *The Rural Life of England*, London, 1862, pp. 237–39.

84. Grey, p. 147.

85. R. Malcolmson, *Population Recreations in English Society, 1700–1850*, Cambridge, 1973, pp. 54–55.

86. John Latimer, *The Annals of Bristol in the Eighteenth Century*, n.p., 1893, pp. 168–69, 279.

87. "The Colliers' Pay Week," *Come All Ye Bold Miners, Ballads and Songs of the Coalfields*, ed. A. L. Lloyd, London, 1952, p. 33.

88. Fictionalized scene from Thomas Hughes' *Tom Brown's Schooldays*, London, 1906, p. 35.

89. G. R. Taylor, *The Angel Makers*, New York, 1974, p. 4.

90. Bamford, p. 128; Pinchbeck, p. 273.

91. W. Sykes, *Rambles and Studies in Old South Wales*, London, 1881, pp. 232–34.

92. On the active participation of women in various kinds of social protest, see Dorothy Thompson, "Women and Nineteenth Century Radical Politics: A Lost Dimenion," *The Rights and Wrongs of Women*, eds. J. Mitchell and A. Oakley, Harmondsworth, 1979, pp. 112–38.

93. Davies, p. 230.

94. *Folklore Journal*, II (1884–85), p. 122.

95. N. McKendrick, "Home Demand and Economic Growth: A new View of the Role of Women and Children in the Industrial Revolution," *Historical Perspectives: Studies in English Thought and Society in Honour of J. H. Plumb*, London, 1974, pp. 172–84.

96. Jones, "Folk Lore of Ceiriog Valley," fol. 82.

97. W. Rhys Jones Papers, 244, National Library of Wales.

98. Jones, "Folk Lore of Ceiriog Valley," fols. 84–85.

99. John Hutchins, *The History and Antiquities of the County of Dorset*, London, 1863, pp. 808, 820–21; J. H. Bettey, *The Island and Royal Manor of Portland*, Weymouth, 1970, passim; Robert Douch, "Customs and Traditions of the Isle of Portland, Dorset," *Antiquity*, XXIII (1949), pp. 140–52. For a fictionalized account of the tradition, see Thomas Hardy, *Two on a Tower*.

100. J. S. Udal, *Dorsetshire Folklore*, Hertford, 1922, p. 199.

101. Jonas Hanway, *The Defects of Policy in the Cause of Immorality*, London, 1775, p. 163; Hanway, *A Candid Historical Account of the Hospital for Reception of Exposed and Deserted Young Children*, London, 1759, p. 43.

102. Charles Kent, "The Land of the 'Babes in the Wood,' " n.p., n.d., p. 75, Folklore Collection, Norfolk Central Library.

103. *The Victorian Working Class: Selections of Letters to the Morning Chronicle*, eds. P. E. Razzell and R. W. Wainwright, London, 1973, p. 57.

104. Ibid., p. 34.

105. Peter Laslett, *Family Life and Illicit Love in Earlier Generations*, Cambridge, 1977, chapter iii.

106. Laslett, *Bastardy and its Comparative History*, pp. 29–41.

107. This will be discussed at length in Chapter 7. For Culcheth, see Gandy, pp. 245ff; Jones, "Besom Wedding," pp. 150–51.

108. See pp. 43–50 above.

109. Laslett, "The Bastardy Prone Sub-society," *Bastardy and its Comparative History*, pp. 217–46.

110. Newman, pp. 149ff.; Levine, chapter ix; Gandy, pp. 175–200.

111. Levine, pp. 139–44.

112. Levine, p. 147; Joan W. Scott and Louise Tilly, *Women, Work and Family*, New York, 1978, p. 120.
113. Hampson, pp. 167–75; Blanch Berryman, ed., *Mitcham Settlement Examinations, 1784–1814*, Surrey Record Society, Guildford, 1973, pp. x–xi; Ashby, pp. 74ff., 99.
114. N. Michelson, *The Old Poor Law in East Yorkshire*, Hull, 1953, pp. 12–13; Canon Hume, "Rural Life and Manners—the Neighborhood of Bidstone and Upton—a Hundred Years Ago," *Transactions of the Historic Society of Lancashire and Cheshire*, 3rd Series, III (1874–75), p. 166.
115. Alun Davies, "The Old Poor Law in an Industrializing Parish: Aberdare," *Welsh History Review*, VIII, no. 3 (June 1977), pp. 301–2; Davies, "The New Poor Law in a Rural Area, 1834–50," *Credigion*, VIII (1978), pp. 245–90.
116. Ashby, pp. 97–99.
117. Quoted in *Parliamentary Papers* (1838), VII, part 1, p. 362.
118. *A Calender of Merioneth Quarter Sessions Rolls*, ed. Keith William-Jones, Aberystwyth, 1965, p. xlxxx; Mark Blaugh, "Myth of the Old Poor Law," *Economic History Review*, XXIII (1963), p. 74; Howitt, p. 163.
119. Levine, p. 144.
120. Barbara Taylor, *Eve and the New Jerusalem: Socialism and Feminism in the Nineteenth Century*, New York, 1983, p. 194.
121. G. Robertson Owen, "Illegitimacy in Islington, 1558–1820," *Devon and Cornwall Notes and Queries*, XXI (1968–70), pp. 220–21.
122. Jones, "Folklore of the Ceiriog Valley," fo.l 84.
123. Addy, p. 122; *Notes and Queries*, 9th Series, IV (September 30, 1899), p. 266. On the use of the term "misfortune," see *English Dialect Dictionary*, IV, London, 1903, p. 128.
124. Gandy, pp. 167, 260–89; C. Stella Davies, *North Country Bred*, London, 1963, p. 23; *The Rector and His Flock: Francis Fulford*, Bassingbourne, 1980, p. 59.
125. Stone, p. 637.
126. Bamford, p. 192.
127. D. Parry-Jones, *My Own Folk*, Llandysul, 1977, p. 120; Trefor Owen, *Welsh Folk Customs*, Cardiff, 1978, pp. 168ff.; also G. Roberts, *The History and Antiquities of the Borough of Lyme Regis and Charnworth*, London, 1934, p. 161. Thompson argues that rough music protected women in a period when they had lost the protection of family and clergy. " 'Rough Music' et charivari: Quelques réflexions complémentares," *Le Charivari*, eds. J. LeGoff and J-C. Schmitt, Paris, 1981, p. 282.
128. David Williams, *The Rebecca Riots*, Cardiff, 1955, p. 55.
129. Parry-Jones, p. 121.
130. Enid Porter, "Folklore of the Fenlands," *Folk-Lore* 72 (1971), p. 592; also Porter, *Cambridgeshire Customs of Folklore*, pp. 8–9.
131. Quoted in Gordon Home, *The Evolution of an English Town*, London, 1915, p. 214.
132. Edward P. Thompson, " 'Rough Music': Le Charivari anglais," *Annales Economies Societies Civilisations*, 27, no. 2 (March–April 1972), pp. 304ff.
133. Violet Alford, "Rough Music or Charivari," *Folk-Lore* 70 (December 1959), pp. 505–8.
134. Thompson, pp. 301–4.
135. *Notes and Queries*, 2nd Series, X (December 15, 1860), pp. 476–77.
136. Trefor Owen, *Welsh Folk Customs*, Cardiff, 1978, p. 169.

137. Charles Redwood, *The Vale of Glamorgan*, London, 1839, pp. 289–95; Owen, p. 170; G. J. Williams, "Glamorgan Customs in the Eighteenth Century," *Gwerin*, I, pp. 106–7.
138. Wirt Sykes, *Rambles and Studies in Old South Wales*, London, 1881, p. 231.

Chapter 5

1. Lawrence Stone, *The Family, Sex and Marriage in England, 1500–1800*, New York, 1977, pp. 271–92, 316–17; Christopher Hill "Clarissa Harlowe and Her Times," *Puritanism and Revolution*, London, 1958, pp. 367–94; Randolf Trumbach, *The Rise of the Egalitarian Family: Aristocratic Kinship and Domestic Relations in Eighteenth Century England*, New York, 1978, chapter ii.
2. For the early Victorian period, see Leonore Davidoff, *The Best Circles: Society, Etiquette and The Season*, London, 1973, pp. 49ff. Victorian attitudes dominated provincial society until World War I. See Vera Brittain, *Testament of Youth*, New York, 1980, pp. 43–49.
3. Stone, p. 318.
4. Ibid., p. 276.
5. Stone, pp. 270–88; Trumbach, pp. 97–113.
6. Stone, pp. 242–44.
7. C. D. P. Nicholson, *The Genealogical Value of Early English Newspapers*, n.p., 1934, passim.
8. Henri Misson, *Memoirs and Observations in His Travels over England (1697)*, London, 1719, p. 183.
9. *How They Lived*, III, ed. A. Briggs, Oxford, 1969, p. 267.
10. Misson, p. 352.
11. On the ring, see John Evans, *English Posies and Posy Rings*, London, 1931, p. xxvi; "The Wedding Ring," *The Antiquary*, III (1881), pp. 22–23, 70–71; William Jones, *Finger-Ring Lore*, London, 1898, pp. 155–74, 283–97; see also Trumbach, pp. 113–17.
12. Quoted from the unpublished papers of John Sanders, *Gloucestershire Notes and Queries*, II (1884), pp. 276–78.
13. Misson, p. 352.
14. Stone, p. 335.
15. Ibid., p. 336.
16. Misson, p. 353.
17. See above, Chapter 1.
18. John Sykes, *Local Record: Or Historical Register*, I, Newcastle upon Tyne, 1866, p. 364.
19. W. H. Howse, *Radnorshire*, Hereford, 1949, p. 149; "Llangattock Parish Scrapbook," *Brycheiniog*, VIII (1961), p. 133.
20. An eighteenth-century Quaker wedding of some elegance is described in *Journal of the Friends Historical Society*, XVI, no. 2 (1919), p. 58.
21. Patrick Joyce, *Work, Society and Politics: The Culture of the Factory in Later Victorian England*, New Brunswick, 1980, p. 184.
22. Clara Alcock's journal, V, manuscript collection C21/2/2, Manchester Central Library.
23. Elizabeth M. Wright, *Rustic Speech and Folklore*, Oxford, 1913, p. 270.
24. Christopher Lasch, "The Suppression of Clandestine Marriage in England: The Marriage Act of 1753," *Salmagundi*, no. 26 (Spring 1974), pp. 60–109.

25. *Archbishop Herring's Visitation Returns of 1743*, Yorkshire Archeological Society Record Series (1929), LXXII (1929), p. 100.
26. "An Act for the Better Preventing of Clandestine Marriages," 26, George II, chapter II.
27. William Cobbett, *The Parliamentary History of England*, XV, London, 1813, p. 59.
28. Ibid., pp. 16, 19.
29. Ibid., p. 21.
30. Ibid., p. 18.
31. Ibid., pp. 20, 59–60.
32. Ibid., p. 40.
33. Ibid., p. 41.
34. J. S. Burn, *The Fleet Registers*, London, 1833, p. 100.
35. "Claverhouse," *Irregular Border Marriages*, London and Edinburgh, 1934, pp. 22–29.
36. Roger Lee Brown, "Clandestine Marriages in London, especially within the Fleet Prison and the Effect in Hardwicke's Act, 1753," unpublished M.A. thesis, University of London, 1972, p. 96.
37. J. C. Cox, *The Parish Registers of England*, London, 1910, p. 92.
38. John Bossy, *The English Catholic Community, 1570–1850*, London, 1975, pp. 136–40; Michael Watt, *The Dissenters*, Oxford, 1978, pp. 329–31.
39. W. Blackstone, *Blackstone's Commentaries*, I, S. Hackensack, New Jersey, 1969, p. 428; for later debates on the Marriage Act, see Ronald Paulson, *Representations of Revolution, 1789–1820*, New Haven, 1983, pp. 116, 143.
40. *Notes and Queries*, 2nd Series, V (April 10, 1858), p. 306.
41. *Leicestershire and Rutland Notes and Queries*, I (1891), p. 230.
42. *Folk-Lore*, 44 (1933), p. 290.
43. T. F. Thiselton Dyer, *Old English Social Life as Told by the Parish Registers*, London, 1898, p. 230; J. Vaux, *Church Folklore*, London, 1894, p. 100.
44. W. Crooke, "The Lifting of the Bride," *Folk-Lore*, XIII (1902), p. 230.
45. W. W. Bladen, "Notes on the Folklore of North Staffordshire, Chiefly collected at Stone," *Transactions of the North Staffordshire Field Club*, XXV (1901), p. 155.
46. D. D. Dixon, "Old Wedding Customs in Upper Coquetdale and Alndale, Northumberland," *Newcastle Courant* (December 1888). Copy in the Newcastle City Library.
47. *Byegones*, 2nd Series, III (June 28, 1893), p. 108.
48. Crooke, p. 229.
49. Ibid., p. 229.
50. Transcript 408, Paul Thompson and Thea Vigne, Family Life and Work Experience Before 1918, Oral History Archive, University of Essex. (Henceforth cited as Family Life and Work Experience Archive.)
51. *Byegones*, 2nd Series, I (October 30, 1890), p. 249.
52. *Notes and Queries*, 6th Series, XII (September 5, 1885), p.
53. *Byegones*, 2nd Series, II (October 23, 1889), p.
54. *Notes and Queries*, 11th Series, VIII (September 13, 1913), p. 209.
55. Margaret Baker, *The Folklore and Customs of Love and Marriage*, Aylesbury, 1974, p. 37.
56. Transcript 420, Family Life and Work Experience Archive.
57. Richard Williams, "History of the Parish of Llanbrgynmair," *Montgomer-*

gyshire Collections, XXII (1888), p. 323; *Notes and Queries*, 2nd Series, V (February 27, 1858), , pp. 178–79.

58. *Notes and Queries*, 9th Series, VII (April 6, 1901), p. 273; IX (May 17, 1902), p. 386; X (July 26, 1902), p. 66.
59. Dixon, p. 12.
60. Iona and Peter Opie, *The Lore and Language of Schoolchildren*, Oxford, 1959, pp. 303–4.
61. *Notes and Queries*, 7th Series, X (December 6, 1890) p. 445.
62. Transcript 302, Family Life and Work Experience Archive.
63. *Notes and Queries*, 4th Series, II (October 10, 1868), p. 434.
64. Edwin Grey, *Cottage Life in a Hertfordshire Village*, Harpenden, 1977, p. 153; on Lincolnshire, see Vaux, p. 109.
65. Carmarthen case, 1897, reported in *Byegones*, 2nd Series, V (May 19, 1897), p. 116.
66. Sabine Baring-Gould, *Old Country Life*, London, 1890, p. 275.
67. Recollections of Miss E. M. Briggs, Sheffield, Center for English Cultural Tradition and Language collections.
68. Grey, pp. 152–53.
69. Transcript 420, Family Life and Work Experience Archive.
70. Grey, pp. 155–57.
71. Lawson, *Letters to the Young on Progress in Pudsey*, Stanninglen, 1887, p. 20.
72. Flora Thompson, *Lark Rise to Candleford*, Harmondsworth, 1974, p. 170.
73. Grey, p. 157; Lawson, p. 19.
74. This began to decline in the mid-eighteenth century. See Davies, *Folk-Lore of West and Mid-Wales*, Abevystwyth, 1911, p. 39; John C. Jeaffreson, *Brides and Bridals*, I, London, 1872, p. 269; Dixon, p. 13.
75. Grey, p. 158.
76. Transcript 237, Family Life and Work Experience Archive.
77. Hird's Diary, fol. 42, Blakeborough Manuscripts, Sheffield University.
78. Richard Blakeborough, "A Country Wedding," fol. 7, Sheffield University.
79. Richard Blakeborough, "A Collection of Valentines," fol. 16, Sheffield University.
80. Blakeborough, "A Country Wedding," fol. 7.
81. Blakeborough, "Collection of Valentines," fol. 17.
82. George Calvert's manuscript notes, fol. 37, Calvert Manuscripts, Leeds University.
83. Ibid., n.p.; also text of "Board School Miss," ca. 1790, found in Blakeborough Notebooks, Sheffield.
84. David Naitby's diary, fol. 33, Blakeborough Manuscripts, Sheffield University.
85. Calvert's manuscript notes, fol. 16, Calvert Manuscripts, Leeds.
86. Richard Blakeborough, *Wit, Character, Folklore and Customs of the North Riding of Yorkshire*, Salburn-by-the-Sea, 1911, p. 96.
87. W. Henderson, *Notes on the Folk-Lore of the Northern Counties of England and the Borders*, London, 1879, p. 42.
88. Naitby's diary, fol. 17, Blakeborough Manuscripts, Sheffield.
89. Blakeborough, "A Collection of Valentines," fol. 16.
90. Blakeborough, "A Country Wedding," fol. 13; E. Gutch, *Country Folklore: East Riding of Yorkshire*, London, 1912, p. 129; Blakeborough, *Wit*, pp. 97–98.

91. Trefor Owen, "West Glamorgan Customs," *Folk-Life*, III (1965), p. 53.
92. John Brand, *Observations on Popular Antiquities*, London, 1877, p. 384.
93. Lydia Fish, *The Folklore of the Coal Mines of the Northeast of England*, Norwood, Pennsylvania, 1975, p. 45.
94. George Henwood, *Cornwall's Mines and Miners*, Truro, 1972, p. 68.
95. Newcastle Broadside Collection, Newcastle Library, L 029.3.
96. Edward Chicken, "The Collier's Wedding," *Come All Ye Bold Miners*, ed. A. L. Lloyd, London, 1952, pp. 51–62.
97. *Dalesman*, January 1976, p. 774.
98. *Cupid's Pupils*, pp. 232–33.
99. Ibid., pp. 201–2.
100. Ibid., p. 186.
101. "Claverhouse," p. 135; Jones, p. 283; and John Aston, *Social England under the Regency*, II, London, 1890, p. 301.
102. *Come All Ye Bold Miners*, pp. 51–62.
103. This change was already evident earlier, see K. Wrightson, "Alehouses, Order and Reformation in Rural England, 1590–1660," *Class Relations and Cultural Forms*, eds. E. and S. Yeo, London, 1979, pp. 1–27.
104. *Come All Ye Bold Miners*, pp. 51–62.
105. *Gentleman's Magazine*, 1784, p. 343; Trefor M. Owen, *Welsh Folk Customs*, Cardiff, 1978, pp. 159–61.
106. Davies, p. 18.
107. *Byegones*, 2nd Series, 1901–2, p. 109; Brand, pp. 383–84.
108. Owen, *Welsh Folk Customs*, pp. 161–62. For another *rammas*, see David Thomas Collection, B 75, National Library of Wales. Italics are mine.
109. T. Owen, "Some Aspects of Bidding in Cardiganshire," *Ceredigion*, IV, no. 1 (1960), pp. 37–46.
110. Brand, pp. 383–84.
111. *Gentleman's Magazine*, 1791, p. 1103; Peter Roberts, *The Cambrian Popular Antiquities*, Norwood, Pennsylvania, 1973, p. 160.
112. *Byegones*, Series, I, 1872, p.
113. *Notes and Queries*, 7th Series, VI (December 15, 1888), p. 477.
114. Wright, p. 272; *Notes and Queries*, 13th Series, CLXVIII (May 25, 1935), p. 376.
115. A. C. Atkinson, *A Glossary of Cleveland Dialect*, London, 1868, pp. 71–72.
116. *Notes and Queries*, 13th Series, (May 25, 1935), p. 376.
117. See Chapter 4.
118. F. Eden, *The State of the Poor* (1797), quoted in Brand, pp. 386–87.
119. W. Howells, *Cambrian Superstitions*, London, 1831, p. 169; on other popular forms of commercialization, see J. Brewer et al. *The birth of consumer society: the commercialization of eighteenth century England*, Bloomington, 1982, chapter II.
120. William Hone, *Table Book*, I, London, 1837, p. 431.
121. Ibid., II, p. 2374.
122. This was in 1807. See W. Rollinson, *Life and Tradition in the Lake District*, London, 1974, p. 58.
123. Walter T. McIntire, *Lakeland and the Borders*, Carlisle, 1948, p. 212; Brand, p. 586.
124. A. Craig Gibson, "Ancient Custom and Superstitions in Cumberland,"

Transactions of the Historic Society of Lancashire and Cheshire, X (1857–58), p. 103.

125. R. U. Sayce, "Popular Enclosures and the One-Night House," *Montgomeryshire Collections*, XLVII, part 2 (1942), pp. 109–17.

126. Brand, pp. 333–45; on Cumberland, see *Monthly Chronicle of North Country Lore* (March 1890), p. 130; William Fleming, "A Furness Diary," *The Countryman*, 55, no. 4 (1958), p. 702; William Howitt, *The Rural Life of England*, London, 1862, p. 236.

127. W. Rhys Jones, "Besom Wedding," *Folk-Lore*, no. 34 (1928), pp. 159–60; surnames were not used much in the Yorkshire dales until the mid-nineteenth century, see Howitt, p. 243.

128. For a discussion of envy, see G. M. Foster, "Anatomy of Envy: A Study of Symbolic Behavior," *Current Anthropology*, VIII, no. 2 (April 1972), pp. 165–202.

Chapter 6

1. John Graunt, *Natural and Political Observations Mentioned in a Following Index, and Made upon the Bills of Mortality*, London, 1662, pp. 44–45, quoted in R. R. Kuczynski, "British Demographers' Opinions on Fertility, 1660–1760," *Political Arithmetic: A Symposium of Population Studies*, ed. L. Hogben, London, 1938, pp. 312–13.

2. William Brakenridge, "A Letter to George Lewis Scot, Concerning the Present Increase of the People in Britain and Ireland," in *Political Arithmetic*, p. 316.

3. Quoted in Leonore Davidoff, Jean L'Esperance, and Howard Newby, "Landscape with Figures: Home and Community in English Society," *The Rights and Wrongs of Women*, eds. J. Mitchell and Ann Oakley, Harmondsworth, 1979, p. 149.

4. Roger Finlay, *Population and Metropolis: The Demography of London, 1580–1650*, Cambridge, 1981, chapter vii; Vivien Brodsky Elliott, "Mobility and marriage in pre-industrial England," unpublished Ph.D. dissertation, University of Cambridge, 1979, pp. 264ff.

5. Steve Lee Rappaport, "Social Structure and Mobility in Sixteenth Century London," unpublished Ph.D. dissertation, Columbia University, chapter v, p. 31.

6. Ibid., chapter v, p. 30.

7. Ibid., chapter v, p. 31.

8. Ibid.

9. For clandestine marriage in London, see Finlay, p. 60.

10. Vivien Brodsky Elliott, "Single Women in the London Marriage Market: Age, Status, and Mobility, 1598–1619," *Marriage and Society: Studies in the Social History of Marriage*, ed. R. B. Outhwaite, New York, 1981, pp. 81–100.

11. Keith Thomas, *Religion and the Decline of Magic*, New York, 1971, pp. 233–34, 308–22; Michael MacDonald, *Mystical Bedlam: Madness, Anxiety, and Healing in Seventeenth-Century England*, Cambridge, 1981, pp. 88–102.

12. Elliott, p. 95.

13. Ibid., p. 97

14. Finlay, p. 149.
15. Lawrence Stone, *The Family, Sex and Marriage in England, 1500–1800*, New York, 1977, pp. 615–19.
16. Ibid., pp. 639–40.
17. Finlay, p. 149. On the prevalence of abortion in the early modern period, see Angus McLaren, "Reproductive Rituals: The Patterning of Human Fertility in England, 1500–1800," unpublished manuscript, chapter iv.
18. For the marriage pattern in a more traditional artisanal/market town, see Alan Armstrong, *Stability and Change in an English Country Town: A Social Study of York, 1801–1851*, Cambridge, 1974, pp. 161–62. Figures on rural/urban nuptiality for the nineteenth century found in *Registrar General's Annual Reports*.
19. On the eighteenth-century backgrounds of the upper-class "white wedding," see Randolf Trumbach, *The Rise of the Egalitarian Family: Aristocratic Kinship and Domestic Relations in Eighteenth Century England*, New York, 1978, pp. 113–17; D. Crozier, "Kinship and Occupational Succession," *Sociological Review*, New Series, XIII (1965), pp. 15–43; Michael Anderson, *Family Structure in Nineteenth Century Lancashire*, Cambridge, 1971, pp. lllff.
20. J. R. Gillis, *Youth and History: Tradition and Change in European Age Relations, 1770–Present*, New York, 1974, pp. 42–54; Gareth Stedman Jones, "Working Class Culture and Working Class Politics in London, 1870–1900: Notes on the Remaking of a Working Class Culture," *Journal of Social History*, VII, no. 4 (Summer 1974), p. 486.
21. Francis Place, quoted in M. Dorothy George, *London in the Eighteenth Century*, New York, 1925, p. 168.
22. J. R. Gillis, "Servants, Sexual Relations, and the Risks of Illegitimacy in London, 1801–1900," *Feminist Studies*, V, no. 1 (Spring 1979), pp. 142–73.
23. Henry Mayhew, *London Labour and the London Poor*, III, London, 1864, p. 233.
24. Contemporary attitudes are reviewed by Harold Perkin, *The Origins of Modern English Society, 1780–1880*, London, 1969, pp. 149–51. Charles Dickens' treatment of Stephen Blackpool's failed marriage is one of the few sympathetic fictional accounts. *Hard Times*, New York, 1961. Benjamin Disraeli's colorful account of a common-law marriage in *Sybil*, London, 1927, p. 194, was entirely made up. See Sheila Smith, "Willenhall and Wodgate: Disraeli's Use of Blue Book Evidence," *Review of English Studies*, XIII (1962), pp. 379–80.
25. Quoted in Eileen Yeo's Introduction to *The Unknown Mayhew*, eds. E. Yeo and E. P. Thompson, New York, 1972, p. 88.
26. P. Gaskell, *The Manufacturing Population of England* (1833), p. 147, quoted in Perkin, p. 150.
27. Finlay, p. 19.
28. Sally Alexander, "Women's Work in Nineteenth Century London: A Study of the Years, 1820–50," *The Rights and Wrongs of Women*, p. 65; Gareth Stedman Jones, *Outcast London*, part I, Oxford, 1971.
29. Anderson, p. 129.
30. F. Engels, quoted in Perkin, p. 149.
31. Anderson, p. 131.
32. From testimony given in 1840, cited in Perkin, p. 151.
33. Anderson, pp. 51–55, 102; for a similar situation in Oldham, see John Foster, *Class Struggle and the Industrial Revolution*, London, 1974, pp. 94–99.

34. Anderson, pp. 132–34.
35. Armstrong, pp. 161–62; Anderson, pp. 161–62.
36. Peter Laslett, "Introduction," *Bastardy and its Comparative History*, eds. Peter Laslett, Karla Oosterveen, and Richard M. Smith, Cambridge, 1980, pp. 30, 35; also Perkin, pp. 152–53.
37. Mr. Bounderby's answer to Stephen Blackpool's questioning of the divorceless marriage law is "The institutions of your country are not your piece-work, and the only thing you have got to do is mind your piece-work." Charles Dickens, *Hard Times*, p. 82.
38. J. Liddington and J. Norris, *One hand tied behind us* London, 1978, pp. 58–59, 74–75, 95, 259.
39. Alexander, p. 65.
40. Alexander, p. 76; John Rule, *The Experience of Labour in Eighteenth Century Industry*, London, 1981, pp. 30–38. Rule estimates that in the eighteenth century only 5 to 6 percent of the population were really self-employed. The term "master" had already come to mean mastery of a skill rather than full economic independence.
41. *Unknown Mayhew*, p. 118.
42. George, p. 168.
43. Quoted in Alexander, p. 103.
44. 1840 Parliamentary Report on Handloom Weaving, quoted in G. Talcott Griffith, *Population Problems in the Age of Malthus*, Cambridge, 1926, p. 119; George, p. 169.
45. *48th Annual Registrar General's Report*, 1886, p. ix.
46. George, p. 199.
47. Alexander, p. 104.
48. "A Present for a Servant Maid" (1743), quoted in George, p. 168.
49. Alexander, p. 99.
50. Daniel Defoe, writing in 1705, cited in George, p. 157; also Perkin, pp. 92–93. On the level of affluence, see J. Brewer et al., *The birth of consumer society: commercialization in eighteenth-century England*, Bloomington, 1982, chapter VI.
51. *Unknown Mayhew*, pp. 105–6.
52. Ibid., p. 114.
53. E. A. Wrigley, "A Simple Model of London's Importance in Changing English Society and Economy, 1650–1750," *Past & Present*, no. 37 (July 1967), pp. 47–65.
54. George, p. 153.
55. "The Weaver and the Factory Maid," *A Touch on the Times: Songs of Social Change 1770 to 1914*, ed. Roy Palmer, Harmondsworth, 1974, p. 133.
56. William Cole, *The Bletchley Diary of Reverend William Cole, 1765–67*, ed. F. G. Stokes, London, 1931, p. 41.
57. Ivy Pinchbeck, *Women, Workers and the Industrial Revolution*, New York, 1925, p. 109.
58. Ibid., p. 38.
59. An example of this is found in a Foundling Hospital petition, 1828/49. (Henceforth all petitions cited with year and number of petition.)
60. Foundling Hospital petition, 1823/191.
61. Ann Kussmaul, *Servants in Husbandry in Early Modern England*, Cambridge, 1981, pp. 83–85, 121–26.

62. Peter Laslett, "Parental Deprivation in the past: a note on orphans and stepparenthood in English History," in Laslett's *Family Life and illicit love in earlier generations*, Cambridge, 1977, pp. 160–72.
63. Foundling Hospital petition, 1825/8.
64. Foundling Hospital petition, 1833/22.
65. Foundling Hospital petition, 1831/36.
66. G. R. Quaife, *Wanton Wenches and Wayward Wives: Peasants and Illicit Sex in Early Seventeenth Century England*, New Brunswick, 1979, pp. 98–123; K. Wrightson, "Infanticide in Early 17th C. England," *Local Population Studies*, 15 (Autumn 1975), pp. 16–17.
67. *Chelmsford Chronicle*, January 1, 1808.
68. Foundling Hospital petitions, 1840/12; 1820/4.
69. Anderson, chapter x.
70. Foundling Hospital petition, 1816/11.
71. Anderson, pp. 99–103, 118–121.
72. Finlay, pp. 141ff.
73. Foundling Hospital petition, 1828/36.
74. Foundling Hospital petition, 1812/9.
75. Ibid.
76. Foundling Hospital petition, 1830/33.
77. Gillis, "Servants," pp. 158–60.
78. Foundling Hospital petition, 1834/22.
79. G. S. Jones, *Outcast London*, pp. 39–40.
80. Ibid., pp. 40–41.
81. Foundling Hospital petition, 1823/139.
82. That was the amount his servant lover borrowed from her mistress, Foundling Hospital petition, 1850/5.
83. Foundling Hospital petition, 1825/6.
84. Foundling Hospital petition, 1835/38.
85. Foundling Hospital petition, 1841/139.
86. Gillis, "Servants," p. 145.
87. Foundling Hospital petition, 1818/3.
88. Gillis, "Servants," pp. 158–62.
89. Testimony from 1840, quoted in G. T. Griffith, p. 124.
90. This pattern is evident in the petitions to the Foundling Hospital.
91. Place Papers, Add MS 25144, fol. 177, British Museum.
92. Ibid., fol. 182.
93. Ibid., fol. 187.
94. *Munby: Man of Two Worlds*, ed. Derek Hudson, London, 1974, p. 103; Place Papers, Add MS 35144, fol. 229.
95. Place Papers, Add MS 35144, fols. 219–220.
96. As illustrated by various Foundling Hospital petitions.
97. Francis Place, *The Autobiography of Francis Place, 1771–1854*, ed. Mary Thrale, Cambridge, 1972, p. 77.
98. Ibid., p. 76.
99. Ibid., p. 101.
100. *Master and Artisan in Victorian England: The Diary of William Andrews and the Autobiography of Joseph Gutteridge*, ed. V. Chancellor, London, 1969, p. 713.
101. Foundling Hospital petition, 1812/12.

102. Foundling Hospital petition, 1812/1.
103. Foundling Hospital petition, 1810/8.
104. Alexander, p. 102.
105. Quoted in Elliott, p. 305.
106. *The New Guide to Matrimony*, n.p., n.d., found in chapbook collection, Newcastle Central Library, L398.5.
107. Place, *Autobiography*, p. 101.
108. *41st Annual Report of Registrar General*, 1883.
109. Gillis, "Servants," pp. 155–56.
110. Ibid., p. 155.
111. Foundling Hospital petition, 1839/26. On the various means of contraception available, see McLaren, "Reproductive Rituals," chapter iii; also Angus McLaren, *Birth Control in Nineteenth-Century England*, New York, 1978, pp. 31–35, 78–87.
112. Anderson, p. 149; Stella Davies, *North Country Bred: A Working Class Chronicle*, London, 1963, pp. 22ff.; Bill Williamson, *Class Culture and Community*, London, 1982, p. 209.
113. Foundling Hospital petition, 1804/1.
114. Foundling Hospital petition, 1806/2.
115. Foundling Hospital petition, 1811/7.
116. Foundling Hospital petition, 1823/5.
117. Foundling Hospital petition, 1822/18.
118. Foundling Hospital petition, 1838/1.
119. Foundling Hospital petition, 1828/36.
120. Gillis, "Servants," pp. 156, 164–65.
121. *Unknown Mayhew*, p. 148.
122. Ibid., pp. 169–71.
123. Foundling Hospital petition, 1834/4, 1844/5, 1845/3; Gillis, "Servants," p. 156.
124. Foundling Hospital petition, 1849/119.
125. Foundling Hospital petitions, 1809/4, 1818/1. For example of fear of swearing a child, see 1808/7.
126. Foundling Hospital petitions, 1828/8, 1823/138.
127. Samuel Bamford, *Passages in the Life of a Radical and Early Days*, London, 1905, p. 192.
128. Foundling Hospital petition, 1817/6.
129. Foundling Hospital petitions, 1831/6, 1818/9, 1816/6.
130. Quoted in Iris Minor, "Working Class Women and Matrimonial Law Reform 1890–1914," *Ideology and the Labour Movement*, eds. David Martin and David Rubinstein, London, 1979, p. 113. See also Havelock Ellis, *Studies in the Psychology of Sex*, VI, Philadelphia, 1924, pp. 388–89.
131. Booth Collection, A vol. XXXII, fols. 12–13, London School of Economics.
132. Gillis, "Servants," p. 165.
133. *Unknown Mayhew*, p. 120.
134. Foundling Hospital petition, 1839/123.
135. Foundling Hospital petitions, 1836/6, 1829/11, 1809/12, 1811/1, 1811/4.
136. Foundling Hospital petition, 1817/6.
137. John Feriar, *Medical Histories and Reflections*, London, 1795, pp. 207–8, quoted in McLaren, "Reproductive Rituals," chapter iv, p. 10; on the costs of family, see Gillis, "Servants," p. 154.

138. Nancy Tomes, "A 'Torrent of Abuse': Crimes of Violence between Working-Class Men and Women in London, 1840–1875," *Journal of Social History*, XI, no. 3 (Spring 1978), p. 332.
139. See Chapter 11 for contemporary situation.
140. *Unknown Mayhew*, p. 88.
141. Foundling Hospital petitions, 1828/6, 1833/27.
142. Foundling Hospital petition, 1822/10.
143. Foundling Hospital petitions, 1818/1, 1825/4, 1817/6.
144. *45th Annual Report of the Registrar General*, 1884.
145. Edward P. Thompson, *Making of the English Working Class*, New York, 1966, p. 56.
146. D. J. Steel, *National Index of Parish Registers*, I, London, 1968, pp. 62–63.
147. Edward Coke, *Religious Rites Made Free to the Poor*, London, n.d., Fulham Papers 101, Lambeth Palace Library.
148. From the reports of the London City Mission, 1844–48, cited in Barbara Taylor, *Eve and the New Jerusalem: Socialism and Feminism in the Nineteenth Century*, New York, 1983, pp. 194–95.
149. *27th Annual Report of the Registrar General*, 1866, p. vii; *Monthly Chronicle of North Country Lore and Legend* (June 1888), p. 280.
150. Transcript no. 225, Family Life and Work Experience Archive. Man married in 1904.
151. G. S. Jones, "Working Class Culture," p. 153.
152. "Marriage in Low Life," *Chambers Journal*, XII (July-December 1859), p. 399.
153. Ibid.
154. J. Watt, *The Facts of the Cotton Famine*, London, 1866, p. 7; Joseph Lawson, *Letters to the Young on Progress in Pudsey*, Stanninglen, 1887, pp. 19–20; Helen Bosanquet, *Rich and Poor*, London, 1898, p. 133.
155. "Marriage in Low Life," p. 399.

Chapter 7

1. Dafydd Ifans, "Lewis Morris ac Afrerion Priodi yng Ngheredigion," *Ceredigion*, VIII, no. 2 (1972), p. 201; *Cymru Fu*, April 14, 1888.
2. Barbara Taylor, *Eve and the New Jerusalem: Socialism and Feminism in the Nineteenth Century*, New York, 1983, p. 119.
3. On the conservatism of the major dissenting bodies, see D. J. Steel, *National Index of Parish Registers*, II, London, 1973, pp. 550–52; for eighteenth-century radical nonconformity, see J. F. C. Harrison, *The Second Coming: Popular Millenarianism, 1780–1850*, New Brunswick, 1979, pp. 25–29.
4. Christopher Hill, *The World Turned Upside Down: Radical Ideas during the English Revolution*, Harmondsworth, 1979, pp. 380–81.
5. J. Leonard Wadding, *The Bitter Sacred Cup: The Wednesbury Riots, 1743–44*, London, 1976, pp. 24–25.
6. John F. Ede, *History of Wednesbury*, Birmingham, 1962, pp. 150–56, 201–14; F. W. Hackwood, *Wednesbury, Ancient and Modern*, n.p., 1902, passim.
7. T. F. Thiselton Dyer, *Old English Social Life as Told by the Parish Registers*, London, 1898, p. 139; F. W. Hackwood, *The Bridal Book*, London, p. 90.
8. Entry to 1798 register, cited in M. R. Austin, "Religion and Society in Derbyshire during the Industrial Revolution," *The Derbyshire Archeological Journal*, XCIII (1973), pp. 85–86.

9. On the character of dissent, see Alan Everitt, *Patterns of Rural Dissent: The Nineteenth Century*, Leicester, 1972, passim; and James Obelkevich, *Religion and Rural Society: South Lindsey, 1825–1875*, Oxford, 1976, pp. 127–37.

10. Reverend W. Sharp, writing in 1813, cited by M. R. Austin, "The Church of England in the County of Derbyshire, 1772–1832," unpublished D.Phil. dissertation, London University, 1969, p. 146.

11. Robert Malcolmson, " 'A set of ungovernable people': The Kingswood Colliers in the Eighteenth Century," *An Ungovernable People: The English and Their Law in the seventeenth and eighteenth centuries*, ed. John Styles and John Brewer, New Brunswick, 1980, p. 91.

12. Eric Evans, "Some Reasons for the Growth of Rural Anti-Clericalism, 1750–1830," *Past & Present*, 66 (February 1975), pp. 84–109.

13. *London City Mission Magazine*, XVI (January 1851), p. 16; XVIII (June 1853), p. 83. I am indebted to Dr. Barbara Taylor for this reference.

14. See Chapter 3.

15. Fulham Papers, 438, Lambeth Palace Library.

16. Horace Walpole to Henry Seymour Conway, May 24, 1753, quoted in William Cobbett, *The Parliamentary History of England*, XV, London, 1813, pp. 32–33.

17. R. B. Outhwaite, "Age of Marriage in England from the late Seventeenth to the Nineteenth Centuries," *Transactions of the Royal Historical Society*, 5th Series, XXII (1973), p. 62.

18. Steel, I, p. 728.

19. *27th Annual Registrar General's Report*, 1866, p. viii.

20. Ibid.; Olive Anderson, "The Incidence of Civil Marriage in Victorian England and Wales," *Past & Present*, 69 (November 1975), pp. 68–69, 73–78.

21. Edward Coke, *Religious Rites Made Free to the Poor*, Fulham Papers 101, Lambeth Palace Library; and 1883 Middlesex Visitation, Fulham Papers 503, Lambeth Palace Library.

22. 1858 Middlesex Visitation, Fulham Papers 461, Lambeth Palace Library.

23. Visitation to St. Thomas, Bethnal Green, Fulham Papers 461.

24. 1883 Middlesex Visitation, Fulham Papers 508, Lambeth Palace Library.

25. Coke, n.p.; 1905 Visitation to St. John's, Notting Hill, MS 17895, box 2, Guildhall Library, London.

26. Visitations to Shoreditch and St. John's, Finsbury, 1905, MS 17885, box 1, Guildhall Library, London.

27. 1905 Visitation, MS 17885, box 2, Guildhall Library, London.

28. Harwich returns, 1772 Visitation, Fulham Papers 438, Lambeth Palace Library.

29. 1905 Visitation to St. Johns, Hampstead, MS 17895, box 2, Guildhall Library, London.

30. Report of the Select Committee of the House of Lords appointed to inquire into the Deficiency of Means of Spiritual Instruction and Places of Divine Worship in the Metropolis, *Parliamentary Papers* (1857–58), IX, p. 450.

31. Harold Smith, "Marriage from Outside," *Essex Review*, LXII (1933), pp. 204ff.

32. "Claverhouse," *Irregular Border Marriages*, London and Edinburgh, 1934, pp. 131–32.

33. *27th Annual Registrar General's Report*, 1866, p. vii; *Monthly Chronicle of North Country Lore and Legend*, June 1888, p. 280.

34. *Notes and Queries*, 8th Series, IX (May 16, 1896), p. 389.

35. "Claverhouse," pp. 26–27; *Notes and Queries*, 7th Series, IX (March 8, 1890), p. 186.
36. H. Neville, *A Corner in the North*, Newcastle, 1909, p. 96.
37. Ibid., p. 107.
38. Ibid., pp. 107–8.
39. J. Barnes, *Observations on Clandestine or Irregular Marriages with a Short Account of the Laws, Both of England and Scotland*, Berwick, 1812; *27th Annual Registrar General's Report*, 1866, p. vii; also *Monthly Chronicle of North Country Lore and Language*, June 1888, pp. 230, 320; *Notes and Queries*, 4th Series, X (August 10, 1872), p. 111. For runaway marriages as late as the 1920s, see *Notes and Queries*, 13th Series, 1926, p.
40. William Rhys Jones (Gwenith Gwyn), Manuscript 2593/24, Welsh Folk Museum.
41. William Rhys Jones, "A Besom Wedding in the Ceiriog Valley," *Folk-Lore*, XXXIX (1928), pp. 153–54.
42. T. Gwynn Jones, *Welsh Folklore and Folk Custom*, London, 1930, p. 185; William Rhys Jones, "Lore of Courtship and Marriage," Jones MSS 236, vol. 94, National Library of Wales. (Translation from Welsh by Miss Blodwen Evans.)
43. Jones, "Lore of Courtship and Marriage," fol. 95.
44. Jones, "Besom Wedding," p. 155.
45. Jones, "Lore of Courtship and Marriage," fol. 93.
46. Ibid., fol. 96.
47. Ibid.
48. Jones, "A Besom Wedding," p. 157.
49. Jones, "Lore of Courtship and Marriage," fol. 83.
50. Ibid., fol. 97.
51. Ibid., fol. 84.
52. Ibid., fol. 99.
53. Ibid., fol. 98; W. R. Jones, "Folklore of the Ceiriog Valley," no pagination, Jones MSS 244, National Library of Wales.
54. Cited in Jones, "Besom Wedding," p. 162; Elias Owen, *Some Old Stone Crosses in the Vale of Clywd*, London, 1886, p. 63.
55. Ifans, p. 201; Leonard T. Davies and A. Edwards, *Welsh Life in the Eighteenth Century*, London, 1939, p. 231.
56. *Notes and Queries*, 10th Series, IX (March 14, 1908), p. 201; IX (May 23, 1908), p. 416.
57. *Notes and Queries*, 11th Series, I (June 18, 1910), p. 485; J. S. Burn, *The Fleet Registers*, London, 1833, p. 100. Also Peter Linebaugh, "The Picaresque Proletarian in Eighteenth Century London," paper delivered at Rutgers University, New Jersey, May 1983.
58. Judith Walkowitz, *Prostitution and Victorian Society: Women, Class, and the State*, Cambridge, 1980, pp. 203–5.
59. Terry Coleman, *The Railway Navvies*, London, 1965, p. 22.
60. Ibid., pp. 181–96.
61. O. Anderson, "The Incidence of Civil Marriage in Victorian England and Wales," *Past and Present*, no. 69 (November 1975), pp. 66–71.
62. Enid Porter, *Cambridgeshire Customs and Folklore*, London, 1969, pp. 3–4; Henry R. Stiles, *Bundling: Its Origins, Progress and Decline in America*, privately printed, 1871, pp. 22–27, 76–77, 90ff., 139–40.

63. As used in the song, "Navvy on the Line," *A Touch on the Times: Songs of Social Change, 1770–1914*, ed. Roy Palmer, Harmondsworth, 1974, pp. 40–41.

64. Jones, "Besom Wedding," p. 163.

65. S. O. Addy, *Household Tales with other Traditional Remains, Collected in the Counties of York, Lincoln, Derby and Nottingham*, London, 1895, p. 102.

66. Ruth L. Tongue, *Somerset Folklore*, London, 1965, p. 143; J. Harvey Bloom, *Folk-Lore, Old Customs and Superstition in Shakespeare's Land*, London, 1929, p. 10.

67. Robert Roberts, *The Classic Slum: Salford Life in the First Quarter of the Century*, Harmondsworth, 1973, p. 47. My informant on the current language of South Yorkshire is Professor Robin Fox.

68. *Notes and Queries*, 5th Series, V (March 4, 1876), p. 186.

69. Addy, p. 122.

70. "Claverhouse," p. 135; J. S. Burn, *History of the Parish Registers in England* 2nd ed., London, 1862, p. 154; *Notes and Queries*, 2nd Series, X (October 13, 1860), p. 290.

71. Testimony in a bigamy case, heard in the Central Criminal Court of London in 1850, *Old Bailey Sessions Papers*, June 14, 1850.

72. Coke, n.p.

73. C. S. Burne, *Shropshire Folklore: A Sheaf of Gleanings*, London, 1883–86, p. 295.

74. A "grass widow" was used to indicate either a wife separated from her husband or an unwed mother. *Cupid's Pupils: From Courtship to Honeymoon: Being the Recollections of a Parish Clerk*, London, 1899, p. 59.

75. Autobiographical account in *Working Women and Divorce: An Account of Evidence Given on Behalf of the Women's Cooperative Guild before the Royal Commission on Divorce*, London, 1911, p. 63.

76. M. D. George, *London in the Eighteenth Century*, London, 1925, p. 199.

77. Communication from Georg von Bunsen, published in *Zeitschrift für Ethnologie*, XIX (1887), p. 376.

78. *Notes and Queries*, 9th Series, IV (September 30, 1899), p. 266.

79. Henry Mayhew, *London Labour and the London Poor*, I, London, 1861–62, pp. 20, 475.

80. Ibid., pp. 27, 42.

81. Ibid., pp. 36, 45.

82. Ibid., pp. 177, 370.

83. Quoted in Ivy Pinchbeck, *Women Workers and the Industrial Revolution, 1750–1850*, New York, 1930, p. 285.

84. Lynn Hollen Lees, *Exiles of Erin: Irish Migrants in Victorian London*, Ithaca, 1979, p. 152.

85. *Report of His Majesty's Commissioners for Inquire into the Poor Laws*, 1834, p. 99.

86. G. R. W. Baxter, *Book of the Bastilles*, London, 1841, p. 571.

87. The story of Blind Dick is told by D. Parry Jones, *My Own Folk*, Llandysil, 1970, p. 119; also Ivor Winters, *Chepstow Parish Records*, Chepstow, 1955, p. 57.

88. *The Rector and His Flock: Francis Fulford*, Blassingbourn, 1980, p. 32.

89. Records Relating to the Population Act 1811, Add MS 6896, fols. 71, 95, 114.

90. William Rhys Jones, "Living Tally," MS 2593/24, Welsh Folk Museum; *Notes*

and Queries, 7th Series, X (September 20, 1890), pp. 229, 297; Jones "Besom Wedding," p. 184.

91. *English Dialect Dictionary*, VI, London, 1905, p. 24.
92. Anthea Newman, "An evaluation of bastardy recordings in an East Kent Parish," *Bastardy and its Comparative History*, eds. Peter Laslett, Karla Oosterveen, Richard M. Smith, Cambridge, 1980, pp. 141–56.
93. Jones, "Folk Lore of the Ceiriog Valley," Jones MSS 244, National Library of Wales, n.p.
94. Ibid., n.p.
95. Ibid.; Jones, "The Lore of Courtship and Marriage," fol. 83.
96. Jones, "Folk Lore of the Ceiriog Valley."
97. David Levine, *Family Formation in an Age of Nascent Capitalism*, New York, 1977, pp. 40–43.
98. Jones, "Folk Lore of the Ceiriog Valley," fol. 87.
99. G. N. Gandy, "Illegitimacy in a Handloom Weaving Community: Fertility Patterns in Culcheth, Lancashire, 1781–1860," unpublished D.Phil. dissertation, Oxford University, 1978, pp. 167–69.
100. Flora Thompson, *Lark Rise to Candleford*, Harmondsworth, 1974, pp. 138, 344.
101. A. C. Bickley, "Some Notes on a Custom at Woking, Surrey," *Home Counties Magazine*, IV (1902), pp. 25–29; Hill, p. 110.
102. Arthur Locke, *A Short History of Woking*, n.p. and n.d., Woking Library.
103. Bickley, p. 28.
104. Quoted in *Denham Tracts*, I, reprint edition, Nedelen, Lichtenstein, 1967, p. 21. On the practice of slanging neighboring communities, see John J. Scott, "A Description and preliminary discussion of the rhymed blason populaire tradition in England," *Lore and Language*, II, no. 2 (January 1975), pp. 9–22.
105. Bickley, p. 25.
106. Jones, "Folk Lore of the Ceiriog Valley," fol. 88.
107. Evidence concerning common-law marriages from the case records of the National Children's Home, case nos. 653, 654, 595. Archives of the National Children's Home, London.
108. Burne, p. 295.
109. *Byegones*, II (October 1874), p. 128.
110. *Working Women and Divorce*, p. 63.
111. Burne, p. 295.
112. G. R. Prynne, *Thirty-five Years of Mission Work in a Garrison and Seaport Town*, Plymouth, 1883, p. 15. My thanks to Judith Walkowitz for this reference.
113. Clippings relating to "leasing" found in box 12, Folklore Society Archive, University of London.
114. W. W. Bladon, "Notes on the Folk Lore of North Staffordshire, chiefly collected in Stone," *Transactions of the North Staffordshire Field Club*, XXV (1901), p. 155; T. Gwynn Jones, *Welsh Folklore and Folk-Customs*, London, 1930, p. 184. For evidence from bigamy trials, see records of cases before the Central Criminal Court of London, published as *Old Bailey Sessions Papers*.
115. *Birmingham Journal*, February 5, 1853.
116. *Notes and Queries*, 1st Series, VII (June 18, 1853), p. 603.
117. *Old Bailey Sessions Papers*, sampled every ten years, confirm this impression.

118. Steel, I, p. 325.

119. G. T. Lawley, "Wife Selling in Staffordshire," *Midland Weekly News*, January 6 and 13, 1894, no pagination. Cited henceforth as Lawley.

120. Keith Thomas, "The Double Standard," *Journal of the History of Ideas*, XX, no. 2 (1959), pp. 195–216. A general survey of wife sales is provided by Samuel Pyeatt Menefee, *Wives for Sale: An Ethnographic Study of British Popular Divorce*, New York, 1981. Menefee's study appeared after this chapter had been written and, for the most part, it confirms the argument offered here.

121. Lawley.

122. *Gloucestershire Notes and Queries*, III (1887), p. 675.

123. *Aris's Birmingham Gazette*, March 1, 1790; Lawley.

124. *Notes and Queries*, 3rd Series, IV (December 5, 1863), p. 450.

125. Lawley.

126. *Cambridgeshire Chronicle*, May 26, 1781, p. 3.

127. Ibid., May 15, 1852, p. 5.

128. Lawley.

129. *Sarah Farley's Bristol Journal*, July 11, 1784.

130. Sabine Baring-Gould, *Devonshire Characters and Strange Events*, London, 1908, p. 61.

131. Lawley.

132. F. W. Hackwood, *Staffordshire Customs, Superstitutions, and Folklore*, Wakefield, 1924, pp. 72–73.

133. W. H. Howse, *Radnorshire*, Herefore, 1949, pp. 217–18.

134. Lawley.

135. For a report of "luck money" in a wife sale, see the instance at Barton on Humber, March 12, 1847. I owe this reference to the kindness of Mr. Rex C. Russell. Also see Palmer, pp. 196–98.

136. Lawley.

137. Case in South Wales, 1882. *Notes and Queries*, 6th Series, V (August 19, 1882), p. 152.

138. Howse, p. 218.

139. *Notes and Queries*, 6th Series, IV (August 13, 1881), p. 133.

140. Baring-Gould, pp. 59–60.

141. *Notes and Queries*, 6th Series, V (February 4, 1882), p. 98.

142. This happened in 1812. William Fleming, "A Furness Diary," *The Countryman*, LV, no. 3 (1958), p. 428.

143. Hackwood, pp. 72–73.

144. W. H. Thorton, "Devonshire Matrimonial Market," *Devon Notes and Queries*, IV (1907), pp. 54–55.

145. *Papers and Reports Read before the Halifax Antiquarian Society*, II (1904–5), p. 4 *Notes and Queries*, III (June 20, 1863), p. 486.

146. This happened in Lancashire in 1870. *Notes and Queries*, 4th Series, VI (November 26, 1870), p. 455.

147. Ibid., 6th Series, V (February 4, 1882), p. 98.

148. *Cambridgeshire Chronicle*, May 15, 1852, p. 5.

149. Case in Croyden, 1815. E. R. Yarham, "Wives to Market," *The Amateur Historian*, VI, no. 5 (1963), p. 189.

150. Boston Quarter Sessions, February 12, 1819. My thanks to Rex C. Russell for this case.

151. Cited in Pinchbeck, p. 311.
152. *Notes and Queries*, 6th Series, III (June 18, 1881), p. 487.
153. Ibid., 4th Series, X (October 5, 1872), p. 271.
154. Baring-Gould, pp. 63, 69.
155. Spilsby evidence provided by Rex C. Russell.
156. For the case of a couple married in 1802 and separated by sale in 1827, see William Andrews, *Curiosities of the Church*, London, 1890, p. 159; also *Notes and Queries*, 3rd Series, IV (December 5, 1863), p. 450.
157. From the 1870s, in West Norfolk, *Folk-Lore*, 50 (1939), p. 72.
158. Menefee, especially chapters iv–vi.
159. B. Frith, ed., *Marriage Allegations in the Diocese of Gloucester, 1681–1700*, II, Publication of Bristol and Gloucester Archeological Society, n.p. and n.d., pp. x–xv.
160. Newman, p. 151.
161. If the whole life cycle is taken into account, the total incidence of of common-law arrangements of one kind or another would be much higher than the incidence at any one point in time.
162. Anon., "The Marriage Ceremony," *Nottingham Review*, May 16, 1843, p. 4.
163. *The Crisis*, May 24, 1834 and July 12, 1834; *New Moral World*, November 15, 1834.
164. "Marriage Ceremony."
165. Harrison, pp. 15ff.
166. Harrison, pp. 22, 28. See also E. D. Andrews, *The People Called Shakers*, New York, 1953, pp. 12–16.
167. Harrison, pp. 166–67.
168. Ibid., p. 173
169. Ibid., p. 107
170. Ibid., pp. 98–99.
171. Ibid., p. 121.
172. Ibid., pp. 236–37.
173. Ibid., p. 253.
174. Ibid., pp. 140–48, 188–90.
175. J. Wilson and W. Ricketson, *Thomas Paine*, Boston, 1978, pp. 22, 28; Eric Foner, *Tom Paine and Revolutionary America*, New York, 1976, pp. 3, 16.
176. Thomas Paine, *Rights of Man*, ed. H. Collins, Harmondsworth, 1983, pp. 269–70.
177. Sheila Rowbotham, *Women, Resistance, and Revolution*, New York, 1974, pp. 44–46.
178. Taylor, pp. 81–82.
179. Edward P. Thompson, *Making of the English Working Class*, New York, 1966, p. 163.
180. Taylor, pp. 25, 32.
181. Ibid., p. 15.
182. Rowbotham, p. 45.
183. Craig Calhoun, *The Question of Class Struggle: Social Foundations of Popular Radicalism during the Industrial Revolution*, Chicago, 1982, pp. 105–15. Also Angus McLaren, *Birth Control in Nineteenth Century England*, New York, 1978, chapter iii; and Thomas Laqueur, "The Queen Caroline Affair: Politics as Art in the Reign of George IV," *Journal of Modern History*, 54, no. 3 (September 1982), pp. 417–66.

184. Quoted in Taylor, p. 34.

185. Ibid., p. 39.

186. Ibid., pp. 39–40.

187. Ibid., p. 48.

188. Ibid., p. ix.

189. Quoted in Taylor, p. 53.

190. *Crisis*, May 18, 1833; also Robert Owen, *Lectures on the Marriages of the Priesthood of the Old Immoral World*, 4th ed., Leeds, 1840, pp. 88–89.

191. Taylor, p. 54.

192. Ibid., pp. 255–57 and chapter viii, passim.

193. Ibid., p. 245.

194. *Crisis*, January 4, 1834.

195. Taylor, p. 191.

196. Ibid., p. 213.

197. Ibid., p. 214.

198. Ibid., p. 213.

199. Ibid., p. 224.

200. Eileen Yeo, "Robert Owen and Radical Culture," *Robert Owen: Prophet of the Poor*, eds. S. Pollard and J. Salt, London, 1971, p. 98.

201. Raymond Lee Muncy, *Sex and Marriage in Utopian Communities*, Bloomington, 1973, p. 58.

202. *New Moral World*, March 29, 1845; Taylor, pp. 209–10; Yeo, pp. 100–101.

203. Taylor, p. 225.

204. *New Moral World*, March 9, 1839, cited in Taylor, p. 198.

205. William Lovett, *Life and Struggles of William Lovett, in His Pursuit of Bread, Knowledge and Freedom*, London, 1967, p. 41.

206. Taylor, chapter ix.

Chapter 8

1. Robert Roberts, *The Classic Slum: Salford Life in the First Quarter of the Century*, Harmondsworth, 1973, p. 47.

2. From William Rhys Jones (Gwenith Gwyn), Manuscripts 2593/4, Welsh Folk Museum; also Roberts, p. 23.

3. On middle-class views of marriage and sensuality, see Peter Gay, *Education of the Senses: The Bourgeois Experience, Victoria to Freud*, New York, 1984, pp. 109–33; on illegitimacy, see Peter Laslett, *Family Life and illicit love in earlier generations*, Cambridge, 1977, p. 113.

4. William Rhys Jones, "Besom Wedding in the Ceiriog Valley," *Folk-Lore*, LXXXVII (1928), p. 156; George Gandy, "Illegitimacy in a Handloom Weaving Community: Fertility Patterns in Culcheth, Lancashire, 1781–1860," unpublished D.Phil. thesis, Oxford University, 1978, pp. 412–414; Barbara Taylor, *Eve and the New Jerusalem: Socialism and Feminism in the Nineteenth Century*, New York, 1983, p. 205.

5. Charles Booth, *Life and Labour of the People of London: Religious Influences*, I, London, 1902, p. 55; also Booth Collection, Series A, vol. 23, fol. 13, London School of Economics.

6. Booth, p. 55.

7. Olive Anderson, "Incidence of Civil Marriage in Victorian England and

Wales," *Past & Present*, 69 (November 1975), pp. 71–87; *69th Annual Registrar General's Report*, 1906; *71st Annual Registrar General's Report*, 1908.

8. David C. Marsh, *The Changing Social Structure of England and Wales, 1871–1971*, London, 1965, pp. 34–35; *Royal Commission on Population: Report*, London, 1964, pp. 46–47; F. Musgrove, *Youth and the Social Order*, London, 1964, pp. 78–81.

9. Mill, *The Subjection of Women*, and Tennyson, *The Princess*, both cited in Walter E. Houghton, *The Victorian Frame of Mind, 1830–1870*, New Haven, 1957, pp. 342, 349.

10. Evidence from Mr. A. Blott, representative of the Poor Man's Lawyer organization of London. Evidence of the Divorce Commission, *Parliamentary Papers*, XVIII (1912–13), p. 201.

11. Flora Thompson, *A Country Calendar and Other Writings*, Oxford, 1979, p. 193.

12. Music hall song by Marie Lofus, "Girls, We Would Never Stand It," quoted in Gareth Stedman Jones, "Working Class Culture and Working Class Politics in London, 1870–1900," *Journal of Social History*, VII, no. 4 (Summer 1974), p. 491.

13. On general demographic trends, see Angus McLaren, *Birth Control in Nineteenth Century England*, New York, 1978, pp. 215–28; and Richard A. Soloway, *Birth Control and the Population Question in England, 1877–1930*, Chapel Hill, 1982, chapter ii; J. A. Banks, *Prosperity and Parenthood: A Study of Family Planning among the Victorian Middle Classes*, London, 1954.

14. Archbishops Visitation Returns, 1905, MS 17895, Guildhall Library, London.

15. Ibid.

16. Ibid.

17. William Rhys Jones (Gwenith Gwyn), Manuscripts 2593/24, Welsh Folk Museum.

18. Divorce Commission, XVIII, p. 394.

19. On sailors' wives, see Booth Collection, A, XXII, fol. 12, London School of Economics; also police reports in Booth Collection, B346. Evidence by a West Ham bailiff to the Divorce Commission, XVIII, pp. 113–14.

20. Divorce Commission, XIX, pp. 26–28.

21. Anderson, pp. 71–77.

22. Quoted in Margaret Hewitt, *Wives and Mothers in Victorian Industry*, London, 1958, p. 55.

23. Reports on rough areas in Bromley, Bow, and Poplar, in Booth Collection A32, fol. 13, London School of Economics.

24. Booth, p. 46.

25. Reports to the National Relief Fund: Unmarried Wives Subcommittee, Violet Markham Papers, Section I, no. 12, London School of Economics.

26. National Children's Home, Case No. 3471.

27. C. Stella Davies, *North Country Bred: A Working Class Chronicle*, London, 1963, p. 153.

28. From Transcript 29, Paul Thompson and Thea Vigne, Family Life and Work Experience Before 1918, Oral History Archive, University of Essex. (Henceforth cited as Family Life and Work Experience Archive.)

29. Divorce Commission, XVIII, p. 41.

30. Booth Collection Parish Notes A, vol. 32, n.p., London School of Economics

31. Divorce Commission, XVIII, p. 63.

32. Ibid., p. 211.
33. Proceedings of the Central Criminal Court, London, October 19, 1880, *Old Bailey Sessions Papers.*
34. Ibid., June 13, 1860.
35. All is from the file of the Prince of Wales Fund for Unmarried Mothers, Violet Markham Papers, Section I, no. 13, London School of Economics. Most of these women were from Glasgow, where the Trades Union Council made a vigorous campaign on their behalf.
36. Laslett, pp. 112–20; Angus McLaren "Women's Work and Regulation of Family Size," *History Workshop Journal,* 4 (1977), pp. 72–79. References to suggested or attempted abortions begin to appear in the case records of the London Foundling Hospital only in the 1850s. For the particular case noted above, see Foundling Hosptial petition, 1889/83.
37. Foundling Hospital petition, 1889/78.
38. Winifred Foley, *Child in the Forest,* London, 1977, p. 253.
39. Report of the Commissioners of Inquiry for South Wales, *Parliamentary Papers,* XVI (1844) p. 177. They were farm workers in Harverfordwest.
40. The consciousness of homosexuality and a new homophobia is discussed by Jeffrey Weeks, *Coming Out: Homosexual Politics in Britain, from the Nineteenth Century to the Present,* London, 1977, part I.
41. On the effect of welfare policy on women, see Patricia Thane, "Women and the Poor Law in Victorian and Edwardian England," *History Workshop Journal,* VI (Autumn 1978), pp. 29–51; Jane Lewis, *The Politics of Motherhood: Child and Maternal Welfare in England, 1900–1939,* London, 1980, passim.
42. U. R. Q. Henriques, "Bastardy and the New Poor Law," *Past & Present,* 37 (July 1967), p. 111.
43. Annual Report of the Poor Law Commissioners of England and Wales, I (1835), p. 57; and VI (1840), pp. 175ff.
44. Anthea Newman, "An evaluation of bastardy records in an east Kent parish," *Bastardy and its Comparative History,* eds. Peter Laslett, Karla Oosterveen, Richard M. Smith, Cambridge, 1980, p. 151.
45. David Levine, *Family Formation in an Age of Nascent Capitalism,* New York, 1977, p. 134.
46. Carol C. Pearce, "Expanding Families: Some Aspects of Fertility in a mid-Victorian Community," *Local Population Studies,* 10 (Spring 1973), pp. 22–36; P. E. H. Hair, "Bridal Pregnancy in Rural England in Earlier Centuries," *Population Studies,* XX, part 2 (November 1966), pp. 233–44; Levine, p. 133–34.
47. Booth, Parish Notes A, vol. 32, n.p., London School of Economics.
48. See Appendix.
49. "My Grandfather's Days," song of the late 1830s, from Roy Palmer, *A Touch on the Times: Songs of Social Change,* Harmondsworth, 1974, pp. 83ff.
50. Foundling Hospital petition, 1896/11.
51. J. Brownlow, *Thoughts and Suggestions Having Reference to Infanticide,* London, 1864, p. 44.
52. Treatment of infanticide remained quite lenient throughout the eighteenth and much of the nineteenth century. R. W. Malcolmson, "Infanticide in the Eighteenth Century," *Crime in England, 1550–1800,* ed. J. S. Cockburn, London, 1977, pp. 187–206; and David Philips, *Crime and Authority in Vic-*

torian England: The Black Country, 1835–1860, London, 1977, p. 261. Mothers applying to the Foundling Hospital were twenty-four times more likely to have used the workhouse after 1850 than before.

53. Brownlow, p. 45; for earlier practices, see Keith Wrightson, "Infanticide in Early 17th Century England," *Local Population Studies*, XV (Autumn 1975), pp. 20–22.

54. Report from the Select Committee on the Protection of Infant Life, *Parliamentary Papers*, VII (1871), p. v.

55. Ibid., p. 12. From evidence of Dr. E. Hart before the Committee.

56. Lawrence Stone, *The Family, Sex and Marriage in England, 1500–1800*, New York, 1977, pp. 475–78. Leniency is evident in the infanticide trials surveyed in *Old Bailey Sessions Papers* during nineteenth century.

57. Louise Tilly and Joan Scott, *Women, Work and Family*, New York, 1978, pp. 151–52.

58. Mark Ebery and Brian Preston, *Domestic Service in Late Victorian and Edwardian England, 1871–1914*, Reading Geographical Papers, 42 (1976), pp. 17–19, 35ff.

59. Figures from Francois Bedarida, *A Social History of England, 1851–1975*, New York, 1979, p. 270; Ann Oakley, *Subject Women*, New York, 1981, pp. 145–47.

60. Quoted from Mrs. Gaskell's *Mary Barton*, in Neil McKendrick, "Home Demand and Economic Growth: A New View of the Role of Women and Children in the Industrial Revolution," *Historical Perspectives: Studies in Thought and Society in Honour of J. H. Plumb*, ed. N. McKendrick, London, 1974, p. 167.

61. Sally Alexander, "Women's Work in Nineteenth Century London: A Study of the Years 1820–50," *The Rights and Wrongs of Women*, Harmondsworth, 1977, pp. 93–97.

62. Ibid., pp. 80–83; *The Unknown Mayhew*, ed. E. P. Thompson and E. Yeo, New York, 1972, pp. 429ff; Taylor, pp. 101–9.

63. Alexander, pp. 81–82.

64. Taylor, p. 111.

65. *Unknown Mayhew*, pp. 169–70; Elizabeth Roberts, "Working Wives and Their Families," *Population and Society in Britain, 1890–1980*, ed. T. Barker and M. Drake, New York, 1982, pp. 143–51.

66. J. G. Gillis, *Youth and History: Continuity and Change in European Age Relations, 1770–Present*, New York, 1974, pp. 122–28.

67. *Unknown Mayhew*, p. 412.

68. Ebery and Preston, chapter ii; for domestic servants, see Eric Richards, "Women in the British Economy since about 1700: An Interpretation," *History*, 29 (October 1974), pp. 347–48; Leonore Davidoff, "Mastered for Life: Servant and Wife in Victorian and Edwardian England," *Journal of Social History*, 7 (1974), pp. 406–22; Theresa M. McBride, *The Domestic Revolution: The Modernization of Household Service in England and France, 1820–1920*, London, 1976, passim; Pamela Horn, *The Rise and Fall of the Victorian Servant*, New York, 1975; Frank E. Huggett, *Life Below Stairs*, New York, 1977; John Burnett, *Useful Toil*, London, 1974, pp. 164–67.

69. The subject of domestic service and sexual relations is treated at length in John Gillis, "Servants, Sexual Relations, and the Risks of Illegitimacy in London, 1801–1900," *Feminist Studies*, V, no. 1 (Spring 1979), pp. 142–73.

70. Quoted in Phyllis Cunningham, *Costume of Household Servants from the Middle Ages to 1900*, London, 1974, p. 128.
71. Francis Sheppard, *London 1808–1870: The Infernal Wen*, Berkeley, 1971, p. 372.
72. Flora Thompson, *Lark Rise to Candleford*, Harmondsworth, 1974, p. 139.
73. Foley, p. 222.
74. Paul Thompson, *The Edwardians: The Remaking of British Society*, Bloomington, 1975, pp. 100ff.; Huggett, pp. 65ff.; Davidoff, passim.
75. Booth, *Life and Labour*, 2nd Series, IV, pp. 214ff.; Anderson, p. 131; Gillis, *Youth and History*, p. 124.
76. Anderson, p. 131.
77. Richards, pp. 346ff.; E. Roberts, pp. 145–46.
78. Tilly and Scott, chapters iv–vi.
79. Gillis, *Youth and History*, pp. 118–31.
80. Anna Davin, "Imperialism and Motherhood," *History Workshop Journal*, V (Spring 1978), pp. 32ff.; also Davin, " 'A Centre of Humanizing Influence': The Schooling of Working Class Girls under the London School Board (1870–1902)," unpublished paper, given at Social History Seminar, Rutgers University, 1981, passim.
81. Ebery and Preston, p. 17.
82. Peter N. Stearns, "Working Class Women in Britain, 1890–1914," *Suffer and Be Still*, ed. M. Vicinus, Bloomington, 1972, pp. 100–20; Lynn Lees, "Getting and Spending: The Family Budgets of English Industrial Workers in 1890," *Consciousness and Class Experience in Nineteenth Century Europe*, ed. J. Merriman, New York, 1979, pp. 173–83.
83. Davin, "Imperialism and Motherhood," pp. 13–15, 33–36.
84. This is based on my forthcoming analysis of the case records of the National Children's Home, London.
85. Records of the National Children's Home, Case no. 3808.
86. National Children's Home, Case No. 5462.
87. National Children's Home, Case No. 4004.
88. Geoffrey Crossick, "Social Structure and Working Class Behavior: Kentish London, 1840–1880," unpublished D.Phil. thesis, University of London, 1976, pp. 122ff.; D. B. Viles "The Building Trades in London, 1835–60," unpublished D.Phil. thesis, University of London, 1975, pp. 30ff.
89. Crossick, pp. 110–20.
90. Foundling Hospital petitions, 1841/143, 1861/103.
91. Crossick, pp. 199–225; also Brian Preston, *Occupations of Father and Son in Mid-Victorian England*, Reading Geographical Papers, no. 56, 1977, pp. 16ff.
92. Report of Police Concerning Hackney Wick, Booth Collection, Series B346, fol. 70, London School of Economics; Gillis, *Youth and History*, pp. 122ff.
93. Ellen Ross, " 'Fierce Questions and Taunts': Married Life in Working-Class London, 1870–1914," *Feminist Studies*, VIII, no. 3 (Fall 1982), pp. 585ff.
94. Evidence given to Divorce Commission, *Parliamentary Papers*, XVIII (1912–13), p. 14. On the conditions of marriage in a south London working-class community, see Maud Pember Reeves, *Round about a Pound a Week*, rev. ed., London, 1979, chapter xi.
95. Francis Place Papers, Add MS 27825, fols. 75, 145, British Museum.
96. *The Autobiography of Francis Place*, ed. Mary Thrale, Cambridge, 1972, p. 116.
97. Divorce Commission, p. 386.
98. R. Roberts, pp. 14–31.

99. Foley, p. 46.
100. B. Seebohm Rowntree, *Poverty: A Study of Town Life*, London, 1914, p. 171.
101. Ellen Ross, "Survival Networks: Women's Neighbourhood Sharing in London before World War One," *History Workshop Journal*, 15 (Spring 1983), pp. 4–27.
102. Anderson, pp. 53–56; Ross, "Survival Networks," p. 9, 14–15.
103. Ibid., p. 7.
104. R. Roberts, pp. 93–94.
105. Ross, "Survival Networks," pp. 10–11.
106. R. Roberts, pp. 53–54.
107. Fred Willis, quoted in G. S. Jones, "Working Class Culture," p. 486.
108. Mrs. A1P, fol. 52, Roberts Collection.
109. Ross, "Fierce Questions," p. 581.
110. Ibid., p. 582.
111. Nancy Tomes, "A 'Torrent of Abuse': Crimes of Violence between Working-Class Men and Women in London, 1840–1875," *Journal of Social History*, XI no. 3 (Spring 1978), pp. 330–34; R. Roberts, p. 56.
112. M. Loane, *From Their Point of View*, London, 1908, p. 34.
113. Lady Bell, *At the Works: A Study of a Manufacturing Town*, London, 1907, p. 115; Loane, p. 33.
114. Divorce Commission, pp. 292–94, 394.
115. R. E. Moore of the Poor Man's Lawyer organization, Divorce Commission, pp. 72, 201.
116. Transcript nos. 96, 292, Family Life and Work Experience Archive; E. Roberts, pp. 147–48.
117. Tilly and Scott, chapter vi; G. S. Jones, "Working Class Culture," pp. 485–91; E. Roberts, pp. 147–48.
118. Quoted in M. Anderson, *Family Structure in Nineteenth Century Lancashire*, Cambridge, 1971, p. 77; see also Carol Dyhouse, *Girls Growing Up in Late Victorian and Edwardian Britain*, London, 1981, pp. 5, 31–32.
119. National Children's Home, Case No. 4740a; a similar situation found in Foundling Hospital petition 1879/12.
120. National Children's Home, Case No. 4821a.
121. A Davin, "Imperialism," p. 53. See R. Soloway on the revival of fears about the stability of the family, especially pages 146–49.
122. C. Penswick Smith, *Revival of Mothering Sunday*, Nottingham, 1921, pp. 46–78.
123. Hymn is quoted in full in Vivien P. Warren, "Some Aspects of Mothering Sunday: With Particular Reference to Nottingham," unpublished M.A. thesis, University of Leeds, 1966, p. 28, Library of Institute of Dialect and Folk Life Studies.
124. Church-sponsored Mothering Sundays declined in the 1930s and revived again in the 1950s, this time with the aid of commercial greeting card companies. In the 1960s older people still spoke of Mothering Sunday, but younger generations now knew it as Mother's Day, apparently a postwar American importation. Research undertaken by the students at the Institute of Dialect and Folk Life Studies at Leeds found women most involved with honoring mothers. They also discovered a certain resentment about the commercialization of the occasion. See Warren, pp. 29ff.; also Peter Gregson, "The Observance of Mothering Sunday," unpublished B. A. thesis, Leeds University, 1966, pp. 22ff., Institute of Dialect and Folk Life Studies.

125. Broadsides of these songs found in Baring-Gould Collection, LR 27a2, II, fols. 231ff., British Museum.
126. "It's Naughty but It's Nice," Ibid., VII, fol. 115.
127. "Sweet Temper'd Wife," ibid., II, fol. 230.
128. Palmer, pp. 150–52; M. Anderson, pp. 70ff.; Dyhouse, p. 31.
129. Recollections of Older People, Essex Record Office, nos. 25/585, 25/248.
130. Ross, "Fierce Questions," pp. 578ff.
131. Comment by a woman contributing to *Working Women and Divorce: An Account of Evidence Given on Behalf of the Women's Cooperative Guild before the Royal Commission on Divorce*, London, 1911, p. 27.
132. M. Anderson, pp. 56, 126–28; P. Willmott and M. Young, *Family and Kinship in East London*, Harmondsworth, 1954, pp. 104–18; R. Roberts, passim.
133. Foundling Hospital petition, 1866/250.
134. Quote from Alexander Paterson, *Across the Bridges*, London, 1911, pp. 210–11. On the difference between the kind of sentimental "momism" that is current today and the kind of substantial matrifocality found in other times and places, see Nancy Turner, "Matrifocality in Indonesia, Africa, and among Black Americans," *Women, Culture, and Society*, eds. Michelle Zimbalist Rosaldo and Louise Lamphere, Stanford, 1974, pp. 132–33.
135. Transcript no. 213, Family Life and Work Experience Archive.
136. Foundling Hospital petition 1868/237.
137. Foundling Hospital petition 1884/83.
138. Foundling Hospital petitions 1886/11, 1885/66.
139. Foundling Hospital petition 1870/11.
140. Booth Collection A, XXXII, Report on Poplar.
141. Foundling Hospital petition 1884/94.
142. Foundling Hospital petition 1884/69.
143. Booth, *Life and Labour: Religious Influences*, p. 56.
144. For cases of ostracism, see Foundling Hospital petitions, 1856/167, 1861/103, 1864/198.
145. National Children's Home, Case No. 2707.
146. Foundling Hospital petition 1874/62.
147. Foundling Hospital petitions 1878/94, 1884/8.
148. Foundling Hospital petition 1896/11.
149. Foundling Hospital petition 1854/47.
150. Foundling Hospital petition 1871/136.
151. Foundling Hospital petition 1874/77.
152. Foundling Hospital petitions 1886/52, 1888/113.
153. Ivy Pinchbeck and Margaret Hewitt, *Children in English Society*, II London, 1973, pp. 582–610.
154. Michael Young and Peter Willmott, *Family and Kinship in East London*, Harmondsworth, 1962, part I.
155. Richard Hoggart, *The Uses of Literacy*, Harmondsworth, 1958, pp. 33–34.
156. Ibid., p. 31.

Chapter 9

1. Jonathan Raban, *Soft City*, London, 1974, p. 160.
2. Robert Bocock, *Ritual in Industrial Society: A Sociological Analysis of Ritualism in Modern England*, London, 1974, pp. 47–48; Sally F. Moore and Bar-

bara G. Myerhoff, "Introduction: Secular Ritual: Forms and Meanings," *Secular Ritual*, eds. S. F. Moore and B. G. Myerhoff, Assen/Amsterdam, 1977, p. 24.

3. See John R. Gillis, *Youth and History: Tradition and Change in European Age Relations, 1770–Present*, New York, 1974, chapters iii and iv.

4. Gillis, pp. 118–28; Peter Stearns, "Working-Class Women in Britain, 1890–1914," *Suffer and Be Still*, ed. M. Vicinus, Bloomington, 1973, pp. 101–5, 109–12.

5. Gillis, p. 152.

6. From old people's memoirs, collected at Essex Record Office nos. T/2 25/248, T/2 25/336, T/2 25/401.

7. Quoted in Standish Meacham, *A Life Apart: The English Working Class 1890–1914*, London, 1977, p. 176.

8. From Transcript 51, Paul Thompson and Thea Vigne, Family Life and Work Experience Before 1918, Oral History Archive, University of Essex. (Henceforth cited as Family Life and Work Experience Archive.)

9. Transcript 232, Family Life and Work Experience Archive.

10. Mrs. O1P, Elizabeth Roberts Collection, Lancaster University. (Henceforth cited as Roberts Collection.)

11. H. W. Harwood, "As Things Wer: A Social History of the Upper Calder Valley," *Transactions of the Halifax Antiquarian Society*, 1968, p. 23.

12. *The Times of Our Lives*, London, 1983, p. 148; Transcript 302, Family Life and Work Experience Archive.

13. *The Times of Our Lives*, p. 148; Transcript 320, Family Life and Life Experience Archive.

14. Transcript 279, Family Life and Work Experience Archive. Robert Roberts noted that Salford residents were very aware of the potential for incest when a daughter took over her mother's position. Robert Roberts, *The Classic Slum: Salford Life in the First Quarter of* the Century, Harmondsworth, 1973, p. 44.

15. Transcript 16, Family Life and Work Experience Archive.

16. Transcript 348, Family Life and Work Experience Archive.

17. Transcript 125, Family Life and Work Experience Archive.

18. Transcript 25 and 90, Family Life and Work Experience Archive.

19. Michael Young and Peter Willmott, *Family and Kinship in East London*, Harmondsworth, 1954, p. 40; Richard Hoggart, *Uses of Literacy*, Harmondsworth, 1975, pp. 51–52.

20. M. Kerr, *The People of Ship Street*, London, 1958, p. 44.

21. Mrs. B1B, fol. 24, Roberts Collection.

22. Mrs. B2P, fol. 11, Roberts Collection.

23. Transcript 362, Family Life and Work Experience Archive.

24. Mr. F1P, fol. 9, Roberts Collection; Transcript 29, Family Life and Work Experience Archive.

25. Mrs. B1P, fol. 9, Roberts Collection.

26. Mr. D2P, fol. 47, Roberts Collection.

27. Mr. B8P, fol. 11, Roberts Collection.

28. Transcript 178, Family Life and Work Experience Archive. For other cases of middle-class control, see Transcript 13 and Mr. B7P, Roberts Collection.

29. Transcript 337, Family Life and Work Experience Archive.

30. *Times of Our Lives*, p. 149.

31. Transcript 85, Family Life and Work Experience Archive.
32. Roberts, *Classic Slum*, fol. 42.
33. Ibid., p. 42.
34. Ibid., p. 44.
35. Stephen Humphries, *Hooligans or Rebels?: An Oral History of Working Class Childhood and Youth, 1889–1930*, Oxford, 1981, chapters ii-iv; Gillis, p. 120.
36. Roberts, *Classic Slum*, p. 44.
37. Mrs. D1P, fol. 16, Roberts Collection.
38. Roberts, *Classic Slum*, p. 47; for more on gossip, see Mrs. A1P, fol. 38, Roberts Collection; and Flora Thompson, *Lark Rise to Candleford*, Harmondsworth, 1974, p. 487.
39. Transcript 38, Family Life and Work Experience Archive; B. Spinley, *The Deprived and the Privileged: Personality Development in English Society*, London, 1953, p. 77.
41. Transcript 317, Family Life and Work Experience Archive.
42. C. E. B. Russell and Lilian M. Rigby, *Working Lads' Clubs*, London, 1908, p. 266; Transcript 350, Family Life and Work Experience Archive.
43. Transcript 313, Family Life and Work Experience Archive; Mr. B1B, p. 92, Roberts Collection.
44. On the rituals of rebellion, see Victor Turner, *The Ritual Process: Structure and Anti-Structure*, Chicago, 1969, p. 179.
45. R. Roberts, *Ragged Schooling*, London, 1978, p. 182.
46. Peter Willmott, *Adolescent Boys of East London*, Harmondsworth, 1969, pp. 52–53; R. Hoggart, *Uses of Literacy*, Harmondsworth, 1969, pp. 51–52.
47. Gillis, pp. 95–118.
48. F. Thompson, p. 340; Fred Mercer, "Edwardian Preston," p. 79–82, Roberts Collection.
49. Mrs. C5P, fol. 29, Roberts Collection.
50. Meacham, p. 66. Based on Transcripts 39, 51, 162, Family Life and Work Experience Archive.
51. Reginald Bray, quoted in Meacham, p. 160; P. Thompson, *The Edwardians: The Remaking of British Society*, Bloomington, 1975, p. 61.
52. P. Thompson, p. 61. On breeching, see George Ewart Evans, *From Mouths of of Men*, London, 1976, pp. 100–104.
53. Elizabeth Roberts, "Learning and Living—Socialization outside School," *Oral History*, III, no. 2 (Autumn 1975), p. 16; F. Thompson, p. 152.
54. Derek Thompson, "Courtship and Marriage in Preston between the Wars," *Oral History*, III, no. 2 (Autumn 1975), p. 39; Meacham, pp. 160–61; P. Thompson, pp. 64–65.
55. Roberts, *Ragged Schooling*, pp. 51, 161; Charles Booth Collection A, vol. 35, fol. 5, London School of Economics.
56. Roberts, *Classic Slum*, pp. 54–55.
57. Roberts, *Ragged Schooling*, pp. 161–62.
58. For a mining community in the 1950s, see Norman Dennis, F. Henriques, and C. Slaughter, *Coal Is Our Life*, London, 1956, pp. 221–25.
59. Roberts, *Ragged Schooling*, p. 162; Humphries, pp. 136–37.
60. Roberts, *Classic Slum*, p. 155.
61. Ibid., p. 156.
62. Humphries, p. 190; Gillis, p. 62.
63. Humphries, p. 191.

64. Geoffrey Pearson, *Hooligan: A History at Respectable Fears*, New York, 1984, chapters ii and iii.
65. P. Thompson, p. 65.
66. Meacham, 192; Humphries, p. 137.
67. Folk Life file E4, Acc 797, Institute of Dialect and Folk Life Studies, Leeds University.
68. Booth Collection A, vol. 33, London School of Economics.
69. D. Thompson, p. 39.
70. *Notes and Queries*, 13th Series, CLXVI (April 7, 1934), p. 241; CLXVI (April 21, 1934), p. 283.
71. C. E. B. Russell, *Manchester Boys*, Manchester, 1905, pp. 115–16.
72. Humphries, pp. 136–37.
73. Mr. F1P, fol. 34, Roberts Collection.
74. D. Thompson, p. 42.
75. Ibid., p. 43.
76. Ibid., p. 44.
77. Thompson, pp. 69–70.
78. Humphries, p. 140.
79. M. Sterner, "Folklore of Worsly, Lancashire," unpublished paper, Leeds University, 1975, Library Institute of Dialect and Folk Life, EII Cj.
80. Booth Collection, vol. A36, London School of Economics.
81. D. Thompson, p. 41.
82. Humphries, p. 140.
83. Mr. F1P, fol. 34, Roberts Collection.
84. Transcript 346, Family Life and Work Experience Archive.
85. Mrs. F1P, fol. 41, Roberts Collection.
86. D. Thompson, p. 42.
87. Frances Rust, *Dance in Society*, London, 1969, pp. 80–96.
88. Kerr, p. 207.
89. W. Somerset Maugham, *Liza of Lambeth*, New York, pp. 114–15.
90. Willmott, p. 43.
91. Ibid., p. 95.
92. Brian Jackson, *Working Class Community*, London, 1968, p. 157.
93. D. Thompson, p. 42; Willmott, pp. 51–58.
94. Roberts, *Ragged Schooling*, p. 162.
95. Mr. F1P, fol. 12, Roberts Collection.
96. Roberts, *Classic Slum*, p. 57.
97. Humphries, p. 136.
98. Judith Walkowitz, *Prostitution and Victorian Society*, Cambridge, 1980, pp. 244–45; Sally Alexander, *St. Giles's Fair: Popular Culture and the Industrial Revolution in 19th Century Oxford*, Oxford, 1969; Edward J. Bristow, *Vice and Vigilance: Purity Movements in Britain since 1700*, London, 1977, part iii.
99. Gillis, p. 148.
100. Mrs. W4P, fol. 12, Roberts Collection.
101. Humphries, p. 140.
102. Mr. F1P, fol. 80, Roberts Collection.
103. D. Thompson, p. 43.
104. Peter Laslett, Karla Oosterveen, and R. W. Smith, *Bastardy and Its Comparative History*, Cambridge, 1980, pp. 17–18; Rachel Pierce, "Marriage in

the Fifties," *Sociological Review*, NS, no. 11, 1963, p. 221; Eustace Chesser, *Women: A Popular Edition of the Chesser Report*, London, 1958, p. 91; Robert Leete, *Changing Patterns of Family Formation and Dissolution in England and Wales, 1964–76*, London, 1979, pp. 38–40. On premarital pregnancy rates, see P. E. H. Hair, "Bridal Pregnancy in Rural England in Earlier Centuries," *Population Studies*, XX, part 2 (November 1966), p. 236.

105. Willmott, pp. 54, 58.
106. Roberts, *Ragged School*, pp. 85–86; Jeffrey Weeks, *Coming Out: Homosexual Politics in Britain, from the Nineteenth Century to the Present*, London, 1979, pp. 39–40; Gillis, pp. 113–14.
107. Roberts, *Ragged Schooling*, p. 162.
108. Walter Greenwood, *Love on the Dole*, Garden City, 1934, p. 41.
109. Dennis, Henriques, and Slaughter, p. 231; on romantic literature, see Jacqueline Sarsby, *Romantic Love and Society*, Harmondsworth, 1983, chapter V.
110. Roberts, *Ragged Schooling*, p. 182.
111. Spinley, p. 87.
112. F. Thompson, p. 486; Humphries, p. 137.
113. Geoffrey Gorer, *Exploring English Character*, London, 1955, pp. 84–85.
114. Flora Thompson recounts the story of two old men living together who were subject to vicious attacks, p. 498. On the harassment of old maids, see Roberts, *Ragged Schooling*, p. 81. On the homophobia of the time, see Weeks, chapters i–iii.
115. This was the way Bethnal Green boys of the 1950s talked about their engagements. Willmott, pp. 43–53; also Transcript 302, Family Life and Work Experience Archive; Bill Williamson, *Class Culture and Community*, London, 1982, p. 145.
116. Transcript 302, Family Life and Work Experience Archive; Elizabeth Laverack, *With This Ring: 100 Years of Marriage*, London, 1979, p. 32.
117. Ibid., p. 32.
118. Transcript 360, Family Life and Work Experience Archive.
119. Transcript 350, Family Life and Work Experience Archive.
120. *Times of Our Lives*, p. 151.
121. Matrimonial Survey, 1947, Mass Observation Archive, Sussex University. (Henceforth Matrimonial Survey, 1947.)
122. Transcript 90, Family Life and Work Experience Archive.
123. Transcript 253, Family Life and Work Experience Archive.
124. Transcript 274, Family Life and Work Experience Archive.
125. Transcript 218, Family Life and Work Experience Archive.
126. Pilot Questionnaire, 1947, Family Planning 3C, Mass Observation Archive.
127. C. Stella Davies, *North Country Bred: A Working Class Chronicle*, London, 1963, p. 144.
128. Mr. B7P, fols. 33–34, Roberts Collection.
129. Transcript 348, Family Life and Work Experience Archive.
130. *Times of Our Lives*, pp. 148, 152.
131. Lorraine Barler, "A Study of Certain Marriage Customs, 1974–75," unpublished paper, p. 43, Institute of Dialect and Folk Life Studies, Leeds University.
132. Ibid., p. 45.

133. Transcript 348, Family Life and Work Experience Archive.
134. L. Warren, "Birth, Marriage, Death," unpublished M.A. thesis, Leeds University, 1967, p. 26; also Barler, pp. 40ff., 50–53, 67; *Maternity: Letters from Working Women*, ed. M. L. Davies, New York, 1978, p. 24.
135. Gorer, pp. 95–97.
136. Ibid., p. 98.
137. Ibid., pp. 94, 104, 111.
138. Ibid., p. 99.
139. Ibid., pp. 94–116; Laslett, Oosterveen, and Smith, pp. 16–19; Karen Dunnell, *Family Formation 1976*, London, 1979 pp. 6–7, 50–59; Michael Schofield, *The Sexual Behavior of Young People*, Harmondsworth, 1968, part II.
140. Greenwood, p. 41.
141. Roberts, *Ragged Schooling*, p. 162.
142. Mr. F1P, fol. 80, Roberts Collection.
143. Willmott and Young, *Family and Kinship*, pp. 70–73.
144. Transcript 2, Family Life and Work Experience Archive; and Matrimonial Survey, 1947.
145. Transcript 10, Family Life and Work Experience Archive.
146. Comment by male, age 44, Pilot Questionnaire, 1947.
147. Transcript 51, Family Life and Work Experience Archive.
148. Transcript 40, Family Life and Work Experience Archive.
149. Willmott and Young, pp. 44–61.
150. Transcript 383, Family Life and Work Experience Archive.
151. Transcript 134, Family Life and Work Experience Archive.
152. Mrs. B1P, no pagination, Roberts Collection.
153. Kerr, p. 41.
154. Transcript 85, Family Life and Work Experience Archive.
155. Roberts, *Classic Slum*, p. 57.
156. Dennis, Henriques, and Slaughter, pp. 222–23; Jackson, p. 157.

Chapter 10

1. On the invention of "tradition," see Eric Hobsbawm and Terence Ranger, eds, *The Invention of Tradition*, Cambridge, 1983; also Leonore Davidoff, Jean L'Esperance, and Howard Newby, "Landscape with Figures: Home and Community in English Society," *Rights and Wrongs of Women*, ed. Juliet Mitchell and Ann Oakley, Harmondsworth, 1971, pp. 139–175; David Cannadine, "The Transformation of Civic Ritual in Modern Britain," *Past & Present*, 94 (1982), pp. 107–30.
2. *Notes and Queries*, 8th Series, IX (May 23, 1896), p. 406; IX (June 13, 1896), p. 475; X (July 18, 1896), p. 59; X (August 8, 1896), p. 126.
3. Ibid., 12th Series, IX (September 10, 1921), p. 209.
4. T. D. Thiselton Dyer, *Folk-lore of Shakespeare Land*, New York, 1883, p. 331; Flora Thompson, *A Country Calendar and other writings*, Oxford, 1979, pp. 85–86.
5. *Notes and Queries*, 2nd Series, VII (September 3, 1859), p. 186.
6. Transcript 296, Paul Thompson and Thea Vigne, Family Life and Work Experience Before 1918, Oral History Archive, University of Essex. (Henceforth cited as Family Life and Work Experience Archive.)

7. Rachel Pierce, "Marriage in the Fifties," *Sociological Review, New Series,* no. 11 (1963), p. 219.

8. Pilot Questionnaire on Marriage, 1947, Family Planning Box 3c, Mass Observation Archive, Sussex University. (Henceforth cited as Pilot Questionnaire, 1947.)

9. See Jacqueline Sarsby, *Romantic Love and Society,* Harmondsworth, 1983, chapter V; for attitudes at the time of World War II, see *Britain and Her Birth Rate: A Report by Mass Observation,* London, 1945, pp. 62–63.

10. *Britain and Her Birth Rate,* p. 63; Geoffrey Gorer, *Exploring English Character,* London, 1955, pp. 65, 71, 151.

11. Pilot Questionnaire, 1947; Gorer, p. 132.

12. Peter Willmott and Michael Young, *Family and Kinship in East London,* Harmondsworth, 1954, p. 23.

13. Richard Soloway, *Birth Control and the Population Problem in England, 1877–1930,* Chapel Hill, 1982, part II.

14. Gorer, p. 132; *Britain and Her Birth Rate,* p. 60; Pilot Questionnaire, 1947.

15. *Disinherited Youth: A Report on the 18 + Age Group,* Edinburgh, 1943, p. 73.

16. Richard Hoggart, *Uses of Literacy,* Harmondsworth, Penguin, 1969, p. 51.

17. *Royal Commission on Population Report,* London, 1949, pp. 22–23.

18. Iris Minor, "Working Class Women and Matrimonial Law Reform, 1890–1914," *Ideology and the Labour Movement,* eds. D. Martin and D. Rubinstein, London, 1979, p. 113.

19. Louise Tilly and Joan Scott, *Women, Work and Family,* New york, 1978, pp. 71–72; François Bedarida, *A Social History of England, 1851–1975,* New York, 1979, p. 270; Ann Oakley, *Subject Women,* New York, 1981, pp. 146–47.

20. Diana Gittens, *Fair Sex: Family Size and Structure in Britain, 1900–39,* New York, 1982, pp. 73ff.

21. John R. Gillis, *Youth and History: Tradition and Change in European Age Relations, 1770–Present,* New York, 1974, pp. 131, 136–37.

22. H. Seebohm Rowntree, *Poverty: A Study of Town Life,* London, 1914, p. 174; Rowntree, *Poverty and Progress: A Second Social Survey of York,* London, 1941, pp. 289–90.

23. Michael Young and Peter Willmott, *The Symmetrical Family,* New York, 1973, p. 361.

24. Lorraine Barler, "A Study of Certain Marriage Customs, 1974–5," unpublished paper, Leeds University, Library of Institute of Dialect and Folk Life Studies, pp. 50–53; Diana Leonard, *Sex and Generation: A Study of Courtship and Weddings,* London, 1980, pp. 124–28.

25. Willmott and Young, *Family and Kinship,* pp. 34, 40.

26. Dorothy Scannell, *Mother Knew Best, An East End Childhood,* London, 1974, p. 176; Barler, p. 48.

27. Transcript 302, Family Life and Work Experience Archive.

28. Standish Meacham, *A Life Apart: The English Working Class, 1890–1914,* London, 1977, p. 64.

29. Transcript 408, Family Life and Work Experience Archive.

30. Norman Dennis, Fernando Henriques, and Clifford Slaughter, *Coal Is Our Life,* London, 1956, p. 223.

31. Information from Miss East of Bolton, recorded 1970, from Leeds Classified File, E II b (G) d, Institute of Dialect and Folk Life Studies, Leeds University.

32. George Monger, "A Note on Wedding Customs in Industry Today," *Folk-Lore*, 82 (1971), p. 315; G. A. Dyer, "Wedding Customs in the Office: A Note," *Lore and Language*, III, no. 1 (July 1979), pp. 73–77; Transcript 90, Family Life and Work Experience Archive.

33. H. Taylor, unpublished paper, p. 23, Folk Life File E II 4, Acc. 797, Institute of Dialect and Folk Life Studies, Leeds University.

34. Transcripts 362 and 408, Family Life and Work Experience Archive; L. Warren, "Birth, Marriage, Death," unpublished M.A. thesis, 1967, Leeds University, p. 34; L. Barler, "A Study of Certain Marriage Customs, 1974–5," unpublished paper, Institute of Dialect and Folk Life Studies, Leeds University, p. 35.

35. Gorer, p. 84.

36. Mr. O2P, fol. 49, Elizabeth Roberts Collection, Lancaster University. (Henceforth cited as Roberts Collection.)

37. Transcripts 362 and 420, Family Life and Work Experience Archive.

38. Pilot Questionnaire, 1947.

39. Quoted from a woman of unskilled working-class background, aged 60, in 1944, Mass Observation survey of attitudes toward family planning, Family Planning Box 2, file A, Mass Observation Archive, Sussex University.

40. Leonard, *Sex and Generation: A Study of Courtship and Weddings*, London, 1980, pp. 210–13.

41. Charles Booth, Parish Notes a, vol. 32, Booth Collection, London School of Economics.

42. Transcript 17, Family Life and Work Experience Archive.

43. Leonard, p. 50; Elizabeth Laverack, *With This Ring: 100 Years of Marriage*, London, 1979, p. 78.

44. Avril Lansdell, *Wedding Fashions, 1860–1980*, Aylesbury, 1980, pp. 30ff., 69.

45. Transcript 360, Family Life and Work Experience Archive.

46. *The Times of Our Lives*, p. 152; Transcripts 349 and 274, Family Life and Work Experience Archive.

47. Mrs. D1P, p. 32, Roberts Collection; Scannell, p. 176, Transcript 350, Family Life and Work Experience Archive.

48. Quoted in K. C. Rosser and C. C. Harris, *The Family and Social Change*, London, 1974, p. 258.

49. Sam Fitten, "Watching the Wedding," *Gradely Lancashire*, Stalybridge, 1929, no pagination; Transcript 360, Family Life and Work Experience Archive.

50. Mrs. B2P, fol. 10, Roberts Collection; also Mr. S1P, fol. 40; Mrs. A3B and Mr. F1P, fol. 64, Roberts Collection.

51. Leonard, pp. 130–38; Lansdell, p. 69.

52. Leonard, p. 132.

53. Transcript 360, Family Life and Work Experience Archive.

54. Fictitious name added, Transcript 162, Family Life and Work Experience Archive.

55. Transcript 8, Family Life and Work Experience Archive.

56. Transcripts 362 and 420, Family Life and Work Experience Archive; on the evolution of wedding photographs, see Laverack, pp. 101–9.

58. Willmott and Young, *Family and Kinship*, pp. 61–63.

59. *Folk-Lore*, 55 (1944), p. 28.

60. Wheatly, Oxfordshire, *Folk-Lore*, 40 (1929), p. 83.

61. Alwyn D. Rees, *Lefe in a Welsh Countryside*, Cardiff, 1950, p. 90.

62. L. Warren, p. 46; Transcripts 357 and 392, Family Life and Work Experience Archive.
63. Transcript 408, Family Life and Work Experience Archive.
64. Rees, p. 90.
65. Transcript 311, Family Life and Work Experience Archive.
66. Transcript 302, Family Life and Work Experience Archive.
67. Transcripts 237, 336, 107, and 420, Family Life and Work Experience Archive; Laverack, p. 131.
68. Mrs. D1P, fol. 31, and Mr. F1P, fol. 64, Roberts Collection; Rees, p. 90.
69. Willmott and Young, *Family and Kinship*, p. 63.
70. Fictitious name added, Mr. D2P, fol. 50, Roberts Collection.
71. Ellen M. Holtzman, "Marriage, Sexuality, and Contraception in the British Middle Class, 1918–1939," unpublished Ph.D. dissertation, Rutgers University, 1982, passim; also Ruth Hall, *Dear Dr. Stopes, Sex in the 1920s*, London, 1978, pp. 13–46; Pierce, p. 235.
72. Mr. D2P, fol. 21, Roberts Collection.
73. Derek Thompson, "Courtship and Marriage in Preston between the Wars," *Oral History*, III, no. 3 (Autumn 1975), p. 40.
74. Transcript 302, 349, and 356, Family Life and Work Experience Archive; Meacham, p. 65.
75. Pierce, p. 223.
76. Mr. C1P, fol. 94, Roberts Collection; Transcripts 18, 215, and 348, Family Life and Work Experience Archive. On clandestine marriage in World War I, see *Local Population Studies*, no. 26 (Spring 1981), pp. 58–59.
77. Margaret Powell, *Below Stairs*, London, 1958, p. 147; Meacham, p. 65; Frank Ormerod, *Lancashire Life and Character*, London and Manchester, 1915, pp. 124–25.
78. Transcript 38, Family Life and Work Experience Archive.
79. Married in 1915, Transcript 336, Family Life and Work Experience Archive.
80. Married in 1917, Transcript 348, Family Life and Work Experience Archive.
81. Transcript 195, Family Life and Work Experience Archive.
82. Mr. P7P, fol. 21, Roberts Collection.
83. Mrs. D3P, fol. 30, Roberts Collection.
84. Mrs. P1P, fol. 89, Roberts Collection; on civil marriages, see Transcripts 68 and 117, Family Life and Work Experience Archive.
85. Married in 1910, Transcript 389, Family Life and Work Experience Archive.
86. D. Thompson, p. 41; Transcript 68, Family Life and Work Experience Archive.
87. Transcript 248, Family Life and Work Experience Archive.
88. Mrs. M6B, fol. 108, Roberts Collection.
89. Transcript 29, Family Life and Work Experience Archive.
90. Pierce, p. 221.
91. Pilot Questionnaire, 1947; Transcript 78, Family Life and Work Experience Archive.
92. O. R. McGregor, *Divorce in England: A Centenary Study*, London, 1957, chapter iv.
93. Quoted in Minor, p. 113.
94. Richard Leete, *Changing patterns of family formation and dissolution in England and Wales, 1964–76*, London, 1979, p. 62.
95. Fictitious name added, Mr. M4P, Roberts Collection.
96. Gorer, p. 83.

97. Willmott and Young, *Family and Kinship*, p. 61.
98. W. Greenwood, *Love on the Dole*, Garden City, 1934, p. 40.
99. Meacham, p. 193.
100. Mrs. C5P, fol. 30, Roberts Collection; Meacham, p. 66.
101. Willmott and Young, *Family and Kinship*, pp. 56–58; *Maternity: Letters from Working Women*, ed. M. L. Davies, New York, 1978, p. 46.
102. Willmott and Young, *Family and Kinship*, pp. 35–60.
103. Ibid., 108 and chapter iii.
104. Transcript 68, Family Life and Work Experience Archive.
105. Willmott and Young, *Family and Kinship*, p. 139.
106. Ibid., 150; in a study of rural Herefordshire in the late 1960s the same pattern was discovered among working-class couples. Ann Whitehead, "Sexual Antagonism in Herefordshire," *Dependence and Exploitation in Work and Marriage*, eds. D. Leonard Barker and Sheila Allen, New York, 1976, pp. 169–203.
107. Willmott and Young, *Family and Kinship*, pp. 114–54.
108. Matrimonial Survey, 1947, Mass Observation Archive, Sussex University. (Henceforth cited as Matrimonial Survey, 1947.)
109. Pilot Questionnaire, 1947.
110. Matrimonial Survey, 1947; Gorer, p. 138.
111. Matrimonial Survey, 1947.
112. Ibid.; Gorer, pp. 154, 158.
113. *Britain and Her Birthrate*, p. 71; McGregor, p. 55.
114. Fictitious name added, Transcript 72, Family Life and Work Experience Archive.
115. Transcript 40, Family Life and Work Experience Archive.
116. Gorer, p. 148.
117. Ibid., p. 155.
118. Transcript 335, Family Life and Work Experience Archive; Gorer, pp. 155–61.
119. Roberts, *Classic Slum*, p. 56.
120. Transcript 72, Family Life and Work Experience Archive.
121. Pilot Questionaire, 1947.
122. Roberts, *Classic Slum*, p. 157.
123. Elizabeth Roberts, "Working Class Women in the North West," *Oral History*, V no. 2 (Autumn 1977), pp. 12–13.
124. Households with kin seemed to have peaked sometime in the late 1940s or 1950s. See Richard Wall, "The Household: Demographic and Economic Change in England, 1650–1970," *Family Forms in Historic Europe*, eds. Richard Wall, Jean Robin, and Peter Laslett, Cambridge, 1983, p. 496.
125. Matrimonial Survey, 1947.
126. Sexual Survey, 1949, Sexual Behavior, Box 9, File B, Mass Observation Archive, Sussex University; also Matrimonial Survey, 1947.
127. Gorer, p. 82.

Chapter 11

1. "Love and Marriage," 1950s hit song quoted in A. Bicat, "Fifties Children: Sixties People," *The Age of Affluence, 1951–1964*, eds. V. Bogdona and R. Skidelsky, London, 1970, p. 323.

2. Richard Leete, *Changing patterns of family formation and dissolution in England and Wales, 1964–76*, London, 1979, pp. 12–13; Karen Dunnell, *Family Formation 1976*, London, 1979, pp. 7–8; Mary Ann Glendon, *State, Law and Family: Family Law in Transition in the United States and Western Europe*, Amsterdam, 1977, pp. 78–105. For most recent figures, see *Social Trends*, 14 (1984), p. 34.

3. Edward Shorter, *The Making of the Modern Family*, New York, 1975, p. 280.

4. Leete, pp. 18ff.; Joan Busfield and Michael Paddon, *Thinking about Children: Sociology and Fertility in Post-War England*, Cambridge, 1977, pp. 8–13.

5. Dunnell, pp. 5–6.

6. Leete, pp. 18ff.; Busfield and Paddon, pp. 8–13.

7. John R. Gillis, *Youth and History: Tradition and Change in European Age Relations, 1770–Present*, New York, 1974, pp. 185–206; F. Musgrove, *Youth and the Social Order*, London, 1964, pp. 80ff.

8. Gillis, p. 191.

9. Joan W. Scott and Louise A. Tilly, *Women, Work, and Family*, New York, pp. 214–225.

10. Gillis, chapter v.

11. Geoffrey Gorer, *Sex & Marriage in England Today*, London, 1971, p. 24; Michael Schofield, *The Sexual Behaviour of Young People*, Harmondsworth, 1968, pp. 41–56.

12. Gorer, p. 30.

13. Jeremy Seabrook, *City Close-Up*, London, 1971, p. 157.

14. Quoted in Judy Payne, "Talking about Children: An Examination of Accounts about Reproduction and Family Life," *Journal of Biosocial Science*, X, no. 4 (October 1978), p. 370.

15 . In her study of working-class Swansea couples, Diana Leonard found little cohabitation, but a strong sense of betrothal as a distinctive phase, with its own rights and obligations. Leonard, *Sex and Generation: A Study of Courtship and Weddings*, London, 1980, chapter v.

16. Ibid., p. 117; see also Elizabeth Laverack, *With This Ring: 100 Years of Marriage*, London, 1979, p. 25.

17. Derek Thompson, "Courtship and Marriage in Preston between the Wars," *Oral History*, III, no. 2 (Autumn, 1975), p. 43.

18. Glendon, pp. 97–99, 102–5.

19. Dunnell, p. 8.

20. Glendon, p. 81.

21. Leete, pp. 62–63.

22. Mary Scott, "Getting Uptight About White," *Guardian*, August 26, 1971, quoted in Leonard, *Sex and Generation*, p. 1.

23. Leonard, *Sex and Generation*, pp. 21, 209.

24. Ibid., pp. 207–9.

25. On the expenditures, see *The Manchester Guardian*, February 14, 1980.

26. Leonard, *Sex and Generation*, pp. 193–95.

27. Lansdell, pp. 98–105.

28. Diana Leonard, "A Proper Wedding," *The Couple*, ed. M. Corbin, Harmondsworth, 1978, p. 69.

29. The mandating of equal relations between husband and wife can be traced from the 1880s onward. See T. E. James, "The English Law of Marriage," *A Century of Family Law, 1857–1957*, London, 1957, pp. 11–14; Glendon, pp. 192–96;

Albie Sachs and Joan Hoff Wilson, *Sexism and the Law: A Study of Male Beliefs and Legal Bias in Britain and the United States*, London, 1978, p. 143.

30. R. H. Graveson, quoted in James, p. 21.
31. Ibid., p. 220.
32. Glendon, p. 104.
33. While it is true that the state has been reluctant to intervene directly in the family, it has been increasingly insistent that women be responsible for children. For the redefinition of "motherhood," see Jane Lewis, *The Politics of Motherhood, Child and Maternal Welfare in England, 1900–1939*, London, 1980, especially chapters i–iii.
34. Ann Oakley, *Subject Women*, New York, 1981, pp. 230–32.
35. Hannah Gavron, *The Captive Wife: Conflicts of Housebound Mothers*, Harmondsworth, 1968, p. 20; Dennis Marsden, *Mothers Alone: Poverty and the Fatherless Family*, Harmondsworth, 1973, part I, passim.
36. Cohabiting women are still denied supplementary benefits. Ann Oakley, "Conventional Families," *Families in Britain*, London, 1982, p. 135; also Linda McDowell, "City and Home: Urban Housing and the Sexual Division of Space," *Sexual Divisions: Patterns and Processes*, eds. M. Evans and C. Ungerson, London, 1983, pp. 142–63; *New Society*, no. 1047 (December 8, 1982), p. 427.
37. Scott and Tilly, pp. 214–25; Oakley, *Subject Women*, pp. 150–62.
38. Marsden, pp. 32–40, 170ff.; Oakley, *Subject Women*, 151–59, 172–73, 293–95.
39. As cited in Gavron, p. 63.
40. Dunnell, p. 77.
41. J. Peel and G. Carr, *Contraception and Family Design*, Edinburgh, 1975, pp. 103–6.; also Jacqueline Sarsby, *Romantic Love and Society*, Harmondsworth, 1983, chapter vii.
42. J. Joseph, "A research note on attitudes to work and marriage of 600 adolescent girls," *British Journal of Sociology*, 12 (1961), p. 182.
43. A. Oakley, *Becoming a Mother*, Oxford, 1979, pp. 263–64.
44. Busfield and Paddon, pp. 116, 121, 135–36.
45. Juliet Miller, "The Misery of an Infertile Marriage," *Sunday Times*, January 28, 1978, cited in Oakley, *Subject Women*, p. 226.
46. Leonard, *Sex and Generation*, pp. 241–43; Payne, p. 371.
47. Same teacher as cited above. Frank Musgrove and Roger Middleton, "Rites of Passage and the Meaning of Age in Three Contrasted Social Groups: Professional Footballers, Teachers, and Methodist Ministers," *British Journal of Sociology*, XXXII, no. 1 (March 1981), p. 46.
48. For some men fatherhood is also a confirmation of masculinity; see Payne, p. 370.
49. Leonard, *Sex and Generation*, pp. 126–45.
50. Gavron, p. 65.
51. Ibid., p. 63.
52. Busfield and Paddon, p. 134. Also Leonard, *Sex and Generation*, pp. 208–10; and Dunnell, pp. 15, 20–24, 32–33.
53. Busfield and Paddon, pp. 9–16.
54. Ibid., p. 16.
55. Ibid., B. Thornes and J. Collard, *Who Divorces?*, London, 1979, pp. 89ff.
56. The term is used by Gorer, p. 62 and by Peter Willmott and Michael Young in *The Symmetrical Family*, New York, 1973, chapter iii.

57. Gorer, pp. 75–76. Men are the ones who insist that there is such a thing as a maternal instinct. See Payne, p. 370.
58. Leonard, *Sex and Generation*, pp. 247–52; middle-class couples are more ideologically disposed to equal roles, but their behavior is often as conventional as the working class.
59. Leonard, *Sex and Generation*, pp. 243–45. See R. and R. Rapoport, "British Families in Transition," *Families in Britain*, London, 1982, p. 485.
60. Ibid., pp. 242–43.
61. Oakley, *Subject Women*, pp. 163–86.
62. Gavron, p. 137.
63. Ibid., pp. 98–100. For other studies, see John Mogey, *Family and Neighbourhood: Two Studies of Oxford*, London, 1956; Peter Willmott and Michael Young, *Family and Class in a London Suburb*, London, 1960.
64. Gavron, pp. 11–13, 96; Busfield and Paddon, p. 123.
65. Thornes and Collard, pp. 131, 139.
66. Gavron, p. 100.
67. Gavron found that twenty-five percent of wives had no friends; forty percent had just one or two. Ibid., pp. 98, 105.
68. Ibid., p. 98.
69. Quoted from Busfield and Paddon, p. 156. See also Gavron, p. 137.
70. Gavron, p. 67.
71. Gorer, p. 97.
72. Ibid., p. 85.
73. Gavron, p. 131.
74. Sarsby, chapter v.
75. Thornes and Collard, chapter v; Jack Dominian, "Families in Divorce," *Families in Britain*, London, 1982, pp. 263–71.
76. Thornes and Collard, chapter vii, and p. 104.
77. Gavron, p. 89.
78. H. Feldman, "The Effects of Children on the Family," *Family Issues of Employed Women in Europe and America*, ed. A. Michal, Leiden, 1971.
79. Thornes and Collard, pp. 89ff.; R. Chester, ed., *Divorce in Europe*, Leiden, 1977, pp. 69–96.
80. Christine Delphy and Diana Leonard, "The Family as an Economic System," unpublished paper, 1980; also Marsden, pp. 24–25, 77–103; Oakley, "Conventional Families," p. 136.
81. Thornes and Collard, p. 141.
82. The American experience of the transition suggests most couples find it quite difficult. See Georgia Dullea, "Marriage Versus Living Together," *New York Times*, February 14, 1983; and Philip Blumstein and Pepper Schwartz, *American Couples*, New York, 1983.
83. Robert Brain, *Friends and Lovers*, New York, 1976, p. 246. On some of the contradictions in contemporary advice literature, see Ellen Ross, " 'The Love Crisis': Couples Advice Books of the Late 1970s," *Signs*, VI, no. 1 (1980), pp. 109–22.
84. William Thompson and Anna Wheeler, 1825, quoted in Barbara Taylor, *Eve and the New Jerusalem: Socialism and Feminism in the Nineteenth Century*, New York, 1983, p. ix.
85. From *Vincication of the Rights of Woman*, 1792, quoted in Brain, p. 12.

Bibliography

I. Archives and Unpublished Materials

Bodleian Library
    Percy Manning Collection
British Museum
    Francis Place Papers
    Records Relating to the Population Act 1811
Center for English Cultural Tradition and Language, University of Sheffield
    Blakeborough Manuscripts
    David Naitby's diary
Essex Record Office
    Recollections of Older Persons
Essex University
    Paul Thompson and Thea Vigne, Family Life and Work Experience Before
    1918, Oral History Archive
Folk Lore Society Library, University of London
    Archives
Gloucestershire Record Office
    Fairford Petty Sessions Papers
Greater London Record Office
    Foundling Hospital Collection
Guildhall Library, City of London
    Visitation records
Institute of Dialect and Folk Life Studies, Leeds University
    Calvert Manuscripts
Lambeth Palace Library, London
    Fulham Papers
Lancaster University
    Elizabeth Roberts Oral History Collection
London School of Economics
    Charles Booth Collection

Violet Markham Papers
Manchester Central Library
    Clara Alcock's Journal
    Fred Leary Collection
National Children's Home, London
    Archives
National Library of Wales
    David Thomas Collection
    William Rhys Jones Papers
Newcastle City Library
    Broadside Collection
Queen Charlotte's Hospital, London
    Archives
University of Sussex
    Mass Observation Archives
Welsh Folk Museum, St. Fagans
    Evan Jones Notebooks
    William Rhys Jones Manuscripts
    Katrin Stevens Notes

II. Published Primary Materials

A. Ballads and Popular Songs

A Touch on the Times: Songs of Social Change 1770–1914, ed. Roy Palmer, Harmondsworth, 1974.

The Common Muse: An Anthology of Popular British Ballad Poetry, 15th to 20th Century, ed. V. de Sola Pinto and A. E. Rodway, Harmondsworth, 1956.

B. Diaries, Account Books, Scrapbooks

"Diary of the Journey of the most illustrious Philip Julius, Duke of Stettin-Pomerania through England, 1602," *Transactions of the Royal Historical Society*, VI (1892).

"Llangattock Parish Scrapbook," *Brycheiniog*, VIII (1961).

Master and Artisan in Victorian England: The Diary of William Andrews and the Autobiography of Joseph Gutteridge, ed. V. Chancellor, London, 1969.

Rural Economy in Yorkshire in 1641, being the Farming and Account Books of Henry Best of Elmswell in East Riding, Surtees Society, no. 33, 1857.

C. Judicial and Administrative Records

Annual Reports of the Poor Law Commissioners of England and Wales.

Annual Reports of the Registrar General.

Admonition to Parliament of 1572, eds. W. H. Frere and C. E. Douglas, London, 1907.

Archbishop Herring's Visitation Returns, 5 vols., Yorkshire, 1928–31.

Calendar of Merioneth Quarter Sessions Rolls, ed. Keith William-Jones, Aberystwyth, 1965.

Churchwarden's Presentments in Oxfordshire Peculiars, ed., S. A. Peyton, Oxfordshire Record Society, X (1928).

Court Leet Records of the Manor of Manchester, I, Manchester, 1884.

Depositions taken before the Mayor and Aldermen of Norwich, 1549–1563, ed. W. Rye, Norwich, 1905.

Early Essex Town Meetings, ed. F. G. Emmison, London and Colchester, 1970.

English Historical Documents, c 500–1042, ed. D. Whitelock, New York, 1955.

Old Bailey Sessions Papers.

Parish Registers and Parochial Documents of the Archdeaconry of Winchester, ed. W. A. Fearon and J. F. William, London, 1909.

Portmote or Court Leet Records of Salford, 1597–1669, ed. J. G. de T. Mandley, Manchester, 1902.

Portsmouth Record Series: Borough Sessions Papers, 1653–1688, London, 1971.

Warwick County Records, VIII, Warwick, 1953.

D. Newspapers and Journals

Aris's Birmingham Gazette

Byegones

Cambridgeshire Chronicle

Cheshire Notes and Queries

The Crisis

Cymru Fu

Devon and Cornwall Notes and Queries

The Gentleman's Magazine

Gloucestershire Notes and Queries

Jacksons Oxford Journal

Leicestershire and Rutland Notes and Queries

Lincolnshire Notes and Queries

London City Mission Magazine

Monthly Chronicle of North Country Lore and Legend

The New Moral World

New Society

Notes and Queries

Notes and Queries for Somerset and Dorset

Nottingham Review

Oxford and District Folklore Society Annual Record

Sarah Farley's Bristol Journal

Sussex County Magazine

Yorkshire Gazette

E. Parliamentary Papers

Evidence Given to the Royal Commission on Divorce and Matrimonial Causes, 1912–13, XVIII

First Report of the Commissioners (Mines), 1842, XVI

General Report on the Agricultural Labourer: Wales, 1893–4, XXXVI

Report from the Select Committee on the Protection of Infant Life, 1871, VII

Report of His Majesty's Commission to Inquire into the Poor Laws

Report of the Commissioners of Inquiry for South Wales, 1844, XVI

III. Other Significant Published Materials

Addy, S. O. "Garland Day in Castleton." *Folk-Lore,* 12 (1901), pp. 406–7.

Addy, S. O. *Household Tales with other Traditional Remains.* London, 1895.

Alexander, Sally. *St. Giles' Fair: Popular Culture and the Industrial Revolution in 19th Century Oxford.* Oxford, 1969.

Alexander, Sally. "Women's Work in Nineteenth Century London: A Study of the Years, 1820–50," *The Rights and Wrongs of Women*, eds. J. Mitchell and A. Oakley. Harmondsworth, 1979.

Alford, Violet. "Rough Music and Charivari." *Folk-Lore*, 70 (1959), pp. 505–18.

Anderson, Michael. *Family Structure in Nineteenth Century Lancashire*. Cambridge, 1971.

Anderson, Olive. "The Incidence of Civil Marriage in Victorian England and Wales." *Past & Present*, 69 (November 1975), pp. 50–87.

Andrews, E. D. *The People Called Shakers*. New York, 1953.

Andrews, William. *Curiosities of the Church*. London, 1890.

Anson, Peter. *Fisher Folklore*. London, 1965.

Anton, A. E. " 'Handfasting' in Scotland." *The Scottish Historical Review*, XXVII, no. 24 (October 1958), pp. 89–102.

Ariès, Philippe. *Centuries of Childhood: A Social History of Family Life*. New York, 1965.

Armstrong, Alan. *Stability and Change in an English Country Town: A Social Study of York, 1801–1851*. Cambridge, 1974.

Ashby, A. W. "One Hundred Years of Poor Law Administration in a Warwickshire Village." *Oxford Studies in Social and Legal History*, III. Oxford, 1912.

Ashley, M. *The Stuarts in Love*. London, 1963.

Ashton, John. *Social England under the Regency*. London, 1890.

Ashton, T. S. "Coal Miners in the 18th Century." *Economic History*, I (1928), pp. 307–34.

Atkinson, J. C. *A Glossary of Cleveland Dialect*. London, 1868.

Atkinson, J. C. *Forty Years in a Moorland Parish: Reminiscences and Researches in Danby in Cleveland*. London, 1891.

Aubrey, John. *Remains of Gentilism and Judaisme*. London, 1881.

Austin, M. R. "Religion and Society in Derbyshire during the Industrial Revolution." *The Derbyshire Archeological Journal*, XCIII (1973), pp. 75–89.

Austin, M. R. "The Church of England in the County of Derbyshire, 1772–1823," unpublished Ph.D. dissertation, University of London, 1969.

Babb, Lawrence. "The Physiological Conception of Love in the Elizabethan and Early Stuart Drama." *Publications of the Modern Language Association*, LVI, no. 4 (December 1941), pp. 1020–55.

Baker, Margaret. *The Folklore and Customs of Love and Marriage*. Aylesbury, 1974.

Balfour, M. C., and N. W. Thomas. *Examples of Printed Folklore concerning Northumberland*. London, 1904.

Bamford, Samuel. *Passages in the Life of a Radical and Early Days*. London, 1905.

Baring-Gould, Sabine. *A Book of Folklore*. London, n.d.

Baring-Gould, Sabine. *Devonshire Characters and Strange Events*. London, 1908.

Baring-Gould, Sabine. *Further Reminiscences*. New York, 1925.

Baring-Gould, Sabine. *Old Country Life*. London, 1890.

Barler, Lorraine. "A Study of Certain Marriage Customs, 1974–5." Unpublished paper, Institute of Dialect and Folk Life Studies, Leeds University.

Barnes, J. *Observations on Clandestine or Irregular Marriages with a Short Account of the laws, both of England and Scotland*. Berwick, 1812.

Barnes, W. "The Diary of William Whiteway." *Proceedings of the Dorset Natural History and Archeological Field Club*, XIII (1892), pp. 285–311.

Barrett, Michele, and Mary McIntosh. *The Anti-Social Family*. London, 1982.

Baxter, G. R. W. *Book of the Bastilles*. London, 1842.

Bedarida, François. *A Social History of England, 1851–1975*. New York, 1979.

Bell, Lady. *At the Works: A Study of a Manufacturing Town.* London, 1907.

Belmont, Nicole. "The Symbolic Function of the Wedding Procession in Popular Rituals of Marriage." *Ritual, Religion and the Sacred,* eds. R. Forster and O. Ranum. Baltimore, 1982.

Bernard, Jessie. *The Future of Marriage.* New York, 1973.

Berryman, Blanch, ed. *Mitcham Settlement Examinations, 1784–1814,* Surrey Record Society. Guildford, 1973.

Bettey, J. H. "Marriages of Convenience by Copyholders in Dorset in the Seventeenth Century." *Dorset Natural History and Antiquarian Field Club,* 98 (1978), pp. 1–5.

Bettey, J. H. *The Island and Royal Manor of Portland.* Weymouth, 1970.

Bicat, A. "Fifties Children: Sixties People." *The Age of Affluence, 1951–1964,* eds. V. Bogdona and R. Skidelsky. London, 1970.

Bickley, A. C. "Some Notes on a Custom at Woking, Surrey." *Home Counties Magazine,* IV (1902), pp. 25–29.

Bird, S. R. "Some Early Breach of Promise Cases." *The Antiquary,* VI (November 1881).

Blackstone, William. *Blackstone's Commentaries.* South Hackensack, New Jersey, 1969.

Bladen, W. W. "Notes on the Folklore of North Staffordshire, Chiefly Collected at Stone." *Transactions of the North Staffordshire Field Club,* XXV (1901).

Blakeborough, Richard. *Wit, Character and Folklore and Custom of North Riding of Yorkshire.* Salburn-by-the-Sea, 1911.

Blaugh, Mark. "Myth of the Old Poor Law." *Economic History Review,* XXVII (1963), pp. 151–85.

Bloom, J. Harvey. *Folk-Lore, Old Customs and Superstition in Shakespeare's Land.* London, 1929.

Blumstein, Philip, and Pepper Schwartz. *American Couples.* New York, 1983.

Bocock, Robert. *Ritual in Industrial Society.* London, 1974.

Booth, Charles. *Life and Labour of the People of London,* 8 vols. London, 1892–96.

Bosanquet, Helen. *Rich and Poor.* London, 1898.

Bossy, John. "Blood and Baptism: kinship, community and Christianity in western Europe from the 14th to the 17th Centuries." *Sanctity and Secularity: The Church and the World,* ed. D. Baker. Oxford, 1973.

Bossy, John. *The English Catholic Community, 1570–1850.* London, 1975.

Bouce, Paul-Gabriel. *Sexuality in Eighteenth-Century Britain.* Manchester, 1982.

Bourne, George. *Lucy Bettesworth.* London, 1913.

Bowman, Winifred M. *England in Ashton-under-Lyne.* Atricham, 1960.

Boyd, K. *Scottish Church Attitudes to Sex, Marriage and the Family, 1850–1914.* Edinburgh, 1980.

Bradley, Leslie. "Common Law Marriage: A Possible Case of Under-registration." *Local Population Studies,* no. 11 (Autumn 1973), pp. 43–44.

Brain, Robert. *Friends and Lovers.* New York, 1976.

Brand, John. *Observations on Popular Antiquities.* London, 1877.

Brinkworth, E. R. C. *The Archdeacon's Court: Liber Actorum, 1585.* Oxfordshire Record Society, 1946.

Bristow, Edward J. *Vice and Vigilance: Purity Movements in Britain since 1700.* London, 1977.

Britain and Her Birth Rate: A Report by Mass Observation. London, 1945.

Brittain, Vera. *Testament of Youth.* New York, 1980.

Brown, Roger Lee. "Clandestine Marriages in London, Especially within the Fleet Prison, and the Effect of Hardwicke's Act, 1753." Unpublished M.A. thesis, University of London, 1972.

Brown, Theo. "The 'Stag-Hunt' in Devon." *Folk-Lore*, 63 (1952), pp. 104–9.

Brownlow, J. *Thoughts and Suggestions Having Reference to Infanticide*. London, 1864.

Brushfield, T. N. "On Obsolete Punishments." *Journal of the Architectural, Archeological and Historic Society of Cheshire*, part vi (1857–9), pp. 203–34.

Bunsen, Georg von. "Communication." *Zeitschrift für Ethnologie*, XIX (1887), p. 376.

Burguière, Andre. "The Marriage Ritual in France: Ecclesiastical Practices and Popular Practices." *Ritual, Religion and the Sacred*, eds. R. Forster and O. Ranum. Baltimore, 1982.

Burke, Peter. "Popular Custom in Seventeenth Century London." *The London Journal*, III, no. 2 (1977), Pp. 143–62.

Burn, J. S. *The Fleet Registers*. London, 1831.

Burn, J. S. *History of the Parish Registers in England*, 2nd ed. London, 1862.

Burn, J. S. "Sponsalia." *Collectanea Topographica Genealogica*, III (1836).

Burne, C. S. *Shropshire Folklore: A Sheaf of Gleanings*. London, 1883–6.

Burnett, John. *Useful Toil*. London, 1974.

Burnley, J., *Phases of Bradford Life*. London, 1889.

Busfield, Joan, and Michael Paddon. *Thinking about Children: Sociology and Fertility in Post-War England*. Cambridge, 1977.

Cairncross, John. *After Polygamy Was Made a Sin: The Social History of Christian Polygamy*. London, 1974.

Calhoun, Arthur W. *A Social History of the American Family*, 3 vols. Cleveland, 1917–19.

Calhoun, Craig. *The Question of Class Struggle: Social Foundations of Popular Radicalism during the Industrial Revolution*. Chicago, 1982.

Cannadine, David. "The Transformation of Civic Ritual in Modern Britain." *Past & Present*, 94 (1982), pp. 107–30.

Capes, W. W. *Scenes of Rural Life in Hampshire*. London, 1901.

Capp, Bernard. *Astrology and the Popular Press: English Almanachs, 1500–1800*. London, 1979.

Carrington, F. A. "On Certain Ancient Wiltshire Customs." *Wiltshire Archeological and Natural History Magazine*, I (1854), pp. 68–91.

Cawte, E. C. "Parsons Who Rode the Stang." *Folk-Lore*, 74 (1963), pp. 399–401.

Chambers, J. D. *Nottinghamshire in the Eighteenth Century*. London, 1932.

Chambers, J. D. "The Vale of Trent, 1670–1800." *Economic History Review Supplement*, III, London, 1957.

Chambers, R. E. *The Book of Days*, 2 vols, London, 1862–4.

Chesser, Eustace. *Women: A Popular Edition of the Chesser Report*. London, 1958.

Chester, Robert, ed. *Divorce in Europe*. Leiden, 1977.

Chisenhale-Marsh, U.B., "Folk Lore in Essex and Herts." *Essex Review*, V (1896), pp. 143–159.

Choice Notes from 'Notes and Queries.' London, 1959.

Clark, Anna. "A Double Violation: The Experience and Language of Rape in England, 1815–1845." Unpublished paper, Women's History Seminar, Rutgers University, 1983.

Clark, Peter. "The Migrant in Kentish Towns, 1580–1640," *Crisis and Order in English Towns, 1500–1700*, eds. P. Clark and Paul Slack. London, 1972.

"Claverhouse." *Irregular Border Marriages*. London and Edinburgh, 1934.

Cobbett, William. *The Parliamentary History of England*. London, 1813.

Coke, Edward. *Religious Rites Made Free to the Poor*. London, n.d.

Cole, William. *The Bletchley Diary of Rev. William Cole, 1765–67*, ed. F. G. Stokes. London, 1931.

Coleman, Terry. *The Railway Navvies*. London, 1965.

Collett, Clara. "Report on the Money Wages of Indoor Domestic Servants." *Parliamentary Papers*, 1899, XXXXIII, pp. 15–30.

Cook, M., ed. *Diocese of Exeter in 1821*. Devon Record Society, 1960.

Cooper, J. P. "Patterns of Inheritance and Settlement by Great Landowners from the Fifteenth to the Eighteenth Centuries." *Family and Inheritance: Rural Society in Western Europe, 1200–1800*, eds. Jack Goody, Joan Thirsk, E. P. Thompson. Cambridge, 1978.

Coulton, G. G. *Medieval Village, Manor and Monastery*. New York, 1960.

Courtney, M. A. *Cornish Feasts and Folk-Lore*. Penzance, 1890.

Cox, J. C., *The Parish Registers of England*. London, 1910.

Crooke, W. "Lifting of the Bride." *Folk-Lore*, XII (1902), pp. 226–51.

Crossick, Geoffrey. "Social Structure and Working Class Behavior: Kentish London, 1840–1880." Unpublished D.Phil. dissertation, University of London, 1976.

Crozier, D. "Kinship and Occupational Succession." *Sociological Review*, NS, XIII (1965), pp. 15–45.

Cunningham, Phyllis. *Costume of Household Servants from the Middle Ages to 1900*. London, 1974.

Cupid's Pupils, London, 1899.

Davidoff, Leonore. *The Best Circles: Society, Etiquette and The Season*. London, 1973.

Davidoff, Leonore. "Mastered for Life: Servant and Wife in Victorian and Edwardian England." *Journal of Social History*, VII (1974), pp. 406–22.

Davidoff, Leonore, Jean L'Esperance, and Howard Newby. "Landscape with Figures: Home and Community in English Society." *The Rights and Wrongs of Women*, eds. J. Mitchell and A. Oakley. Harmondsworth, 1979.

Davies, Alun. "The New Poor Law in a Rural Area, 1834–50." *Credigion*, VIII (1978), pp. 245–90.

Davies, Alun. "The Old Poor Law in an Industrializing Parish: Aberdare." *Welsh History Review*, VIII, no. 3 (June 1977), pp. 285–311.

Davies, C. Stella. *North Country Bred*. London, 1963.

Davies, J. C. *Folk-Lore of West and Mid-Wales*. Aberystwyth, 1911.

Davies, K. " 'The Sacred Condition of Equality'—How Original Were Puritan Doctrines of Marriage." *Social History*, V (1977), pp. 563–80.

Davies, Leonard T., and A. Edwards. *Welsh Life in the Eighteenth Century*. London, 1939.

Davin, Anna. " 'A Centre of Humanizing Influence': The Schooling of Working Class Girls under the London School Board (1870–1902)." Unpublished paper, given at Rutgers University, 1981.

Davin, Anna. "Imperialism and Motherhood." *History Workshop Journal*, V (Spring 1978), pp. 9–66.

Davis, Natalie Z. "The Reasons of Misrule." *Society and Culture in Early Modern France*. Stanford, 1975.

Davis, Natalie Z. "Women on Top." *Society and Culture in Early Modern France*. Stanford, 1975.

Denham Tracts, reprint edition. Nedelen, Lichtenstein, 1967.

Dennis, Norman, F. Henriques, and C. Slaughter. *Coal Is Our Life*. London, 1956.

Disinherited Youth: A Report on the 18+ Age Group. Edinburgh, 1943.

Dixon, D. D. "Old Wedding Customs in Upper Coquetdale and Alndale, Northumberland." *Newcastle Courant*, December 1888.

Dixon, D. D. *Whittingham Vale, Northumberland: Its History, Traditions and Folklore*. Newcastle, 1895.

Dominian, J. "Families in Divorce," *Families in Britain*. London, 1982.

Douch, R. "Customs and Traditions of the Isle of Portland, Dorset. *Antiquary*, XXVII (1949), pp. 140–52.

Downward Paths: An Inquiry into the Causes Which Contributed to the Making of a Prostitute, London, 1916.

Dunnell, Karen. *Family Formation 1976*. London, 1979.

Dupâcquier, J., et al., eds. *Marriage and Remarriage in Populations of the Past*. London, 1981.

Dyer, G. A. "Wedding Customs in the Office: A Note." *Lore and Language*, III, no. 1 (July 1979), pp.

Dyer, T. B. Thiselton. *Folk-lore of Shakespeare's Land*. New York, 1883.

Dyer, T. B. Thiselton. *Old English Social Life as Told by the Parish Registers*. London, 1898.

Dyhouse, Carol. *Girls Growing Up in Late Victorian and Edwardian Britain*. London, 1981.

Ebery, Mark, and Brian Preston. *Domestic Service in Late Victorian and Edwardian England, 1871–1914*. Reading Geographical Papers no. 42, 1976.

Ede, John F. *History of Wednesbury*. Birmingham, 1962.

Edwards, H. *A Collection of Old English Customs and Curious Bequests and Charities*. London, 1842.

Elliott, Vivien B. "Mobility and Marriage in Pre-industrial England." Unpublished Ph.D. dissertation, Cambridge University, 1979.

Elliott, Vivien B. "Single Women in the London Marriage Market: Age, Status, and Mobility, 1598–1619." *Marriage and Society: Studies in the Social History of Marriage*, ed. R. B. Outhwaite. New York, 1981.

Ellis, Havelock. *Studies in the Psychology of Sex*, VI. Philadelphia, 1924.

Ellison, D., ed. *The Rector and His Flock*. Bassingbourne, 1980.

Elworthy, E. F. *West Somerset Word-Book*. London, 1886.

Emmison, F. G. *Elizabethan Life: Morals and Church Courts*. Chelmsford, 1973.

Evans, Eric. "Some Reasons for the Growth of Rural Anti-Clericalism, 1750–1830." *Past & Present*, 66 (February 1975), pp. 84–109.

Evans, George Ewart. *From Mouths of Men*. London, 1976.

Evans, George Ewart. *Pattern under the Plough*. London, 1966.

Evans, George Ewart. *Where Beards Wag All: The Relevance of the Oral Tradition*. London, 1970.

Evans, John. *English Posies and Posy Rings*, London, 1900.

Everitt, Alan. "Farm Labourers," *The Agrarian History of England and Wales*, IV. Cambridge, 1967.

Everitt, Alan. *Patterns of Rural Dissent: The Nineteenth Century*. Leicester, 1972.

Extracts from Leeds Intelligencer and Leeds Mercury, 1769–1776, ed. G. Denison Lamb. Leeds, 1838.

Festy, P. "Aspects demographiques de la Formation de la Famille en Europe Occidentale." *Marriage and Cohabitation in Contemporary Societies*, eds. J. M. Eekelaar and Sanford Katz. Toronto, 1980.

Finlay, Roger. *Population and Metropolis: The Demography of London, 1580–1650.* Cambridge, 1981.

Fish, Lydia. *The Folklore of the Coal Mines of the North of England.* Norwood, Pennsylvania, 1975.

Fitten, Sam. "Watching the Wedding," *Gradely, Lancashire.* Stalybridge, 1929.

Flandrin, Jean-Louis. *Families in Former Times: Kinship, Household and Sexuality.* Cambridge, 1979.

Fleming, William. "A Furness Diary." *The Countryman*, 55, no. 4 (1958), p. 428.

Foley, Winifred. *Child in the Forest.* London, 1977.

Foster, G. M. "Anatomy of Envy: A Study of Symbolic Behavior." *Current Anthropology*, VIII, no. 2 (April 1972), pp. 165–202.

Foster, John. *Class Struggle and the Industrial Revolution.* London, 1974.

Fox, Vivien C., and Martin H. Quitt. *Loving, Parenting and Dying: The Family Cycle in England and American Past and Present.* New York, 1980.

Friedan, Betty. *The Second Stage.* New York, 1981.

Furnivall, F. J. *Child-Marriages, Divorces, and Ratifications in the Diocese of Chester.* London, 1897.

Gandy, G. N. "Illegitimacy in a Handloom Weaving Community: Fertility Patterns in Culcheth, Lancashire, 1781–1860." Unpublished D.Phil. dissertation, Oxford University, 1978.

Gavron, Hannah. *The Captive Wife.* Harmondsworth, 1968.

Gay, Peter. *Education of the Senses: The Bourgeois Experience, Victoria to Freud.* New York, 1984.

van Gennep, Arnold. *The Rites of Passage.* Chicago, 1960.

George, M. Dorothy. *London in the Eighteenth Century.* New York, 1925.

Gibson, A. Craig. "Ancient Customs and Superstitions in Cumberland." *Transactions of the Historic Society of Lancashire and Cheshire*, X (1857–8), pp. 97–110.

Giesen, D. *Grundlagen und Entwicklung des englischen Eherechts in der Neuzeit bis zum Beginn des 19. Jahrhunderts.* Bielefeld, 1973.

Gillis, John R. "Conjugal Settlements: Resort to Clandestine and Common Law Marriage in England and Wales, 1650–1850," *Disputes and Settlements: Law and Human Relations in the West*, ed. J. Bossy. Cambridge, 1983.

Gillis, John R. "Peasant, Plebeian, and Proletarian Marriage in Britain, 1600–1900," *Proletarianization and Family History*, ed. D. Levine. Forthcoming.

Gillis, John R. "Servants, Sexual Relations, and the Risks of Illegitimacy in London, 1801–1900." *Feminist Studies*, V, no. 1 (Spring 1979), pp. 142–73.

Gillis, John R. *Youth and History: Tradition and Change in European Age Relations, 1770 to Present.* New York, 1975.

Gittens, D. *Fair Sex: Family Size and Structure in Britain, 1900–39.* New York, 1982.

Glamorgan County History, IV, Cardiff, 1974.

Glendon, Mary Ann. "The New Marriage and the New Property," *Marriage and Cohabitation in Contemporary Societies*, eds. J. M. Eekelaar and S. Katz. Toronto, 1980.

Glendon, Mary Ann. *State, Law and Family: Family Law in Transition in the United States and Western Europe.* Amsterdam, 1977.

Goode, William J. "The Theoretical Importance of Love." *American Sociological Review*, XXIV, no. 1 (February 1959), pp. 38–47.

Goody, Jack. *The development of the family and marriage in Europe*. Cambridge, 1983.

Gorer, Geoffrey. *Exploring English Character*. London, 1955.

Gorer, Geoffrey. *Sex & Marriage in England Today*. London, 1971.

Gottlieb, Beatrice. "The Meaning of Clandestine Marriage." *Family and Sexuality in French History*, eds. R. Wheaton and T. Harveven. Philadelphia, 1980.

Gough, Richard. *The History of Myddle*. Harmondsworth, 1981.

Gregson, Peter. "The Observance of Mothering Sunday." Unpublished B.A. thesis, Leeds University, 1966.

Grey, Edwin. *Cottage Life in a Hertfordshire Village*. Harpenden, 1977.

Griffith, G. Talcott. *Population Problems in the Age of Malthus*. Cambridge, 1926.

Grose, Francis. *A Provincial Glossary*, rev. ed. London, 1811.

Gutch, E. *Country Folklore: North Riding of Yorkshire, York and the Ainsty*. London, 1901.

Habakkuk, H. J. *Population Growth and Economic Development since 1750*. Leicester, 1971.

Hackwood, F. W. *The Bridal Book*. London, n.d.

Hackwood, F. W. *Staffordshire Customs, Superstitions, and Folklore*, 2nd ed. Wakefield, 1974.

Hackwood, F. W. *The Wednesbury Papers*. Wednesbury, 1884.

Haigh, Christopher. *Reformation and Resistance in Tudor Lancashire*. Cambridge, 1975.

Haines, Michael. *Fertility and Occupation: Population Patterns in Industrialization*. New York, 1979.

Hair, P. E. H. "Bridal Pregnancy in Rural England in Earlier Centuries." *Population Studies*, XX, part 2 (November 1966), pp. 233–44.

Hajnal, John. "European marriage patterns in perspective," *Population in History*, eds. D. V. Glass and D. E. C. Eversley. Chicago, 1965.

Hale, William H., ed. *A Series of Presentments and Proceedings in Criminal Causes, 1475–1640, from the Act-Books of the Ecclesiastical Courts of the Diocese of London*. London, 1947.

Hall, Ruth. *Dear Dr. Stopes, Sex in the 1920s*. London, 1979.

Hampson, E. *The Treatment of Poverty in Cambridgeshire, 1597–1834*. Cambridge, 1934.

Hanway, J. *A Candid Historical Account of the Hospital for Reception of Exposed and Deserted Young Children*. London, 1759.

Hanway, J. *The Defects of Policy in the cause of Immorality*. London, 1775.

Harland, J., and T. T. Wilkinson. *Lancashire Legends*. London, 1873.

Harwood, H. W. "As Things Were: A Social Study of the Upper Calder Valley." *Transactions of the Halifax Antiquarian Society*, 1968, pp. 17–25.

Harrison, J. F. C. *The Second Coming: Popular Millenarianism, 1780–1850*. New Brunswick, 1979.

Hearnshaw, F. J. C. *Leet Jurisdiction in England*. Southhampton, 1908.

Hecht, J. J. *The Domestic Servant Class in Eighteenth Century England*. London, 1956.

Helmholtz, R. H. *Marriage Litigation in Medieval England*. Cambridge, 1974.

Henderson, William. *Notes on the Folk-Lore of the Northern Counties and Borders*. London, 1879.

Henriques, U. R. Q. "Bastardy and the New Poor Law." *Past & Present*, no. 37 (July 1967), pp. 103–129.

Henwood, G. *Cornwall's Mines and Miners*. Truro, 1972.

Hewitt, Margaret. *Wives and Mothers in Victorian Industry*. London, 1958.

Hewitt, Sarah. *Nummits and Crummits: Devonshire Customs, Characteristics and Folklore*. London, 1900.

Hey, David. *An English Rural Community: Myddle under the Tudors and the Stuarts*. Leicester, 1974.

Hill, Christopher. "Clarissa Harlowe and Her Times," *Puritanism and Revolution*. London, 1958.

Hill, Christopher. *Economic Problems of the Church*. Oxford, 1956.

Hill, Christopher. *Society and Puritanism in Pre-Revolutionary England*, 2nd ed. London, 1967.

Hill, Christopher. *The World Turned Upside Down: Radical Ideas during the English Revolution*. Harmondsworth, 1975.

Hobsbawm, Eric, and Terence Ranger, eds. *The Invention of Tradition*. Cambridge, 1983.

Hobsbawm, Eric, and George Rudé. *Captain Swing*. New York, 1968.

Hoggart, Richard. *Uses of Literacy*. Harmondsworth, 1969.

Holdsworth, W. S. *History of English Law*, 17 vols. London, 1922–72.

Hole, Christina. *A Dictionary of British Folk Customs*. London, 1976.

Hole, Christina. *Traditions and Customs of Cheshire*. London, 1937.

Holtzman, Ellen M. "Marriage, Sexuality and Contraception in the British Middle Class, 1918–1939." Unpublished Ph.D. dissertation, Rutgers University, 1982.

Homans, George. *English Villagers in the Thirteenth Century*. New York, 1975.

Home, Gordon. *The Evolution of an English Town*. London, 1915.

Hone, William. *Table Book*. London, 1837.

Horn, Pamela. "The Bucks Straw Plait Trade in Victorian England." *Records of Buckinghamshire*, XIX (1971–77), pp. 42–54.

Horn, Pamela. *The Rise and Fall of the Victorian Servant*. New York, 1975.

Houghton, Walter E. *The Victorian Frame of Mind, 1830–1870*. New Haven, 1957.

Houlbrooke, Ralph. *Church Courts and the People during the English Reformation*. Oxford, 1979.

Howard, G. E. *The History of Matrimonial Institutions*, 4 vols. London, 1904.

Howell, Cicely. "Peasant inheritance customs in the Midlands, 1280–1700," *Family and Inheritance: Rural Society in Western Europe, 1200–1800*, eds. J. Goody, J. Thirsk, and E. P. Thompson. Cambridge, 1978.

Howells, W. *Cambrian Superstitions*. London, 1831.

Howitt, William. *Rural Life of England*. London, 1862.

Howse, W. H. *Radnorshire*. Hereford, 1949.

Huggett, Frank E. *Life Below Stairs*. New York, 1977.

Hughes, Thomas. *Tom Brown's School Days*. London, 1906.

Huizinga, Johann. *Homo Ludens: A Study of the Play-Element in Culture*. Boston, 1950.

Hume, Ganon. "Rural Life and Manners—The Neighborhood of Bidstone and Upton—A Hundred Years Ago." *Transactions of the Historic Society of Lancashire and Cheshire*, 3rd Series, III (1874–75), pp. 131–68.

Humphries, Stephen. *Hooligans or Rebels?: An Oral History of Working Class Childhood and Youth, 1889–1930*. Oxford, 1981.

Hunt, W. *The Puritan Moment*. Cambridge, 1983.

Hutchins, John. *The History and Antiquities of the County of Dorset*, I. London, 1863.

Ifans, Dayffd. "Lewis Morris ac Afrerion Priodi ygn Ngheredigion." *Ceredigion*, VIII, no. 2 (1972), pp. 194–200.

Ingram, M. "Ecclesiastical Justice in Wiltshire, 1600–1640." Unpublished D.Phil. thesis, Oxford University, 1976.

Ingram, M. "Le Charivari dans L'Angleterre du XVIᵉ et du XVIIᵉ siècle." In J. Le Goff and J.-C. Schmitt, *Le Charivari*. Paris, 1981.

Ingram, M. "Spousals Litigation in the English Ecclesiastical Courts, 1340–1640." In *Marriage and Society*, ed. R. B. Outhwaite. New York, 1981.

Jackson, Brian. *Working Class Community*. London, 1968.

James, T. E. "The English Law of Marriage," *A Century of Family Law, 1857–1957*. London, 1957.

Jeaffreson, John C. *Brides and Bridals*. London, 1872.

Jenkins, David. *The Agricultural Community in South-West Wales at the Turn of the Twentieth Century*. Cardiff, 1971.

Jenkins, Geraint H. *Literature, Religion and Society in Wales, 1660–1730*. Cardiff, 1978.

Johnson, James T. *A Society Ordained by God: English Puritan Marriage Doctrine in the First Half of the Seventeenth Century*. Nashville, 1970.

Johnston, J. A. "The Probate Inventories and Wills of a Worcestershire Parish, 1676–1775." *Midland History*, I, no. 1 (Spring 1971), pp. 20–33.

Jollie, H. *Sketch of Cumberland Manners and Customs*. Carlisle, 1811.

Jones, D. Parry. *My Own Folks*, Lladysul, 1972.

Jones, E. W. "Medical Glimpses of Early 19th Century Cardignshire." *National Library of Wales Journal*, XIV (1965–66), pp. 260–75.

Jones, Gareth Stedman. *Outcast London*. Oxford, 1971.

Jones, Gareth Stedman. "Working Class Culture and Working Class Politics in London, 1870–1900: Notes on the Remaking of a Working Class Culture." *Journal of Social History*, VII, no. 4 (Summer 1974), pp. 460–508.

Jones, G. P. "Illegitimacy in Ten Northern Parishes." Unpublished paper, Cambridge Group for the Study of the History of Population and Social Structure Library.

Jones, G. P. "Illegitimacy in Withersback, 1671–1812." Unpublished paper, Cambridge Group Library.

Jones, R. Tudor. "Religion in Post-Restoration Brecknockshire, 1660–68." *Brycheiniog*, VIII (1962), pp. 16–48.

Jones, T. Gwynn. *Welsh Folklore and Folk Custom*. London, 1930.

Jones, William. *Finger-Ring Lore*. London, 1898.

Jones, William Rhys. "Besom Wedding in the Ceiriog Valley." *Folk-Lore*, 34 (1928), pp. 149–60.

Jones-Baker, Doris. *The Folklore of Hertfordshire*. London, 1977.

Joseph, J. "A Research note on attitudes to work and marriage of 600 adolescent girls." *British Journal of Sociology*, 12 (1961), pp. 176–83.

Joyce, Patrick. *Work, Society and Politics: The Culture of the Factory in Later Victorian England*. New Brunswick, 1980.

Kerr, Madeline. *The People of Ship Street*. London, 1958.

Kitteringham, Jennie. "Country Work Girls in Nineteenth Century England," *Village Life and Labour*, ed. R. Samuel. London, 1975.

Kuczynski, R. R. "British Demographers' Opinions on Fertility, 1660–1760," *Political Arithmetic*, ed. L. Hogben. London, 1938.

Kussmaul, Ann. *Servants in Husbandy in Early Modern England*. Cambridge, 1981.

Kussmaul-Cooper, Ann. "The Mobility of English Farm Servants in the 17th and 18th Centuries." Unpublished paper, Cambridge Group for the Study of the History of Population and Social Structure Library.

Lansdell, Avril. *Wedding Fashions, 1860–1980*. Aylesbury, 1983.

Lasch, Christopher. "The Suppression of Clandestine Marriage in England: The Marriage Act of 1753." *Salmagundi*, no. 26 (Spring 1974), pp. 60–109.

Laslett, Peter. "Parental deprivation in the past: a note on orphans and step-parenthood in English history," *Family Life and illicit love in earlier generations*. Cambridge, 1977.

Laslett, Peter. *The World we have lost*. New York, 1965.

Laslett, P., Karla Oosterveen, and R. W. Smith, eds. *Bastardy and Its Comparative History*. Cambridge, 1980.

Latimer, John. *The Annals of Bristol*, 2 vols. Bristol, 1893.

Laverack, Elizabeth. *With This ring: 100 Years of Marriage*. London, 1979.

Lawley, G. T. "Wife Selling in Staffordshire." *Midland Weekly News*, January 6 and 13, 1894.

Lawson, Joseph. *Letters to the Young on Progress in Pudsey during the Last Sixty Years*. Stanninglen, 1887.

Layton, W. T. "Changes in the Wages of Domestic Servants during Fifty Years." *Journal of the Royal Statistical Society*, 71 (1908), pp. 515–24.

Lees, Lynn. *Exiles of Erin: Irish Migrants in Victorian London*. Ithaca, 1979.

Lees, Lynn. "Getting and Spending: The Family Budgets of English Industrial Workers in 1890," *Consciousness and Class Experience in Nineteenth Century Europe*, ed. J. Merriman. New York, 1979.

Leete, Robert. *Changing Patterns of family formation and dissolution in England and Wales, 1964–76*. London, 1979.

Leffingwell, Arthur. *Illegitimacy and the Influence of the Seasons upon Conduct*. New York, 1892.

Leifchild, J. R. *Cornwall: Its Miners and Mines*. London, 1855.

Leites, Edmund. "The Duty to Desire: Love, Friendship, and Sexuality in Some Puritan Theories of Marriage." *Journal of Social History*, XV, no. 3 (Spring 1982), pp. 383–408.

Leonard, Diana. "A Proper Wedding," *The Couple*, ed. M. Corbin. Harmondsworth, 1978.

Leonard, Diana. *Sex and Generation: A Study of Courtship and Weddings*. London, 1980.

Leonard, Diana, and Christine Delphy. "The Family as an Economic System." Unpublished paper.

Lesthaeghe, Ron. "A Century of Demographic and Cultural Change in Western Europe: An Exploration of Underlying Dimensions." *Population and Development Review*, IX, no. 3 (September 1983), pp. 411–36.

Levine, David. *Family Formation in an Age of Nascent Capitalism*. New York, 1977.

Levine, David. "Production, Reproduction and the Proletarian Family in England, 1500–1851," *Proletarianization and Family History*, ed. D. Levine. Forthcoming.

Levine, David, and Keith Wrightson. "The social context of illegitimacy in early modern England," *Bastardy and its Comparative History*, eds., Peter Laslett, Karla Oosterveen, and R. M. Smith. Cambridge, 1980.

Lewis, Jane. *The Politics of Motherhood: Child and Maternal Welfare in England, 1900–1939.* London, 1980.

Liddall, M. G. "The St. Pancras Vestry: A Study in the Administration of a Metropolitan Parish, 1760–1835." Unpublished Ph.D. dissertation, Rutgers University, 1981.

Liddington, Jill, and J. Norris. *One Hand Tied Behind Us: The Rise of the Woman's Suffrage Movement.* London, 1978.

Linebaugh, Peter. "The Picaresque Proletarian in Eighteenth Century London." Unpublished paper, Rutgers University, 1983.

Lloyd, A. L., ed. *Come All Ye Bold Miners: Ballads and Songs of the Coal Fields.* London, 1952.

Loane, M. *From Their Point of View.* London, 1908.

Locke, Arthur. *A Short History of Woking*, n.p., n.d.

Lovett, William. *Life and Struggles of William Lovett, in His Pursuit of Bread, Knowledge, and Freedom.* London, 1967.

Lowe, Roger. *The Diary of Roger Lowe*, ed. William L. Sachse. New Haven, 1938.

MacDonald, Michael. *Mystical Bedlam: Madness, Anxiety, and Healing in Seventeenth Century England.* Cambridge, 1981.

Macfarlane, Alan. *The Family Life of Ralph Josselin: A Seventeenth Century Clergyman.* New York, 1977.

Macfarlane, Alan. "The Informal Social Control of Marriage in Seventeenth Century England," in V. Fox and M. Quitt, *Loving, Parenting, and Dying.* New York, 1980.

Macfarlane, Alan. *The Origins of English Individualism: The Family, Property and Social Transition.* Oxford, 1978.

Machyn, Henry. *The Diary of a Resident of London.* London, 1847.

Malcolmson, Robert. "Infanticide in the Eighteenth Century," *Crime in England, 1550–1800*, ed. J. S. Cockburn. London, 1977.

Malcolmson, Robert. *Life and Labour in England, 1700–1780.* New York, 1981.

Malcolmson, Robert. *Popular Recreations in English Society, 1700–1850.* Cambridge, 1973.

Malcolmson, Robert. " 'A set of ungovernable people:' the Kingswood colliers in the eighteenth century," *An Ungovernable People: The English and their Law in the seventeenth and eighteenth centuries*, J. Brewer and J. Styles. New Brunswick, 1980.

"Marriage in Low Life." *Chambers Journal*, XII (July–December 1859), pp. 399–440.

Marsden, Dennis. *Mothers Alone: Poverty and the Fatherless Family.* Harmondsworth, 1973.

Martin, J. M. "Marriage and Economic Stress in the Felden of Warwickshire during the Eighteenth Century." *Population Studies*, XXXI (1977), pp. 519–36.

Marwick, Arthur. *The Deluge: British Society and the First World War.* Harmondsworth, 1967.

Maternity: Letters from Working Women, ed. M. L. Davies. New York, 1978.

Mayhew, Henry. *London Labour and the London Poor*, 3 vols. London, 1864.

Mayhew, Henry. *The Unknown Mayhew*, eds. E. Yeo and E. P. Thompson. New York, 1972.

McBride, Theresa M. *The Domestic Revolution: Modernization of Household Service in England and France, 1820–1920*. London, 1976.

McCauley, A. *History and Antiquities of Claybrook*, n.p., 1791.

McCulloch, A. "Alternative Households," *Families in Britain*. London, 1982.

McDowell, L. "City and home: Urban housing and the sexual division of space," *Sexual Divisions: Patterns and Processes*, eds. M. Evans and C. Ungerson. London, 1983.

McGrath, P. "Notes on the History of Marriage Licences," *Gloucestershire Marriage Allegations, 1637–1680*, ed. B. Frith. Gloucester, 1960.

McGregor, O. R. *Divorce in England: A Centenary Study*. London, 1957.

McIntire, W. T. "Gretna Green Marriages." *The Genealogists Magazine*, IX, no. 3 (September 1940), pp. 77–83.

McIntire, W. T. *Lakeland and the Borders*, Carlisle, 1948.

McKendrick, N. "Home Demand and Economic Growth: A New View of the Role of Women and Children in the Industrial Revolution," *Historical Perspectives: Studies in English Thought and Society in Honour of J. H. Plumb*. London, 1974.

McLaren, Angus. *Birth Control in Nineteenth Century England*. New York, 1978.

McLaren, Angus. "Reproductive Rituals: The Patterning of Human Fertility in England, 1500–1800." Forthcoming book.

McLaren, Angus. "Women's Work and Regulation of Family Size." *History Workshop Journal*, 4 (1977), pp. 71–80.

Meacham, Standish. *A Life Apart: The English Working Class, 1890–1914*. London, 1977.

Medick, Hans. "The Proto-industrial family economy: The structural function of household and family during the transition from peasant society to industrial capitalism." *Social History*, III (1976), pp. 291–315.

Menefee, Samuel Pyeatt. *Wives for Sale: An Ethnographic Study of British Popular Divorce*. New York, 1981.

Miller, Juliet. "The Misery of an Infertile Marriage." *Sunday Times*, January 28, 1978.

Minor, Iris. "Working Class Women and Matrimonial Law Reform 1890–1914," *Ideology and the Labour Movement*, eds. David Martin and David Rubinstein. London, 1979.

Minors, Tom. "Quaint Marriage Customs in Old Cornwall." *Old Cornwall*, I, n.d.

Misson, Henri. *Memoirs and Observations in His Travels over England (1697)*. London, 1719.

Monger, George. "A Note on the Similarities between Some Wedding Customs in England and France." *Lore and Language*, II, no. 1 (July 1974), pp. 36–38.

Monger, George. "A Note on Wedding Customs in Industry Today." *Folk-Lore*, 82 (1971), pp. 314–16.

Moore, A. Percival. "Marriage Contracts or Espousals in the Reign of Queen Elizabeth." *Reports and Papers of the Associated Architectural Societies of 1909*.

Moore, S., and B. Myerhoff. *Secular Ritual*. Assen/Amsterdam, 1977.

Morris, S. Meeson. "Obsolete Punishments of Shropshire." *Shropshire Archeological and Natural History Society*, IX (1885), pp. 84–113.

Mortimer, R. S. "Marriage Discipline of Early Friends." *Journal of Friends Historical Society*, 48, no. 4 (1957), pp. 175–95.

Moss, Fletcher. *Folk-Lore*. Manchester, 1898.

Munby, Arthur. *Munby: Man of Two Worlds*, ed. Derek Hudson. London, 1974.

Muncy, Raymond Lee. *Sex and Marriage in Utopian Communities*. Bloomington, 1973.

Muncy, R. W. *The Romance of the Parish Registers*. London, 1933.

Musgrove, Frank. *Youth and the Social Order*. London, 1964.

Musgrove, Frank, and Roger Middleton. "Rites of passage and the meaning of age in three contrasted social groups: professional footballers, teachers, and Methodist Ministers." *British Journal of Sociology*, XXII, no. 1 (March 1981), pp. 39–55.

Neff, W. F. *Victorian Working Women*. New York, 1929.

Nelson, Benjamin. *The Idea of Usury: From Tribal Brotherhood to Universal Otherhood*. Princeton, 1949.

Neville, H. M. *A Corner in the North*. Newcastle, 1909.

New Guide of Matrimony, n.p., n.d.

Newman, Anthea. "An Evaluation of bastardy recordings in an east Kent parish," *Bastardy and its Comparative History*, eds. Peter Laslett, Karla Oosterveen, and R. M. Smith. Cambridge, 1980.

Newman, R. C. *A Hampshire Parish: Bramschott and Liphook*, Petersfield, England, 1976.

Nicholls, H. B. *Nicholl's Forest of Dean*, rev. ed. Whitsable, 1966.

Nicholls, W. *History and Tradition of Ravenstonedale, Westmoreland*. Manchester, 1877.

Nicholson, C. D. P. *The Genealogical Value of Early English Newspapers*, n.p., 1934.

Nissel, M. "Families and Social Change since the Second World War." *Families in Britain*. London, 1982.

Oakley, Ann. *Becoming a Mother*. Oxford, 1979.

Oakley, Ann. "Conventional Families," *Families in Britain*. London, 1982.

Oakley, Ann. *Subject Women*. New York, 1981.

Obelkevich, James. *Religion and Rural Society: South Lindsey, 1825–75*. Oxford, 1976.

O'Donovan, Katherine. "The Male Appendage—Legal Definitions of Women," *Fit Work for Women*, ed. Sandra Burman. London, 1979.

Old Yorkshire, ed. W. Smith, I. London, 1881.

Opie, Iona and Peter. *Children's Games in Street and Playground*. Oxford, 1969.

Opie, Iona and Peter. *Lore and Language of School Children*. Oxford, 1959.

Orme, E. "Conditions of Work in the Nail, Chain, and Bolt Making Industries in the Black Country," Royal Commission on Labour, *Parliamentary Papers*, 1893, XXVI.

Ormerod, Frank. *Lancashire Life and Character*. London and Manchester, 1915.

Outhwaite, R. B. "Age of Marriage in England from the late Seventeenth to the Nineteenth Centuries." *Transactions of the Royal Historical Society*, 5th Series, XXII (1973), pp. 55–70.

Owen, Elias. *Some Old Stone Crosses of the Vale of Clwyd*. London, 1886.

Owen, E. Robertson. "Illegitimacy in Islington, 1558–1820." *Devon and Cornwall Notes and Queries*, XXI (1968–70).

Owen, G. D. *Elizabethan Wales: The Social Scene*. Cardiff, 1962.

Owen, Robert. *Lectures on the Marriages of the Priesthood and the Old Immoral World*, 4th ed. Leeds, 1840.

Owen, Trefor. "Some Aspects of Bidding in Cardiganshire." *Ceredigion*, IV no. 1 (1960), pp. 37–46

Owen, Trefor. *Welsh Folk Customs*. Cardiff: National Museum of Wales, 1978.

Owen, Trefor. "West Glamorgan Customs." *Folk-Life*, III (1965).

Ozment, Steven. *When Fathers Ruled: Family Life in Reformation Europe*. Cambridge, 1983.

Paine, Thomas. *The Rights of Man*, ed. H. Collins. Harmondsworth, 1983.

Palmer, Roy. *The Rambling Soldier*. Harmondsworth, 1977.

Paterson, Alexander. *Across the Bridges*. London, 1911.

Paulson, Ronald. *Representations of Revolution, 1789–1820*. New Haven, 1983.

Payne, Judy. "Talking about Children: An Examination of Accounts about Reproduction and Family Life." *Journal of Biosocial Science*, X, no. 4 (October 1978), pp. 367–74.

Peacock, A. J. *Bread or Blood: A Study of the Agrarian Riots in East Anglia in 1816*. London, 1965.

Peacock, A. J. "Village Radicalism in East Anglia, 1800–50," *Rural Discontent in 19th Century Britain*, ed. J. Dunabin. New York, 1974.

Pearce, Carol C. "Expanding Families: Some Aspects of Fertility in a Mid-Victorian Community." *Local Population Studies*, X (Spring 1973), pp. 22–36.

Pearson, Geoffrey. *Hooligan: A History of Respectable Fear*. New York, 1984.

Peel, J., and G. Carr. *Contraception and Family Design*. Edinburgh, 1975.

Pepys, Samuel. *Diary of Samuel Pepys*, ed. H. B. Wheatley. New York, 1896.

Perkin, Harold. *The Origins of Modern English Society, 1780–1880*. London, 1969.

Peterson, M. Jeanne. "The Victorian Governess: Status Incongruence in Family and Society." *Victorian Studies*, XIV, no. 1 (September 1970), pp. 7–26.

Philips, David. *Crime and Authority in Victorian England: The Black Country, 1835–60*. London, 1977.

Phythian-Adams, C. *Desolation of a City: Coventry and the Urban Crisis of the Late Middle Ages*. Cambridge, 1979.

Phythian-Adams, C. *Local History and Folklore*. London, 1975.

Pierce, Rachel. "Marriage in the Fifties." *Sociological Review*, NS, no. 11, (1963), pp. 215–48.

Pinchbeck, Ivy. *Women Workers and the Industrial Revolution, 1750–1850*. New York, 1925.

Pinchbeck, Ivy, and Margaret Hewitt. *Children in English Society*, 2 vols. London, 1969–73.

Place, Francis. *The Autobiography of Francis Place, 1771–1854*, ed. Mary Thrale. Cambridge, 1972.

Porter, Enid. *Cambridgeshire Customs and Folklore*. London, 1979.

Porter, Enid. "Folklore of the Fenlands." *Folk-Lore*, 72 (1971), pp. 584–98.

Porter, Enid. *The Folklore of East Anglia*. London, 1974.

Porter, Roy. "Mixed Feelings: The Enlightenment and Sexuality in Eighteenth Century Britain," *Sexuality in Eighteenth-Century Britain*, ed. Paul-Gabriel Bouce. Manchester, 1982, pp. 1–27.

Poster, Mark. *Critical Theory of the Family*. New York, 1978.

Powell, Margaret. *Below Stairs*. London, 1958.

Power, Eileen. *Medieval People*. New York, 1963.

Preston, B. *Occupations of Father and Son in Mid-Victorian England*. Reading Geographical Papers, no. 56 (1977).

Pruett, John N. *Clergy under the Later Stuarts: The Leicestershire Experience*. Chicago, 1978.

Prynne, G. R. *Thirty-Five Years of Mission Work in a Garrison and Seaport Town*. Plymouth, 1883.

Purvis, J. *Tudor Parish Documents of the Diocese of York*. Cambridge, 1948.

Quaife, G. R. *Wanton Wenches and Wayward Wives: Peasants and Illicit Sex in early seventeenth century England.* New Brunswick, 1979.

Raban, Jonathan. *Soft City.* London, 1975.

Radford, E. and M. A. *Encyclopedia of Superstition.* London, 1961.

Raine, J., ed. *Depositions and Other Ecclesiastical Proceedings from the Courts of Durham.* Surtees Society, XXVI, 1845.

Rapoport, Robert and Rhona. "British Families in Transition," *Families in in Britain.* London, 1982.

Rappaport, Steve. "Social Structure and Mobility in Sixteenth Century London." Unpublished Ph.D. dissertation, Columbia University, 1982.

Razzell, P. E., and R. W. Wainwright. *The Victorian Working Class: Selections of Letters to the Morning Chronicle.* London, 1973.

Redford, A. *The History of Local Government of Manchester.* London, 1939.

Redwood, Charles. *The Vale of Glamorgan.* London, 1839.

Rees, Alwyn. *Life in a Welsh Countryside.* Cardiff, 1975.

Reeves, Maud Pember. *Round about a Pound a Week,* rev. ed. London, 1979.

Renshaw, Walter C. "Notes from the Act-Book of the Archdeaconry Court of Lewes." *Sussex Archeological Collection.* XLIX (1906), pp. 47–65.

Reynel, C. *The True English Intent.* London, 1674.

Richards, Eric. "Women in the British Economy since about 1700: An Interpretation." *History,* 29 (October 1974), pp. 337–57.

Richards, M. E. *Gloucestershire Family History.* Gloucester, 1979.

Richardson, Sheila J. " 'The Servant Question': A Study of the Domestic Labor Market, 1851–1911." Unpublished M.Phil. thesis, University of London, 1967.

Rigby, A. *Alternative Realities: a study of communes and their members.* London, 1974.

Rigby, A. *Communes in Britain.* London, 1974.

Roberts, Elizabeth. "Learning and Living—Socialization outside School." *Oral History,* III, no. 2 (Autumn 1975), pp.

Roberts, Elizabeth. "Working Class Women in the North West." *Oral History,* V, no. 2 (Autumn 1977), pp.

Roberts, Elizabeth. "Working Wives and Their families," *Population and Society in Britain, 1890–1980,* eds. T. Barker and M. Drake. New York, 1982.

Roberts, G. *The History and Antiquities of the Borough of Lyme Regis and Charnworth.* London, 1934.

Roberts, Peter. *The Cambrian Popular Antiquities.* Norwood, Pennsylvania, 1973.

Roberts, Robert. *The Classic Slum: Salford Life in the First Quarter of the Century.* Harmondsworth, 1973.

Roberts, Robert. *A Ragged Schooling.* London, 1978.

Rollinson, W. *Life and Tradition in the Lake District.* London, 1974.

Ross, Ellen. " 'Fierce Questions and Taunts': Married Life in Working Class London, 1870–1914." *Feminist Studies,* VIII, no. 3 (Fall 1982), pp. 576–602.

Ross, Ellen. " 'The Love Crisis': Couples Advice Books of the Late 1970s." *Signs,* VI, no. 1 (1980), pp. 109–22.

Ross, Ellen. "Survival Networks: Women's Neighborhood Sharing in London before World War One." *History Workshop Journal,* 15 (Spring 1983), pp. 4–27.

Rosser, K. C., and C. C. Harris. *Family and Social Change.* London, 1974.

Rovie, David. "Mining Folk of Fife," *County Folklore,* VIII. London, 1914.

Rowbotham, Shiela. *Women, Resistance, and Revolution.* New York, 1974.

Rowntree, B. Seebohm. *Poverty and Progress: A Second Social Survey of York.* London, 1931.

Rowntree, B. Seebohm. *Poverty: A Study of Town Life*. London, 1914.

Rowse, A. L. *A Cornish Childhood*. London, 1942.

Rule, John. *The Experience of Labour in Eighteenth Century Industry*. London, 1981.

Russell, C. E. B. *Manchester Boys*. Manchester, 1905.

Russell, C. E. B. and Lilian M. Rigby. *Working Lad's Clubs*. London, 1908.

Rust, Frances. *Dance in Society*. London, 1969.

Sachs, Albie, and Joan Hoff Wilson. *Sexism and the Law: A Study of Male Beliefs and Legal Bias in Britain and the United States*. London, 1978.

Sarmela, Matti. *Reciprocity Systems of the Rural Society in the Finnish Karelian Culture Area*. Folklore Fellows Communications, no. 207, Helsinki, 1969.

Sarsby, Jacqueline. *Romantic Love and Society*. Harmondsworth, 1983.

Sayce, R. "Popular Enclosures and the One-Night House." *Montgomeryshire Collections*, XLVII, part 2 (1942), pp. 109–119.

Scannell, Dorothy. *Mother Knew Best, An East End Childhood*. London, 1974.

Schofield, Michael. *The Sexual Behavior of Young People*. Harmondsworth, 1968.

Scott, George R. *Curious Customs of Sex and Marriage*. London, 1953.

Scott, Joan W., and Louise Tilly. *Women, Work, and Family*. New York, 1978.

Scott, John J. "A Description and Preliminary Discussion of the Rhymed Blason Populaire Tradition in England." *Lore and Language*, II, no. 2 (January 1975), pp. 9–22.

Scourfield, E. "Fact Finding in a Welsh Rural Community." *Folk-Life*, X (1972), pp. 60-66.

Scourfield, E. "References to Y Ceffyl Pren (the Wooden Horse) in South-West Wales." *Folk-Lore* 87 (1976), pp. 60–62.

Seabrook, Jeremy. *City Close-Up*. London, 1971.

Segalen, Martine. *Love and Power in the Peasant Family*. Oxford, 1983.

Sharp, J. A. *Defamation and Sexual Slander in Early Modern England: The Church Courts at York*. Borthwick Papers, no. 58. York, 1980.

Sheppard, Francis. *London 1808–1870: The Infernal Wen*. Berkeley, 1971.

Shorter, Edward. *The Making of the Modern Family*. New York, 1975.

Skinner, John. *Journal of a Somerset Rector 1803–34: John Skinner*, eds. H. and P. Cooms. Bath, 1971.

Smith, C. Penswick. *Revival of Mothering Sunday*. Nottingham, 1921.

Smith, Edward. *Foreign Visitors in England*. London, 1889.

Smith, Harold. "Marriages from Outside." *The Essex Review*, LXII (1933), pp. 203–4.

Smith, Norah, "Sexual Mores and Attitudes in Enlightenment Scotland," *Sexuality in eighteenth-century Britain*, ed. P. G. Bouce. Manchester, 1982.

Smith, Richard M. "Population and its Geography in England, 1500–1730," *An Historical Geography of England and Wales*, eds. R. A. Dodghson and R. A. Butlin. London, 1978.

Smith, Richard M. "Some reflections on the evidence for the origins of the European marriage pattern," *The Sociology of the Family*, ed. C.C. Harris. Monograph Series of the Sociological Review, 28 (1980).

Smith, William. *Morley: Ancient and Modern*. London, 1886.

Smith-Rosenberg, Carroll. "The Female World of Love and Ritual: Relations Between Women in Nineteenth Century America." *Signs*, I (Autumn 1975), pp. 1–29.

Smout, T. C. "Scottish Marriage, Regular and Irregular, 1500–1940," *Marriage and Society*, ed. R. B. Outhwaite. New York, 1981.

Snell, Keith. "Agricultural Seasonal Unemployment, the Standard of Living and Women's Work in the South and East, 1690–1860." Unpublished paper, Cambridge Group for the Study of the History of Population and Social Structure Library.

Social Trends. London, 1982.

Soloway, R. A. *Birth control and the population question in England, 1877–1930*. Chapel Hill, 1982.

Soly, Hugo, and Catharina Lis. "Policing the Early Modern Proletariat, 1450–1850," *Proletarianization and Family Life*, ed. David Levine. Forthcoming.

Spargo, J. W. *Juridical Folklore in England, illustrated by the cucking-Stool*. Durham, North Carolina, 1944.

Spinley, B. M. *The Deprived and the Privileged: Personality Development in English Society*. London, 1953.

Spurford, Margaret. "Peasant inheritance customs and land distribution in Cambridgeshire from the sixteenth to the eighteenth centuries," *Family and Inheritance: Rural Society in Western Europe, 1200–1800*, eds. J. Goody, J. Thirsk, and E. P. Thompson, Cambridge, 1978.

Stearns, Peter N. "Working Class Women in Britain, 1890–1914," *Suffer and Be Still*, ed. M. Vicinus. Bloomington, 1972.

Steel, D. J. *National Index of Parish Registers*, 12 vols. London, 1968– .

Sterner, M. "Folklore in Worsley, Lancashire." Unpublished paper, Leeds University Institute of Dialect and Folk Life Studies.

Stiles, Henry. *Bundling: Its Origins, Progress and Decline in America*. Mount Vernon, New York, 1937.

Stoianovich, Traian. "Gender and Family: Myths, Models and Ideologies." *The History Teacher*, XV, no. 1 (November 1981), pp. 67–117.

Stone, Lawrence. *The Family, Sex and Marriage in England, 1500–1800*. New York, 1977.

Stone, Lawrence. "Literacy and Education in England, 1640–1900," *Past & Present*, 42 (February 1969), pp. 69–139.

Storm-Clark, Christopher. "The Miners, 1870–1970: A Test Case for Oral History." *Victorian Studies*, XV, no. 1 (September 1971), pp. 49–74.

Stott, Mary. "Getting Uptight about White." *Guardian*, August 26, 1971.

Swinburne, Henry. *A Treatise on Spousals or Matrimonial Contracts*. London, 1686.

Sykes, John. *Local Record: or Historical Register*. Newcastle upon Tyne, 1866.

Sykes, Wirt. *Rambles and Studies in Old South Wales*. London, 1881.

Tanner, Nancy. "Matrifocality in Indonesia, Africa, and among Black Americans," *Women, Culture and Society*, eds. M. Z. Rosaldo and L. Lamphere. Stanford, 1974.

Taylor, Barbara. *Eve and the New Jerusalem: Socialism and Feminism in the Nineteenth Century*. New York, 1983.

Taylor, Gordon Rattray. *The Angel Makers: A Study of the Psychological Origins of Historical Change, 1750–1850*. New York, 1974.

Tebbutt, C. F. *Bluntisham-cum-Earith, Huntingdonshire*. St. Noets, 1941.

Tebbutt, C. F. *Huntingdonshire Folk Lore*. St. Noets, 1951.

Thane, Patricia. "Women and the Poor Law in Victorian and Edwardian England." *History Workshop Journal*, VI (Autumn 1978), pp. 29–51.

Thirsk, Joan. "Younger Sons in the Seventeenth Century," *History*, LIV (1969), pp. 358–70.

Thomas, Keith. "Age and Authority in Early Modern Britain." *Proceedings of the British Academy*, LXII (1976), pp. 209–45.

Thomas, Keith. "The Double Standard." *Journal of History of Ideas*, XX, no. 2 (1959), pp. 195–216.

Thomas, Keith. "The Place of Laughter in Tudor and Stuart England." *Times Literary Supplement*, January 21, 1977, pp. 77–81.

Thomas, Keith. "The Puritans and Adultery: The Act of 1650 Reconsidered," *Puritans and Revolutionaries: Essays in Seventeenth Century History Presented to Christopher Hill*, eds. D. Pennington and K. Thomas. Oxford, 1978.

Thomas, Keith. *Religion and the Decline of Magic*. New York, 1971.

Thomas, Keith. "Women and the Civil War Sects," *Crisis in Europe, 1560–1660*, ed. T. Aston. Garden City, 1965.

Thompson, Derek. "Courtship and Marriage in Preston between the Wars." *Oral History*, III, no. 2 (Autumn 1975), pp. 39–44.

Thompson, Dorothy. "Women and Nineteenth Century Radical Politics: A Lost Dimension," *The Rights and Wrongs of Women*, eds. J. Mitchell and A. Oakley. Harmondsworth, 1979.

Thompson, Edward P. *Making of the English Working Class*. New York, 1966.

Thompson, Edward P. " 'Rough Music' et charivari: Quelques réflections complémentares," *Le Charivari*, eds. J. LeGoff and J.–C. Schmitt. Paris, 1981.

Thompson, Flora. *A Country Calendar and other writings*. Oxford, 1979.

Thompson, Flora. *Lark Rise to Candleford*. Harmondsworth, 1974.

Thompson, Paul. *The Edwardians: The Remaking of British Society*. Bloomington, 1975.

Thompson, Roger. *Women in Stuart England and America*. London, 1974.

Thornes, Barbara, and Jean Collard. *Who Divorces?* London, 1979.

Thornton, W. H. "Devonshire Matrimonial Market." *Devonshire Notes and Queries*, IV (1907), pp. 54–55.

Thrupp, John. *The Anglo-Saxon Home*. London, 1862.

Tibbutt, S. M. "Knitting Stockings in Wales—A Domestic Craft." *Folk-Life*, XVI (1978), pp. 61–73.

Tindall, Gillian. *A Handbook of Witches*. London, 1965.

Todd, M. "Humanists, Puritans and the Spiritual Household." *Church History*, 49 (1980), pp. 18–34.

Toll, Terry. "Childbirth and Health Care Throughout Time: Maternal Mortality in England, 1750–1920." Unpublished paper delivered to American Association for the History of Medicine, 1977.

Tomes, Nancy. "A 'Torrent of Abuse': Crimes of Violence between Working Class Men and Women in London, 1840–1875." *Journal of Social History*, XI, no. 3 (Spring 1978), pp. 328–45.

Tongue, Ruth. *Somerset Folklore*. London, 1965.

Treatis of Feme Coverts or the Lady's Law. London, 1732.

Trost, Jan. "The Choice Not to Marry: Married and Unmarried Cohabitation in Sweden," *The Couple*, ed. Marie Corbin. Harmondsworth, 1977.

Trumbach, Randolf. "Kinship and Marriage in Early Modern France and England: Four Books." *Annals of Scholarship*, II, no. 4 (1981), pp. 113–28.

Trumbach, Randolf. "London's Sodomites: Homosexual Behavior and Western Culture in the Eighteenth Century." *Journal of Social History*, XI (Fall 1977), pp. 1–33.

Trumbach, Randolf. *The Rise of the Egalitarian Family: Aristocratic Kinship and Domestic Relations in Eighteenth Century England.* New York, 1978.

Turner, E. S. *History of Courting.* London, 1954.

Turner, Thomas. *The Life and Times of Thomas Turner of East Hoathley,* ed. D. K. Worcester. New Haven, 1948.

Turner, Victor. *The Ritual Process: Structure and Anti-Structure.* Chicago, 1969.

Turner, Victor. *Schism and Continuity in an African Society.* Manchester, 1957.

Udal, J. S. *Dorsetshire Folklore.* Hertford, 1922

Udal, J. S. "Witchcraft in Dorset." *Proceedings of the Dorset Natural History and Field Club,* XIII (1892), pp. 41–49.

Vann, Richard T. "Nurture and Conversion in the Early Quaker Family," *Journal of Marriage and the Family,* XXXI, no. 4 (1969), pp. 639–43.

Vann, Richard T. *The Social Development of English Quakerism, 1655–1755.* Cambridge, 1969.

Vaux, J. *Church Folklore.* London, 1894.

Viles, D. B. "The Building Trades in London, 1835–60." Unpublished D.Phil. dissertation, University of London, 1975.

Vincent, David. *Bread, Knowledge, Freedom: a study of nineteenth century working class autobiography.* London, 1981.

Vincent, David. "Love and Death and the nineteenth century working class." *Social History,* V, no. 2 (May 1980), pp. 223–47.

Wadding, J. Leonard. *The Bitter Sacred Cup: The Wednesbury Riots, 1743–44.* London, 1976.

Wales, John W. "St. Valentine's Day." *The Antiquary,* V (February 1982), pp.

Walford, Edward. *Old and New London.* London, n.d.

Walker, R. B. "Religious Change in Cheshire, 1750–1850." *Journal of Ecclesiastical History,* XVII, no. 1 (1966), pp. 71–94.

Walkowitz, Judith. "The Making of an Outcast Group: Prostitutes and Working Women in Nineteenth Century Plymouth and Southhampton," *Suffer and Be Still,* ed. M. Vicinus. Bloomington, 1972.

Walkowitz, Judith. *Prostitution and Victorian Society: Women, Class, and the State.* Cambridge, 1980.

Wall, Richard. "The Household: demographic and economic change in England, 1650–1970," *Family Forms in historic Europe,* eds. R. Wall, J. Robin, and P. Laslett. Cambridge, 1983.

Walzer, Michael. *The Revolution of the Saints: A Study in the Origins of Radical Politics.* Cambridge, 1965.

Warren, L. "Birth, Marriage, Death." Unpublished M.A. thesis, Leeds University, Institute of Dialect and Folk Life Studies, 1967.

Warren, Vivien P. "Some Aspects of Mothering Sunday: With Particular Reference to Nottingham." Unpublished M.A. thesis, Leeds University, Institute of Dialect and Folk Life Studies.

Watt, Michael. *The Dissenters.* Oxford, 1978.

Watts, John. *The Facts of the Cotton Famine.* London, 1866.

"Wedding Ring." *The Antiquary,* III (1881), pp. 22–23, 70–71.

Weeks, Jeffrey. *Coming Out: Homosexual Politics in Britain, from the Nineteenth Century to the Present.* London, 1977.

Weeks, Jeffrey. *Sex, Politics and Society: The Regulation of Sexuality since 1800.* London, 1981.

Weeks, W. S. *The Clithero District.* Clithero, n.d.

Westermarck, Edward A. *History of Human Marriage*, 3 vols. New York, 1922.

Wharton, C. "The Folklore of South Warwickshire." Unpublished Ph.D. dissertation, Leeds University Institute of Dialect and Folk Life Studies, 1974.

Whitehead, "Sexual Antagonism in Herefordshire." *Dependence and Exploitation in Work and Marriage*, eds. D. Leonard-Barker and Sheila Allen. New York, 1976.

Wikman, Robert K. *Die Einleitung der Ehe*. Abo, 1937.

Williams, A. Baily. "Courtship and Marriage in Late Nineteenth Century Montgomeryshire." *Montgomeryshire Collections*, II, part i (1950), pp. 116–27.

Williams, David. *The Rebecca Riots: A Study of Agrarian Discontent*. Cardiff, 1955.

Williams, G. J. "Glamorgan Customs in the Eighteenth Century." *Gwerin*, I (1956–57), pp. 99–108.

Williams, Glanmore. *The Welsh Church from Conquest to Reformation*. Cardiff, 1962.

Williams, Richard. "History of the Parish of Llanbrgynmair." *Montgomergyshire Collections*, XXII (1883), pp. 35–69.

Williamson, Bill. *Class, Culture and Community*. London, 1982.

Willmott, Peter. *Adolescent Boys of East London*. Harmondsworth, 1966.

Willmott, Peter, and Michael Young. *Family and Kinship in East London*. Harmondsworth, 1954.

Willmott, Peter, and Michael Young. *The Symmetrical Family*. New York, 1973.

Winters, Ivor. *Chepstow Parish Records*, Chepstow, 1955.

Woodforde, James. *The Diary of a Country Parson*, 5 vols. London, 1924–31.

Working Women and Divorce: An Account of Evidence Given on Behalf of the Women's Cooperative Guild before the Royal Commission on Divorce. London, 1911.

Wright, A. R. *British Calendar Customs*, 3 vols. London, 1936–40.

Wright, Elizabeth M. *Rustic Speech and Folk-Lore*. London, 1913.

Wrightson, Keith. "Alehouses, Order, and Reformation in Rural England, 1590–1660," *Class Relations and Cultural Forms*, eds. E. and S. Yeo. London, 1979.

Wrightson, Keith. *English Society, 1580–1680*. New Brunswick, 1982.

Wrightson, Keith. "Infanticide in Early 17th Century England." *Local Population Studies*, 15 (Autumn 1975), pp. 10–22.

Wrightson, K. "The nadir of English illegitimacy in the seventeenth century," *Bastardy and its Comparative History*, eds., Peter Laslett, Karla Oosterveen, and R. M. Smith. Cambridge, 1980.

Wrightson, Keith, and David Levine. *Poverty and Piety in an English Village: Terling, 1525–1700*. New York, 1979.

Wrigley, E. A. "Clandestine Marriage in Tetbury in the late Seventeenth Century." *Local Population Studies*, no. 10 (Spring 1973), pp. 15–21.

Wrigley, E. A. "A Simple Model of London's Importance in Changing English Society and Economy, 1650–1750," *Past & Present*, no. 37 (July 1937), pp. 47–65.

Wrigley, E. A., and R. S. Schofield. *The Population History of England, 1541–1871*. Cambridge, 1981.

Wynn, John. "A Report on the Deanry of Penllyn and Edeirnion by Rev. John Wynne, 1730." *The Merioneth Miscellany*, no. 3 (1955), pp. 4–41.

Yarham, E. "Wives to Market." *The Amateur Historian*, VI, no. 5 (1963), pp. 190–93.

Yeo, Eileen. "Robert Owen and Radical Culture," *Robert Owen: Prophet of the Poor*, eds. S. Pollard and J. Salt. London, 1971.

Index

Abandonment, 241, 246
Abortion, 163, 180, 238
Addison, Joseph, 136
Addy, Sidney O., 202
Adolescence, 262, 267. *See also* Youth
Adoption, 128, 130
Adultery, 13, 78–79, 81, 257, 303
Adultery Act of 1650, 100
Adulthood, 288, 291, 315
Affiliation orders, 182, 258
Agricultural Revolution, 111–14, 145, 169–70
Almondbury, 91
Anglesey, 200
Anglo-Saxons, 17
Anti-clericalism, 151, 191–92, 205, 235
Antinomianism, 102–3, 190–92
Apprentices, 164–65, 262
Ariès, Philippe, 3
Aristocracy, 12–13, 135–36, 138–39
Artisans, 15, 109, 162, 164–69, 174–75; and marriage, 13, 168; and secularism, 235
Ash-next-Sandwich, 115, 206, 219, 239
Ashton, 44
Ashton-under-Lyne, 79
Astrologers, 162–63
Aubrey, John, 17, 58

Baby farmers, 241
Bamford, Samuel, 121, 124–25, 130
Banns, 52–54, 142–43, 232, 292–93
Baptists, 102, 191
Baring-Gould, Sabine, 27, 145
Barking, 99
Barrow, 299

Bastards: term for, 129–30. *See also* Illegitimacy
Bath, 211
Baxter, Richard, 101
Bedale, 147–50
Bedding, 63, 69
Bedfordshire, 26
Beggar weddings, 88, 98. *See also* Bride-ales; Penny weddings
Beke, John and Margory, 20
Berkshire, 94, 115
Besom weddings, 198–200, 202–3. *See also* Common-law marriage
Best, Henry, 31, 38, 43, 61
Bethnal Green, 193, 240, 246, 255, 263, 267, 274, 277, 283, 287, 292, 295–96, 300–301
Betrothal, 20, 43, 46–47, 50, 52, 114–15, 128–29, 136; changes in, 179–81; legality of, 16, 20, 309; puritan view of, 21; as rite of passage, 47–50; and sexuality, 308–9. *See also* Trothplight
Bettesworth, Lucy, 114
Bewcastle, 216
Bidding, 71; bidding letter, 155; bidding wedding, 153–56
Bigamy, 99–100, 209–11, 236
Big weddings, 56–57, 70, 109, 145–47, 227, 286. *See also* Wedding
Bilston, 211
Birkby, 62
Birmingham, 113, 166, 191, 210–11, 219, 227
Birth, 156–57, 172
Birth control, 238, 288, 297
Black Country, 118

Blackpool, 297
Blackstone, William, 142
Blake, William, 222
Blakeborough, Richard, 66, 150
Blason populaire, 28, 122
Bocock, Robert, 7
Bolton, 291
Booth, Charles, 232, 257
Bottom drawer, 263
Bourne, Henry, 26
Bradford, 39, 67, 139, 222
Brain, Robert, 5, 320
Brakenridge, William, 161
Brampton, 143
Braughing, 19
Breconshire, 94, 97
Brideales, 98
Bride seat, 75
Bridestowe, 68
Bride wain, 74, 156
Bristol, 213
Brownists, 208
Buchan, Luckie, 221
Buckinghamshire, 119, 169, 171
Bullinger, Heinrich, 20
Bundling, 30–31, 109, 114, 120–21
Bunyan, John, 88
Burney, Fanny, 137
Burnley, 144
Burns, 21
Burntwood, 213

Caernarvonshire, 198
Calvert, George, 149
Cambridgeshire, 68, 99, 114, 131, 205, 213
Camerton, 119
Canon law, 84
Capitalism, 111–14, 117, 163–69
Capras, William, 210–11
Cardiganshire, 31, 59, 73–74
Carlile, Richard, 222
Carlisle, 193, 196
Carmarthen, 87
Carmarthenshire, 153–55
Catholics, 205, 298
Ceffyl pren, 77, 80, 125, 130, 132; *See also*
    Rough music
Ceiriog, 110, 118, 122, 125–28, 198–99,
    206–9, 231
Celibacy, 11, 15, 110, 162–63, 220, 234
Chaperonage, 136, 264
Chappelsmith, Margaret, 226–27
Chastity, 136, 164, 226, 239, 292
Cheltenham, 227
Cheshire, 25, 31, 38, 121, 201, 206, 208

Chester, 33
Chesterfield, 213
Chicken, Edward, 151
Children: attitudes toward, 126, 287; of
    cohabiting couples, 310; and divorce,
    302; effects on marriage, 316–17, 319;
    employment of, 11, 166; naming of, 159;
    rearing of, 314
Chorley, 272
Christmas, 24–25
Church ales, 86–87. *See also* Brideales
Church control of marriage, 18–19
Church courts, 51, 55
Churching, 300
Civil marriage, 56, 89, 92, 189, 193, 232,
    235, 297–99, 310–11
Clacton, 297
Clandestine marriage, 92–98, 193–95; in
    cities, 194; and civil marriage, 193–94,
    196, 235; and clergy, 93–94, 96; clients,
    95–96; by laymen, 94; opposition to,
    140; and premarital pregnancy, 97; as
    substitute for betrothal, 97–98; in twen-
    tieth century, 297–99
Clare, John, 27–28
Class differences: 85–86, 89, 98–99, 104–5,
    128–30, 135, 148–50, 187–89, 239, 261,
    267, 274, 285–86, 293–97, 304, 308, 313,
    316–17
Cleaver, Robert, 46, 52
Clergy: responses to Harwicke Act, 142;
    role in weddings, 18–19, 152; use of
    magic, 19–20
Cleveland, 62, 130
Cobbett, William, 122
Cock-and-Hen Clubs, 177, 248
Cohabitation: attitudes toward, 304, 307;
    by class, 309; contemporary, 310; levels
    of, 307; premarital, 181–82, 186
Cold Aston, 54, 73
Coldstream Bridge, 195–96
Colquhoun, Patrick, 186
Common-law divorce, 198, 209–19, 232;
    rites of, 209–11. *See also* Wife sales
Common-law marriage, 186, 197–209, 232;
    conditions for, 206–9; decline of, 234–35;
    incidence of, 110–11; rites of, 203;
    words for 203–4
Conjugality: concept of, 3–5, fragility of,
    251; ideal of, 232, 252, 307–8, 313; limits
    of, 301, 318, 320; myth of, 5, 313, 321;
    purtian idea of, 14, 101; ritual expres-
    sion in weddings, 294, 311
Coolstrin court, 133–34 *See also* Rough
    music
Coppe, Abiezer, 102

Cormortha, 87. *See also* Church ales
Cornwall, 39, 68–69, 120, 127, 151, 159, 234, 243, 263, 281
Costermongers, 165, 185, 204
Couples, 11, 15–16
Courtship: calender of, 25–29, 123–24, 176–79, 271, 279; clandestine, 36, 121, 266; at dances, 27, 273–74; gifts, 38; in groups, 276–77; length of, 280; locations of, 29, 123, 176, 271–73; parental control of 21, 256–58, 262–64, 282–84; polygamous character, 37, 273; ritualization of, 260–61, 308; rural, 161–62; terms for, 29, 271, 279; times for, 29–30; urban, 176–79. *See also* Monkey ranks
Couvade, 159
Coventry, 15, 25, 69, 121, 174, 176, 178
Cowper, William, 161
Coxwold, 67
Crosse, Robert, 100
Cradley Heath, 118
Cuckolds, 78
Culcheth, 110, 118, 127–28, 206–8, 231
Cumberland, 27, 31, 72–74, 143, 150, 156–59, 192, 195, 208, 216
Curtesy, 19

Dancing, 27–28, 124, 176, 273; in hogs trough, 72
Davies, Stella, 280
Defamation suits, 34
Defoe, Daniel, 140
Denbighshire, 156
Deptford, 171
Derbyshire, 54, 68, 92, 147, 191, 262, 296
Desertion, 99, 246
Devil's Bridge, 153
Devon, 60, 66, 68, 113, 127, 173, 201, 214–15, 220
Diarying, 121
Dissent, 100–104, 105; disobedience to the marriage law, 219; and Hardwicke Act, 142; marriage discipline, 190
Divination, 226
Divorce, 98–100, 199, 223, 225–27, 246, 299, 302–3, 319
Dolgelly, 121
Domesticization, 245, 300, 318
Donington-on-Bain, 143
Dorchester, 16
Dorking, 217
Dorset, 16, 123, 127
Dower, 19
Dow purse, 62–63, 137
Dowry, 48–49, 62, 147, 283

Ducking, 72–73
Durham, 25, 48, 122, 156
Dyer, T. B. Thiselton, 285

East Anglia, 113, 263
Easter, 79
Easter Monday and Tuesday, 24–25, 123
Edale, 191
Eden, Frederick, 156
Effeminacy, 269
Effingham, 217
Elopement, 92–93, 95–96, 171, 199
Enfield, 234
Engagement, 279, 284; gifts at, 290; as rite of passage, 282–82; saving during, 281, 283; sexuality during, 282. *See also* Betrothal
Engels, Friedrich, 166
Envy, 66, 72
Ernest money, 29
Essex, 26, 62, 87–90, 93, 98–99, 113, 143–44, 262
Exeter, 173, 216–17
Eyre, Adam and Susan, 82

Fairs, 176, 248
Familists, 102
Family: division of labor, 248, 251, 287–88, 302, 316; extended, 116; income, 114, 166, 243, 247, 317; nuclear, 14, 82, 105, 140, 184, 224, 228, 314; shared activities of, 301, 316
Feme covert, 51, 183, 204
Feminism, 221, 223–28, 321
Feminization, 267, 274
Ferryside, 77
Fertility, 127
Fetching the bride, 58–60, 146, 150, 189, 293
Finglin night, 271, 279
Fisher folk, 123
Fleet, the, 92, 95–98, 142
Foley, Winifred, 238, 244
Folklore, 7, 285
Footings: at banns, 54; in courtship, 39, 122–23; at weddings, 61–62, 65–66, 68–69, 143, 189. *See also* Joking; Pitchering
Ford, 143, 195–96
Forest of Dean, 117, 144
Forman, Simon, 162
Foundling Hospital, 171, 179–80, 237–40, 322
Fox, George, 103
Fox, Henry, 141

Frampton, 89
Franklin, William, 103
Free thinking, 190–92. 222–24
Friendship, 34–35, 37, 42, 321
Froome, 68
Furness, 216

Gadbury, Mary, 103
Games, 23, 28, 30, 176–77
Gandy, G. N., 208
Garment making, 168, 242–43
Garters, 33, 63, 138, 147; opposition to,
    147–50; race for, 64, 152
Gaudy loup, 143
Gavron, Hannah, 316–17
Generational relations, 15–16, 85, 101–2,
    178–79, 255–58, 262–67
Gifts: at betrhothal, 43–44; in courtship
    30–33; at weddings, 87, 138, 153–54, 296
Giving away the bride, 60, 145–46, 150,
    293
Glamorgan, 27, 74, 93, 133
Gloucestershire, 68, 70, 92, 113, 137, 211,
    219
Go-betweens, 34, 36, 38, 42, 48, 51
Godwin, William, 222–23
Gorer, Geoffrey, 302, 304, 308, 316
Gosport, 291
Gossip, 125, 265
Gouge, William, 21
Gough, Richard, 46, 54
Grass widows, 204. *See also* Common-law
    divorce
Graunt, John, 161
Graveley, 122
Great Yarmouth, 53
Greenleigh, 301, 317
Greenwich, 247
Greenwood, Walter, 278
Gretna Green, 195–96
Grey, Edwin, 145, 147
Grindletonians, 102
Guising, 79
Guns, 145
Gutteridge, Joseph, 121, 178
Gwadhoodwr, 153. *See also* Bidding
Gwas caru, 30. *See also* Go-betweens
Gwyn, Gwenith, 198–99, 207

Haldane, George, 141
Half-married, 98
Hampshire, 115, 173
Handfasting, 17, 44, 50. *See also* Betrothal

Hardwicke Act, 140–42, 190, 192
Hardy, Thomas, 132
Harlowe, Clarissa, 104
Havering, 194
Helmsley, 78
Hen parties, 291
Henpecking, 78–80
Hereford, 214–15
Herefordshire, 93, 122
Hickson, Emily, 210–11
Hill, Christopher, 14, 104
Hiring fairs, 28–29
Hodson, William, 226
Hoggart, Richard, 258–59, 288
Holland, John, 103
Holy Trinity (Minores), 92
Home, 287, 300
Homosexuality, 11, 131, 239
Homosocial relationships, 11–12, 34, 261,
    267, 270, 274, 317
Honeymoon, 138–39, 147, 189, 296, 311
Horsham, 28
Household, 13, 22, 75, 81–82, 112, 128,
    146–47, 167, 184, 225–26, 281, 316–17
Housekeeping, 300, 316–17
Housing, 289, 297, 300–301, 311
Hull, 251
Husband, 57, 81
Hustlers, 67

Illegitimacy, 13, 37, 110, 112, 115, 125,
    127–28, 199, 208, 231, 237, 315, 325; ef-
    fects of New Poor Law on, 239–41;
    terms for, 129–30; 163, 186
Industrial Revolution, 109, 165–69, 241–44.
    See also Proto-industrialization
Infanticide, 241
Inheritance, 15, 37, 111–12, 164, 169–70,
    245, 254–55, 318
Irish, 205
Isle of Portland, 50, 70, 125–27

Jealousy, 71–72, 251, 303, 318
Jews, 140, 142
Johnson, Samuel, 81
Joking, 48, 54, 79, 296
Josselin, Ralph, 47, 98
Jumping: brides, 65–66, 143; brush and
    steel, 202; grooms, 70

Kendal, 39
Kent, 70, 206

Kingswood, 192
Kinship, 18, 35, 116–17, 154, 159, 174, 184, 208, 297, 300–301
Kissing, 19, 673, 143
Knitting, 120

Laborers, 112–14, 145–46
Lake District, 50
Lamberton Toll, 195
Lancashire, 13, 36, 44, 118–19, 159, 167, 182, 206–8, 219, 231, 235, 270, 294
Laurence Street Chapel, 219, 227
Lawless churches, 90, 92–93
Leasing, 210–11, 215. *See also* Common-law divorce
Leave taking, 60, 150
Lee, Ann, 191, 220
Legitimation, 19, 310
Leicester, 77
Leicestershire, 46, 93, 207
Leominster, 77
Leonard, Diana, 310
Licenses, 53, 90–92, 192–93
Life cycle, 15, 35, 245, 254, 261–62, 288, 316
Lifting: on Easter Monday and Tuesday, 25; at weddings, 64–66, 70
Lilly, William, 162
Lincolnshire, 54, 89, 130, 143, 145, 205–6, 217, 285, 296
Littleport, 114
Little weddings, 8–9, 84, 200–201, 310. *See also* Wedding
Liverpool, 50
Living tally, 203, 206. *See also* Common-law marraige
Llanelly, 144
Llangollen, 200
Lollardy, 100
London, 13, 23, 63, 68–69, 70, 80, 90, 92–93, 96, 98, 113, 136, 138, 139, 161, 177–78, 203–5, 231–32, 234–36, 240–52, 254–59, 263, 272–73, 294, 300, 312
London City Misson, 192, 231
Love: attitudes toward, 12, 40, 73, 287; potions, 266; romantic, 278, 318; sickness, 73; spoons, 31; tokens, 31
Lovett, William, 227
Lowe, Roger, 22, 30, 31, 36–38, 40–44, 50, 61
Lyme Regis, 93

Magic: of church, 44, 70; of gifts, 33; rings, 62; times, 71; at weddings, 71

Maidstone, 53
Malinowski, Bronislaw, 16
Malthusianism, 225
Manchester, 87–88, 139, 187, 191, 193–94, 227, 269–70, 302
Manor courts, 78–79
Manor custom, 19
Margate, 263
Marloe Magna, 90
Marriage: age of, 110, 112, 232, 244, 289, 307–8; Anglo-Saxon, 17–18; church ceremony, 62, 152; companionate, 135, 232–33, 259, 301–2; law, 313–15; legal age, 86; lines, 235; medieval, 18–19; plebeian, 159–60; politics of, 16; porch, 18; private, 135–38, 145–46; prohibitions, 71, 88–89; rates, 307–8, 310; residency requirements, 194; rituals, 161–62; seasonality, 179
Marvel, Andrew, 80
Masculinity, 183–84, 243, 256; proving, 250–251, 268, 275
Mass, 19
Matriarchy, 265
Matrifocality, 252, 293, 317
May Day, 24–27, 123–24
Mayhew, Henry, 165, 168, 181, 204, 243
Maying, 24
Men: aggressiveness of, 125; attitudes toward marriage, 287–88, 301–2, 315; attitudes toward weddings, 286; concepts of love, 278; dependency on marriage, 252; education, 245; employment, 245, 289; leisure, 249, 288, 317. *See also* Family; Patriarchy
Menea Fen, 226
Menses, 267
Merioneth, 129
Metal workers, 118
Methodists, 121, 149, 191, 220
Middle classes: seventeenth century, 85, 104–5; eighteenth century, 135–39; nineteenth century, 164, 187, 232–33; twentieth century, 264, 285, 293, 311, 316–317
Middleton, 124–25
Middlewich, 144
Middling sort, 14
Midlands, 25–26, 60, 192, 201, 208
Midsummer games, 23–24
Migration, 169–73, 234
Mill, John Stuart, 232
Milton, John, 55–56
Miners, 117, 119–20, 123, 150–51
Mint, The, 92

Misson, Henry, 137–38
Monkey ranks, 271–72
Monkhouse, John, 115
Montgomeryshire, 53
Morecombe, 139
Morley, 122
Mormons, 222
Morris, Lewis, 58, 154, 190, 200
Morrison, Frances, 226–27
Morrison, James, 227
Mother-daughter relations, 249, 251, 255, 263, 284, 292, 297, 301, 317
Motherhood, 238, 248, 252–55, 300, 313, 315, 318
Mothering Sunday, 253
Mother-in-laws, 251, 255, 283
Munby, Arthur, 23, 177
Myddle, 54

Naitby, David, 149
Navvies, 201–2
National Children's Home, 246
Newcastle, 71, 150–51
Newgate Prison, 92
Newman, Anthea, 219
Nicolaitans, 191
Night visiting, 30–31. *See also* Bundling
Norfolk, 53, 60, 99, 127
North Bovey, 216
Northhamptonshire, 117
Northumberland, 63, 65–66, 69, 143, 150, 156, 195–96, 208
Norwich, 24–25, 99
Nottingham, 219, 253
Nottinghamshire, 92
Nugent, Robert, 141

Oakington, 213, 215–16
Oldham, 166
One-night houses, 158–59
Orators, 18, 45
Orbiston, 225
Orphans, 21, 170, 246
Owen, Robert, 224–28
Owenism, 224–228
Oxford, 270, 276
Oxfordshire, 28, 55, 90, 147, 208, 233, 244, 266, 298

Paine, Thomas, 222–23
Palm Sunday, 176

Parental authority, 22, 37, 86, 118–19, 121, 150, 178–79, 283, 309
Parenthood, 314
Parkins, Eleanor, 16
Patriarchy, 47, 61, 81–83, 104, 117, 119, 140, 150, 187, 265, 316
Patricians, 135–39
Patrifocal, 255, 293
Peasants, 13, 15, 109, 111–12
Peeping Toms, 39
Peers, 42–43, 60, 66–67, 75, 80–81, 268–70, 282, 290–91
Penance, 78, 131
Penny weddings, 98, 156, 158. *See also* public bridals
Pepys, Samuel, 24, 26, 63, 69, 71
Petting stones, 65–66
Pickering, 131
Pitchering, 39
Place, Francis, 164, 176–77, 248
Plebeians, 117, 152–60
Plough Monday, 79
Plymouth, 210, 217, 234, 252, 276
Polygamy: in courtship, 13, 23; in marriage, 99–100, 102
Poor Law, 113, 129, 205, 239
Population, 11–13, 23, 109–10, 161–62, 232, 277, 288–89, 307
Portsmouth, 76
Pregnancy, 125, 300
Premarital pregnancy, 52, 110–11, 120, 179–80, 231, 277, 299
Presbyterians, 196
Preston, 139, 166, 251, 255, 263, 265, 267, 271–73, 276, 293–95, 298, 300, 309
Privacy, 194
Private spousals, 44–45
Proletariat, 13, 166–67
Prostitution, 163, 201
Proto-industrialization, 116–21
Proverbs, 43, 46, 60–63, 319
Poverty, 245, 247, 249
Proving, 127
Public bridals, 152–59. *See also* Beggar weddings; Penny weddings
Pudsey, 28–29, 147
Puritanism, 14, 46, 52, 56, 62, 86
Pwython, 58. *See also* Gifts

Quakers, 102, 104, 139, 140
Quantocks, 203
Queen Caroline Affair, 223

Queenswood, 224
Quintain, 58

Raban, Jonathan, 261
Radnorshire, 139
Ranters, 101–2
Rebecca Riots, 130–31
Receptions, 294–95
Redwood, Charles, 133
Remarriage, 110
Rhythu, 122, 126
Rice, 144–45
Riding the stang, 80, 131–33. *See also* Rough music
Rings, 62, 137, 203–4, 279
Rites of passage, 20–21, 76, 311
Ritual, 6–7, 17, 23, 39–40, 260–61, 269–70, 285–86, 319, 321. *See also* Courtship; Wedding
Roberts, Robert, 265, 278, 284
Rochester, 76
Rouchfoucauld, Duc de la, 136
Roping, 66–67, 143–44
Rough music: aimed at seducers, 130–31; by butcher boys in London, 68, 138; calendar of, 79; change in targets, 131; in maritial discipline, 77–81; in twentieth century, 296; at weddings, 67, 70; women's role in, 125, 130. *See also* Riding the stang; Skimmington
Rowntree, H. Seebohm, 289

St. Bartholomew's Fair, 176
St Benet Paul's Wharf, 90
St. James (Dukes Palace), 92
St. James the Great, 193
Sailors, 201, 234, 252
Salford, 87, 231, 249, 255, 265, 269, 276, 284, 288, 303–4
Sammenboende, 309
Savoy Chapel, 142
Scannell, Dorothy, 293, 297
Scilly Isles, 79
Scotland, 151, 158, 195–96, 221, 323n.
Sowthrawelde, 55
Seabrook, Jeremy, 309
Seekers, 58
Self-divorce, 99. *See also* Common-law divorce
Self-marriage, 18. *See also* Common-law marriage
Separation, 82, 99, 163, 218–19

Servants: domestic, 165, 174–75, 244–5; in husbandry, 15, 35
Sex ratios, 174, 234, 288
Sexuality: anxiety about, 275–76, 296; attitudes toward, 126, 288; ignorance of, 268–69; in marriage, 251; premarital, 38, 114–16, 126–28, 282, 320; restraints on, 277; and shame, 300; and seventeenth-century radicalism, 100–105
Shakers, 220
Shaming, 79. *See also* Joking; Rough music
Sharples, Elizabeth, 222
Sheffield, 15, 122, 202–3, 217
Shepshed, 117, 128, 207
Shipham, 45
Shoemaking, 168
Shorter, Edward, 3
Shropshire, 72, 204–4, 210
Shrove Tuesday, 79–80
Single mothers, 314. *See also* Illegitimacy
Single parents, 314
Sittings, 123. *See also* Courtship
Skimmington, 80, 132. *See also* Rough music
Skinner, John, 115, 119, 121
Skirbeck, 217
Smith, C. Penwick, 253
Social drama, 6, 73, 76
Socialism, 224–28
Soldiers, 218, 237, 246, 253
Somerset, 34, 54, 68, 80, 90, 93, 144, 203
Southcott, Joanna, 219–21
Southhampton, 201
Spence, Thomas, 222–23
Spilsby, 217
Spinsters, 234, 238
Spitalfields, 174, 185
Spousals. *See* Betrothals
Spurrings, 54, *See also* Banns
Stafell, 74
Staffordshire, 25, 72, 174, 191, 210, 213
Stag hunt, 68
Stag parties, 290–91
Status reversal, 79–81. *See also* Rough music
Stockton, 89
Stone, Lawrence, 3–4, 138
Stones, 17
Stopes, Marie, 296
Stowe, John, 80
Stratford-upon-Avon, 92, 193
Strawplaiting, 119
Stubbes, Philip, 88
Suburbanization, 301, 318

Surrey, 208
Sussex, 51, 68, 109, 171, 281
Swansea, 309, 317
Sweden, 309
Swedenborgians, 220
Sweeps, 204
Swinburne, Henry, 16
Sykes, Wirt, 134

Tailors, 168, 242–43
Taylor, Jeremy, 100
Tennyson, Alfred Lord, 232
Terling, 45, 88–89, 112, 127, 240
Thaxted, 285
Thomas, Keith, 71
Thompson, Edward P., 132
Thompson, Flora, 208, 233, 244, 267
Thompson, William, 224–25, 320
Threshold rites, 75, 124
Throwing: rice 144–45, 285; shoes, 60, 145, 285; sods, 145, 285; stocking, 69
Tom Brown's School Days, 124
Tower of London, 92
Townshend, Charles, 141
Tradition, 285–86
Trothplight, 17–18. *See also* Betrothal
Trotman, Dorothea, 137–38
Turner, Thomas, 31, 109
Turner, Victor, 47, 73
Tysoe, 113, 115, 129
Ty un nos, 159. *See also* One-night houses

United States, 224, 310
Upton St. Leonards, 70
Urbanization, 162–63
Uxbridge, 234

Vagabonds, 13, 23
Valentines, 278
Valentine's Day, 23–25, 123–25
Vale of Clwyd, 72
Van Gennep, Arnold, 84
Vaughan, Amelia and James, 227
Virility, 126, 250–51, 267. *See also* Masculinity

Wakes, 28
Wales, 25–26, 30–31, 47, 50, 58, 60–61, 66, 71–73, 77, 87, 93, 109, 120, 123, 125, 129–30, 134, 144–45, 150, 153–59, 174,

183, 190, 192, 196, 198, 202, 204–9, 219, 231, 234–35, 264, 266, 296
Warwickshire, 92, 113, 129
Weavers, 117–18, 168–69
Webbe, Thomas, 102
Wedding: bells, 60, 70, 143; church, 286, 292–93; costume, 187, 293–94, 311–13; days, 71, 150, 187; favors, 58, 61, 75; feast, 74, 146; as female event, 294; guns at, 60, 70; horse, 60; houses 19; medieval, 55; patrician, 138–39, 187; peasant and artisan, 57–73; plebeian, 152–59; politics, 297; processions, 60, 69, 145; propitiary rites at, 72–73; puritan attitudes toward, 55; quiet, 297, 310–11; riding, 58, 60, 145; and school children, 144; throwing coins at, 67, 143; and trades, 60–70; urban, 187–88; white, 286–87, 294, 311–13. *See also* Big weddings
Wednesbury, 25, 191, 214
Weds, 17–18
Wesley, John, 191, 220
West Germany, 310
West Ham, 55, 66
Westmoreland, 210
Whitehaven, 216
Whiteway, William, 16
Whittingham, 143
Whitton, 234
Widowers, 253, 299
Widows, 299
Wife, 57, 81, 118
Wifebeating, 185, 249, 303
Wife sales, 211–19
Willmott, Peter, 274
Wiltshire, 53, 172
Witchcraft, 71–72
Women: aggressiveness, 125, 130; attitudes toward children, 315; attitudes toward marriage, 287, 301–2, 315–16; attitudes toward weddings, 286; bargaining power, 175–83; class differences, 317; education, 245; employment, 113, 118, 165–66, 242–46, 252, 289, 308, 317; and housekeeping, 249; independence, 121; initiative in courtship 28, 37, 48, 270, 278–79; leisure, 249, 318; magical powers, 125–26; notions of love, 278; respectability, 248; sexuality, 130; sexual radicalism, 102–3; sharing, 185–86, 249. *See also* Family; Feminization; Motherhood
Whately, William, 22
Winstanley, Gerrard, 100–103

Woking, 79, 132, 208–9
Wollstonecraft, Mary, 222–23, 321
Wolverhampton, 166
Woodforde, James, 115
Woodhead, 201
Woolwich, 247
Worcestershire, 89
Working class: divisions within, 247–52,
    271–72; *See also* Plebeians; Proletariat
Worsley, 272
Wrightson, Keith, 21
Wroe, John, 222
Wynne, William, 94

Yarmouth, 88
Yarmouth Beach, 277

York, 71, 164, 167, 289
Yorkshire, 31, 33, 53, 64–69, 72, 74, 78,
    91, 93, 99, 109, 120, 122–23, 125, 129–31,
    133, 137, 143–44, 147–51, 201, 203–4,
    206, 215–17, 222, 298
Youth: and adolescence, 262; attitudes to-
    ward marriage, 304, 314; employment,
    262–63; groups, 22, 269–70; homosocia-
    bility of, 261, 308; mobility, 262; organi-
    zations, 276; relations with parents,
    262–64; rural, 34–35; sexuality, 308; sta-
    tus of, 15 34–35, 119; violence of, 269–70